THE NAVAL HISTORY OF GREAT BRITAIN

VOLUME THE SIXTH

THE RIGHT HON. ADMIRAL VISCOUNT DUNCAN.

FROM A PAINTING BY H. P. DANLOUX

Engraved by W. Greatbach.

THE
NAVAL HISTORY
OF
GREAT BRITAIN

FROM THE DECLARATION OF WAR BY FRANCE
IN 1793
TO THE ACCESSION OF GEORGE IV.

BY

WILLIAM JAMES

*A NEW EDITION, WITH ADDITIONS AND NOTES
BRINGING THE WORK DOWN TO 1827*

VÉRITÉ SANS PEUR

IN SIX VOLUMES
VOL. VI.

London
MACMILLAN AND CO., Limited
NEW YORK: THE MACMILLAN COMPANY
1902

All rights reserved

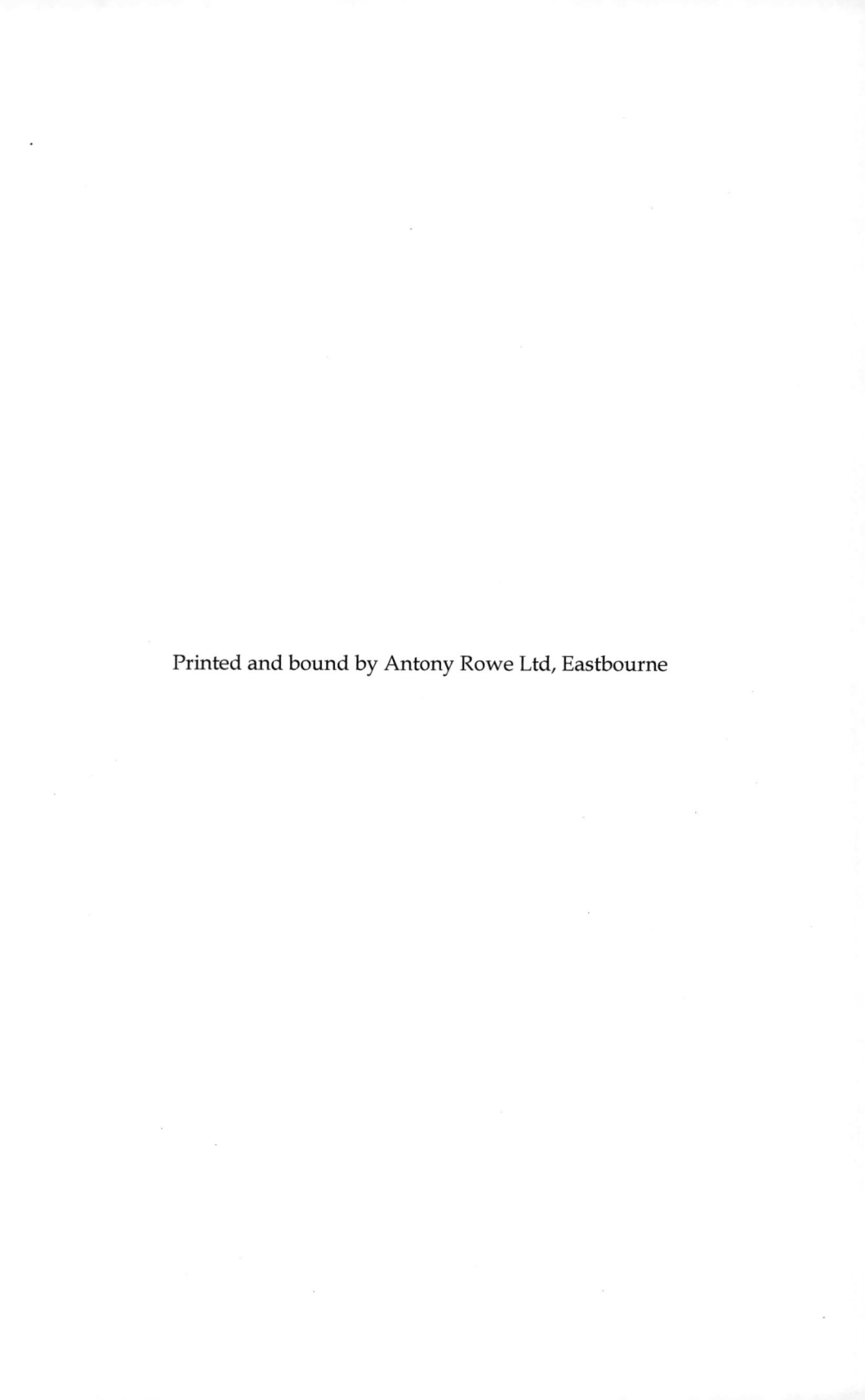

Printed and bound by Antony Rowe Ltd, Eastbourne

CONTENTS.

VOL. VI.

1813 (*in continuation*).

BRITISH AND FRENCH FLEETS, 1—Sir Edward Pellew and Comte Emerian, 3.

LIGHT SQUADRONS AND SINGLE SHIPS, 4—Blazer and Brevdrageren in the Elbe, ibid.—Albacore and Gloire, 6—Linnet and Gloire, 7—Alphea and Renard, 9—Telegraph and Flibustier, 10—Scylla and Royalist with Weser, 12—Andromache and Trave, 14—Thunder and Neptune, ibid.—Snap and five French luggers, 15—Sir George Collier off North Coast of Spain, ibid.—Boats of Undaunted at Carri, 17—Of Volontaire at Morgion, ibid.—Of Repulse, &c., at same place, ibid.—Of Berwick and Euryalus at Cavalarie, 18—Capture of Ponza, 19—Captain Hall and Neapolitan gun-boats, ibid.—Boats of Bacchante and Weasel near Cape Otranto, 21—Bacchante at Karlebego, 22—Her boats at Gela-Nova, 23—Weasel and French gun-boats near Zirana, 24—Boats of Kingfisher at Melara, 26—Of Havannah at Vasto, &c., ibid.—Of Apollo and Weasel at St. Cataldo, 27—Capture of islands of Augusta and Curzola, ibid.—Boats of Apollo and Cerberus, near Corfu, &c., ibid.—Saracen at Zapano, 29—Boats of Elizabeth and Eagle at Goro, Omago, &c., ibid.—Capture of Fiume, 31—Also of Porto-Ré, Farasina, &c., ibid.—Capture of Rovigno, Ragosniza, and Triest, ibid.—Bacchante and Saracen at Castel-Nuova, 33—Boats of Swallow off d'Anzo, ibid.—Of Edinburgh and squadron at same place, 34—Boats of Furieuse at Marinelo, 35—Of Revenge at Palamos, ibid.—Of Undaunted at Port-Nouvelle, ibid.—Boats of Swiftsure and French privateer, 36—Amelia and Aréthuse, ibid.—Bonne Citoyenne and Hornet, 45—Peacock and Hornet, 46—Shannon and Chesapeake, 50—Alexandria and President, 70—Dominica and Decatur, 74—Boxer and Enterprise, 75—Pelican and Argus, 78—Boat attacks, &c., in Chesapeake bay, 83—Capture of the Lottery schooner, ibid.—Lieutenant Polkinghorne at the Rappahannock, 84—Rear-admiral Cockburn at Frenchtown, &c., 85—Capture of Surveyor schooner, 90—Junon and American gun-boats, ibid.—Unsuccessful attack on Craney island, 91—British at Hampton, 94—Rear-admiral Cockburn at Ocracoke, 95—Capture of Asp, 96—Martin and

vi   CONTENTS.

American gun-boats in the Delaware, 97 — Valiant and Acasta with the United States and Macedonian, 99—Attempt to destroy Ramillies by an explosion vessel, 100—British and Americans on Canadian lakes, 101—Operations on lake Ontario, ibid.—Same on lake Erie, ibid.—Captain Barclay and Commodore Perry, 109—Captain Everard on la e Champlain, 115.

1814.

BRITISH AND FRENCH FLEETS, 116—State of the British navy, ibid.—Sir Edward Pellew, and the Baron Cosmao-Kerjulien, 117—Boyne and Romulus, 118—Concluding operations in the Adriatic, 119—Surrender of Cattaro, Ragusa, &c., ibid.—Also of Spezzia and Genoa, ibid.—Passage of the Adour and peace with France, 120.

LIGHT SQUADRONS AND SINGLE SHIPS, 122—Capture of the Iphigénie and Alcmène, ibid.—Severn with Etoile and Sultane, 124—Creole and Astrea with Etoile and Sultane, ibid.—Hebrus and Etoile, 128—Niger and Tagus with Cérès, 131—Eurotas and Clorinde, 133—Primrose and Marlborough packet, 142—Majestic with Atalante and Terpsichore, 144—Loire and President, 147—Phœbe and Essex, 150—Orpheus and Frolic, 156—Epervier and Peacock, 158—Reindeer and Wasp, 161—Avon and Wasp, 165—Landrail and Syren, 167—Ballahou and Perry, ibid.—Boat attacks, &c., in Chesapeake bay, 168—Captain Barrie and Commodore Barney's flotilla, ibid.—Rear-admiral Cockburn at Leonard's town, 171—At Nominy ferry, &c. ibid.—Defensive preparations at Washington, 174—Destruction of Commodore Barney's flotilla, 175—Battle of Bladensburg, 177—Capture of Washington, 179—Captain Gordon at Alexandria, 181—Death of Sir Peter Parker, 187—Attack on Baltimore, ibid.—Sir Thomas Hardy and Commodore Decatur, 193—Captain Coote at Pettipague, 196—Lieutenant Garland at Wareham, ibid.—Pique and Constitution, 199—Junon and Tenedos with Constitution, 200—Expedition to the Penobscot, 201—British and Americans on Canadian lakes, 202—Operations on lake Ontario, 204—Attack on Oswego, ibid.—On vessels at Sandy creek, 206—Operations on Lake Huron, 208—Capture of schooners Tigress and Scorpion, ibid.—Capture of schooners Somers and Ohio on lake Erie, 210—British and Americans on lake Champlain, 212—British boats and General Armstrong privateer, 223.

1815.

BRITISH AND FRENCH FLEETS, 225—State of the British navy, ibid.—Buonaparte's return from Elba, 226—His surrender, and conveyance to St. Helena, 227—Rivoli attacks and captures Melpomène, ibid.—Pilot engages Légère, ibid.—Proceedings at Martinique, 229.

LIGHT SQUADRONS AND SINGLE SHIPS, 230—Expedition to New Orleans, ibid.—Attack on Fort Bowyer and destruction of Hermes, 231—Captain

CONTENTS. vii

Lockyer and American gun-boats, 233—Boat attacks on coast of Georgia, 235—Rear-admiral Cockburn at Cumberland island, 236—Endymion and President, 239—St. Lawrence and Chasseur, 247—Levant and Cyane with Constitution, 248—Third chase and escape of the Constitution, 252— Penguin and Hornet, 261—Nautilus and Peacock, 266—Piratical vessels, 269—Cameleon and Tripoli, 274.

1816.

STATE OF THE BRITISH NAVY, 276—American expedition to Algiers, ibid. ENGLAND AND THE BARBARY STATES, 278—Battle of Algiers, 279.

1817 to 1820.

STATE OF THE BRITISH NAVY, 292—New classification of the ships, ibid.— British and American 74s, 293—Sir Robert Sepping's improvements, &c., 298—New plan of ship-building by Captain Hayes, 300

1824.

THE BURMESE WAR, 302.

1827.

THE BATTLE OF NAVARIN, 358.

APPENDIX 381
    Annual Abstracts 397
    Notes to Annual Abstracts 403

DIAGRAM.

Action of the Shannon and Chesapeake 60

NAVAL HISTORY OF GREAT BRITAIN.

BRITISH AND FRENCH FLEETS.

Owing to a deficiency of seamen and the disaffected state of those that remained, the Scheldt fleet, numerically strong as it was, gave, during this year, very little trouble to those that blockaded it; nor did the Brest squadron, or fleet, as it now might almost be called, make any attempt to put to sea. On the 27th of August the newly-formed port of Cherbourg was opened, with great pomp, under the eyes of the empress Marie-Louise; and on the 12th of October the 80-gun ship Zélandais, the first line-of-battle ship constructed at Cherbourg, was launched: another was also getting ready with all possible despatch. Since the 28th of May the French 74-gun ship Régulus, from Rochefort, had anchored in the river of Bordeaux; and, according to the French accounts, she was the first ship of her class that had ever entered the Gironde.

Toulon was now the only French port to be looked to for any operations of importance between the fleets of England and France. The British Mediterranean fleet remained in the able hands of Vice-admiral Sir Edward Pellew, and the fleet in Toulon was still under the command of Vice-admiral the Comte Emeriau. The flag of the latter was flying on board the 130-gun ship Impérial, and the flag of the second in command, the Baron Cosmao-Kerjulien, on board the Wagram, of the same force. On the 15th of August the 130-gun ship Héros was launched; making the sixth three-decker in the port. Not being able to discover the launching of any three-decker in Toulon named Impérial, we consider that the Austerlitz had recently changed her name; especially as, at the latter end of 1812, the flag of Vice-admiral Emeriau was flying on board of her. The addition of the Héros makes the total number of line-of-battle ships 21; all, except the Héros and Montebello, at anchor in the inner and outer roads, in company with ten 40-gun frigates and one 20-gun corvette. On the stocks there were two 80s, and one 74, the latter in a very forward state.

Although a dearth of seamen, owing to the draughts sent away to the army, prevented the Toulon fleet, as a body, from making any serious attempt to put to sea during the year 1813, large divisions of it, when the wind would serve also for returning, frequently weighed from the road, and exercised in manœuvring between the Capes Brun and Carquaranne. In the latter part of October the British fleet was blown off its station by a succession of hard gales, which lasted eight days; and it was only on the evening of the 4th of November, that the inshore squadron, consisting of the 74-gun ships Scipion, Mulgrave, Pembroke, and Armada, Captains Henry Heathcote, Thomas James Maling, James Brisbane, and Charles Grant arrived off Cape Sicie. The main body of the British fleet at this time consisted of the

Gun-ship.		
120 { Caledonia	{	Vice-admiral (r.) Sir Edward Pellew, Bart. Rear-admiral (w.) Israel Pellew. Captain Jeremiah Coghlan.
Hibernia		,, Thomas Gordon Caulfield.
112 San-Josef	{	Rear-admiral (b.) Sir Richard King, Bart. Captain William Stewart.
100 Royal George		,, T. Fras. Ch. Mainwaring.
98 { Boyne		,, George Burlton.
Prince of Wales		,, John Erskine Douglas.
Union		,, Robert Rolles.
Barfleur		,, John Maitland.
74 Pompée		,, Sir James Athol Wood.

On the 5th, at 9 h. 30 m. A.M., Vice-admiral Comte Emeriau, in the Impérial, with, according to the French accounts, 12, and according to Sir Edward Pellew's letter, 14 sail of the line, six frigates, and the Victorie schooner, got under way with a strong east-north-east wind, and stood to the usual spot for exercise. Captain Heathcote's squadron was off Cape Sicie; and the main body of the British fleet, consisting, as already shown, of nine sail of the line, had just hove in sight from the southward, standing under close-reefed topsails to reconnoitre the port. At 11 h. 30 m. A.M., just as the French advanced squadron, of five sail of the line and four frigates, under Rear-admiral the Baron Cosmao, had got a little to the south-east of Cape Sepet, the wind suddenly shifted to north-west. This unexpected occurrence, while it set the French ships to trimming sails to get back into port, afforded to the leading British ships a prospect of cutting off some of the leewardmost of the former, the names of which were as follows:—

Gun-ship.		
130	Wagram	{ Rear-admiral le Baron Cosmao-Kerjulien. { Captain François Legras.
74	{ Agamemnon { Ulm { Magnanime { Borée	,, Jean-Marie Letellier. ,, C.-J.-César Chaunay-Duclos. ,, Laurent Tourneur. ,, Jean Michel Mahé.
Gun-frigate.		
40	{ Pauline { Melpomène { Pénélope { Galatée	,, Etienne-Stanislaus Simiot. ,, Charles Beville. ,, Edme-Louis Simonot. ,, Jean-Bapt. Bonafoux-Murat.

The British in-shore squadron immediately stood for the French rear; and at 34 minutes past noon the leading British ship, the Scipion, opened a fire from her larboard guns upon the nearest French ships, which were then standing on the opposite or starboard tack; as did also, in succession, the Mulgrave, Pembroke, Armada, and Pompée (who had just joined), as they followed the Scipion in line astern. At 40 minutes past noon, having passed over, the Scipion wore, to bring her starboard broadside to bear; and in two minutes afterwards the first French shot that took effect carried away part of the Pembroke's wheel. The five British 74s, having wore round and come to, continued the cannonade with their starboard broadsides, and were then not more than a mile distant from the shore near Cape Sepet.

At 45 minutes past noon the advanced squadron filled and stood on; and at 1 P.M. the Caledonia, Boyne, and San-Josef, who were far ahead of the remainder of their fleet, stood in-shore athwart the bows of the former. In four minutes the Caledonia opened a heavy fire from her larboard guns upon the sternmost French ship, the Wagram; who, being then on the starboard tack, returned the fire with her larboard guns. The Boyne and San-Josef, as they arrived in succession, also got into action with the French rear. Having reached the wake of the Wagram, the Caledonia wore, and came to on the starboard tack, still engaging; but the French ships, having the weather-gage, in a few minutes got out of gun-shot, and the firing, in which the batteries had slightly participated, ceased.

The casualties on either side, arising from this skirmish, were not of any serious amount. The Caledonia received one shot through her mainmast and three or four in her hull; had a shroud and some backstays cut, and her launch and barge destroyed, with three seamen slightly wounded. One unlucky shot, which fell on the San-Josef's poop, struck off the leg of each of two fine young officers, Lieutenant of marines William Clarke, and midshipman William Cuppage, and slightly wounded one marine and one seaman. The Boyne and Scipion had each one man wounded slightly; and the latter had another killed by an accident. The Pembroke had three men slightly wounded by shot, and the Pompée two men slightly burnt by accident; total, 12 wounded by the enemy's fire, and one killed and two slightly wounded by accident. The Armada escaped without any loss, but one of the enemy's shot passed through the bows of her launch and lodged in the booms.

The Agamemnon appears to have been the greatest sufferer among the French ships: she had her masts, rigging, and sails a good deal damaged, and received several shot in her hull, by which nine men were slightly wounded. The Wagram also suffered, but in a less degree, and had only two men wounded. A shot, that entered the roundhouse of the Borée, wounded two seamen, and carried away the wheel; a splinter from which slightly wounded Captain Mahé. The Ulm had one man severely and another slightly wounded. Of the four advanced frigates, the Pénélope and Melpomène were the most engaged: both received damage in their sails, rigging, and hull, and the latter had one man wounded; making the total loss on the French side 17 wounded. Leaving a small squadron off Toulon, Sir Edward Pellew soon afterwards steered for Minorca, and on the 15th of the same month anchored in Port Mahon. On the 5th of December the French fleet in Toulon received an accession of force in the new 74-gun ship Colosse; and the close of the year left Comte Emeriau still at his anchorage in the road.

Light Squadrons and Single Ships.

On the 14th of March, Lieutenant Francis Banks, of the Blazer gun-brig, commanding the small British force stationed off the island of Heligoland, having received information of the distressed state of the French at Cuxhaven and of the entrance of the Russians into Hamburgh, took the Brevdrageren gun-brig, Lieutenant Thomas Barker Devon, under his orders, and proceeded to the river Elbe, with the hope of intercepting such of the enemy's gun-vessels as might attempt to make their escape.

Early on the morning of the 15th the two brigs entered the river, and found the French flotilla of 20 gun-vessels stationed at Cuxhaven in the act of being destroyed. On the 16th, by invitation from the shore, Lieutenant Banks landed, and with a detachment of 32 troops, which he had embarked at Heligoland, took possession of the batteries of Cuxhaven, and on the next day concluded a treaty with the civil authorities, by which it was agreed that the British flag should be hoisted in conjunction with the colours of Hamburgh.

On the 20th, while the two gun-brigs were lying at anchor off Cuxhaven, Lieutenant Devon volunteered, with a boat from each brig, to go up the river in quest of a privateer of which information had just been received. Accordingly, in the night, taking with him the Brevdrageren's gig, containing a midshipman and eight men, and the six-oared cutter of the Blazer, containing 11 men commanded by Mr. William Dunbar, her master, Lieutenant Devon proceeded to execute the service he had undertaken.

On the 21st, at daylight, the two boats found themselves off the Danish port of Brunsbuttel, situated about 30 miles up the river, and close to two large galliots at anchor. Under the supposition that these were merchant-vessels, Lieutenant Devon, followed by the cutter at some distance, advanced to examine them. On the near approach of the gig, the two vessels were found to be gun-boats; the nearest of which instantly hoisted Danish colours, hailed, and opened a fire, which, luckily for the people in the gig, passed over their heads. In this critical situation, Lieutenant Devon considered that there was no safety but in resolutely boarding. He accordingly dashed alongside, and, in the smoke of the second discharge, which passed as harmlessly as the first, and amidst a degree of confusion among the Danes caused by the explosion of some cartridges Lieutenant Devon, his brother, midshipman Frederick Devon (a youth only 12 years of age), and eight men, captured, without the slightest casualty, the Danish gun-boat Jonge-Troutman, commanded by Lieutenant Lutkin of the Danish navy, and mounting two long 18-pounders and three 12-pounder carronades, with a crew of 26 men; of whom two were wounded.

Mr. Dunbar arriving up, the prisoners were secured under the hatches, the cable cut, and sail made after the other galliot, the commander of which, on seeing the fate of his commodore, had cut and steered for Brunsbuttel, about four miles distant. The prize-galliot soon gained upon her late consort; and, the wind being light, the Blazer's cutter was despatched to cut off the fugitive from her port. This Mr. Dunbar gallantly accomplished, and with his 11 men captured, without opposition, the Danish gun-boat Liebe, of the same force as the Jonge-Troutman, and commanded by Lieutenant Writt, also of the Danish navy. This, it must be owned, was altogether a very gallant exploit, and Lieutenant Devon well merited the praises that were bestowed upon him for his conduct on the occasion.

Early in the month of October, Captain Arthur Farquhar, of the 18-pounder 36-gun frigate Desirée, arrived at Heligoland, and assumed the command of the British naval force on that station. By this time the French had regained possession of Cuxhaven. After performing several important services up the Weser and Ems, Captain Farquhar, on the 30th of November, with a small squadron of gun-brigs and gun-boats, successfully co-operated with a Russian force in an attack upon the heavy batteries that defended Cuxhaven. Crossing the Elbe, Captain Farquhar afterwards ascended to Gluckstadt, and co-operated with a detachment of the Crown Prince of Sweden's army in reducing that important fortress. On the 5th of January, 1814, after an investment of 16, and a bombardment of six days, Gluckstadt surrendered by capitulation.

The British squadron which, besides the Desirée, was employed on the occasion, appears to have been, the 10-gun schooner-sloop Shamrock, Captain John Marshall; brig-sloop (late gun-brig) Hearty, Captain James Rose; gun-brigs Blazer, Lieutenant Francis Banks; and Redbreast, Lieutenant Sir George Morat Keith; and gun-boats, No. 1, Lieutenant David Hanmer; No. 2, master's mate Thomas Riches; No. 3, Lieutenant Charles Henry Seale; No. 4, Lieutenant Andrew Tullock; No. 5, midshipman John Hallowes; No. 8, Lieutenant Richard Roper; No. 10, Lieutenant Francis Darby Romney: and No. 12, Lieutenant John Henderson. Captain Farquhar, in his despatch, speaks also in high terms of Captain Andrew Green, who commanded a party of seamen and marines on shore, and of his assistants, Lieutenants Charles Haultain and John Archer, and midshipman George Richardson; likewise of Lieutenant Joshua Kneeshaw. The loss sustained by the flotilla amounted to three men killed and 16 wounded, including Captain Rose, midshipman Richard Hunt, and captain's clerk John Riches.

On the 16th of December, 1812, the French 40-gun frigate Gloire, Captain Albin-René Roussin, sailed from Havre, with a very strong south-east wind, which carried her as far as the

Lizard, and there left her, on the afternoon of the 17th, entirely becalmed. On the 18th, at daylight, the Gloire found herself nearly in the midst of nine vessels, the greater part of them evidently merchantmen. Two of the number, however, were vessels-of-war: the nearest was the British 18-gun ship-sloop Albacore (twenty-six 32, and eight 12 pounder carronades and two long sixes, with a crew of 121 men and boys), Captain Henry Thomas Davies; and, about four miles to the westward of her, was the 14-gun brig-schooner Pickle, Lieutenant William Figg. At 8 A.M. the Gloire, who had been standing on the starboard tack, wore with a light air of wind, and edged away for the Albacore, then bearing from north-east by north. Each ship soon ascertained that the other was an enemy; and at 9 A.M. the Gloire hauled to the wind on the larboard tack, and made all sail to escape. Judging by this, probably, that the apparent French 40-gun frigate was an armée en flûte or large store-ship, Captain Davies crowded sail in chase, followed at some distance by the Pickle; the latter and the Albacore making repeated signals, to apprise the vessels in sight of the presence of an enemy.

At 10 h. 12 m. A.M., having by carrying down the breeze arrived within carronade range on the French frigate's weather-quarter, the Albacore opened her fire; whereupon the Gloire hoisted French colours and fired in return, hauling up a little, to bestow a raking broadside upon her unequal antagonist. To avoid this the Albacore tacked. The breeze soon afterwards fell to nearly a calm; and at 11 A.M., finding her antagonist much too strong for her, the Albacore discontinued the action, with her fore spring-stay shot away, her rigging a good deal damaged, and, what was the worst of all, with the loss of one lieutenant (William Harman) killed, and six or seven men wounded. Strange to say, the French frigate herself did not seem disposed to renew the action, but wore and made all sail to the westward.

At 1 P.M., the Pickle having closed and a light breeze having sprung up from the southward, the Albacore again made sail, and at 3 P.M. was joined in the chase by the 12-gun brig-sloop (late gun-brig) Borer, Captain Richard Coote and 4-gun cutter Landrail, Lieutenant John Hill. At 5 P.M. the Albacore began firing her bow-chasers; as, on coming up, did two out of her three (for the Landrail to have fired her 12-pounder carronades would have been a farce) formidable consorts. To this alarming cannonade, the Gloire replied with her stern-chasers, and continued running from the "escadrille," as if each of her four pursuers had been a frigate like herself. Thus the chase continued, but without any firing after 7 p.m., until midnight on the 19th; when this dastardly French frigate, who, it appears, did not have a man hurt on the occasion, had run herself completely out of sight. Captain Davies merited great praise for his gallantry and perseverance; and there cannot be a doubt that, by the boldness of the Albacore in chasing and attacking the Gloire, several merchant-vessels were saved from capture.

On the following day, the 20th, the Gloire captured the Spy armed store-ship, from Halifax, Nova Scotia, and, disarming her, sent her to England as a cartel. Captain Roussin then steered for the coast of Spain and Portugal, and on the 28th, off the rock of Lisbon, was chased for a short time by two ships-of-war. On the 1st of February he arrived to windward of Barbadoes, and returned soon afterwards to Europe. On the 25th, in the chops of the Channel, the wind blowing a gale with a raging sea, the Gloire fell in with the British 14-gun brig Linnet, Lieutenant John Tracey. Bearing up under her foresail and close-reefed maintopsail, the Gloire, at 2 h. 30 m. p.m., arrived within hail of the Linnet and ordered her to strike. Instead of doing so, the brig boldly crossed the bows of the French frigate, and, regardless of a heavy fire which the latter commenced, got to windward of her. As the Gloire out-sailed the Linnet on every point, all that Lieutenant Tracey could now do, was to endeavour to out-manœuvre her. This he did by making short tacks; well aware that, owing to her great length, the frigate could not come about so quickly as a brig of less than 200 tons. In practising this manœuvre, the Linnet had to cross the bows of the Gloire a second and a third time (the second time so near as to carry away the frigate's jib-boom), and was all the while exposed to her fire; but which, owing to the ill-direction of the shot from the roughness of the sea, did no great execution. At length, at 3 h. 30 m. p.m., having succeeded in cutting away some of the Linnet's rigging, the Gloire got nearly alongside of her; but the resolute lieutenant would not yet haul down the British colours. The Linnet suddenly bore up athwart the hawse of the frigate; and the Gloire, had she not as suddenly luffed up, must, Captain Roussin says, have passed completely over the brig. Being now under the guns of the Gloire, two of the latter's broadsides carried away the fore-yard, gaff, and bowsprit of the Linnet, and compelled the brig to surrender. Such seamanship and intrepidity, on the part of

Lieutenant Tracey, show where the Gloire would have been had he encountered her in a frigate. To do M. Roussin justice, he complimented his prisoner highly for the skill and perseverance he had shown; and all must allow, that the captain of the Gloire was an excellent judge of the best means to effect an escape.

On the 27th the Gloire and her prize anchored at Brest; and Lieutenant Tracey and his officers and crew remained as prisoners until the spring of the ensuing year. On the 31st of May, 1814, a court-martial was held on board the Gladiator at Portsmouth, to try the late officers and crew of the Linnet for her loss. On that occasion, Lieutenant Tracey received, with an honourable acquittal, the most unqualified praise for his conduct; and in 11 days afterwards, as we see by the list, was deservedly made a commander.

On the 17th of April, in the morning, the British 16-gun brig-sloop Mutine, Captain Nevinson De Courcy, cruising in the bay of Biscay, discovered and chased a strange ship on her lee-bow. At 2 P.M. the ship, which was the Invincible privateer, of Bayonne, Captain Martin Jortis, mounting 16 guns (twelve French 18-pounder carronades and four long sixes), with a crew on board of 86 men, partly Americans, hoisted French colours, and commenced a fire from her stern-guns; which disabling the Mutine in her sails and rigging, occasioned her to drop astern. The Mutine immediately commenced refitting herself, and at 8 h. 40 m. again arrived within gun-shot; when the Invincible hoisted a light and opened a fire from her broadside. In this way the running fight was maintained until 10 h. 45 m. P.M.; when, the ship having had her maintopgallantmast and jib shot away, the Mutine was enabled to close. Still it was not until after a spirited resistance of 50 minutes, which made it 11 h. 30 m. P.M., that the Invincible hauled down her colours. The Mutine is represented to have had two men wounded in the action, but the loss, if any, sustained by the Invincible appears to have been omitted in Captain De Courcy's letter.

On the 9th of September, at 3 P.M., the British schooner Alphea, of eight 18-pounder carronades, and 41 men and boys, Lieutenant Thomas William Jones, fell in with and chased the French 14-gun privateer schooner Renard, Captain De Roux, belonging to Cherbourg, and acknowledged to have had on board a crew of 50 men. At midnight the Alphea commenced firing her chase-guns; and at 1 A.M. on the 10th a close and spirited action commenced. After a while, the Alphea, by the calm and the heavy swell that prevailed, became forced under the bows of the Renard. The crew of the privateer immediately threw into the Alphea several hand-grenades, and made an attempt to board, but were gallantly repulsed by the crew of the British schooner; which latter then poured in a most destructive fire of grape-shot, that swept the whole of the Renard's forecastle. A second boarding attempt was made, and the Frenchmen were again beaten off.

The two schooners soon afterwards burst the grapplings by which they had been held together, and separated to a short distance; both still maintaining a furious cannonade. At 3 h. 30 m. A.M., owing in a great measure to the number of hand-grenades which had been thrown into her, the Alphea blew up, and along with her, perished the whole of her gallant crew. Three or four men were seen on a piece of the wreck, but the Renard having had her jolly-boat sunk by shot, as it was towing astern, and her launch cut to pieces as it lay on the booms, could render no assistance; nor could the poor fellows find their way to the privateer, although repeatedly hailed to do so, as they had lost their eyesight by the explosion.

The loss on board the Renard, as acknowledged by her officers, amounted to five men killed and 31 badly wounded, including the captain with the loss of an arm, and three of his lieutenants. There was also a fourth-lieutenant, who took the command when Captain Le Roux was wounded. It is not unlikely, therefore, that the "50 men" refer to the sailors only, and that, officers included, the Renard had from 70 to 80 men. As mounting "14 guns," this schooner must have been about 200 tons measurement; whereas the Alphea, one of the Bermudian vessels, was only 111 tons. The execution admitted to have been done by the Alphea to her antagonist was highly creditable to the gunnery of the British crew, and renders it probable that, had not the fatal accident happened, the Alphea would have made a prize of the Renard, although the latter was so much superior to her in force. It was, indeed, a lamentable occurrence; and, to heighten the misfortune, Lieutenant Jones was a very deserving officer.

In the early part of October the French brig-corvette Flibustier, mounting fourteen 24-pounder carronades and two long sixes or eights, and commanded by Lieutenant de vaisseau Jean-Jacques-Léonore Daniel, lay at St.-Jean-de-Luz, about three leagues north-east of the bar of Bayonne, watching an opportunity to put to sea, with treasure, arms, ammunition, salt provisions, and a few troops for the garrison of Santona. The near approach of the Marquis of Wellington's army at last made it necessary to move; and, taking advantage of the dark and stormy state of the weather, the Flibustier, at midnight, on the 12th, attended three "trincadores," or armed fishing-boats, weighed and stood alongshore to the south-west. At daylight on the 13th the French brig, then lying becalmed close under the heights near the mouth of the Bayonne river, was seen and chased by the British schooner Telegraph, of twelve 12-pounder carronades, Lieutenant Timothy Scriven, also by the 18-gun brig-sloop Challenger, Captain Frederick Vernon, and 12-gun brig Constant, Lieutenant John Stokes; the latter about six, the former upwards of eight miles distant in the offing.

Favoured by a partial breeze, the Telegraph rapidly approached the Flibustier, who had by this time anchored under the distant protection of some batteries; and at 6 h. 45 m. P.M. the schooner commenced cannonading the brig in a raking position ahead. The Flibustier returned the Telegraph's broadside with such of her guns as would bear. The action continued in this way until about 7 P.M.; when finding the two British brigs in the offing approaching to take a part in the combat, the French brig set herself on fire. The schooner continued discharging her guns for about half an hour longer. Lieutenant Scriven then ceased firing, and sent his boats to endeavour to save the vessel, whose crew had already reached the shore in their boats. The schooner's boat got on board; and so, it is believed, did some boats from the Challenger and Constant, but too late to save the Flibustier; which at about 8 h. 10 m. P.M. exploded, in sight of the English and French armies encamped on the east side of the Adour. The Telegraph had not a man hurt, nor, as it appears, a spar or a shroud shot away.

For his gallantry in advancing to attack a force so much superior to his own, Lieutenant Scriven was promoted to the rank of commander; and the Telegraph, by his continuing to be captain of her, became a sloop-of-war. Lest we should appear to have underrated the force of the Flibustier, we are bound to state, that the official account of her destruction assigns her a force of 16 carronades and two nines, with a brass howitzer, and four brass 3-pounders. The swivels and howitzer she may have mounted; but we doubt if the Flibustier carried more than 14 carronades, chiefly because we know not of a single instance (the Abeille, as already stated, had been a foreign-built vessel[1]),

[1] See vol. v., p. 253.

in which a regular French brig-corvette mounted more than 16 guns, similar to the Oreste, and a great many others that have appeared in these pages. Moreover, very little time was allowed for the British to take an accurate account of the force of the Flibustier.

On the 30th of September the two Franco-Batavian 40-gun frigates Trave and Weser, Captains Jacob Van-Maren and Paul-Roelof Cantz-Laar, put to sea from the Texel, on a cruise off the Western Isles. On the 16th of October a violent gale of wind dismasted both frigates, and separated them from each other. On the 18th, towards 1 A.M., latitude 47° 30' north, longitude 9° 18' west, the British 18-gun brig-sloop Scylla, Captain Colin Macdonald, fell in with the Weser, then with the loss of her main and mizen masts and foretopmast, steering east by north, on her way to Brest. After hailing the frigate several times, the Scylla received a broadside from her. On this the brig made sail ahead. At daylight both vessels hoisted their colours; but Captain Macdonald judged it not prudent to attack a ship that, although crippled in her masts, was so decidedly his superior in guns and men, especially as the Scylla might herself get crippled, and, in the severe state of the weather, be thereby prevented from keeping sight of the frigate; a service on which the brig now assiduously employed herself.

On the 19th, at daylight, having passed the night in burning blue-lights, firing guns, and throwing up rockets, to indicate that she was in chase of an enemy, the Scylla found herself alone, the thick weather obscuring the Weser from her view. Steering, during that day and night, a course deemed the most likely to rejoin the French frigate, the Scylla, at daylight on the morning of the 20th, fell in with the British 18-gun brig-sloop Royalist, Captain James John Gordon Bremer. The latter, volunteering, the two brigs, with the wind from the south-west, bore away to seek and engage the enemy, then supposed to be in the east-north-east. At 9 h. 30 m. A.M. the Weser was discovered in the north-east and chased; latitude at noon 48° 28 north, longitude 6° 18' west. At 3 h. 30 m. P.M. the two brigs opened their fire, the Royalist stationing herself on the frigate's starboard-bow, and the Scylla on her starboard-quarter. At 5 P.M., being much cut up in their sails and rigging, and the Scylla having her mainmast shot through, and the Royalist five men badly wounded, the two brigs hauled off to repair their damages.

Since 1 h. 30 m. P.M. a sail had been observed to leeward.

This was the British 74-gun ship Rippon, Captain Sir Christopher Cole, using her utmost efforts to take a part in the action. Captain Macdonald now detached Captain Bremer to reconnoitre the ship to leeward. The Royalist accordingly bore up, and the Scylla continued following the French frigate. On the 21st, at a little before daylight, the Royalist spoke the Rippon, and again made all sail on a wind to close the Scylla and frigate. At 9 h. 30 m. A.M. the Scylla, taking a raking position, recommenced firing at the Weser; and the Royalist placing herself on the latter's larboard-bow, soon joined in the action. In 10 minutes, finding that the Rippon was nearly within gun-shot on her lee-quarter, and that all hopes of escape were at an end, the Weser fired her larboard-guns at the Royalist, and, standing on towards the Rippon, hauled down her colours. A boat from the Royalist immediately boarded the French frigate; and the Rippon, on arriving up, took the prize in tow, and conducted her to Falmouth.

In this creditable performance on the part of the two brigs, the Scylla had two seamen wounded, and the Royalist two seamen killed, her first-lieutenant (James Waring), master (William Wilson, severely), five seamen, one marine, and one boy wounded; total, on board the two brigs, two killed and 11 wounded. As a proof that the carronades of the brigs had produced some effect, the Weser, out of a crew of 340 men and boys, had four men killed and 15 wounded.

On the morning of the same day on which the Weser was captured, the British brig-sloop Achates, of fourteen 24-pounder carronades and two sixes, Captain Isaac Hawkins Morrison, standing to the south-south-east with the wind at south-west, fell in with the Trave, upon her weather-beam. The Achates immediately made sail in chase, and, as soon as she had forereached sufficiently, wore and stood for the French frigate. At 7 h. 50 m. A.M. the Achates gallantly engaged the Trave in passing, and received in return a fire that much injured her sails and rigging. At 8 A.M. a large ship was discovered bearing down. The Achates immediately hauled towards her and made the private signal; but the stranger, instead of answering it, tacked from the brig and hauled close to the wind. In the mean time the Trave had bore up to the eastward. At noon, latitude 46° 37' north, longitude 7° 26' west, the Achates was again near enough to exchange shots with the Trave, and continued engaging in an advantageous position on her quarter, until about 8 P.M.; when dark and squally weather concealed the Trave from her view. In this very spirited as well as skilful attack, Captain Morrison had the good fortune not to lose a man; but the fire of the Achates had wounded two seamen belonging to the Trave.

Favoured by the darkness, the French frigate continued her course without further interruption, until, on the afternoon of the 23rd, she encountered the British 18-pounder 36-gun frigate Andromache, Captain George Tobin. At 3 h. 30 m. p.m. the Trave opened a fire from her stern-chasers, but the Andromache did not return it until 4 h. 15 m. p.m.; by which time she had gained a position on the French frigate's weather-quarter. The fire which the Andromache now commenced was so close and well directed, that in a quarter of an hour the Trave hauled down her colours. Indeed, had the latter been an efficient instead of a dismasted ship, further resistance would have been vain, as the British 24-pounder 38-gun frigate Eurotas, Captain John Phillimore, was approaching in the north-east. Out of her 321 men and boys, the Trave had one seaman killed, her captain, second-lieutenant, two midshipmen (one mortally), and 24 seamen wounded. The Andromache's loss consisted of only two wounded, but one was her first-lieutenant, Thomas Dickinson, severely.

Both the Weser and Trave, being new frigates, one of 1081, the other of 1076 tons, were added to the British navy. It was considered rather singular, that frigates of that size should have been armed upon the quarter-deck and forecastle with carronades of so light and ineffective a caliber as 18-pounders. Of these, each frigate mounted 16, making, with her 28 long 18-pounders, 44 guns.

On the 9th of October, at 8 h. 30 m. a.m., the Owers light bearing north-north-east, the British bomb-vessel Thunder, Captain Watkin Owen Pell, being on her way from Spithead to Woolwich, observed a large armed lugger to windward under easy sail. His vessel being of a class likely to effect more by decoying than chasing an enemy, Captain Pell altered his course towards the shore and took in his studding-sails. The bait took, and the lugger, which was the Neptune, of Dunkerque, mounting 16 guns, with a crew on board of 65 men, bore up in chase. At 10 h. 30 m. a.m., having arrived on the Thunder's larboard-quarter, the French captain hailed the supposed merchantman to bring to, and strike.

With her numerous crew all ready, the Neptune then put up her helm, to lay her anticipated prize on board. The Thunder at the same moment put her helm down, and had barely time to fire her four carronades and a volley of musketry, when the lugger fell on board. A portion of the British crew were on her decks in a trice; and, after a severe conflict, in which four Frenchmen were killed and 10 wounded, including one mortally and five very severely, the Thunder made a prize of the Neptune, and that with so slight a loss as two men wounded.

On the 1st of November in the morning, St. Vallery on the coast of France bearing south-south-east distant five miles, the 16-gun brig-sloop Snap, Captain William Bateman Dashwood, discovered five French armed luggers, three in the north-west close to windward, and two considerably to leeward. The Snap immediately wore and stood for the three weathermost luggers, but Captain Dashwood had very soon the mortification to observe their separation, and then their escape by superior sailing. At 9 A.M. the Snap bore up in pursuit of the two leewardmost vessels, and after using various deceptions, enticed one alongside. The British brig immediately opened her fire, and, at the end of a 10 minutes' cannonade, captured, without the loss of a man, the French privateer Lion, of Boulogne, mounting 16 guns, with 69 men; of whom the captain and four men were killed, and six severely wounded.

The British squadron, stationed off the north coast of Spain to assist the patriots, was under the command of Captain Sir George Ralph Collier, of the 38-gun frigate Surveillante. In the early part of May the force detached off the port of Castro de Urdeales consisted of the brig-sloops Lyra, Captain Robert Bloye, and Royalist and Sparrow, Captains James John Gordon Bremer and Joseph Needham Tayler. Although everything was done by the three commanders and their respective officers and crews, in landing guns and bringing them into operation, the French force in the neighbourhood was too powerful to be resisted. By great exertions the garrison, consisting of about 1150 men, was embarked on board the brigs and conveyed to Bermeo. The loss sustained by the little squadron, in the service it had performed, amounted to 10 wounded, including Lieutenant Samuel Kentish and midshipman Charles Thomas Sutton (leg amputated) of the Royalist.

The principal object now was to blockade the port, and prevent the French garrison from getting any supplies. This was so effectually done, that on the 22nd of June, after committing upon the inhabitants enormities of the most revolting description, the French evacuated the town and retired to Santona.

The Sparrow having just at this moment arrived off the port, Captain Tayler very properly garrisoned the castle; and such was the precipitate flight of the French commandant, on observing the approach of the British brig, that he fled without destroying the artillery or powder.

On the 10th of July, at 10 A.M., the breaching batteries, raised by the army of General Graham on the Chope sand-hills, were opened against the walls of St. Sebastian; and a detachment of seamen was landed from Sir George Collier's squadron to co-operate in the attack, under the orders of the first-lieutenant of the Surveillante, Dowell O'Reilly. The loss sustained by this detachment, up to the evening of the 21st of July, amounted to two seamen killed, Lieutenant Robert Graham Dunlop, and five seamen wounded. The squadron stationed off St. Sebastian consisted, besides the Surveillante, Lyra, and Sparrow, of the 38-gun frigates Révolutionnaire and Présidente, Captains John Charles Woolcombe and Francis Mason, brig-sloops Beagle, Despatch, and Challenger, Captains John Smith, James Galloway, and Frederick Vernon, schooners Holly and Juniper, and two gun-boats.

On the 31st of August two divisions of boats from the squadron, placed under the orders of Captains Galloway and Bloye, was sent to make a demonstration on the back of the rock of St. Sebastian. The plan succeeded, and a large proportion of the garrison was diverted from the defence of the breach which, on the preceding day, had been made in the walls. The men-of-war brigs also weighed with a light breeze, and stood into the harbour. At 11 A.M. the assault by the breach took place, and at 1 h. 30 m. P.M. the town was entered and possessed; but the citadel still held out. Captain Smith of the Beagle was slightly wounded, also three or four of the seamen. On the 8th of September the breaching and mortar batteries opened a most ruinous fire upon the castle of La Motte, or citadel of St. Sebastian; and in a very short time General Rey, the governor, sent out a flag of truce to propose terms of capitulation, which were immediately agreed to. In addition to the ships already named, there were present co-operating in the attack, the 18-pounder 36-gun frigate Magicienne, Captain the Hon. William Gordon, and the gun-brig Constant, Lieutenant John Stokes. Among the naval officers who distinguished themselves on the occasion, Captain Sir George Collier names Lieutenant the Hon. James Arbuthnot of the Surveillante; also midshipmen Digby Marsh, George Harvey, Henry Bloye, and William Lawson.

On the 18th of March the British 38-gun frigate Undaunted, Captain Thomas Ussher, chased a tartan under the battery of Carri, situated about five leagues to the westward of Marseille. Light winds preventing the ship from getting up, Lieutenant Aaron Tozer offered his services to destroy the battery. The boats under his orders, assisted by Mr. Robert Clennan the master, acting Lieutenant Thomas Salkeld and Lieutenant of marines Harry Hunt, pushed off accordingly to execute the service. The British landed, and in a few minutes afterwards carried the battery, mounting four 24-pounders, a 6-pounder field-gun, and a 13-inch mortar; and this although the French troops were strongly posted behind palisadoes, and stood until the marines were in the act of charging bayonets, when they turned and suffered a severe loss. The guns at the battery were all destroyed, the tartan brought out, and the boats returned to the ship with no greater loss than two men killed and one wounded.

On the 30th, while the Undaunted was in company with the 38-gun frigate Volontaire, Captain and senior officer the Hon. Granville George Waldegrave, and the 18-gun brig-sloop Redwing, Captain Sir John Gordon Sinclair, 14 merchant-vessels were discovered at anchor in the harbour of Morgion, situated between Marseille and Toulon. Lieutenant Isaac Shaw, first of the Volontaire, assisted by Lieutenants of marines William Burton, and Harry Hunt, proceeded with the boats of the three ships, to endeavour to cut out the convoy.

On the 31st, in the morning, Lieutenant Shaw and his party landed at Sourion, and, marching over the hills at daylight, carried the two batteries of the place in the rear, after a partial resistance from 40 French troops stationed at them. Five 36-pounders in one battery, and two 24-pounders in the other, were thrown into the sea, one mortar well spiked, and all the ammunition destroyed. The boats, under Lieutenant Dey Richard Syer, although elsewhere opposed by two field-pieces, brought out 11 vessels, tartans and settees, laden with oil, and destroyed some others. The whole service was accomplished with so slight a loss as one marine killed, and two marines and two seamen wounded. The names of no other officers present, than those above given, appear in Captain Waldegrave's letter, except midshipman Charles Wyvill, on whom great praise is bestowed.

On the 2nd of May, Captain Robert Hussey Moubray, of the 74-gun ship Repulse, detached 100 marines from that ship, under Captain Edward Michael Ennis, along with the marines of the Volontaire and Undaunted, to destroy some newly-erected works in the vicinity of Morgion; while the boats of the squadron, under Lieutenant Isaac Shaw, first of the Volontaire, covered by the launches with their carronades and by the brig-sloop Redwing, brought out some vessels that were in the harbour. The detachment of marines landed, and drove a detachment of French troops to the heights in the rear of the harbour; where they were kept in check until the vessels were secured, and the batteries, on which were found nine gun-carriages and a 13-inch mortar, were blown up and destroyed. On this occasion Lieutenant Shaw was wounded; and in the boats two men were killed and three wounded. The vessels brought out were six in number, all laden, but small.

Between the 10th and 15th of May, through the judicious management of Captain Charles Napier of the 18-pounder 36-gun frigate Euryalus, the French coasting trade, to and from Toulon to the eastward, was collected in Cavalarie road, to the number of upwards of 20 sail. Judging this convoy to be a proper object of attack, Captain Edward Brace, of the 74-gun ship Berwick, detached for the purpose the boats of the two ships under the orders of Lieutenant Henry Johnston Sweedland, assisted by Lieutenant Alexander Sandiland, first of the Euryalus, and, among others, by midshipmen John Monk and Maurice Crawford, containing, along with a detachment of seamen, the whole of the marines of the 74 and frigate, commanded by Captain William T. I. Matthews.

On the morning of the 16th the united detachments landed, and in 20 minutes were in possession of the batteries, and had begun to open a fire from them upon the retreating enemy. The French national xebec Fortune, carrying 10 long 8-pounders and four swivels, with a crew of 95 men, commanded by Lieutenant Félix-Marie-Louis-Anne-Joseph-Julien Lecamus, tried to effect her escape; but the Euryalus, pushing close in, cut her off. The French crew then abandoned her, leaving her, with a hole made through her bottom by a shot from one of her guns and a train laid to her magazine, at anchor with a spring on her cable, under the fire of the Euryalus, the captured fort, and the launches. The vessel was promptly boarded by a division of the boats, and just in time to preserve her from blowing up or sinking. The vessels found in the harbour amounted to 22, of different descriptions. The whole were either taken or destroyed ; and the object of the enterprise was fully accomplished, with no greater loss than one marine killed and one seaman missing.

On the 18th of August an attack was made upon the batteries of Cassis, a town between Marseille and Toulon, by the Undaunted frigate, Redwing brig, and 16-gun brig-sloop Kite, Captain the Hon. Robert Cavendish Spencer, accompanied by a detachment of boats from the three first-named vessels, and from the Caledonia, Hibernia, Barfleur, and Prince of Wales line-of-battle ships, part of Sir Edward Pellew's fleet. Owing to light winds, the Undaunted could not take up the anchorage that Captain Ussher intended; but the Redwing and Kite, in spite of a fire from four batteries that protected the entrance of the bay, swept themselves in, and took a most judicious position for covering the marines; who, led by Captain Jeremiah Coghlan, of the Caledonia, carried the citadel battery by escalade. The marines then drove the French before them, at the point of the bayonet, and pursued them through the batteries to the heights that commanded the town. The boats, under the direction of Captain Sir John Sinclair of the Redwing, then entered the mole, across the entrance to which two heavy gun-boats were moored, and captured them, a third gun-boat, and 24 merchant-settees and tartans.

The loss sustained by the British in executing this dashing enterprise was rather serious, amounting to four marines killed, one lieutenant (Aaron Tozer), one petty officer, and 14 marines wounded. In his official letter, Captain Ussher mentions, besides those already named, the following officers as having behaved with distinguished gallantry: Lieutenants Joseph Robert Hownam and Joseph Grimshaw, Captains of marines Thomas Sherman and Thomas Hussey, and Lieutenants of marines Harry Hunt, Robert Turtliff Dyer, William Blucke, John Maule, Thomas Reeves, Alexander Jarvis, Edward Mallard, and Samuel Burdon Ellis. Lieutenant Hunt, it appears, was the first who entered the citadel battery, by a ladder, under a galling fire.

On the 26th of February, in the morning, the British 12-pounder 32-gun frigate Thames, then Captain Charles Napier, and 18-pounder 36-gun frigate Furieuse, Captain William Mounsey, having on board Lieutenant-colonel Coffin and the second battalion of the 10th regiment of foot, bore up for the narrow entrance (about a quarter of a mile across) to the harbour of the island of Ponza on the coast of Naples; and, giving and receiving a fire from the batteries on each side, anchored close across the mole-head. Colonel Coffin and the troops were then landed, and pushed for a tower into which the enemy had retreated. The appearance of the troops, aided by the severe fire of the ships, induced the governor to hoist a flag of truce. This led to a capitulation, and the island on the same day surrendered to the arms of his Britannic majesty. Nor did the British lose a single man in either service, although the batteries mounted ten 24 and 18 pounders and two 9-inch mortars; and although the Thames was hulled three times and the Furieuse twice, besides having their sails and rigging a good deal cut.

A convoy of 50 sail of armed vessels, chiefly Neapolitan gun-boats, having assembled at Pietra-Nera on the coast of Calabria, to be ready to transport to Naples timber and other government property, Captain Robert Hall, who commanded the Sicilian flotilla stationed at Messina, volunteered, with two divisions of gun-boats and four companies of the 75th regiment, under the command of Major Stewart, supplied by Lieutenant-general Lord William Bentinck at Palermo, to destroy the enemy's works. On the night of the 14th of February, Captain Hall proceeded to the attack; but, owing to light and contrary winds, the boats did not arrive at Pietra-Nera until nearly daylight on the 15th; when Major Stewart, with about 150 men, and an auxiliary party of seamen, commanded by Lieutenant Francis Le Hunte, landed, and, without waiting for the remainder of the force intended be be employed, pushed up a height, the possession of which a complete battalion, with two troops of cavalry and two pieces of artillery, were prepared to dispute.

Assisted by a corporal's detachment of the rocket corps, the British troops charged the height in the most determined manner, and succeeded only after as determined a resistance, the French colonel-commandant, Roche, and most of his officers, being killed or made prisoners, and the height literally covered with dead. The division of the flotilla under Captain Imbert had by this time commenced a most destructive cannonade on the batteries; which held out with such obstinacy, that Captain Hall was obliged to order them to be successively stormed. This service was performed by Lieutenant Le Hunte, with a party of seamen, in a very gallant style. At 8 A.M. everything was in the possession of the assailants; the most valuable of the enemy's vessels and timber launched, and the rest on fire. Upwards of 150 French were killed and wounded, and 163 made prisoners, including several of the principal officers. Major Stewart, whose behaviour is highly praised by Captain Hall, fell by a musket-shot while in company with the latter, pushing from the shore after the troops had embarked. The loss on the part of the navy amounted to only one boatswain and one seaman killed and seven seamen wounded.

On the 6th of January, at daybreak, as the British 38-gun frigate Bacchante, Captain William Hoste, and 18-gun brig-sloop Weasel, Captain James Black, were lying becalmed about five leagues to the south-east of Cape Otranto, at the mouth of the Adriatic, five gun-vessels were discovered; three in the south-west, steering towards Otranto, and two in the south-east, steering to the eastward. Ordering, by signal, the Weasel to attend to the latter, Captain Hoste sent the Bacchante's boats, under the command of Lieutenant Donat Henchy O'Brien, assisted by Lieutenants Silas Thomas Hood and Frank Gostling, Lieutenant of marines William Haig, master's mates George Powell and James M'Kean, and midshipmen the Hon. Henry I. Rous and William Waldegrave, Thomas Edward Hoste, James Leonard Few, and Edward O. Pocock, in pursuit of the division in the south-west. At 8 A.M. Lieutenant O'Brien in the barge captured the sternmost gun-boat, mounting two guns, one French 12, and one 6 pounder, both on pivots, and manned with 36 men, commanded by the senior French officer of the three, all of whom were enseignes de vaisseau.

Leaving, to take possession of the prize, the first gig, commanded by midshipman Thomas Edward Hoste, Lieutenant O'Brien pushed on after the two remaining gun-vessels, then sweeping with all their strength towards the coast of Calabria. Sending his prisoners below, and fastening the hatches over them, young Hoste, with his seven men, in the most gallant manner, loaded and fired the bow-gun at the retreating gun-boats; which, in a little time, were also captured. This dashing enterprise, with Lieutenant O'Brien's usual good fortune, was achieved without any loss, although the shot from the gun-vessels cut the oars from the men's hands as the boats were pulling towards them. For his gallantry on the above and several other occasions, Lieutenant O'Brien was promoted to the rank of commander.

The Weasel not being able to overtake her two gun-vessels, two of her boats under Lieutenant Thomas Whaley and midshipman James Stewart, and a boat belonging to the Bacchante under master's mate Edward Webb, proceeded in chase. The

Bacchante's boat, taking the lead, soon overtook, and, although she carried only a 3-pounder in the bow with 18 men, captured, in spite of a warm opposition, the sternmost French gun-boat, armed the same as that already described, and having 40 men actually on board. Leaving the captured vessel to be taken possession of by the boats astern, Mr. Webb pushed after the remaining gun-boat, and carried her in the same gallant manner, and with equal impunity as to loss.

On the 14th of February, early in the morning, the Bacchante sent her barge, armed with a 12-pounder carronade, and manned with 23 officers and men under Lieutenant Hood, in chase of a vessel seen by the night-glass to be sweeping and steering for Otranto. After pouring in a destructive fire of round shot and musketry, Lieutenant Hood, assisted by Lieutenant of marines William Haig and master's mates William Lee Rees and Charles Bruce, boarded and carried the French gun-vessel Alcinous, of two long 24-pounders and 45 men, last from Corfu. The only person hurt on the British side was Lieutenant Hood, who received a severe contusion on the loins by a fall; so severe, indeed, that this gallant young officer became eventually deprived of the use of both his legs. The loss on the French side amounted to two killed and nine wounded, and the gun-boat was so shattered by the carronade, that she had three feet water in her hold. As soon, therefore, as the prisoners were removed, it was found necessary to set the prize on fire.

Notwithstanding that an officer of acknowledged merit is now walking on crutches, in consequence of an incurable lameness produced by the wound he received in this truly gallant enterprise, no other notice was taken in the London Gazette of Captain Hoste's letter on the subject, than a statement, that two letters, dated on the 14th of February, had been received: " One, reporting the capture, off Otranto, of l'Alcinous French gun-boat, carrying two guns and 32 men, and of eight trading-vessels under her convoy from Corfu; the other, stating the capture of la Vigilante French courier gun-boat, from Corfu to Otranto with despatches, and having on board, as passenger, the general of artillery Corda and his staff."

On the 11th of May, receiving information that a convoy of enemy's vessels were lying in the channel of Karlebago, Captain Hoste proceeded thither; but, on account of a contrary wind and strong current, the Bacchante did not arrive there until the morning of the 15th. As the port of Karlebago afforded excellent shelter for enemy's vessels, Captain Hoste resolved to destroy the works that defended it. The governor refusing to accede to the terms offered, the Bacchante anchored within pistol-shot of the battery, which mounted eight guns; and, after a good deal of firing, a truce was hung out, and the place surrendered at discretion. The marines, and a detachment of seamen under Lieutenant Hood, landed and took possession. The guns of the place were embarked, the public works destroyed, and the castle blown up; and the Bacchante retired with the loss of four seamen severely wounded, two of them with their arms shot off.

On the 12th of June, at daylight, the Bacchante discovered an enemy's convoy under the town of Gela-Nova, on the coast of Abruzza. As the frigate was six or seven miles to leeward of them, with a light breeze and a strong current against her, Captain Hoste detached the boats under Lieutenant Hood, with discretionary orders, either to attack the convoy or to wait till the Bacchante arrived. Lieutenant Hood took with him Lieutenant Frank Gostling, acting Lieutenant Edward Webb, Lieutenants of marines Charles Holmes and William Haig, master's mate William Lee Rees, and midshipmen James Rowe, Thomas Edward Hoste, Francis George Farewell, the Hon. William Waldegrave, Thomas William Langton, James M'Kean, and Samuel Richardson.

Lieutenant Hood found the enemy much stronger than had been expected, consisting of seven large gun-boats, mounting each one long 18-pounder in the bow, three smaller gun-vessels, with a 4-pounder in the bow, and 14 sail of merchant-vessels, four of which also had guns in the bow: and the shore astern of the vessels was lined with troops intrenched on the beach, having with them two field-pieces. "This," says Captain Hoste, "was the force opposed to a frigate's boats; but no disparity of numbers could check the spirit of the brave officers and men employed on this service. The attack was determined on instantly, and executed with all the gallantry and spirit which men accustomed to danger and to despise it have so frequently shown; and never was there a finer display of it than on this occasion." The boats, as they advanced, were exposed to a heavy fire of grape and musketry; and it was not until they were fairly alongside the gun-boats that the crews of the latter slackened their fire: they were then driven from their vessels with great loss. The troops on the beach, stated by the prisoners to amount to 100 men, fled on the first fire, and their two field-pieces were destroyed by the British marines. In performing this very brilliant exploit, the boats of the Bacchante sustained a loss of two seamen and one marine killed, and five seamen and one marine wounded.

On the 22nd of April, at daybreak, the brig-sloop Weasel, cruising about four miles to the east-north-east of the island of Zirana, discovered and chased a convoy, close to the main land, making for the ports of Trau and Spalatro. As the brig approached, the vessels separated in different directions, the greater part, with 10 gun-boats, bearing up for the bay of Boscalina. These the Weasel continued to chase under all sail; and at 5 h. 30 m. A.M. they anchored in a line about a mile from the shore, hoisted French colours, and commenced firing at her. The wind blowing strong from the south-east, which was directly into the bay, the sails and rigging of the brig were considerably damaged before she could close. At 6 A.M., however, the Weasel anchored with springs, within pistol-shot of the gun-boats; and a furious action commenced. At the end of 20 minutes the latter cut their cables, ran closer in, and again opened their fire. This increased distance not suiting her carronades, the Weasel cut her cable, ran within half pistol-shot of the gun-boats, and recommenced the action. Three large guns, at the distance of 30 yards from each other, and 200 or 300 musketry, on the heights immediately over the British brig, now united their fire to that of the gun-boats. The engagement continued in this way until 10 A.M.; when three of the gun-boats struck their colours, two were driven on shore, and one was sunk.

The remaining four gun-boats were now reinforced by four more from the eastward; who anchored outside the Weasel, and commenced firing at her. This obliged the brig to engage on both sides, but the outer gun-boats afterwards ran in and joined the others; all of whom now placed themselves behind a point of land, so that the Weasel could only see their masts from her deck. Here the gun-boats commenced a most destructive fire, their grape-shot striking the brig over the land in every part. At this time the Weasel's crew, originally short by the absence of several men in prizes, was so reduced, that she could with difficulty man four guns; the marines and a few of the seamen firing musketry, her grape being all expended. The action lasted in this way until 3 P.M., when the gun-boats discontinued their fire. At the expiration of 40 minutes the engagement recommenced, and continued, without intermission, until 6 h. 30 m. P.M., when the firing entirely ceased on both sides,

The Weasel was now in a very critical situation: she was but a few yards from a lee-shore, almost a complete wreck, with the whole of her running, and the greater part of her standing-rigging cut to pieces, most of her sails shot from the yards, her masts shot through in several places, her anchors all destroyed or rendered unserviceable, her hull pierced with shot, five of which had entered between wind and water, and her two pumps shot away between the decks, so that the crew could with difficulty keep the brig free by constantly bailing at both hatches. In addition to all this, the Weasel had already lost 25 men in killed and wounded. Captain Black, nevertheless, after dark, sent his boats, and destroyed, besides the gun-boats that had struck and gone on shore, eight of the convoy; the boats bringing away some of the enemy's anchors, by the aid of which the brig was enabled to warp herself out.

On the 23rd, at daybreak, having warped herself about a mile from the land, the Weasel was again attacked by the gun-boats, who, taking a raking position, annoyed the brig much; especially as, her last cable being half shot through and the wind blowing strong in, she could not venture to bring her broadside to bear upon them. All this day and night the Weasel continued warping out from the shore, but very slowly, her people being reduced in numbers and exhausted with fatigue. On the 24th, at noon, the French opened a battery, which they had erected, on a point of the bay close to which the Weasel was obliged to pass; and at 1 P.M. the gun-boats pulling out in a line astern, recommenced their fire. The wind was now moderate, and shortly afterwards it fell calm. At 5 P.M. the gun-boats, having got within range, received the contents of the brig's larboard broadside and sheered off; but, owing to the calm, the Weasel was unable to follow up her advantage, and they effected their escape.

In this very gallant, and, considering the extrication of the vessel from such a host of difficulties, admirably conducted enterprise, the Weasel had her boatswain (James Toby), three seamen, and one marine killed, and her commander badly wounded by a musket-ball through the right hand; but with a modesty that did him honour, Captain Black would not suffer the surgeon to insert his name in the official report. The brig's remaining wounded consisted of her first-lieutenant (Thomas Whaley, severely), one master's mate (William Simkin, severely), one midshipman (James Stewart), 19 seamen, and two marines wounded. The loss sustained on the part of the French gun-boats, and at the batteries on shore, could not be ascertained, but must have been severe.

On the 2nd of February, at daylight, Faro bearing south-south-east distant six miles, the British 18-gun ship-sloop Kingfisher, Captain Ewell Tritton, discovered several trabaccolos near Melara steering to the southward. There being little wind, Captain Tritton detached the cutter and pinnace, under Acting-lieutenant George H. Palmer and Mr. John Waller the gunner, to intercept the vessels. After a five hours' chase, the two boats succeeded in capturing one trabaccolo, and in running nine on shore near St. Catharine's, in the island of Corfu, five of which were totally destroyed. In executing this service, the two boats were exposed to a heavy fire of musketry from the heights, and from a one-gun battery, and sustained a loss, in consequence, of two men killed and seven severely wounded.

On the 6th of January, at 2 P.M., a division of the boats of the 18-pounder 36-gun frigate Havannah, Captain the Hon. George Cadogan, placed under the orders of Lieutenant William Hamley, attacked and carried the French gun-boat, No. 8, of one long 24-pounder and 35 men, although the vessel was prepared in every respect, and was supported by musketry from the shore to which she had been made fast. Lieutenant Hamley had no expectation of meeting an armed vessel, until, upon opening the creek in which the gun-boat lay, the boats were fired upon, and desired by the troops drawn up on the beach to surrender. Three merchant-vessels were taken at the same time; and the British loss amounted to one master's mate (Edward Percival) killed and two seamen wounded.

On the 22nd of March the boats of the Havannah, under the same commanding officer, assisted by Lieutenant of marines William Hockly, captured, under the town of Vasto, a large trabaccolo, mounting three long French 8-pounders, and destroyed a similar vessel laden with oil. On the 26th, Lieutenant Hamley, assisted again by Lieutenant Hockly, captured five armed trabaccolos and five feluccas laden with salt, near the town of Fortore. In both instances, the vessels were hauled aground, and were under the protection of a strong body of military and some guns on the beach. No greater loss, notwithstanding, was sustained by the British in either enterprise than two men slightly wounded. On the 17th of June, in the morning, the boats of the same frigate, still commanded by Lieutenant Hamley, landed and brought off, from under the town of Vasto and from the fire of eight guns, 10 sail of merchant-vessels; and that with no greater loss than three men slightly wounded.

On the 21st of December, 1812, the British 38-gun frigate Apollo, Captain Bridges Watkinson Taylor, accompanied by the brig-sloop Weasel, chased a trabaccolo under the protection of the tower of St. Cataldo. As this tower was reputed to be the strongest between Brindisi and Otranto, Captain Taylor resolved to attempt its destruction. The boats of the two vessels were accordingly detached on that service, under the orders of Lieutenants George Bowen and Michael Quin. The enemy became so much discouraged at having Murat's Neapolitan colours cut down by the first shot from the Apollo's barge, that the tower was carried without the assistance of the ships or the slightest loss. It contained a telegraph, three carriage-guns, and three swivels, and was blown up.

On the 18th of January, 1813, Rear-admiral Thomas Francis Freemantle, the British commander-in-chief in the Adriatic, detached the Apollo, accompanied by the Esperanza privateer and four gun-boats, having on board 250 troops under Lieutenant-colonel Robertson, to attack the island of Augusta. On the 29th the island surrendered; and Captain Taylor bestows great praise upon Lieutenant Bowen, first, and Mr. Thomas Ullock, purser, of the Apollo, who served on shore; also, for their gallantry in the frigate's barge, launch, and yawl, midshipmen William Henry Brand, William Hutchinson, and William David Folkes. Colonel Robertson having left a garrison in Augusta, the Apollo and small vessels sailed, on the 1st of February, for the neighbouring island of Curzola; and, on the same night, 160 soldiers, 70 seamen, and 50 marines, with a howitzer, landed at Port Bufalo, and surprised and carried a hill that commanded the town. Finding that, notwithstanding the British had got their field-guns to this spot, and that the advance was already in possession of the suburbs, the enemy appeared determined to hold out, Captain Taylor took off the Apollo's seamen, and on the morning of the 3rd attacked and silenced the sea-batteries. This led to an immediate capitulation. The loss to the British on the occasion amounted to two seamen killed and one slightly wounded, and the Apollo had her mainmast badly wounded and her rigging much cut.

On the night of the 11th of April, Captain Taylor sent three boats of the Apollo, and two belonging to the 32-gun frigate Cerberus, Captain Thomas Garth, cruising in company, to take temporary possession of the Devil's island near the north entrance of Corfu; by which the boats captured a brig and trabaccolo going into Corfu with grain. On the 14th the two frigates chased a vessel, which, on its falling calm, escaped into Malero. Perceiving that the five boats were proceeding to attack her, and fearing from the natural strength of the island that they would not succeed, Captain Taylor sent to desire that the boats would wait until the Apollo came up. The message, however, arrived too late, and Lieutenant Edward Hollingsworth Delafosse, first of the Cerberus, and Mr. Ullock, purser, of the Apollo, were wounded. On the arrival of the Apollo, Captain Taylor landed the marines; who, after some skirmishing, captured the island, and found eight vessels laden with grain, but scuttled.

On the 24th of April, at daylight, observing a felucca run into St. Cataldo and disembark troops, Captain Taylor landed 30 marines under Lieutenants John Tothill and Colin Campbell, who, by a steady charge, dislodged them from a strong position, made 26 prisoners, and killed one and wounded several. The boats in the mean time brought out the vessel, and the whole service was executed without loss.

On the 17th of May, while cruising off Otranto the Cerberus discovered an enemy's vessel close to the land a little to the southward of Brindisi; and which, upon being chased, ran herself on shore under a martello tower. Captain Garth immediately despatched three boats belonging to the Cerberus, under Lieutenant John William Montagu, and two belonging to the Apollo, under Lieutenant William Henry Nares, to attempt to bring out the vessel. This, after receiving her fire, they accomplished without any loss, and drove some of the enemy's troops, who had come down to protect her, a considerable way up the country. The vessel was armed with a 6-pounder in the bow and a swivel. On the next morning the boats brought off a gun from a martello tower a little further to the southward.

On the 27th, observing a canopy collected in Otranto, which it was thought would push for Corfu the first north-west wind, Captain Garth, on the following morning, took a station off Faro, to endeavour to intercept them, and sent the barge and pinnace of the Cerberus and the barge and gig of the Apollo, under Lieutenants Montagu and Nares, close in shore. At about 1 A.M. the vessels came out, protected by eight gun-boats. Notwithstanding this strong force, and that they were aided by three more gun-boats from Faro, and the cliffs covered with French troops, the four British boats attacked them in the most determined and gallant manner. Lieutenant Nares, in the Apollo's barge, boarded and carried one gun-boat, and midshipman William Hutchinson, in the Apollo's gig, actually boarded and carried another before the barge of the Cerberus could get alongside. In boarding another gun-boat, Mr. Thomas Richard Suett, master's mate of the Cerberus, was shot through the heart. This, with one seaman killed, and one marine dangerously wounded, was the extent of the British loss. The gun-boats taken had each a 9-pounder in her bow and two 4-pounders abaft, and were carrying troops to Corfu. Four of the convoy were also taken.

On the 17th of June, at 9 p.m., Captain John Harper, of the 18-gun brig-sloop Saracen, accompanied by Lieutenant William Holmes and Lieutenant of marines Edward Hancock, put off with his boats containing 40 men, and at 11 p.m. landed upon the island of Zapano. After a difficult march of three miles, Captain Harper surprised and took prisoners a corporal's guard that was in advance. Pushing for the guard-house and commandant's quarters, he then carried the whole by the bayonet, without loss, and took 36 prisoners, including the commanding officer of the two islands of Zapano and Mezzo. The remaining 16 officers and men of the garrison effected their escape.

On the 29th of April the boats of the 74-gun ships Elizabeth and Eagle, Captains Edward Leveson Gower and Charles Rowley, under the orders of Lieutenants Mitchell Roberts and Richard Greenaway, assisted, among others, by Lieutenant Thomas Holbrook, fell in, off Goro, with a convoy of seven armed merchant-vessels, laden with oil. Four of them were captured, and the remaining three ran themselves on shore into a tremendous surf, under the protection of a two-gun battery, two schooners, and three settee gun-boats, that opened a most galling fire. Notwithstanding all these difficulties, one of the vessels was brought off, and another destroyed, without a casualty.

On the 8th of June, observing three vessels, supposed to contain powder, within the town of Omago on the coast of Istria, Captain Gower, after the two ships had fired for some time, detached the marines, under Captain John Hore Graham and Lieutenants Thomas Price and Samuel Lloyd, who soon drove the enemy, consisting of 100 French soldiers, out of the town; while the boats of the Elizabeth and Eagle, under Lieutenants Mitchell Roberts, Martin Bennett, Richard Greenaway, and William Hotham, destroyed a two-gun battery and brought out four vessels. This service was executed with no greater loss than one man wounded.

On the 20th, at daybreak, Captain Gower caused to be landed at Dignano, opposite to the Prioni islands, 50 seamen from the Elizabeth, under the orders of Lieutenants Roberts and Bennett, and the marines under Captain Graham and Lieutenant Price; who, assisted by Lieutenant Henry Richard Bernard with a division of armed boats, took possession of the town, and made prisoners of the French troops within it, without the slightest loss.

On the 3rd of July, in the morning, Rear-admiral Fremantle, with the 74-gun ships Milford (flag), Captain John Duff Markland, Elizabeth, and Eagle, Bacchante frigate, and gun-brig Haughty, Lieutenant James Harvey, got under way, with a light breeze at south-west, from an anchorage about four miles from Fiume; and, leaving a detachment of boats and marines with the Haughty to storm the battery at the mole-head as soon as the guns were silenced, proceeded to attack the sea-line batteries of the town, mounting 15 heavy guns. A shift of wind to the south-east, aided by a strong current from the river, broke the ships off, and the Eagle could not fetch the second battery, opposite to which she anchored; and against which she presented so well-directed a fire, that the fort soon became silenced.

This being communicated by telegraph, Rear-admiral Fremantle made the signal to storm; when Captain Rowley, leading in his gig the first detachment of marines, took possession of the fort and hoisted English colours; while Captain Hoste, with the marines of the Milford, took and spiked the guns of the first battery, which had been under the fire of the Milford and Bacchante, and early evacuated. Leaving a party of seamen to turn the guns of the second battery against the others, Captain Rowley, without losing time, boldly dashed on through the town, although annoyed by the enemy's musketry from the windows of the houses, and a field-piece placed in the centre of the great street: but the marines, headed by Lieutenants Samuel Lloyd and Edmund Nepean, and the seamen from the boats, proceeded with such firmness, that the French troops retreated before them, drawing the field-piece until they came to the square, where they made a stand, taking post in a large house. At this time the boats under Captain Markland, with their carronades, opened upon the gable end of it with such effect, that the French gave way at all points, and forsook the town in every direction. Captain Hoste, with his division, followed close to Captain Rowley; and, on their junction, the two captains took possession of the two batteries, along with the field-piece, stores, and shipping; but no prisoners were made, the governor and every officer and man of the garrison having run away.

Considering that the number of troops in the town, besides the natives, was about 350, the loss on the British side, in amounting to only one marine killed, and Lieutenant Lloyd and five seamen and marines wounded, was comparatively trifling. Although the town was stormed in every part, such was the prudent management of Captains Rowley and Hoste, that not an individual was plundered, nor was anything taken away, except what was afloat and in the government stores. Ninety vessels were captured. More than half of these were restored to the proprietors; 13, laden with oil, grain, powder, and merchandise, were sent to Lissa, and the remainder destroyed. The guns on the batteries were rendered useless, and 500 stands of arms and 200 barrels of powder were brought off.

On the 5th the British squadron moved from Fiume to Porto-Ré; at which place Captains Hoste and Markland landed with the marines, and found the forts abandoned by the enemy. The boats went up to Bocca-Ré, where a convoy of 13 sail had been scuttled; and, after rendering the guns, 10 in number, useless, and destroying the carriages and works, the two captains returned to their respective ships.

On the 7th, at 11 A.M., the Eagle attacked the fortress of Farasina, mounting five 18-pounders. After some resistance, the works were stormed and carried, under cover of the ship's fire, by a party of seamen and marines, under the command of Lieutenants Greenaway and Hotham and Lieutenant of marines Samuel Lloyd. The guns were disabled and the works laid in ruins; and at 2 P.M. the party re-embarked, with no greater loss than midshipman John Hudson slightly wounded.

On the 2nd of August, in the evening, while the Eagle and Bacchante were sailing along the coast of Istria, a convoy of 21 sail was seen at anchor in the harbour of Rovigno. Conceiving the capture of the vessels feasible, an attack was determined on; and, the Bacchante leading in, the two ships opened their fire on the batteries. After some resistance, the batteries were abandoned; whereupon Captain Hoste landed with a detachment of seamen and marines, drove the enemy out of the town, disabled the guns, and destroyed or brought off the whole of the vessels; and that with so slight a loss as one marine wounded.

On the 4th of August, in the evening, the boats of the 74-gun ship Milford and brig-sloop Weasel, under Captain Black of the latter, accompanied by Lieutenant John Grant, and Lieutenant of marines Kenyon Stevens Parker, left the Milford about seven leagues from the island of Ragosniza, and, having passed the sea-battery within pistol-shot unperceived, landed at the back of the island. At daylight on the 5th, the French troops were saluted with a cheer from the British at the top of the hill; who, quickly descending, entered the battery at the rear, where it was open, and carried it without much resistance. Six 24-pounders and two 7½-inch mortars were mounted on the battery. These were disabled, a newly-erected signal-tower demolished, and the seamen and marines returned on board without any loss.

On the 5th of October, Rear-admiral Fremantle, with the Milford, Eagle, and some smaller vessels, arrived off and blockaded the port of Triest, while a detachment of Austrian troops from the main body under General Count Nugent invested the town by land. On the 10th the French unexpectedly opened a masked battery of two guns upon the Milford, whose stern was towards the shore. Captain Markland in a few minutes got a spring upon the cable, and in a quarter of an hour disabled both guns, and killed two and wounded seven of the men stationed at them, while not a man was hurt on board the Milford. On the same day Captain Markland landed with the marines and two field-pieces; and on the 11th General Nugent returned from Gorizia, having obliged the viceroy to pass the Isongo. It was then determined to lay siege to the castle. By the 16th the British had 12 guns in two batteries, which opened their fire and continued it nearly the whole day. Towards evening the French were driven from the windmill, and the Austrians took possession of the fort, and of two howitzers advanced there. The fire was continued with increased effect until the 29th, when Colonel Rabie, the French commanding officer, surrendered on a capitulation.

Captain Rowley commanded one of the batteries on shore, and was accompanied by Lieutenants William Hotham **and** Charles Moore, and midshipman Edward Hibbert. Captain Fairfax Moresby, of the brig-sloop Wizard, also commanded a battery, and, having been ordered to form another battery of four 32-pounders within breaching distance, he did so in the course of 56 hours, under every disadvantage of weather, and without any other assistance than 50 men from the Milford and 20 from his own sloop. Mr. William Watts, acting-master of the

Wizard, and who was severely wounded, is also spoken highly of in the rear-admiral's despatch; as is likewise Captain David Dunn, of the armed en flûte 32-gun frigate Mermaid. Captain Markland, as has been already mentioned, was also on shore in command of the marines. The loss of the British on this occasion amounted to 10 seamen and marines killed, and 35 wounded, including Mr. Watts, and a midshipman of the Wizard, Edward Young.

On the 12th the Bacchante arrived off Ragusa, and was joined by the Saracen and three gun-boats, with a detachment of the garrison of Curzola on board: and, from the information of Captain Harper and the insurrection of the Bocchese, Captain Hoste lost no time in proceeding to Castel-Nuova. On the 13th, in the morning, the Bacchante and Saracen forced the passage between that castle and the fort of Rosas, and after some firing, secured a capital anchorage for the squadron about three miles above Castel-Nuova. At 10 P.M., Captain Hoste detached Captain Harper with the two Sicilian gun-boats, the launch and barge of the Bacchante and the boats of the Saracen, to capture the enemy's armed naval force represented to be lying between the island of St. George and the town of Cattaro.

On going through the passage of Cadone, the boats received a heavy but ineffectual fire from the island of St. George; and at midnight, when within four miles of Cattaro, Captain Harper found the enemy's four gun-boats in a state of revolt, and instantly took possession of them. He then landed and summoned the inhabitants, who immediately, at his request, armed *en masse* against the French. Having brought about this change, Captain Harper hoisted the English and Austrian flags on board the four captured gun-boats, and manning them with part English, proceeded down to attack the island of St. George. On the 13th, at 6 A.M., a heavy and well-directed fire was opened from the gun-boats under the command of Lieutenant Frank Gostling of the Bacchante, upon the island, and returned from the batteries. In 15 minutes, however, the French were driven from their guns, and were eventually compelled to surrender at discretion. The possession of this island was of great importance, as it commands the narrow channel to the narrow branch of the river that leads up to Cattaro.

On the 16th of September, at daylight, the British 18-gun brig-sloop Swallow, Captain Edward Reynolds Sibly, being well in-shore between the river Tiber and D'Anzo, discovered a brig and xebec between herself and the latter harbour. Captain Sibly immediately despatched after them three of the Swallow's boats, under the orders of Lieutenant Samuel Edward Cook, assisted by master's mate Thomas Cole and midshipman Henry Thomas. After a row of two hours, the boats overtook, close under D'Anzo, the French brig Guerrier, of four guns and 60 stands of small arms; and notwithstanding that numerous boats and two gun-vessels had been sent from D'Anzo to her assistance, and kept the brig in tow until the British were alongside, Lieutenant Cook and his party gallantly carried her; but, in doing so, he sustained a loss in his own boat, of two seamen killed and four severely wounded.

On the 5th, in the morning, the 74-gun ship Edinburgh, Captain the Hon. George Heneage Lawrence Dundas, 38-gun frigates Impérieuse, Captain the Hon. Henry Duncan, and Resistance, Captain Fleetwood Broughton Reynolds Pellew, sloops Swallow, Eclair and Pylades, the two latter commanded by Captains John Bellamy and James Wemyss, assembled off the port D'Anzo, where lay a convoy of 29 vessels, which for several days past had been watched by Captain Duncan. The necessary arrangements having been made by that officer for the attack, Captain Dundas merely added the force of the Edinburgh to it. The place was defended by two batteries, mounting two heavy guns each, on a mole, a tower to the northward of this with one gun, and a battery to the southward with two guns, to cover the mole.

At 1 h. 30 m. P.M., everything being prepared, the ships bore up, and took their stations as follows: The Impérieuse and Resistance against the mole batteries; the Swallow against the tower; the Eclair and Pylades against the battery to the southward, and the Edinburgh supporting the two last-named ships. Soon after the ships had opened their fire, which they did together by signal, a detachment of seamen, under Lieutenant Eaton Travers, of the Impérieuse, and the marines under Captain Thomas Mitchell, landed in the best order close under the southern battery, which Lieutenant Travers instantly carried, driving the French in all directions. Lieutenant David Mapleton having also taken possession of the mole-head, the convoy, 20 of which were laden with timber for the arsenal at Toulon, were brought out without any loss. Before leaving the place, the British blew up all the works; and the ships received no greater injury than a few shot in their hulls and some damaged rigging. It appears that Captain Duncan had gained some very material information respecting the strength of D'Anzo by a gallant exploit performed a few nights previously by Lieutenant Travers; who, at the head of a single boat's crew, stormed, carried, and destroyed, a tower mounting one gun, and brought off the guard as prisoners.

On the 14th of October, at 1 P.M., the 36-gun frigate Furieuse, running along the coast towards the island of Ponza, observed, in the harbour of Marinelo, situated about six miles to the eastward of Civita Vecchia, a convoy of 19 vessels, protected by two gun-boats, a fort of two long 24-pounders, and a strong fortified tower and castle. It appearing practicable to cut them out, Lieutenants Walter Croker and William Lester, and Lieutenants of marines James Whylock and William Davis, gallantly volunteered to storm the fort on the land side, while the frigate anchored before it. This service was promptly executed; and, after a few broadsides from the Furieuse, the battery was carried, and the guns spiked, by the party on shore.

The French troops retreated to the strong position of the castle and tower overlooking the harbour; whence they kept up a constant fire of musketry through loopholes, without the possibility of being dislodged, although the Furieuse weighed and moved in, so that the whole fire of the ship was directed upon it. Nothing could damp the ardour of the party on shore, who, together with Lieutenant Lester in the boats, lost not a moment in boarding and cutting the cables of 16 vessels under a most galling fire. Two of the vessels sank at the entrance of the harbour, but the remaining 14, deeply laden, were brought out. The loss to the British in performing this service, which was over in three hours, amounted to two men killed and 10 wounded.

On the 8th of November, at 8 h. 30 m. P.M., the boats of the 74-gun ship Revenge, Captain Sir John Gore, under the orders of Lieutenant William Richards, assisted by Lieutenant Thomas Blakiston, Captain of marines John Spurin, and master's mates and midshipmen Thomas Quelch, William Rolfe, Henry Fisher, Benjamin Mainwaring, John Harwood, Valentine Munbee, George Fraser, Robert Maxwell, Charles M. D. Buchanan, and John P. Davey, were sent into the harbour of Palamos, to endeavour to cut out a French felucca privateer. At 11 P.M. Lieutenant Richards and his party boarded and carried the privateer, without having a man hurt, and by 1 A.M. on the 9th had brought her alongside the Revenge.

On the 9th Captain Ussher sent the boats of the Undaunted, under the orders of Lieutenant Joseph Robert Hownam, assisted by Lieutenant Thomas Hastings and Lieutenant cf marines Harry Hunt, also the boats of the Guadeloupe brig, under Lieutenant George Hurst and Mr. Alexander Lewis the master, into Port-Nouvelle. The batteries were stormed and carried in the most gallant manner, and two vessels captured and five destroyed, without a casualty.

On the 26th of November, off Cape Rousse, island of Corsica, the boats of the British 74-gun ship Swiftsure, Captain Edward Stirling Dickson, under the orders of Lieutenant William Smith, the 4th, were detached in pursuit of the French privateer schooner Charlemagne, of eight guns and 93 men, who was using every exertion by sweeping to effect her escape. On the approach of the boats, the privateer made every preparation for resistance, and reserved her fire till the boats had opened theirs; when the schooner returned it in the most determined manner for some minutes, until the boats got close alongside. The British then boarded the Charlemagne on the bow and quarter and instantly carried her; but not without a serious loss, having had one midshipman (Joseph Douglas) and four seamen killed, and two lieutenants (Rose Henry Fuller and John Harvey, the latter mortally), one lieutenant of marines (James Robert Thompson), one midshipman (—— Field), and 11 seamen wounded.

On the 25th of November, 1812, the two new French 40-gun frigates Aréthuse, Commodore Pierre-François-Henry-Etienne Bouvet, and Rubis, Captain Louis-François Ollivier, sailed from Nantes on a cruise. In January these two frigates, accompanied by a Portuguese prize-ship, the Serra, steered for the coast of Africa, and on the 27th, when off Tamara, one of the Isles de Los, the Rubis, who was ahead, discovered and chased a brig, which was the British gun-brig Daring, Lieutenant William R. Pascoe. The latter, when at a great distance, taking the Rubis for an English frigate, sent his master in a boat to board her. On approaching near, the boat discovered her mistake and endeavoured to make off, but was captured. The Daring was now aware of her perilous situation, and crowded sail for Tamara, followed by the Rubis; whom the lightness of the breeze delayed so much, that the brig succeeded in running on shore and her crew in setting her on fire. The two French frigates, at 6 P.M., came to an anchor in the road of Isle de Los. Here Captain Bouvet learnt, that Sierra Leone was the rendezvous of two British frigates and several sloops-of-war; that one of the former had recently quitted the coast, and that the remaining frigate, reported to him as larger and stronger than either of his own, still lay at anchor in the river.

In the course of six days, the French commodore refitted his ships, and supplied them with water and provisions for six months. Having also sent to Sierra Leone to exchange the few prisoners in his possession, consisting, besides the boat's crew of the Daring, of the master and crew of a merchantman he had taken, Captain Bouvet, on the 4th, weighed and made sail with his two frigates. At 4 P.M. the Aréthuse, who was ahead, struck on a coral bank, but forcing all sail, got off immediately, with no greater damage than the loss of her rudder. The two frigates then re-anchored, but driving in a gale of wind, were obliged, at 3 A.M. on the 5th, to get under sail; the Aréthuse contriving a temporary rudder while her own was repairing.

At daylight, when the gale had abated, the Aréthuse found herself lying becalmed within four leagues north-east of the island of Tamara; and Captain Bouvet was surprised to discover his consort still among the islands, covered with signals, which the distance precluded him from making out, but which were judged to be of melancholy presage. At 8 A.M. the Aréthuse anchored in 12 fathoms. At 11 A.M. the Rubis was observed to fire several guns, and at noon to have the signal flying, that the pumps were insufficient to free her. Captain Bouvet immediately sent his longboat with two pumps; but at 2 A.M. on the 6th the officer returned, with information that the Rubis had struck on the rocks, and that her crew were removing to the Portuguese ship. At daylight, by which time she had repaired and reshipped her rudder, the Aréthuse discovered a large ship to windward. This was the British 38-gun frigate Amelia, Captain the Hon. Frederick Paul Irby, from Sierra Leone.

It was at 3 h. 30 m. P.M. on the 29th of January, that Lieutenant Pascoe and a part of his crew joined the Amelia, then moored off Free Town, Sierra Leone, bringing information, that he had left "three French frigates" at anchor in Isle de Los road. The Amelia began immediately to bend sails and clear for action, and in the evening was joined by the Hawk merchant-schooner, with some more of the Daring's men. On the morning of the 30th the Amelia's launch-carronade was put on board the Hawk, and Lieutenant Pascoe, having volunteered, was despatched in her to reconnoitre the French ships.

On the 2nd of February, at noon, Lieutenant Pascoe returned, with intelligence of the names of the two French frigates and their prize; and also of Captain Bouvet's intention to proceed immediately to sea, to intercept the British homeward-bound trade. On the 3rd, at 8 A.M., the cartel-cutter, noticed as having been despatched by Captain Bouvet, arrived with prisoners, including the crew of the Daring's boat: and at 10 h. 30 m. the Amelia, with a debilitated crew, for whose recovery she was about to proceed to England, got under way, and made sail, against a west-south-west wind, for the Isles de Los, in the hope of falling in with some British cruiser that might render the match more equal, and prevent the two French frigates from molesting several merchant-vessels that were daily expected at Sierra Leone.

On the 5th, at 8 A.M., the Amelia got a sight of Isle de Los: and at 8 P.M., when standing to the north-east, and then distant three leagues west-north-west of Tamara, she observed a strange sail in the north-east, or right ahead, making night-signals. Supposing this vessel to be one of the French frigates, the Amelia tacked to the westward, the wind now blowing fresh from the north-west. On the 6th, at daylight, the Amelia again tacked to the north-east, and at 9 A.M. spoke the Princess Charlotte government-schooner from Sierra Leone, the vessel that had been making signals the preceding night. At 9 h. 30 m. A.M. the French ships were observed in the north-east, at anchor off the north end of Tamara: one, the Aréthuse, considerably to the northward of the other, who appeared to be unloading the prize, but was really removing into the latter her own crew. At 10 A.M. Captain Irby despatched the Princess Charlotte to Sierra Leone, with directions for any British ship-of-war that might arrive there to repair immediately to him. The Amelia then bore away to Tamara to reconnoitre the enemy.

At 2 h. 30 m. P.M. the two French frigates were observed to interchange signals; and at 3 h. 20 m. the Aréthuse weighed and made sail on the starboard tack, with a moderate breeze at south-south-west. The Amelia thereupon shortened sail, and hauled to the wind on the same tack as the Aréthuse. In a few minutes the latter tacked to the westward, to avoid a shoal, and the Amelia did the same. At 6 P.M. the Aréthuse bore from the Amelia north-north-east distant six miles; at which time the Rubis, as supposed, but probably the Serra, was observed to have her topsails hoisted. At 6 h. 30 m. P.M. the north end of Tamara bore from the Amelia east-south-east distant five leagues. At 8 P.M. the Amelia lost sight of the Aréthuse; and at

8 h. 30 m., in order to keep off shore during the night, Captain Irby tacked to the south-south-west, with the wind from the westward. At 6 h. 45 m. A.M. on the 7th the Amelia discovered the Aréthuse about eight miles off in the south-east; but a calm, which came on at 8 A.M., kept both frigates stationary. At noon a light breeze sprang up from the west-north-west: whereupon the Aréthuse stood towards the Amelia, on the larboard tack, under all sail; the latter making sail also, in the hope to draw the Aréthuse from her consort, still supposed to be in a condition to follow and assist her.

At 5 P.M., finding the wind beginning to fall, and conceiving that he had drawn the Aréthuse to a sufficient distance from her consort, Captain Irby shortened sail, wore round, and, running under his three topsails with the wind on the starboard-quarter, steered to pass, and then to cross the stern of, the Aréthuse; who was standing, under the same sail, close hauled on the larboard tack. To avoid being thus raked, Captain Bouvet, at 7 h. 20 m. P.M., tacked to the south-west, and hoisted his colours; as the Amelia previously had hers. It was now a fine moonlight night, with the wind very moderate, and the sea nearly as smooth as a millpond. At 7 h. 45 m. P.M., just as the Amelia had arrived within pistol-shot upon her starboard or weather-bow, the Aréthuse opened her fire, which was immediately returned. After about three broadsides had been exchanged, the maintopsail of the Amelia, in consequence of the braces having been shot away, fell aback. Owing to this accident, instead of crossing her opponent as she intended, the Amelia fell on board of her; the jib-boom of the Aréthuse carrying away the Amelia's jib and stay, and the French ship's bumpkin or anchor-fluke, part of the British ship's larboard forecastle barricade.

The Aréthuse now opened a heavy fire of musketry from her tops and mast-heads, and threw several hand-grenades upon the Amelia's decks, hoping, in the confusion caused by such combustibles, to succeed in an attempt to board; for which purpose several of the Aréthuse's men had stationed themselves in her fore-rigging. A man was now seen on the spritsail-yard of the Aréthuse, making strenuous efforts to get on board the Amelia. Scarcely had the poor fellow called out, "For God's sake, don't fire, I am not armed!" when a musket-ball from a British marine dropped him in the water. It was afterwards ascertained, that one of the crew of the Aréthuse, a Hamburgher, had formerly belonged to the Amelia, having been taken out of one of her prizes on the coast of Spain, and forced to enter on board the French frigate. It appears that the man was so desirous to get back to his ship, that he requested a settler at the Isle de Los to secrete him till an opportunity offered of his reaching Sierra Leone. The probability therefore is, that the man so shot, while upon the spritsail-yard of the Aréthuse, was the unfortunate Hamburgher.

Finding that, owing in a great degree to the steady and well-directed fire kept up by the Amelia's marines, her object could not be accomplished, the Aréthuse threw all aback and dropped clear. In doing this, her spritsail-yard knocked Lieutenant William Reeve, who had been invalided from the Kangaroo sloop, from the break of the forecastle into the waist. Setting her maintopgallant and middle staysails (her jib for the time being disabled), the Amelia endeavoured again to get her head towards the bow of the Aréthuse. The Amelia at length did so, but, in attempting a second time to cross her antagonist, a second time fell on board of her; and the two ships now swang close alongside, the muzzles of their guns almost touching. This was at about 9 h. 15 m. P.M., and a scene of great mutual slaughter ensued. The two crews snatched the sponges out of each other's hands through the portholes, and cut at one another with the broadsword. The Amelia's men now attempted to lash the two frigates together, but were unable, on account of the heavy fire of musketry kept up from the Aréthuse's decks and tops, a fire that soon nearly cleared the Amelia's quarter-deck of both officers and men. Among those who fell on the occasion were the first and second lieutenants (John James Bates and John Pope), and a lieutenant of marines. Captain Irby was also severely wounded, and obliged to leave the deck to the command of the third-lieutenant, George Wells; who, shortly afterwards, was killed at his post, and Mr. Anthony De Mayne, the master, took the command.

The mutual concussion of the guns at length forced the two frigates apart; and, in the almost calm state of the weather, they gradually receded from each other, with, however, their broadsides still mutually bearing, until 11 h. 20 m. P.M.; when both combatants, being out of gun-shot, ceased firing. Each captain thus describes this crisis. Captain Irby says: "When she (the Aréthuse) bore up, having the advantage of being able to do so, leaving us in an ungovernable state, &c." Captain Bouvet says: "At eleven o'clock the fire ceased on both sides; we were no longer within fair gun-shot, and the enemy, crowding sail, abandoned to us the field of battle."—" A onze heures, le feu cessa de part et d'autre ; nous n'étions plus à bonne portée, et l'ennemi se couvrit de voiles, nous abandonnant le champ de battaille."[1]

The damages of the Amelia, although, chiefly on account of the smooth state of the sea, they did not include a single fallen spar, were very serious ; the frigate's masts and yards being all badly wounded, her rigging of every sort cut to pieces, and her hull much shattered. But her loss of men will best show how much the Amelia had suffered. Of her proper crew of 265 men, and 30 (including, as if 18 were not already enough, 12 established supernumerary) boys, and her 54 supernumerary men and boys, composed chiefly of the Daring's crew, the Amelia and her three lieutenants (already named), second-lieutenant of marines (Robert G. Grainger), Lieutenant Pascoe, late commander of the Daring, one midshipman (Charles Kennicott), the purser of the Thais (John Bogue, of his second wound), 29 seamen, seven marines, and three boys killed, her captain (severely), Lieutenant Reeve, invalided from the Kangaroo sloop, the master (already named), first-lieutenant of marines (John Simpson), purser (John Collman), boatswain (John Parkinson, dangerously), one master's mate (Edward Robinson), four midshipmen (George Albert Rix, Thomas D. Buckle, George Thomas Gooch, and Arthur Beever), 56 seamen (two mortally), 25 marines (three mortally), and three boys wounded ; total, 51 killed and died of their wounds, and 90 wounded, dangerously, severely, and slightly.

The Aréthuse, as well as her opponent, left off action with her masts standing ; but they were all more or less wounded, and her rigging was much cut. Her hull must also have suffered considerably ; as her acknowledged loss, out of a crew, including the boat's crew of the Rubis, of at least 340 men and boys, amounted to 31 killed, including 11 of her officers, and 74 wounded, including nearly the whole of her remaining officers.

The guns of the Amelia (late French Proserpine) were the same as those mounted by the Java, with an additional pair of 32-pounder carronades, or 48 guns in all. The guns of the Aréthuse were the same, in number and caliber, as the Java mounted when captured as the French Renommée.[2] Although

---

[1] Mon. April 29. An English translator of Captain Bouvet's letter has rendered "Nous n'étions plus à bonne portée" by "We were no longer in good condition.' See Naval Chronicle, vol. xxix., p. 385.
[2] See vol. v., p. 290.

the total of men and boys on board the Amelia would be 349, yet, if we are to allow for the number of her men that were unable to attend their quarters, and for the feeble state of many of the remainder, among whom, including the Daring's, there were nearly 40 boys, 300 will be an ample allowance. The Aréthuse has been represented to have had a crew of 375 or 380 men, but we do not believe she had a man more of her proper crew than 330; making, with the boat's crew of the Rubis, 340. The Aréthuse was the sister-frigate of the Renommée: consequently the tonnage of the Java will suffice.

Comparative Force of the Combatants.

		Amelia.	Aréthuse.
Broadside-guns	No.	24	22
	lbs.	549	463
Crew	No.	300	340
Size	tons	1059	1073

Here was a long and bloody action between two (taking guns and men together) nearly equal opponents, which gave a victory to neither. Each combatant withdrew exhausted from the fight; and each, as is usual in the few cases of drawn battles that have occurred, claimed the merit of having forced the other to the measure. But it must now be clear, from the Amelia's damaged state, that Captain Bouvet was mistaken when he said, that she crowded sail to get away; it is much more probable, as requiring no other effort than shifting the helm, that the Aréthuse, as Captain Irby states, bore up.

Viewing the relative effectiveness of the two crews, one debilitated by sickness, the other, as admitted, in the full vigour of health; considering that, although both frigates sustained an almost unparalleled loss of officers, the captain of one of them only was obliged to give up the command; considering, also, the difference in the numerical loss, 141 and 105, a difference mainly attributable, no doubt, to the fatigued state of the Amelia's crew at the latter part of the action; we should say, that the Aréthuse, had she persevered, or could she, being to leeward, have done so, would, in all probability, have taken the British frigate. In saying this, we are far from placing every French 40-gun frigate upon a par with the Aréthuse; she was excellently manned, and was commanded by one of the best officers in the French navy. The chief part of the crew of the Aréthuse may, it is true, have been conscripts, but then they were conscripts of the year 1807, and were under an officer capable, if any officer was so, of making them good seamen.

With respect to Captain Irby, his critical situation, without reference to the state of his crew, must not be overlooked. The Amelia commenced, gallantly commenced, the action, under the impression that another French frigate, also equal in force to herself, was, although out of sight, at no great distance off. If, then, there was a probability of the approach of the Rubis when the action began, how must that probability have been heightened after the action had lasted three hours and a half, both ships remaining nearly stationary the whole time, and the wind, when it afterwards sprang up, drawing from the eastward, the direction in which the Rubis had been last seen? In addition to all this, the Amelia had on board a considerable quantity of gold dust, belonging to merchants in England. Upon the whole, therefore, both frigates behaved most bravely; and, although he had no trophy to show, each captain did more to support the character of his nation than many an officer who has been decorated with the chaplet of victory.

Previously to quitting the action of the Amelia and Aréthuse, we would request the boasters in the United States of America to compare the execution here done by an 18-pounder French frigate, with the best performance of one of their huge 24-pounder frigates; bearing in mind, that it was done against an opponent, not only equal to herself in force, but equally able to manœuvre by the possession of her masts; that it was done in a fair side-to-side action, neither frigate, during the three hours and a half's engagement, having had an opportunity to give one raking fire. It will, no doubt, also strike Commodores Decatur and Bainbridge, that, so far from constantly evading the close assaults of his antagonists, Captain Bouvet remained nearly in the same position from the commencement of the battle to its termination.

Both frigates found ample employment, during the remainder of the night, in clearing the decks of the dead and wounded, and in securing their damaged masts. At daylight on the 8th they were about five miles apart, the Aréthuse to the eastward of the Amelia, and both nearly becalmed. On a light breeze springing up, the Amelia, having bent a new foresail and fore-topsail, made sail before it to the southward, on her way to Madeira and England; and the Aréthuse stood back to Isle de Los, to see what had become of Captain Ollivier and his people

On the morning of the 10th the Aréthuse was joined by the Serra, with the late crew of the Rubis, stated then to consist of 300 men.

Taking half the number on board his frigate, Captain Bouvet, with the Serra in tow, steered for France. On reaching the latitude of Madeira, however, Captain Bouvet removed every man out of the Serra, and destroyed her, as she retarded the Aréthuse in her voyage. On the 18th of March, in latitude 33° 30' north, longitude 40° west, the French frigate fell in with and boarded the Mercury and another cartel, having on board the surviving officers and crew of the late British frigate Java; and on the 19th of April, after having made in the whole about 15 prizes, the Aréthuse anchored in St. Malo; as on the 22nd of the preceding month had the Amelia at Spithead.

Another pair of French 40-gun frigates had been nearly the same route as the Aréthuse and Rubis, but, during a two months and a half's cruise, had not encountered a single hostile vessel-of-war. The Hortense and Elbe, Captains Pierre-Nicolas Lahalle and Jules Desrostours, sailed from Bordeaux on the 7th of December, 1812; and steering for the coast of Africa, anchored on the 4th of January between the Bissagot islands, a little to the northward of Sierra Leone. They sailed soon afterwards, cruised a short time off the Azores, and on the 15th of February succeeded in entering Brest.

While, in the early part of December, 1812, the United States frigate Constitution, Commodore Bainbridge, and ship-sloop Hornet, of eighteen 32-pounder carronades and two long 12-pounders, Captain James Lawrence, were waiting at St. Salvador, to be joined by the Essex, an occurrence happened which the characteristic cunning of Americans turned greatly to their advantage. In the middle of November the British 20-gun ship Bonne-Citoyenne, of eighteen 32-pounder carronades and two long 9-pounders, Captain Pitt Barnaby Greene, having, while coming from Rio de la Plata, with half a million sterling on board, damaged herself greatly by running on shore, entered the port of St. Salvador to land her cargo and be hove down.

When the ship was keel-out, the two American ships arrived in the port. The American consul and the two American commanders now laid their heads together to contrive something which, without any personal risk to any one of the three, should contribute to the renown of their common country. What so likely as a challenge to Captain Greene? It could not be accepted; and then the refusal would be as good as a victory to Captain Lawrence. Accordingly, a challenge for the Hornet to meet the Bonne-Citoyenne was offered by Captain Lawrence, through the American consul, to the British consul, Mr. Frederick Landeman; Commodore Bainbridge pledging his honour to be out of the way, or not to interfere.

Without making the unpleasant avowal that his government, upon this occasion, had reduced the vessel he commanded from a king's cruiser to a merchant-ship, Captain Greene transmitted, through the consular channel, an animated reply; refusing a meeting "upon terms so manifestly disadvantageous as those proposed by Commodore Bainbridge." Indeed, it would appear, as if the commodore had purposely inserted the words, "or not interfering," lest Captain Greene, contrary to his expectation, should accept the challenge. For, had the two ships met by agreement, engaged, the Constitution looked on without interfering, and the British ship been the conqueror, the pledge of honour, on the part of both American commanders, would have been fulfilled; and can any one for a moment imagine, that Commodore Bainbridge would have seen the Bonne-Citoyenne carry off a United States ship-of-war, without attempting her rescue? It was more than his head was worth. Where was the guarantee against recapture, which always accompanies a serious proposal of this sort, when a stronger force, belonging to either party, is to preserve a temporary neutrality? The bait, therefore, did not take; the specie remained safe; and the American officers were obliged to content themselves with all the benefit they could reap from making a boast of the circumstance. This they did; and, to the present hour, the refusal of the Bonne-Citoyenne to meet the Hornet stands recorded in the American naval archives, as a proof of the former's dread, although the "superior in force," of engaging the latter. The two ships, as has just been seen, were equal in guns, and not very unequal in crews; the Hornet having 171 men and two boys, the Bonne-Citoyenne, including 21 supernumeraries, 141 men and nine boys. But this inferiority was in a great degree compensated by the pains which Captain Greene had taken to teach his men the use of their guns.

After the Constitution had sailed for Boston as already stated,[1] the Hornet continued blockading the Bonne-Citoyenne and her dollars until the arrival, on the 24th of January, of the British 74-gun ship Montagu, Captain Manley Hall Dixon, bearing the

[1] See vol. v., p. 421.

flag of Rear-admiral Manley Dixon. The American sloop, on being chased, ran for the harbour; but, night coming on, the Hornet wore, and, by standing to the southward, dexterously evaded her pursuer. Escorted by the Montagu, the Bonne-Citoyenne, with her valuable cargo on board, put to sea on the 26th of January; and on the 22nd of February, in latitude 5° 20′ south, longitude 40° west, the rear-admiral left Captain Greene to pursue his voyage alone. Some time in the month of April, having stopped at Madeira by the way, the Bonne-Citoyenne arrived in safety at Portsmouth.

After escaping from the Montagu, the Hornet hauled her wind to the westward, and on the 14th of February, when cruising off Pernambuco, captured an English brig, with about 23,000 dollars in specie on board. Having removed the money and destroyed the prize, Captain Lawrence cruised off Surinam until the 22nd; then stood for Demerara, and on the 24th chased a brig, but was obliged to haul off on account of the shoals at the entrance of Demerara river. Previously to giving up the chase, the Hornet discovered a brig-of-war, with English colours flying, at anchor without the bar. This was the brig-sloop Espiègle, of sixteen 32-pounder carronades and two sixes, Captain John Taylor, refitting her rigging.

At 3 h. 30 m. P.M., while beating round Caroband bank to get at the Espiègle, the Hornet discovered a sail on her weather-quarter bearing down for her. This was the British brig-sloop Peacock, of sixteen 24-pounder carronades and two sixes, Captain William Peake; who had only sailed from the Espiègle's anchorage the same day at 10 A.M. At 4 h. 20 m. P.M. the Peacock hoisted her colours; and at 5 h. 10 m., having kept close to the wind to weather the Peacock, the Hornet tacked for that purpose and hoisted her colours. At 5 h. 25 m., in passing each other on opposite tacks, within half pistol-shot, the ship and brig exchanged broadsides. After this, the Peacock wore to renew the action on the other tack; when the Hornet, quickly bearing up, received the Peacock's starboard broadside; then, at about 5 h. 35 m., ran the latter close on board on the starboard quarter. In this position the Hornet poured in so heavy and well-directed a fire, that at 5 h. 50 m., having had her commander killed, and being with six feet water in the hold, and cut to pieces in hull and masts, the Peacock hoisted from her fore-rigging an ensign, union down, as a signal of distress Shortly afterwards her mainmast went by the board.

Both the Hornet and Peacock were immediately anchored; and every attempt was made to save the latter, by throwing her guns overboard, by pumping and bailing her, and stopping such shot-holes as could be got at; but all would not do, and in a very few minutes after she had anchored, the Peacock went down in five and a half fathoms water, with 13 of her men, four of whom afterwards got to the foretop and escaped, as well as three men belonging to the Hornet. An American lieutenant and midshipman, and the remainder of the Hornet's men on board the Peacock, with difficulty saved themselves by jumping, as the brig went down, into a boat which was lying on her booms. Four of the Peacock's seamen had just before taken to her stern boat; in which, notwithstanding it was much damaged by shot, they arrived in safety at Demerara.

Of her 110 men and 12 boys, the Peacock lost, about the middle of the action, her young and gallant commander and four seamen killed, her master, one midshipman, the carpenter, captain's clerk, and 29 seamen and marines wounded; three of the latter mortally, but the greater part slightly. The principal damages of the Hornet are represented to have been one shot through the foremast, and her bowsprit slightly wounded by another: her loss, out of a crew of 163 men and two boys, the Americans state at one seaman killed, and two slightly wounded; also one mortally, and another severely burnt by the explosion of a cartridge.

The Hornet had three lieutenants, a lieutenant of marines, and a great show of full grown young midshipmen; and her men were all of the usual class of "American" seamen. Her established complement was 170, but she had on board, as was frequently the case in American ships-of-war, three supernumeraries. On the other hand, eight men were absent in a prize. This reduced the Hornet's crew to 165; among whom we will suppose, although none were discoverable, there were three boys. The Hornet, it will be observed, mounted one gun more of a side than the Wasp, and the latter was 434 tons: the former, therefore, could not well have been less than 460 or 470 tons.

Comparative Force of the Combatants.

		Peacock.	Hornet.
Broadside-guns	No.	9	10
	lbs.	192	297
Crew (men only)	No.	110	162
Size	tons	386	460

This is what the Americans, now for the first time pretending to believe, that "24-pounders are as good as 32s," call an equal match; or rather, as a brass swivel or two were stuck upon the capstan, or somewhere about the quarter-deck, of the Peacock, by way of ornament, these and the boat-carronade were reckoned in, and the Hornet was declared to have gained a victory over a superior British force.

If, in their encounter of British frigates, the Americans were so lucky as to meet them with crippled masts, deteriorated powder, unskilful gunners, or worthless crews, they were not less fortunate in the brigs they fell in with. There was the Frolic, with her main-yard gone and topmasts sprung; and here is the Peacock, with 24 instead of 32-pounder carronades, the establishment of her class, and with a crew that, owing to the nature of their employment ever since the brig had been commissioned, in August, 1807, must have almost forgotten that they belonged to a man-of-war. The Peacock had long been the admiration of her numerous visitors, for the tasteful arrangement of her deck, and had obtained, in consequence, the name of the yacht. The breechings of the carronades were lined with white canvas, the shot-lockers shifted from their usual places, and nothing could exceed in brilliancy the polish upon the traversing bars and elevating screws. If carronades, in general, as mounted in the British service, are liable to turn in-board or upset, what must have been the state of the Peacock's carronades after the first broadside? A single discharge from them, in exercise, would have betrayed the very defective state of their fastenings; and the feelings of Englishmen might then have found some relief in the skill, as well as gallantry, evinced in the Peacock's defence. The firing of the Hornet was admirable, and proved that her men, to the credit of Captain Lawrence and his officers, had been well taught what use to make of their guns: at the same time, it must be admitted, that the Peacock, Frolic, and all the brigs of their class were mere shells; especially when compared with such a ship as the Hornet, whose scantling was nearly as stout as that of a British 12-pounder frigate.

The wreck of the Peacock was visible for a long time after the action, and bore from Point Spirit, which is about six miles to the eastward of the entrance to Demerara river, north-east by east distant six leagues; making the distance between the Espiègle and Peacock, during the action, nearly 24 miles. This confirms the statement of Lieutenant Frederick Augustus

Wright, the late senior lieutenant of the Peacock, that the Espiègle "was not visible from the look-outs stationed at the Peacock's mast-heads for some time previous to the commencement of the action, and gives rather an awkward appearance to Captain Lawrence's statement, that the Espiègle lay about six miles in-shore of him, and "could plainly see the whole of the action." If another confirmation were wanted, it is to be found in the log of the Espiègle; by which it appears, that, although pieces of wreck passed her on the morning of the 25th, Captain Taylor did not know that an action had taken place until informed, the same afternoon, by the governor of Demerara, of the Peacock's destruction.

It was fortunate, perhaps, for the character of the British navy that the disordered state of her rigging prevented the Espiègle from sailing out to engage the ship, which, at noon on the day of action, she plainly saw, and continued to see for nearly an hour, until the Hornet tacked and stood to the south-east; as, at the court-martial subsequently held upon him, Captain Taylor was found guilty of having "neglected to exercise the ship's company at the great guns." It seemed hard, however, to punish the Espiègle's commander for a piece of neglect, which prevailed over two-thirds of the British navy; and to which the admiralty, by their sparing allowance of powder and shot for practice at the guns, were in some degree instrumental.

Much good as, we flatter ourselves, we have done to the cause of truth, by analyzing the American accounts of their naval actions with the English, the inattention of a contemporary may throw some doubt upon the accuracy of our statement respecting the relative force of the parties in the case that has just been detailed. Captain Brenton, with a particularity not common with him, states, that "the force of the Peacock was sixteen 32-pound carronades and two long sixes.[1] Admitting that neither our former work on the subject, published some years ago, nor the first edition of the present work, and into which we know our contemporary has occasionally dipped, was deemed of sufficient authority, what has Captain Brenton to say to Lieutenant Wright's letter, published in all the London papers? Nay, what objection has he to offer to the official statement of Captain Lawrence himself, "She (the Peacock) mounted sixteen 24-pound carronades and two long nines?"

The counter-statement of our contemporary, it is true, may

[1] Brenton, vol. v., p. 111.

have little weight in this country; but not so in the United States—not so among a people whom we are, and long have been, labouring so hard to convince of the inutility, even in a profit-and-loss point of view, of telling a falsehood. There the high rank and presumed practical experience of the author, and his long list of kings, princes, *princesses*, dukes, and officers of the navy, for subscribers, will produce their full effect: the Americans will be convinced that, in the hurry of the moment, Captain Lawrence made a mistake respecting the force of his prize. By-the-by, Captain Brenton is not the only British officer who has given the Peacock 32-pounder carronades: a post-captain, who, about 18 months ago, volunteered to correct the misstatements of a very captivating writer, both for and against the Americans, did the same. That the established armament of the Peacock's class was 32-pounders, there cannot be a doubt; any more than that the brig, being new and built of oak, was well able to bear them. But Captain Peake probably considered that 24-pounders gave a lighter appearance to his deck, and took up less room. We know not what other reason to assign for the change.

We left in the port of Boston the three American frigates Constitution,[1] President, and Congress.[2] A fourth, the 36-gun frigate Chesapeake, Captain Samuel Evans, sailed from Boston on the 17th of December, 1812; ran down past Madeira, the Canaries, and Cape-de-Verds; thence on the equator between longitudes 16° and 25°, where the American frigate cruised six weeks. The Chesapeake afterwards steered for the coast of South America, and passing within 15 leagues of Surinam, was on the same spot on which the Hornet had, the day previous, sunk the Peacock. The frigate then cruised off Barbadoes and Antigua, and, steering homewards, passed between Bermuda and the Capes of Virginia. Standing to the northward, the Chesapeake passed within 12 leagues of the Capes of Delaware and 20 of New York, and on the 18th of April, 1813, re-entered Boston by the eastern channel; having, during her 115 days' cruise, recaptured one merchant-vessel and captured four, been chased by a British 74 and frigate, and chased on her part, for two days, a British brig-sloop.

Among the captains of British 38-gun frigates who longed, ardently longed, for a meeting with one of the American 44s, was Captain Philip Bowes Vere Broke, of the Shannon. This desire was not founded on any wish for a display of personal

[1] See vol. v., p. 422.   [2] Ibid., p. 404.

valour, but in order to show to the world what apparent wonders could be effected, where the ship and the crew were in all respects fitted for battle. It was not since the late American war that Captain Broke had begun to put his frigate in fighting order, and to teach his men the art of attack and defence. From the day on which Captain Broke had joined her, the 14th of September, 1806, the Shannon began to feel the influence of her captain's proficiency as a gunner and zeal for the service.

The laying of a ship's ordnance, so that it may be correctly fired in a horizontal direction, is justly deemed a most important operation; as upon it depends, in a great measure, the true aim and destructive effect of every future shot she may fire. On board the Shannon, at her first outfit, this was attended to by Captain Broke in person; and his ingenious mode of laying ships' ordnance has since received the highest commendation. By draughts from other ships, and the usual means to which a British man-of-war is obliged to resort, the Shannon got together a crew; and, in the course of a year or two, by the paternal care and excellent regulations of Captain Broke, an undersized, not very well disposed, and, in point of age, rather motley, ship's company became as pleasant to command as they would have been dangerous to meet. In August, 1811, the Shannon sailed for the coast of North America; and, had this frigate, in the excellent order in which she was kept, met the Constitution in August, 1812, we verily believe —— But the Shannon and Constitution did not meet; therefore the thing was not tried.

On the 21st of March, 1813, accompanied by the Tenedos, of the same force, and kept in nearly the same order, Captain Hyde Parker, the Shannon sailed from Halifax on a cruise in Boston bay. On the 2nd of April the two frigates reconnoitred the harbour of Boston, and saw the President and Congress, the latter quite, and the former nearly ready for sea. The Constitution was at this time undergoing a large repair; and her decks were being lowered, to render her more snug, and give her a smaller, and more inviting appearance. Captains Broke and Parker having resolved, if in their power, to bring the President and Congress to action, the Shannon and Tenedos took a station to intercept them. It was in this interval that the Chesapeake escaped into the port in the manner related; and on the 1st of May, foggy weather and a sudden favourable shift of wind, enabled the President and Congress to elude the vigilance of the two British frigates and put to sea.

Captains Broke and Parker very soon discovered the chance they had missed, and sadly disappointed they were. There now remained in Boston only the Constitution and Chesapeake. The first, as has been stated, was undergoing a serious repair; but the Chesapeake had only to get in her main and mizen masts, and would be ready for sea in a week or two. Having obtained a furlough to enjoy his share of prize-money, Captain Evans was succeeded in the command of the Chesapeake by Captain James Lawrence, the late fortunate, highly applauded, and, we readily admit, truly gallant commander of the Hornet.

As two frigates were not required to attack one, and as the appearance of such a superiority would naturally prevent the Chesapeake from putting to sea, Captain Broke, on the 25th of May, took a supply of water and provisions from the Tenedos, and detached her, with orders to Captain Parker not to rejoin him before the 14th of June; by which time, it was hoped, the business would be over. On the 26th the Shannon recaptured the brig Lucy, and on the 29th the brig William, both of Halifax. Aware of the state of incapacity to which some of the British frigates on the station had reduced themselves, by manning and sending in their prizes, Captain Broke destroyed all he captured. We believe he had sacrificed not fewer than 25 sail of prizes, to keep the Shannon in a state to meet one or the other of the American frigates. Being resolved to have a meeting with the Chesapeake, nothing but the circumstance of the two recaptures belonging to Halifax could induce Captain Broke to weaken the Shannon's crew by sending them in. The master of the Lucy, assisted by five recaptured seamen belonging to some ship on the station, carried in that vessel; and a midshipman and four of the Shannon's men took charge of the William. On the 29th, in the afternoon, the Shannon boarded the Nova Scotia privateer brig Sir John Sherbrooke, and took from her 22 Irish labourers, whom the brig, three days before, with 30 more (then volunteers on board herself), had recaptured in a prize belonging to the American privateer Governor Plumer; bound, when the latter fell in with her, from Waterford to Burin, Newfoundland.

Before we proceed further, let us show what guns were mounted by the two frigates, whose mutual animosity was on the eve of being quenched by the capture of one of them. On her main deck, the Shannon was armed the same as every other British frigate of her class, and her established guns on the quarter-deck and forecastle were 16 carronades, 32-pounders, and four long 9-pounders, total 48 guns. But Captain Broke had since had mounted a 12-pounder boat-carronade through a port purposely made on the starboard side of the quarter-deck, and a brass long 6 pounder, used generally as an exercise gun, through a similar port on the larboard side; besides which there were two 12-pounder carronades, mounted as standing stern-chasers through the quarter-deck stern-ports. For these last four guns, one 32-pounder carronade would have been more than an equivalent. However, as a 6-pounder counts as well as a 32-pounder, the Shannon certainly mounted 52 carriage-guns. The ship had also, to be in that respect upon a par with the American frigates, one swivel in the fore, and another in the main top.

The armament of the Chesapeake, we have already on more than one occasion described: she had at this time, as afterwards found on board of her, 28 long 18-pounders on the main deck, and 20 carronades, 32-pounders, and one long shifting 18-pounder, on the quarter-deck and forecastle, total 49 guns; exclusively of a 12-pounder boat-carronade, belonging to which there was a very simple and well-contrived elevating carriage for firing at the tops, but it is doubtful if the gun was used. Five guns, four 32-pounder carronades and one long 18-pounder, had, it was understood, been landed at Boston. Some have alleged, that this was done by Captain Lawrence, that he might not have a numerical superiority over his antagonists of the British 38-gun class: others say, and we incline to be of that opinion, that the reduction was ordered by the American government, to ease the ship, whose hull had already begun to hog, or to arch in the centre.

On the 1st of June, early in the morning, having received no answer to several verbal messages sent in, and being doubtful if any of them had even been delivered, Captain Broke addressed to the commanding officer of the Chesapeake a letter of challenge, which, for candour, manly spirit, and gentlemanly style stands unparalleled. The letter begins: "As the Chesapeake appears now ready for sea, I request you will do me the favour to meet the Shannon with her, ship to ship, to try the fortune of our respective flags." The Shannon's force is thus described: "The Shannon mounts 24 guns upon her broadside, and one light boat-gun, 18-pounders upon her main deck, and 32-pound carronades on her quarter-deck and forecastle, and is manned with a complement of 300 men and boys (a large proportion of the latter), besides 30 seamen, boys, and passengers, who were taken out of recaptured vessels lately." After fixing the place of meeting, and providing against all interruption, Captain Broke concludes thus: "I entreat you, sir, not to imagine that I am urged by mere personal vanity to the wish of meeting the Chesapeake; or that I depend only upon your personal ambition for your acceding to this invitation. We have both nobler motives. You will feel it as a compliment if I say, that the result of our meeting may be the most grateful service I can render to my country; and I doubt not that you, equally confident of success, will feel convinced, that it is only by repeated triumphs in *even combats* that your little navy can now hope to console your country for the loss of that trade it can no longer protect. Favour me with a speedy reply. We are short of provisions and water, and cannot stay long here."

This letter Captain Broke intrusted to a Captain Slocum, a discharged prisoner, then about to proceed, in his own boat, to Marblehead, a port a few miles north of Boston. Shortly afterwards the Shannon, with colours flying, stood in close to Boston lighthouse, and lay to. The Chesapeake was now seen at anchor in President roads, with royal yards across and apparently ready for sea. The American frigate presently loosed her foretopsail, and, shortly afterwards, all her topsails, and sheeted them home. The wind, blowing a light breeze from west by north, was perfectly fair. At about 30 minutes past noon, while the men of the Shannon were at dinner, Captain Broke went himself to the mast-head, and there observed the Chesapeake fire a gun, and loose and set topgallantsails. The American frigate was soon under way, and made more sail as she came down, having in her company numerous sailing pleasure-boats, besides a large schooner gun-boat, with, we believe, Commodores Bainbridge and Hull, and several other American naval officers on board. While at the Shannon's mast-head, Captain Broke saw that Captain Slocum's boat had not reached the shore in time for the delivery of his letter of challenge to the commander of the Chesapeake. Notwithstanding this, there cannot be a doubt, that Captain Lawrence had obtained the consent of Commodore Bainbridge (whose orders from the government at Washington were to despatch the Chesapeake to sea as soon as she was ready), to sail and attack the Shannon, in compliance with one or more of the verbal challenges which had been sent in. It was natural for the conqueror of the Peacock to wish for an opportunity to capture or drive away a British ship that had repeatedly lay to off the port, and, in view of all the citizens, had used every endeavour to provoke the Chesapeake to come out and engage her.

At 0 h. 55 m. P.M., Cape Ann bearing north-north-east half-east distant 10 or 12 miles, the Shannon filled, and stood out from the land under easy sail. At 1 P.M. the Chesapeake rounded the lighthouse under all sail; and at 3 h. 40 m. P.M. hauled up, and fired a gun, as if in defiance; or, perhaps, to induce the Shannon to stop, and allow the gun-vessel and pleasure-boat spectators an opportunity of witnessing how speedily an American, could "whip" a British frigate. Presently afterwards the Shannon did haul up, and reefed topsails. At 4 P.M. both ships, now about seven miles apart, again bore away: the Shannon with her foresail clewed up, and her maintopsail braced flat and shivering, that the Chesapeake might overtake her. At 4 h. 50 m. the Chesapeake took in her studding-sails, topgallant-sails, and royals, and got her royal-yards on deck. At 5 h. 10 m. P.M., Boston lighthouse bearing west distant about six leagues, the Shannon again hauled up, with head to the southward and eastward, and lay to, under topsails, topgallant-sails, jib, and spanker.

At 5 h. 25 m. the Chesapeake hauled up her foresail, and, with three ensigns flying, one at the mizenroyalmast-head, one at the peak, and one, the largest of all, in the starboard main rigging, steered straight for the Shannon's starboard quarter. The Chesapeake had also, flying at the fore, a large white flag, inscribed with the words: "SAILORS' RIGHTS AND FREE TRADE;" upon a supposition, perhaps, that this favourite American motto would paralyze the efforts, or damp the energy of the Shannon's men. The Shannon had a union-jack at the fore, an old rusty blue ensign at the mizen-peak, and, rolled up and stopped, ready to be cast loose if either of these should be shot away, one ensign on the main stay and another in the main rigging. Nor, standing much in need of paint, was her outside appearance at all calculated to inspire a belief of the order and discipline which reigned within.

At 5 h. 30 m. P.M., to be under command, and ready to wear if necessary, in the prevailing light breeze, the Shannon filled her main topsail and kept a close luff; but, at the end of a few minutes, having gathered way enough, she again shook the wind out of the sail, and kept it shivering, and also brailed up her driver. Thinking it not unlikely that the Chesapeake would pass under the Shannon's stern, and engage her on the larboard side, Captain Broke divided his men, and directed such as could not fire with effect to be prepared to lie down as the enemy's ship passed. But, either overlooking or waving this advantage,

Captain Lawrence, at 5 h. 40 m., gallantly luffed up, within about 50 yards, upon the Shannon's starboard quarter, and, squaring his main-yard, gave three cheers.

The Shannon's guns were loaded thus: the aftermost main-deck gun with two round shot and a keg containing 150 musket-balls, the next gun with one round and one double-headed shot, and so alternately along the broadside.[1] The Captain of the 14th gun, William Mindham, had been ordered to fire, the moment his gun would bear into the Chesapeake's second main-deck port from forward. At 5 h. 50 m. P.M. the Shannon's aftermost main-deck gun was fired, and the shot was seen to strike close to the port at which it had been aimed.[2] In a second or so the 13th gun was fired; then the Chesapeake's bow-gun went off; and then the remaining guns on the broadside of each ship as fast as they could be discharged.

At 5 h. 53 m. P.M., finding that, owing to the quantity of way in the Chesapeake, and the calm she had produced in the Shannon's sails, he was ranging too far ahead; and, being desirous to preserve the weather-gage in order to have an opportunity of crippling the Shannon by his dismantling shot, Captain Lawrence hauled up a little.[3] At 5 h. 56 m., having had her jib-sheet and foretopsail-tie shot away, and her helm, probably from the death of the men stationed at it, being for the moment unattended to, the Chesapeake came so sharp to the wind as completely to deaden her way; and the ship lay, in consequence, with her stern and quarter exposed to her opponent's broadside. The shot from the Shannon's aftermost guns now took a diagonal direction along the decks of the Chesapeake; beating in her stern-ports, and sweeping the men from their quarters. The shot from the Shannon's foremost guns, at the same time, entering the Chesapeake's ports from the main mast aft, did considerable execution.[4] At 5 h. 58 m. an open cask of musket-cartridges, standing upon the Chesapeake's cabin-skylight for the use of the marines, caught fire and blew up, but did no injury whatever. Even the spanker-boom, directly in the way of the explosion, was barely singed.

As the Shannon had by this time fallen off a little, and the manœuvres of the Chesapeake indicated an intention to haul

---

[1] [Sir Howard Douglas, in 'Naval Gunnery,' says he was informed by the first-lieutenant of the Shannon that this was an error, for no kegs of musket-balls and no double-headed shot were used, but the maindeck guns were loaded alternately with two round shot and with one round shot and grape.—H. Y. POWELL.]

[2] See diagram at p. 60.

[3] Ibid.

[4] Ibid. But in this position the engraver has not copied the drawing quite so faithfully as he might have done.

away, Captain Broke ordered the helm to be put a-lee; but scarcely had the Shannon luffed up in obedience to her helm than the Chesapeake was observed to have stern way, and to be paying round off. The Shannon immediately shifted her helm a-starboard, and shivered her mizentopsail, to keep off the wind again, and delay the boarding, probably until her guns had done a little more execution among a crew, supposed to be at least a fourth superior in number. At that moment, however, the Shannon had her jib-stay shot away; and her head-sails being becalmed, she went off very slowly. The consequence was, that, at 6 P.M., the Chesapeake fell on board the Shannon, with her quarter pressing upon the latter's side, just before her starboard main-chains. The Chesapeake's foresail being at this moment partly loose, owing to the weather clue-garnet having been shot away from the bits, the American frigate forged a little ahead, but was presently stopped, by hooking, with her quarter-port, the fluke of the Shannon's anchor stowed over the chess-tree.

Captain Broke now ran forward; and observing the Chesapeake's men deserting the quarter-deck guns, he ordered the two ships to be lashed together, the great guns to cease firing, the main-deck boarders to be called, and Lieutenant George Thomas L. Watt, the first-lieutenant, to bring up the quarter-deck men, who were all boarders. While zealously employed outside the bulwark of the Shannon, making the Chesapeake fast to her, the veteran boatswain, Mr. Stevens (he had fought in Rodney's action), had his left arm hacked off with repeated sabre cuts, and was mortally wounded by musketry. The midshipman commanding on the forecastle, Mr. Samwell, was also mortally wounded. Accompanied by the remaining forecastle party, about 20 in number, Captain Broke, at 6 h. 2 m. P.M., stepped from the Shannon's gangway-rail, just abaft the fore-rigging, on the muzzle of the Chesapeake's aftermost carronade, and thence, over the bulwark, upon her quarter-deck. Here not an officer or man was to be seen. Upon the Chesapeake's gangways, about 25 or 30 Americans made a slight resistance. These were quickly driven towards the forecastle, where a few endeavoured to get down the fore hatchway, but, in their eagerness, prevented each other. Several fled over the bows; and, while part, as it is believed, plunged into the sea, another part reached the main deck through the bridle-ports. The remainder laid down their arms and submitted. Lieutenant Watt, with several quarter-deck men, and serjeant Richard Molyneux, corporal George Osborne, and the first division of marines; also Lieutenant Charles Leslie Falkiner, third of the Shannon, with a division of the main-deck boarders, quickly followed Captain Broke and his small party. Lieutenant Watt, just as he had stepped on the Chesapeake's taffrail, was shot through the foot by a musket-ball fired from the mizentop, and dropped on his knee upon the quarter-deck; but quickly rising up, he ordered Lieutenant of marines James Johns to point one of the Shannon's 9-pounders at the enemy's top. In the mean time Lieutenant Falkiner and the marines, with the second division of which Lieutenant John Law had now arrived, rushed forward; and, while one party kept down the men who were ascending the main hatchway, another party answered a destructive fire still continued from the main and mizen tops. The Chesapeake's main top was presently stormed by midshipman William Smith (now lieutenant *e*) and his top-men, about five in number; who either destroyed or drove on deck all the Americans there stationed. This gallant young man had deliberately passed along the Shannon's fore-yard, which was braced up to the Chesapeake's main-yard, which was nearly square; and thence into her top. All further annoyance from the Chesapeake's mizen top had also been put a stop to by another of the Shannon's midshipmen, Mr. Cosnahan, who, from the starboard main-yard arm, had fired at the Americans, so fast as his men in the top could load the muskets and hand them to him.

After the Americans upon the forecastle had submitted, Captain Broke ordered one of his men to stand sentry over them, and then sent most of the others aft where the conflict was most going on. He was in the act of giving them orders to answer the fire from the Chesapeake's maintop (this was just before Mr. Smith's gallant and successful exploit), when the sentry called lustily out to him. On turning round, the captain found himself opposed by three of the Americans; who, seeing they were superior to the British then near them, had armed themselves afresh. Captain Broke parried the middle fellow's pike, and wounded him in the face; but instantly received from the man on the pikeman's right, a blow with the but-end of a musket, which bared his skull, and nearly stunned him. Determined to finish the British commander, the third man cut him down with his broadsword, but, at that very instant, was himself cut down by Mindham, the Shannon's seaman, already known to us Captain Broke was not the only sufferer upon this occasion: one of his men was killed, and two or three were badly wounded. Can it be wondered, if all that were concerned in this breach of faith fell victims to the indignation of the Shannon's men? It was as much as Captain Broke could do, to save from their fury a young midshipman, who, having slid down a rope from the Chesapeake's foretop, begged his protection. Mr. Smith, who had just at that moment descended from the maintop, assisted Mindham and another of the Shannon's men in helping the captain on his legs. While in the act of tying a handkerchief round his commander's head, Mindham, pointing aft, called out, "There, sir, there goes up the old ensign over the yankee colours." Captain Broke saw it hoisting (with what feelings may well be imagined), and was instantly led to the Chesapeake's quarter-deck, where he seated himself upon one of the carronade-slides.

The act of changing the Chesapeake's colours had proved fatal to a gallant British officer, and to four or five fine fellows of the Shannon's crew. We left Lieutenant Watt, just as, having raised himself on his legs after his wound, he was hailing the Shannon, to fire at the Chesapeake's mizentop. He then called for an English ensign; and, hauling down the American ensign, bent, owing to the halliards being tangled, the English flag below instead of above it. A few seconds before this, the Chesapeake's quarter gallery had given way, and the two ships were gradually separating. Observing the American stripes going up first, the Shannon's people re-opened their fire; and directing their guns with their accustomed precision at the lower part of the Chesapeake's mizenmast, killed their own first-lieutenant (a grape-shot took off the upper part of his head) and four or five of their comrades. Before the flags had got half-way to the mizen-peak, they were lowered down and hoisted properly; and the aggrieved and mortified men of the Shannon ceased their fire.

An unexpected fire of musketry, opened by the Americans who had fled to the hold, killed a fine young marine, William Young. On this, Lieutenant Falkiner, who was sitting on the booms, very properly directed three or four muskets, that were ready, to be fired down. Captain Broke, from his seat upon the carronade-slide, told Lieutenant Falkiner to summon the Americans in the hold to surrender, if they desired quarter. The lieutenant did so. The Americans replied, "We surrender;" and all hostilities ceased. The Shannon was now about 100 yards astern of the Chesapeake, or rather upon her larboard quarter. To enable the Shannon to close, Captain Broke ordered the Chesapeake's mainyard to be braced flat aback, and her foresail to be hauled close up. Almost immediately afterwards Captain Broke's senses failed him from loss of blood; and the Shannon's jolly-boat just then arriving with a fresh supply of men, he was conveyed on board his own ship.

Between the discharge of the first gun, and the period of Captain Broke's boarding, 11 minutes only elapsed; and in four minutes more, the Chesapeake was completely his. The following diagram will explain the few evolutions there were in this quickly-decided action:—

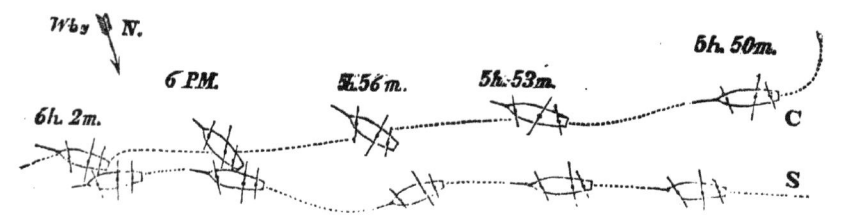

Now for the damage and loss of men sustained by the respective combatants. Five shot passed through the Shannon; one only below the main deck. Of several round shot that struck her, the greater part lodged in the side, ranged in a line just above the copper. A bar-shot entered a little below the water-mark, leaving a foot or 18 inches of one end sticking out. Until her shot-holes were stopped, the Shannon made a good deal of water upon the larboard tack; but, upon the other, not more than usual. Her fore and main masts were slightly injured by shot; and her bowsprit (previously sprung) and mizenmast were badly wounded. No other spar was damaged. Her shrouds on the starboard side were cut almost to pieces; but, from her perfect state aloft, the Shannon, at a moderate distance, appeared to have suffered very little in the action.

Out of a crew, including eight recaptured seamen and 22 Irish labourers two days only in the ship, of 306 men and 24 boys, the Shannon lost, besides her first-lieutenant, her purser (George Aldham), captain's clerk (John Dunn), 13 seamen, four marines, three supernumeraries, and one boy killed, her captain (severely), boatswain (William Stevens, mortally), one midshipman (John Samwell, mortally), and 56 seamen, marines, and supernumeraries wounded: total, 24 killed and 59 wounded.

The Chesapeake was severely battered in her hull, on the larboard quarter particularly. A shot passed through one of her transoms, equal in stoutness to a 64-gun ship's; and several shot entered the stern windows. She had two main-deck guns and one carronade entirely disabled. One 32-pounder carronade was also dismounted, and several carriages and slides broken. Her three lower masts, the main and mizen masts especially, were badly wounded. The bowsprit received no injury; nor was a spar of any kind shot away. Her lower rigging and stays were a good deal cut; but neither masts nor rigging were so damaged that they could not have been repaired, if necessary, without the ships going into port.

Out of a crew of at least 381 men and five boys or lads, the Chesapeake, as acknowledged by her surviving commanding officer, lost her fourth-lieutenant (Edward I. Ballard), master (William A. White), one lieutenant of marines (James Broom), three midshipmen, and 41 petty officers, seamen, and marines killed, her gallant commander and first-lieutenannt (both mortally), her second and third lieutenants (George Budd and William L. Cox), acting chaplain (Samuel Livermore), five midshipmen, her boatswain (mortally), and 95 petty officers, seamen, and marines wounded; total, 47 killed and 99 wounded, 14 of the latter mortally. This is according to the American official account; but, it must be added, that the total that reported themselves, including several slightly wounded, to the Shannon's surgeon, three days after the action, were 115; and the Chesapeake's surgeon wrote from Halifax, that he estimated the whole number of killed and wounded at from 160 to 170.

Of the Chesapeake's guns we have already given a full account: it only remains to point out, that the ship had three spare ports of a side on the forecastle, through which to fight her shifting long 18-pounder and 12-pounder boat-carronade. The former is admitted to have been used in that way; but, as there is some doubt whether the carronade was used, we shall reject it from the broadside force. This leaves 25 guns, precisely the number mounted by the Shannon on her broadside. The accuracy of Captain Broke's statement of his ship's force is, indeed, worthy of remark: he even slightly overrated it, because he represented all his guns of a side on the upper deck, except the boat-gun, as 32-pounder carronades, when two of the number were long nines.

This will be the proper place to introduce an account of some of the extraordinary means of attack and defence to which, in their naval actions with the British, the fears of the Americans had compelled them to resort. Among the Chesapeake's "round and grape" (the only admitted cannon-shot used on board an

American ship), were found double-headed shot in abundance; also bars of wrought iron, about a foot long, connected by links, and folded together by a few rope-yarns, so as, when discharged from the gun, to form an extended length of six feet. Other bars, of twice the length, and in number from three to six, were connected at one end by a ring: these, as they flew from the gun, expanded in four points. The object of this novel artillery was to cut away the shrouds, and facilitate the fall of the masts; and the plan was, to commence the action with the bar and chain shot, so as to produce, as early as possible, that desirable result: after which the American ship could play round her antagonist, and cut her to pieces with comparative impunity.

So much for the *matériel* of her opponent; nor was his *personnel* forgotten. The canister-shot of the Chesapeake, when opened, were found to contain, in the centre, angular and jagged pieces of iron and copper, broken bolts, and copper and other nails. The musket-cartridges, as we formerly noticed, contained each three buck-shot loose in the powder; and several rifled-barrel pieces were found among the small-arms. As British seamen were well known to be terrible fellows for getting on board an enemy, something was to be done to check them in their advance. Accordingly, a large cask of unslacked lime was brought on board the Chesapeake, and placed on the forecastle with the head open, in order that the American crew might scatter the lime by handfuls over the assailants. A bag of the same was placed in the foretop. We do not, however, believe, that Captain Lawrence had any hand in this contrivance. One of the Shannon's early shot struck the cask, and scattered the contents, as if in retribution, over the faces and into the eyes of the projectors. We ourselves saw the remains of the lime on and about the Chesapeake's forecastle: we recollect also observing, that the quarter-deck and forecastle barricades of the American frigate were lined with strong netting, to catch the splinters.

Lieutenant Budd, when called upon to certify as to the number of men with which the Chesapeake went into action, swore to 381; but even admitting his own account of the killed and mortally wounded to be correct, the Chesapeake certainly had five men more. For instance, the prisoners out of the ship, mustered at Halifax, including 91 severely and slightly wounded, and four that were sick, amounted to 325; which number, added to 61, the acknowledged amount of the killed and mortally wounded, makes 386. This was three short of the number, appearing by the Chesapeake's books to have been victualled by her on the morning of the action, and as many as 54 short of the regular complement established upon the ship. Several of the Chesapeake's petty officers, indeed, after their arrival at Melville island prison, near Halifax, confessed that 30 or 40 hands, principally from the Constitution, came on board; but whose names, in the hurry and confusion, were not entered in the purser's books. In confirmation of several men having joined the ship a very short time before the action, a number of bags and hammocks were found lying in the boats stowed over the booms; and, in direct proof that some of the Constitution's men were on board the Chesapeake, three or four of the Guerrière's Americans, who, after that ship's capture, had enlisted on board the Constitution, were among the prisoners taken out of the Chesapeake, and were immediately recognised by their former shipmates, now, as stated before, serving on board the Shannon. But, as the American officer swore that the Chesapeake commenced action with only 381 men, we shall give her no more; and, although not above one boy, that would rate as such in a British ship, was to be seen on board the Chesapeake, we shall allow her five.

In one of the lockers of the Chesapeake's cabin, was found a letter dated in February, 1811, addressed by Robert Smith, Esq., then secretary at war, to Captain Samuel Evans at Boston, directing him to open houses of rendezvous for manning the Chesapeake, and enumerating the different classes, or ratings, at a total of 443. The Chesapeake was manned in April, 1811; and as, in the American naval service, the men enlist for two years and sign articles for that period, the ship would require to be remanned in April, 1813, the very month, as we have seen, in which the Chesapeake returned to Boston. The greater part of the crew then re-entered; and, as may be supposed, a very large proportion of those who accepted their discharge were, or rather had been, British men-of-war's men. In order to fill up the deficiency, four houses of rendezvous were opened. The moment a man declared himself a candidate, he received a dollar, and accompanied an officer to the ship. There he was examined as to his knowledge of seamanship, age, muscular strength, &c., by a board of officers, consisting of the master, surgeon, and others: if approved, the man signed the articles and remained where he was; if rejected, he returned to the shore with a dollar in his pocket. So fastidious was the committee of inspection, that frequently, out of five boat-loads of men that would go cfl to the ship in the course of the day, three would come back, not eligible. The features of the American war would have borne a very different aspect, could British ships have been manned in a similar way.

As far as appearance went, the Chesapeake's was a remarkably fine crew; and a clear proof of the stoutness of the men was afforded, when, in the middle of the night after the action, in consequence of a strong manifestation of a desire to retake the ship, the irons, which the Americans had got ready for the wrists of the Shannon's crew, and which, to the number of 360, were stowed in a puncheon, with the head off, standing under the half-deck, came to be put upon the wrists of the Chesapeake's crew. None of the Americans found them too large, and many, when not allowed to choose such as fitted them, complained that the manacles hurt them on account of their tightness.

Among the 325 prisoners, whose names were set down in the agent's book at Halifax, about 32, including the gunner, were recognised as British seamen. This fellow was an Irishman, and went by the name of Matthew Rogers; by which name, but with, of course, a blank for his birth-place, he stands in the Washington "Register" formerly noticed by us. It is probable that, had the Chesapeake been taken when Captain Evans commanded her, five times 32 traitors would have been found on board of her. Nay, the men who, when the first party from the Shannon rushed on board, leaped from the Chesapeake's bows into the water were, it is natural to conjecture, deserters from British ships-of-war. That they were not all Americans, the following anecdote will prove. One of the Shannon's men, when in the act of cutting down one of the Chesapeake's men, was stopped by the imploring ejaculation, "Would you, Bill?" "What, Jack!" "Ay, Bill, but it won't do; so here goes." Overboard the poor fellow sprang, and was seen no more. This man's name was John Waters, a fine young Bristolian, who had deserted from the Shannon, when at anchor in Halifax harbour, on the 3rd of the preceding October. We naturally turn to the return of loss at the foot of the American official account; but we search in vain for the name of "John Waters." It is true that he most likely went by another name; but, as it is customary to report men who fall or leap overboard, or who are not actually slain or wounded in the action, under the head of "Missing," and no such head appearing in the American returns, we conclude that all the men of the Chesapeake, whose shame-stricken consciences prompted them to commit self-destruction in the manner of poor Waters, were purposely omitted. We are therefore more than ever convinced that, when she commenced engaging the Shannon, the Chesapeake had on board upwards of 400 men. But, as we said before, the American sworn amount only shall be introduced into the

Comparative Force of the Combatants.

		Shannon.	Chesapeake.
Broadside-guns	No.	25	25
	lbs.	538	590
Crew (men only)	No.	306	376
Size	tons.	1066	1135

It is clear from this statement, that the "superiority of force," little as it may have been, was on the side of the Chesapeake. That we will not, for a moment, dwell on; nor shall the American star and chain shot, and hogshead of lime, be allowed to disturb the equality and fairness of the action. But Captain Broke did something more than capture an American frigate of equal force: he sought and commenced the attack close to an American port filled with armed vessels, and beat his ship in 11, and captured her in 15 minutes: thereby proving, that the bard, who eight months before had sung,

> And, as the war they did provoke,
> We'll pay them with our cannon;
> The first to do it will be BROKE,
> In the gallant ship the SHANNON,[1]

was not a false prophet.

Thus was the spell broken; and we may remark, that the Chesapeake was not finally subdued by a superiority in that quality which constituted the forte of the Shannon, her gunnery. No, it was by boarding; by Captain Broke's quick discernment in catching, and his promptitude and valour in profiting by, the critical moment, when the Chesapeake's men were retreating from their quarters. Gallant, truly gallant, was the behaviour of Captain Lawrence. His first-lieutenant, Augustus Charles Ludlow, emulated his commander; and both deserved a better crew than the Chesapeake's; a crew that (oh, woful addition!) consisted, within about a twelfth part, of native Americans.

Owing to Captain Broke's incapacity from his wound, Lieutenant Provo William Parry Wallis, second of the Shannon, took

[1] Naval Chronicle, vol. xxviii, p. 422.

charge of her, and Lieutenant Falkiner, third of the Shannon, remained in charge of the Chesapeake. Having repaired the damage done to their respective rigging, and the Shannon having fished her mizenmast, the two frigates made sail for Halifax; and on the 6th, at 3 h. 30 m. P.M., the prize, followed by her captor, passed along the wharfs of the town, amidst the cheers of the inhabitants, as well as of the crews of the ships-of-war that were lying in the harbour. Captain Lawrence had died on board the Chesapeake of his wounds two days before; and Captain Broke, in a state of severe suffering from his wounds, was removed from the Shannon to the house of the commissioner, Captain the Hon. Philip Wodehouse.

Lieutenants Wallis and Falkiner were both deservedly made commanders. Of the acting-master, Henry Gladwell Etough, Captain Broke in his official letter speaks in high terms; also of Lieutenants of marines James Johns and John Law, and midshipmen William Smith, Hugh Cosnahan, John Samwell, Henry Martin Leake, Douglas Clavering, George Raymond, and David Littlejohn: likewise of Mr. Aldham the purser, and Mr. Dunn the clerk, both of whom were killed at the head of the small-arm men. Mr. Etough, and Messrs. Smith and Cosnahan, were promoted to lieutenants. For his important achievement, and, in respect to its effect on the public mind, a most important achievement it was, Captain Broke was created a baronet; he received, also, the formal thanks of the board of admiralty, and the warm congratulations of every well-wisher to England: and his trophy, the Chesapeake, in a name by which, coupled with that of the Shannon, she will long be remembered both in England and America, was added to the British navy.

As a matter of course, a court of inquiry was held, to investigate the circumstances under which the Chesapeake had been captured. Commodore Bainbridge was the president of the court; and the following is the first article of the very "lengthy" report published on the subject: "The court are unanimously of opinion, that the Chesapeake was gallantly carried into action by her late brave commander; and no doubt rests with the court, from comparison of the injury respectively sustained by the frigates, that the fire of the Chesapeake was much superior to that of the Shannon. The Shannon, being much cut in her spars and rigging, and receiving many shot in and below the water-line, was reduced almost to a sinking condition, after only a few minutes' cannonading from the Chesapeake; whilst the

Chesapeake was comparatively uninjured. And the court have no doubt, if the Chesapeake had not accidentally fallen on board the Shannon, and the Shannon's anchor got foul in the after-quarter-port of the Chesapeake, the Shannon must have very soon surrendered or sunk." Some very singular admissions of misconduct in the officers and crew follow; and then the report proceeds as follows : " From this view of the engagement, and a careful examination of the evidence, the court are unanimously of opinion, that the capture of the late United States frigate Chesapeake was occasioned by the following causes : the almost unexampled early fall of Captain Lawrence, and all the principal officers ; the bugleman's desertion of his quarters, and inability to sound his horn; for the court are of opinion, if the horn had been sounded when first ordered, the men being then at their quarters, the boarders would have promptly repaired to the spar-deck, probably have prevented the enemy from boarding, certainly have repelled them, and might have returned the boarding with success ; and the failure of the boarders on both decks, to rally on the spar-deck, after the enemy had boarded, which might have been done successfully, it is believed, from the cautious manner in which the enemy came on board."

It was certainly very "cautious" in Captain Broke to lead 20 men on board an enemy's ship, supposed to be manned with a complement of 400; and which, at the very moment, had at least 270 men without a wound about them. The court of inquiry makes, also, a fine story of the firing down the hatchway. Not a word is there of the "magnanimous conquered foe" having fired from below, in the first instance, and killed a British marine. Captain Broke will long have cause to remember the treatment he experienced from this "magnanimous conquered foe." So far, indeed, from the conduct of the British being "a most unwarrantable abuse of power after success," Lieutenant Cox of the Chesapeake, in the hearing of several English gentlemen, subsequently admitted that he owed his life to the forbearance of one of the Shannon's marines. When the American officers arrived on board the Shannon, and some of them were finding out reasons for being "taken so unaccountably," their first-lieutenant, Mr. Ludlow, candidly acknowledged that the Shannon had beaten them heartily and fairly.

Although it would not do for an official document, like that we have just been quoting, to contain an admission that any portion, any influential portion at least, of the crew of an American ship-of-war consisted of British seamen, the journalists, pamphleteers, and historians of the United States did not scruple to attribute to the defection of the latter, the unfortunate issue of the business with the Chesapeake. "There are no better sailors in the world," says an American writer, "than our own; and it seems hard that the war should be carried on for nothing but British sailors' rights, and that those same sailors should desert us in the moment of conflict. Cowardice is a species of treason. If renegado Englishmen are permitted to fight under our flag, it becomes prudent not to mix our own people with them to be destroyed; for, at the critical moment when the boarders were called, the foreigners all ran below, while not a native American shrank from the conflict." A writer in a Boston paper, after he has insisted that the "native Americans" on board the Chesapeake "fought like heroes," and that the British part of the crew "behaved treacherously," very naturally asks, "Can any of your correspondents inform us whether any Americans were on board the Shannon?" We may answer, Yes, there were some (prisoners), in her hold; although not so many, by several scores, as were in the hold of the Chesapeake, in a very few seconds after the Shannon's boarders sprang upon her quarter-deck.

But, had the Chesapeake, instead of 32, mustered 100, British men-of-war's men in her crew, we have not a doubt that the same result would have ensued. However expert and courageous these renegades may be when sheltered behind a bulwark, they become paralyzed with shame, they sink into the veriest cowards in nature, when opposed face to face to their shipmates of former days, their partners in scenes which they *can* remember with credit. The American commanders have tact enough to see this; hence arises the preference they give to a cannonade engagement; hence the repugnance they invariably show, unless with a twofold superiority, to grapple with their British antagonists.

Previously to our dismissing the action of the Shannon and Chesapeake, we shall confer a service on the profession, by stating as much as we know of the means taken by Captain Broke, to endow his men with that proficiency at the guns, the effects of which were so decisive and astonishing. Every day, for about an hour and a half in the forenoon, when not prevented by chase or the state of the weather, the men were exercised at training the guns, and, for the same time in the afternoon, in the use of the broadsword, pike, musket, &c. Twice a week the crew fired at targets, both with great guns and musketry; and

Captain Broke, as an additional stimulus beyond the emulation excited, gave a pound of tobacco to every man that put a shot through the bull's eye. As the Shannon was always clear for action, and had on deck a sufficient quantity of ammunition for two or three broadsides, it was impossible to take her by surprise; nor could the officers well complain of the want of a few of their cabin conveniences, when the cabin of their chief was so completely stripped of everything which was not absolutely indispensable, of everything that could not be removed at a moment's notice.

The Chesapeake's late captain was buried at Halifax on the 8th, with military honours such as a post-captain in the British navy of less than three years' standing would be entitled to; and, unlike poor Captain Lambert at St. Salvador,[1] Captain Lawrence was followed to his grave by all the naval captains in port. Lieutenant Ludlow died of his wounds while at Halifax, and was also buried with military honours. On the 10th of August a cartel arrived from Boston, and applied for and carried away the remains of the late captain of the Chesapeake and his first-lieutenant, to be deposited, with suitable ceremony, in their own country.

On the 1st of May, as already stated,[2] Commodore Rodgers, with the President and Congress frigates, the latter still commanded by Captain Smith, sailed from President roads, Boston, on his third cruise. On the 2nd the two American frigates fell in with and chased the British 18-gun brig-sloop Curlew, Captain Michael Head; but, by knocking away the wedges of her masts, and using other means to increase her sailing, the brig effected her escape. On the 8th, in latitude 39° 30' north, longitude 60° west, the Congress, whether by intention or accident is not stated, parted company.

The commodore now proceeded alone; pleased, no doubt, at the prospect thus afforded him, of rivalling his brother commodores in the capture, single-handed, of a "large-class" British frigate, and, like each of them, of being hailed on his return as one of the first of naval conquerors. The President cruised along the eastern edge of the Grand Bank of Newfoundland, so as to cross the tracks of the West India, Halifax, Quebec, and St. John's trade. Having reached latitude 48° without meeting anything, the commodore stood to the south-east, and cruised off the Azores until the 6th of June; when, learning from an American merchant-vessel, that she had, four days

[1] See vol. v., p. 421.   [2] See p. 54.

previous, passed a homeward-bound West India fleet, the President crowded sail to the north-east. Commodore Rodgers, however, was too late; and, even had the President got among the merchant-ships, the admirable sailing of their escort the Cumberland 74, Captain Thomas Baker, might have made the commodore regret that he had acted upon the information of his countryman.

On the 13th of June, being then in latitude 46° north, longitude 28° west, the disappointed commodore resolved to shape a course towards the North Sea, in the hope of falling in with vessels bound from St. George's Channel to Newfoundland; but, to his "astonishment," no prize fell in his way. The President subsequently made the Shetland islands, and on the 27th of June put into North Bergen for provisions and water. Water was all the commodore could obtain; and, provided with a supply of that wholesome article, the President quitted North Bergen on the 2nd of July, and stretched over towards the Orkney islands; and thence towards the North Cape, for the purpose of intercepting a convoy of 25 or 30 sail, which the commodore had understood would leave Archangel about the middle of the month, under the protection of two British brig-sloops.

On the 19th of July, when off the North Cape, in company with the privateer-schooner Scourge, of New York, and in momentary expectation of meeting the Archangel fleet, Commodore Rodgers was driven from his station by, in the language of his official letter, "a line-of-battle ship and a frigate," but, in the language of truth, by the British 12-pounder 32-gun frigate Alexandria, Captain Robert Cathcart, and 16-gun ship-sloop Spitfire, Captain John Ellis. As the commodore is very brief in his account of this meeting, we shall take our narrative from the logs of the two British ships. On the day in question, at 2 h. 30 m. P.M., latitude at noon (the mean of the two ships' reckonings) 71° 52' north, longitude 20° 18' east, the Alexandria and Spitfire, standing south-east by south, with a light wind from the northward, discovered a frigate and a large schooner in the north-north-east. The two British ships immediately hauled up in chase, and at 5 h. 30 m. P.M. tacked to the west-north-west, making the Russian as well as English private signals. At 6 h. 15 m. the President and her consort, who had hitherto been standing towards the two British ships, tacked from them to the north-west, under all sail, followed by the Alexandria and Spitfire. At 7 h. 30 m. P.M. the Spitfire was within five miles of the President, who then bore from her north-north-west. In order that there may be no doubt of identity in this case, we subjoin a brief extract or two from the letter of Commodore Rodgers. "At the time of meeting with the enemy's two ships, the privateer-schooner Scourge, of New York, had fallen in company."—"I stood towards them until, making out what they were, I hauled by the wind upon the opposite tack to avoid them."

The lightness of the night in these latitudes enabling the British frigate and sloop to keep sight of their enemy, no interruption occurred in the chase. On the 20th, at 4 h. 30 m. P.M., finding that the Spitfire, as well as the President, was gaining upon her, the Alexandria cut away her bower-anchor. At 4 h. 40 m. the Scourge parted company from the President, who was now nearly hull-down from the leading British ship. A schooner being unworthy game when a frigate was in sight, the Alexandria and Spitfire continued in pursuit of the President. "Their attention," says the commodore, "was so much engrossed by the President, that they permitted her (the Scourge) to escape, without appearing to take any notice of her."

At 6 P.M., when the Alexandria bore from the Spitfire full two miles south-south-east, the President bore north distant only six miles. From this time the American frigate continued gaining upon the Spitfire until 1 h. 10 m. P.M. on the 21st; when, thick weather comin on, the latter lost sight both of her consort and her chase. The discharge of four guns, however, by the Alexandria, enabled the Spitfire to close. The two British ships again making sail, the sloop, at 2 h. 15 m. P.M., again got sight of the President, in the west-south-west, and at 4 P.M. was once more within six miles of her; which, says the commodore, "was quite as near as was desirable." The chase continued, during the remainder of the 21st, to the advantage of the American frigate, until 8 A.M. on the 22nd, when the Spitfire, a fourth time, got within six miles of the President; who again, by the most strenuous efforts, began increasing her distance.

At 6 P.M., when nearly hull-down from the little persevering sloop, and quite out of sight from the Alexandria, the President fired a gun, hoisted an American ensign at her peak, and a commodore's broad pendant at her main, and hauled upon a wind to the westward. Captain Ellis continued gallantly to stand on, until, at 6 h. 40 m. P.M., Captain Cathcart, who was then eight miles in the east-north-east of his consort, considerately signalled the Spitfire to close. As soon as the latter had done so, sail was again made; and the chase continued throughout that night, and until 10 A.M. on the 23rd; when the President had run completely out of sight of both "the line-of-battle ship and the frigate," or, as an American historian says, of the "two line-of-battle ships,"[1] which had so long been pursuing her.

Among the prisoners on board the President at the time of the chase, were the master and mate of the British snow Daphne, of Whitby. According to the journal of these men, published in the newspapers, they, as well as many of the President's officers and men, were convinced that the chasing ships were a small frigate and a sloop-of-war. They describe, in a ludicrous manner, the preparations on board the President, to resist the attack of this formidable squadron. During each of the three days a treble allowance of grog was served out to the crew, and an immense quantity of star, chain, and other kinds of dismantling shot got upon deck, in readiness for action. It appears also that, when the Eliza Swan whaler hove in sight a few days afterwards, she was supposed to be a large ship-of-war, and the ceremony with the grog and dismantling shot was repeated. After a very cautious approach on the part of the President, the chase was discovered to be a clump of a merchantman, and made prize of accordingly.

In the above, as the American commodore accurately states it, "80 hours' chase," what a contrast appears in the gallantry of one party, and the pusillanimity of the other. Will any one pretend that the flight of Commodore Rodgers was all the effect of delusion? What! mistake a ship of 422 tons for a frigate, and a frigate of 662 tons for a "line-of-battle ship"? Well was it for the commodore that he did not belong to the British navy. Well was it, too, for Captains Cathcart and Ellis, that the Alexandria sailed so ill; for it was physically impossible that she and the Spitfire should have come off victorious. Yet, that gallantry, which had urged their captains to the pursuit of so formidable a ship, a ship known by her ensign and broad pendant to be a similar frigate to those that had captured, in succession, the Guerrière, Macedonian, and Java, would have impelled them to stand by each other, until both ships had either been buried in the deep, or become the trophies of the American commodore.

Overjoyed at his escape, Commodore Rodgers determined to

---

[1] Naval Monument, p. 230.

quit a region where constant daylight afforded an enemy so many advantages over him: he therefore crowded sail to the westward. On the 2nd of August, after the President had been four or five days in a good position for intercepting the trade passing in and out of the Irish Channel, a rumour of "superior force in that vicinity," another "line-of-battle ship and frigate" probably, rendered it expedient for the commodore to shift his cruising-ground. He then made the circuit of Ireland; and, getting into the latitude of Cape Clear, steered for the banks of Newfoundland. Here Commodore Rodgers was near being gratified with the sight of a real line-of-battle ship and frigate, the Bellerophon 74, Captain Edward Hawker, bearing the flag of Vice-admiral Sir Richard Goodwin Keats, and the Hyperion 36, Captain William Pryce Cumby.

With this intelligence, the President bent her course towards the United States; and on the 23rd of September, when a little to the southward of Nantucket, succeeded in decoying and capturing the British 5-gun schooner Highflyer, tender to the San-Domingo 74, and commanded by her second-lieutenant, William Hutchinson. That was not all. Owing to a great deal of cunning on one side, and a tolerable share of imbecility on the other, Commodore Rodgers obtained the stations of the different British men-of-war on the American coast; and taking his measures accordingly, was enabled, on the same day, to enter unobserved the harbour of Newport, Rhode-island.

The Congress frigate continued cruising, without effecting any thing of consequence, until the middle of December; when Captain Smith succeeded in reaching, unobserved as it also appears, the harbour of Portsmouth, New Hampshire. One of her officers, when writing to a friend announcing his return, says: "The Congress has 410 of her crew on board, all in good health: she lost four men by sickness, and has manned a prize with a few others." The officer's friend carried this letter to a newspaper editor, and he gave it immediate insertion. There cannot therefore be a doubt, that the Congress had quitted port with at least 425 men; and the Congress and Chesapeake were of the same class. Some months after the arrival of the Congress at Portsmouth, the Tenedos cruised off the port; and, during a long blockade, Captain Parker used every means in his power to induce the Congress to come out and engage him. But the fate of the Chesapeake had put a stop to the future cruises of the American 18-pounder frigates, and the Congress, after a while, was disarmed and laid up.

On the 5th of August, off the southern coast of the United States, the British schooner Dominica, of 12 carronades, 12-pounders, and two sixes, with, as an extra gun, a 32-pounder carronade upon a traversing-carriage, Lieutenant George Wilmot Barretté, having under her convoy the king's packet Princess Charlotte, bound from St. Thomas's to England, fell in with the French, or rather, the Franco-American, privateer-schooner Decatur, of six 12-pounder carronades and one long 18-pounder traversing-carriage, commanded by the celebrated Captain Dominique Diron.[1] We have no other details than those furnished by the American papers; but we suppose that Lieutenant Barretté, the moment he discovered the privateer approaching, hauled off from the packet to meet her.

Commencing the attack from to-windward, at a distance that best suited her long 18-pounder, the Decatur gradually closed with the Dominica, and made an attempt to board, but was repulsed. A second attempt met the same fate; but, after the contest had lasted three-quarters of an hour, the Decatur ran her jib-boom through the Dominica's mainsail, when a third attempt, made by the whole of the French crew, succeeded; that is, the privateer's men gained a footing upon the Dominica's deck. Here a sanguinary conflict ensued; in which Lieutenant Barretté, although he had been wounded early in the action by two musket-balls in the left arm, fought in the most gallant manner, and, refusing to surrender, was killed. Emulating the example of their youthful commander (he was not 26), the remaining officers and men made a noble resistance against double their numbers. Owing to the crowded state of the Dominica's deck from the presence of the boarders, and the valour of the British crew in persisting to struggle with the latter, fire-arms became useless, and cutlasses and cold shot were the chief weapons used. At length, the Dominica's brave crew became diminished to about a dozen effective men and boys; and the Decatur's, then six times more numerous, hauled down the British colours.

Of her 67 men and nine boys, the Dominica had her commander, master (Isaac Sacker), purser (David Brown), two midshipmen (William Archer and William Parry), and 13 seamen and boys killed and mortally wounded, and 47 severely and slightly wounded, including every other officer (her sub-lieutenant was absent) except the surgeon and one midshipman. One of her boys, not 11 years old, was wounded in two places. Poor

[1] See vol. iv., p. 182.

child! it would have suited thee better to have been throwing dumps than "cold shot;" to be gamboling in the nursery, rather than "contending for victory" upon a man-of-war's deck. Out of a crew of at least 120 men, the Decatur had four killed and 15 wounded.

It appears that Captain Diron, by his masterly manœuvres, prevented the Dominica from making any effectual use of her guns, relying for success upon the arm in which he knew he was almost doubly superior. The Dominica was captured by a privateer, certainly, but under circumstances that reflected an honour rather than a disgrace upon the British character. The following paragraph forms a part of Captain Diron's account in the Charleston papers; nor have we been able to discover a contradiction to the serious charges it contains: "During the combat, which lasted an hour, the king's packet Princess Charlotte remained a silent spectator of the scene; and, as soon as the vessels were disengaged from each other, she tacked and stood to the southward."

On the 5th of September, at daylight, as the British brig-sloop (late gun-brig), Boxer, of 12 carronades, 18-pounders, and two sixes, Captain Samuel Blyth, was lying at anchor near Penguin point, a few miles to the eastward of Portland in the United States, the American gun-brig Enterprise, of 14 carronades, 18-pounders, and two nines, Lieutenant-commandant William Burrows, was seen in the south-south-east. At 7 h. 30 m. P.M., leaving her surgeon, two of her midshipmen, and an army officer, a passenger, on shore at Manhegan, "shooting pigeons," the Boxer got under way, and, at 8 h. 30 m., hoisting three English ensigns, bore up for the Enterprise, then standing on the larboard tack. At 9 A.M. the latter tacked and stood to the southward. At 9 h. 30 m., when the two brigs were about four miles apart, it fell calm; and at 11 h. 30 m. a breeze sprang up from the southward, which placed the American brig to windward. At 2 P.M. the Enterprise made sail on a wind, to try her rate of sailing with the Boxer; and, in half an hour, having clearly ascertained his advantage in this respect, as well as that the Boxer was inferior in size and force, Lieutenant Burrows hoisted three American ensigns, and firing a shot of defiance, bore up to engage.

At 3 h. 15 m. P.M. the Boxer, being on the starboard tack, fired her starboard broadside, and immediately received the larboard broadside of the Enterprise in return; the two brigs then not more than half pistol-shot apart. In the very first broadside, an 18-pound shot passed through Captain Blyth's body, and shattered his left arm. The command of the Boxer then devolved upon her only lieutenant, David M'Creery. At about the same time a musket-ball fired from the Boxer mortally wounded Captain Burrows. At 3 h. 30 m. P.M. the Enterprise, now commanded by Lieutenant Edward R. M'Call, ranged ahead, and, rounding to on the starboard tack, raked the Boxer with her starboard guns, and shot away her maintopmast and foretopsail-yard. The American brig then set her foresail, and, taking a position on the starboard bow of her now wholly unmanageable antagonist, continued pouring in successive raking fires until 3 h. 45 m., when the Boxer surrendered.

The Boxer was much cut up in hull and spars, and, out of her 60 men (12 absent) and six boys, lost, besides her commander, three men killed, and 17 men wounded, four of them mortally. The Enterprise suffered very little injury in her hull and spars; but her rigging and sails were a good deal cut. Out of her 120 men and three boys the American brig lost one man killed, her commander, one midshipman (both mortally), and 11 men wounded, one of the latter mortally.

The established armament of the Boxer was 10 carronades; and that number, with her two six-pounders, was as many as the brig could mount with effect or carry with ease. But when the Boxer was refitting at Halifax, Captain Blyth obtained two additional carronades: had he taken on board, instead of them, 20 additional seamen, the Boxer would have been a much more effective vessel. Against the English 18-pounder carronade, complaints have always been made, for its lightness and unsteadiness in action; but the American carronade of that caliber is much shorter in the breech, and longer in the muzzle: therefore it heats more slowly, recoils less, and carries farther. The same is the case, indeed, with all the varieties of the carronade used by the Americans; and they, in consequence, derive advantages in the employment of that piece of ordnance not possessed by the English, whose carronades are notoriously the lightest and most inefficient of any in use. If the English carronade, especially of the smaller calibers, had displayed its imperfections, as these pages have frequently shown that the English 13-inch mortar was in the habit of doing, by bursting after an hour or two's firing, the gun must either have been improved in form, or thrown out of the service. While on the subject of carronades, we may remark, that even the few disadvantages in the carronade, which the Americans have not been able entirely to obviate, they have managed to lessen, by using not only stouter, but double, breechings; one of which, in case the ring-bolt should draw, is made to pass through the timberhead.

Although it was clearly shown, by the number of prisoners received out of her, that the Boxer commenced the action with only 66 men and boys, Captain Isaac Hull was so officious as to address a letter to Commodore Bainbridge at Boston, purposely to express his opinion, that the British brig had upwards of "100 men on board; for," says Captain Hull, "I counted upwards of 90 hammocks." As the American public did not know that, in the British service, every seaman and marine has two hammocks allowed him, this statement from one of their favourite naval officers produced the desired effect all over the republic, Washington not excepted.

The Boxer measured 181 tons and a fraction, the Enterprise at least 245 tons; and, while the bulwarks of the latter were built of solid oak, those of the former consisted, with the exception of one timber between each port, of an outer and an inner plank, pervious to every grape-shot that was fired. As a proof of the difference in the size of the two vessels, the mainmast of the Enterprise was 15 inches more in circumference than that of the Boxer, and her mainyard upwards of 10 feet longer.

We will, however, admit that, but for the twofold disparity in their crews, these two vessels would have been a tolerably fair match. It was not in number of men only that the disparity existed; an acting-master's mate, Hugh James, and three seamen, as proved at the court-martial assembled to try the surviving officers and crew for the loss of the Boxer, deserted their quarters in the action. So that, as the two midshipmen were absent, Lieutenant M'Creery was the only officer left after the death of the captain, and the latter, it will be recollected, was killed in the first broadside; whereas the Enterprise, after her gallant commander fell, had still remaining two lieutenants, one or two master's mates, and four midshipmen. Her crew, also, had evidently been well practised at the guns; but the Boxer's men appear to have known very little what use to make of their guns. The sentence of the court-martial refers particularly to this disgraceful circumstance. Upon the whole, the action of the Boxer and Enterprise was a very creditable affair to the Americans; but, excepting the Frolic's action, and that was a case *sui generis*, it was the first engagement in which an

American vessel had succeeded against a British vessel nearly equal to her in guns; and, even in this case, the American vessel was doubly superior in crew, better formed in every respect, nearly a third larger, and constructed, as we have already stated, of much stouter scantling.

On the 7th of September the gallant commanders of the two brigs were buried at Portland with military and civic honours; and the few surviving officers of the Boxer, to testify their regard for their late commander, caused a tombstone, with a suitable inscription, to be placed over his grave. None of the praises lavished upon the "fine brig-of-war Boxer" could gain her a place among the national vessels of the United States. She was put up to auction, and sold for a merchant-brig; for which service only, and that in peaceable times, she was ever calculated.

On the 12th of August, at 6 h. 30 m. A.M., the British 18-gun brig-sloop Pelican, Captain John Fordyce Maples, anchored in Cork from a cruise. Before the sails were furled, Captain Maples received orders to put to sea again, in quest of an American sloop-of-war, which had been committing serious depredations in St. George's Channel, and of which the Pelican herself had gained some information on the preceding day. At 8 A.M., having supplied herself with a few necessary stores, the Pelican got under way, and beat out of the harbour against a very strong breeze and heavy sea, a proof of the earnestness of her officers and crew.

On the 13th, at 7 h. 30 m. P.M., when standing to the eastward with the wind at north-west, the Pelican observed a fire ahead, and a brig standing to the south-east. The latter was immediately chased under all sail, but was lost sight of in the night. On the 14th, at 4 h. 45 m. A.M., latitude 52° 15′ north, longitude 5° 50′ west, the same brig was seen in the north-east, separating from a ship which she had just set on fire, and steering towards several merchantmen in the south-east. This active cruiser was the United States brig-sloop Argus, Captain William Henry Allen, standing close hauled on the starboard tack, with the wind a moderate breeze from the southward. The Pelican was on the weather-quarter of the Argus, bearing down under a press of sail to close her; nor did the latter make any attempt to escape, her commander, who had been first-lieutenant of the United States in her action with the Macedonian, being confident, as it afterwards appeared, that he could "whip any English 22-gun" (as all the British 18-gun brigs were called in America) sloop-of-war in 10 minutes. Let us now show the force of each of these anxious candidates for the laurel crown.

The Pelican mounted the usual establishment of her class, 16 carronades, 32-pounders, and two long sixes, with a 12-pounder boat-carronade. But, unfortunately, Captain Maples, when recently at Jamaica, had taken on board two brass 6-pounders. As there were no broadside ports for them, these surplusage guns were not thrown into the hold along with the ballast, but were mounted through the sternports, to the perpetual annoyance of the man at the helm, without a redeeming benefit in contributing, in the slightest degree, to the brig's actual force. Of her established complement of 120 men and boys, the Pelican had on board 101 men and 12 boys; and, among her absentees, was her second-lieutenant. The Argus mounted 18 carronades, 24-pounders, and two long English 12-pounders, the same we believe that had belonged to the Macedonian. On quitting the United States upon this cruise, the Argus mustered 157 men and boys; but she had since manned so many prizes as to reduce her crew to 127, or, as acknowledged by her officers, 125, a number that included about three lads or boys.

At 4 h. 30 m. A.M., being unable to get the weather-gage, the Argus shortened sail, to give the Pelican the opportunity of closing. At 5 h. 55 m. A.M., St. David's Head bearing east distant about five leagues, the Pelican hoisted her colours. The Argus immediately did the same, and at 6 A.M., having wore round, opened her larboard guns within grape-distance; receiving in return the starboard broadside of the Pelican. In about four minutes Captain Allen was severely wounded, and the main braces, main springstay, gaff, and trysail-mast of the Argus were shot away. At 6 h. 14 m. the Pelican bore up, to pass astern of the Argus; but the latter, now commanded by Lieutenant William Henry Watson, adroitly threw all aback, and frustrated the attempt, bestowing at the same time a well-intended, but ineffective raking fire. At 6 h. 18 m., having shot away her opponent's preventer-brace and main topsail-tie, and thus deprived her of the use of her after-sails, the Pelican passed astern of and raked the Argus, and then ranged up on her starboard quarter, pouring in her fire with destructive effect. In a short time, having by this vigorous attack had her wheel-ropes and running-rigging of every description shot away, the Argus became entirely unmanageable, and again exposed her stern to the broadside of the Pelican; who, shortly afterwards, passing the broadside of the Argus, placed herself on the latter's starboard-bow. In this position the British brig, at 6 h. 45 m. A.M., boarded the American brig, and instantly carried her, although the master's mate of the Pelican, Mr. William Young. who led the party, received his death-wound from the foretop of the Argus, just as he had stepped upon her gunwale. Even this did not encourage the American crew to rally; and two or three among those who had not run below hauled down the colours.

On board the Pelican, one shot had passed through the boatswain's and another through the carpenter's cabin. Her sides were filled with grape-shot, and her rigging and sails much injured: her foremast and maintopmast were slightly wounded, and so were her royal-masts; but no spar was seriously hurt. Two of her carronades were dismounted. Out of her 101 men and 12 boys, the Pelican lost, besides the master's mate, Mr. Young, slain in the moment of victory, one seaman killed, and five slightly wounded, chiefly by the American musketry and langridge; the latter to the torture of the wounded. Captain Maples had a narrow escape: a spent canister-shot struck, with some degree of force, one of his waistcoat buttons, and then fell on the deck.

The Argus was tolerably cut up in her hull. Both her lower masts were wounded, although not badly, and her fore-shrouds on one side were nearly all destroyed; but, like the Chesapeake, the Argus had no spar shot away. Several of her carronades were disabled. Out of her 122 men and three boys, to appearance a remarkably fine ship's company, the Argus had six seamen killed, her commander, two midshipmen, the carpenter, and three seamen mortally, her first-lieutenant and five seamen severely, and eight others slightly wounded; total, six killed and 21 wounded.[1]

We shall not, of course, reckon as a part of the Pelican's broadside force the two 6-pounders in her stern-ports, nor, for the reason formerly stated, the 12-pounder boat-carronade. Although a trifle shorter on deck than the Pelican, the Argus carried her 10 guns of a side with ease; first, because, being of a smaller caliber, they took up rather less room, and next, because her tiller worked on the 'tween decks, and admitted her aftermost port to be carried nearer to her stern by several feet. The American writers dwelt upon the number of prizes which the Argus had previously made, partly with the view of raising

---

[1] [In 'Naval Occurrences' it says total 24.—H. Y. POWELL.]

an inference, that she had reduced her ammunition to an inadequate amount. The fact is that, after her action with the Pelican, the Argus had more powder left than was supplied to the Pelican at her first outfit; and the American brig's round, grape, and canister-shot, exclusive of bars of iron, old iron, rusty nails, bayonets lashed together with rope-yarn, and other species of American langridge, weighed 22 cwt. With respect, also, to muskets, pistols, swords, and pikes, nearly twice as many were found on board the Argus, as were allowed to a British brig-sloop of the Pelican's class.

The Argus was built at Boston in the year 1799 or 1800: she measured 298 tons American, or 316 English; and her qualifications as a cruiser called forth the following encomium from the editor of the National Intelligencer: "She is admitted to be one of the finest vessels in the service of her class, and the model of such a vessel is certainly inestimable." But the Argus at that time had not been captured by the British. In point of length, the two brigs were the same, within about four feet in favour of the Pelican; who had also three feet more beam, and consequently was of greater measurement by nearly 70 tons. But, while the main yard of the Pelican was 54 feet 7 inches in length, that of the Argus was 55 feet 2 inches. In point of scantling the Argus had also the advantage in a slight degree.

Comparative Force of the Combatants.

		Pelican.	Argus.
Broadside-guns	No.	9	10
	lbs.	262	228
Crew (men only)	No.	101	122
Size	tons.	385	316

We will set the Americans a good example by freely admitting, that there was here a superiority against them; but then, even after she had captured the Argus, the Pelican was in a condition to engage and make prize of another American brig just like her. The slight loss incurred on one side in this action is worth attending to, not only by the boasters in the United States, but by the croakers in Great Britain.

Despatching his prize, with half her crew, including the wounded, and a full third of his own, in charge of the Pelican's first and only lieutenant, Thomas Welsh, to Plymouth, Captain Maples himself, with the remaining half of the prisoners, proceeded to Cork, to report his proceedings to Admiral Thornborough. On the 16th the Argus arrived at Plymouth; and soon afterwards, for the promptitude, skill, and gallantry which he had displayed, Captain Maples was most deservedly posted. Captain Allen had his left thigh amputated by his own surgeon; and, notwithstanding every attention, died on the 18th of August, at Mill Prison hospital. On the 21st he was buried with high military honours, and attended to his grave by all the navy, marine, and army officers in the port.

A court of inquiry was of course held on the surviving officers and crew of the Argus, for the loss of their vessel. The court declared, "it was proved that, in the number of her crew, and in the number and caliber of her guns, the Pelican was decidedly superior to the Argus." How it was "proved" that the Pelican had more men than the Argus, or what was the number that either vessel carried, the court did not deem it worth while to state. Nor does Lieutenant Watson in his official letter, and which doubtless was before the court, make the slightest allusion to any superiority on the part of the Pelican in number of men. But the court was not aware, perhaps, that Lieutenant Watson, and the two officers next in rank to him, had solemnly sworn, in a British prize-court, that the Argus went into action with 125 men. Lieutenant Watson officially enumerates the Pelican's guns, boat-carronade and all, at 21; and, many months before the sitting of the court, that officer, Lieutenant William Henry Allen the younger, and the brig's master, had sworn that the Argus mounted 20 guns; a very "decided" superiority certainly. Upon the whole, we must conclude that these American courts of inquiry are less scrupulous about the truth than the expediency of the decisions they pronounce; and yet some persons may consider it not very wise in the Americans, looking back on their previous boastings, to make the "caliber of guns" a subject of investigation.

Unfortunately, the capture of frigate after frigate by the Americans could not persuade the British government that the United States were in earnest about going to war. Hence, instead of one of the 10 or 12 dashing flag-officers, whose names have recently figured in these pages, being sent out to fight the Americans into compliance, a superannuated admiral, whose services, such as they were, bore a very old date, arrived, early in March, 1813, in Chesapeake bay, to try the effect of diplomacy and procrastination. Had not Sir John Warren's second in command, Rear-admiral Cockburn, been of a more active turn, the inhabitants of that very exposed part of the American sea-frontier, the coast around the bay in which the two admirals had cast anchor, would scarcely have known, except by hearsay, that war existed. But, before we proceed to give an account of the proceedings of Rear-admiral Cockburn in the rivers at the head of the Chesapeake, we have to relate a boat-attack that took place a few weeks previous to his arrival on the American coast.

On the 8th of February, at 9 A.M., while a British squadron, consisting of the 18-pounder 36-gun frigates Maidstone and Belvidera, Captains George Burdett and Richard Byron, and 38-gun frigates Junon and Statira, Captains James Sanders and Hassard Stackpoole, was at anchor in Lynhaven bay, a schooner was observed in the north-west, standing down Chesapeake bay. Immediately the boats of the Belvidera and Statira were detached in chase. Shortly afterwards, on Captain Byron's making the signal, that the chase was superior to the boats, a fresh force of boats was sent, making nine in all, under the command of Lieutenant Kelly Nazer.

On seeing the boats approaching her, the schooner, which was the Lottery, of six 12-pounder carronades and 28 men, Captain John Southcomb, from Baltimore bound to Bordeaux, made all sail to escape; but soon found herself becalmed. At 1 P.M. she opened from her stern-chasers a well-directed fire upon the headmost boats, or those first detached. These rested on their oars until their comrades came up; when the whole rushed forward, and, through a very animated fire of round and grape, boarded the schooner, but did not carry her until after a most obstinate resistance, in which Captain Southcomb was mortally wounded, and 18 of his men also wounded, many of them dangerously. The British sustained a loss comparatively slight, having had only one man killed and five wounded.

This was a very gallant resistance on the part of the Lottery; and Captain Southcomb, until he died, was treated with the greatest attention by Captain Byron, on board of whose frigate he had been brought. Captain Byron then sent the body of the Lottery's late commander on shore, with every mark of respect due to the memory of a brave officer; and he afterwards received a letter of thanks from Captain Charles Stewart of the American 18-pounder 36-gun frigate Constellation, at an anchor in St. James river leading to Norfolk, watching an opportunity to put to sea. The Lottery was a fine schooner of 225 tons, pierced for 16 guns, and afterwards became the Canso in the British service.

Just as Sir John Warren, with the 74-gun ships San-Domingo, bearing his flag, Captain Charles Gill, and Marlborough, bearing

Rear-admiral Cockburn's flag, Captain Charles Bayne Hodgson Ross, accompanied by the Maidstone and Statira frigates and Fantome and Mohawk brig-sloops, had arrived abreast of the river Rappahannock, in their way up the Chesapeake, five large armed schooners were discovered, and were immediately chased into the river by the frigates and smaller vessels. It now falling calm, the boats of the two line-of-battle ships and frigates, consisting of the San Domingo's pinnace, with 23 officers and men and a 12-pounder carronade, under Lieutenant James Polkinghorne and midshipman Robert Amyett Newman, Maidstone's launch, with 21 officers and men and a 12-pounder carronade, under Lieutenant Matthew Liddon, Marlborough's barge and cutter, with 40 officers and men, under Lieutenant George Constantine Urmston and James Scott, and Statira's cutter with 21 officers and men, under Lieutenant George Bishop, total 105 officers and men were immediately detached in pursuit.

After rowing 15 miles, Lieutenant Polkinghorne found the four schooners, which were the Arab, of seven guns and 45 men, Lynx, of six guns and 40 men, Racer, of six guns and 36 men, and Dolphin of 12 guns and 98 men, drawn up in line ahead, and fully prepared to give him a warm reception. He, notwithstanding, dashed at them. The Arab was boarded and carried by the Marlborough's two boats; the Lynx hauled down her colours just as the San Domingo's pinnace arrived alongside; and the Racer was carried by Lieutenant Polkinghorne, after a sharp resistance. The guns of the Racer were then turned upon the Dolphin; and the latter was gallantly boarded and carried by the Statira's cutter and Maidstone's launch.

The loss sustained by the British in this very gallant boat-attack amounted to one seaman and one marine killed, Lieutenant Polkinghorne, another lieutenant (William Alexander Brand), one lieutenant of marines (William Richard Flint), one midshipman (John Sleigh), and seven seamen and marines wounded. The loss sustained by the Americans was six men killed and 10 wounded. The captured schooners were very fine vessels, and of large dimensions for schooners, each measuring from 200 to 225 tons. The Racer and Lynx, under the names of Shelburne and Musquedobit, were afterwards 14-gun schooners in the British service. Because, probably, these four formidable schooners were only privateers, the gallantry of Lieutenant Polkinghorne in capturing them with a force so decidedly inferior, did not obtain him a commander's rank until upwards of 14 months afterwards.

Rear-admiral Cockburn was now directed, with a squadron of small vessels, to penetrate the rivers at the head of the bay, and endeavour to cut off the enemy's supplies, as well as to destroy his foundries, stores, and public works; particularly a depôt of flour, military and other stores, ascertained, by the information of some Americans, to be at a place called French-town, situated a considerable distance up the river Elk. Accordingly on the evening of the 28th of April, taking with him the brigs Fantome and Mohawk, and the Dolphin, Racer, and Highflyer tenders, the rear-admiral moved towards the river. Having anchored the brigs and schooners as far within the entrance as could be effected after dark, the rear-admiral took with him in the boats of his little squadron, commanded by Lieutenant George Augustus Westphal, first of the Marlborough, 150 marines, under Captains Marmaduke Wybourn and Thomas Carter, and five artillerymen, under Lieutenant Robertson, of that corps, and proceeded to execute his orders.

Having, owing to ignorance of the way, entered the Bohemia, instead of keeping in the Elk river, the boats did not reach the destined place till late on the following morning. This delay enabled the inhabitants of French-town to make arrangements for the defence of the stores and town, for the security of which a six-gun battery had lately been erected. As soon as the boats approached within gun-shot of it, a heavy fire was opened upon them. Disregarding this, however, the marines quickly landed; and the American militia fled from the battery to the adjoining woods. The inhabitants of the town, which was situated at about a mile distant, having, as far as could be ascertained, taken no part in the contest, were not in the slightest degree molested; but a considerable quantity of flour, of army-clothing, saddles, bridles, and other equipments for cavalry; also various articles of merchandise, and the two stores in which they had been contained, together with five vessels lying near the place, were entirely consumed. The guns of the battery, being too heavy to be carried away, were disabled; and the boats departed, with no other loss than one seaman wounded in the arm by a grape-shot. The Americans lost one man killed by a rocket, but none wounded.

The rear-admiral's system, and which he had taken care to impart to all the Americans captured by, or voluntarily coming on board the squadron, was to land without offering molestation to the unopposing inhabitants, either in their persons or properties; to capture or destroy all articles of merchandise and munitions of war; to be allowed to take off, upon paying the full market price, all such cattle and supplies as the British squadron might require; but, should resistance be offered, or menaces held out, to consider the town as a fortified post, and the male inhabitants as soldiers; the one to be destroyed, the other, with their cattle and stock, to be captured.

As the boats in their way down the Elk were rounding Turkey point, they came in sight of a large estate, surrounded by cattle. The rear-admiral landed; and, directing the bailiff, or overseer, to pick out as many oxen, sheep, or other stock, as were deemed sufficient for the present use of the squadron, paid for them to the full amount of what the bailiff alleged was the market price. Not the slightest injury was done; or, doubtless one of the industrious American historians would have recorded the fact. Having learnt that cattle and provisions, in considerable quantity, were at Specucie Island, the rear-admiral, with the brigs and tenders, proceeded to that place. In his way thither, it became necessary to pass in sight of Havre de Grace, a village of about 60 houses, situated on the west side of the Susquehanna, a short distance above the confluence of that river with the Chesapeake. Although the British were a long way out of gun-shot, the Americans at Havre de Grace, as if inspired by the heroism of their townsman, Commodore Rodgers, fired at them from a six-gun battery, and displayed to their view, as a further mark of defiance, a large American ensign. This determined the rear-admiral to make that battery and town the next object of attack. In the meanwhile he anchored off Specucie Island. Here a part of the boats landed, and obtained cattle upon the same terms as before. A complaint having been made that some of the subordinate officers had destroyed a number of turkeys, the rear-admiral paid the value of them out of his own pocket. The Americans, as they were driving the cattle to the boats, jeered the men, saying, "Why do you come here? Why don't you go to Havre de Grace? There you'll have something to do." About this time a deserter gave the people at Havre de Grace, who had already been preparing, notice of the intended attack.

After quitting Specucie Island, the rear-admiral bent his course towards Havre de Grace; but the shallowness of the water admitting the passage of boats only, the 150 marines and the five artillerymen embarked at midnight on the 2nd of May, and proceeded up the river. The Dolphin and Highflyer tenders attempted to follow in support of the boats, but shoal water compelled them to anchor at the distance of six miles from the point of attack. By daylight the boats succeeded in getting opposite to the battery; which mounted six guns, 12 and 6 pounders, and opened a smart fire upon the British. The marines instantly landed to the left; which was a signal to the Americans to withdraw from their battery. Lieutenant Westphal, having in the mean time stationed his rocket-boat close to the battery, now landed with his boat's crew, turned the guns upon the American militia, and drove them to the extremity of the town. The inhabitants still keeping up a fire from behind the houses, walls, and trees, Lieutenant Westphal, by the admiral's orders, held out a flag of truce, and called upon them to desist. Instead of so doing, these "unoffending citizens" fired at the British lieutenant, and actually shot him through the very hand that was bearing the flag of truce. After this, who could wonder if the British seamen and marines turned to the right and to the left, and demolished everything in their way? The townspeople themselves had constructed the battery; and yet not a house in which an inhabitant remained was injured. Several of the inhabitants, principally women, who had fled at first, came again into the town and got back such articles as had been taken. Some of the women actually proceeded to the boats; and, upon identifying their property, obtained its restoration.

Many of the inhabitants who had remained peaceably in their houses, as a proof that they were well informed of the principle upon which Sir George Cockburn acted, frequently exclaimed to him: "Ah, sir, I told them what would be the consequence of their conduct. It is a great pity so many should suffer for a headstrong few. Those who were the most determined to fire upon you the other day, saying it was impossible you could take the place, were now the first to run away." Several of the houses that were not burnt did, in truth, belong to the chief agents in those violent measures which had caused such severity on the part of the British; and the very townspeople themselves pointed out the houses. Lieutenant Westphal, with his remaining hand, pursued and took prisoner an American captain of militia; and others of the party brought in an ensign and several privates, including an old Irishman, named O'Neill. After embarking the six guns from the battery, and taking or destroying about 130 stands of small-arms, the British departed from Havre de Grace.

One division of boats, headed by the rear-admiral, then proceeded to the northward in search of a cannon-foundry, of which some of the inhabitants of Havre de Grace had given information. This was found, and quickly destroyed; together with five long 24-pounders, stationed in a battery for its protection; 28 long 32-pounders, ready for sending away; and eight long guns, and four carronades, in the boring-house and foundry. Another division of boats was sent up the Susquehanna; and returned, after destroying five vessels and a large store of flour.

On the night of the 5th of May, the same party of British marines and artillerymen again embarked in the boats, and proceeded up the river Sassafras, separating the counties of Kent and Cecil, towards the villages of George-town and Frederick-town, situated on opposite sides of the river, nearly facing each other. Having intercepted a small boat with two of the inhabitants, Rear-admiral Cockburn halted the detachment, about two miles from the town; and then sent forward the two Americans in their boat, to warn their countrymen against acting in the same rash manner as the people of Havre de Grace had done; assuring them that, if they did, their towns would inevitably experience a similar fate; but that, on the contrary, if they did not attempt resistance, no injury should be done to them or their towns; that vessels and public property only would be seized; that the strictest discipline would be maintained; and that whatever provision, or other property of individuals, the rear-admiral might require for the use of the squadron, would be instantly paid for in its fullest value. The two Americans agreed in the propriety of this; said there was no battery at either of the towns; that they would willingly deliver the message, and had no doubt the inhabitants would be peaceably disposed.

After waiting a considerable time, the rear-admiral advanced higher up; and, when within about a mile from the towns, and between two projecting points of land which compelled the boats to proceed in close order, a heavy fire was opened upon them from one field-piece, and, as conjectured, 300 or 400 militia, divided and intrenched on the opposite sides of the river. The fire was promptly returned, and the rear-admiral pushed on shore with the marines; but, the instant the American militia observed them fix their bayonets, they fled to the woods, and were neither seen nor heard of afterwards. All the houses, excepting those whose owners had continued peaceably in them, and taken no part in the attack, were forthwith destroyed; as were four vessels lying in the river, together with some stores of sugar, of lumber, of leather, and other merchandise. On this occasion, five of the British were wounded. One of the Americans, who entreated to have his property saved, wore military gaiters; and had, no doubt, assisted at the firing upon the British. Agreeably to his request, however, his property was left untouched.

On his way down the river, the rear-admiral visited a town situated on a branch of it. Here a part of the inhabitants actually pulled off to him; and, requesting to shake hands, declared he should experience no opposition whatever. The rear-admiral accordingly landed, with the officers, and, chiefly out of respect to his rank, a small personal guard. Among those that came to greet him on his landing, were observed two inhabitants of George-town. These men, as well as an inhabitant of the place who had been to George-town to see what was going on, had succeeded in persuading the people to adopt, as their best security, a peaceable demeanour. Having ascertained that there were no warlike stores nor public property, and obtained, upon payment of the full value, such articles as were wanted, the rear-admiral and his party re-embarked. Soon afterwards a deputation was sent from Charles-town, on the north-east river, to assure the rear-admiral, that the place was considered as at his mercy; and, similar assurances coming from other places in the upper part of the Chesapeake, the rear-admiral and his light squadron retired from that quarter.

Persons in England may find it difficult to consider, as soldiers, men neither embodied nor dressed in regimentals. That circumstance has not escaped the keen discernment of the American government. Hence the British are so often charged, in proclamations and other state papers, with attacking the "inoffensive citizens of the republic." The fact is, every man in the United States, under 45 years of age, is a militiaman; and, during the war, attended in his turn, to be drilled or trained. He had always in his possession either a musket or a rifled-barrel piece; knew its use from his infancy; and with it, therefore, could do as much execution in a smock frock or plain coat as if he wore the most splendid uniform. These soldiers in citizens' dresses were the men whom Rear-admiral Cockburn so frequently attacked and routed; and who, when they had really acted up to the character of non-combatants, were invariably spared, both in their persons and properties. The rear-admiral wished them, for their own sakes only, to remain neutral; but General Hull, in his famous proclamation, prepared with so much care at Washington, invited the Canadian people to become open traitors to their country; and visited, upon the heads of those that refused, all "the horrors and calamities of war."

On the 12th of June the boats of the 18-pounder 32-gun frigate Narcissus, Captain John Richard Lumley, containing about 40 men, under the command of Lieutenant John Crerie, first of that ship, and of Lieutenant of marines Patrick Savage, were despatched up York river, in the Chesapeake, to cut out the United States schooner Surveyor, mounting six 12-pounder carronades. Captain Samuel Travis, the American commander, had furnished each of his men with two muskets; and they held their fire until the British were within pistol-shot. The Americans then opened; but the boats pushed on, and finally carried the vessel by boarding, with the loss of three men killed, and six wounded. Captain Travis had five men wounded. His crew amounted to only 16; and so gallant was their conduct, as well as that of their commander, in the opinion of Lieutenant Crerie, that that officer returned Captain Travis his sword, accompanied by a letter, not less complimentary to him than creditable to the writer.

Admiral Warren, who had quitted the Chesapeake for Bermuda, returned to his command early in June, bringing with him, according to newspaper account, a detachment of battalion-marines, 1800 strong, 300 of the 102nd regiment, 250 of the Independent Foreigners, or Canadian chasseurs, and 300 of the royal marine-artillery; total 2650 men. On the 18th of June the Junon frigate anchored in Hampton roads, and Captain Sanders despatched his boats to capture or destroy any vessels that might be found at the entrance of James river. Commodore John Cassin, the naval commanding officer at Norfolk, observing this, directed the 15 gun-boats of that station to be manned with an additional number of seamen and marines from the Constellation frigate, then moored at the navy-yard, also with 50 infantry from Craney Island, and despatched them under the command of Captain Tarbell, to attempt the capture or destruction of the Junon.

It was not till about 4 P.M. on the 20th, that this formidable flotilla, armed with upwards of 30 guns, half of which were long 32 and 24 pounders, and manned with, at least, 500 men, commenced its attack upon the Junon, then lying becalmed. Captain Sanders warmly returned their fire with his long 18-pounders, hoping that they would soon venture to approach within reach of his carronades. This the gun-boats carefully avoided; and between them and the frigate, a distant cannonade, very slightly injurious to either party, was maintained for about three-quarters of an hour. A breeze now sprang up; which enabled the 18-pounder 36-gun frigate, Barrosa, Captain William Henry Shirreff, and the 24-gun ship Laurestinus, Captain Thomas Graham, lying about five miles off, to get under way, in the hope to have a share in the amusement. The Junon, also, was at this time under sail, using her best efforts to give a more serious complexion to the contest; but Commodore Cassin, who, as he assures us, was in his boat during the whole of the action, considering that the flotilla had done enough to entitle him to display both his fighting and his epistolary qualifications, very prudently ordered the 15 gun-boats to make the best of their way back to Norfolk.

The appearance of the two frigates and sloop in Hampton roads soon brought to Norfolk and its vicinity as many as 10,000 militia; and the works recently constructed there were all manned, ready for defending that important post. At Hampton, also, a militia force had assembled; and batteries were erecting, in case that town should prove the object of attack. On the 20th of June 13 sail of British ships, consisting of three 74s, a 64 armée en flûte, four frigates, and five sloops, transports, and tenders, lay at anchor, the nearest within seven, the furthest off within 13, miles of Craney island. An assemblage of boats at the sterns of several of the ships, on the afternoon of that day, gave no very unequivocal notice to the people on shore, that some expedition was on foot. Accordingly, Craney island being rather weakly manned, the commanding officer at Norfolk sent 150 of the Constellation's seamen and marines to a battery of 18-pounders on the north-west, and about 480 Virginia militia to reinforce a detachment of artillery stationed with two 24 and four 6 pounders on the west, side of the island. Captain Tarbell's 15 gun-boats were also moored in the best position for contributing to the defence of the post.

After two days' parade of boats and bustle among the British ships, a division of 17 or 18 boats, at daylight on the morning of the 22nd, departed with about 800 men, under Major-general Beckwith, round the point of Nansemond river, and landed them at a place called Pig's point, near to the narrow inlet separating the main from Craney island. Owing to some error in the arrangements, unexpected obstacles presented themselves. An attack from that quarter being therefore considered hopeless, and the position itself not tenable, the troops, in the course of the day, re-embarked and returned to the squadron.

A second division of boats, 15 in number, containing a detachment of 500 men from the 102nd regiment, Canadian chasseurs, and battalion-marines, and about 200 seamen, the whole under the command of Captain Samuel John Pechell, of the San-Domingo, arrived, at about 11 A.M., off the north-west side of the island, directly in front of the battery manned by the Constellation's men. Great difference of opinion prevailed among the officers engaged in the expedition, about the propriety of making the attack at that time of tide, it being then the ebb. Captains John Martin Hanchett, of the Diadem, the Hon. James Ashley Maude, of the Nemesis, and Romilly of the engineers, were decidedly against it. Captain Pechell was for it; and he, being the senior officer, carried his point. Captain Hanchett then volunteered to lead the boats to the attack; which he was permitted to do. Captain Hanchett's boat was the Diadem's launch, carrying a 24-pounder carronade, the only boat so armed in the division. He had taken his station about 60 yards ahead of the other boats; and was pulling, under a very heavy and long-continued fire from the batteries, directly in front of them, when his boat unfortunately took the ground, at the distance of about 100 yards from the muzzles of the enemy's guns. Captain Hanchett, who had been previously standing up in his boat, animating his men to hasten forward, had wrapped round his body a union-jack, and prepared to wade on shore to storm the American battery.

At that instant one of the seamen, having plunged his boat-hook over the side, found three or four feet of slimy mud at the bottom. A check being thus effectually given to a daring enterprise, in which all were so ready to join, Captain Hanchett waved his hat for the boats astern to keep afloat. In the hurry of pulling and the ardour of the men, this warning was disregarded; and one or two of the boats grounded. Two others, owing to their having received some shot that had passed through the sails of the Diadem's launch, sank.

In the meanwhile, the Americans at the battery, well aware of the shoal, had anticipated what had happened; and, feeling their own security, poured in their grape and canister with destructive effect. A 6-pound shot, which had passed through a launch on the starboard side of Captain Hanchett's boat, and killed and wounded several men, struck that officer on the hip, and he instantly fell; but was quickly on his legs again. While he was assisting to save the men that were struggling in the water, in consequence of their boat having been sunk, a langridge shot entered his left thigh. While, also, the men from the sunken boats, and who consisted chiefly of the Canadian chasseurs, or Independent Foreigners, were struggling for their lives in the water and mud, the Constellation's marines, and the American infantry, waded a short distance into the water, and deliberately fired at them. Huddled together, as the boats were when they struck the ground, and that within canister range of a battery which kept upon them an incessant fire of more than two hours' duration, it required no very expert artillerists to sink three of the boats, and to kill three men and wound 16; especially when aided by the muskets of those humane individuals who waded into the water to fire at the drowning crews. Including 10 seamen, 62 were officially reported as missing. Of these, it appears, 40 gained the shore, and "deserted" to the Americans. As more than that number of missing appear to have belonged to the two foreign companies, this creates no surprise; especially, as the only alternative left to the men was to become prisoners of war.

The policy of attacking Craney island, as a means of getting at Norfolk, whither the Constellation frigate had retired for shelter on the first arrival of the British in the Chesapeake, has been much questioned; but there can be only one opinion, surely, about the wisdom of sending boats, in broad daylight, to feel their way to the shore, over shoals and mud-banks, and that in the very teeth of a formidable battery. Unlike most other nations, the Americans in particular, the British, when engaged in expeditions of this nature, always rest their hopes of success upon valour rather than numbers. But still, had the veil of darkness been allowed to screen the boats from view, and an hour of the night chosen when the tide had covered the shoals with deep water, the same little party might have carried the batteries; and a defeat as discreditable to those that caused, as honourable to those who suffered in it, might have been converted into a victory. As it was, the affair of Craney island, dressed up to advantage in the American official account, and properly commented upon by the government-editors, was hailed throughout the union as a glorious triumph, fit for Americans to achieve.

On the night of the 25th of June, the effective men of the 102nd regiment, Canadian chasseurs, and battalion-marines; also, three companies of ship's marines, the whole amounting to about 2000 men, commanded by Major-general Beckwith, embarked in a division of boats, placed under the orders of Rear-admiral Cockburn, and covered by the brig-sloop Mohawk, and the launches of the squadron. About half an hour before daylight on the 26th, the advance, consisting of about 650 men, with two 6-pounders, under Lieutenant-colonel Napier, landed two miles to the westward of Hampton, a town about 18 miles from Norfolk, and separated from it by Hampton roads. Shortly afterwards, the main body, consisting of the royal marine-battalion under Lieutenant-colonel Williams, landed; and the whole moved forward. As might be expected, the town, and its seven pieces of cannon, fell into the hands of the British, after a trifling loss of five killed, 33 wounded, and 10 missing. The Americans admit a loss of seven killed, 12 wounded, 11 missing, and one prisoner.

A subject next presents itself for relation, upon which it is painful to proceed. As soon as the Americans were defeated, and driven from Hampton, the British troops, or rather, the foreign troops, for they were the principals, forming part of the advanced force, commenced perpetrating upon the defenceless inhabitants acts of rapine and violence, which unpitying custom has, in some degree, rendered inseparable from places that have been carried by storm; but which are as revolting to human nature, as they are disgraceful to the flag that would sanction them. The instant these circumstances of atrocity reached the ears of the British commanding officer, orders were given to search for, and bring in, all the Canadian chasseurs distributed through the town; and, when they were so brought in, a guard was set over them. The officers could do no more: they could not be at every man's elbow, as he roamed through the country in search of plunder; and plunder the soldier claims as a right, and will have, when the enemy has compelled him to force his way at the point of the bayonet.

No event of the war was so greeted by the government editors as the affair at Hampton. All the hireling pens in the United States were put in requisition, until tale followed tale, each outdoing the last in horror. The language of the brothel was exhausted, and that of Billingsgate surpassed, to invent sufferings for the American women, and terms of reproach for their "British" ravishers. Instances were not only magnified, but multiplied, tenfold; until the whole republic rang with peals of execration against the British character and nation. A few of the boldest of the anti-government party stood up to undeceive the public; but the voice of reason was drowned in the general clamour, and it became as dangerous, as it was useless, to attempt to gain a hearing. The "George-town Federal-Republican," of July 7, a newspaper published just at the verge of Washington city, and whose editor possessed the happy privilege of remaining untainted amidst a corrupted atmosphere, contained the following account: "The statement of the women of Hampton being violated by the British, turns out to be false. A correspondence, upon that subject and the pillage said to have been committed there, has taken place between General Taylor and Admiral Warren. Some plunder appears to have been committed, but it was confined to the French troops employed. Admiral Warren complains, on his part, of the Americans having continued to fire upon the struggling crews of the barges after they were sunk."

On the 11th of July, Sir John Warren detached Rear-admiral Cockburn, with the Sceptre 74, into which ship he had now shifted his flag, the Romulus, Fox, and Nemesis, frigate armed en flûte, the Conflict gun-brig, and Highflyer and Cockchafer tenders, having on board the 103rd regiment, of about 500 rank and file, and a small detachment of artillery, to Ocracoke harbour, on the North-Carolina coast, for the purpose of putting an end to the commerce carried on from that port by means of inland navigation, and of destroying any vessels that might be found there. During the night of the 12th, the squadron arrived off Ocracoke bar; and, at 2 A.M. on the 13th, the troops were embarked in their boats; which, accompanied by the Conflict and tenders, pulled in three divisions towards the shore. Owing to the great distance and heavy swell, the advance division, commanded by Lieutenant Westphal, first of the Sceptre, did not reach the shoal-point of the harbour, behind which two large armed vessels were seen at anchor, until considerably after daylight: consequently, the enemy was fully prepared for resistance.

The instant the British boats doubled the point, they were fired upon by the two vessels; but Lieutenant Westphal, under cover of some rockets, pulled directly for them, and had just got to the brig's bows, when her crew cut the cables and abandoned her. The schooner's colours were hauled down by her crew about the same time. The latter vessel proved to be the Atlas letter of marque, of Philadelphia, mounting 10 guns, and measuring 240 tons· the former the Anaconda letter of marque, of New York, mounting 18 long 9-pounders, and measuring 387 tons. In the course of the morning the troops were landed, and took possession of Ocracoke and the town of Portsmouth, without the slightest opposition. The inhabitants behaved with civility, and their property, in consequence, was not molested. After remaining on shore for two days, Rear-admiral Cockburn, with the troops and seamen, re-embarked without loss or molestation. Not, as it would appear, because he had performed the service intrusted to him, but, on account of his "not feeling himself competent to the attack on Newburn, now that its citizens were preparing to receive him." No sooner had the British soldiers and seamen departed, than the American militia flocked to the post; thus presenting us with a new system of military defence. Both the prizes were afterwards added to the British navy, the Anaconda, by her own name, as an 18-gun brig-sloop, and the Atlas, by the name of St. Lawrence, as a 14-gun schooner.

On the 11th of July, at 9 A.M., the two United States gun-vessels Scorpion and Asp got under way from Yeocomico river, but soon afterwards were chased back by the British brig-sloops Contest, Captain James Rattray, and Mohawk, Captain the Hon. Henry Dilkes Byng. The two brigs then came to anchor off the bar; and, seeing that one of the two enemy's vessels, a schooner, was considerably in the rear of her consort, Captain Rattray despatched in pursuit of her the cutter of each brig, under the orders of Lieutenant Roger Carley Curry, assisted by Lieutenant William Hutchinson, and by midshipmen George Morey, —— Bradford, and Caleb Evans Tozer.

Lieutenant Curry pushed up the narrow inlet of Yeocomico, and, when about four miles from the entrance, found the American schooner, which was the Asp, of one long 18-pounder, two 18-pounder carronades and swivels, hauled up close to the beach, under the protection of a large body of militia. The British boats, however, persevered in their attack, and after a smart struggle, in which they had two men killed and Lieutenant Curry and five men wounded, carried the vessel. The American commanding officer, Lieutenant Segourney was killed, and nine out of his 25 in crew were either killed or wounded. The British set fire to the Asp, but not effectually, as the Americans afterwards extinguished the flames and preserved the vessel.

In the month of July, Captain Saunders, with his frigate the

Junon, and the ship-sloop Martin, Captain Henry Fleming Senhouse, of 16 carronades, 24-pounders, and two long nines, was stationed in Delaware bay. On the 29th, about 8 A.M., the Martin grounded on the outer ridge of Crow's shoal, within two and a half miles from the beach; and, it being a falling tide, could not be floated again before the return of flood. The water ran so shoal, that it became necessary to shore the ship up; and the same cause prevented the Junon from afterwards anchoring nearer to the Martin than a mile and three quarters. This afforded to the flotilla of American gun-boats and block-vessels then in the Delaware, a fine opportunity to destroy the British sloop. They accordingly, 10 in number, advanced, and deliberately took up an anchorage at about a mile and three quarters distant, directly on the Martin's beam, on the opposite side to the Junon, and so as to bring the latter in a line with the sloop. Thus, by anchoring at the distance of three miles from the frigate, which, it was well known, could not approach nearer on account of the shoals, the American gun-boats had no force but the Martin's to contend with.

All this while, crowds of citizens, on foot, on horseback, and in carriages, were hastening to the beach, in the hope to see verified, in the speedy destruction of the Martin, the wonderful accounts they had heard of American prowess on the ocean. The Martin got her topgallantmasts struck, and her sails furled; and, although he despaired of saving his ship from so formidable a force, Captain Senhouse resolved to defend her to the last extremity. The gun-boats commenced the fire, and the Martin returned it, at first with her carronades; but, finding they could not reach, Captain Senhouse had the two 9-pounders transported from their ports, one to the topgallant-forecastle, the other to the poop. Between these two guns, and all the guns of the American flotilla, was the fire maintained for nearly two hours, without the slightest injury to the Martin. At about 2 P.M. the sternmost gun-boat in the line having separated a little from the rest, Captain Sanders made a signal for the boats manned and armed. Accordingly, three boats were despatched from the Martin, containing 40 officers and men, and four from the Junon, containing 100 officers and men, the whole under the orders of the Junon's First-lieutenant Philip Westphal. On the approach of the boats, the gun-vessels turned their fire from the Martin against them, but at too great a distance to be effective. The single gun-boat, which was the principal object of attack, kept up a spirited fire, but was quickly boarded and overpowered

The British boats, in this affair, lost three killed and mortally wounded, and four slightly wounded; the gun-boat, seven wounded. The last discharge from the gun, mounted on board the gun-boat, broke its carriage. That prevented the British from returning the fire of the remaining gun-boats, which had dropped down in line, hoping to retake the prize; but which the captors towed off in triumph. As, in their attempt to save their companion, the gun-boats passed the bow of the Martin, the sloop fired upon them with effect; and the Junon opened her fire, but her shot scarcely fell beyond the Martin.

Some of the gun-boats having grounded, the remainder anchored for their mutual protection. The tide had drifted the ships' boats, as well as the captured vessel, to a considerable distance. The gun-boats that had grounded, got off, and the whole, as if to renew the attack upon the change of tide, anchored within two miles and a half of the Martin, now weakened by the absence of 40 of her best hands. However, at 5 P.M., to the surprise of the Martin's officers and crew; and, as it afterwards appeared, to the extreme mortification of the spectators on the shore, this formidable flotilla weighed and beat up, between the Martin and the shore, without further molesting her, and arrived in safety, soon afterwards, at their station near the mouth of the river.

The force that attacked the Martin, consisted of eight gun-boats and two block-vessels. The latter were sloops of 100 tons each, which had been coasters. Their sides had been raised, heavy beams laid across, and the whole planked in, on the top, on each side, and at the ends; leaving only loopholes for musketry (through which pikes might be used in repelling boarders), and three ports of a side: in these were mounted six long 18-pounders. The covering extended the whole length of the vessel, and was large enough to contain 60 men, the number stated as the complement of each. The gun-boats were sloop-rigged vessels, averaging about 95 tons, and mounted each a long 32, and a 4-pounder on traversing-carriages, with a complement of 35 men, the exact number found on board the prize. Each gun-boat, and block-vessel was commanded by an experienced merchant-master: and the whole flotilla by Master-commandant Samuel Angus, of the United States navy.

On the 24th of May the frigate United States, still commanded by Commodore Decatur, accompanied by the 18-pounder 36-gun frigate Macedonian, Captain Jacob Jones, and 18-gun ship-sloop Hornet, Captain James Biddle, all provisioned and stored for a cruise in the East Indies, quitted the harbour of New York through Long-island Sound, the Sandy-hook passage being blockaded by a British force. Having found in his ship a disposition to *hog*, Commodore Decatur had put on shore six of his carronades; thus reducing the force of the United States from 54 to 48 guns. It was however asserted, and we believe stated, in the New York papers, that the commodore had taken on board eight medium or columbiad 32-pounders, and sent an equal number of 24-pounders from his four 'midship ports on each side to the Macedonian: and that of the latter's eight long 18-pounders removed to make room for the 24s, two were mounted on board the Hornet in lieu of her 12-pounders.

Just as the United States, towards evening, arrived abreast of Hunt's-point, her mainmast was struck by lightning. The electric fluid tore away the commodore's broad pendant and cast it upon the deck; it then passed down the after-hatchway, through the wardroom, into the doctor's cabin, put out his candle and tore up his bed, and, entering between the skin and ceiling of the ship, ripped off two or three sheets of copper just at the water's edge. No further trace of it could be discovered. The Macedonian, who was about 100 yards astern of the United States, on seeing what had happened, hove all aback, to save herself from the justly dreaded explosion of the latter. Fortunately, not a man was hurt on the occasion. Commodore Decatur soon afterwards anchored under Fisher's island, near the entrance of New London river, to be ready for a start the first opportunity.

On the 1st of June, very early in the morning, the American squadron got under way and stood out to sea; but at 9 A.M., just as they were clearing the Sound, the ships were discovered by the British 74-gun ship Valiant, Captain Robert Dudley Oliver, and 18-pounder 40-gun frigate Acasta, Captain Alexander Robert Kerr. The two British ships gave chase, and the three American ships put back; both parties hauling to the wind under all sail. At about 1 h. 30 m. P.M. the American squadron bore up for New London; and the United States and Hornet, being too deep for their trim, started their water and threw overboard a part of their provisions. At 2 h. 15 m., P.M., being far ahead of the Valiant, and just within gun-shot of the United States, the Acasta fired a bow-chaser at the latter, just as the Macedonian was rounding New London lighthouse. The United States returned the shot with one from her stern. Instead, however, of bringing-to and trying to cut off the British frigate from her consort, as many of the spectators on shore expected to see done, Commodore Decatur stood on, and anchored with his squadron in the river. Having shortened sail, the Acasta hauled to the wind, and tacked, and soon afterwards, with the Valiant, anchored off Gardner's island, distant about 12 miles from New London.

Having no persons on board acquainted with the navigation of the Sound, the British ships, particularly the 74, chased with much less effect than they otherwise would. It was not, of course, known to Captain Oliver, that he might even have followed the American squadron into New London; and that, had the United States and her companions ascended the river beyond his reach, he might, with very little risk, there being no battery of any consequence, have placed the Valiant and Acasta against the town, and blown the houses about the ears of the inhabitants, if they refused to deliver up the ships.

For several weeks previous to this event, the New York and Boston papers had been filled with panegyrics on their "naval heroes," whose valour they depicted as impetuous, amounting almost to rashness. Some of the papers, as if a little ashamed of what they had said, now added "a rasée" to the two British ships, and gave that as a reason that the American commodore suffered his squadron to be chased into New London.

In a week or two afterwards two merchants of New York, encouraged by a promise of reward from the American government, formed a plan for destroying the British 74-gun ship Ramillies, Captain Sir Thomas Masterman Hardy, as she lay at anchor off Fisher's island. A schooner named the Eagle was laden with several casks of gunpowder, having trains leading from a species of gunlock, which, upon the principle of clockwork, went off at a given period after it had been set. Above the casks of powder, and in full view at the hatchway, were some casks of flour, it being known at New York that the Ramillies was short of provisions, and naturally supposed that Captain Hardy would immediately order the vessel alongside, in order to get the ship's wants supplied.

Thus murderously laden, the schooner sailed from New York and stood up the Sound. On the 25th, in the morning, the Eagle approached New London, as if intending to enter that river. The Ramillies detached a boat, with 13 men under Lieutenant John Geddes, to cut her off. At 11 A.M. Lieutenant Geddes boarded the schooner, and found that the crew, after having let go her only anchor, had abandoned their vessel and fled to the shore. The lieutenant brought the fatal prize near to the Ramillies, and Sir Thomas ordered him to place the vessel alongside of a trading sloop, which had been recently captured and lay a short distance off. The lieutenant did as he was ordered; and at 2 h. 30 m. P.M., while he and his men were in the act of securing her, the schooner blew up with a tremendous explosion. The poor lieutenant, and 10 of the fine fellows who were with him, perished; and the remaining three men escaped only with being shockingly scorched.

We shall not trust ourselves to comment upon this most atrocious proceeding. In the following remarks on the subject by a contemporary, we perfectly concur: " A quantity of arsenic among the food would have been so perfectly compatible with the rest of the contrivance, that we wonder it was not resorted to. Should actions like these receive the sanction of governments, the science of war, and the laws of nations, will degenerate into the barbarity of the Algerines; and murder and pillage will take place of kindness and humanity to our enemies." [1]

The northern frontier of the United States, as is almost too well known to need repetition, bounds on the British provinces of Upper and Lower Canada. The line, or barrier, as far as we need take notice of it, consists of a rapid river, the St. Lawrence, and the navigable lakes Ontario, Erie, and Huron. From Quebec to Kingston, which stands at the entrance of Lake Ontario, the distance is about 180 miles, but the water communication is interrupted by shoals and rapids. Lake Ontario is about 180 miles long and 50 broad, and is navigable for ships of any burden. The strait of Niagara, in length about 36 miles, but interrupted at one part by its famous falls, connects Ontario with Lake Erie; which is about 220 miles in length, and about 40 broad, and is also navigable for large ships. Of Lake Huron, it will suffice to say, that it is connected with Erie by the river Detroit; on which river stands the British post of Amherstburgh, distant just 800 miles from Quebec.

The regular force, scattered over the Canadas at the breaking out of the war, consisted of between 4000 and 5000 men, chiefly fencible and veteran or invalid troops. The British commander-in-chief was Lieutenant-general Sir George Prevost. Ontario was the only lake that contained any armed vessels belonging to the British. These consisted of the Royal George, a ship of 340 tons, mounting 20 guns, a brig of 14 guns, and two or three smaller vessels; all manned by Canadians, and commanded by a provincial officer, named Earle. The force of the Americans on this lake, at the commencement of the war, con-

[1] Brenton, vol. v., p. 120.

sisted of only one solitary brig, the Oneida, of 16 guns, commanded by Lieutenant Melancthon Thomas Woolsey, of the national navy. The principal port of the British was Kingston; that of the American's, Sackett's Harbour.

On the 15th of July, 1812, Commodore Earle, with his squadron, appeared off Sackett's Harbour, with the avowed intention of taking or destroying the Oneida; but a fire from two or three guns, mounted on a point of land near the harbour's mouth, was sufficient to deter the Canadian (we will not call him British) commodore from attempting that, with his five vessels, which the Royal George alone, well manned and appointed, might easily have accomplished. Emboldened by the dastardly behaviour of his opponent, Lieutenant Woolsey fitted out a captured British merchant-schooner with one long 32-pounder and two sixes; and, manning her with about 30 seamen and a company of riflemen to act as marines, sent her, under the command of Lieutenant Henry Wells, to Ogdensburg, on the St. Lawrence. On her way thither, the Julia encountered, and actually beat off without losing a man, the Moira of 14, and the Gloucester of 10 guns.

Notwithstanding the glaring incompetency of Earle, Sir George Prevost neither removed nor censured him. About this time the British 20-gun ship Tartarus, Captain John Pasco, arrived at Quebec from Halifax; and, had the governor-general of British America but given his sanction to the measure, the captain would have laid his ship up, and, with his officers and men, have proceeded straight to Kingston, and superseded Earle in the command of the squadron. Instead of this, an attempt was made to hire sailors at Quebec, at one-half of the wages which the merchants were giving; as if sailors could be of any use without an officer capable or willing (for we believe Earle, as well as Sir George, was born on the wrong side of the boundary line) to lead them against the enemy.

In the month of October, 1812, Commodore Isaac Chauncey arrived at Sackett's Harbour, as commander-in-chief; and, having brought with him a number of officers, and between 400 and 500 prime sailors, from the Atlantic frontier, was enabled, by the 6th of November, to appear on the lake with the Oneida and six fine schooners, mounting altogether 48 guns, including several long 24 and 32 pounders; and many of the guns being mounted on pivot or traversing carriages, were as effective as double the number. With this comparatively formidable force, Commodore Chauncey chased the Royal George into Kingston, cannonaded the town and batteries, and possessed the entire command of the lake. On the 26th of November the Madison, a fine ship of 600 tons, pierced to carry 24 guns on a flush deck, was launched at Sackett's Harbour; and, as soon as she was fitted, the commodore shifted his broad pendant to her. Soon afterwards Sir George Prevost ordered two ships-of-war to be built, to mount 24 guns each; one at Kingston, the other at York, an unprotected port at the opposite extremity of the lake.

On Lake Erie, while the Americans possessed only one armed vessel, the Adams, a small brig mounting six 6-pounders, the British colonial authorities, by hiring or purchasing some merchant-vessels and arming them, had assembled a force consisting of one ship of 280 tons, the Queen Charlotte, mounting 16 light carronades, a brig of 10 guns, a schooner of 12, and three smaller vessels, mounting between them seven guns. These six vessels were manned by 108 Canadians, and subsequently by 160 soldiers in addition. On the 16th of July, at the surrender of Detroit, the Adams fell into the hands of the British, and was afterwards named the Detroit, and sent down the lake, manned by a small Canadian crew. Early in the month of October, 1812, the American government sent Lieutenant Jesse D. Elliot, and between 50 and 60 petty-officers and seamen, to superintend the construction of some schooners at Black Rock. On the 9th Lieutenant Elliot, with the whole of his seamen and about 50 soldiers, boarded and carried the Detroit, and a merchant-brig, the Caledonia, of one or two swivels, in her company. The former the Americans were afterwards obliged to burn, to save her from falling into the hands of a detachment of soldiers from Fort Erie; but the Caledonia and her valuable cargo, they carried safe to Black Rock.

On the 25th of April, 1813, having received a reinforcement of seamen, Commodore Chauncey sailed from Sackett's Harbour with his fleet, now augmented to 10 vessels, on board of which was a body of troops under General Dearborn, to attack the port of York, and destroy the ship-of-war there building. The Americans landed and drove away the few British troops at the post; but, previously to their retreat, the latter saved the Americans the trouble of burning the ship on the stocks, by destroying her themselves. Commodore Chauncey took away a considerable quantity of naval stores and a small unserviceable 10-gun brig, the Gloucester, and returned to Sackett's Harbour in triumph.

On the 6th of May the British troop-ship Woolwich, Captain Thomas Ball Sullivan, arrived at Quebec from Spithead, having on board Captain Sir James Lucas Yeo, four commanders of the navy, eight lieutenants, 24 midshipmen, and about 450 picked seamen, sent out by government expressly for service on the Canada lakes. Such was the zeal of the officers and men to get to the scene of action, that they departed, the same evening, in schooners for Montreal. In four or five days they reached Kingston; and, although the number of seamen was not half enough to man the vessels in the harbour, now augmented by the 24-gun ship Wolfe, launched on the 5th or 6th of May, Sir James Yeo, with the aid of the provincial sailors already on the lake, and of a few companies of soldiers, was ready, by the end of the month, to put to sea with two ships, one brig, and three schooners, besides a few small gun-boats.

Sir George Prevost now allowed himself to be persuaded to embark 750 troops on board the squadron, for the purpose of making an attack upon Sackett's Harbour; but, to mar the successful issue of the plan, he resolved to head the troops himself. On the 27th of May, when an excellent opportunity was afforded by the absence of the American squadron at the opposite end of the lake, the British squadron, in high glee, sailed from Kingston, and with a fair wind stood across to the enemy's depôt. At noon the squadron arrived off Sackett's Harbour, and lay-to, with everything in readiness for the troops to disembark. Sir George hesitated, looked at the place, mistook trees for troops, and blockhouses for batteries, and ordered the expedition to put back.

Just as the ships had turned their heads towards Kingston, and, with the wind now changed, were beginning to sail before it, about 50 Indians brought off a party of American soldiers from the shore near Sackett's Harbour. Encouraged by this, Sir George permitted the squadron to begin working its way back to the American port. On the morning of the 29th some of the lighter vessels got close to the shore, and the troops were landed. They drove the Americans like sheep, compelled them to set fire to the General Pike, a new frigate on the stocks, the Gloucester, captured at York, and a barrack containing, among other valuable articles, all the naval stores taken on the same occasion. At this moment some resistance unexpectedly made at a log-barrack caused the British commander-in-chief to sound a retreat. The indignant, the victorious, officers and men were obliged to obey the fatal bugle, and the British retired to their vessels; and the Americans, as soon as they could credit their senses, hastened to stop the conflagration. The General Pike, being built of green wood, was saved; but the Gloucester, and the barrack containing the stores, were entirely consumed.

That Sir George Prevost was as fond of writing official letters as he was of substituting the first personal pronoun for the third, has already appeared in these pages;[1] but, in the present instance, contrary to all precedent, he required his adjutant-general, Colonel Edward Baynes, to pen the despatch. That obedient gentleman did so; and the European public scarcely knows at this hour through whose fault it was that Sackett's Harbour was not taken from the Americans in May, 1813. The Canadian public, besides being in the secret, were less surprised at the result of the enterprise; because they knew that Sir George, a few months before, had rejected an excellent opportunity of marching across the ice to Sackett's Harbour, and destroying the whole American lake-navy at a blow.

On the 3rd of June, Sir James Yeo sailed from Kingston with his squadron, composed of the ship Wolfe, of 23 guns and 200 men, ship Royal George, of 21 guns and 175 men, brig Melville, of 14 guns and 100 men, schooners, Moira, of 14 guns and 92 men, Sidney Smith, of 12 guns and 80 men, and Beresford, of eight guns and 70 men, together with a few gun-boats. On the 8th, at daylight, the squadron arrived in sight of the American camp at Forty-mile creek; but, as it was calm, the only vessels that could get close to the shore were the Beresford, Captain Francis Brockell Spilsbury, and the gun-boats, commanded by Lieutenant Charles Anthony, first of the Wolfe. A spirited attack by the schooner and gun-boats compelled the American troops to make a precipitate retreat, and all their camp equipage, provisions, and stores fell into the hands of the British. Sir James then landed the troops that were on board his squadron, and steered to the westward. On the 13th he captured two American schooners and some boats containing supplies. Receiving information from the prisoners, that there was a depôt of provisions at Genesse river, Sir James proceeded thither; and, landing some seamen and marines, brought off the whole. On the 19th he took another supply of provisions from Great Sodus, and on the 29th re-anchored in Kingston.

All this while Commodore Chauncey was waiting at Sackett's Harbour for the General Pike to be got ready for sea. At length, towards the latter end of July, that fine ship was armed, manned,

[1] See vol. v., p. 71.

and stored. The Pike alone was nearly a match for the whole of Sir James Yeo's squadron: she measured about 850 tons, and mounted 26 long 24-pounders on a flush deck, another 24-pounder on a pivot-carriage upon her forecastle, and a second, similarly mounted, upon her quarter-deck; and her crew, including some soldiers serving as marines, amounted to 400 men. With this ship, the Madison, Oneida, and 11 fine schooners, Commodore Chauncey sailed from Sackett's Harbour for the head of the lake. On the 8th of August, in the morning, while the American fleet lay at anchor off Fort Niagara, the British squadron hove in sight; and, that a better opinion may be formed of the situation of the parties, we will state the force of each. The British had six vessels, mounting 92 guns; of which two were long 24-pounders, 13 long 18-pounders, five long 12 and 9 pounders, and 72 carronades of different calibers, including six 68-pounders; and the vessels were manned with 717 officers and men. The Americans, by their own admission, had 14 vessels, armed, also by their admission, with 114 guns; of which, seven were long 32-pounders, 32 long 24-pounders, eight long 18-pounders, 19 long 12 and 9 pounders, and 48 carronades, 40 of which were 32 and 24 pounders. Nearly one-fourth of the long guns and carronades were on pivot-carriages, and were consequently as effective in broadside as twice the number. The 14 American vessels, thus armed, were manned with 1193 officers and men.

Commodore Chauncey immediately got under way, and stood out, with his 14 vessels, formed in line-of-battle; but, as the six British vessels approached, the American vessels, after discharging their broadsides, wore and stood under their batteries. Light airs and calms prevented Sir James Yeo from closing; and during the night, in a heavy squall, two of the American schooners, the Hamilton and Scourge, upset, and their crews unfortunately perished. On the 9th the two parties were again in sight of each other, and continued manœuvring during that and the succeeding day. On the 10th, at night, a fine breeze sprang up, and Sir James Yeo immediately took advantage of it, by bearing up to attack his powerful opponent; but, just as the Wolfe got within gun-shot of the Pike and Madison, these two powerful American ships bore up, fired their stern-chase guns, and made sail for Niagara; leaving two fine schooners, the Julia and Growler, each armed with one long 32 and one long 12 pounder on pivots, and manned with a crew of 40 men, to be captured without an effort to save them. With his two prizes, and without the loss of a man, and with no greater injury to his ships than a few cut ropes and torn sails, Sir James Yeo returned to Kingston.

The "United States Gazette," of September 6, gave a letter from one of the General Pike's officers. The writer, having previously stated the American force at two ships, one brig, and 11 schooners, says: "On the 10th, at midnight, we came within gun-shot, every one in high spirits. The schooners commenced the action with their long guns, which did great execution. At half-past 12, the Commodore fired his broadside, and gave three cheers, which was returned from the other ships, the enemy closing fast. We lay by for our opponent, the orders having been given not to fire until she came within pistol-shot, though the enemy kept up a constant fire. Every gun was pointed, every match ready in hand, and the red British ensign plainly to be descried by the light of the moon—when, to our utter astonishment, the commodore wore, and stood S.E., leaving Sir James Lucas Yeo to exult in the capture of two schooners, and in our retreat; which was certainly a very fortunate one for him." No wonder an order soon afterwards issued from Washington, that no officer should write, with the intention of publication, accounts of the operations of the fleet and army. Sir James could not have had his assertions more ably supported than they were by the Pike's officer. The latter was mistaken, however, as to any "execution" having been done by the American squadron. The captured schooners of course made no resistance; although the American editors trumped up a story about their desperate defence,—how they tore and ripped up the enemy, &c.

The Pike's officer has described two other "chases;" differing chiefly from the last, in no loss having been suffered, or even shot fired. He says: "We proceeded directly for Sackett's Harbour; where we victualled and put to sea, the next day after her arrival, August 14. On the 16th we discovered the enemy again, again hurried to quarters, again got clear of the enemy by dint of carrying sail, and returned to Sackett's Harbour. On the 18th we again fell in with the enemy steering for Kingston, and we reached the harbour on the 19th. This is the result of two cruises; the first of which, by proper guidance, might have decided in our favour the superiority on the lake, and consequently in Canada." This is what many of the American editors called "chasing the British commander all round the lake." Commodore Chauncey, although he had lost four of his 14 vessels, appeared in September with 11 sail; having brought out with him the Schooner Elizabeth, of about the same force as the Growler or Julia, and the new schooner Sylph, mounting, at that time, four long 32-pounders upon pivot-carriages, and four long sixes. This schooner was described by the Americans as upwards of 400 tons. She was afterwards converted into a brig.

On the 11th of September, while the British squadron lay becalmed off Genessee river, the American fleet of 11 sail, by the aid of a partial wind, succeeded in getting within range of their long 24 and 32 pounders; and during five hours cannonaded the British, who did not fire a carronade, and had only six guns in all the squadron that could reach the enemy. At sunset a breeze sprang up from the westward, when Sir James steered for the American fleet; but the American commodore avoided a close meeting, and thus the affair ended. It was so far unfortunate for Sir James Yeo, that he had a midshipman (William Ellery) and three seamen killed and seven wounded. In his official letter on the subject of this action, Commodore Chauncey most uncandidly says: "I was much disappointed that Sir James refused to fight me, as he was so much superior in point of force, both in guns and men, having upwards of 20 guns more than we have, and heaves a greater weight of shot."

Another partial engagement took place on the 28th of September. Commodore Chauncey, having the weather-gage, kept his favourite distance, and one of his shot carried away the Wolfe's maintopmast; which, in its fall, brought down the mizentopmast and cross-jack yard. It was this, and not, as Mr. Clark says, "a manœuvre of the commodore's," that "threw the British in confusion." Even with this great advantage, Commodore Chauncey would not venture within carronade-range. Mr. Clark, in describing this action, speaks of the British "frigate" Wolfe, upon which he had previously mounted "36 guns." Only two shot from the Americans did any material damage; the one already mentioned, and another that struck the Royal George's foretopmast, which fell, upon her anchoring. Mr. Clark says: "Prudence forbad any further pursuit on the part of the Americans;" and the editor of the "History of the War," another American publication, adds: "The commodore was obliged to give up the chase; his ship was making water so fast, that it required all his pumps to keep her clear, and others of his vessels were much damaged. The General Pike suffered a considerable loss of men; among whom were 22 killed or wounded by the bursting of a gun." Other American accounts stated the commodore's loss in men at upwards of 60 killed and wounded. It was therefore the damages and loss sustained by the American squadron, and not the " British batteries on Burlington heights," upon which not a musket was mounted, that " obliged the commodore to give up the *chase*." The effect produced by Sir James's few long guns gave a specimen of what his carronades would have done, and his opponent allowed them to be used.

In the month of May, 1813, Captain Robert Heriot Barclay was appointed to the command of the British flotilla on this lake; an appointment which had been declined by Captain William Howe Mulcaster, another of Sir James Yeo's commanders on account of the exceedingly bad equipment of the vessels. These, owing to the loss of one of them, now consisted of five; and they were not equal in aggregate tonnage or force to a British 20-gun ship. With a lieutenant, and 19 rejected seamen of the Ontario squadron, Captain Barclay, towards the middle of June, joined his enviable command; and, with the aid of the seamen he had brought, a ship was forthwith laid down at Amherstburgh, intended to be of 305 tons, and to mount as many as 18 guns.

Since the latter end of March, Captain Oliver Hazard Perry, of the United States navy, had arrived at the port of Erie, with a numerous supply of officers and seamen, to equip a flotilla; and, by the time Captain Barclay arrived, the American force consisted of one brig, the Caledonia, six fine schooners, and one sloop, mounting 15 heavy long guns, all on traversing-carriages. Two brigs, of about 460 tons each, to mount 18 carronades, 32-pounders, and two long twelves, had also been laid down at Presqu'isle, and were in a state of some forwardness. The destruction of these vessels on the stocks, would have enabled the British to maintain the ascendancy on the lake, and would have averted the fatal blow that was afterwards struck in this quarter. Colonel Proctor, the British commanding officer at Amherstburgh, saw this; as well as the facility with which the thing might be done, if Sir George Prevost would send him the long promised supply of troops, and about 100 sailors. He wrote letter after letter to Sir George on the subject, but all in vain. The latter, when he had exhausted his excuses, became petulant and rude. The two American brigs were launched; and, although they had to pass a bar, with their guns and stores out, and almost on their beam-ends, the Niagara and Lawrence, by the beginning of August, were riding on the lake, in readiness for action.

By the latter end of August, the Detroit, as the new ship was named, was launched; and the next difficulty was to get guns for her. For this, the fort of Amherstburgh was stripped, and 19, of four different calibers, were obtained. It will convey some idea of the expense of hastily fitting vessels at this distance from home, to mention, that every round shot costs one shilling a pound for the carriage from Quebec to Lake Erie, that powder was ten times as dear as at home, and that, for anchors, their weight in silver would be scarcely an over-estimate. But, were the Americans on this lake any better off? In five days an express reaches Washington. It would, under the most favourable circumstances as to weather and despatch in office, take as many months to get an article ordered from England, or even permission to stir a peg out of the common routine of service. The American vessels were therefore completely at home, while the British vessels were upwards of 3500 miles from home; penned up in a lake on the enemy's borders, inaccessible by water, and to which the land-carriage, for heavy articles, ordnance and naval stores especially, was most difficult and tedious.

Early in September, Captain Barclay received a draught of seamen from the Dover troop-ship; and many of these would have scarcely rated as "ordinaries" on board the regular ships-of-war. He had now 50 British seamen to distribute among two ships, two schooners, a brig, and a sloop, armed altogether with 63 carriage-guns. It must have been the incredibility of this that induced some of the British journals, in their account of the proceedings on this lake, to state "150," instead of 50 seamen. It is asserted, on the express authority of Captain Barclay himself, that no more than 50 seamen were at any time on board the Lake Erie flotilla; the complements having been made up by Canadian peasants and soldiers, men that, without disparagement to either, were sorry substitutes for British sailors. On the other hand, the ships of the Americans, as their newspapers informed us, were equipped in the most complete manner; and through the same channel we learned, that large draughts of seamen had repeatedly marched to Lake Erie from the sea-board. The best of riflemen were to be obtained on the spot. What else was required to render the American ships in these waters quite as effective as the best appointed ships on the ocean?

On the 9th of September, Captain Barclay was lying, with his little squadron, in the port of Amherstburgh, anxiously waiting the arrival of a promised supply of seamen. Almost surrounded by hostile shores, his people on half-allowance of food, not another day's flour in store, a large body of Indians, whose friendship would cease with the least abridgment in their accustomed supply, close in his rear; alike hopeless of succour and of retreat, what was Captain Barclay to do? Impelled by dread of famine, and, not improbably, of Indian treachery too, he sailed out in the evening to risk a battle with an enemy's fleet, whose force he knew was nearly double his own.

The following statement will place the fact of superiority beyond a doubt:—

British.				*Americans.*			
Long guns.		No.	No.	Long guns.		No.	No.
24-pounders	. . .	2		32-pdrs. all on pivots	.	3	
18 ,,	on pivot	1		24 ,,	ditto	.	4
12 ,,	2 on pivots	8		12 ,,	4 ditto	.	8
9 ,,	ditto	12					
6 ,,	. . .	8					
4 ,,	. . .	2					
2 ,,	. . .	2					
			— 35				— 15
Carronades.				Carronades.			
24 ,,	. . .	15		32 ,,	2 ditto	.	38
18 ,,	. . .	1		24 ,,	ditto	.	1
12 ,,	. . .	12					
			— 28				— 39
	Total	. .	63		Total	. .	54
Half of guns not on pivots	.	29		Half of guns not on pivots.	.	20	
Pivot guns	. . .	5		Pivot guns	. . .	14	
Broadside-guns . . .	{ No.	34		Broadside-guns . .	{ No.	34	
	{ lbs.	459			{ lbs.	928	

But this is supposing that the two squadrons were fitted in an equal manner; whereas, however incredible it may appear, before they could fire a single great gun on board the Detroit, the men were obliged to discharge a pistol at the touch-hole! By adding 80 Canadians, and 240 soldiers from the Newfoundland and 41st regiments, to the 50 British seamen, the crew of Commodore Barclay's squadron is made to amount to 345;[1] whereas Commodore Perry had picked crews to all his vessels, particularly on board the Lawrence and her sister-brig, and his total of men amounted to at least 580.

[1] [The total of 345 does not add up quite correctly, but in 'Naval Occurrences' the number of soldiers is given as rather less.—H. Y. POWELL.]

On the 10th, soon after daylight, Commodore Barclay discovered the American squadron at anchor in Put-in bay, and immediately bore up, with the wind from the south-west, to bring the enemy to action. Commodore Perry thereupon got under way to meet the British; who, at 10 A.M., by a sudden shift of wind to south-east, were thrown to leeward of their opponents. Commodore Barclay, who carried his broad pendant on board the Detroit, so stationed his vessels that those which were the nearest to an equality of force in the two squadrons might be opposed together. The schooner Chippeway, commanded by master's mate J. Campbell, was in the van. Then came, in succession, the Detroit and Queen Charlotte, the latter commanded by Captain Robert Finnis, brig Hunter, Lieutenant George Bignell, schooner Lady Prevost, Lieutenant Edward Buchan; and the sloop Little Belt, by whom commanded we are not aware, brought up the rear.

At about 11 h. 45 m. A.M. the action began; and the Detroit became closely engaged with the Lawrence, Captain Perry's brig, supported by the schooners Ariel and Scorpion. Although the matches and tubes of the Detroit were so defective that pistols were obliged to be fired at the guns to set them off, the seamen, Canadians, and soldiers plied their guns so well that, in the course of two hours, they knocked the Lawrence almost to pieces, and, after driving Commodore Perry out of her, compelled her to surrender; but, having sailed with only one boat, and that being cut to pieces, the Detroit could not take possession of the American brig, and the latter, as soon as she had dropped out of gun-shot, rehoisted her colours.

In the mean time the Queen Charlotte, with her 24-pounder carronades, had been opposed by the Niagara, supported, as the Lawrence had been, by two schooners with heavy long guns. In a few minutes Captain Finnis was killed; and his successor in the command, Lieutenant John Stokes, was struck senseless by a splinter. The next officer, provincial Lieutenant Irvine, was without any experience, and therefore comparatively useless. The Queen Charlotte soon afterwards struck her colours. From having kept out of the range of the Charlotte's carronades, the Niagara was a fresh vessel, and to her Captain Perry proceeded. As soon as he got on board, the American commodore, accompanied by some of his schooners, bore down, and took a raking position athwart the bows of the already disabled Detroit. In a short time Lieutenant John Garland, first of the Detroit, was mortally, and Captain Barclay himself most severely, wounded. The command then devolved upon Lieutenant George Inglis; who fought his ship in the most determined manner, until, out of the 10 experienced British seamen on board, eight were killed or wounded, and every hope of success or of escape had fled: he then ordered the colours of the Detroit to be struck The Hunter and Lady Prevost surrendered about the same time; as did the Chippeway and Little Belt, as soon as some of the American vessels overtook them on their retreat.

The loss on the British side amounted to three officers and 38 men killed, and nine officers and 85 men wounded. The officers killed were, Lieutenant S. J. Garden, of the Newfoundland regiment, and John Garland, the first-lieutenant, on board the Detroit; and the captain of the Queen Charlotte. The officers wounded were Captain Barclay most dangerously in his left or remaining arm, Mr. John M. Hoffmeister, purser of the Detroit, Lieutenant John Stokes, and midshipman James Foster, of the Queen Charlotte, Lieutenants Edward Buchan and Francis Roulette, and master's mate Henry Gateshill, of the Lady Prevost, and master's mate J. Campbell, commanding the Chippeway. The loss on the American side, as taken from Captain Perry's letter, amounted to 27 killed and 96 wounded, including 22 killed and 61 wounded on board the Lawrence.

The fact of this brig having surrendered is admitted by Captain Perry himself, in the following words: "It was with unspeakable pain, that I saw, soon after I got on board the Niagara, the flag of the Lawrence come down, although I was perfectly sensible that she had been defended to the last, and that to have continued to make a show of resistance, would have been a wanton sacrifice of her brave crew. But the enemy was not able to take possession of her, and circumstances soon permitted her flag again to be hoisted." The chief fault to be found with Captain Perry's letter is, that it does not contain the slightest allusion to the bravery of Captain Barclay, or the inferiority of his means of resistance.

As the Americans are by this time pretty well ashamed of all the bombastic nonsense circulated by the press of the United States, day after day during many months of the war, on the subject of Captain Perry's "Nelsonic" victory, we shall not rake the trash up again; but we fear that the professional, and therefore presumably correct, dictum of a contemporary, that "in number and weight of guns, the two squadrons were nearly equal,"[1] will make the Americans imagine, that they really had

Brenton, vol. v., p. 132.

some ground for their extravagant boasting. However, on referring again to our contemporary's account, we feel satisfied that little harm will arise; for, should the evident partiality that is shown to Sir George Prevost miss being seen, the statement, that "both the Detroit and Queen Charlotte struck to the United States ship St. Lawrence, Captain Perry," will satisfy the American reader that Captain Brenton knew very little about the action he was attempting to describe.

On the 16th of September, 1814, Captain Barclay, and his surviving officers and men, were tried by a court-martial on board the Gladiator at Portsmouth, for the loss of the late Erie flotilla, and the following was the sentence pronounced: "That the capture of his majesty's late squadron was caused by the very defective means Captain Barclay possessed to equip them on Lake Erie; the want of a sufficient number of able seamen, whom he had repeatedly and earnestly requested of Sir James Yeo to be sent to him; the very great superiority of the enemy to the British squadron; and the unfortunately early fall of the superior officers in the action. That it appeared that the greatest exertions had been made by Captain Barclay, in equipping and getting into order the vessels under his command; that he was fully justified, under the existing circumstances, in bringing the enemy to action; that the judgment and gallantry of Captain Barclay in taking his squadron into action, and during the contest, were highly conspicuous, and entitled him to the highest praise; and that the whole of the other officers and men of his majesty's late squadron conducted themselves in the most gallant manner; and did adjudge the said Captain Robert Heriot Barclay, his surviving officers and men, to be most fully and honourably acquitted." Rear-admiral Edward James Foote, president.

Notwithstanding this flattering testimonial, notwithstanding the severity of his wounds, wounds by one of which his right arm had been entirely lost, many years before the Lake Erie defeat, and by two others, received in that action, his remaining arm had been rendered permanently motionless, or nearly so, and a part of his thigh cut away, Captain Barclay was not confirmed as a commander until the 19th of November, 1813; and was only promoted to post-rank in 1824.

The first naval event of the late war upon Lake Champlain, a lake, all, except about one-twentieth part, within the boundaries of the United States, occurred on the 3rd of June, 1813. Two American armed sloops appeared in sight of the British garrison at Isle-aux-noix. Three gun-boats immediately got under way to attack them; and the crews of two batteaux and of two row-boats were landed to annoy the enemy in the rear, the channel being very narrow. After a contest of three hours and a half, the two sloops surrendered. They proved to be the Growler and Eagle, mounting 11 guns, and having a complement of 50 men, each; both under the command of Lieutenant Sidney Smith, of the United States navy. The British had three men wounded; the Americans, one man killed, eight severely wounded, and, including the latter, 99 prisoners. No British naval officer was present. The feat was performed by detachments of the 100th regiment, and royal artillery, under the direction of Major Taylor, of the former.

On the 1st of August, some officers and seamen having arrived from Quebec, Captain Thomas Everard, late of the 18-gun brig-sloop Wasp, with the two prize-sloops, three gun-boats, and several batteaux, containing about 1000 troops under the command of Colonel Murray, entered the American port of Plattsburg. Here the colonel landed with his men; and, after driving away the American militia at the post, destroyed all the arsenals, block-houses, barracks, and stores of every description, together with the extensive barracks at Saranac. The two enterprising officers then proceeded off Burlington and Swanton, in Vermont; where they seized and destroyed several sloops laden with provisions, and did other considerable injury. At this time the United States troops at Burlington, distant only 24 miles from Plattsburg, under the command of Major-general Hampton, amounted to about 4000 men. Although a letter written by an inhabitant of Burlington, and published in most of the American papers, declares that the British troops "did no injury whatever to private property," an American historian states thus: "They (the British) wantonly burned several private store-houses, and carried off immense quantities of the stock of individuals."[1]

As a proof that a little energy on the part of the Americans might have averted the Plattsburg misfortune, it appears by a statement, published in the United States within three weeks after the above affair happened, that the American naval force on Lake Champlain then consisted of the President, of 12 guns, the Commodore Preble and Montgomery of 11 guns each, the Frances, of 6 guns, two gun-boats, of one 18-pounder each, and six scows, of one 12-pounder each.

[1] Sketches of the War, p. 156.

BRITISH AND FRENCH FLEETS.

The remarks which we ventured to submit, when commencing with the important operations of the preceding year, have left us little to do in ushering the present year into notice, beyond pointing to the usual Annual Abstract,[1] and to the prize and casualty lists attached to it.[2]

The number of commissioned officers and masters, belonging to the British navy at the beginning of the year 1814, was,

Admirals	65
Vice-admirals	68
Rear-admirals	76
,, superannuated 29	
Post-captains	798
,, superannuated 37	
Commanders, or sloop-captains	628
,, superannuated 50	
Lieutenants	3285
Masters	674

And the number of seamen and marines, voted for the service of the year, was 140,000 for seven, and 90,000 for six lunar months of it.[3]

Although we can afford to say very little on the subject, it may be necessary to state that, during the preceding year, in consequence of treaties among them, Russia, Prussia, Austria, Denmark, and Sweden, allied themselves with England, Spain, and Portugal, against France. A counter-revolution took place in Holland, and the prince of Orange landed there from England

---

[1] See Appendix, Annual Abstract, No. 22.   [2] See Appendix, Nos. 1 and 2.
[3] See Appendix, No. 3.

and was proclaimed sovereign prince of the United Netherlands. Before the present year was many days old, Murat deserted his old benefactor, and made peace with England. All these events, many of which are highly interesting to the historical reader, will be found amply detailed in other works exclusively devoted to the subject: our business is with occurrences that take place upon a different element, and to them we return.

On the 12th of February a French squadron, of three sail of the line and three frigates, under the command of Rear-admiral the Baron Cosmao-Kerjulien, sailed from Toulon to meet a newly-built French 74 expected from Genoa. Matters in France were getting so near to a crisis, that the Moniteur could find no room in its pages for an account which, otherwise, would have been allowed a conspicuous place: hence, we can give the names of only one line-of-battle ship and one frigate, the Romulus and Adrienne. On the 13th, at a few minutes after daybreak, this squadron, then steering to the southward, was discovered by Sir Edward Pellew's fleet. At 7 h. 55 m. A.M. the six French ships tacked together, and, with a strong east wind, steered for Porquerolles on their return to Toulon. At 10 h. 30 m. A.M. the ships entered the bay of Hyères by the Grande-Passe, and, in about an hour afterwards, quitted it by the Petite-Passe, still under all sail.

The British fleet, consisting of the following 15 sail of the line, besides the Unité frigate and Badger brig-sloop, was also under all sail, advancing to cut off the French squadron from the road of Toulon, towards which it was now steering:

Gun-ship.		
120	Caledonia	Vice-admiral (r.) Sir Edward Pellew, Bart. Rear-admiral (w.) Israel Pellew. Captain Edward Lloyd Graham.
	Hibernia	Vice-admiral (w.) Sir William Sidney Smith. Captain Thomas Gordon Caulfield.
112	San-Josef	Rear-admiral (b.) Sir Richard King, Bart. Captain William Stewart.
100	Royal George	,, T. Fras. Ch. Mainwaring.
98	Boyne	,, George Burlton.
	Ocean	,, Robert Plampin.
	Prince of Wales	,, John Erskine Douglas.
	Union	,, Robert Rolles.
	Barfleur	,, John Maitland.
74	Duncan	,, Robert Lambert.
	Indus	,, William Hall Gage.
	Berwick	,, Edward Brace.
	Swiftsure	,, Edward Stirling Dickson.
	Armada	,, Charles Grant.
	Aboukir	,, George Parker.

At 30 minutes past noon the leading ship of the British fleet, the Boyne, opened a fire upon the second French ship from the rear (believed to have been the Adrienne frigate), which was immediately returned by the squadron, then running before the wind, at the rate of 10 knots, for Cape Carquaranne. The Boyne carried a press of sail, in the hope of cutting off or driving on shore the sternmost French ship, the Romulus: but the latter kept so close to the shore, as to render the attempt impracticable, without the Boyne herself going on shore. The Boyne, therefore, had no alternative but to lay close alongside the French 74; who, as well as her five companions, was now steering straight for Cape Brun. A steady and well-directed fire, within half pistol-shot distance, was maintained by the Boyne; but to which the Romulus scarcely returned a shot, until she got abreast of Pointe Sainte-Marguerite. Being by this time nearly unrigged by the Boyne's fire, the Romulus now hauled dead-in, to run on shore between the batteries of Brun and Sainte-Marguerite. At this instant, Sir Edward Pellew, in the Caledonia, who was close astern of the Boyne, waved to Captain Burlton to haul out. No sooner had the Boyne made a movement in obedience to this order, than the Romulus, putting her helm a-starboard, shot round Cape Brun, and, notwithstanding a broadside from the Caledonia, and her evidently disabled state from the Boyne's previous fire, succeeded in entering the road of Toulon; where the remaining ships of the French squadron were just about to anchor.

The French batteries, particularly those of Cape Brun and Cape Sepet, opened a very heavy and destructive fire upon the Boyne as she stood out to the southward. The Boyne at length got clear; and the Caledonia, running up alongside of her, greeted the Victory's sister-ship, who had just acted so nobly in emulation of her, with three hearty cheers; a salute which the men of the Boyne were not slow in returning. The fire from the French batteries and ships, particularly the former, had shot away the Boyne's mizentopsail yard, and main and spring stays, greatly damaged her running-rigging and sails, badly wounded her foremast, fore-yard, and bowsprit, disabled two of her guns, and struck her hull in several places under water. Her loss on the same occasion amounted to one midshipman (George Terry) and one seaman killed, one midshipman (Samuel Saunders), 32 seamen, six marines, and one boy wounded; total, two killed and 40 wounded. The Caledonia received no damage; and her loss was confined to one seaman killed by an explosion.

The Romulus is acknowledged to have sustained a loss, in killed and badly wounded, of 70, and the Adrienne of 11. The Romulus, undoubtedly, was manœuvred in a very skilful manner; and her captain, whose name we regret not being able to give, deserved credit, as well for that, as for his bravery in not striking his colours to so powerful an opponent as the Boyne. According to the French papers, the 74 from Genoa succeeded in entering Toulon on the following day, the 14th; making 23 sail of the line, including six three-deckers, afloat in the road and harbour, besides two or three two-deckers on the stocks.

On the 5th of January, after a 10 days' cannonade, the fortress of Cattaro in the Adriatic, surrendered to the British 38-gun frigate Bacchante, Captain William Hoste, and the 18-gun brig-sloop Saracen, Captain John Harper. The loss on the occasion was comparatively trifling, amounting to only one seaman killed, and Lieutenant of marines William Haig, slightly wounded. Captain Hoste, in his letter to Rear-admiral Fremantle on the subject, speaks in high terms of the following officers: Captain Harper, Lieutenants John Hancock and Charles Robert Milbourne, acting Lieutenant William Lee Rees, Mr. Stephen Vale, the Bacchante's master, Lieutenant Haig, and midshipman Charles Bruce. On the 28th Ragusa surrendered to the Bacchante and Saracen, and to a body of British and Austrian troops who were besieging the fortress; and on the 13th of February, the island of Paxo surrendered, without resistance, to the British 38-gun frigate Apollo, Captain Bridges Watkinson Taylor, and a detachment of troops under Lieutenant-colonel Church.

In the course of January and February, indeed, by the active and gallant exertions of the different ships composing the squadron of Rear-admiral Fremantle in the Adriatic, aided by detachments of Austrian troops, every place belonging to the French in Dalmatia, Croatia, Istria, and the Frioul, with all the islands in that sea, surrendered to the allies; as, in the month of March and April, did Spezzia and Genoa to a small squadron under the command of Sir Josias Rowley, aided by a detachment of British troops and a division of Sicilian gun-boats. At Genoa the British gained possession of the French 74-gun ship Brilliant ready for launching, another 74 in frame, and four brig-corvettes, of which the Renard that had engaged the Swallow was one. The Brilliant was a ship of 1883 tons, and, being built of good oak, became an acquisition to the British navy; in which she still continues under the name of Genoa.

In order to co-operate with the British army under the Marquis of Wellington, which, on the 20th of February, had reached the banks of the Adour, a small squadron had been stationed off the mouth of the river, under the command of Rear-admiral Charles Vinicombe Penrose; who, to get nearer to the scene of operations, had embarked on board the 24-gun ship Porcupine, Captain John Coode. On the morning of the 23rd, which was as early as the ships and the boats collected for the service could arrive off the river, the latter were detached to endeavour to find a passage through the tremendous surf that beats over the bar. At this time the British troops were seen from the ships, crossing over to the north side of the river, but greatly in want of the boats intended for their assistance. Thus stimulated, Captain Dowell O'Reilly, of the 10-gun brig-sloop Lyra, in a Spanish-built boat selected as the most safe for the purpose, and having with him the principal pilot, was the first to make the attempt to cross the bar, but the boat overset. Captain O'Reilly, however, and we believe the whole boat's crew were so fortunate as to gain the shore. Lieutenant John Debenham, in a six-oared cutter, succeeded in reaching the beach; but, as it was scarcely possible that one boat in 50 could then have crossed, the other boats returned, to await the result of the next tide. The tide being at length at a proper height, and all the vessels well up for the attempt, several boats drew near the bar, but hauled off again, until at last Lieutenant George Cheyne, of the 10-gun brig-sloop Woodlark, in a Spanish boat, with five British seamen, crossed the surf and ran up the river. The next was a prize-boat, manned from a transport, closely followed by a gun-boat, commanded by Lieutenant John Cheshire, who was the first that hoisted the British colours in the Adour. The remainder of the boats and vessels followed in rapid succession, "the zeal and science of the officers triumphing over all the difficulties of the navigation;" but this arduous and most perilous undertaking was not accomplished without a heavy loss of life. Captain Elliot of the brig-sloop Martial, Mr. Henry Bloye, master's mate of the Lyra, and 11 seamen of the Porcupine, Martial, and Lyra, drowned: three transport boats lost, number of men unknown; also a Spanish chasse-marée, the whole of which perished in an instant.

The British army afterwards crossed the Adour and invested Bayonne; and, early in March, a detachment under Marshal Beresford moved forward towards Bordeaux. On the 21st, Rear-admiral Penrose, with the 74-gun ship Egmont, to which he had now shifted his flag, anchored in the Gironde. On the 2nd of April, Captain Coode of the Porcupine, who had ascended the Gironde above Pouillac, detached his boats under the orders of Lieutenant Robert Graham Dunlop, in pursuit of a French flotilla which was observed proceeding down from Blaye to Tallemont. On the approach of the boats, the flotilla ran on shore; and about 200 troops from Blaye lined the beach to protect the vessels; but Lieutenant Dunlop, landing with a detachment of seamen and marines, drove the French with great loss into the woods, and remained until the tide allowed the greater part of the vessels to be brought off. One gun-brig, six gun-boats, one armed schooner, three chasse-marées, and an imperial barge, were captured; and one gun-brig, two gun-boats, and one chasse-marée burned. This service was performed with the loss of two seamen missing, and 14 seamen and marines wounded.

On the evening of the 6th the 74-gun ship Centaur, Captain John Chambers White, anchored in the Gironde, in company with the Egmont; and preparations were immediately made for attacking the French 74-gun ship Régulus, three brig-corvettes, and other vessels lying near her, as well as the batteries that protected them; but at midnight the French set fire to the Régulus and her companions, and the whole were destroyed. Before the 9th the batteries of Pointe Coubre, Pointe Nègre, Royan, Sonlac, and Mèche were successively entered and destroyed by a detachment of seamen and marines under Captain George Harris of the 38-gun frigate Belle-Poule.

The entry of the allies into Paris on the 31st of March, and the preliminary treaty entered into between England and France on the 24th of April, put a temporary stop to the miseries of war in Europe. Louis XVIII. landed at Calais from Dover the same day; and on the 28th of April Napoleon embarked at Fréjus in Provence on board the British 38-gun frigate Undaunted, Captain Thomas Ussher, who, on the 4th of May, landed his passenger in safety at Porto-Ferraro in the Isle of Elba.

In the succeeding August the Scheldt fleet was divided in the following manner: 12 sail of the line were allowed to be retained by France; three were restored to Holland, as having formerly belonged to her; and seven others were also given to her, to be held in trust, until the congress at Vienna should decide how they were to be disposed of. The ships, generally, were a good deal broken in the sheer, and having been constructed of green wood, were in bad condition. The nine sail of the line, including two three-deckers on the stocks, were to be broken up.

Light Squadrons and Single Ships.

On the 20th of October, 1813, the two French 40-gun frigates Iphigénie and Alcmène, Captains Jacques-Léon Emeric and Alexandre Ducrest de Villeneuve, sailed from Cherbourg on a six months' cruise. The two frigates proceeded first off the Western Isles, and then to the coast of Africa; where they captured two guineamen, laden with elephants' teeth, &c. After taking out the most valuable parts of the cargoes, Captain Emeric burnt the ships. From Africa the Iphigénie and Alcmène sailed to the Canary Isles, in the vicinity of which they took six other prizes. On the 16th of January, at 7 A.M., when cruising off these islands, the two French frigates fell in with the British 74-gun ship Venerable, Captain James Andrew Worth, bearing the flag of Rear-admiral Philip Charles Durham, on his way to take the chief command at the Leeward Islands, 22-gun ship Cyane, Captain Thomas Forrest, and prize-brig Jason, a French letter-of-marque captured 17 days before, and now, with two guns (having thrown 12 overboard in chase) and 22 men, in charge of Lieutenant Thomas Moffat, belonging to the Venerable.

The two frigates, when first descried, were in the north-east; and the Cyane, the wind then blowing from the east-south-east, was ordered to reconnoitre them. Having shortened sail and hauled to the wind on the starboard tack, the Cyane, at 9 A.M., ascertained that they were enemies, and made a signal to that effect to the Venerable, who immediately went in chase. The chase continued throughout the day, so much to the advantage of the 74, that, at 6 h. 15 m. P.M. the Venerable arrived within hail of the Alcmène, the leewardmost frigate. After having hailed twice in vain, the Venerable opened her guns as they would bear; when the French frigate immediately put her helm up, and, under all sail, laid the British 74 on board, Captain Villeneuve, as was understood, expecting that his commodore, in compliance with a previous agreement, would second him in the bold attempt. According to another statement, and which has more the air of probability, the object of the Alcmène in bearing up was to cross the 74's bows, and by disabling her bowsprit and foremast, to deprive her of the means of pursuit. Whether Captain Emeric had agreed to co-operate or not, the Iphigénie now hauled sharp up, and left the Alcmène to her fate. A very short struggle decided the business, and before 6 h. 25 m. the French colours were hauled down by the British boarders, headed by Captain Worth. The conflict, although short, had been severe, especially to the Alcmène; who, out of a crew of 319 men and boys, lost two petty officers and 30 seamen killed, and 50 officers and men wounded, including her gallant commander. The Venerable's loss consisted of two seamen killed and four wounded.

During the time that had thus elapsed, and the additional time required to shift the prisoners and repair the trifling injury done to the 74's rigging by the frigate's attempt to board, the Cyane and Jason had gone in chase of the Alcmène's fugitive consort. At 10 P.M. the little Jason, having outrun the Cyane in the chase, commenced firing at the Iphigénie with her two guns, both of which Lieutenant Moffat had now got on the brig's larboard side. Such was the slow sailing of the Iphigénie, or the unskilfulness of those that manoeuvred her, that at 45 minutes past midnight the Cyane got near enough to open a fire from her bow-guns, and received in return a fire from the frigate's stern-chasers, which cut her rigging and sails a good deal. At 4 h. 30 m. A.M., on the 17th, the Cyane gallantly fired three broadsides at the French frigate, but soon found the latter too heavy for her, and dropped astern. At 5 h. 45 m. A.M. Captain Forrest despatched the brig in search of the admiral, and continued his pursuit of the Iphigénie; who shortly afterwards hauled close to the wind on the larboard tack, and fired three broadsides at the Cyane, nearly all the shot of which, fortunately for the latter, either went over her masts or between them. At 9 A.M. the Iphigénie bore up and steered south-west, still followed by the Cyane.

The chase thus continued, the latter losing sight occasionally and again recovering it, during the remainder of the 17th, and the whole of the 18th and 19th. In the evening of the latter day the Cyane dropped astern; but the Venerable was now fast coming up, and, at daylight on the 20th, was within two miles of the French frigate. The Venerable, from whose mast-head the Cyane was now not to be seen, presently opened a fire from her bow-guns, and received in return a fire from the stern and quarter guns of the Iphigénie. Having thrown overboard her boats and cut away her anchors without effect, the French frigate, at 8 A.M., discharged her starboard broadside and struck her colours

Neither the Venerable nor the Iphigénie appears to have suffered any loss from the other's fire: and the Cyane, whose gallantry and perseverance in the chase were so creditable to Captain Forrest, seems also to have escaped without loss. The same good fortune attended the Jason; who with her two guns (6-pounders probably), gave so good an earnest of what Lieutenant Moffat would have done, had he commanded a vessel that mounted 20. The Iphigénie and Alcmène, being nearly new frigates, were both added to the British navy; the first under the name of Gloire, the latter under that of Dunira, afterwards changed to Immortalité.

In the latter end of October, 1813, the two French 40-gun frigates Etoile and Sultane, Captains Pierre-Henri Phillibert and Georges Du-Petit-Thouars, sailed from Nantes on a cruise. On the 18th of January, at 4 A.M., latitude about 24° north, longitude (from Greenwich) 53° west, these two French frigates discovered in the north-west the British 24-pounder 40-gun frigate Severn, Captain Joseph Nourse, escorting a convoy from England to the island of Bermuda, and steering west by north, with the wind a light air from the south-east. At 7 h. 30 m. A.M. the Severn proceeded in chase; and at 8 h. 40 m., finding the strangers did not answer the private signal, the British frigate bore up north by east, and made all possible sail from them, signalling her convoy to take care of themselves.

At 10 h. 30 m. A.M. the Severn commenced firing her stern-chasers at the leading enemy's frigate, and at noon lost sight of her convoy steering to the westward. At 4 h. 5 m. P.M. the headmost French frigate, the Etoile, hoisting her colours and broad pendant, began firing her bow-guns. A running fight now ensued, which, without doing the slightest injury to the Severn, lasted until 5 h. 30 m. P.M.; when the Etoile then distant less than two miles (the Sultane astern of her about one), ceased firing. The chase continued all night, rather to the advantage of the Severn. At 8 A.M. on the 19th the two French frigates gave up the pursuit, and hauled to the wind on the starboard tack.

The Etoile and Sultane afterwards proceeded to the Cape de Verds, and anchored in the port of English Harbour, island of Mayo. On the 23rd of January, at about 9 h. 55 m. A.M., the two British 18-pounder 36-gun frigates Creole, Captain George Charles Mackenzie, and Astrea, Captain John Eveleigh, rounding the south-east end of Mayo on their way from the neighbouring island of Fort-aventura, with the wind at north-east, blowing fresh, discovered over a point of land the mast-heads of the two French frigates, and of two merchant-ships, one brigantine, and one schooner, lying in their company. At 10 h. 15 m. the two British frigates having cleared the point, wore and hauled to the wind on the larboard tack, under their topsails. On a supposition that the strangers, whose hulls were now plainly visible, were Portuguese or Spanish frigates, the Creole hoisted the Portuguese, and the Astrea, by signal from her, the Spanish, private signals. No answer being returned, the strange frigates were considered to be enemies; and at 11 h. 30 m. A.M. the Creole and Astrea wore and made sail for the anchorage in which they lay.

At noon, when the two British frigates were about a mile distant from them, the Etoile and Sultane, having previously hoisted their topsail-yards to the mast-head, cut or slipped, and made sail free on the larboard tack, with a strong wind still from the north-east. The two former now set topgallantsails in chase; and the Astrea, owing to a gust of wind suddenly striking her, had the misfortune to split all three topsails, the mizentopsail very badly, to replace which a fresh sail was soon got into the top. At about 30 minutes past noon the south-west end of the island of Mayo bore from the Creole, the leading British frigate, east-north-east distant four miles. In another quarter of an hour the Creole, both British frigates having previously hoisted their colours, fired a shot ahead of the sternmost French ship, the Sultane, then on the former's lee or starboard bow. The two French frigates immediately hoisted their colours. The Creole continued firing her bow-guns occasionally at the Sultane until 1 P.M.: when the former discharged a few of her larboard-guns, and then, as she ranged up on the Sultane's lee beam, received the French ship's first broadside.

The Astrea also opened her fire in crossing the stern of the Sultane, and then gallantly passed between the latter and the Creole, just as the two ships had exchanged the fourth broadside. After giving and receiving two broadsides, within pistol-shot, the Astrea, at 2 h. 15 m. P.M., stood on to engage the Etoile, then about half a mile ahead of her consort, with her mizen topsail aback. Having extinguished a fire that had caught in the foretopmast staysail and mizen chains, the Creole, at 2 h. 30 m., recommenced the action with the Sultane, and presently shot away her mizenmast. About this time the wadding from the French ship's guns again set the Creole on fire, in the forecastle hammocks and on the booms. The flames were again extinguished, and the action continued for nearly half an hour longer; making about two hours from its commencement. Having now had every brace and bowline, tack, and sheet shot away, her main stay and several of her shrouds cut through, her three masts, particularly her foremast, badly wounded, the Creole put her helm a-lee, and, steering to the north-west in the direction of the island of St. Jago, abandoned the contest.

It took the Astrea, when at 2 h. 15 m., she had quitted the Sultane, until 2 h. 30 m. before she got alongside of the Etoile to leeward. After an exchange of broadsides, the Astrea, having, from the great way upon her, ranged too far ahead, luffed up and raked the Etoile on her starboard bow. The Astrea, just at this moment losing her wheel, fell round off; and the Etoile, wearing, passed close astern of her, separating her from the boat she was towing, and poured in a most destructive raking fire; which cut the Astrea's lower rigging to pieces, shot away both deck-transoms and four quarter-deck beams, burst a carronade, and ripped up the quarter-deck in all directions. Backing round, the Astrea soon got her starboard guns to bear; and the two frigates, each with a fresh side opposed to the other, recommenced the action, yard-arm and yard-arm. In a few minutes Captain Eveleigh fell, mortally wounded by a pistol-shot just below the heart, and was carried below.

The command now devolved upon Lieutenant John Bulford; and the engagement between the Astrea and Etoile continued in this close position, with mutual animation, although it was no cheering sight to the Astrea, at about 3 P.M., to observe her consort, on the starboard tack, apparently a beaten ship, and the Etoile's consort approaching to double the force against herself. At 3 h. 5 m. P.M. the topsail, which lay in the Astrea's mizen top to replace the split one, caught fire, but the flames were soon extinguished. Seeing the near approach of the Sultane, the Astrea would have boarded the Etoile, and endeavoured to decide the contest that way; but the motion of the ships was too great, and the British frigate could only continue to keep her antagonist under her guns to leeward. At 3 h. 30 m. the Sultane, as she passed to leeward, raked the Astrea, and did her considerable damage. In five minutes the Sultane wore from the Astrea, and stood before the wind, leaving the latter and the Etoile still in close action.

At 3 h. 45 m. the Etoile also wore round on the starboard

tack; and in five minutes afterwards the Astrea's mizenmast, with the topsail a second time in flames, went by the board, carrying some of the firemen with it. In a short time after she had wore and ceased firing, the Etoile stood towards her consort, who was waiting for her under easy sail; and the Astrea, having by this time had the whole of her lower and topsail braces shot away, and being otherwise greatly damaged in rigging and sails, was in too unmanageable a state to follow. At 4 h. 15 m. the Sultane's maintopmast went over the side;[1] and the Astrea, having soon afterwards partially refitted herself, wore round on the starboard tack with her head towards San-Jago. At this time the Creole was not visible to the Astrea; and the two French frigates were about four miles distant in the south-west, steering south by west. At 4 h. 30 m. P.M. the Creole was discovered under the land, standing into Porto-Praya bay; where at 4 h. 45 m. she anchored, and where, in about an hour afterwards, the Astrea joined her.

The principal damages of the Creole have already been related: her loss, out of a complement of 284 men and boys, amounted to one master's mate, seven seamen, and two marines, killed, and 26 petty officers, seamen and marines wounded. The Astrea, besides the loss of her mizenmast and the damage done to her rigging and sails, had her fore and main masts wounded, and was a good deal struck about the stern and quarter. Her loss, out of the same complement as the Creole's, consisted of her commander and eight seamen and marines killed, and 37 petty officers, seamen, and marines wounded, four of them dangerously and 11 severely; making the loss on board the two British frigates 19 killed and 63 wounded. The two remaining masts of the Sultane, and all three masts of the Etoile, were badly wounded: and, that their hulls escaped no better is most likely, because the acknowledged loss on board of each, out of a complement of 340 men and boys, was about 20 men killed and 30 wounded, or 40 killed and 60 wounded between them.

Here were two pairs of combatants, about as equally matched, considering the character of the opponent parties, as could well be desired; and who fought so equally, as to make that a drawn battle, which, under other circumstances, might have ended decisively. Had the Creole, having already witnessed the fall of the Sultane's mizenmast, been aware of the tottering state of that

[1] The logs of the Creole and Astrea concur in stating it to have been the mainmast that fell, but both ships were mistaken.

frigate's maintopmast, Captain Mackenzie would not, we presume, have discontinued the engagement, simply for the preservation of his wounded foremast; especially when the Creole's main and mizen masts were still standing, as well as all three of her topmasts, and when, by his early retirement, he was exposing to almost certain capture a crippled consort. No frigate could have performed her part more gallantly than the Astrea; but two such opponents, as the one that had so long been engaging her, were more than she could withstand. Fortunately for the Astrea, both French frigates had seemingly had enough of fighting; and the Etoile and Sultane left their sole antagonist in a state not less of surprise than of joy at her extraordinary escape.

On the 26th of March, at 9 A.M., these two frigates (the Sultane with jury topmasts and mizenmast), when about 12 leagues to the north-west of the Isle de Bas, steering for Saint Malo, in thick weather, with a moderate breeze at south-west, fell in with the British 18-pounder 36-gun frigate Hebrus, Captain Edmund Palmer, and 16-gun brig-sloop Sparrow, Captain Francis Erskine Loch. The latter was so near to the French frigates that, in crossing them, she received seven or eight shot from each; which greatly damaged her rigging and sails, killed her master, and wounded one seaman. The brig now tacked towards the Hebrus, who was on her weather-quarter, standing on the larboard tack. The latter, as she passed the French frigates to windward on the opposite tack, exchanged distant broadsides with them, and fired her weather or larboard guns as a signal to her consort, the 74-gun ship Hannibal, Captain Sir Michael Seymour. At 9 h. 30 m. A.M., the Hebrus again tacked, and in 10 minutes afterwards, on the fog clearing, observed the Hannibal coming down under a press of canvas. At 10 A.M., being joined by the 74, the Hebrus crowded sail after the two French frigates, then bearing from her south-east by east distant about four miles. At 11 A.M. the wind suddenly shifted to the north-north-west, and blew very fresh. On this the two French frigates, finding their pursuers rapidly approaching, separated: the Sultane changed her course to east by north, and the Etoile hauled up to south-east. Directing by signal the Hebrus, as the best sailing-ship, to chase, in company with the Sparrow, the most perfect frigate, the Hannibal herself went in pursuit of the other.

At 2 P.M. the Hebrus lost sight of the Hannibal and Sultane, and at 5 P.M. of the Sparrow; and the Etoile then bore from her south-east by east, distant three miles. Soon afterwards the

Etoile gradually hauled up to east-north-east, but was still gained upon by the Hebrus. About midnight the French frigate reached the Race of Alderney; when, the wind getting more northerly, the Hebrus came up fast, and took in her studding-sails. At 1 h. 35 m. A.M. on the 27th, having run the length of Point Jobourg, the Etoile was obliged to attempt rounding it almost within the wash of the breakers. At 1 h. 45 m., while, with her courses hauled up, the Hebrus was following close upon the larboard quarter of the Etoile as the latter wore round the point, the French frigate opened a fire upon the British frigate's starboard bow. This fire the Hebrus quickly returned within pistol-shot distance, running athwart the stern of the Etoile, to get between her and the shore; and that so closely, that her jib-boom passed over the French ship's taffrail. The Hebrus was now in eight fathoms water, and the land within musket-shot on her starboard beam. At 2 h. 20 m. A.M., while crossing the bows of the Hebrus to get again inside of her, the Etoile shot away the British frigate's foretopmast and foreyard, and crippled her mainmast and bowsprit, besides doing considerable injury to her rigging, both standing and running.

It had been nearly calm since the commencement of the action, but at 3 A.M. a light breeze sprang up from the land. Taking advantage of this, the Hebrus succeeded in pouring several raking fires into her antagonist, and at 3 h. 45 m. shot away her mizenmast by the board. At 4 A.M. the Etoile ceased firing; and, after a close and obstinate combat of two hours and a quarter, hailed to say that she had struck. No sooner was possession taken of the prize, than it became necessary to turn the heads of both ships off the shore, as well to prevent them from grounding as to get beyond the reach of a battery, which, having been unable in the darkness of the morning to distinguish one frigate from another, had been annoying them both with its fire. The tide fortunately set the ships round Pointe Jobourg, and at 7 A.M. they anchored in Vauville bay, about five miles from the shore.

Although the principal damages of the Hebrus were in her masts and rigging, her hull had not wholly escaped, as is evident from her loss; which, out of a crew of about 284 men and boys, amounted to one midshipman (P. A. Crawley) and 12 seamen killed, and 20 seamen, 2 marines, and three boys wounded; four of the number dangerously, and six severely. The Etoile's principal damages lay in her hull, which was extremely shattered, leaving her at the close of the action with four feet water in the hold: her loss, in consequence, out of 327 men and boys (including the wounded in the former action), amounted to 40 killed and 73 wounded.

The guns of the Hebrus, one of the new yellow-pine frigates, were the same as those of the Belvidera.[1] The Etoile mounted 44 guns, including 14 carronades, 24-pounders, and two 8-pounders on the quarter-deck and forecastle. Of her acknowledged crew of 327, we shall allow 12 for the badly wounded, and not yet recovered, of the action of the 26th of January.

Comparative Force of the Combatants.

		Hebrus.	Etoile.
Broadside-guns	No.	21	22
	lbs.	467	463
Crew	No.	284	315
Size	tons.	939	1060

As the crew of the Hebrus was quite a new ship's company, with scarcely a single draught from any other ship, while the crew of the Etoile had been formed out of the united ships' companies of the Aréthuse and Rubis, and had, even since fought a creditable, if not a victorious action with an equal force, a great share of credit is due to Captain Palmer, his officers, and crew, for the successful result of this action; considering, especially, how near it was fought to the French shore, and how critically circumstanced the Hebrus was, both during its continuance and at its termination. We formerly concluded, that the stock of ammunition on board the Etoile must have been considerably diminished when she fell in with the Hebrus; but it has since been proved to us, that, after her capture by the latter, the Etoile had a considerable quantity of powder and shot left: consequently we erred in our supposition, and are extremely gratified that the inaccuracy has been pointed out in time to be corrected in these pages. We must not omit to mention, that Captain William Sargent, of the navy, who was a passenger on board the Hebrus during the action, evinced much skill and intrepidity; as is very handsomely acknowledged by Captain Palmer in his official letter.

The Hannibal was not long in overtaking the disabled frigate of which she went in chase. At 3 h. 30 m. P.M. on the 26th the Sultane hoisted her colours and fired a gun. At 4 h. 15 m., having received two chase shot from the Hannibal, as an earnest of what would presently follow, the French frigate, keeping

[1] See vol. v., p. 360.

away a little, discharged her starboard broadside and surrendered.

The leaks of the Etoile, from the well-directed shot of the Hebrus, were so serious, that the ship could not be kept free on a wind, so as to reach Portsmouth: Lieutenant Robert Milborne Jackson, the prize-master, was therefore obliged to bear away for Plymouth; where, on the 29th, the prize anchored in safety. The Sultane was carried to Portsmouth; and both the latter and her late consort, being new frigates, were added to the British navy, the Sultane in her own name, and the Etoile under the name of Topaze. The first-lieutenant of the Hebrus, Mr. Jackson, who, besides his good conduct in the action, had, as we have seen, some difficulty in getting his charge into port, was promoted to the rank of commander.

On the 5th of January, at 10 A.M., the island of St. Antonio, one of the Cape de Verds, bearing south-east by south distant eight or nine leagues, the British 38-gun frigate Niger, Captain Peter Rainier, and 18-pounder 36-gun frigate Tagus, Captain Philip Pipon, with a convoy in company, steering to the westward, discovered nearly ahead the French 40-gun frigate Cérès, Captain Hyacinth-Yves-Potentien le baron de Bougainville; which, in company with the Clorinde, of the same force, Captain Réné-Jean-Marie Denis-Lagarde, the senior officer, had sailed from Brest in the early part of December. Both British frigates proceeded in chase with a light breeze from the east-south-east, the Niger leading. Towards evening the Cérès gained in the pursuit; but, on the Niger's throwing overboard 800 shot, the latter got near enough, at 11 P.M., to fire three shot from her bow-chasers.

On the 6th, at 1 h. 30 m. A.M., the Niger fired two more shot, which the Cérès returned from her stern-guns. As the day opened, the wind drew to the north-east; which so favoured the Tagus that, at 7 h. 30 m. A.M., she passed the Niger, and was gaining fast upon the French frigate. At 8 h. 15 m., desirous to try a different point of sailing, the Cérès shortened sail and hauled to the wind on the starboard tack. As a proof that the French frigate gained little by this, in half an hour the Tagus got within gun-shot, and, hoisting her colours, opened a fire, which the Cérès, hoisting hers, presently returned. A running fight now commenced between the Tagus and Cérès, and continued until 9 h. 30 m. A.M.; when, having had her maintopmast shot away, the French frigate fired a broadside and surrendered. At this time, owing to some damage done to the rigging of the Tagus by her opponent's stern-chasers, the Niger had headed her consort, and was in the act of opening a heavy fire upon the Cérès.

Besides the loss of her maintopmast, the rigging and sails of the Cérès were a good deal cut, and some of her lower masts injured. The damages of the Tagus were confined to her rigging and sails; and neither the French nor the English sustained a greater loss than one man wounded. Being a fine new frigate of 1074 tons, the Cérès was added to the British navy, under the name of Seine, a Ceres being already in the service.

It is uncertain on what day, previous to the capture of the Cérès, her consort, the Clorinde, parted company; but we find the latter on the 25th of February, in latitude 47° 40' north, longitude (from Greenwich) 9° 30' west, on her way to Brest, after a tolerably successful cruise. It was at 2 P.M., when standing close hauled on the starboard tack, with the wind at south-west by south, that the Clorinde was descried by the British 24-pounder 38-gun frigate Eurotas, Captain John Phillimore, then on the former's weather-beam steering by the wind on the larboard tack. The Eurotas quickly bore up in chase; and at 2 h. 30 m. P.M. the Clorinde, whose national character and force was by this time ascertained, also bore up, under a press of sail.

While the chase is going on, we will proceed to point out some peculiarities in the armament of one of these ships, a knowledge of which will be necessary to render fully intelligible the details we have to give of the action fought between them. At the commencement of the year 1813, under the head of "British and American Navies," we stated that, among the means taken to meet the large American frigates on equal terms, some of the British 38-gun class were mounted with medium 24-pounders, and allowed an increased complement of men. The first two frigates so fitted were the Cydnus and Eurotas, both built of red pine and recently launched. The Cydnus was fitted with the 24-pounder of General Blomefield, measuring 7 ft. 6 in., and weighing about 40 cwt.; and the Eurotas, after having, by mistake we believe, received on board a set of long or 49 cwt. 24s, was fitted with the 24-pounder of Colonel Congreve, measuring only 7 ft. 6 in., and intended to weigh 41 cwt. 1 qr. 12 lbs., but actually weighing only 40 cwt. 2 qrs. 21 lbs. With 28 of these guns on the main deck, 16 carronades, 32-pounders, two long nines, and the usual 18-pounder launch-carronade, on the quarter-deck and forecastle, as her regular establishment, and with, we are inclined to think, one additional 24-pounder upon General Blomefield's principle, the Eurotas, commanded by Captain John Phillimore (promoted from the Diadem troop-ship, which he had commanded since June, 1810), sailed from the Nore in the middle of the month of August, bound off Brest.

On the 30th the Eurotas joined the blockading squadron, which was under the command of Commodore Pulteney Malcolm, in the 100-gun ship Queen Charlotte, Captain Robert Jackson. On some day in September (we believe the 14th) Captain Phillimore invited the commodore and all the captains of the squadron on board the Eurotas to witness a trial of her 24-pounders. The guns were tried eight times, with the full allowance of powder, and double-shotted; and they stood remarkably well. Commodore Malcolm said he should like to have Colonel Congreve's 24-pounders on the Queen Charlotte's second and third decks; and every one of the captains went away pleased with the gun. The following captains, with the exception of one or two, but which we cannot say, were present at this successful trial of the guns of the Eurotas: Captains Willoughby Thomas Lake, Robert Lambert, Thomas Elphinstone, Sir Michael Seymour, Henry Vansittart, George M'Kinley, George Tobin, George Harris, and Robert Jackson. Captain Phillimore subsequently declared that, if well manned, he could fight both sides of the Eurotas with ease; was delighted with the guns in a gale of wind; and found that, when the Eurotas was carrying a press of sail off Ushant, the guns did not work in the least, nor the ship seem to feel the smallest inconvenience from them.[1] On the 25th of November the Eurotas sent six of her 24-pounders on board the Cydnus, and received in exchange the same number of the latter's guns; but on the 5th of the ensuing February, when the two ships again met, the Eurotas received back her six 24s, and returned to the Cydnus those belonging to her. We must now show what ensued between the Eurotas and the French frigate Clorinde; whose force, it may be necessary to state, was 28 long 18-pounders, 14 carronades, 24-pounders, and two long 8-pounders, total 44 guns.

At 4 P.M. the wind shifted to the north-west and fell considerably; but the Eurotas, nevertheless, gained in the chase. At about the same time the Clorinde, then not quite four miles distant in the east-north-east, suddenly shortened sail, and endeavoured to cross the hawse of her pursuer. This only

[1] For a copy of a letter from Captain Phillimore, stating most of these particulars, see Appendix, No. 4.

hastened the junction; and at 4 h. 45 m. the Eurotas fired a shot and hoisted her colours, as did also the Clorinde. At 5 P.M., having bore up, the Eurotas passed under the stern of the Clorinde and discharged her starboard broadside. Then, luffing up under the Clorinde's quarter, the British frigate received so close and well-directed a fire, that in the course of 20 minutes, and just as she had reached the larboard bow of her antagonist, her mizenmast fell by the board over the starboard quarter; and, nearly at the same time, came down the fore-topmast of the Clorinde.

The French frigate now, shooting ahead, endeavoured to cross the bows of the Eurotas, with the intention of raking her. To evade this, and at the same time lay her antagonist on board, the Eurotas put her helm hard a-port and luffed up; but, being obstructed in her manœuvre by the wreck of the mizenmast, she could only pass close under the stern of the Clorinde, and pour in her larboard broadside. The two frigates again got side by side, and cannonaded each other with redoubled fury. At 6 h. 20 m. P.M. the Eurotas, then close on her opponent's starboard beam, had her mainmast shot away; and which, fortunately for her, fell over the starboard or unengaged quarter. Almost at the same instant the mizenmast of the Clorinde came down. At 6 h. 50 m., the two ships being nearly in the same relative position, the foremast of the Eurotas fell over the starboard bow; and in a minute or two afterwards the mainmast of the Clorinde shared the same fate. The Eurotas was now quite, and the Clorinde almost, unmanageable. At 7 h. 10 m. P.M., being then on the larboard bow of the Eurotas, the Clorinde set the remains of her foresail and her fore staysail and stood to the south-east, out of gun-shot.

Captain Phillimore, who since the early part of the action had been dangerously wounded in the shoulder by a grape-shot (the loss of blood from which, according to a published statement,[1] had caused him to faint three times on deck), now consented to go below; and the command of the Eurotas devolved upon Lieutenant Robert Smith. The boats' masts were immediately stepped on the booms, and the sails set, to endeavour, with a light westerly breeze, to keep after the enemy, still in the south-east. The wreck of the masts were also cleared away, and preparations made for getting up jury-masts; and in the meanwhile the ship laboured much, owing to her dismasted state and a heavy swell from the westward

[1] Naval Chronicle, vol. xxxi., p. 184.

By great exertions throughout the night, the Eurotas, at 5 A.M. on the 26th, got up a spare maintopmast for a jury mainmast and at 6 h. 15 m., a foretopmast for a jury foremast, and a rough spar for a mizenmast; the Clorinde still preserving the same line of bearing as on the preceding evening, but having increased her distance to nearly six miles. At 11 h. 30 m. A.M. Lieutenant Smith spoke the English merchant-schooner Dungarvon, from Lisbon bound to Port Glasgow, and requested her master to keep between the Eurotas and Clorinde, and, in the event of the Eurotas not overtaking the Clorinde before night, to show a light and fire guns. At noon the Eurotas and Clorinde were about eight miles apart; but in so different a state with respect to ability to renew the action, that while the latter had only partially cleared away the wreck of her main and mizen masts, the former had jury-courses, topsails, staysails, and spanker set, going with a northerly wind, six and a half knots through the water, and evidently gaining in the chase.

But at this moment, Captain Phillimore justly observes, "to the great mortification of every one on board" the Eurotas, two sail were descried on the lee bow. The nearest of these was the British 18-pounder 36-gun frigate Dryad, Captain Edward Galwey; the other the 16-gun brig-sloop Achates, Captain Isaac Hawkins Morrison. At 1 h. 15 m. P.M. the Clorinde hoisted French colours aft and English forward, and despatched a boat to the Dryad, who then shortened sail and hove to to receive it. The purport of Captain Denis-Lagarde's communication, as it has appeared in print, was to require terms before he would surrender. The doubt expressed by the French officers as to the ship in sight to windward being that which had reduced the Clorinde to such a state, was far from unreasonable; considering that, not only had a night intervened, but the ship now seen was masted, rigged and under sail, where the ship engaged the evening before had been left as bare as a hulk. The French lieutenant was quickly sent back to the Clorinde to get ready her "resources," and the Dryad filled and stood towards her, to give her an opportunity of trying the effect of them. At 1 h. 35 m. P.M., having placed herself on the Clorinde's quarter, the Dryad fired one shot into her; when the French frigate hauled down her colours, and was taken immediate possession of. At this time the Eurotas was between four and five miles off to windward, and the Achates about the same distance from the Clorinde to leeward.

Out of a complement on board of 329 men and boys, the

Eurotas had two midshipmen (Jeremiah Spurking and Charles Greenway), one first-class volunteer (John T. Vaughan), 13 seamen, four marines, and one boy killed, her commander (very severely), one lieutenant of marines (Henry Foord), one midshipman (John R. Brigstock), 30 seamen, and six marines wounded; total, 21 killed and 39 wounded. Out of a crew on board numbering, according to the depositions of Captain Denis-Lagarde and his two principal officers, 344 men and boys, the Clorinde had 30 officers and men killed and 40 wounded. From the great proportion of killed, it is probable that the severely wounded only are here reckoned. They may have amounted to 20 more; making the killed 30, and the wounded 60.

In the letter which Captain Galwey, with a proper feeling, permitted Captain Phillimore to write, the latter states, that the Clorinde had "a complement of 360 picked men," and that "M. Gerrard," one of the French officers, calculated their loss at 120 men. With respect to the complement, judging by the number of men usually found on board frigates of the Clorinde's class, and allowing, if necessary, that some may have been absent in prizes, we consider the sworn amount, 344, and that for which the head-money was afterwards paid, as likely to be the most correct. In regard to the alleged declaration of "M. Gerrard," unless the slightly wounded were in a very unusual proportion, the statement extracted from the Dryad's log is more to be depended upon; especially, as it specifies both killed and wounded, and accords exactly, as we shall proceed to show, with the number and distribution of the prisoners. Owing to there being three British men-of-war in company, it is natural to suppose that all the prisoners would be taken out of the French ship, with the exception of the badly wounded. Accordingly, out of the 314 assumed survivors of the French crew, the Dryad received on board 125, the Eurotas 92, and the Achates 57; leaving on board the Clorinde, by a singular coincidence, the exact number stated by the French officers as the amount of their wounded. Every one of those officers, not left in the Clorinde, appears to have been on board the Dryad; among whom we find Captain Denis-Lagarde, M. Joseph Lemaître, his first, and M. Vincent Moulac, his second lieutenant; but we do not see in the list the name of "Gerrard," nor any name resembling it. This person, therefore, was probably one of the wounded left on board the Clorinde.

Although we are by no means satisfied that the Eurotas did not mount one of General Blomefield's 24-pounders in addition to her established armament already particularized, we shall not include that gun, nor, of course, the 18-pounder launch carronade, in the following

Comparative Force of the Combatants.

		Eurotas.	Clorinde.
Broadside-guns	No.	23	22
	lbs.	601	463
Crew	No.	329	344
Size	tons	1084	1083

Had the Eurotas been armed the same as the generality of her class, this would have been a remarkably fair match; but the British ship's 24-pounders destroyed the equilibrium. Yet, with a distance which would even have suited carronades, and with the exclusive advantage of two raking fires, those 24-pounders did not do so much execution, in proportion to the time they were acting, as had been done on many other occasions by an equal number of 18s. The ship, it is true, had not been quite 10 months in commission, and had not had her guns on board many days over six months; but even the shorter of those two periods was long enough for the men to have been taught as much of practical gunnery as should have enabled them, in a close action of nearly two hours with an inferior antagonist, to have done greater execution, in reference to what they themselves suffered, than appears to have been inflicted by the Eurotas upon the Clorinde.

But, deficient as the crew of the Eurotas may have been at their guns, they were by no means so at the various other duties of their calling. The quickness with which the seamen refitted their ship was as great a proof of their spirit as it was of their skill; and, contrasted with the evidently unprepared state of the Clorinde, 18 hours after the battle, showed, in a very clear manner, the superiority of a British over a French crew. It was the capability to go ahead and manœuvre, thus given, that would again, in a short time, have brought the Eurotas alongside of the Clorinde; and it was a perfect readiness to renew the action, with, owing to the preceding day's two hours' practice at the guns, an actual increase of power, that would have made the Clorinde the prize of the Eurotas, even had the Dryad not interposed her unwelcome presence.

The arrival of the Dryad and Achates, although it certainly robbed the Eurotas of her trophy, went a very little way towards dignifying the surrender of the Clorinde; who, notwithstanding her captain's previous threat, did not fire a shot in return for the one discharged at her by the Dryad. We formerly expressed a belief, that the Achates alone would have produced the same result; but, much as was to be expected from the tried gallantry of the brig's commander, we now, looking at the number of unwounded prisoners received out of the Clorinde, and the impunity with which her principal officers escaped, think otherwise. Nor do we feel disposed to award so much credit to M. Denis-Lagarde as we formerly did; not only because of the tameness of his surrender, but because, with so many officers and men in an effective state, he ought, in the 18 hours that had elapsed, to have cleared away his wreck, and partially refitted his ship. The dismasted state of the Eurotas, and her serious loss in men, prove that the French crew knew in what way to handle their guns; and considering how long the Clorinde had been in commission, and how many months of the time at sea,[1] we must suppose that her men were competent to perform the other duties of men-of-war's men, had their officers issued the proper directions. With good management, therefore, the Clorinde might have effected her escape before the Dryad and Achates fell in with her; and, even had the prevailing westerly wind begun to blow strong, soon after the close of the action, and lasted through the night, the probability is, that the French frigate, unrefitted as she was, would still have gained a port of France.

Taking the prize in tow, the Dryad proceeded with her to Portsmouth; and the Clorinde was afterwards added to the British navy by the name of Aurora, a Clorinde (also a French frigate) being already in the service. For his gallantry in this action, and his unremitting exertions in getting the ship cleared, masted, and under sail in so short a space of time, Lieutenant Robert Smith, first of the Eurotas, was deservedly promoted to the rank of commander. A litigation afterwards took place on the subject of the head-money for the crew of the Clorinde; and it was at length decreed to the Dryad, as having been the actual captor.

With the exception of the particulars entered into respecting the guns of the Eurotas, and respecting the state of the prisoners received out of the Clorinde, the above account of the action between these frigates is essentially, and almost verbally, the same as that given in the preceding edition of this work. The accuracy of that account having been publicly impugned, we

[1] See vol. v., pp. 48, 282.

are bound, either to admit that we are misinformed on the subject, or to bring forward such proofs as will place beyond the reach of further contradiction the validity of our statements. As far as we have been able to glean them, the following are the principal, if not the only objections that were raised: 1. That the Eurotas' 24-pounders were experimental guns, and proved defective in some (but what, we cannot say) particular, when tried in the action. 2. That the crew of the Eurotas *had been* taught how to fire with precision; consequently, that the comparatively slight execution done by the Eurotas to the Clorinde did not arise from the inexpertness of her men, but from the ineffectiveness of her guns. Unfortunately, the newspapers of the day used their endeavours to circulate a much more important objection than either of these; no less than that the main-deck guns of the Eurotas were 18, and not 24 pounders. Let us hasten to do Captain Phillimore the justice to state, that he never made, although we do not remember that he contradicted, an assertion which could have been so easily refuted. A contemporary saw the paragraph, and, putting aside the newspaper, kept it until he could give the statement again to the public, with a post-captain's name as a voucher for its accuracy, in the following words: "A frigate-action, of an interesting nature, was fought in February, 1814, between the Eurotas, a British ship, of 44 guns, 18-pounders, and La Clorinde, of the same force."[1]

Taking the two serious objections in the order in which they are stated, we shall begin with the quality of the guns. As far as a trial before the action could speak for the Congreve 24-pounders, we have already shown, that Captain Phillimore himself, Commodore Malcolm, and several experienced post-captains, were "delighted with them." Now for their behaviour in the action. The moment we learnt that Captain Phillimore had a complaint to allege against the guns, for some ill quality or deficiency that discovered itself in the action between the Eurotas and Clorinde, we turned again to the official letter. Finding no complaint there, we once more looked into the ship's log; knowing that there at least a minute of the circumstance ought to have been noted down. Not a word could we discover on the subject. We then took the pains to ascertain, if any official report, complaining of the guns, had reached the navy board. Except an application, made in March, to have the breeching-bolts of the carronades, and the cat-heads of the

[1] Brenton, vol. v., p. 139.

Eurotas made different from those of any other ship in the service, and a refusal of both requests, we could find no correspondence between Captain Phillimore and the commissioners of the navy.

Pursuing our inquiries, we at last discovered that, on the 15th of March, 1814, an examination took place of the officers of the Eurotas on the very subject on which we desired information; and the following (all we have been able to procure) is a transcript of what purports to be the testimony of the second-lieutenant of the Eurotas, Richard Wilcox Graves: "That, when the said guns were tried at Sheerness against the common 24-pounder long gun, they seemed to carry the shot, both double and single, as far as the latter; that they bounded a little more than the long gun, but not dangerously so; that they can be worked with two men less than the common long gun, are easier to train, and embrace a larger range or circle; that, in the action, one bolt only was drawn on the main deck, and one seizing broken, the latter of which might have been badly made, that, upon the main deck, two shot were fired from each gun in the first three rounds, and one round and one grape during the remainder of the action; that the quantit of gunpowder was 8 lb., which was considered 2 lb. too much, no difference of range being perceived when the guns were fired with only 6 lb.; that there is only one gun on board the Eurotas, similar to those on board the Cydnus, upon Lieutenant-general Blomefield's principle, on account of there not being a complete set at Woolwich when the Eurotas was fitted out."

From the time of her action, except to land them when docked to have her damages repaired, the Eurotas retained these same guns, until Captain James Lillicrap paid the ship off on the 6th of January, 1816; when the Eurotas landed her "28 Congreve's 24-pounders" at the arsenal at Woolwich. Consequently, there could have been no well-grounded complaint against the guns, otherwise the board of admiralty would not have suffered the Eurotas again to go to sea with them on board. On the contrary, the lords of the admiralty were so pleased with the report made of the 40 cwt. Congreve 24-pounder, after a series of experiments tried at Sutton Heath, that, in the latter end of the year 1813, they ordered 300 more of the same description of gun to be cast; and, as a proof that the behaviour of the guns in the action of the Eurotas with the Clorinde, rather confirmed than lessened the previous good opinion entertained of them, the board of admiralty, on the 28th of April, 1815, ordered that all the first-rate ships in the British navy should thenceforward be established, upon their upper or third decks, with the Congreve 24-pounder.

After this full exposition of the perfect adequacy of the Eurotas' 24-pounders to perform, in a close contest especially, quite as well as any guns of the same caliber, we might answer the second objection, by simply pointing to the execution done by English 24 and 32, against French 18 and 24 pounders, and *vice versâ*, as unfolded in our detailed account of this action; but we shall not blink the question: we stated, that the ship's company of the Eurotas had not been sufficiently practised at the guns, and we are prepared to prove our assertion. We must premise that, at the time the Eurotas was commissioned and armed with 24-pounders, three American 24-pounder frigates had recently captured three English 18-pounder frigates, and that with such impunity as to indicate that the art of gunnery had been much neglected in the British navy. The degree of attention paid by a captain to the exercise of his men, which would be commendable in 1811, would scarcely deserve any praise at all in 1813. And even in the latter part of 1813, a captain of a 38-gun frigate, armed in the usual manner of her class, might allege, as some excuse for not troubling himself more than he had been accustomed to do about the expertness of his crew at the guns, that the board of admiralty had issued an order, that no British 18-pounder frigate was voluntarily to engage one of the 24-pounder frigates of America. But here was a frigate, fitted out purposely to be a match for one of those frigates; and we have not a doubt that, before he fell in with the Clorinde, Captain Phillimore expressed a strong desire to encounter the Constitution. Under these circumstances, no pains should have been spared to make the crew of the Eurotas expert cannoneers. We have seen the means that Captain Broke took to teach his men how to point their guns with effect, and we have seen in what a short space of time those guns, thus skilfully directed, tore to pieces an equal antagonist.

Knowing that it is customary to minute down in the log when the men are exercised at great guns and small arms, we naturally turn for information to the log of the Eurotas, and find that, from the 13th of August to the 25th of February, the crew were so exercised, including thrice in firing at a mark, 24 times; which is at the rate of about once in eight days, or, admitting we may have overlooked an entry or two, once a week. It is evident, however, from the statement we have already given, that when the day of trial came, the English crew failed in accomplishing as much as might have been expected of them. But, that the men wanted neither zeal nor capacity, has already appeared in the quickness with which they refitted their ship, to go again in pursuit of their enemy. Some persons have urged as an excuse for the crew of the Eurotas, that a heavy sea was raging, which prevented them from pointing their guns with precision; forgetting, that the crew of the Clorinde laboured under precisely the same inconvenience. We need not refer to many pages back to show what was performed, about a month afterwards, by a British frigate with 18-pounders, and two guns less of a side than the Eurotas, against a French frigate equal in force to the Clorinde; and the Hebrus was not put in commission until five months after the Eurotas, and was not by any means so well manned, the principal part of the latter's crew having been draughted from the Quebec, Arethusa, and Cornelia frigates.

We trust that we have now completely established the accuracy of our former statement, that the guns of the Eurotas, in her action with the Clorinde, did not perform so well as they ought; and that the fault lay, not in the guns themselves, but in the manner in which they were handled. In conclusion, we beg to observe, that, if the slight superiority in execution which the Eurotas' 24-pounders proved themselves to possess over the 18-pounders of the Clorinde, were not clearly shown to have arisen from adventitious circumstances,[1] with what face could we, as we so strenuously have done, deny to the Americans the greater part of the credit which they take to themselves, for having, with their 24-pounder frigates, so completely beaten the 18-pounder frigates of England? Why was the armament of the Eurotas changed from 18 to 24-pounders, if not to give the ship an increase of force?

On the 12th of March, at 2 P.M., latitude 43° 16′ north, longitude 10° 56′ west, the British 18-gun brig-sloop Primrose, Captain Charles George Rodney Phillott, while lying to on the larboard tack with the wind from the north-east by east, discovered, and at 2 h. 30 m. made sail after, a vessel on the lee bow, standing to the south-west. This vessel was the British brig-packet Duke of Marlborough, Captain John Bull, from Falmouth with a mail, bound to Lisbon. At 4 h. 20 m. P.M., observing that the strange brig had altered her course to avoid her, the Primrose fired a gun and hoisted her colours, a small

[1] [Sir H. Douglas says that the 24-pounders, after repeated firing, *bounded* very inconveniently.—H. Y. POWELL.]

blue ensign, at the gaff-end, and continued in chase. Shortly afterwards, when the Marlborough was about seven miles distant, the blue ensign was hauled down, and, that the stranger might see it more distinctly, a large red one hoisted in its stead. At 6 h. 50 m. P.M. the Primrose fired a shot at the strange brig, which, from her yawing about, was supposed to be a captured English merchantman; anything, in short, but a king's packet, as she had no lower studding-sails or royals set.

On first observing herself chased by the Primrose, whom she took for an American privateer, the Marlborough had hoisted the private signal, but the end-on position of the two vessels, their distance apart, and the circumstance of the flags being only half the established size, prevented the Primrose from making them out. After being up about two hours, by which time the Primrose had approached to within five miles, the private signal was hauled down, and the ensign and pendant only kept flying. As soon as it became dark the private night-signal was made, or rather was attempted to be made, for it appears that no one on board the packet, except the gunner, knew the difference between a blue light and a false fire. At 7 h. 55 m. P.M., the Marlborough opened a fire from one of her two brass 9-pounders out of the stern-ports, which was so well directed, that it cut some of the rigging about the bowsprit and foremast of the Primrose, and passed through her main course. The fire was repeated from both stern guns, and continued to be destructive to the rigging and head-sails of the Primrose; who, from the breeze freshening, was now fast approaching.

At 8 h. 15 m. P.M., ranging up on the Marlborough's larboard quarter, at the distance of about 100 yards, the Primrose shortened sail; and Captain Phillott hailed once, and his second-lieutenant, who had a loud voice, twice. The only answer returned, was the discharge of three guns, and immediately afterwards of the packet's whole broadside; whereby the master, Mr. Leech, and two men were mortally, and three slightly wounded on board the Primrose. The latter now began firing as her guns could be brought to bear; but, owing to the manœuvres of the Marlborough, the Primrose found a difficulty in firing with any effect. The Primrose then steered for the packet's quarter to run her on board, but was prevented from doing so by a boom or spare-yard that had been rigged out from her stern. The sloop's head-braces being at the same time shot away, her head-sails came aback, and she was unable for the present to close. Quickly refitting herself, the Primrose again made sail, and, closing, re-opened her fire. That of the Marlborough soon slackened; and, on Captain Phillott again hailing, the painful truth came out, that his antagonist was a British packet.

The damages received by the Marlborough, as admitted by Captain Bull and his officers, were of a very serious nature. Two 32-pound shot had passed through just below the water's edge; and the packet, in consequence, had three and a half feet water in the hold, and by its rapid increase, was reduced to nearly a sinking state. Her masts also were much injured, and her standing and running-rigging nearly all shot away. Her loss, on this unfortunate occasion, amounted to Adjutant Andrews of the 60th regiment, and another passenger, killed, and the master and nine or ten men wounded. Except a shot through her mainmast, the principal damage sustained by the Primrose has already been related: her loss amounted to one seaman killed, her master (Andrew Leech, dangerously), one master's mate (Peter Belcher severely), and 12 seamen and marines wounded. At the request of Captain Bull, the carpenter of the Primrose and one of his mates were sent on board the Marlborough, to assist in stopping her leaks.

The facts above detailed differ materially from those we inserted in the first edition of this work; but we shall be exonerated from blame when we mention, that our first statement was grounded upon an apparently authentic account, already before the English public; and which account, owing probably to the absence of the Primrose on a foreign station, was not contradicted. The minutes of a court of inquiry, held upon Captain Phillott, on the subject of this unfortunate rencounter, have since been put into our hands; and it is thus that we have been enabled to give the only correct account of the transaction which has appeared in print.

On the 2nd of February, at 8 P.M., latitude at noon that day 36° 41' north, longitude 22° 11' west, the British 56-gun ship Majestic,[1] Captain John Hayes, steering east-half-north with the wind a moderate breeze from the south-south-east, on the lookout for the American frigate Constitution, which had sailed from Boston bay on the 1st of January, discovered on her weatherbow a ship, evidently a cruiser, standing towards her. In about 20 minutes the stranger, which, as afterwards ascertained, was the American privateer Wasp, of Philadelphia, mounting 20 guns, found her mistake; and wearing, stood to the north-east under all the canvas she could set. The Majestic made sail in chase,

[1] See vol. v., p. 427. But the Majestic mounted only one 12-pounder chase-gun.

and continued the pursuit until daylight on the 3rd; when, having got within four miles of the Wasp, she descried, about three leagues off in the south-south-east, three ships and one brig, of a very suspicious appearance, the ships especially. At 7 A.M. the Majestic made the private signal, and, receiving no answer, shortened sail to reconnoitre the strangers. These were not, as conjectured, an American squadron, but the two French 40-gun frigates Atalante and Terpsichore, from Lorient on the 8th of January, and their prizes, a large richly-laden Spanish ship, captured the day previous, named the San-Juan-de-Baptista, carrying 20 guns and 50 men, and an unarmed merchant-brig. At 7 h. 30 m. the four vessels stood towards the Majestic. Having again made the private signal without effect, Captain Hayes, at 8 h. 30 m. A.M., gave up the chase of the Wasp, and hauled to the wind on the larboard tack, with a light breeze from the north-north-east, more distinctly to make out the character of the strangers in the south.

At 9 A.M. the Majestic tacked to the westward. At 9 h. 15 m., just as she had got upon the beam of the weathermost ship, which was the Terpischore, the latter made to her consort the signal for an enemy. Captain Hayes being determined to force these ships, now clearly seen to be large frigates, to show their colours, the Majestic, at 10 A.M., tacked, hoisted her colours, and bore up for the Terpsichore. In five minutes the latter shortened sail, for the Atalante, who was some distance astern, to close; and on the Majestic's evincing an increased eagerness to get alongside of her, the Terpsichore wore and stood towards her tardy companion, with the signal flying, "The enemy is inferior to us." The French commodore answered this with, "Make more sail." Thinking his signal had been misunderstood, Captain Breton repeated it, but merely obtained a repetition of the answer to his first signal.

As soon as the Terpsichore had joined the Atalante, which was at about 11 h. 30 m. A.M., the two frigates, formed in line ahead, with the Lima ship and merchant-brig on the weather-bow, seemed resolved to withstand an attack. But the Majestic, by her bold approach, extinguished the last remnant of resolution in the poor commodore; and at 11 h. 45 m., the Atalante crowded sail nearly before the wind to the south-south-east. In a minute or two the Terpsichore, hoisting French colours, followed her consort. Both French ships carried their larboard studding-sails; and the Atalante, ludicrously enough, still kept the signal flying, "Make more sail." The armed ship and merchant-brig, meanwhile, had hauled up to the eastward, also under a press of canvas.

Towards noon the wind freshened, and the Majestic gained upon the Terpsichore. At 2 h. 15 m. P.M. the latter opened a fire from her stern chase-guns. At 3 P.M., being in a good position, going at the rate of 10 knots an hour, the Majestic commenced firing her bow-guns with considerable effect, almost every shot striking. After a running fight, which lasted until 4 h. 49 m. P.M., the Terpsichore fired a few of her aftermost guns at the Majestic, who was then within musket-shot distance, and struck her colours, but did not shorten sail. The Majestic, in consequence, fired another shot or two; when, at 4 h. 56 m., the French frigate let all fly and brought to. The wind increasing and the prize being in a state of confusion, Captain Hayes felt himself obliged to stay by her, and to suffer the other frigate, with the ship and brig, to escape. The sea, indeed, got up so very fast, that out of 317 prisoners, 100 only could be removed; and, in effecting that, the jolly-boat was stove and two of the prisoners drowned. The previous loss on board the Terpsichore, out of a crew of 320 men and boys, amounted to three men killed and six wounded. The Majestic did not lose a man.

We much regret our inability to give the name of the senior officer of these two French frigates, the captain of the Atalante. We should like to hold up to contempt the officer who could tamely suffer his consort to be cannonaded by an enemy's ship for one hour and three-quarters, when in a very few minutes he might have placed himself within a few yards of the attacking force. Not a single shot did he bestow, even in defence of a prize that, besides her valuable cargo, had on board 600,000 dollars in specie.[1] Captain François-Désiré Breton deserved a braver commodore; for no one surely will say, the two French 40-gun frigates (without reckoning the 20-gun ship) ought not

---

[1] The captain of the Atalante's name was Mallet; he was chased into Concarneau bay, on the 25th of March, 1814, by the Menelaus, Captain Sir Peter Parker. On the 26th, Lieutenant Seagrove and midshipman Frederic Chamier were sent in with a flag of truce, conveying a challenge to Monsieur Mallet, inviting him to weigh, and not to allow a frigate of equal force to keep him skulking behind the rocks and batteries of Concarneau; but, as has been shown before, the French captain was not very eager for any combat. He returned the following answer:—

" Monsieur,—La frégate l'Atalante, que je commande ne peut sortir d'un Port Français que par un ordre de mes chefs; je le réclamerai, mais je ne peux pas assurer que je l'obtiendrai.

" J'ai l'honneur, &c.,

"MALLET,

" Capitaine de frégate,
" Chevalier en la Légion d'Honneur

" à Monsieur,
Le Baronet Peter Parker."

to have attacked the Majestic. Admitting that the nature of her metal would have justified a retreat, Monsieur whoever he was should at least have waited till he had ascertained whether that metal was light or heavy.

The conduct of the Majestic, in unhesitatingly bearing down to the attack, even when the want of colours and the haze of the weather rendered it doubtful whether two of the four strangers were not American frigates, places the gallantry of Captain Hayes in a conspicuous light. Even had they been the Constitution and Essex, as Captain Hayes, before the Terpsichore showed her colours (one frigate, from her style of painting, appearing much larger than the other), conjectured they were, so excellent a crew had the Majestic, and so well skilled were they in fighting the powerful guns which this fine ship mounted, that the result would scarcely have been doubtful: at all events, the captain and his officers would have considered such a meeting as the most fortunate epoch of their professional lives.

On the 14th of February, off Lorient, the prize to these French frigates the San-Juan, was recaptured by the British 38-gun frigate Menelaus, Captain Sir Peter Parker, the Rippon 74, Captain Sir Christopher Cole, in sight. On the same, or the preceding day, the Atalante succeeded in entering the port, towards which the Lima ship was steering when fallen in with, Lorient.

On the 5th of December, 1813, the American frigate President, Commodore Rodgers, sailed from Providence, Rhode Island, upon her third cruise; but not unseen, for the British frigate Orpheus, Captain Hugh Pigot, obtained a distant view of her, and hastened with the information to her consort, the 74-gun ship Albion, Captain John Ferris Devonshire. On the 25th, in latitude 19° north, longitude 35° west, the President fell in with, chased, and on making them out to be frigates, and concluding them to be British, ran from, the two French 40-gun frigates Nymphe and Méduse, from Brest upon a cruise since the latter end of November. Had these ships really been British, the President would have had a narrow escape, the headmost frigate having thrown several shot over her. By altering her course in the night, the American frigate at last got clear, and, steering to the south-west, cruised to windward of Barbadoes until the 16th of January. The commodore then ran off Cayenne; thence off Surinam, Berbice, and Demerara, and between the islands of Tobago and Grenada; thence across the Caribbean sea, along the south-east side of Porto-Rico, through the Mona Passage, and down the north side of Jamaica.

Striking soundings off St. Augustine, the President, on the 11th of February, passed Charlestown; and, on arriving off the Delaware, fell in with, in a fog, "a large vessel, apparently a man-of-war." This ship "disappearing," the President stood on to the northward. "From the Delaware," says the commodore, in his letter to the secretary of the American navy, "I saw nothing, until I made Sandy Hook, when I again fell in with another of the enemy's squadrons; and, by some unaccountable cause, was permitted to enter the bay, although in the presence of a decidedly superior force, after having been obliged to remain outside seven hours and a half, waiting for the tide."

The "decidedly superior force" is thus explained in a letter from one of the President's officers: "After passing the light, saw several sail, one large sail to windward; backed our maintopsail, and cleared ship for action. The strange sail came down within gun-shot, and hauled her wind on the starboard tack. We continued with our maintopsail to the mast three hours, and, seeing no probability of the 74-gun ship's bearing down to engage the President, gave her a shot to windward, and hoisted our colours; when she bore up for us, reluctantly. When within half gun-shot, backed her maintopsail. At this moment all hands were called to muster aft, and the commodore said a few, but impressive words, though it was unnecessary; for, what other stimulant could true Americans want, than fighting gloriously in the sight of their native shore, where hundreds were assembled to witness the engagement? Wore ship to engage; but, at this moment, the cutter being discovered coming back, backed again to take in the pilot, the British 74 (strange as it must appear) making sail to the southward and eastward. Orders were given to haul aboard the main and fore tacks, to run in; there being then in sight from our deck a frigate and gun-brig. The commander of the 74 had it in his power, for five hours, to bring us at any moment to an engagement, our maintopsail to the mast during that time."[1]

"It was," adds the American writer who was so fortunate as to be favoured with a copy of this genuine American epistle, "afterwards ascertained, that the ship, which declined the battle with the President, was the Plantagenet 74, Captain

[1] Naval Monumnet, &c., p. 235.

Lloyd. The reason given by Captain Lloyd for avoiding an engagement was, that his crew were in a state of mutiny." Another American historian says: "Captain Lloyd, after returning to England, accounted for his conduct by alleging a mutiny in his ship, and had several of his sailors tried and executed on that charge."[1] We are here forcibly reminded of the old Munchausen story, where one man declares that he drove a nail through the moon, and his companion, determined both to back and to outdo him, swears he clenched it.

To Captain Lloyd's regret, even had the Constitution been in company with the President, the Plantagenet (whose crew was one of the finest and best disposed in the service), at noon on the 18th of February, the day on which this "strange" event happened, was in latitude 25° 27' north, longitude 43° 45' west, steering east-south-east, or towards Carlisle bay, Barbadoes. No: it was the British 38-gun frigate Loire, Captain Thomas Brown, that lay off the Hook. At 9 h. 40 m. A.M. the Loire first descried the President in the north-north-west, and, with the wind from the west-south-west, made all sail in chase; but at 10 h. 30 m., making out the President to be what she was, the Loire shortened sail and hauled to the wind. The fact is, that out of her complement of 352 men and boys, the Loire had 75 of her best men, including of course several officers and petty-officers absent in prizes; and, of the remaining 277, nearly 20 were boys, and about 40 too sick to attend their quarters: consequently, the effective crew of the Loire did not exceed 220 men. Had the Loire been fully manned, we may readily infer what course Captain Brown would have pursued; and, as his complement was ample, and he had been particular in exercising his men at the guns, if the President, contrary to what her movements indicated, had waited to engage, Commodore Rodgers, in all probability, would have found the conquest of a British 18-pounder frigate, by an American 44, not so easy a task as he had been led to expect.

We formerly noticed the sailing, on the 27th of October, 1812, of the United States 32-gun frigate Essex, Captain David Porter, from Delaware bay, on a cruise in the Pacific, conjointly with the Constitution and Hornet.[2] Not finding either of these ships at the appointed rendezvous, Captain Porter resolved to proceed alone round Cape Horn; and on the 14th of March, 1813, having previously captured the British packet Nocton, and taken out of her 11,000*l*. sterling in specie, the Essex

[1] Sketches of the War, &c., p. 240. [2] See vol. v. p. 408.

arrived at Valparaiso, on the coast of Chili. Captain Porter here refitted and provisioned his frigate, and then cruised along the coast of Chili and Peru, and among the Gallapagos islands, until October; by which time he had captured 12 British whale-ships.

Having taken several American seamen out of a Peruvian corsair, and decoyed several British seamen out of his prizes, Captain Porter armed and manned two of the whale-ships as cruisers. One of them, late the Atlantic, but newly named the Essex Junior, was armed with 20 guns (10 long 6-pounders and ten 18-pounder carronades), and manned with a crew, officers included, of 95 men; and Lieutenant John Downes, who had the command of her, taking under his charge the Hector, Catherine, and Montezuma, proceeded with them to Valparaiso. On the return of the Essex Junior from this service, the Essex, with the remaining three prizes (three having been sent to America, and two given up to the prisoners), steered for the island of Nooaheevah, one of the Marquesas. Here Captain Porter completely repaired the Essex; and, sailing thence on the 12th of December, in company with the Essex Junior, returned, on or about the 12th of January, 1814, to Valparaiso.

On the 8th of February, at 7 A.M., the British 18-pounder 36-gun frigate Phœbe, Captain James Hillyar, accompanied by the 18-gun ship-sloop Cherub, Captain Thomas Tudor Tucker, when standing in towards the harbour of Valparaiso, in quest of the Essex and the three ships which Captain Porter was represented to have armed, discovered the Essex Junior off the port, and, shortly afterwards, the Essex herself and two of her three prizes, the Montezuma and Hector, at anchor within it. At 11 h. 15 m. A.M. Captain Hillyar spoke the Essex; and at 11 h. 30 m. the Phœbe and Cherub anchored at no great distance from her. The established force of the Phœbe was precisely what we supposed it to be in May, 1811;[1] but, profiting by the example of the Americans, Captain Hillyar had since mounted one swivel in the fore, two in the main, and one in the mizentop of the Phœbe, and had also fitted her 18-pounder boat-carronade, and another carronade, a 12-pounder, as broadside guns. The force of the Cherub was 18 carronades, 32-pounders, on the main deck, and on the quarter-deck and forecastle six carronades, 18-pounders, and two sixes. The 46 guns of the Essex have already been described.[2]

On the 9th, at 9 A.M., Captain Porter began his attempts

See vol. v., p. 290. [2] Ibid., p. 362.

upon the loyalty of the Phœbe's seamen, by hoisting at his fore topgallantmast-head a white flag with the motto, "FREE TRADE AND SAILORS' RIGHTS." This, in a little while, the Phœbe answered, with the St. George's ensign, and the motto, "GOD AND COUNTRY, BRITISH SAILORS' BEST RIGHTS: TRAITORS OFFEND BOTH." On this the crew of the Essex manned her rigging and gave three cheers, which the Phœbe's crew presently returned. On the 12th, Captain Porter's motto mania returned, and the Essex hoisted a flag inscribed with the words, "GOD, OUR COUNTRY, AND LIBERTY: TYRANTS OFFEND THEM."

On the 15th, at 7 A.M., the Essex Junior was towed out of the harbour. At 8 A.M. the Phœbe and Cherub weighed and stood after her; and at noon, finding she could not escape, the Essex Junior returned to the anchorage, passing ahead of the Phœbe within pistol-shot. On the 23rd, when the two British ships were cruising in the bay, the Essex weighed and stood out, but in about an hour resumed her station in the harbour. On the 25th, Captain Porter had his prize, the Hector, towed out to sea and set fire to. On the 27th, at about 6 h. 45 m. P.M., when the Phœbe was about four miles west-north-west of the anchorage, and the Cherub about six miles north by west of her, the Essex and Essex Junior got under way with a light breeze from the westward, and stood out towards the British frigate. On seeing them approach, the Phœbe backed her maintopsail and hoisted her colours. At this moment, by a mere accident as it appears, a gun went off from the Phœbe's windward side. This was at once interpreted by Captain Porter into a challenge. At 7 h. 20 m. P.M., as the Phœbe was in the act of wearing to bring her starboard guns to bear, the Essex and Essex Junior hauled to the wind on the starboard tack, and the former fired one gun to windward. Soon after this little flourish, Captain Porter and his lieutenant stood for the anchorage, followed by Captain Hillyar under all sail.

Beyond a second attempt of the Essex Junior to escape, made and frustrated on the 3rd of March, nothing further of consequence happened until the 28th of the month, when the Essex put in practice a well-concerted plan for freeing herself from the further annoyance of her watchful enemy. It was the intention of Captain Porter, as he himself states, to allow the Phœbe and Cherub to chase the Essex out of the bay, in order to afford to the Essex Junior the opportunity of getting to sea; and, if the plan succeeded, the two American ships were to effect their junction at the Marquesas. The wind being, as it usually is, to the southward, any scheme that would draw the two British ships to the north-east or the lee side of the bay, could not fail to favour the escape of the two American ships. Accordingly, from about midnight to past 1 A.M. on the 28th, a quantity of blue-lights and rockets were burnt and thrown up in the north-east and in the north. The Phœbe and Cherub, as may be supposed, chased in those directions; but, finding no answer returned to the lights they each hoisted, the two captains suspected who were the makers of the signals, and again hauled to the wind. Daylight found the Essex and Essex Junior at their moorings, and the two British ships rather too close to the port to justify the American ships in attempting their escape.

A fresh south-south-east wind now blew, and so increased towards 3 P.M., that the Essex parted her larboard cable, and dragged her starboard anchor out to sea. Sail was presently set upon the ship; and seeing a prospect of passing to windward of his two opponents, Captain Porter began to chuckle at his good fortune in having been blown out of the harbour. Just, however, as the Essex was rounding the point at the west end of the bay, the accomplishment of which would have set Captain Porter free, a heavy squall struck the ship and carried away her maintopmast. The Essex now bore up, followed by both British ships, and at 3 h. 40 m. anchored within half a mile of the shore, in a small bay about a mile to the eastward of Point Caleta. The Essex then hoisted one motto-flag at the fore, and another at the mizen topgallantmast-head, and one American ensign at the mizen peak, and lashed a second in the main rigging. Not to be outdone in decorations, the two British ships hoisted their motto-flags, with a handsome display of ensigns and union-jacks.

At 4 P.M., when the Phœbe was standing towards the starboard-quarter of the Essex, at about a mile distant, a squall from the land caused the ship to break off, and prevented her from passing, as had been Captain Hillyar's intention, close under the American frigate's stern. At 4 h. 10 m., having fetched as near as the wind would permit, the Phœbe commenced firing her starboard guns, but with very little effect, owing to the great distance. In five minutes more the Cherub, who lay on the Phœbe's starboard-quarter, opened her fire; the Essex returning the fire of both ships with three long 12-pounders run out of her stern-ports. At 4 h. 30 m. P.M. the two British ships, being very near the shore, ceased firing, and wore round on the larboard tack. While the Phœbe was wearing, a shot from the Essex passed through several folds of her mainsail, as it hung in the clew-garnets, and prevented it from being reset in the strong wind which was then blowing. Her jib-boom was also badly wounded, and her fore, main, and mizen stays shot away. Having, besides increasing her distance by wearing, lost the use of her jib, mainsail, and mainstay, the Phœbe was now at too great a distance to fire more than one or two random shot. At 4 h. 40 m. the Phœbe tacked towards the Essex; and Captain Hillyar soon afterwards informed Captain Tucker, by hailing, that it was his intention to anchor, but that the Cherub must keep under way.

On closing the Essex at 5 h. 35 m., the Phœbe recommenced a fire from her bow-guns, which was returned by the former, the weather at this time nearly calm. In about 20 minutes the Essex hoisted her flying-jib, cut her cable, and, under her foresail and foretopsail, endeavoured to run on shore. This exposed her to a tolerably warm carronade from the Phœbe; but the Cherub, owing to the baffling winds, was not able to get near. Just as the Essex had approached the shore within musket-shot, the wind shifted from the land, and paid her head down upon the Phœbe. That not being a course very desirable to Captain Porter, the Essex let go an anchor, and came to within about three-quarters of a mile of the shore.

The object now was to get the specie and other valuables in the ship removed on shore; and, as the boats of the Essex had been nearly all destroyed, it was considered fortunate that Lieutenant Downes was present with the three boats from the Essex Junior. A portion of the British subjects belonging to the crew took this opportunity of effecting their escape; and others, alarmed by Captain Porter's report that "flames were bursting up each hatchway," flames of which not a trace could afterwards be discovered, leaped overboard to endeavour to reach the shore. In the midst of all this confusion, at about 6 h. 20 m. P.M., the Essex hauled down her numerous flags, and was taken possession of just in time to save the lives of 16 of her men who were struggling in the waves: 31 appear to have perished, and between 30 and 40 to have reached the shore.

The damages of the Phœbe were trifling. She had received seven 32-pound shot between wind and water, and one 12-pound shot about three feet under water. Her main and mizen masts, and her sails and rigging, were rather seriously injured. Out of her crew of 278 men, and 22 boys, total 300, the Phœbe had her first-lieutenant (William Ingram) and three seamen killed, four seamen and marines severely, and three slightly wounded. The Cherub's larboard foretopsail-sheet was shot away, and replaced in five minutes: several of her lower shrouds were cut through, also the maintopmast-stay, and most of the running rigging; and three or four shot struck her hull. One marine killed, her commander severely, and two marines slightly wounded, was all the loss which that ship sustained; making the total loss on the British side five killed and 10 wounded. When the Essex was boarded by the British officers, buckets of spirits were found in all parts of the main deck, and most of the prisoners were in a state of intoxication. This decided proof that "American sailors want no grog" accounts for the Phœbe and Cherub having sustained their principal injury during the first three broadsides. Afterwards, the firing of the Essex became very irregular; and nearly all her shot went over the British ships.

The damages of the Essex were confined to her upper works, masts, and rigging. "The battered state of the Essex," says Captain Porter, "will, I believe, prevent her ever reaching England." There is strong reason to believe that the greater part of the Essex Junior's crew came on board the Essex, and returned when the colours were about to be struck; but we shall consider the American frigate to have commenced action with only 260 men, and five lads or boys. Out of this number, the Essex, as far as is borne out by proof (the only safe way where an American is concerned), had 24 men killed, including one lieutenant, and 45 wounded, including two acting-lieutenants and the master. But Captain Porter, thinking by exaggerating his loss both to prop up his fame and account for the absentees of his crew at the surrender, talks of 58 killed and mortally wounded, 39 wounded severely, and 27 slightly. How then did it happen that 23 dead (Lieutenant Wilmer had been previously knocked overboard and drowned) were all that were found on board the Essex, or that were reported as killed to the British? As only 42 wounded were found in the Essex, and only three were acknowledged to have been taken away by Lieutenant Downes, what became of the remaining 21? The loss, too, as we have given it, is quite as much as from the damages of the Essex one might suppose that she had sustained. But it is Captain Porter, the author of the "Journal of a Cruise into the Pacific, &c.," who has made these extraordinary statements; therefore, no more need be said about them.

For having done what was done, no merit is claimed by the two British captains. They had heard so much of American prowess, that they expected little short of being blown out of the water; and yet, after the Essex had struck, the Phœbe, without the assistance of the Cherub, was ready to tackle with another American frigate of the same force. On the 31st of May the Phœbe and Essex, the latter commanded by Lieutenant Charles Pearson, set sail for England; and on the 13th of November, having stopped some time at Rio Janeiro, the two ships anchored in Plymouth sound. Lieutenant Pearson was immediately promoted to the rank of commander.

Let us now endeavour to trace what became of the 12 whale-ships captured by the Essex. On the 25th of July, 1813, Captain Porter despatched home the Georgiana armed with 16 guns, manned with a lieutenant and about 40 men, and laden with a full cargo of spermaceti oil, which would be worth, in the United States, about 100,000 dollars. She was captured in the West Indies, by the 18-pounder 36-gun frigate Barrossa. The Policy, laden also with a full cargo of oil, was retaken by the Loire frigate; and the New Zealander, having on board "All the oil of the other prizes," by the Belvidera. The Rose and Charlton were given up to the prisoners. The Montezuma, it is believed, was sold at Valparaiso. The Hector and Catherine, with their cargoes, were burnt at sea. The Atlantic, afterwards called the Essex Junior, was disarmed by the orders of Captain Hillyar, and sent to America as a cartel. The Sir Andrew Hammond was retaken by the Cherub; the Greenwich, burnt by the orders of the American officer in charge of her; and the Seringapatam, taken possession of by her American crew. The mutineers carried her to New South Wales; whence she was brought to England, and delivered up to her owners, on payment of salvage. Thus have we the end of all the "prizes taken by the Essex in the Pacific, valued at 250,000 dollars;" and, as another item on the debit side of Captain Porter's account, the Essex herself became transferred to the British navy.

At the risk of being charged with impiety, we must express a wish that, instead of announcing his success in the words: "It pleased the Almighty Disposer of events to bless the efforts of my gallant companions, and my personal, very humble ones, with victory," Captain Hillyar had stated, in a plain manner, the surrender of the Essex, and left the public to judge by what means, others than the well-directed 18-pounders of the Phœbe, the comparatively unimportant event had been brought about. It was only a few months before, that an American commander announced his success over a Lilliputian British fleet on Lake Erie, in the following words: "It has pleased the Almighty to give to the arms of the United States a signal victory over their enemies on this lake." We remember, also, when looking over the log-books of British ships, and some hundreds have passed under our inspection, once coming to the words, "Mustered the crew and read prayers for the victory." And what was the "victory?" Why, the success of three ships over one, and that not until after the sacrifice of nearly 100 lives. In our view of the matter, appeals to the Deity on such occasions of blood and carnage are, to say the least of them, quite at variance with the spirit of true religion.

The best part of Captain Hillyar's public letter is, we think, the following passage: "The defence of the Essex, taking into consideration our superiority of force, the very discouraging circumstance of her having lost her maintopmast, and being twice on fire, did honour to her brave defenders, and most fully evinced the courage of Captain Porter, and those under his command. Her colours were not struck until the loss in killed and wounded was so awfully great, and her shattered condition so seriously bad, as to render further resistance unavailing." Captain Hillyar penned this encomium two days after the action, and nothing could better evince the goodness of his heart; but he soon found that he had praised the unworthy. As one proof among many that could be adduced, Captain Porter, in a letter dated in July, accuses Captain Hillyar of acting towards him with "perfidy." Yet the conduct of this same slanderer of a gallant British officer, of this same Captain David Porter, of whom few in his own country will venture to speak well, is declared by our contemporary to have been "perfectly honourable."[1]

Early in the month of February the first launched of the American "18-gun" ship-sloops, of which we formerly gave some account,"[2] the Frolic, commanded by master-commandant Joseph Bainbridge, sailed from Portsmouth, New Hampshire. On the 20th of April, at daylight, latitude 24° 12' north, longitude 81° 25' west, the Frolic fell in with the British 18-pounder 36-gun frigate Orpheus, Captain Hugh Pigot, and 12-gun schooner Shelburne, Lieutenant David Hope. When the chase commenced, both British ships were to leeward; but, in an

[1] Bj :nton, vol. v., p. 161.   [2] See vol. v., p. 433.

hour or two, the schooner weathered the American ship. At a few minutes past noon the Orpheus, then on the Frolic's lee-quarter, standing upon the opposite tack, fired two shot, both of which fell short. However, they produced as good an effect as if they had struck the American ship between wind and water; and, in about half an hour, just as the Shelburne was closing her, down went the "star-spangled banner" and its stripes from the Frolic's mizen-peak. As soon as the Orpheus, who was but an indifferent sailer, could get near enough to take possession of her, this fine American sloop-of-war was found with 171 officers and men, all "high-minded Americans," on board.

According to the report of the British officers, this gentle surrender was attended with a circumstance in other respects disgraceful to the Frolic's officers and crew. The locks of the great guns were broken, and the muskets, pistols, pikes, swords, bar and chain shot, &c., were thrown overboard, together with the pendant that was struck! A Nassau paper of the 25th of April adds: "The purser's store-room was next sacked; then the men got into the gun-room and the captain's cabin, and pillaged them. In short, the ship, we are told, bore the semblance of a town given up to the pillage of soldiery." Perhaps these gentlemen were determined that as their ship had not behaved like a man-of-war, they would destroy all appearance of her having been one.

We should not have hesitated to call a French, or even a British captain, who had acted as master-commandant Joseph Bainbridge of the United States navy did in this instance act, a ———; but we will not again soil our pages with a name that, in the few instances in which it occurs, has not, we trust, been wrongfully applied. The court of inquiry which sat upon the Frolic's loss "honourably acquitted" the officers and crew. One excuse was, that the lee guns of the American ship had been thrown overboard. So they were, but not until long after the Orpheus had begun chasing her. Captain Bainbridge might as well have urged that he had no locks, pistols, &c., because he and his crew had destroyed and thrown them overboard just before possession was taken.

The master-commandant, who performed this exploit, is the brother of the commodore, who did so much for the national glory by capturing the Java; and, from his great interest (a sway that even republics can feel), the former is now a captain. Let, then, Captain Joseph Bainbridge, if the subject be not a sickening one to him, turn over these pages, and count how many instances he can find of conduct like his own. Enough of such a character: suffice it, that the British became possessed, at an easy rate, of a finer 22-gun ship than any they had previously owned; a vessel with excellent quarters, and of extraordinary large scantling. The Frolic, or Florida, as she was newly named, came into British possession very opportunely for elucidating the merits of the three actions which we have next to record.

On the 23rd of February the British 18-gun brig-sloop Epervier, Captain Richard Walter Wales (sixteen 32, and two 18-pounder[1] carronades), cruising off Cape Sable, captured, without opposition, the American privateer-brig Alfred, of Salem, mounting 16 long 9-pounders, and manned with 108 men; the British 38-gun frigate Junon, Captain Clotworthy Upton, in sight about 10 miles to leeward. On his way to Halifax with his prize, Captain Wales discovered that a part of his crew had conspired with the late crew of the Alfred, to rise upon the British officers, and carry one vessel, if not both, into a port of the United States. As the readiest mode to frustrate the plan, Captain Wales persevered against a gale of wind, and on the 25th arrived at Halifax. He immediately represented to the commanding officer of the port, the insufficiency of the Epervier's crew for any service; and, in particular, expressed his doubts about their loyalty, from the plot in which they had recently been engaged. However, the affair was treated lightly; and on the 3rd of March the Epervier, without a man of her crew being changed, sailed, in company with the Shelburne schooner, for the "protection" of a small convoy bound to Bermuda and the West Indies.

Having reached her outward destination in safety, the Epervier, on the 14th of April, sailed from Port Royal, Jamaica, on her return to Halifax; and, as if the reputation of her officers and of the flag she bore was not enough for such a crew as the Epervier's to be intrusted with, the brig took on board at Havana, where she afterwards called, 118,000 dollars in specie. On the 25th of April the Epervier sailed from Havana, in company with one of the vessels, an hermaphrodite brig bound to Bermuda, which she had convoyed from Port Royal. On the 29th, at about 7 h. 30 m. A.M., latitude 27° 47' north, longitude 80° 7' west, a ship under Russian colours, from Havana bound to

---

[1] These Captain Wales had taken on board at Halifax, in lieu of the two long sixes and launch-carronade.

Boston, joined the Epervier, then steering north by east, with the wind about east-south-east. Shortly afterwards a large ship was discovered in the south-west, apparently in chase of the convoy. At 9 A.M. the Epervier hauled to the wind on the larboard tack, so as to keep between her convoy and the stranger; whom we may at once introduce as the United States ship-sloop Peacock, of 20 carronades, 32-pounders, and two long 18s, Captain Lewis Warrington, from New York since the 12th of March.

No answer being returned to the brig's signals, the English ensign and pendant flying on board the Peacock did not remove the suspicions of her being an enemy; and accordingly the Epervier made the signal to that effect to her convoy. At 9 h. 40 m. A.M. the Peacock, who had approached rapidly on account of the wind having veered to the southward, hauled down the English colours, and hoisted the American flag at almost every mast and stay. At 10 A.M., when within half gun-shot of the Epervier, the Peacock edged away, as if to bring her broadside to bear in a raking position. This the brig evaded by putting her helm up, until close on the Peacock's bow, when she rounded to and fired her starboard guns. With this their first discharge, the three aftermost carronades became unshipped by the fighting-bolts giving way. The guns, however, were soon replaced; and having, when she got abaft the beam of her opponent, tacked and shortened sail, the Epervier received the broadside of the Peacock, as the latter kept away with the wind on the larboard beam. Although the first fire of the American ship produced no material effect, a continued discharge of star and bar shot cut away the rigging and sails of the brig, and completely dismantled her. Just as the Epervier, by a well-directed fire, had brought down her opponent's foreyard, several of the carronades on the larboard side behaved as those on the starboard side had done, and continued to upset, as often as they were replaced and discharged.

In the midst of this confusion, the main boom, having been shot away, fell upon the wheel, and the Epervier, having had her head-sails all cut to pieces, became thrown into a position to be raked; but, fortunately for the brig, the Peacock had too much head-way, to rake her with more than two or three shot. Having by this time shot away the brig's maintopmast, and rendered her completely unmanageable, the Peacock directed the whole of her fire at her opponent's hull, and presently reduced the Epervier's three waist guns to the disabled state of the others. At 11 A.M., as if the defects in the fighting-bolts were not a sufficient disaster, the breeching-bolts began to draw. There being no immediate remedy here, an effort was made to get the brig round, in order to present a fresh broadside to the enemy; but it was found impracticable, without falling on board the Peacock.

As a last resource, and one which British seamen are generally prompt to execute, Captain Wales called the crew aft, to follow him in boarding; but these gentlemen declined a measure so fraught with danger. The Epervier having now one gun only wherewith to return the fire of the 11 guns of her antagonist; being already with four feet and a half water in her hold, and her crew falling fast beneath the heavy and unremitting fire of the Peacock, no alternative remained but to strike the colours, to save the lives of the few remaining good men in the vessel. This was done at 11 h. 5 m. A.M., after the firing had lasted an hour; during three-quarters of which the vessels lay close together, and during more than half of which, owing to the defects in the brig's armament, the successful party had it all to himself.

Besides the damages already detailed, the Epervier had her fore-rigging and stays shot away, her bowsprit badly wounded, and her foremast cut nearly in two and left tottering, and which nothing but the smoothness of the water saved from falling. Her hull, as may be imagined, was pierced with shot-holes on the engaged or larboard side, both above and below water. The brig's loss, out of a crew of 101 men and a passenger, and 16 boys, amounted to eight killed and mortally wounded, and 15 wounded severely and slightly, including among the former her very gallant first-lieutenant, John Hackett; who, about the middle of the action, had his left arm shattered, and received a severe splinter-wound in the hip, but who yet would hardly suffer himself to be carried below. Captain Warrington states, we believe with truth, that the Peacock's principal injury was the wound in her foreyard. Not a shot, by his account, struck the ship's hull; and her loss, in consequence, out of a crew of 185 picked seamen, without a boy among them, amounted to only two men wounded, neither of them dangerously.

A statement of comparative force would, in this case, be next to a nullity; as how could we, with any show of reason, confront eight carronades that overset the moment they were fired with 10 carronades that remained firm in their places to the last. For any damage that such a vessel as the Epervier could have done to her, the Peacock might almost as well have fought with the unarmed Russian ship that had just quitted the former's company, and then have boasted, as Captain Warrington did, how many shot the Peacock placed in her antagonist's hull, and how free from any she escaped in her own.

At the time she engaged the Peacock, the Epervier had but three men in a watch, exclusively of petty officers, able to take helm or lead; and two of her men were each 70 years of age! She had some blacks, several other foreigners, lots of disaffected, and few even of ordinary stature: in short, the crew of the Epervier was a disgrace to the deck of a British man-of-war. Had, instead of this, the Epervier been manned with a crew of choice seamen, equal in personal appearance to those received out of the Chesapeake and Argus, after they had been respectively carried by boarding, we might have some faith in Captain Porter's assertion, that British seamen were not so brave as they had been represented. But, shall we take the Epervier's crew as a sample of British seamen? As well might we judge of the moral character of a nation by the inmates of her jails, or take the first deformed object we meet, as the standard of the size and shape of her people.

We must be allowed to say that, had the Epervier's carronades been previously fired in exercise, for any length of time together, the defect in the clinching of her breeching-bolts, a defect common to the vessels of this and the smaller classes, nearly all of them being contract-built, would have been discovered, and perhaps remedied. Even one or two discharges would have shown the insufficiency of the fighting-bolts. We doubt, however, if any teaching at the guns could have amended the Epervier's crew: the men wanted, what nature alone could give them, the hearts of Britons.

On the 28th of June, at daylight, latitude 48° 36' north, longitude 11° 15' west, the British 18-gun brig-sloop Reindeer, Captain William Manners, steering with a light breeze from the north-east, discovered and chased in the west-south-west the United States ship-sloop Wasp, Captain Johnston Blakeley. The latter was the sister-ship to the Peacock, and armed every way the same. The Reindeer, built of fir in 1804, was a sister-brig to the Epervier, but not so heavily armed, having, on account of her age and weakness, exchanged her 32-pounder carronades for 24-pounders; 16 of which, with two sixes and a 12-pounder boat-carronade, formed her present armament.

By 1 P.M. the two vessels had approximated near enough to

ascertain that each was an enemy; and, while one manœuvred to gain, the other manœuvred to keep, the weather-gage. At 2 P.M. the Wasp hoisted her colours, and fired a gun to windward; and immediately the Reindeer, whose colours had been previously hoisted, fired a gun also to windward, as an answer to the challenge. At 3 h. 15 m. P.M., being distant about 60 yards on the Wasp's starboard and weather quarter, the Reindeer opened a fire from her boat-carronade mounted upon the top-gallant forecastle. This she repeated four times; when at 3 h. 26 m., putting her helm a-lee, the Wasp luffed up and commenced the action with the after-carronade and the others in succession. The Reindeer returned the fire with spirit, and a close and furious engagement ensued.

After the mutual cannonade had lasted about half an hour, the Reindeer, owing to her disabled state, fell with her bow against the larboard quarter of the Wasp. The latter immediately raked her with dreadful effect; and the American riflemen in the tops picked off the British officers and men in every part of the deck. It was now that Captain Manners showed himself a hero. The calves of his legs had been partly shot away early in the action; yet did he keep the deck, encouraging his crew, and animating, by his example, the few officers remaining on board. A grape or canister shot passed through both his thighs: he fell on his kness, but quickly sprang up; and, although bleeding profusely, resolutely refused to quit the deck. Perceiving at this time the dreadful slaughter which the musketry in the Wasp's tops was causing among his crew, this gallant young officer called out to them, "Follow me, my boys, we must board." While with that object in view climbing into the Reindeer's rigging, two balls from the Wasp's maintop penetrated his skull, and came out beneath his chin. Placing one hand on his forehead, and with the other convulsively brandishing his sword, he exclaimed' "O God!" and dropped lifeless on his own deck!

> "To live with fame
> The gods allow to many; but to die
> With equal lustre is a blessing Heaven
> Selects from all the choicest boons of fate,
> And with a sparing hand on few bestows."
> *Glover.*

Having lost, besides her captain, nearly the whole of her officers and more than half her men, the Reindeer was wholly unable to oppose the Wasp's overwhelming numbers. Accordingly, at about 4 P.M., the American crew rushed on board, and received possession of their hard-earned trophy from Mr. Richard Collins, the captain's clerk, the senior officer alive on deck.

In a line with her ports, the Reindeer was literally cut to pieces: her upper-works, boats, and spare spars were one complete wreck. Her masts were both badly wounded; particularly her foremast, which was left in a tottering state. Out of her crew of 98 men and 20 boys, the brig had her commander, purser (John Thomas Barton), and 23 petty officers, seamen, and marines killed, her first and only lieutenant on board (Thomas Chambers), one master's mate (Matthew Mitchell), one midshipman (Henry Hardiman), her boatswain (all badly), and 37 petty officers, seamen, and marines wounded; total, 25 killed and 42 wounded, 27 of the number dangerously and severely. One of the men was wounded in the head by a ramrod; which, before it could be extracted, required to be sawed off close to the skull. The man, notwithstanding, recovered. After receiving this desperate wound, he, like his gallant chief, refused to go below; saying to those who begged him to leave his gun, "If all the wounded of the Reindeer were as well able to fight as I am, we should soon make the American strike."

The sails and rigging of the Wasp were a good deal cut. "Six round shot and many grape," Captain Blakeley says, struck her hull. We should imagine, from the Wasp's acknowledged loss, that a few more had either perforated her thick sides, or entered at her port-holes. One 24-pound shot passed through the centre of the foremast: and yet it stood: a tolerable proof of its large dimensions. Out of 173 men and two boys in complement, the Wasp had two midshipmen and nine seamen and marines killed and mortally wounded, and 15 petty officers, seamen, and marines wounded severely and slightly. Doubtless, a great part of the Wasp's loss arose from the determined efforts of the Reindeer's crew to board; but how, taking the relative numbers as they at first stood, could 98 men succeed against 173?

Comparative Force of the Combatants.

		Reindeer.	Wasp.
Broadside-guns	No.	9	11
	lbs.	198	338
Crew (men only)	No.	98	173
Size	tons	385	539

Notwithstanding this decided disparity of force, the weaker

party was the assailant; nor can the British commander be accused of rashness, both vessels being "sloops-of-war." The force employed by the Wasp, stationed upon a floating body, varying a trifle in construction, would have entitled the Reindeer to seek her safety in flight. But, had she run from the Wasp, Mr. Madison would have exulted as much, in announcing that a British ship had been chased, as captured, by an American ship "of the same class;" and even Britons would have considered the act as a stigma upon the national character. This may be pronounced one of the best-fought sloop-actions of the war. The British crew had long served together, and Captain Manners was the idol and delight of his men. They were called the pride of Plymouth. Gallant souls! they wanted but as many more like themselves as would have brought them in number within a fourth of their opponents; and the Americans would have had to rue the day that the Wasp encountered the Reindeer.

On the 29th, in the afternoon, on a breeze springing up, the foremast of the prize went by the board; and on the same evening, finding the Reindeer too much shattered to keep the sea, and too old and worthless, had she been otherwise, to be worth carrying into port, Captain Blakeley set fire to and destroyed her. The Wasp then steered for Lorient, to refit and renovate her crew, and on the 8th of July anchored in that port.

It will appear surprising, that an action so pregnant with circumstances calculated to excite the sympathy of the brave of all nations, an action in the conduct of it from first to last so highly honourable to the character of the British navy, as that of the Reindeer and Wasp, should be altogether omitted by an English naval historian; by a writer, especially, who claims the honour to belong to that very profession of which the gallant Manners was a member. But every friend to the memory of the youthful hero, every well-wisher to the cause of the British navy, will rejoice to find, that Captain Brenton has not even glanced at the action of the Reindeer and Wasp, when he discovers that, in the Avon's case (to which we shall come presently), the Wasp is described as a "brig, mounting eighteen 32-pounder carronades and two sixes, with 140 men.[1] Recollecting the mistake about the force of the Peacock, the Hornet's opponent,[2] we have not a doubt that Captain Brenton would have made a similar mistake respecting the Reindeer; and then, what with under-

[1] Brenton, vol. v., p. 141.   [2] See p. 49.

rating the force on one side, and overrating it on the other, the merits of the action would have been entirely changed.

On the 27th of August the Wasp, thoroughly refitted and manned, sailed from Lorient to resume her cruise; and on the 1st of September, at 7 P.M., latitude 30° north, longitude 11° west, going free on the starboard tack, with the wind at south-east, Captain Blakeley fell in with the British 18-gun brig-sloop Avon (sixteen 32-pounder carronades and two sixes), Captain the Hon. James Arbuthnot, nearly ahead, steering about south-west. At 7 h. 34 m. P.M. the Avon made night-signals to the Wasp; which the latter at 8 P.M. answered with a blue light on the forecastle. At 8 h. 38 m. the Avon fired a shot from her stern chase-gun; and still running on to the south-west, fired a second shot from her starboard and lee side. At 9 h. 20 m., being then on the weather-quarter of the Avon, the Wasp was hailed by the latter, "What ship is that?" and answered by the question, "What brig is that?" The Avon replied with her name, but it was not heard on board the Wasp. The former again asked, "What ship is that?" and was told to heave-to and she would be informed. The question was repeated, and answered to the same effect. An American officer then went forward on the Wasp's forecastle, and ordered the Avon to heave-to; but the latter declined doing so, and at 9 h. 25 m. P.M. set her larboard foretopmast studding-sail.

At 9 h. 26 m. P.M. the Wasp fired her 12-pounder carronade: whereupon the Avon commenced the action by a discharge from her larboard guns. The Wasp then kept away, and, running under the brig's lee, at 9 h. 29 m., opened her broadside. Almost the first fire from the American ship, consisting of star and bar shot, cut away, with other parts of her rigging, the slings of the brig's gaff; and on the immediate fall of the latter, the boom-mainsail covered the quarter-deck guns on the side engaged, the only ones that would at this time bear. Shortly afterwards the brig's mainmast fell by the board. Thus rendered completely unmanageable, the Avon lost all advantage to be derived from manœuvring; and, what with the wreck lying upon some of her guns, and the upsetting of others from the usual defects in their fastenings, the brig could make little or no return to the animated fire maintained by the Wasp; who, on this occasion (recollecting what she had lately suffered by allowing the British an opportunity to board), fought much more warily than in her action with the Reindeer.

At 10 h. 12 m. P.M., according to Captain Blakeley's minutes, but at a time much nearer 11 P.M., as will presently be proved, the Wasp hailed the Avon, to know if she had surrendered, and received an answer in the affirmative. When, says Captain Blakeley, " on the eve of taking possession," the Wasp discovered " a sail close on board of her." This sail was the British 18-gun brig-sloop Castilian (same force as Avon), Captain David Braimer. It was exactly at 11 P.M. that the Castilian came near enough to ascertain that one vessel was a dismasted brig (supposed to be the Avon), and the other a ship. The Castilian immediately chased the Wasp, then without either light or ensign. After having hailed several times without effect, the Castilian, at 11 h. 40 m. P.M., fired her lee guns into, or rather, as it proved, over, the weather quarter of the Wasp; who, although this second opponent had only cut away her lower main cross-trees and damaged her rigging, did not return a shot, but made all sail before the wind.

Repeated signals of distress having by this time been made by the Avon, the Castilian tacked and stood towards her; and on closing, at 11 h. 55 m., Captain Braimer was informed by Captain Arbuthnot, that the Avon was sinking fast. The Castilian immediately hoisted out her boats to save the people; and at 1 A.M. on the 2nd, just as the last boat had pushed off from the Avon, the British brig went down: an irrefragable proof, that she had not surrendered until every hope of success or escape had vanished. Hoisting in her boats, the Castilian filled and made sail to the north-east, in search of the Wasp; but the latter had already run out of sight. As a reason for this, Captain Blakeley has alleged that he discovered two other vessels, besides the Castilian, in chase of him.

Out of her 104 men and 13 boys, the Avon lost her first-lieutenant (John Prendergrast) and nine seamen and marines killed and mortally wounded, her commander, second-lieutenant (John Harvey), one midshipman (John Travers), and 29 seamen and marines wounded severely and slightly. According to Captain Blakeley, the Wasp received only four round shot in her hull, and, out of her acknowledged complement of 173 men, had but two killed and one wounded. The gallantry of the Avon's officers and crew cannot, for a moment, be questioned; but the gunnery of the latter appears to have been not a whit better than, to the discredit of the British navy, had frequently before been displayed in combats of this kind. Nor, from the specimen given by the Castilian, is it likely that she would have performed any better.

The Wasp, unfortunately for her brave officers and crew, never reached a port of the United States: she foundered, as is supposed, between the 15th, when she was off Madeira, and the end of September. To the merit justly due to the captain of the Wasp, for his conduct in his two successful actions, America must be contented to divide her claim; as Captain Blakeley was a native of Dublin, and, with some English and Scotch, did not, it may be certain, neglect to have in his crew a great many Irish. The construction of so fine a ship as the Wasp, and the equipment of her as an effective man-of-war, is that part of the merit, and no small part either, which belongs exclusively to the United States.

On the 12th of July the British cutter Landrail, of four 12-pounder carronades and 19 men and boys, commanded by Lieutenant Robert Daniel Lancaster, in her way across the British Channel with despatches, was chased by the American privateer schooner Syren; and maintained with her a running fight of one hour and 10 minutes, and a close action, within pistol-shot, of 40 minutes, in all two hours. The Landrail then surrendered, with the loss of seven men wounded. Her sails were riddled with shot-holes, and her hull much struck. The Syren, whose force was one long 18-pounder on a travelling-carriage, four long 6-pounders and two 18-pounder carronades, with a crew of 75 men, had three men killed, and 15 wounded, including some of her principal officers; a tolerable proof of the execution that may be done by two 12-pounder carronades, if well pointed. The action certainly reflects great credit on Lieutenant Lancaster and his ship's company, or rather, his boat's crew.

Although the Landrail had not even room for another gun beyond the four she mounted, the American historians, in the first instance, gave her 10 guns, and afterwards, by way of amending their statement, 8 guns; at which the Landrail now stands in their prize-lists. The Landrail was recaptured on her way to the United States, and carried into Halifax, Nova Scotia; consequently her valuable services as a cruiser were not lost to the British navy.

Much about the time that the Landrail encountered the Syren, the Ballahou of the same class as the former, but rigged as a schooner, and commanded by Lieutenant Norfolk King, fell in with the American privateer schooner Perry, and, after a chase of 60 minutes, 10 of which they closely engaged, was captured It is not known what loss was sustained on either side. The prize was carried into Wilmington, North Carolina. The Ballahou's original armament consisted of four carronades, 12-pounders; but, according to the American papers, two only were mounted, the remaining two having been placed in the hold on account of bad weather. Her complement, admitting all to have been on board, was 20 men and boys. In an American prize-list now lying before us, the Ballahou appears with 10 guns. The Perry mounted five guns, one, a long 18 or 24 pounder, upon a pivot, and had a complement of 80 men. The Landrail and Ballahou were each under 76 tons; the Syren and Perry of at least 180 tons each.

After 15 or 16 precious months had been wasted in the experiment, the British government discovered that Admiral Sir John Warren was too old and infirm to carry on the war as it ought to be carried on against the Americans. Sir John was therefore recalled, and in the summer of 1814 Vice-admiral Sir Alexander Cochrane arrived at Bermuda to take the command on the coast of North America. During the preceding winter the command of the British forces in the Chesapeake had been intrusted to Captain Robert Berrie, of the 74-gun ship Dragon. In the latter end of May, Rear-admiral Cockburn in the 74-gun ship Albion (into which he had shifted his flag from the Sceptre), Captain Charles Bayne Hodgson Ross, arrived in the bay and relieved Captain Barrie. The first operation of any importance in the bay of Chesapeake, after Rear-admiral Cockburn's arrival, was an attack upon a strong American flotilla fitted out at Baltimore, and intrusted to the command of a brave officer of the revolutionary war, Commodore Joshua Barney, a native of Ireland. This flotilla consisted of the commodore's vessel, the Scorpion sloop, mounting eight carronades and a heavy long gun upon a traversing-carriage, and 16 gun-boats, with one long gun in the bow and another in the stern, the largest of the vessels carrying 32-pounders and 60 men, and the smallest, 18-pounders and 40 men.

The first sight gained of this flotilla, by the British, was on the 1st of June, when it was proceeding from Baltimore, past the mouth of the river Patuxent, to "scour the bay." The British vessels consisted of the St. Lawrence schooner, of 13 guns, and 55 men, and the boats, in number seven, of the Albion and Dragon, under the command of Captain Barrie. The Americans had the honour of seeing this trifling force retreat before them to the Dragon, then at anchor off Smith's point. That ship got under way, and, with the schooner and the boats, proceeded in chase; but the shallowness of the water shortly compelled the Dragon to re-anchor. In the mean time the flotilla had run for shelter into the Patuxent. By way of inducing Commodore Barney to separate his force, Captain Barrie now detached two boats to cut off a schooner under Cove point; but, not considering that his orders to give protection warranted such a risk, Commodore Barney allowed the vessel to be burnt in his sight.

On the 6th the flotilla retreated higher up the Patuxent: and, being joined on the day following by the 38-gun frigate Loire, Captain Thomas Brown, and 18-gun brig-sloop Jasseur, Captain George Edward Watts, Captain Barrie proceeded up the river with them, the St. Lawrence, and the boats of the two 74s. The flotilla retreated about two miles up St. Leonard's creek, where it could be reached by boats only; but the force of the latter was not equal to the attack. Captain Barrie endeavoured, however, by a discharge of rockets and carronades from the boats, to provoke the American vessels, which were moored in a close line abreast across the channel, to come down within reach of the guns of the ship, brig, and schooner, at anchor near the mouth of the creek. At one time the American flotilla got under way, and chased the boats to a short distance, and then returned to their moorings. With a view to force the flotilla to quit its station, detachments of seamen and marines were landed on both sides of the river, and the American militia, estimated at 300 or 400, retreated before them to the woods. The marines destroyed two tobacco-stores, and several houses converted into military posts; but still the flotilla remained at its moorings.

On the 15th of June the 32-gun frigate Narcissus, Captain John Richard Lumley, joined the little squadron; and Captain Barrie, taking with him 12 boats, containing 180 marines, and 30 of the black colonial corps, proceeded up the river to Benedict. Here the men disembarked, and drove into the woods, without a struggle, a number of militia, who left behind a part of their muskets and camp equippage, as well as a 6-pounder field-piece. After spiking the latter, and destroying a store containing tobacco, the British again took to their boats, except five or six men, who had probably strayed too far into the woods.

After quitting Benedict, Captain Barrie ascended the river to Lower Marlborough, a town about 28 miles from the capital of the United States. The party landed and took possession of the place; the militia, as well as the inhabitants, flying into the woods. A schooner, belonging to a Captain David, was captured, and loaded with tobacco. After this, having burnt, at Lower Marlborough and at Magruders, on the opposite side of the river, tobacco-stores containing 2800 hogsheads, and loaded the boats with stock, the detachment re-embarked. The Americans collected a force, estimated at about 350 regulars, besides militia, on Holland's cliffs; but some marines, being landed, traversed the skirts of the heights, and re-embarked without molestation, the American troops not again showing themselves till the boats were out of gun-shot.

The blockade of Commodore Barney's flotilla, and the depredations on the coasts of the Patuxent, by Captain Barrie's squadron, caused great inquietude at Washington. At length an order reached the American commodore, directing him to destroy the flotilla, in the hope that the British, having no longer such a temptation in their way, would retire from a position so near to the capital. The order was suspended, owing to a proposal of Colonel Wadsworth, of the engineers; who, with two 18-pounders upon travelling-carriages, protected by a detachment of marines and regular troops, engaged to drive away the two British frigates from the mouth of the creek. The colonel established his battery behind an elevated ridge, which sheltered him and his men; and on the morning of the 26th of June a simultaneous attack by the gun-boats and battery was made upon the Loire and Narcissus. Owing to the effect of the colonel's hot shot, the impracticability of bringing a gun to bear upon his position from either frigate, and the want of a sufficient force to storm and carry the battery, Captain Brown retreated with the Loire and Narcissus to a station near Point Patience; and, with the exception of two barges, which put back, disabled apparently by the shot from the frigates, the American flotilla moved out of the creek, and ascended the Patuxent. The frigates sustained no loss on this occasion; but Commodore Barney admits a loss of one midshipman and three men killed and seven men wounded.

On the 4th of July the 40-gun frigate Severn, Captain Joseph Nourse, joined the Loire and Narcissus; and Captain Nourse immediately despatched Captain Brown, with the marines of the three ships, 150 in number, up St. Leonard's creek. Here two of Commodore Barney's barges were found scuttled, owing to the damage they had received in the action with the frigates. The barges and several other vessels were burnt, and a large tobacco-store destroyed. Soon after this, the British quitted the Patuxent.

On the 19th of July, Rear-admiral Cockburn, having been joined by a battalion of marines, and a detachment of marine artillery, proceeded up the river Potomac, for the purpose of attacking Leonard's town, the capital of St. Mary's county, where the 36th United States regiment was stationed. The marines of the squadron under Major George Lewis were landed, whilst the boats pulled up in front of the town; but, on discovering the marines, the enemy's armed force quitted the place, and suffered the British to take quiet possession. A quantity of stores belonging to the 36th regiment, and a number of arms of different descriptions, were found there and destroyed; and a quantity of tobacco, flour, provisions, and other articles, were brought away in the boats, and in a schooner which was lying off the town. Not a musket being fired, nor an armed enemy seen, the town was spared.

A body of militia having assembled at a place called Nominy ferry, in Virginia, a considerable way up Nominy river, Rear-admiral Cockburn, on the 21st, proceeded thither, with the boats and marines; the latter commanded by Captain John Robyns, during the illness of Major Lewis. The enemy's position was on a very commanding eminence, projecting into the water; but, some marines having been landed on its flank, and they being seen getting up the craggy side of the mountain, while the main body was disembarking at the ferry, the Americans fell back, and, although pursued for several miles, escaped with the loss of a few prisoners. The Americans had withdrawn their field-artillery, and hid it in the woods; fearing that, if they kept it to use against the British, they would not be able to retreat with it quickly enough to save it from capture. After taking on board all the tobacco and other stores found in the place, with a quantity of cattle, and destroying all the store-houses and buildings, the rear-admiral re-embarked; and dropping down to another point of the Nominy river, observed some movements on shore. Upon this he again landed with the marines. The Americans fired a volley, but, on the advance of the marines, fled into the woods. Everything in the neighbourhood was therefore destroyed or brought off; and, after visiting the country in several other directions, covering the escape of the negroes who were anxious to join him, the rear-admiral quitted the river, and returned to the ships with 135 refugee negroes, two captured schooners, a large quantity of tobacco, dry goods, and cattle, and a few prisoners.

On the 24th of July the rear-admiral went up St. Clement's

creek, in St. Mary's county, with the boats and marines, to examine the country. The militia showed themselves occasionally, but always retreated when pursued; and the boats returned to the ships without any casualty, having captured four schooners, and destroyed one. The inhabitants remaining peaceably in their houses, the rear-admiral did not suffer any injury to be done to them, excepting at one farm, from which two musket-shot had been fired at the admiral's gig, and where the property was, in consequence, destroyed.

On the 26th the rear-admiral proceeded to the head of the Machodic river, in Virginia, where he burnt six schooners, whilst the marines marched, without opposition, over the country on the banks of that river; and, there not remaining any other place on the Virginia or St. Mary's side of his last anchorage, that the rear-admiral had not visited, he, on the 28th, caused the ships to move above Blackstone's island; and, on the 29th, proceeded with the boats and marines, up the Wicomoco river. He landed at Hamburgh and Chaptico; from which latter place he shipped a considerable quantity of tobacco, and visited several houses in different parts of the country; the owners of which living quietly with their families, and seeming to consider themselves and the neighbourhood to be at his disposal, the rear-admiral caused no further inconvenience to them, than obliging them to furnish supplies of cattle and stock for the use of his forces, for which they were liberally paid.

On the 2nd of August the squadron dropped down the Potomac, near to the entrance of the Yocomico river, which the rear-admiral entered on the following day, with the boats and marines, and landed with the latter. The enemy had here collected in great force, and made more resistance than usual, but the ardour and determination of the rear-admiral's gallant little band carried all before it; and, after forcing the enemy to give way, the marines followed him 10 miles up the country, captured a field-piece, and burnt several houses, which had been converted into depôts for militia arms, &c. Learning afterwards that General Hungerford had rallied his men at Kinsale, the rear-admiral proceeded thither; and, although the position of the Americans was extremely strong, they had only time to give the British an ineffectual volley before the latter gained the height, when the Americans again retired with precipitation, and did not re-appear. The stores found at Kinsale were then shipped without molestation; and, having burnt the store-houses and other places, with two old schooners, and destroyed two batteries, the rear-admiral re-embarked, bringing away five prize schooners, a large quantity of tobacco, flour, &c., a fieldpiece, and a few prisoners. The American General Taylor was wounded and unhorsed, and escaped only through the thickness of the wood and bushes, into which he ran. The British had three men killed, and as many wounded. Thus 500 British marines, and 200 seamen and marine-artillery, penetrated 10 miles into the enemy's country, and skirmished, on their way back, surrounded by woods, in the face of the whole collected militia of Virginia, under Generals Hungerford and Taylor; and yet, after this long march, carried the heights of Kinsale in the most gallant manner.

Coan river, a few miles below Yocomico, being the only inlet on the Virginia side of the Potomac that the rear-admiral had not visited, he proceeded on the 7th to attack it, with the boats and marines. After a tolerably quick fire on the boats, the enemy went off precipitately, with the guns. The battery was destroyed, and the river ascended; in which three schooners were captured, and some tobacco brought off. On the 12th the rear-admiral proceeded up St. Mary's creek, and landed in various parts of the country about that extensive inlet; but without seeing a single armed person, although militia had formerly been stationed at St. Mary's factory for its defence, the inhabitants of the state appearing to consider it wiser to submit than to attempt opposition. On the 15th of August the rear-admiral again landed within St. Mary's creek; but found, in the different parts of the country, the same quiet and submissive conduct on the part of the inhabitants, as in the places visited on the 12th.

Some hints thrown out by the British commissioners at the conference at Ghent, coupled with the rumoured destination of British troops shipping in the ports of France, induced the American commissioners to intimate to their government, that an attack upon the federal city would probably be made in the course of the summer of 1814. This notice reached Mr. Madison on the 26th of June; and, on the 1st of July, he submitted to his council a plan for immediately calling 2000 or 3000 men into the field, and holding 10,000 or 12,000 militia and volunteers, of the neighbouring states, in readiness to reinforce that corps. On the next day he created into a military district the whole state of Maryland, the district of Columbia, and that part of Virginia north of the Rappahannock river, embracing an exposed coast of nearly 1000 miles ; vulnerable at every point, and intersected by many large rivers, and by the Chesapeake bay. On the 4th of July, as a further defensive preparation, the President made a requisition to the several states of the union, for 93,500 militia, as authorized by law ; designating their respective quota, and requesting the executive magistrates of each state, to detach and hold them in readiness for immediate service. Of these 93,500 militia, 15,000 were to be drawn from the tenth military district, or that surrounding the metropolis, for whose defence they were intended.

On the 2nd of June the British 74-gun ship Royal Oak, Rear-admiral Pulteney Malcolm, Captain Edward Dix, accompanied by three frigates, three sloops, two bomb-vessels, five ships armed en flûte, and three transports, having on board a body of troops under Major-general Ross, sailed from Verdon road at the mouth of the Gironde. On the 24th of July the squadron arrived at Bermuda, and there joined Vice-admiral Cochrane, in the 80-gun ship Tonnant. On the 2nd of August, having received on board the Tonnant Major-general Ross and his staff, Sir Alexander sailed, in company with the 18-pounder 36-gun frigate Euryalus, Captain Charles Napier, for Chesapeake bay ; and on the 14th of August arrived, and joined the Albion, Rear-admiral Cockburn, off the mouth of the Potomac. On the next day Major-general Ross, accompanied by Rear-admiral Cockburn, went on shore to reconnoitre.

The rear-admiral's knowledge of the country, as well as the excellent plan he adopted to prevent surprise, enabled the two officers to penetrate further than would otherwise have been prudent. The thick woods that skirt, and the numerous ravines that intersect, the different roads about Washington, offer important advantages to an ambushing enemy. Rear-admiral Cockburn, therefore, in his frequent walks through the country, invariably moved forward between two parties of marines, occupying, in open order, the woods by the roadside. Each marine carried a bugle, to be used as a signal, in case of casual separation, or the appearance of an enemy. It was during the excursion with General Ross, that Rear-admiral Cockburn suggested the facility of an attack upon the city of Washington; and General Ross determined, as soon as the troops should arrive from Bermuda, to make the attempt.

On the 17th of August, Rear-admiral Malcolm arrived with the troops, and joined Vice-admiral Cochrane off the mouth of the Potomac ; and the whole proceeded to the Patuxent, situated about 20 miles further up the bay. In the mean time Captain James Alexander Gordon, of the 38-gun frigate Seahorse, with some vessels of the squadron, had been detached up the Potomac, to bombard Fort Washington, situated on the left bank of that river, about 14 miles below the federal city; and Captain Sir Peter Parker, with the 38-gun frigate Menelaus, had been sent up the Chesapeake, above Baltimore, to create a diversion in that quarter. The direct route to Washington, from the mouth of the Potomac, was up that river, about 50 miles, to Fort Tobacco; thence, over land, by the village of Piscataway, 32 miles, to the lower bridge across the eastern branch of the Potomac; but, as no doubt could be entertained that this bridge, which was half a mile long, and had a draw at the west end, would be defended as well by a body of troops, as by a heavy sloop-of-war and an armed schooner, known to be in the river, a preference was given to the route up the Patuxent, and by Bladensburg; where the eastern branch, in case of the bridge at that spot being destroyed, could be easily forded.

Commodore Barney's gun-boats were still lying in the Patuxent. An immediate attempt against this flotilla offered two advantages; one, in its capture or destruction; the other, as a pretext for ascending the Patuxent, with the troops destined for the attack of the federal city. Part of the ships, having advanced as high up the river as the depth of water could allow, disembarked the troops, about 4000 in number, on the 19th and 20th of August, at Benedict, a small town about 50 miles southeast of Washington. On the 20th, in the evening, Rear-admiral Cockburn, taking with him the armed boats and tenders of the fleet, having on board the marines under Major Robyns, and the marine-artillery under Captain James H. Harrison, proceeded up the river, to attack Commodore Barney's flotilla; and to supply with provisions, and, if necessary, afford protection to the army, as it ascended the right bank. The boats and tenders were separated into three divisions. The first division was commanded by Captains Thomas Ball Sullivan and William Stanhope Badcock; the second, by Captains Rowland Money and James Somervell; and the third, by Captain Robert Ramsay; and the whole was under the superintendence and immediate management of Captain John Wainwright, of the Tonnant. The frigates Severn and Hebrus, Captains Joseph Nourse and Edmund Palmer, accompanied by the brig-sloop Manly, Captain Vincent Newton, had been also directed to follow the boats up the river as far as might prove practicable.

On opening the reach above Pig-point, the rear-admiral, who had just before been joined by Captains Nourse and Palmer with the boats of their two frigates, which they could get no higher than Benedict, discovered Commodore Barney's broad pendant in the headmost vessel, a large sloop, and the remainder of the flotilla extending in a long line astern of her. The British boats now advanced as rapidly as possible: but, on nearing the flotilla, the sloop bearing the broad pendant was observed to be on fire, and soon afterwards blew up; as did 15 out of the 16 remaining gun-boats. The one in which the fire had not taken was captured. The rear-admiral found 13 merchant-schooners, which had been under Commodore Barney's protection. Of these, such as were not worth bringing away, were destroyed. The remainder were moved to Pig-point, to receive on board the tobacco which had been there found.

The destruction of this flotilla secured the right flank of the army under Major-general Ross; who, on the afternoon of the 22nd, with the troops, arrived and encamped at the town of Upper Marlborough, situated about four miles up the western branch of the Patuxent. The men, therefore, after having been nearly three months on board ship, had, in less than three days, marched 40 miles; and that in the month of August, when the sultriness of the climate could scarcely be tolerated. While General Ross and his men were resting themselves at Upper Marlborough, General Winder and his army, now joined by Commodore Barney and the men of his flotilla, were lying at their encampment at the long Old Fields, only eight miles distant. On the next morning the American troops were reviewed by Mr. Madison, "their commander-in-chief, whose martial appearance gladdened every countenance and encouraged every heart."[1] Soon after the review, a detachment from the American army advanced along the road to Upper Marlborough; and, after exchanging a few shots with the British skirmishers, fell back to the main body.

On the 23rd, in the morning, Rear-admiral Cockburn, having left at Pig-point, directly opposite to the western branch, the marines of the ships under Captain Robyns, and two divisions of the boats, crossed over with the third division to Mount Calvert; and proceeded by land to the British encampment at Upper Marlborough. The little opposition experienced by the army in its march from Benedict, and the complete success that had attended the expedition against Commodore Barney's flotilla

[1] Wilkinson's Mem., vol. i., p. 766.

determined Major-general Ross to make an immediate attempt upon the city of Washington, distant from Upper Marlborough not more than 16 miles. At the desire of the major-general, the marine and naval forces at Pig-point were moved over to Mount Calvert; and the marines, marine-artillery, and a proportion of the seamen under Captains Palmer and Money, joined the army at Upper Marlborough.

As if by concert, the American army retired from the long Old Fields, about the same time that the British army advanced from Upper Marlborough; and the patroles of the latter actually occupied, before midnight, the ground which the former had abandoned. The American army did not stop until it reached Washington; where it encamped for the night near the navy-yard. On the same evening upwards of 2000 troops arrived at Bladensburg from Baltimore. On the 24th, at daylight, General Ross put his troops in motion for Bladensburg, 12 miles from his camp; and, having halted by the way, arrived, at about 11 h. 30 m. A.M., at the heights facing the village.

According to a letter of General Armstrong, the American secretary at war, to the editor of the "Baltimore Patriot," General Winder had under his command, including the 15,000 militia he had been directed to call out, as many troops and seamen as would make his total force, when assembled, 16,300 men; but an American writer gives the details of the general's force, in which he includes 600 seamen, and makes the total amount to only 7593 men. Of artillery, the American army had on the field not fewer than 23 pieces, varying from 6 to 18 pounders. This army was drawn up in two lines, upon very commanding heights, on the north of the turnpike-road leading from Bladensburg to Washington; and, as an additional incitement to glory on the part of the American troops, their President was on the field.

The affair (for it hardly deserves the name of battle) of Bladensburg, ended, as is well known, in the rout of the Americans; from whom 10 pieces of cannon were taken, but not above 120 prisoners, owing to the swiftness with which the enemy went off, and the fatigue which the British army, about 1500 of whom only were engaged, had previously undergone. The retreating American troops proceeded, with all haste, towards Washington; and the British troops, including the rear-division, which, just at the close of the short scuffle, had arrived upon the ground, halted to take some refreshment. Had it not been for the American artillery, the loss of the British would have been very trifling. Under these circumstances, the loss, on the part of the army, amounted to one captain, two lieutenants, five sergeants, and 56 rank and file killed, two lieutenant-colonels, one major, one captain, 14 lieutenants, two ensigns, 10 sergeants, and 155 rank and file wounded; total, 64 killed and 185 wounded. The loss sustained by the naval department amounted to only one colonial marine killed, one master's mate (Jeremiah M'Daniel), two sergeants, and three colonial marines wounded; making a total of 65 killed and 191 wounded. The officers of the navy and of the marines, who, besides Rear-admiral Cockburn, were present in the battle, appear to have been Captain Edmund Palmer, with his aide-de-camp, midshipman Arthur Wakefield, Lieutenant James Scott, first of the Albion, acting as Rear-admiral Cockburn's aide-de-camp, Lieutenant John Lawrence, of the marine-artillery, and lieutenant of marines Althestan Stephens.

As soon as the troops were refreshed, General Ross and Rear-admiral Cockburn, with about 1000 men, moved forward from Bladensburg, and at 8 P.M. arrived at an open piece of ground, two miles from the federal city. The troops were here drawn up, while Major-general Ross, Rear-admiral Cockburn, and several other officers, accompanied by a small guard, rode forward to reconnoitre. On arriving opposite to some houses, the party halted; and, just as the officers had closed each other, in order to consult whether or not it would be prudent to enter the heart of the city that night, a volley was fired from the windows of one of two adjoining houses, and from the capitol; which volley killed one soldier, and General Ross's horse from under him, and wounded three soldiers. Rear-admiral Cockburn instantly rode back to the detachment stationed in advance, and soon returned with the light companies. The house was then surrounded; and, after some prisoners had been taken from it, set on fire: the adjoining house fell with it. The capitol, which was contiguous to these houses, and which, according to an American writer, was "capable of being made an impregnable citadel against an enemy, with little artillery, and that of the lighter class," was also set on fire.

We are obliged to pause an instant, in order to correct a very serious misstatement, which, as the book in which it appears with two or three others lay open before us, we at first took to be the splenetic effusion of an American writer. But we owe an apology to the Americans; for the statement emanates from the pen of a British naval officer, and here it is: "A little musketry from one of the houses in the town, which killed the general's horse, was all the resistance they met with. This was quickly silenced; the house burnt, and the people within it put to death."[1] When it is considered who are usually the inmates of a dwelling-house, the statement that "the people within it were put to death," and that for "killing a horse," is calculated to fill the mind with horror, and to call forth execrations against the monsters who could perpetrate such an act. Fortunately for the fame of the general and admiral who presided on the occasion, the account we have just given, and the substance of which we published eight or nine years ago, is a faithful relation of all that occurred.

Scarcely had the flames burst out from the capitol and the two contiguous houses, than an awful explosion announced that the Americans were employed upon the same business in the lower part of the city. By this time the remainder of the British forces from Bladensburg had arrived at the encampment. At 10 h. 30 m., P.M., after a party had been sent to destroy the fort and public works at Greenleaf's point, Major-general Ross, and Rear-admiral Cockburn, each at the head of a small detachment of men, numbering together not more than 200, proceeded down the hill towards the President's palace. Finding it utterly abandoned, and hearing probably that a guard of soldiers, with "two pieces of cannon, well mounted on travelling-carriages,"[2] had been stationed at, and but recently withdrawn from, this the American "commander-in-chief's" head-quarters, Rear-admiral Cockburn directed it to be set on fire. A log-hut, under similar circumstances, would have shared the same fate, and the justice of the measure not been disputed. Why, then, in a country where "equality of rights" is daily preached up, should the palace be held more sacred than the cottage? The loss of the one falls, where it ought, upon the nation at large; the loss of the other, a lamentable case at all times, solely upon the individual proprietor. To the building, containing the treasury and war offices, the torches of the conquerors were next applied. On arriving opposite to the office of the "National Intelligencer," the American government-paper, Rear-admiral Cockburn observed to the inhabitants near him, that he must destroy it. On being told, however, that the adjoining buildings would be likely to take fire, he desisted. The rear-admiral then wishing the inhabitants "good night," and assuring them

---

[1] Brenton, vol. v., p. 166.
[2] Testimony of Mr. William Simmons, before the American committee of investigation.

that private property and persons should be respected, departed to his quarters on the capitol-hill. Early on the next morning the rear-admiral was seen walking about the city, accompanied by three soldiers only. Indeed, General Wilkinson says: "A single sentinel who had been accidentally left on post near the office of the 'National Intelligencer,' kept undisturbed possession of the central part of the metropolis until the next morning; of which there are several living witnesses."[1] At this time, too, it appears an American force of more than 4000 combatants was posted upon the heights of Georgetown, which is a continuation of the city to the westward.

During the morning of the 25th the secretary of state's office was burnt, and the types and printing materials of the government-paper were destroyed. A serious accident had happened to the party sent to Greenleaf's point. Some powder, concealed in a well, accidentally took fire, killing 12, and wounding 30, officers and men. The extensive ropewalks, at some distance from the city, were destroyed by the British; and so was an immense quantity of small arms and heavy ordnance, as well as the great bridge across the Potomac; a very prudent military measure, especially as the Americans had themselves destroyed the two bridges crossing the eastern branch. A party, under Captain Wainwright, destroyed the few stores and buildings in the navyyard, which had escaped the flames of the preceding night. As the British were in haste to be gone, and as the vessels, even if they could have been floated in safety down the Potomac, were not wanted, it was very considerate in the American government to order the destruction of the frigate, of 1600 tons, which was nearly ready to be launched, and of the fine sloop-of-war Argus, ready for sea; and whose 20 carronades, 32-pounders, and two long 18-pounders, would have assisted so powerfully in defending the entrance to the city by the lower bridge.

According to the official estimate of the public property destroyed, the value has been much overrated. It appears not to have exceeded 1,624,280 dollars, or 365,463*l*. sterling. With respect to private property, we have only to quote passages from American prints, to show how that was treated. One newspaper says: "The British officers pay inviolable respect to private property, and no peaceable citizen is molested." A writer from Baltimore, under the date of August 27th, says: "The enemy, I learn, treated the inhabitants of Washington well." That the

[1] Wilkinson, vol. i., p. 791.

British officers did all they could to secure the inhabitants from injury, both in their persons and properties, may also be gathered from the acknowledgment from Mr. Thompson, another American writer, that "the plunder of individual property was prohibited, and soldiers transgressing the order were severely punished."

On the 25th, at 8 P.M., the British left Washington, by the way of Bladensburg. Here such of the wounded as could ride, or be transported in carriages, were provided with 30 or 40 horses, 12 carts and waggons, one coach, and several gigs. With these, preceded by a drove of 60 or 70 cattle, the troops moved leisurely along. On the 29th, in the evening, they reached Benedict, 50 miles from Washington, without a single musket having been fired; and, on the following day, re-embarked in the vessels of the fleet. No complaints that we can discover have been made against the British during their retreat across the country; although, as an American writer has been pleased to say, "General Ross scarcely kept up his order, sufficiently to identify the body of his army."

Of the many expeditions up the bays and rivers of the United States during the late war, none equalled in brilliancy of execution that up the Potomac to Alexandria. This service was intrusted to Captain James Alexander Gordon, of the 38-gun frigate Seahorse, having under his orders the 18-pounder 36-gun frigate Euryalus, Captain Charles Napier, bomb-ships Devastation, Ætna, and Meteor, Captains Thomas Alexander, Richard Kenah, and Samuel Roberts, rocket-ship Erebus, Captain David Ewen Bartholomew, and a small tender, or despatch-boat. On the 17th, at 9 h. 15 m. A.M., the squadron got under way from the anchorage at the entrance of the Potomac, and, without the aid of pilots, began ascending the intricate channel of the river leading to the capital of the United States. On the 18th the Seahorse grounded, and could only get afloat again by shifting her guns to the tenders in company. That done, and the guns returned to their places, the squadron again stood up the river. On the 25th, while passing the flats of Maryland-point, a squall struck the squadron: the Seahorse had her mizenmast sprung; and the Euryalus, just as she had clewed up her sails to be in a state to receive it, had her bowsprit and the head of her foremast badly sprung, and the heads of all three topmasts fairly wrung off. Such, however, was the state of discipline on board the ship, that in 12 hours, the Euryalus had refitted herself, and was again under way ascending the river.

On the 27th, in the evening, after each of the ships had been aground not less than 20 times, and each time obliged to haul themselves off by main strength, and after having for five successive days, with the exception of a few hours, been employed in warping a distance of not more than 50 miles, the squadron arrived abreast of Fort Washington. The bomb-ships immediately began throwing their shells into the fort, preparatory to an attack the next morning by the two frigates. On the bursting of the first shell, the garrison was observed to retreat; but, supposing some concealed design, Captain Gordon directed the fire to be continued. At 8 P.M., however, all doubts were removed by the explosion of the powder-magazine, which destroyed the inner buildings. On the 28th, at daylight, the British took possession of the fort, and of three minor batteries, mounting altogether 27 guns, chiefly of heavy caliber. The guns had already been spiked; and their complete destruction, with the carriages, was effected by the seamen and marines of the squadron. These forts were intended for the defence of Alexandria, the channel to which the British began immediately to buoy. A flag of truce now came off with a proposal to capitulate; and one hardly knows which to admire most, the prudence of Captain Gordon, in postponing his answer to the common council of Alexandria, until, says he, "I was enabled to place the shipping in such a position, as would insure assent to the terms I had decided to enforce," or the peremptory and humiliating conditions which he did enforce. It was in vain that the Americans had sunk their vessels; they must get them up again, and put them in the state in which they were, when the squadron passed the Kettle Bottoms; the owners of the vessels must send on board their furniture without delay; merchandise removed must be brought back; and the merchants load their own vessels, which will be towed off by the captors!

The last article of the capitulation provides, that British officers are to see the terms "strictly complied with." One of the officers sent on this service was midshipman John Went Fraser of the Euryalus, a mere stripling. Having strayed alone to some distance from his boat, two American naval officers rode at, as if to run over him; one, a very powerful man, caught the youth by the shirt-collar and dragged him, almost suffocating, across the pummel of the saddle, galloping off with him. Fortunately the shirt-collar gave way, and the lad fell to the ground. He was quickly upon his legs again, and ran towards a landing-place, where his boat was waiting; the American pursuing him.

The boat and the men in it were hid under a steep bank or wall and, on that account, could not level their carronades at the honourable gentleman as he approached. The instant he saw the boat's crew, he turned pale with fright; and rode off in a contrary direction as fast as his horse could carry him. The American editors thought this a good joke; and very readily informed us, that one of these worthies was the famed Captain David Porter, the other, and he that committed the atrocious and dastardly assault, Master-commandant John Orde Creighton, an American by adoption only, and, we rather think, an Irishman. The first of these officers, for his "brilliant deeds at Valparaiso." had recently been appointed to the new frigate at Washington, whose name, to commemorate the exploits of Captain Porter's favourite ship, had been changed from the Columbia to the Essex, and his gallant brother-horseman had been appointed to the new corvette Argus; both of which ships, it will be recollected, were burnt, and their intended commanders thrown out of employment, by the entry of the British into Washington, a few days previous. This is what infuriated the two heroes, and determined them to sacrifice the first straggling Briton they could find. At the time this outrage was committed, a flag of truce was flying before Alexandria; whose inhabitants, in a body, disavowed the act, reprobating it as became them. Such conduct on their part alone prevented Captain Gordon from enforcing the last article of the treaty.

After the British had retired from Washington, the Americans recovered a little from their panic; and took strong measures to oppose Captain Gordon's return down the Potomac. Commodore Rodgers, with a chosen body of seamen from the Guerrière at Philadelphia, Captains Perry, Porter, and other "distinguished officers," a party of officers and men from the Constellation at Norfolk, the men that had belonged to Commodore Barney's flotilla, regular troops, riflemen, artillerists, and militia, all flocked to the shores of the Potomac, to "punish the base incendiaries." The American newspaper-editors, for some days, feasted their readers with the anticipated destruction of the British squadron. "It is impossible the ships can pass such formidable batteries, commanded by our naval heroes, and manned by our invincible seamen. We'll teach them how to draw up terms of capitulation."

On the 31st, early in the morning, the British 18-gun brig-sloop Fairy, Captain Henry Loraine Baker, after having fought her way up the river passed a battery of five guns and a large military force, joined Captain Gordon with Vice-admiral Cochrane's orders for him to return. On the same day, without waiting to destroy those remaining stores which he had not the means of bringing away, Captain Gordon weighed on his return, accompanied by 21 sail of prizes, many of which, having been sunk by the enemy, had been weighed, masted, hove down, calked, rigged, and loaded, all within three days. Contrary winds again compelled the British to resort to the laborious task of warping the ships down the channel of the river, and a day's delay occurred by the grounding of the Devastation. Taking advantage of this circumstance, the Americans attempted the destruction of the bomb-ship, by means of three fire-vessels and five row-boats, directed in person by Commodore Rodgers; but their object was defeated by the promptitude and gallantry of Captain Alexander, who pushed off with his own boats, and, being followed by those of the other ships, compelled the renowned commodore to face about, and fly under as much alarm towards, as about 13 months before he had fled from, an Alexandria. The cool and steady conduct of midshipman John Moore, of the Seahorse, in towing the nearest fire-vessel on shore, while the others were removed from the power of doing mischief by the smaller boats of the Devastation, is spoken of in high and just terms of commendation by Captain Gordon.

Notwithstanding that the Meteor and Fairy, assisted by the despatch-boat, a prize gun-boat, and a boat belonging to the Euryalus, with a howitzer, had greatly impeded the progress of the Americans in their works, the latter were enabled to increase their battery from five to 11 guns, with a furnace for heating shot. On the 3rd of September, the wind coming to the northwest, the Ætna and Erebus succeeded in getting down to the assistance of the Meteor and her companions. On the 4th the frigates and prizes reached the same spot; but the Devastation, in spite of the utmost exertions in warping her, still remained five miles higher up the river. This was the moment that the Americans made their greatest efforts to effect the destruction of the British squadron. The Erebus, who had been placed by her commander in an admirable position for harassing the workmen employed in the trenches, was attacked by three field-pieces; which, before they were beaten off, did the ship considerable injury. A second attempt was now made to destroy the Devastation by fire-vessels; but, owing to the alacrity with which Captain Baker with the boats of the squadron went to her assistance, the American boats and fire-vessels retreated, and the ship was saved. In consequence of the Americans having sought refuge under some guns in a narrow creek, thickly wooded, and from which it was impossible to dislodge them, Captain Baker sustained a serious loss, including among the killed his second-lieutenant, Charles Dickinson.

On the 5th, at noon, the wind coming fair and every suitable arrangement having been made, the Seahorse and Euryalus anchored within musket-shot of the batteries, while the whole of the prizes passed between the frigates and the shoal. The three bombships, the Fairy and the Erebus, firing as they passed, anchored in a favourable position for facilitating, by means of their force, the further removal of the frigates. At 3 P.M., having completely silenced the fire of the American batteries, the Seahorse and Erebus cut their cables, and the whole squadron proceeded to the next position taken up by the American troops; who had here two batteries mounting from 14 to 18 guns, on a range of cliffs about a mile in extent, and close under which the ships were obliged to pass. It was not intended to make the attack that evening: but, the Erebus grounding within range of the batteries, the frigates and other vessels were necessarily called into action. On this occasion the fire of the Fairy produced the most decisive effect, as well as that of the Erebus, while the Devastation, Ætna, and Meteor threw their shells with admirable precision. In consequence of these vigorous measures, the American batteries, by 8 P.M., were completely silenced. On the 6th, at daylight, the British squadron again got under way; and, so satisfied were the whole of the parties on shore that their opposition was ineffectual, that they allowed the British to pass without further molestation. On the 9th the Seahorse and her companion sailed out of the Potomac, and came to an anchor in safety on the spot whence they had weighed 23 days before.

The toil and fatigue undergone by the officers and men, and the deprivations they so cheerfully submitted to, were equalled only by their gallantry in defeating the batteries on shore, and their skill and perseverance in surmounting the difficulties of a most intricate and dangerous navigation. Happily, the loss in this daring enterprise did not exceed, on board all the vessels, seven killed, including the Fairy's lieutenant already named, and 35 wounded, including Captains Napier and Bartholomew, Lieutenant Reuben Paine, and master's mate Andrew Reid, all slightly. Of the captains and other officers associated with them, and of Lieutenants Henry King, first of the Seahorse, and Thomas Herbert, first of the Euryalus, Captain Gordon, in his official letter, speaks in the highest terms; also of the master of the Seahorse, Mr. Alexander Louthean, "for both finding and buoying the channel of a navigation, which no ship of a similar draught of water had ever before passed with her guns and stores on board." It was stated by a seaman of the Seahorse, who had served on board the President, that that frigate did not accomplish the same task under a period of 42 days, and then not without taking out her guns.

We formerly noticed that Sir Peter Parker, of the Menelaus frigate, had been detached on service up Chesapeake bay. Having but recently arrived on the North American station, Sir Peter was not aware of the ambushing tricks to which a small invading force would be exposed, in a country so filled with woods, ravines, and defiles; and where local knowledge and skill with the rifle were an overmatch for all the valour he could bring against them. Information having reached the ship, then at anchor off Moor's-fields, that 200 American militia were encamped behind a wood distant about a mile from the beach, Captain Parker, at 11 p.m. on the 30th of August, was induced to land with 104 seamen, and 30 marines, in two divisions, one commanded by Lieutenant Henry Crease, with midshipman Henry Finucane, the other by Lieutenant Robert Pearce, and midshipman Frederick Chamier.

It appears that Colonel Read, the commander of the American force, stated that 170 Maryland volunteers, having been apprised of the intended attack, had retired to a small open space, surrounded by woods, distant four or five miles from his first encampment. Thither, having alarmed a small cavalry picket, the heedless seamen and marines, headed by their undaunted chief, proceeded. The enemy, with some pieces of artillery, was found drawn up in line in front of his camp. The British commenced the fire; and, charging, drove the Americans through their camp into the woods. It was about this time that Sir Peter received a mortal wound from a back-shot, which divided the femoral artery, and which occasioned his bleeding to death before medical assistance could be procured. Secure behind the trees, the Americans levelled their pieces with unerring aim; while the British, deceived by the apparent flight of their wary foe, rushed on through the woods, until, bewildered and embarrassed, the survivors of this adventurous band were compelled to retreat to their ship; bringing away, however, the body of their lamented commander, and all their wounded but three. The British suffered a loss of 14 killed, including Sir Peter Parker and midshipman John T. Sandes, and 27 wounded, including both lieutenants of marines, Benjamin George Benyon and George Poe.[1] The Americans, as a proof how little they exposed themselves, sustained a loss of not more than two or three men killed and wounded.

At the head of a narrow bay or inlet of the Patapsco river, and distant from its confluence with the Chesapeake about 14 miles, stands the city of Baltimore, containing about 50,000 inhabitants. It is nearly surrounded by detached hills; one of which, Clinkapin hill, situated on its eastern side, commands the city itself, as well as the approach to it by land from the Chesapeake. Its water approach is defended by a strong fortification, named Fort M'Henry, situated at the distance of about two miles from the city, upon the point of the peninsula that forms the south side of the bay or harbour; which, at its entrance, is scarcely a quarter of a mile in width. As an additional security, the Patapsco is not navigable for vessels drawing more than 18 feet water; and, just within the harbour, is a 14 or a 15 feet bar.

The arrival of troops in the Chesapeake, and the subsequent operations of the British in the Patuxent and Potomac rivers, could not do otherwise than cause serious alarm at Baltimore, distant from Washington but 35 miles. The panic-struck inhabitants believed that the British troops would march across the country, and attack them in the rear, while the squadron was cannonading them in front. The numbers of the British on shore were too small to warrant such an enterprise; but, had it been risked, and had the fleet made a simultaneous movement up the bay, there is little doubt that Baltimore would have capitulated. Fortunately for the city, the military and naval forces within it were becoming hourly more powerful; and, far from desponding, the generals and commodores used their utmost exertions in strengthening the defences and improving the natural advantages of the position. Upon the hills to the eastward and northward of the city, a chain of palisadoed redoubts, connected by breastworks, with ditches in front, and well supplied with artillery, was constructed; and works were

---

[1] Amongst the wounded was James Perrin, the midshipman's servant. He called to Mr. Chamier to give him some water, saying he thought he could hold out till he shot an American. He kept his fatal resolution too well; for, on the approach of a former foe to assist him, he shot him dead, and instantly expired himself.

thrown up and guns mounted at every spot from which an invading force, either by land or water, could meet with annoyance. The Java frigate, of 60 guns, and two new sloops-of-war, of 22 guns each, the Erie and Ontario, were equipping at Baltimore. There were also in the harbour several gun-boats, armed each with a long French 36-pounder, besides a carronade; as well as several private armed vessels. So that the Americans, including their field and regular battery guns, had an immense train of artillery to put in operation against an enemy. As to troops, exclusively of the 16,300 militia, regulars, and flotillamen, which General Winder had been authorised to assemble for the defence of the 10th military district, volunteers were flocking in from Pennsylvania; and the seamen and marines of Commodore Rodgers, and Captains Perry and Porter, had just arrived from the banks of the Potomac.

If any southern town or city of the United States was an object of immediate attack, it certainly was Baltimore. The destruction of the new frigate and sloops, and of the immense quantities of naval stores, at that depôt, would have been seriously felt by the American government. Yet were the British ships, that had on board the troops, waiting in the Patuxent, until the passing of the "approaching equinoctial new moon" would enable them to proceed, with safety, upon the "plans which had been concerted previously to the departure of the Iphigenia," or, in other words, upon the expedition to New Orleans. On the 6th of September came a flag of truce from Baltimore; and instantly all was bustle and alacrity on board the British squadron. The Royal Oak 74, and troop-ships stood out of the Patuxent; and Vice-admiral Cochrane, quitting his anchorage off Tangier island, proceeded with the remainder of the fleet up the bay to North-point, near the entrance of the Patapsco river. On the 10th and 11th the fleet anchored; and, by noon on the 12th, the whole of the troops, marines of the fleet, black colonial marines, and seamen, numbering altogether 3270 rank and file, had disembarked at North-point, in order to proceed to the immediate attack upon Baltimore by land; while some frigates and sloops, the Erebus rocket-ship, and five bomb-vessels, ascended the Patapsco, to threaten and bombard Fort M'Henry, and the other contiguous batteries. The seamen, 600 in number, were under the orders of Captain Edward Crofton, assisted by Captains Thomas Ball Sullivan, Rowland Money, and Robert Ramsay, and the marines under Captain John Robyns.

ATTACK ON BALTIMORE.

Immediately after landing, the British moved forward to the city. On arriving at a line of intrenchments and abattis, thrown up between Black river and Humphries' creek on the Patapsco, and distant about three miles from the point of landing, some opposition was expected; but the American dragoons and riflemen stationed there fled without firing a shot. At this time Major-general Ross and Rear-admiral Cockburn, with a guard of 50 or 60 men, were walking together, considerably ahead of the advanced or light companies, in order to reconnoitre the enemy. At about 10 A.M., after having proceeded about two miles from the entrenchment, and some distance along a road flanked by thick woods, they encountered a division of American infantry, riflemen, cavalry, and artillery, numbering about 370 men. A short skirmish ensued, and the Americans fell back; most of them taking to the woods. After saying to Rear-admiral Cockburn, "I'll return and order up the light companies," Major-general Ross proceeded to execute his purpose. In his way back, alone, by the same road along which he and his party had just passed, the major-general received a musket-bullet through his right arm into his breast, and fell mortally wounded. The firing had at this time wholly ceased; and the expiring general lay on the road, unheeded, because unseen, either by friend or foe, until the arrival at the spot of the light companies, who had hastened forward upon hearing the musketry. Leaving some attendants in charge of the lamented chief, the officer commanding rushed on; and it was then that Rear-admiral Cockburn learned the loss which the army and the country had sustained.

As soon as the British main body, now under the command of Colonel Brooke of the 44th regiment, closed upon the advance, the whole moved forward; and, at about two miles further, and about five from the city, came in sight of the American army, drawn up, with six pieces of artillery, and a body of cavalry, numbering in the whole about 4500 men; and backed, in case of a retreat, by at least 8000 more, and these hourly augmenting, and by heavy batteries in all directions. As the British advanced to the attack, the Americans opened a fire of musketry from their whole line, and a heavy cannonade from their field-pieces, and then retreated to a wood in the rear. From this position the Americans were quickly expelled, chiefly by the bayonet, leaving all their wounded and two of their guns in the possession of the British. The latter, however, were too much fatigued to follow up their victory on that evening.

The British loss amounted to one general-staff, one subaltern, two sergeants, and 35 rank and file killed, seven captains, four subalterns, 11 sergeants, and 229 rank and file wounded, of the army. The navy lost one captain's clerk (Arthur Edmondson), five seamen, and one marine killed, one captain of marines (John Robyns), one lieutenant (Sampson Marshall, severely), one midshipman (Charles Ogle), 30 seamen, and 15 marines wounded; making the total loss of the British on shore amount to 46 killed and 300 wounded. The great disproportion of wounded arose from the employment, by the enemy, of buck-shot; and the magnitude of the loss, altogether, to the enemy's sheltered position. The loss of the Americans upon the field, according to their own account, was 20 killed, 90 wounded, and 47 missing. The last item is evidently erroneous, as the British commanding officer carried away with him about 200 prisoners.

Early on the morning of the 13th, leaving a small guard at a meeting-house, from which the enemy had been driven, to protect the wounded, Colonel Brooke moved forward with the army, and at 10 A.M. occupied a favourable position, about two miles to the eastward of Baltimore. From this point, the stong defences in and around the city were plainly visible; and arrangements were made for storming, during the ensuing night, with the co-operation of the fleet, the American intrenched camp; at which lay General Stricker and his army, now reinforced by Douglas's brigade of Virginia militia, under General Winder, and the United States dragoons, under Captain Bird.

In their way up the Patapsco, several of the frigates and other vessels had grounded; and one or two of the frigates did not get off until the next day. On the 13th, at about 9 P.M., the Meteor, Ætna, Terror, Volcano. and Devastation, bomb-vessels, Captains Samuel Roberts, Richard Kenah, John Sheridan, David Price, and Thomas Alexander, and the Erebus, rocket-ship, Captain David Ewen Bartholomew, came to anchor in a position, from which they could act upon the enemy's fort and batteries, the frigates having already taken their stations outside of all. On the 13th, at daylight, the bombardment commenced upon, and was returned by, Fort M'Henry, the Star Fort, and the water batteries on both sides of the entrance. At about 3 P.M. the four bomb-vessels and rocket-ship weighed, and stood further in; the latter, to give effect to her rockets, much nearer than the others. The forts, which had discontinued their fire on account of the vessels being out of range, now recommenced a brisk cannonade; but which, although persevered in for some hours, did not injure a man on board any of the vessels: two of the bombs only were slightly struck. The close position of the Erebus led the commander-in-chief, whose ship, the Severn, with the other frigates, was at anchor in the river, to imagine that Captain Bartholomew could not maintain his position. The vice-admiral, therefore, sent a division of boats to tow out the Erebus.

On the 13th, in the middle of the night, a division of 20 boats was detached up the Ferry branch, to cause a diversion favourable to the intended assault upon the enemy's intrenched camp at the opposite side of the city. The rain poured in torrents, and the night was so extremely dark, that 11 of the boats pulled, by mistake, directly for the harbour. Fortunately, the lights of the city discovered to the crews their perilous situation, in time for them to get back in safety to their ships. The remaining nine boats, consisting of one rocket-boat, five launches, two pinnaces, and one gig, containing 128 officers, seamen, and marines, under the command of Captain Charles Napier, passed up the Ferry branch to a considerable distance above Fort M'Henry, and opened a heavy fire of rockets and shot upon the shore; at several parts of which they could have landed with ease, had the whole of their force been together. After having, by drawing down a considerable number of troops to the beach, effected their object, the British stood back with their boats. When just opposite to Fort M'Henry, one of the officers caused a rocket to be fired. The consequence was, an immediate discharge of round, grape, and canister, from the fort and water batteries below; by which one of the boats was slightly struck, and a man mortally wounded. Not another casualty occurred.

It appears that, on the evening of the 13th, after the boats had been ordered upon this service, Vice-admiral Cochrane sent a messenger to acquaint Colonel Brooke, that, as the entrance to Baltimore by sea was entirely obstructed by a barrier of vessels, sunk at the mouth of the harbour, defended inside by gun-boats, a naval co-operation against the city and intrenched camp was found impracticable. The heavy rain, at this time falling, greatly increased the difficulty of ascending the steep hill, upon which the camp was situated; and both commanders concurred in the propriety of immediately withdrawing the troops and ships. On the 14th, at 1 h. 30 m. A.M., the British troops commenced retiring, and halted at three miles distance. In the course of the evening they retired three miles further, and encamped for the night. Late on the morning of the 15th, they moved down to North-point; and, in the course of that day, re-embarked, without having experienced, during their slow and deliberate retreat, the slightest molestation from the enemy. Since 7 A.M. on the preceding day, the rocket-ship and bomb-vessels had been called off from the American batteries; which, notwithstanding the long-continued bombardment, lost only four men killed and 24 wounded. The ships afterwards stood down the river, and joined the remainder of the squadron at anchor off North-point.

No Briton but must regret that any plan of "ulterior operations" should have obtruded itself to check the progress of the attack. With respect to naval co-operation, it is well known, that the gallant commanders of the Severn, Euryalus, Havannah, and Hebrus frigates, volunteered to lighten their ships, and lay them close alongside Fort M'Henry. The possession of this fort would have enabled the British to silence the batteries on the opposite side of the bay, and, indeed, have placed the city completely at their mercy. The very advance of the frigates to their stations would probably have led to the destruction of the Java, Erie, and Ontario; and then the British might have retired, "holding in view the ulterior operations of the troops," with something more to boast of than, not merely an empty, but, considering what had been lost by it, a highly disastrous "demonstration."

On the 19th of September Sir Alexander Cochrane, with the Tonnant and Surprise frigate, sailed for Halifax, to hasten the construction of the flat-bottomed boats, intended to be employed in the great expedition on foot; and on the same day, the Albion, Rear-admiral Cockburn, sailed for Bermuda, leaving the Royal Oak, 74, Rear-admiral Pulteney Malcolm, with some frigates and smaller vessels, and the ships containing the troops, at anchor in the river Patuxent. On the 27th the Rear-admiral removed to the Potomac; where, on the 3rd of October, the troops were placed into boats, and sent up Coan river. In their way up, two soldiers were wounded, and Captain Kenah of the Ætna, a gallant young officer, killed, by musketry from the shore. Against so powerful a force, when once landed, the few militia could not be expected to stand: they fired a volley and fled, and the troops advanced past Northumberland court-house, five miles into the interior. After taking and scuttling two or three worthless schooners, and, according to the American editors, plundering the inhabitants, the troops re-embarked, and stood down the river to their ships. The latter soon afterwards descended the Potomac; and on the 14th, taking with him the Royal Oak, Asia, and Ramillies, 74s, one or two frigates, and all the troop-ships and bombs, Rear-admiral Malcolm quitted the Chesapeake for the grand rendezvous at Negril bay, Jamaica.

In our account of the last year's proceedings before the blockaded port of New London, we related the disgraceful attempt made to destroy the British 74-gun ship Ramillies, and her crew of 590 or 600 men, by an explosion-vessel fitted out at New York.[1] We remember frequently hearing it said, that the plan originated with "mercenary merchants;" and it was even hinted, that the projectors were adopted, not native, Americans, the latter being too "high-minded" to countenance such a proceeding. Above all things, no one, who wished to escape a tar-and-feathering, dare have whispered a supposition, that an American naval officer would lend his ear to so dishonourable a mode of freeing himself from the presence of his enemy. Those, the most ready to fly out on these occasions, did not of course recollect the attempt made in the bay of Chesapeake, with the sanction, if not under the direction, of Captain Charles Stewart of the American navy, to blow up the Plantagenet 74, by a torpedo conducted by Mr. Mervine P. Mix, one of the Constellation's midshipmen; nor of a second plan to blow up the Ramillies, projected by that "excellent man," that "ornament to his country,"[2] Commodore Stephen Decatur, but of which, very fortunately, Sir Thomas Hardy received intelligence in time to place him on his guard. Nay, an officer and boat's crew from the Ramillies actually succeeded in capturing one of the crew of the frigate United States, who was to conduct the whale-boat containing the torpedo, and which whale-boat lay for several weeks, waiting a fit opportunity to push off, at Southold on Long island.

The British force at anchor off New London in January, 1814, consisted, besides the Ramillies, of the 24-pounder 40-gun frigate Endymion, Captain Henry Hope, and the 38-gun frigate Statira, Captain Hassard Stackpoole. In the hearing of an American privateer-captain, named Moran, about to quit the Ramillies for the shore, Captains Hope and Stackpoole, happened to express a desire to meet the United States and Macedonian. This soon became known all over New London. Feeling his consequence likely to be lowered in the opinion of the citizens, Commodore Decatur resolved to put in immediate practice an

[1] See p. 100.   [2] Brenton, vol. v., pp. 61, 202.

epistolary stratagem; which, managed as he intended it should be, could not fail to redound to his advantage. On the 14th of January, making the subject of the above-reported conversation the ground of the application, the American commodore sent to Captain Hardy a written proposition for a contest between the United States, of "48 guns and a boat-gun," and the Endymion, of "50 guns," and between the Macedonian, of "47," and the Statira, of "50 guns." Captain Hardy readily consented that the Statira should meet the Macedonian, as they were sister-ships; but, quite contrary, as may be supposed, to the wishes of Captain Hope, he refused to permit the Endymion to meet the United States, because the latter was much the superior in force.

Through the medium of Captain Biddle, the bearer of his proposition, Commodore Decatur had agreed, that the crews of the Endymion and Statira, both of which were short of complement, should be made up from the Ramillies and Borer; and, had it been finally settled that the meeting should take place between the Macedonian and Statira, Sir Thomas Hardy meant, as we have understood, to include himself among the volunteers from the Ramillies to serve on board the latter. This would undoubtedly have been a very hard measure upon Captain Stackpoole; but we do not see how Sir Thomas Hardy, having consented that a ship, other than the one he commanded, should meet in single combat the ship of an enemy, could well have acted otherwise.

When Commodore Decatur wrote his letter about capturing the Macedonian, he did not mention, although he took care to reckon, that ship's boat-gun; but now he tells us, that the 49th gun of the United States is a "12-pound carronade, a boat-gun." We have already shown, that the reduction of that ship's force did not go quite the length it purported to go, and that the Macedonian, although she may have mounted but 47 guns, was more effectively armed than when she mounted 49.[1] The armament of each of the two British ships is easily stated. Until the latter end of the year 1812, when she went into dock at Plymouth, the Endymion mounted, with her 26 long 24-pounders on the main deck, 14 carronades, 32-pounders, on the quarter-deck, and four of the same caliber, and two long nines on the forecastle; total 46 guns. In May, 1813, the Endymion had her quarter-deck barricade continued a few feet further forward, to admit an additional carronade of a side; which, with two additional carronades on the forecastle, and, in lieu of her two 9-pounders, a brass long French 18-pounder as a

[1] See p. 99.

bow chase-gun and for which there was no broadside-port, gave the Endymion 49 guns. Her net complement consisted of 347 men and boys. The Statira mounted the 46 guns of her class, and two light boat-guns, with a net complement (when filled) of 317 men and boys. The crew of the United States was about 480, and the crew of the Macedonian from 430 to 440 men.[1]

Commodore Decatur, however, declined a meeting between the Macedonian and Statira, from the alleged apprehension, that the latter might be over-manned; thereby tacitly admitting, what went rather against the previous claims of himself and his brother conquerors, that three men were better than two. Thus ended this vapouring affair. Commodore Decatur then sent the correspondence to a newspaper-editor; and he and Captain Jacob Jones were bepraised on all sides for the valour they had displayed. According to one of the swaggering statements made on the occasion, Captain Jones harangued his men, and pretended to lament the loss of so fine a ship as the Statira; which, he assured them, would have been their prize in a very short time. He had also the hardihood to tell them, that it was all owing to the refusal of the British, who were "afraid to contend with Americans upon equal terms."

Shortly after this business was broken off, a verbal challenge passed between the commanders of the Hornet and Loup-Cervier, the late American Wasp. The latter vessel soon afterwards foundered at sea, and every soul on board perished: nothing respecting this challenge has therefore been made public on the British side. The American "Port-folio," for November, 1815, in which the "Life of Captain James Biddle" is given, contains some account of it. It is there stated, that "Captain (William Bowen) Mends, of the Loup-Cervier, said that, if Captain Biddle would inform him of the number of souls he commanded, he, Captain Mends, pledged his honour to limit his number to the same; but that Commodore Decatur would not permit Captain Biddle to acquaint Captain Mends with the number of his crew, and meet him on the terms stated: because it was understood that, in that case, the Loup-Cervier would have a picked crew from the British squadron." What do we gather from this? Why, that the Americans, with all picked men on their side, were afraid to meet an equal number of British, because they *might have* picked men on theirs. Commodore Decatur's amended proposition was: "The Hornet shall

---

[1] [Mr. James here seems for once to have been misled; the Macedonian was a smaller frigate than Congress or Chesapeake, and hence the Americans would scarcely put on board of her more than 380 or at most 400 men.—H. Y. POWELL.]

meet the Loup-Cervier, under a mutual and satisfactory pledge, that neither ship shall receive any additional officers or men, but shall go into action with their original crews respectively." Was this fair? The Hornet's "original crew" was 170, including about three boys; the Loup-Cervier's original crew 121, including 18 boys. So that, deducting the boys, the numbers would stand: Americans 167, British 103.

The blockade of the American ships in New London having continued until the season had passed, in which Commodore Decatur could hope to effect his escape, the United States and Macedonian were moved up the river, to the head of navigation for heavy vessels, and there dismantled; and, while Captain Jones and the late crew of the Macedonian proceeded to reinforce the squadron under Commodore Chauncey on Lake Ontario, Commodore Decatur and his ship's company passed into the President, then at anchor in New York, her late distinguished commander and his crew having been transferred to the new 44-gun frigate Guerrière, fitting for sea at Philadelphia, and armed on the main deck with 30 medium 32-pounders.

On the 7th of April, in the evening, Captain the Hon. Thomas Bladen Capel, of the 74-gun ship Hogue, commanding a small British squadron, consisting, besides that ship, of the Endymion and Maidstone frigates, and 14-gun brig-sloop Borer, Captain Richard Coote, despatched six boats, containing 136 men, under the orders of Captain Coote, assisted by Lieutenant Harry Pyne, and Lieutenant of marines Walter Griffith Lloyd, to attempt the capture or destruction of some American vessels near Pettipague point, about 14 miles up Connecticut river. On the 8th Captain Coote and his party reached the point, and, after a slight skirmish with some militia, destroyed all the vessels, 27 in number, afloat or on the stocks within three miles of the place, besides several boats and a considerable quantity of naval stores. Three of the vessels were large privateers, completely equipped and ready for sea; and the aggregate burden of the 27 was upwards of 5000 tons. In the evening, after dark, the boats dropped down the river, without rowing; and the British reached their ships with no greater loss than two men killed and two wounded. For this gallant and important exploit, Captain Coote obtained post-rank, and Lieutenant Pyne his commission as commander.

On the 14th of June, Captain the Hon. Charles Paget of the British 74-gun ship Superb, detached, under the orders of Lieutenant James Garland, all that ship's boats, and two boats from the 18-gun brig-sloop Nimrod, Captain George Hilton, to endeavour to destroy some newly-built ships and other vessels at a place called Wareham, at the head of Buzzard's bay in the state of Connecticut. Lieutenant Garland completely succeeded in his object, without incurring the slightest loss, and destroyed as many ships, brigs, schooners, and sloops, on the stocks and afloat, as measured in the aggregate 2522 tons; also a large cotton manufactory, with its contents, valued at half a million of dollars. The extreme intricacy of the navigation rendered it too hazardous to attempt the enterprise without the assistance of daylight. This, however, would necessarily expose the boats, upon their return down the narrow stream, to a fire of musketry from a numerous militia, which, on the first alarm, had collected from the vicinity. But the foresight and prompt resolution of Lieutenant Garland completely succeeded in obviating the danger that was thus to be apprehended; for, as soon as he had destroyed the vessels and cotton manufactory, he ascertained who were the principal people of the place, and then secured them as hostages for a truce, until the boats were conducted back out of the reach of difficulty. This produced the desired effect, and the hostages were relanded at the first convenient spot.

We have already stated that the American frigate Congress was laid up, and have assigned a reason for her having been so. The only remaining 18-pounder frigate belonged to the United States, except the Macedonian in the mud of New London river, was the Constellation at Norfolk. In the latter end of the year 1813, Captain Stewart was relieved in the command of that frigate by Captain Charles Gordon, and was promoted to the Constitution; which ship had been in a manner rebuilt, and was lying in President road, Boston, ready for sea.

It appears that this American frigate now mounted a pair of carronades fewer than she did in the Java's action.[1] But the Constitution had not left either that pair or the pair of which she had previously disarmed herself, on shore, but had transferred them to the hold; so that, as she had the ports for them, they could be remounted in a very few minutes. To compensate for this slight reduction in her armament, the Constitution had taken on board a furnace for heating shot. Her officers stated, that it would heat shot to a white heat in 15 minutes, but that "hot shot were not to be used in action, unless the ship was assailed by a superior force." What an American captain would pronounce "superior force" may be partly ima-

[1] See vol. v., pp. 376, 410.

gined by the numerous American descriptions of "equal force" to be found in these pages. Upon her capstan the Constitution now mounted a piece resembling seven musket barrels, fixed together with iron bands. It was discharged by one lock; and each barrel threw 25 balls, making 175 shot from the piece within the space of two minutes. What could have impelled the Americans to invent such extraordinary implements of war but fear, downright fear?

Numerically, the Constitution was well manned, having a crew of 480, including three boys; but all the best hands out of her first crew had been draughted to the ships on the lakes, except a few sent on board the Chesapeake. The ship had now, therefore, what the Americans would call a bad crew, but what a British captain, judging from their personal appearance, would consider a tolerably fine ship's company. To give the men increased confidence in case of being boarded, they were provided with leather caps, fitted with narrow plates of iron, crossing at the top, and bending upward from the lower edge of the crown, to prevent a blow from striking the shoulder after having glanced on the head. Another strong symptom of fear; all the effect of the exertions making by the British to meet the Americans on terms not quite so unequal as had been the case in nearly every action in which the latter had come off victorious.

On the 1st of January, 1814, after having suffered herself to be blockaded, for several weeks, by the 38-gun frigate Nymphe, Captain Farmery Predam Epworth, the Constitution escaped to sea unperceived from President road. On the 14th of February, to windward of Barbadoes, Captain Stewart captured and destroyed the British 14-gun schooner Picton; and on the 23rd, when running through the Mona passage on her way homewards, the Constitution fell in with the British 18-pounder 36-gun frigate Pique, Captain the Hon. Anthony Maitland. The Pique (late French Pallas[1]) was a remarkably fine frigate of her class, measuring 1029 tons, and mounted, with her 26 long 18-pounders on the main deck, 16 carronades, 32-pounders, and four long nines on her quarter-deck and forecastle; total 46 guns, with an established complement of 284 men and boys.

When, at about noon, they first discovered each other, the two ships were steering to the north-west, with a light wind right aft. The Pique immediately braced her yards by, to allow the stranger, who was astern under a crowd of sail, to come up. At 4 h. 30 m. P.M. the Constitution took in her studding-sails.

[1] See vol. iii., p. 7.

Observing this, the Pique hauled to the wind on the larboard tack, and, hoisting her colours, made all sail to close. Almost immediately afterwards, and when bearing from the Pique south-east by south distant three miles, the Constitution took a reef in her topsails, hoisted her colours, and hauled to the wind on the starboard tack. The island of Zachee at this time bore from the Pique north by east distant 12 or 13 miles. The change of position of each ship afforded to the other a tolerable idea of the force which would be opposed to her. The Constitution counted 13 ports and a bridle on the Pique's main deck, and saw at once that she was of a class inferior to the Guerrière and Java; and the Pique counted 15 ports and a bridle on the Constitution's main deck, and therefore knew as well that she was one of the large class of American frigates.

We formerly noticed the directions given by the British admiralty, that the 18-pounder frigates were not to seek an engagement with the American 44-gun frigates. A prohibitory order of this kind was in the possession of Captain Maitland; but was of course unknown to his crew. He had the good fortune to command one of the finest ship's companies in the British navy; and, as a proof how much British seamen had been "cowed by the successes of the Americans," the Pique's men, on observing that it was not Captain Maitland's intention to become the assailant, went aft and requested him to bring the American frigate to action. Captain Maitland could do no less than read to them the instructions he had received, but entirely failed in persuading the Pique's crew that there had been any necessity for issuing them. Either just before, or just after, the reading of the captain's orders, the crew refused to take their supper-time grog: alleging as a reason, that they did not want "Dutch courage to fight a Yankee frigate." Although it is true that the Constitution was by no means so well manned as when she took the Java or Guerrière, and that the Pique had about 260 men, who, upon an average, were not more than 26 years of age, and the major part of them good seamen, yet the numerical disproportion was too great; and it was well that Captain Stewart thought the Pique's 18s were 24s, and therefore did not make an effort to bring her to action.

At 8 P.M., owing to thick squally weather, during which the wind shifted to the east-north-east, the two frigates lost sight of each other. At 2 A.M. on the 24th the Pique tacked to the south-east, and, crossing the bows of the Constitution, again discovered her, at the distance of about two miles on her lee beam.

As each stood on her course, the Pique to the south-east, and the Constitution to the north by west, the two ships, by 3 A.M., had run each other quite out of sight. Those who have gone along with us thus far, in unravelling the American accounts, and exposing the little peccadilloes of the writers, professional and non-professional, will feel no surprise at being told, that Captain Stewart declared to his government, and through that channel to the public, that he had chased a British frigate, but that she had escaped from him in the dark.

On the 3rd of April, at 7 A.M., having arrived off the port of Marblehead, in the state of Massachusetts, the Constitution fell in with the two British 38-gun frigates Junon, Captain Clotworthy Upton, and Tenedos, Captain Hyde Parker. The American frigate was standing to the westward, with the wind about north by west, and bore from the two English frigates about north-west by west. The Junon and Tenedos quickly hauled up in chase, and the Constitution crowded sail in the direction of Marblehead. At 9 h. 30 m., finding the Tenedos rather gaining upon her, the Constitution started her water, and threw overboard a quantity of provisions, spars, and other articles. At 11 h. 30 m. she hoisted her colours, and the two British frigates, who were now rather dropping in the chase, did the same. At 1 h. 30 m. P.M. the Constitution came to an anchor in the harbour of Marblehead. Captain Parker, whose ship now bore from Cape Ann north-north-east distant nine miles, was anxious to follow the American frigate into the port, which had no defences; but the Tenedos was recalled by signal from the Junon. A shift of wind to the south-east enabled the Constitution, at 6 P.M., to remove to Salem: where she lay much more secure. A short time afterwards the American frigate found an opportunity of quitting Salem unperceived, and anchored in the harbour of Boston.

On the 26th of August an expedition under the joint command of Lieutenant-general Sir John Coape Sherbrooke, governor of the province, and Rear-admiral Edward Griffith, consisting of the 74-gun ship Dragon, Captain Robert Barrie, frigates Endymion and Bacchante, Captains Henry Hope and Francis Stanfell, 18-gun ship-sloop Sylph, Captain George Dickens, and 10 sail of transports with troops, sailed from Halifax, Nova Scotia, bound to the river Penobscot, near the north-eastern extremity of the coast of the United States. On the 31st, when off the Metinicus islands, the expedition was joined by the 74-gun ship Bulwark, Captain Farmery Predam Epworth, frigate Tenedos,

Captain Hyde Parker, and brig-sloops Rifleman and Peruvian, Captains Joseph Pearce and George Kippen. From the Rifleman intelligence was now received, that the United States ship Adams, of 26 guns, Captain Charles Morris, had a few days before put into Penobscot, and, not deeming herself safe at the entrance of the river, had proceeded to Hamden, a place situated 27 miles higher up, where she had landed her guns and placed them in battery for her protection. The original plan of making Machias on the main coast the first point of attack, was now deviated from, and the general and admiral determined to ascend the river and endeavour to capture or destroy the Adams.

Towards evening the fleet, led by the Tenedos, made sail up the Penobscot with a fair wind, and by daylight on the 1st of September was off the fort and town of Castine. At 8 A.M. the men-of-war and transports came to anchor; and, after a slight show of resistance, Castine surrendered. The service of capturing or destroying the Adams frigate and the batteries erected for her defence was now intrusted to Captain Barrie; who, at 6 P.M., taking with him the Peruvian and Sylph sloops, a tender belonging to the Dragon commanded by acting Lieutenant James Pearson, and the Harmony transport, commanded on this occasion by Lieutenant William Henry Woodin, containing between them about 600 troops under Lieutenant-colonel Henry John, proceeded with the utmost despatch up the Penobscot. Light variable winds, thick foggy weather, and a most intricate channel of which the British were entirely ignorant, made it 2 P.M. on the 2nd before the Peruvian and her consorts arrived off Frankfort. At 5 P.M., having arrived off Ball's-head cone, distant about five miles from Hamden, Colonel John and Captain Barrie landed to reconnoitre; and by 10 P.M. the whole of the troops were also landed. The troops bivouacked for the night amidst an incessant rain; and at 6 A.M. on the 3rd the little party began their march towards Hamden. The larger vessels were kept in the rear in reserve; while the boats, commanded by Lieutenant George Pedlar, first of the Dragon, assisted by Lieutenant the Hon. George James Perceval, of the Tenedos, and Lieutenant Francis Ormond, of the Endymion, and preceded, at the distance of about a quarter of a mile, by a rocket-boat under the immediate direction of Captain Barrie himself, advanced in line with the right flank of the army.

The American militia and crew of the Adams, to the number altogether, as reported, of 1400 men, had taken up a most excellent position on a high hill fronting the town of Hamden, with some field-pieces stationed in the woods on their right. About a quarter of a mile to the southward of the Adams frigate, and calculated to command both the highway by which the troops were advancing and the river, were mounted eight 18-pounders; and 15 more 18-pounders were mounted on a wharf close to the Adams, completely commanding the river, which at that spot was only 600 yards wide. The British force consisted, besides the 600 infantry and artillery under Lieutenant-colonel John, of 80 marines under Captain Thomas Carter of the Dragon, and about as many seamen under Lieutenant James Symonds, Samuel Mottley, and Henry Slade, all of the Bulwark, and Mr. John Spurling, that ship's master.

The moment the British boats arrived within gun-shot, the Americans opened a fire upon them both from the hill and the wharf. This fire was warmly returned, and the rockets evidently threw the enemy into confusion. In the mean time the troops, marines, and seamen had stormed the hill with the utmost gallantry, and the American militia were in full retreat on the road to Bangor. Before the boats could get within grape-shot distance, Captain Morris, finding himself deserted by those who, doubtless, had a few minutes before promised to do wonders, set fire to the Adams. The American militia made so good a use of their legs, that very few were taken prisoners. The only loss sustained on the part of the British was one seaman killed, Captain Gall, of the 29th, and seven privates wounded, and one rank and file missing. Two ships, one of them armed, were destroyed by the Americans at the same time as the Adams. The British immediately hastened on to Bangor, which also surrendered; and there one ship, one brig, three schooners, and a sloop were destroyed. A copper-bottomed brig, pierced for 18 guns, and the Decatur privateer, of 16 guns, were captured, but lost in descending the river. Several vessels, at the different towns on the banks of the river, were found on the stocks, but were all left untouched.

The Adams had been a 32-gun frigate, but was afterwards lengthened, so as to rate as a 36; and then, on account of some defect in her construction, was cut down to a corvette. She measured 725 tons American, or about 783 English. The Adams sailed upon her last cruise with an armament of four long 18-pounders, 20 columbiad, or medium guns of the same caliber, and two long 12-pounders; total 26 guns, and with a complement, according to a prisoner who was some weeks on board of her, of 248 picked seamen, chiefly masters and mates of merchantmen. The Adams, therefore, was one of the most formidable "corvettes" that cruised on the ocean. While in the Irish channel, towards the end of July, she was chased by the 18-pounder 36-gun frigate Tigris, Captain Robert Henderson, and would probably have been caught, had not Captain Morris thrown overboard his quarter-guns and a portion of his stores. Captain Brenton confounds the Adams with the "John Adams," and gives the ship only "20 guns."[1]

As at the close of the preceding year, the military and naval commanders-in-chief, upon the Canadian frontier of the United States, were Lieutenant-general Sir George Prevost and Commodore Sir James Lucas Yeo. On the 15th of April were launched at Kingston, Lake Ontario, the British ships Prince Regent and Princess Charlotte. The first measured 1310 tons and mounted 28 long 24-pounders on the main deck, four long 24-pounders, four carronades, 68-pounders, and 22 carronades, 32-pounders, on the upper or spar deck; total 58 guns, with a complement of 485 men and boys. The last-named ship measured 815 tons, and mounted 24 long[2] 24s on the main deck, and two more, along with fourteen 32 and two 68 pounder carronades on the quarter-deck and forecastle; total 42 guns, with a complement of 315 men and boys. The six 68-pounder carronades were the same mounted in the preceding year on board the Wolfe and Royal George. The latter, now named the Niagara, had replaced the two 68s with two long 18-pounders; the former, now the Montreal, her four, with the same number of 32-pounder carronades. The schooners Moira and Sidney Smith had been altered into brigs, and their names changed to the Charwell and Magnet; as had been the names of the Melville and Beresford to the Star and Netley; but, it is believed, no alterations, beyond those already mentioned, were made in the armaments of any of the British vessels.

Before the end of March, Commodore Chauncey had succeeded in equipping two large brig-sloops, the Jones and Jefferson, each, as acknowledged, of 500 tons American, and therefore of at least 530 tons English. It has been stated, that these brigs carried 42-pounder carronades, and mounted 24 guns each; but they will be considered as having mounted the same as the ships Frolic and Peacock, with the addition of a long 24-pounder upon a traversing-carriage. The Sylph, now a brig, mounted,

---

[1] Brenton, vol. v., p. 171.   [2] Doubtful if not medium.

in lieu of her former armament, 14 carronades, 24-pounders, and two long 12s. On the 1st of May was launched, at Sackett's Harbour, the Superior, of about 1580 tons, mounting 30 columbiad or medium 32-pounders, on the lower or main deck; two long 24s, and 30 carronades, 42-pounders, on the upper or spar deck: total 62 guns, with a complement of 550 men.

Oswego is situated on the river of the same name, near its confluence with Lake Ontario, and is distant from Sackett's Harbour about 60 miles. At the mouth of the river there is a safe harbour, with two fathoms water; the channel to which is completely commanded by a well-built fort, standing near the state warehouses, barracks, and a few houses, upon a commanding height on the eastern shore of the river, having its front towards the lake. On the western bank of the river stands the town, consisting of about 30 houses. As this river afforded the only water communication between New York and Sackett's Harbour, the accumulation of naval stores in the warehouses of Oswego is readily explained, and gave to the post an importance which it would not otherwise possess. On the 3rd of May, in the evening, a detachment of troops, numbering altogether 1080 rank and file, embarked in the vessels of Sir James Yeo's fleet, lying at Kingston; and, early on the following morning, Lieutenant-general Drummond went on board the Prince Regent, as commander of the troops. The squadron, consisting of the Prince Regent, Captain Richard James Lawrence O'Connor, bearing the broad pendant of Sir James Yeo; Princess Charlotte, Captain William Howe Mulcaster; Montreal, Captain Stephen Popham; Niagara, Captain Francis Brockell Spilsbury; Charwell, Captain Alexander Dobbs; Star, Captain Charles Anthony; and Magnet, Captain Henry Collier, immediately stood out of the harbour; but, on account of light and variable winds, did not arrive off Oswego until noon on the following day.

Either suspicion, or direct information, of the attack had led to preparations on the part of the Americans. Since the 30th of April, Lieutenant-colonel Mitchell had arrived from Sackett's Harbour, with 300 heavy and light artillery, and several engineer and artillery officers. The batteries were repaired and fresh picketed, and new platforms laid for the guns; which were four in number, 24, 12, and 6 pounders; besides a 12-pounder, planted *en barbette* close to the lake-shore. The United States schooner Growler, of three heavy guns, Lieutenant George Pearce, was lying in the harbour, preparing, under the superintendence of Captain Woolsey, to conduct to Sackett's Harbour a division of batteaux laden with stores. Arrangements had also been made for assembling the militia of the district; and, no sooner did the British squadron show itself at 6 A.M., on the 5th, than alarm guns were fired, which soon brought to the post upwards of 200 militia; thus making a total force of at least 540 men. By way, also, of making this force appear treble what it was, in the hope thereby to daunt the British, and prevent them from attempting to land, the Americans pitched all their tents upon the opposite, or town side of the river, while they themselves remained in their barracks.

At 3 P.M. the ships lay to within long range of the shore ; and the gun-boats, 11 in number, were sent in, under the orders of Captain Collier, to induce the enemy to show the number and position of his guns. At 4 P.M., by which time the gun-boats had got within point-blank range, the Americans opened their fire, and a mutual cannonade was kept up until 5 h. 30 m. P.M.; when, having effected his object, Captain Collier stood back to the fleet. Preparations were now made for disembarking the troops on that evening, but, about sunset, a heavy gale from the north-west compelled the ships to gain an offing; in which effort four of the boats, their crews being first taken out, were obliged to be cut adrift. As soon as the weather moderated the squadron cast anchor about 10 miles to the northward of the fort.

On the 6th, in the morning, the ships having returned and everything being ready, a division of about 770 men, including 200 seamen, armed with pikes, under Captain Mulcaster, embarked in the boats. Owing to the shoalness of the water off the harbour, the Prince Regent and Princess Charlotte could not approach near enough to cannonade the battery with any effect; but this service was most gallantly performed by the Montreal and Niagara, under a heavy discharge of red-hot shot, which set the Montreal on fire three times. The Magnet took her station in front of the town, on the opposite side of the river ; while the Star and Charwell towed in and covered the boats, containing the troops. The wind was at this time nearly ahead; and the consequent tardiness in the approach of the boats exposed the men to a heavy and destructive fire from the enemy's batteries, and from upwards of 500 regulars and militia, drawn up on the brow of the hill. The British. nevertheless, effected their landing, and instantly formed on the beach. Having to ascend a steep and long hill, the troops suffered extremely from the enemy's fire. No sooner, however, had they reached the summit, than the 300 American regulars retired to the rear of the fort, and the 200 American militia fled, helter-skelter, into the woods. In 10 minutes after the British had gained the height, the fort was in their possession. Lieutenant James Laurie, of the marines, was the first man who entered it; and Lieutenant John Hewett, of the same corps, climbed the flagstaff, under a heavy fire, and struck the American colours, which had been nailed to the mast; more, as it would seem, to give trouble to the British than to evince a determination, on the part of the Americans, of defending the post with any unusual obstinacy.

The British loss in the affair of Oswego was rather severe. It amounted to one captain of marines (William Holtoway), and 14 non-commissioned officers and privates of the royal marines and De Watteville's regiment, and three seamen killed, one captain and one subaltern of De Watteville's, two captains (William Howe Mulcaster, dangerously, and Stephen Popham), one lieutenant (Charles William Griffith Griffin) and one master of the navy (—— Richardson), 51 non-commissioned officers and privates of the royal marines and De Watteville's, and seven seamen wounded; total 18 killed and 64 wounded. The Americans stated their loss at one lieutenant and five men killed, 38 wounded, and 25 missing. The British captured 60 prisoners.

The British carried away with them seven long guns, 32 and 24 pounders, a great quantity of ordnance stores, and large rope, 2400 barrels of provisions, and three schooners. They destroyed three long 24-pounder guns, one long 12, and two long 6s, a schooner, the barracks, and all the other public buildings. One of the schooners was the Growler, late Hamilton. Besides the above, a quantity of cordage, and other naval stores, and three long 32-pounders, were sunk in the river by the Americans themselves. The guns and stores for the new ship Superior, had, unknown to the British, been removed from Oswego previously to the attack; and reached Sackett's Harbour, chiefly by land conveyance. After departing from Oswego, Sir James anchored off Sackett's Harbour, and blockaded a port which Sir George Prevost, with a portion of the large force then concentrated around him at his "camp of instruction" at Chambly ought to have enabled him to attack.

By the capture of a boat from Oswego, containing two long 24-pounders and a 19½ inch cable for the Superior, Sir James became apprised that 18 other boats, similarly laden, were waiting at Sandy-creek for an opportunity of reaching Sackett's Harbour. He accordingly detached Captains Popham and Spilsbury, with 180 seamen and marines, to endeavour to cut out the vessels. On the 30th of May, shortly after daylight, the two captains arrived at, and began ascending the creek; and, when within a quarter of a mile of the enemy, Lieutenant Thomas S. Cox, with the principal part of the marines, was landed on the left bank, and Lieutenant Brown, with the Cohorn and small-arm party, accompanied by Lieutenant Patrick M'Veagh with a few marines, landed on the right bank. Just as the leading British boat, containing a 68-pounder in the bow and a 24-pounder in the stern, had arrived within sight of the American boats, the 68-pounder, the previous fire from which had dispersed a body of Indians from the banks of the river, became disabled, and the boat pulled round to bring the 24-pounder to bear. Considering by this that the British were on their retreat, the Americans to the number of 150 riflemen, 200 Indians, and a large body of militia and cavalry, unexpectedly rushed upon them. The British made a noble resistance, but were at length overpowered and made prisoners. As a proof that Captains Popham and Spilsbury and their party of seamen and marines made an obstinate resistance, their loss amounted to 18 killed, including Mr. Hoare, a master's mate of the Montreal, and 50 dangerously wounded, including Lieutenants Cox and M'Veagh. Captain Popham concludes his official letter on the subject with this paragraph: "The exertions of the American officers of the rifle corps, commanded by Major Appling, in saving the lives of many of the officers and men, whom their own men and the Indians were devoting to death, were conspicuous, and claim our warmest gratitude."

On the 11th of June, the Americans launched at Sackett's Harbour the Mohawk, of about 1350 tons, mounting 28 long 24-pounders on the main deck, two long 24s and 18 carronades, 42-pounders, on the quarter-deck and forecastle; total 48 guns, with a complement of 460 men. This made the British and American forces in this lake stand, in relative broadside force at, British 2752 lbs., and American 4188 lbs., and in number of men at, British 1517, American 2321. In the latter end of July Sir James Yeo raised the blockade of Sackett's Harbour, and returned to Kingston; and on the 1st of August Commodore Chauncey sailed out of port, vexed at the unwillingness of the British to meet him on "equal terms."

Some operations on the upper lakes now demand our attention. The possession of Captain Barclay's fleet had not only given to the Americans the command of Lake Erie, and the large lakes Huron and Superior, leading from it, but had restored to them the immense territory of Michigan, and gained over on their side the five nations of Indians, late the allies of the British. Had the spirit of the Americans, indeed, kept pace with the apathy and neglect, so conspicuous on the part of the British commander-in-chief, the province of Upper Canada could not have held out as it did.

After the capture of the British flotilla on this lake, Captain Perry retired to Lake Ontario, to serve under Commodore Chauncey, and the command on Lake Erie devolved upon Captain Arthur Sinclair. In the month of July, taking with him the two large brigs, Niagara and St. Lawrence, and the Caledonia, Ariel, Scorpion, and Tigress, Captain Sinclair entered Lake Huron, and on the 4th of August failed in an attack upon the British port of Michilimacinac at the head of that lake. Having obtained intelligence that Lieutenant Miller Worsley of the British navy, with the North-west Company's schooner Nancy, was at Nattawassaga, Captain Sinclair, first despatching the St. Lawrence and Caledonia brigs, with a portion of the troops to co-operate with the American army at Fort Erie, proceeded with the remainder to attack a post deemed far less difficult of reduction than the "Gibraltar" (Michilimacinac), from which he and Colonel Croghan had just been repulsed. The Nancy was lying about two miles up the Nattawagassa, under the protection of a block-house, situated on the southeast side of the river; which here runs parallel to, and forms a narrow peninsula with the shore of Gloucester bay. This enabled Captain Sinclair to anchor his vessels within good battering distance of the block-house. A spirited cannonade was kept up between the block-house, where, besides two 24-pounder carronades on the ground, a 6-pounder was mounted, and the three American vessels outside, composed of the Niagara, mounting, as formerly stated, 18 carronades, 32-pounders, and two long 12-pounders, and the Tigress and Scorpion, mounting, between them, one long 12, and two long 24 pounders. In addition to this force, a 5½ inch howitzer, with a suitable detachment of artillery, had been landed on the peninsula. Against these 24 pieces of cannon, and upwards of 500 men, were opposed, one piece of cannon, and 23 officers and seamen.

Further resistance was in vain; and, just as Lieutenant Worsley had prepared a train, leading to the Nancy from the block-house, one of the enemy's shells burst in the latter, and both the block-house and the vessel were presently blown up. Lieutenant Worsley and his men escaped in their boat up the river; and, fortunately, the whole of the North-west Company's richly-laden canoes, bound across the lake, escaped also into French river. Having thus led to the destruction of a vessel, which the American commander had the modesty to describe as "his Britannic Majesty's schooner Nancy," Captain Sinclair departed for Lake Erie; leaving the Tigress and Scorpion to blockade the Nattawassaga, and, as that was the only route by which supplies could be readily forwarded, to starve the garrison of Michilimacinac into a surrender.

After remaining at their stations for a few days, the two American schooners took a trip to the neighbourhood of St. Josephs. Here they were discovered, on the 25th of August, by some Indians on their way to Michilimacinac. On the 31st Lieutenant Worsley and his men arrived at the garrison, bringing intelligence that the two schooners were five leagues apart. An immediate attempt to effect their capture was therefore resolved upon; and on the 1st of September, in the evening, Lieutenant Worsley and his party, composed of Midshipman Dobson, one gunner's mate, and 17 seamen, re-embarked in their boat; and Lieutenant Bulger, of the royal Newfoundland regiment, with two lieutenants, two sergeants, six corporals, and 50 rank and file, of his own corps, one hospital-mate, one bombardier, and one gunner of the royal artillery, with a 3 and 6 pounder, Major Dickson, superintendent of Indian affairs, four others of the Indian department, and three Indian chiefs, making a total of 92 persons, embarked on board three other boats. A body of Indians also accompanied the expedition in their canoes. It was sunset on the 2nd before the boats arrived at the Detour, or entrance of St. Mary's strait; and not until the next day, the 3rd, that the exact situation of the American vessels became known. At 6 P.M. the boats pulled for the nearest vessel, ascertained to be at anchor about six miles off. The Indians, who, as just stated, had quitted Michilimacinac with the expedition, remained three miles in the rear; and at 9 P.M. the schooner appeared in sight. As soon as she discovered the boats, which was not till they had approached within 100 yards of her, the American vessel opened a smart fire from her long 24-pounder and musketry. The boats, however, advanced rapidly; and, two of them boarding her on each side, Lieutenant Worsley carried, in five minutes, the United

States schooner Tigress, of one long 24-pounder on a pivot-carriage, and 28 officers and men. The British loss was two seamen killed, Lieutenant Bulger, and four or five soldiers and seamen wounded; and the American loss, three men, including one or two officers, wounded.

On the 4th, early in the morning, the prisoners were sent in one of the boats, under a guard, to Michilimacinac, and preparations were made to attack the other schooner, which was understood to be at anchor 15 miles further down. On the 5th the Scorpion was discovered working up to join her supposed consort, the American ensign and pendant being still kept flying on board the Tigress. In the evening the Scorpion anchored at the distance of about two miles from the Tigress; who, just as day was dawning on the 6th, slipped her cable, and, running down under her foresail and jib, was within ten yards of the Scorpion before any discovery was made. In five minutes more the deck of the latter was covered by the two lieutenants and their men, and the British flag was hoisted over that of the United States. The Scorpion was manned with 30 officers and men; and carried one long 24, and, in her hold, one long 12 pounder. Her loss amounted to two killed and two wounded; that of the British to one or two soldiers wounded, making the total British loss, in capturing the two vessels, amount to three killed and eight wounded. These two American " gun-boats" averaged, according to British measurement, 100 tons. They had on board abundance of shot, including some 32-pounders, and in small-arms, between them, 64 muskets and 104 cutlasses and boarding-pikes. As a proof of the value of these two schooners, now that they were afloat upon Lake Huron, their hulls and stores were appraised by the proper officers at upwards of 16,000*l.* sterling. In another point of view, they were still more valuable. Commodore Perry's victory left the Americans without an enemy to fear upon the lakes Erie and Huron; and yet do we find, still remaining on board of the four (including two that will be named presently) smallest of his nine vessels, three times as many experienced seamen, as were on board all the " very superior British fleet," which that " illustrious American commodore," after an obstinate struggle, succeeded in capturing.

On the 12th of August the three United States armed schooners, Somers, Ohio, and Porcupine, each with 35 men commanded by a lieutenant, being stationed close to Fort Erie, then in the possession of the Americans, for the purpose of flanking the British army in their approach against it, Captain

Dobbs, of the Charwell, with a detachment of 75 seamen and marines from his vessel and from the Netley, Lieutenant Coples Radcliffe, lying opposite to Fort George, resolved to attempt their capture or destruction. For this purpose the seamen carried the captain's gig upon their shoulders from Queenstown to Frenchman's creek, a distance of 20 miles. From this spot, by the aid of Lieutenant-colonel Nichol, the quarter-master general of the militia, five batteaux, as well as the Charwell's gig, were got across through the woods to Lake Erie, a distance of eight miles. Two of the American schooners, the Somers and Ohio, were presently carried, sword in hand; "and the third," says Captain Dobbs, "would certainly have fallen had not the cables been cut, which made us drift to leeward of her among the rapids." It is almost impossible, without having been on the spot, to form an adequate idea of the rapidity, and of course the danger, of the Niagara stream, as it approaches the cataract.

The British loss was Lieutenant Radcliffe and one seaman killed, and four seamen wounded; the loss on the part of the Americans one seaman killed, three officers and four seamen wounded. When it is considered that, with the Porcupine, the Americans had a force of 92 lbs. weight of metal and 105 men, to oppose to 75 men, without any artillery whatever, the exploit of Captain Dobbs and his brave followers deserves every commendation. It proved that British seamen could find expedients to capture two out of three fine American armed schooners, in waters, where the gig and five batteaux of the conquerors were the only British vessels afloat.

About the middle of October, when the season for cruising on Lake Ontario was almost over, the British succeeded in getting ready their large ship the St. Lawrence, of 2305 tons, and intended to mount 102 guns. A "peep into Kingston," by one of the American light vessels, gave Commodore Chauncey timely notice of this, and he retired to Sackett's Harbour to stir out no more. The Americans now commenced building two "74-gun ships," each of whose broadsides would have about equalled that of the St. Lawrence. To meet this on the part of the British, a 74 was commenced, and a frigate, like the Princess Charlotte, constructed; but, before the lakes were open in the ensuing spring, peace came, otherwise, there is no saying whether the building mania would not have continued, until there was scarcely room on the lake for working the ships.

During the months of June and July, the Quebec papers were

continually announcing the arrival of transports from the Garonne with troops; and those troops, too, such as, under the Marquis of Wellington, had hitherto carried all before them. So satisfied now were the Americans, that Sackett's Harbour would be the first point of attack, even if Sir George had to cross the St. Lawrence, and march overland, that General Izard, on the 1st of September, broke up his encampment at Plattsburg, and marched there with between 3000 and 4000 regulars. If anything could raise British courage beyond its accustomed height, it was, surely, the emulation which existed between the troops that had recently arrived from the Peninsula, and those that had been originally allotted for the defence of the Canadas; the one, highly jealous of the reputation they had already gained, the other, equally so, of their local experience, and of the dressing they had several times given to superior numbers of the very same enemy, against whom the two united bodies were now about to act. Under these circumstances, will any one, except an American, say, that 11,000 of such troops would not have beaten, upon any ground where evolutions could be practised, 17,000 of the best troops which the United States could have brought into the field? A British army, then, of 11,000 men, with a most excellent train of artillery, commanded in chief by Sir George Prevost, and, under him, by officers of the first distinction in the service, left their camp at Chambly, "with a view," says the American official account, "of conquering the country, as far as Crown point and Ticonderoga" on Lake Champlain.

In the early part of August the British naval force on Lake Champlain consisted of the brig-sloop Linnet, of 16 long 12-pounders and 80 men and boys, commanded by Captain Daniel Pring, cutter Chubb, of 10 carronades, 18-pounders, and one long 6-pounder, and 40 men and boys, Lieutenant James M'Ghie, cutter Finch, of six 18-pounder carronades, one medium or columbiad 18-pounder, and one 6-pounder, Lieutenant William Finch, and 10 gun-boats, mounting between them two long 24, and five long 18 pounders, and six 32-pounder carronades, and manned with 294 men and boys, of whom 30 were British seamen: the remainder, as was the case with the greater proportion of the crews of the three larger vessels, consisted of privates of the 39th regiment and Canadian militia, very few of which latter could speak a word of English. This would make a total of 48 guns and 444 men and boys; the greater part, as already stated regular soldiers, and Canadian **militia**.

The American force consisted of the ship Saratoga, mounting on a flush deck eight long 24-pounders, 12 carronades, 32-pounders, and six carronades, 42-pounders; total 26 guns, with a complement of 250 as her regular crew, besides a detachment of the 15th United States infantry acting as marines, making a total of at least 300 men, commanded by Commodore Thomas Macdonough; brig Eagle, Captain Robert Henley, of eight long 18-pounders and 12 carronades, 32-pounders; total 20 guns, and 142 men as her regular crew, and at least 160, including her acting marines; schooner Ticonderoga, Lieutenant-commandant Stephen Cassin, of eight long 12, and four long 18 pounders and five 32-pounder carronades; total 17 guns, and a regular crew of 115, with about 15 acting marines, or 130 men in the whole; sloop Preble, of seven long nine-pounders and 45 men, and 10 gun-boats, mounting between them six long 24, six medium 18, and four long 12 pounders, and manned with 346 men; making a grand total of 86 guns and 981 men, the whole of the latter, excepting the regular troops (about 83 in number) acting as marines, seamen from the American ships-of-war laid up at New London and other ports of the Atlantic frontier.

On the 25th of August a ship, which had been hastily constructed by the British, was launched in the vicinity of Isle-aux-Noirs; and on the 3rd of September Captain George Downie, late of the Montreal on Lake Ontario, accompanied by his first-lieutenant, arrived to take the command of the Confiance, as the new ship was named, as well as of the British squadron on Lake Champlain: which squadron, as soon as the Confiance could be armed and manned, Sir George Prevost had directed to co-operate with the British army, in the intended attack upon Plattsburg and the American shipping lying near it. On the same day that he arrived, Captain Downie detached Captain Pring with the flotilla of gun-boats to protect the left flank of the army; and on the 4th Captain Pring took quiet possession of Isle de la Motte, and constructed a battery of three long 18-pounders to support his position abreast of Little Chazy, where the supplies of the army were ordered to be landed.

The approach of Sir George's army, by Odelltown, to the line of demarcation, was the signal for Major-general Macomb, with the few regulars of General Izard's army left under his command to retire from the neighbourhood of the lines towards Plattsburg; and the latter's abandoned camp was entered by Sir George Prevost on the 3rd of September. From this position the British left division, of about 7000 men, composed of all but the reserve and heavy artillery, moved forward on the 4th, and halted on the 5th, within eight miles of Plattsburg; having taken four days to advance 25 miles along the lake-shore. On the 6th, early in the morning, the left division proceeded on its march, Major-general Power's, or the right column, advancing by the Beckmantown road; and Major-general Brisbane's column, except one wing of De Meuron's regiment, left to keep up the communication with the main body, taking the road that runs parallel to Lake Champlain. At a bridge crossing a creek that intersects this road, the American general had stationed a small force, with two field-pieces, to abattis and obstruct the way. In the meanwhile, the right column, meeting with no impediments to its progress, passed rapidly on, 700 American militia, upon whom, says General Macomb, "the British troops did not deign to fire, except by their flankers and advanced patroles," retreating before it. The rapid advance of Major-general Power secured Major-general Brisbane from any further opposition than such as he might experience from the American gun-boats and galleys. Notwithstanding a heavy fire from their long 24 and 12 pounders, the bridge across the creek was presently reconstructed, and the left column moved forward upon Plattsburg.

The village of Plattsburg contains about 70 houses and stores, and is situated on both side of the river Saranac, close to its confluence with Lake Champlain. The statement in the British official account, that "the column entered Plattsburg," must, therefore, be understood to mean, either the township of that name, or the small portion of the village which was situated on the north side of the stream. It was to the south side that General Macomb, after taking up the planks of the bridge, had retreated; and it was on the elevated ridge of land forming its banks, that the Americans had erected their works. General Macomb mentions three forts, and two blockhouses strongly fortified. One of the latter mounted three guns; and we believe there were from 15 to 20 guns in all, most of them of heavy caliber. There was, also, a large new stone-mill, four stories high, which formed an excellent position for the American riflemen. It was on the evening of the 6th, that the British left division arrived on the north bank of the Saranac. "But," says an American writer, "not all the galleys aided by the armament of the whole flotilla, which then lay opposite Plattsburg, under Commodore Macdonough, could have prevented the capture of Macomb's army, after its passage of the Saranac, had Sir George Prevost pushed his whole force upon the margin of that stream. Like General Drummond, at Erie, he made a pause, in full view of the unfinished works of the Americans, and consumed five days in erecting batteries, and throwing up breastworks, for the protection of his approaches. Of this interval the American general did not fail to avail himself; and kept his troops constantly employed in finishing his line of redoubts." [1] The reader need scarcely be reminded, that this is the same Plattsburg, at which Colonel Murray, with 1000 troops, landed; the river on which it stands, the same Saranac, up which the colonel ascended, three miles, to burn the enemy's barracks; and that those barracks were burnt, while an American regular army, more than twice as strong as General Macomb's, lay encamped in the neighbourhood.[2]

Sir George Prevost knew perfectly well that the Confiance, although afloat and with Captain Downie's pendant flying on board of her, had scarcely men enough to get the rigging over her mast-heads, and that the shipwrights were still at work upon her hull; but he, notwithstanding, urged Captain Downie, both by letter and through the officers of his staff, to co-operate with the army. At length came an insinuation, that "the commander-in-chief hoped Captain Downie allowed himself to be delayed by nothing but the state of the wind." The effects of this upon a spirit like that of the gallant first-lieutenant of the Seahorse in July, 1808,[1] may be partly conceived. On the 8th the wind proved fair; and immediately the Confiance and her consorts moved from Isle-aux-Noirs into Lake Champlain, and anchored abreast of the main body of the British army, to wait until the whole of her crew had arrived from Quebec, and until the carpenters had fitted the ring-bolts for her guns, and the joiners completed the magazine for the reception of the powder, without which those guns could be of no use. On the 9th Captain Downie received a draught of marines, numbering, with a few artillerymen and soldiers, 86 men; and, in the course of that and the following day, the whole of the petty officers and seamen intended for the ship came on board; forming a total of 270 officers, seamen, marines, and boys. The seamen, among whom were 19 foreigners, were men of inferior quality and bad character; who, as the term is, had "volunteered" from their respective ships, or, in plain words, had been dismissed from them in disgrace. Some, indeed, had been liberated from irons, for the very purpose of manning Captain Downie's ship. Ten

[1] Sketches of the War, p. 319.   [2] See p. 115.   [3] See vol. iii., p. 422.

ships-of-war at Quebec had furnished 118 of these "volunteers;" and some transports had lent 25 of their men. The men of the Confiance, therefore, were all strangers to each other and to their officers; and Captain Downie was acquainted with no officer on board his ship but his first-lieutenant, and the latter with none of the other officers.

On the 10th, just as the last draught of the motley crew we have described was ascending the side of the Confiance, while the loud clank of the builder's hammer was still sounding in all parts of the ship, while the guns were being breeched and pointed through the ports, and while powder, for the want of a place fitted for its reception, was lying in a boat alongside, an officer from Sir George Prevost came to solicit the instant co-operation of the British squadron. Relying upon the assurance now given by the commander-in-chief, that the army should attack the works of Plattsburg, while the squadron was attacking the American ships lying in front of them, Captain Downie, in spite of the unprepared state of the Confiance, consented to go into action on the following morning. It was then agreed, that the Confiance, when rounding Cumberland head, which forms the northernmost point of Plattsburg bay, should scale her guns; and that, at that instant, the column of attack should advance to storm the American works. As it could not well be said, that the Confiance mounted any guns at all, until they were placed upon her broadside, and as that had only just been done when the ship was thus on the eve of going into action with a greatly superior force, we have deferred until now giving any account of the Confiance's armament. The ship mounted 26 long 24-pounders on the main deck, also two 32-pounder carronades through her bow, and two of the same through her stern ports. Upon the poop were mounted, *en barbette*, four 24-pounder carronades, and upon the topgallant forecastle, in the same ineffective manner, two 24-pounder carronades, and one long 24 on a traversing-carriage; making a total of 37 guns.

On the 11th at daylight, with the carpenters still working at his ship, Captain Downie made the signal to weigh. This was promptly complied with; and the Confiance, Linnet, Chubb, Finch, and 10 gun-boats, made sail towards Plattsburg bay. At 7 A.M. the American squadron was seen at anchor, in line ahead, abreast of the encampment of General Macomb's army. The Eagle, flanked by five gun-boats, was in the van: then the Saratoga; next to her the Ticonderago: and lastly the Preble, also flanked by five gun-boats. It was Captain Downie's intention to lay the Confiance athwart the hawse of the Saratoga; that the Linnet, supported by the Chubb, should engage the Eagle, and the Finch, with the gun-boats, the Ticonderago and Preble. While the squadron was lying-to, that the commanding officer of each vessel might be informed of the plan of attack, Commodore Downie caused it to be made known to the different crews, that the army would co-operate with them. This was necessary, to inspire the men with confidence, in attacking a force so evidently superior. Lieutenant John Robertson, first of the Confiance, went to her crew while at their quarters, and explained particularly to the men the nature of the co-operation, as he had understood it from Captain Downie.

At 7 h. 40 m. A.M. the British squadron filled and made sail in order of battle; and the moment the Confiance, the leading ship, arrived abreast of Cumberland head, she scaled her guns as had been agreed upon; but the signal was not answered from the army. Sir George Prevost did, however, direct a signal to be made: it was for the army "to cook," instead of to fight; to give the men their breakfasts, instead of to deprive the enemy of the opportunity of taking his. To the honour of the soldiers and the officers in general, they all panted to rush forward; but, in truth, a third part of the troops would have done all that was required, and in two hours from the time the Confiance scaled her guns, would have given a victory to both army and navy, instead of a flight to one, and a defeat to the other. Captain Downie now discovered, too late, the mistake into which his confidence had led him. The Confiance was already in the enemy's bay, and almost within gun-shot of his squadron.

At 8 A.M., favoured by a very light air, amounting almost to a calm, the American row-galleys and gun-boats commenced upon the Confiance a heavy and galling fire. Having by this means had two anchors shot from her bows, the Confiance, at 8 h. 10 m., was obliged to anchor within 400 yards upon the beam, instead of, as had been intended, close athwart the bows, of the Saratoga. The Linnet and Chubb soon afterwards took their allotted stations, something short of that distance; but the cutter presently had her main-boom shot away, and, drifting within the enemy's line, was compelled to surrender. The Finch had the misfortune, while proceeding to her station, to strike on a reef of rocks off Crabb island; where there was an American battery of two guns, which fired at the Finch, and wounded two of her men, the only loss she sustained. All the gun-boats, except the Murray, Beresford, and another, abandoned the object assigned them; that is, ran away, almost as soon as the action commenced. Within 15 minutes after the commencement of the action, fell the British commanding officer, the brave, the lamented Captain Downie. The way in which he met his death is of too extraordinary a nature to be passed over. A shot from the Saratoga struck one of the Confiance's 24-pounders, and threw it completely off the carriage against Captain Downie, who was standing close in the rear of it. He received the blow upon his right groin, and, although signs of life remained for a few minutes, never spoke afterwards. No part of his skin was broken: a black mark, about the circumference of a small plate, was the only visible injury. His watch was found flattened, with the hands pointing to the hour, minute, and second at which the fatal blow had been given.

At length, the greater part of the Confiance's guns on the larboard side having been disabled, Lieutenant Robertson, now the commanding officer, made an effort to wind the ship round, to bring her starboard broadside to bear; but, owing to the loss of her two anchors and the shameful flight of the gun-boats, this object could not be effected. Having nearly the whole of her guns on the engaged side in a similar state to those of the Confiance, the Saratoga let go a stern anchor, cut her bower cable, and, with great ease, winded herself round, so as to bring her larboard broadside to bear upon her antagonist, now lying in a defenceless state; and who, at 10 h. 30 m., after receiving several raking broadsides, hauled down her colours; thus affording the extraordinay instance of a ship being launched, fitted, fought, and captured, within the short space of 16 days.

A few minutes before the Confiance surrendered, unable to withstand the heavy and well-directed fire of the Linnet, the Eagle cut her cable and took up a fresh position between the Ticonderoga and Preble. The attention of the American commodore was now directed to the Linnet; who, although greatly disabled, continued the action with spirit. At 10 h. 45 m. A.M, after having, for upwards of 10 minutes, withstood the whole united force of the American squadron, the Linnet hauled down her colours. As the Finch had been compelled to strike before, and the Chubb, from having her cable cut, very soon after, the action had commenced; and as the gun-boats had all effected their escape, the surrender of the Linnet gave a complete victory to the American squadron.

The brigade of the British army, which was stationed near the banks of the Saranac, on the opposite side of which, as already stated, lay the army, if it deserved such a name, of General Macomb, was commanded by Major-general Brisbane. It appears that, while the action between the squadrons was going on, this portion of the British army, either mistaking or disregarding Sir George's cooking signal, attacked the American works, and not only crossed the Saranac, but brought away some prisoners. This showed at once the practicability of the thing, and only wanted the quiescence, temporary or final, of the commander-in-chief, and the British army would have gained a victory in spite of Sir George Prevost; but who, nevertheless, with the assistance of "Mr. Secretary Brenton" in penning the despatch, would have got all the credit of it. Unfortunately, some one acquainted Sir George with what was going on at the banks of the Saranac; and, learning at the same time that the Confiance had struck her colours, he sent orders to Major-general Brisbane to desist from beating the poor Americans, to leave them in quiet possession of their half-carried works, and hasten after him out of the enemy's territory.

So certain was Commodore Macdonough, that, in a few minutes, the batteries at Plattsburg would be turned against the American squadron, that, before he took formal possession of the prizes, he removed his ships out of gun-shot. Lieutenant Robertson was then conveyed on board the Saratoga, to deliver up his sword. On that occasion, Commodore Macdonough spoke to him as follows: "You owe it, sir, to the shameful conduct of your gun-boats and cutters, that you are performing this office to me; for, had they done their duty, you must have perceived, from the situation of the Saratoga, that I could hold out no longer: and indeed, nothing induced me to keep up her colours, but, seeing from the united fire of all the rest of my squadron on the Confiance, and her supported situation, that she must ultimately surrender." Here is an acknowledgment candid and honourable in the extreme. Can this be the "T. Macdonough," whose signature appears to the two American official accounts of the action?

The loss on board the Confiance amounted to 41 killed, including her captain and another officer, and about 60, including one officer, wounded. The Linnet had her second-lieutenant, boatswain, and eight seamen killed, one midshipman and 13 seamen and marines wounded; the Chubb, six seamen and marines killed, one officer and 15 seamen and marines wounded; and the Finch two seamen and marines wounded; total 57 killed and 92 wounded. The loss on the American side has been officially reported as follows: Saratoga, 28 killed and 29 wounded; Eagle, 13 killed and 20 wounded; Ticonderago, six killed and six wounded; and Preble and the gun-boats, five killed and three wounded; total 52 killed and 58 wounded: a tolerable proof that the British, notwithstanding the many disadvantages under which they laboured, had made a good use of their ill-fitted guns.

Now for a comparative statement of the force engaged in this, viewed in its consequences on both sides of the Atlantic, very important lake action. As the Finch grounded opposite an American battery before the engagement between the squadrons commenced, we shall exclude her from the estimate; and so we shall one-half of the British gun-boat force. Only three of the 10 gun-boats, indeed, came near enough to engage, while all the American gun-boats are admitted to have participated in the action. On the American side, we shall take no notice of the armed sloops Montgomery and President, the batteries on shore, or the "militia ready to assist."

With respect to the Confiance, although she mounted 37 guns, 17 only of them, as has already been shown, could be presented in broadside; and even four of these, on account of there being only a ridge-rope, or rail, along either side of the poop and topgallant forecastle, were disabled after the first discharge. Having no gun-locks on board (they being in the Junon frigate, which did not arrive at Quebec in time), Captain Downie attempted to substitute carronade-locks: which he contrived to fasten to the guns by means of copper hoops. But the plan was not found to answer, and matches were resorted to. Determined that the British should derive no advantage from publishing this fact, an American paper subjoins to an exaggerated account of the Confiance's force in guns, "with locks."

We have enumerated the guns of the Confiance at 37; but we should have stated, that the ship had two long 18-pounders among the ballast in the hold. These Commodore Macdonough, in his official letter, places on the "berth deck;" and in his statement of comparative force, actually carries them out as part of the Confiance's "39 guns." The substance of the following statement having appeared before the American, as well as the British public more than nine years ago, and being, as far as we know, to this hour uncontradicted, we again submit it as the actual

Comparative Force of the Combatants.

		Captain Downie.	Capt. Macdonough.
Vessels	No.	8	14
Broadside-guns	{ No.	38	52
	{ lbs.	765	1194
Crew	Agg. No.	537	950
Size	tons	1426	2540

This, without bringing in aid the shameful abandonment of the enterprise by the commander-in-chief of the Canadas, shows that the squadron under Commodore Downie wanted a full third of being as strong as that under Commodore Macdonough. As was to be expected, however, the Americans claimed it as a victory obtained over a decidedly superior force; and, instead of attributing the retreat of the British army of 11,000 men to the imbecility (to say no worse) of General Sir George Prevost, they ascribed it all to the superior prowess of the American army, of less than 2000 men, under General Alexander Macomb.

Unfortunately, justice was interrupted in its course by the death of Sir George, before he could be tried upon the following charges brought against him by Commodore Sir James Lucas Yeo: 1. For having, on or about the 11th of September, 1814, by holding out the expectation of a co-operation of the army, under his command, induced Captain Downie, late of his majesty's ship Confiance, to attack the American squadron on Lake Champlain, when it was highly imprudent to make such attack without the co-operation of the land forces, and for not having afforded that co-operation. 2. For not having stormed the American works on shore, at nearly the same time that the said naval action commenced, as he had given Captain Downie reason to expect. 3. For having disregarded the signal for co-operation, which had been previously agreed upon. 4. For not having attacked the enemy on shore, either during the said naval action, or after it was ended; whereby his majesty's naval squadron under the command of Captain Downie, might have been saved.

On the 28th of August, 1815, Captain Pring, and the surviving officers and crews late belonging to the British Lake Champlain squadron, were tried by court-martial on board the Gladiator at Portsmouth, and the following was the sentence pronounced: "The court having maturely weighed the evidence, is of opinion, that the capture of H. M. S. Confiance and the remainder of the squadron, by the American squadron, was principally caused by the British squadron having been urged into battle previous to its being in a proper state to meet the enemy; by the promised co-operation of the land-forces not being carried into effect, and by the pressing letters of their commander-in-chief, whereby it appears that he had on the 10th of September, 1814, only waited for the naval attack to storm the enemy's works. That the signal of the approach on the following day was made, by the scaling of the guns, as settled between Captain Downie and Major Coote; and the promised co-operation was communicated to the other officers and crews of the British squadron before the commencement of the action.

"The court, however, is of opinion, that the attack would have been attended with more effect, if a part of the gun-boats had not withdrawn themselves from the action, and others of the vessels had not been prevented by baffling winds from getting into the stations assigned them. That Captain Pring of the Linnet, and Lieutenant Robertson, who succeeded to the command of the Confiance, after the lamented fate of Captain Downie (whose conduct was marked by the greatest valour), and Lieutenant Christopher James Bell, commanding the Murray, and Mr. James Robertson, commanding the Beresford, gun-boats, who appeared to take their trial at this court-martial, conducted themselves with great zeal, bravery, and ability during the action: that Lieutenant William Hicks, commanding the Finch, also conducted himself with becoming bravery; that the other surviving officers and ship's crew, except Lieutenant M'Ghie of the Chubb, who has not appeared here to take his trial, also conducted themselves with bravery; and that Captain Pring, Lieutenant Robertson, Lieutenant Hicks, Lieutenant Bell, and Mr. James Robertson, and the rest of the surviving officers and ship's company, except Lieutenant M'Ghie, ought to be most honourably acquitted, and they are hereby most honourably acquitted, accordingly." On the 18th of the ensuing September, Lieutenant M'Ghie was put upon his trial, and the following was the sentence pronounced upon him: "The court having heard the circumstances, determined that the Chubb was not properly carried into action, nor anchored so as to do the most effectual service; by which neglect, she drifted into the line of the enemy: that it did not appear, however, that there was any want of courage in Lieutenant M'Ghie; and, therefore, the court did only adjudge him to be severely reprimanded."

Upon the American accounts we shall bestow but a few words.

Having seen the effects of Commodore Perry's puritanical epistle, Commodore Macdonough writes his letter in the same mock-religious strain: "The Almighty has been pleased to grant us a signal victory on Lake Champlain, in the capture of one frigate, one brig, and two sloops-of-war of the enemy." The Confiance a "frigate;" and the Chubb and Finch "sloops-of-war"! Yet, according to an American writer, Commodore Macdonough was "a religious man, as well as a hero, and prayed with his brave men on the morning of the victory."[1]

In the very summer preceding the Lake Champlain action, some of the American newspaper editors were blaming Commodore Chauncey for not sailing out of Sackett's Harbour, in the new ships Superior and Mohawk, after the latter had been launched nearly two, and the former upwards of three months. How did that cautious commander answer them? Why, by writing to the secretary of the American navy thus: "I need not suggest to one of your experience, that a man-of-war may appear to the eye of a landsman perfectly ready for sea when she is deficient in many of the most essential points of her armament; nor how unworthy I should have proved myself of the high trust reposed in me, had I ventured to sea in the face of an enemy of equal force, without being able to meet him in one hour after my anchor was weighed." And yet, had poor Captain Downie acted with only half this caution, his fair fame would have been tarnished, and the very service to which he belonged scoffed at, by no less a man than the governor-general of the British North American provinces.

On the 26th of September the British 74-gun ship Plantagenet, Captain Robert Lloyd, 38-gun frigate Rota, Captain Philip Somerville, and 18-gun brig-sloop Carnation, Captain George Bentham, cruising off the Western Isles, discovered at anchor in the road of Fayal the American privateer schooner General Armstrong, of seven guns, including a long 24 or 32 pounder on a traversing-carriage, and about 90 men, Captain Guy R. Champlin. Captain Lloyd sent Lieutenant Robert Faussett, in the Plantagenet's pinnace, into the port, to ascertain the force of the schooner, and to what nation she belonged. Owing to the strength of the tide, and to the circumstance of the schooner getting under way and dropping fast astern, the boat drifted nearer to her than had been intended. The American privateer hailed, and desired the boat to keep off but that was impracticable, owing to the quantity of stern-way on the schooner. The

[1] Naval Monument, p. 155.

General Armstrong then opened her fire, and, before the boat could get out of gun-shot, killed two and wounded seven of her men.

As the captain of the American privateer had now broken the neutrality of the port, Captain Lloyd determined to send in and endeavour to cut out his schooner; which had since come to again with springs close to the shore. Accordingly, at 8 P.M., the Plantagenet and Rota anchored off Fayal-road; and at 9 P.M. four boats from the Plantagenet and three from the Rota, with about 180 seamen and marines, under the command of Lieutenant William Matterface, first of the frigate, pulled in towards the road. The Carnation had been directed to cover the boats in their advance; but owing, as it appears, to the strength of the current and the intricacy of the navigation, the brig did not arrive within gun-shot of the American schooner, and therefore was not of the slightest use. At midnight, after a fatiguing pull against a strong wind and current, the boats got within hail of the General Armstrong, and received from her, and from a battery erected, with a portion of her guns, on the commanding point of land under which she had anchored, a heavy fire of cannon and musketry. In about half an hour, this fire sank two of the boats, and killed or disabled two-thirds of the party that had been detached in them. The remainder returned, and at about 2 A.M. on the 27th reached the Rota.

The loss appears to have been of the following lamentable amount: the Rota's first and third lieutenants (William Matterface and Charles R. Norman), one midshipman, and 31 seamen and marines killed, the Rota's second-lieutenant (Richard Rawle), first-lieutenant of marines (Thomas Park), purser (William Benge Basden), two midshipmen, and 81 seamen and marines wounded. Among the langridge which the Americans fired, were nails, brass buttons, knife-blades, &c.; and the consequence was, that the wounded, as on former occasions recorded in this work, suffered excruciating pain before they were cured. Soon after daylight the Carnation went into the road to destroy the privateer, but the Americans saved the British the trouble by setting fire to her themselves.

BRITISH AND FRENCH FLEETS.

Two circumstances, in the abstract for the commencement of the present year,[1] indicate the return of peace; the small number of line-of-battle cruisers in commission, and the great number of ships sold, taken to pieces, or otherwise removed from the service.[2]

The number of commissioned officers and masters, belonging to the British navy at the beginning of the year 1815, was—

Admirals	70
Vice-admirals	73
Rear-admirals	76
,, superannuated 35	
Post-captains	824
,, superannuated 39	
Commanders, or sloop-captains	762
,, superannuated 60	
Lieutenants	3211
Masters	666

And the number of seamen and marines, voted for the service of the same year, was 70,000 for three, and 90,000 for ten lunar months.[3]

On the 2nd of January, 1815, his royal highness the prince regent was pleased to advance the splendour, and to extend the limits, of the most honourable military order of the bath, "to the end that those officers who have had the opportunity of distinguishing themselves by eminent services during the late war may share in the honours of the said order, and that their

---

[1] See Appendix, Annual Abstract, No. 23. [2] See Appendix, Nos. 5 and 6.
[3] Ibid., No. 7.

names may be delivered down to remote posterity, accompanied by the marks of distinction which they have so nobly earned." The order of the bath was thenceforward to be composed of three classes. The first class was to cons.st of knights grand-crosses, and was limited to 72; of whom 12 might be persons who had rendered eminent services to the state in civil and diplomatic employments. The second class, limited to 180, exclusive of 10 foreign officers holding British commissions, was to consist of knights-commanders; and the third class of companions of the bath.

The qualifications of a companion of the bath are thus defined: "No officer shall be nominated a companion of the said most honourable order, unless he shall have received, or shall hereafter receive, a medal, or other badge of honour, or shall have been especially mentioned by name in despatches published in the London Gazette, as having distinguished himself by his valour and conduct in action against his majesty's enemies, since the commencement of the war in 1803, or shall hereafter be named in despatches published in the London Gazette, as having distinguished himself." This was all very proper; but, suppose the board of admiralty should neglect to publish in the "London Gazette" despatches, incontestably showing, that an officer had "distinguished himself by his valour and conduct in action?" For instance, had Captain Manners of the Reindeer, after having been hewed and hacked as he was, escaped the two bullets that passed through his head, would he not have deserved to be made a companion, at least, if not a knight-commander of the bath? But the account of the Reindeer's action did not appear in the Gazette: therefore Captain Manners, had he survived, would not have been officially qualified to receive an honour, designed by the sovereign for the exclusive reward of gallantry. Nay, there would have been another impediment in the way. The order descends no lower than post-captains; whereas, in the French navy, even an enseigne de vaisseau is deemed eligible to bear an order; and, in a navy-list of a recent date now before us, the names of several of that class appear with an honorary distinction affixed to them.

The sudden return to France of Napoleon from the island of Elba, again sent Lord Exmouth (the new title, which, since the 14th of May, 1814, had been deservedly bestowed upon Sir Edward Pellew) to the Mediterranean; but, before the admiral had well got to his station, the battle of Waterloo was fought, and shortly afterwards the cause of all this new commotion surrendered himself into the hands of the British. The registers and histories of the period will give the particulars of these important events. It will be enough for us to state, that Buonaparte embarked from Elba on the 24th of February in an armed brig, landed on the afternoon of the 1st of March in the gulf of Juan, near Cannes, and on the 21st entered the capital of France amidst the greetings of at least 200,000 of the inhabitants. The battle of Waterloo was fought, as need scarcely be stated, on the 18th of June; and on the 15th of July, finding he could not evade the British cruisers and get to the United States, Buonaparte surrendered himself to Captain Frederick Lewis Maitland, of the Bellerophon 74, lying in Basque roads. The latter ship immediately conveyed her important charge to Torbay, and then to Plymouth; where the Bellerophon arrived on the 26th. On the 7th of August the ex-emperor was removed to the 74-gun ship Northumberland, Captain Charles Bayne Hodgson Ross, bearing the flag of Rear-admiral Sir George Cockburn, K.C.B. On the 8th the Northumberland sailed for the island of St. Helena, and on the 16th of October there safely disembarked the "general" and his few attendants. Europe being thus freed, all parties felt seriously inclined for peace; and on the 20th of November treaties were entered into at Paris between the different powers.

During the short interval of renewed war, that had preceded the execution of these treaties, one or two naval occurrences happened, which require our notice. On the 30th of April, a few miles to the northward of the island of Ischia, the British 74-gun ship Rivoli, Captain Edward Sterling Dickson, after a running fight and brave defence of 15 minutes, captured the French 40-gun frigate Melpomène, Captain Joseph Collet, from Porto-Ferrajo to Naples, to take on board Napoleon's mother. The frigate was very much cut up in hull, masts, and rigging, and had six men killed and 28 wounded. The Rivoli, on the other hand, had only one man mortally, and a few others slightly wounded.

On the 17th of June, at daylight, the British brig-sloop Pilot, of 16 carronades, 32-pounders, and two sixes, Captain John Toup Nicolas, being about 50 miles to the westward of Cape Corse, observed and chased a ship in the east-north-east. This proved to be the French Buonapartean corvette Légère, of 20 carronades, 24-pounders, and two 12-pounders on the main deck, with four or six light guns, probably brass 6-pounders on the quarter-deck, Capitaine de frégate Nicolas Touffet. At 2 P.M.

the Légère hauled towards the Pilot, and, hoisting a tri-coloured pendant and ensign, fired a gun to windward. At 2 h. 30 m., after some manœuvring on both sides to get the weather-gage, the Pilot placed herself close on the Légère's weather-beam, and hoisted her colours. Observing that the corvette was preparing to make sail to pass ahead, and being at the same moment hailed, "Keep further from us," the Pilot fired a shot through the Légère's foresail. A broadside from the French ship immediately followed, and the action commenced within pistol-range. The brig's shot, being from her lee guns and directed low, evidently struck the hull of her opponent in quick succession, while the Légère's shot passed high, and chiefly disabled the Pilot's rigging and sails.

By 4 P.M. the fire of the Légère had considerably slackened, and at 4 h. 30 m. she hauled up her mainsail, and backed her mizentopsail, in order to drop astern. Captain Nicolas endeavoured also to shorten sail; but, having had every brace, bowline, and clue-garnet cut away, the Pilot unavoidably shot ahead. The brig, then, as the only alternative, put her helm up to fire into her opponent's bows. Of this movement on the part of the Pilot, the Légère took immediate advantage, by hauling close to the wind, and making off with all the sail she could carry. The yards of the Pilot being wholly unmanageable, her maintopgallantmast over the side, her maintopsail-yard shot away in the slings, and her stays and the chief part of her standing as well as running rigging cut away, the brig was not in a condition for an immediate pursuit. In about an hour, however, the Pilot got another maintopsail-yard across, and the sail set, and by 7 P.M. was going seven knots by the wind in chase of the French corvette, then bearing on her weather-bow about six miles distant. The Pilot continued the chase until the 18th, at daylight; when, to the mortification of all on board, it was found that the Légère had eluded them in the night.

The principal damages sustained by the Pilot have already been described: her loss amounted to one seaman killed, another mortally wounded, and her first-lieutenant (Keigwin Nicolas, the captain's brother), purser (Thomas Rowe), 10 seamen, and two marines wounded. The damages of the Légère were almost wholly in her hull and lower masts; and her loss is represented to have amounted, out of a crew that probably was not less than 170 men, to 22 killed and 79 wounded, 64 of them severely.

Even half this loss would show that the guns of the Pilot

had been ably managed; **and, indeed,** the action throughout reflects very great credit upon Captain Nicolas, his officers, and brig's company.

According to the following statement, which has appeared in print, the Pilot was better provided against accidents by shot than any of her unfortunate sister-brigs; such as the Avon, Peacock, and others. " On rejoining the Pilot (end of 1814), Captain Nicolas applied to the admiralty to have that sloop altered agreeably to a plan he proposed; and by which a shot-hole could be immediately stopped, between wind and water, in any part of the ship; and which, in the former arrangement of the store and bread rooms was impossible. This, it had been confidently asserted, was the principal cause of the capture of the Avon and Peacock. The admiralty not only complied with his request, but ordered all the 18-gun brigs then under repair at Portsmouth to be fitted on the same plan."[1] It is very probable that some improvement had also been made in the fastenings of the Pilot's carronades.

The news of the landing of Napoleon in France soon became known at the two principal islands of the French in the West Indies. At Martinique, the governor, the Comte de Vaugiraud, was favourable to Louis XVIII.; but the governor of Guadaloupe, Vice-admiral the Comte Linois, so often named in these pages, was a stanch Buonapartist. The British naval and military commanders-in-chief at the Leeward islands were Rear-admiral Sir Philip Charles Durham, K.C.B., and Lieutenant-general Sir James Leith. Some time in the month of June, at the request of the Comte de Vaugiraud, a body of British troops landed at Martinique, to aid him in preserving the island for King Louis; and in the month of August, Sir Philip Durham and Sir James Leith, assisted by the French Royalist comte, landed a body of troops on the island of Guadaloupe. On the 10th of August, after a skirmish, in which the British army lost 16 killed and about 50 wounded, the Comte Linois surrendered the island by capitulation, and was afterwards, with his adjutant-general, conveyed to France by virtue of one of the articles of the treaty.

The treaty of peace between France and the allies, which was signed at Paris on the 30th of May, 1814, and interrupted for a short time as has already been briefly noticed, was again signed at Paris on the 20th of November, 1815. Of this treaty, it will be only necessary for us to state that, by the 8th article, France

[1] Naval Chronicle, vol. xl., p. 427.

received back from Great Britain (not the first time that the latter has ceded by the pen what she had won by the sword) all her colonies, fisheries, factories, and establishments of every kind, as they were possessed by her on the 1st of January, 1792, in the seas, or on the continents, of America, Africa, and Asia; except Tobago and Sainte Lucie, and the Isle of France, Isle Rodrigue, and the Sechelles.

Light Squadrons and Single Ships.

In our account of the unfortunate "demonstration" before the city of Baltimore, we mentioned, as one cause of the abandonment of the enterprise, and of the tepidness with which it had been conducted, an "ulterior object" in the view of the naval commander-in-chief. The ulterior object was the city of New Orleans, the capital of the state of Louisiana. It stands upon the left bank of the river Mississippi, 105 miles, following the stream, and 90 miles, in a direct line, from its mouth. The population of the city, in 1814, was estimated at 23,242 persons. The line of maritime invasion extends from Lake Pontchartrain, on the east, to the river Têche, on the west, intersected by several bays, inlets, and rivers, which furnish avenues of approach to the metropolis. But the flatness of the coast is everywhere unfavourable for the debarkation of troops; and the bays and inlets being all obstructed by shoals or bars, no landing can be effected, but by boats, except up the Mississippi; and that has a bar at its mouth, which shoals to 13 or 14 feet water. There were not, it is true, any American 74s, or 60-gun frigates, building or lying blockaded at New Orleans; but those who suggested the expedition well knew that, as the cotton crops of Louisiana, and of the Mississippi territory, had been for some years in accumulation, the city warehouses contained merchandise to an immense amount. Indeed, considering that New Orleans was the emporium of the annually increasing productions of a great portion of the western states of the republic, the enormous sum of 3,000,000*l.* was perhaps not an over-estimate of what, in the event of even a temporary possession of the city, would have been shared by the captors.

Before we say the little we mean to say on the subject of the attack upon New Orleans, an unsuccessful enterprise upon a small scale in the vicinity, and which, according to chronological order, should have been included in the preceding year's narrative, requires to be briefly noticed. On the 12th of September, 1814, early in the morning, Captain the Hon. Henry William

Percy of the British 20-gun ship Hermes, having under his orders the 20-gun ship Carron, Captain the Hon. Robert Churchill Spencer, and 18-gun brig-sloops Sophie and Childers, Captains Nicholas Lockyer and John Brand Umfreville, anchored off the coast of West Florida, about six miles to the eastward of Mobile-point, for the purpose of making an attack upon Fort Bowyer situated on that point, and mounting altogether 28 guns, including 11 long 32 and 24 pounders. The ships afterwards got under way and stood towards Mobile-point; but, owing to the narrowness of the channel and the intricacy of the navigation, they did not arrive until the afternoon of the 15th in the neighbourhood of the fort.

The Hermes at last gained a station, within musket-shot distance; the Sophie, Carron, and Childers anchoring in a line astern of her. Previously to this, a detachment of 60 marines and 120 Indians, with a 5½-inch howitzer, under the orders of Major Edward Nicolls, had disembarked on the peninsula. Sixty of the Indians, under Lieutenant Castle, were immediately detached, to secure the pass of Bonsecours, 27 miles to the eastward of the fort. The great distance at which the Carron and Childers had unavoidably anchored confined the effective cannonade, on the part of the British, to the Hermes and Sophie; nor was the fire of the latter of much use, as, owing to the rottenness of her timbers, and her defective equipment, her carronades drew the bolts, or turned over at every fire. The Hermes, before she had fired many broadsides, having had her cable cut, was carried away by the current, and presented her head to the fort. In that position the British ship remained from 15 to 20 minutes, while the raking fire from the fort kept sweeping the men from her deck. Shortly afterwards the Hermes grounded, directly in front of the fort. Every means were now used to get the ship afloat, but without effect. All the boats were destroyed except one; and, with that one, Captain Percy removed to the Sophie the whole of his surviving crew, and then set the ship on fire. The Hermes and Sophie alone sustained any loss. The first had 25 men killed and 24 wounded; the other six killed and 16 wounded; total, with one marine killed on shore, 32 killed and 40 wounded. The Americans acknowledged a loss of only four killed and four wounded.

On the 8th of December, Vice-admiral Cochrane, in the Tonnant, with several other ships, arrived and anchored off the Chandeleur islands. On the same day two American gun-boats fired at the 38-gun frigate Armide, Captain Edward

Thomas Troubridge, as, accompanied by the Seahorse frigate and Sophie brig, she was passing down, within the chain of small islands, that run parallel to the shore from Mobile towards Lake Borgne. Three other gun-boats were presently discovered cruising in the lake. On the 10th, 11th, and 12th, the remainder of the men-of-war and troop-ships arrived; the 74s anchoring off Chandeleur islands, and the frigates and smaller vessels between Cat island and the main, not far from the entrance to Lake Borgne. The bayou Catalan, or Bienvenu, at the head of Lake Borgne, being the contemplated point of disembarkation, the distance from the anchorage at Cat island to the bayou 62 miles, and the principal means of transport open boats, it became impossible that any movement of the troops could take place until these gun-boats were destroyed. It was also an object to get possession of them in a serviceable state, that they might assist, as well in transporting the troops, as in the attack of any of the enemy's forts in the route. Accordingly on the night of the 12th, 42 launches, armed with 24, 18, and 12 pounder carronades, and three unarmed gigs, carrying altogether about 980 seamen and marines, under the orders of Captain Lockyer, assisted by Captains Henry Montresor and Samuel Roberts, of the brig-sloop Manly and bomb-vessel Meteor, in three divisions, each commanded by a captain in the order named, pushed off from the Armide.

The American gun-boats, which were the object of attack, consisted of No. 156, mounting one long 24-pounder on a traversing-carriage, four 12-pounder carronades, and four swivels, with 41 men on board, commanded by Lieutenant-commandant Thomas Ap Catesby Jones; No. 23, mounting one long 32-pounder on a traversing-carriage, six long 6-pounders, two 5-inch howitzers and four swivels, with 39 men on board, commanded by Lieutenant Isaac M'Keene; No. 162, one long 24-pounder, four 6-pounders and four swivels, with 35 men, commanded by Lieutenant Robert Spedden; Nos. 5 and 163, each armed with the same carriage-guns No. 23, the first with 36 men, commanded by sailing-master John D. Ferris, the other with 31 men, commanded by sailing-master George Ulick; schooner Seahorse, of one 6-pounder and 14 men, sailing-master William Johnson; and sloop Alligator, of one 4-pounder and eight men; sailing-master Richard S. Sheppard. We have taken the number of men from the American official account: but Captain Lockyer's letter makes the number greater. And, as Lieutenant Jones did certainly misstate the force of his little squadron in guns, there is every probability that he also underrated the number of his men.

On the 13th, at 10 A.M., from his anchorage at the Malheureux islands, Lieutenant Jones discovered the boats advancing towards Passe Christian, as he supposed, to disembark troops. He immediately detached the Seahorse to bay St. Louis, to destroy the stores there; and at 3 h. 30 m. P.M., when the flood-tide made, got under way with the remaining vessels and stood towards the Petites-Coquilles. At about 3 h. 45 m. Captain Lockyer despatched some boats to cut out the Seahorse, who had moored herself advantageously under the protection of two 6-pounders mounted on a commanding point. It appears that, after sustaining a very destructive fire for nearly half an hour, the boats were repulsed; considering his position untenable against a greater force, Mr. Johnson set fire to his vessel and the warehouses containing the stores, and the whole were consumed.

On the 14th, at 1 A.M., Lieutenant Jones moored his five principal gun-vessels with springs on their cables and boarding-netting triced up, in a close line abreast, athwart the narrow channel called Malheureux-island passage, and made every preparation to give the British boats a warm reception. At about 9 h. 30 m. A.M., observing the Alligator trying to rejoin her five consorts at anchor, Captain Lockyer detached Captain Roberts with a few boats to take her. This was speedily accomplished without much opposition. Having arrived within long gun-shot of the enemy, and the men having pulled 36 miles, a great part of the way against a strong current, Captain Lockyer brought the boats to a grapnel and allowed the crews to take their breakfasts. This done, at about 10 h. 30 m. A.M. the boats weighed, and took again to their oars; pulling against a strong current of at least three knots an hour, and being exposed all the while to a heavy and destructive fire of round and grape from the long guns of the American flotilla.

At about noon Captain Lockyer and Lieutenant George Pratt, in the second barge of the Seahorse, closed with the gun-boat of the American commodore; and, after an obstinate struggle, in which the greater part of the officers and men in the boat were either killed or wounded, including among the wounded the captain himself severely, and Lieutenant Pratt mortally, succeeded in boarding her. Seconded, then, by the Seahorse's first barge, commanded by midshipman George Robert White, and by the boats of the Tonnant under Lieutenant James Barnwell

Tattnall, the British soon carried the gun-boat. Lieutenant Tattnall had his boat sunk alongside; but, getting on board another, gallantly pushed on to the attack of the remaining four gun-vessels. Upon these the guns of No. 156 were now turned; and, in the course of five minutes, with the assistance of the second and third divisions of boats under Captains Montresor and Roberts, they were all secured.

The loss on the British side was extremely severe, occasioned, except in the instance of Captain Lockyer's boat and those already named as supporting him in the attack upon No. 256, by the heavy fire opened upon the boats in their tedious advance against the current. Three midshipmen (Thomas W. Moore, John Mills, and Henry Symons), 13 seamen, and one private marine were killed, and one captain (Nicholas Lockyer), four lieutenants (William Gilbert Roberts, John Franklin, Henry Gladwell Etough, and George Pratt, the latter mortally), one lieutenant of marines (James Uniacke), three master's mates (Mark Pettel, James Hunter, and John Sudbury), seven midshipmen (John O'Reilly, Robert Uniacke, Peter Drummond, George Ward Cole, William Grove White, David M'Kenzie, and ——— Pilkington, the latter mortally), 50 seamen, and 11 private marines wounded; total, 17 killed and 77 wounded. The loss on board the American flotilla was comparatively trifling, amounting to six men killed and 35 wounded, including among the latter Lieutenant Jones, the commanding officer, who conducted himself with great bravery. For the gallantry which they displayed on the occasion, Captains Lockyer, Montresor, and Roberts were deservedly made post; and some of the lieutenants and midshipmen also received a step in rank.

The obstacle to a passage through the lakes being now removed, the disembarkation of the troops commenced. On the 16th the first division, consisting of the 85th regiment, landed at Isle-aux-Poix, a small swampy spot, at the mouth of the Pearl river, about 30 miles from the anchorage, and nearly the same distance from the bayou Catalan, or Bienvenu, intended as the point of disembarkation. Various causes delayed the arrival of the boats at the fishermen's village, near the entrance of the bayou, until midnight on the 22nd; at which time the advance, consisting in all of 1688 men, under the command of Colonel Thornton of the 85th regiment, commenced ascending the bayou Mazaut, or principal branch of the Bienvenu; and, at 4 A.M. on the 23rd, landed at the extremity of Villeré's canal, running from the Mazaut towards the Mississippi. We must not, however, trench upon the province of the military historian. We shall, therefore, merely state, that on the 8th of January, 1815, an unsuccessful attack was made by the British army, under Major-general Sir Edward Pakenham, upon the strongly fortified position of the American Major-general Jackson; and that the loss, on the part of the former, amounted to the enormous total, in killed, wounded, and prisoners of nearly 2000 men, including among the killed the brave commander-in-chief. The full details of the action have already appeared in a work devoted exclusively to the subject of the military operations of the late American war; and to that, on account more particularly of the quantity of naval matter yet to be included in this volume, we must beg to refer the reader.[1]

Early in the month of December, Rear-admiral Cockburn, in the Albion, from Bermuda, bringing with him the Orlando frigate and some smaller vessels, arrived in the Chesapeake, but merely to carry away the colonial marines; with whom, on the 14th, the rear-admiral steered towards Amelia Island, in East Florida; having left orders for Captain Barrie to follow, with the Dragon, Hebrus, and Regulus. Captain Barrie accordingly departed soon afterwards, leaving a few frigates and sloops in the Chesapeake; and on the 10th of January arrived off Cumberland island, the southernmost of the chain along the coast of Georgia, and separated by Cumberland-sound from Amelia island.

Rear-admiral Cockburn not having yet arrived, Captain Philip Somerville of the 38-gun frigate Rota, as the senior officer, determined upon employing the two companies of the 2nd West-India regiment, and the detachments of royal marines which had recently arrived on that coast, in a combined attack upon the frontier-town of the state of Georgia, St. Mary's, situated a few miles up the river of that name, dividing the United States from East Florida. On the 13th an attack, with about 700 troops, marines, and seamen, under the command of Captain Barrie, was made on the fort, or key, to the entrance of the river, at Point Petre. This fort mounted two 24, two 18, one 9, and two brass 6 pounders; from which, however, scarcely a single discharge was made, ere the garrison abandoned the post, and fled to the woods in the rear. On the 14th, the combined forces, accompanied by the bomb-vessels Devastation and Terror, Captains Thomas Alexander and John Sheridan, ascended the river to St. Mary's. Contrary to expectation, here, also, no resistance

[1] James's Military Occurrences, vol. ii., p. 355.

was made; and the town, the shipping in the harbour, and the merchandise in the stores, were taken quiet possession of. Soon afterwards an expedition of boats went a considerable distance further up the river, and brought down' the Countess of Harcourt Indiaman, which had been captured and carried in there by a Charlestown privateer; also a beautiful gun-boat, named the Scorpion, a present from the town of St. Mary's to the United States.

On the 15th of January, Rear-admiral Cockburn, who had been blown off the coast by strong north-west gales, arrived and took the command; and on the 22nd, after removing the guns, and destroying the fort and barracks, at Point Petre, the British descended the river to Cumberland island; of which immediate possession was taken. The troops and marines were here encamped; and the rear-admiral established his head-quarters at a very large house, surrounding it with the ordnance brought from Point Petre. On the 22nd of February eight launches, two pinnaces, and one gig, containing 186 officers, seamen, and marines, under the command of Captain Phillott, of the Primrose, assisted by Captain Bartholomew, of the Erebus, ascended the St. Mary's river, without opposition, 120 miles; when a heavy fire of musketry, opening upon them from each side, compelled the British to retreat. While daylight lasted, a spirited fire was kept up by the boats; but, unfortunately, after dark, the men could not be restrained from firing, by which they exposed themselves to the view of the enemy. The river, in some parts, was so narrow, that a couple of stout trees, many of which were on the banks, felled and thrown across, would have completely cut off the retreat of the boats. That not having been done, the boats got back to the island, with four killed, and 25 wounded, including among the latter the two captains; also lieutenant of marines John Fraser, and midshipmen James Everingham and Jonathan Haworth Peel.

Rear-admiral Cockburn remained at his fortified house on Cumberland island, awaiting the arrival of some troops, to aid in making an attack upon the town of Savannah in Georgia; when, on the 25th of February, the American general in the vicinity apprised him that peace had been concluded between the United States and Great Britain. Such was the fact. The treaty had been signed at Ghent on the 24th of December, 1814, and was ratified by the President at Washington on the 18th of February, 1815. Of its terms, we shall merely say, that "Free trade and sailors' rights," the avowed object of the war, remained precisely in the same undefined state, as before it was declared by Mr. Madison and his senate. "Canada," said an American writer at the early part of the war, "must be conquered, or we shall stand disgraced in the eyes of the world. It is a rod held over our heads; a fortress which haughtily frowns upon our country, and from which are disseminated throughout the land the seed of disaffection, sedition, and treason. The national safety and honour and glory are lost, if we do not win this splendid prize." And yet, in spite of Sir George Prevost and his acts, Canada remained unconquered. Although an end had been put to hostile operations on shore, we have still two or three naval actions to record.

We formerly stated, that Commodore Decatur had removed with his crew on board the President frigate at New York. This ship, like the United States and Constitution, had made some reduction in her armament: she had landed two of her 42-pounder carronades; which, we believe, were put on board the brig-sloop the Syren, then fitting for sea in the port. The American government being still determined upon an expedition to the East Indies, a squadron, consisting of the President, Peacock, and Hornet, with the Macedonian and Tom Bowline brigs, laden with stores for their use, was ordered to proceed to the bay of Bengal. On the night of the 18th of November the Hornet, which had been left at New London as a guard-ship, succeeded in eluding the blockading force, and reached New York.

The British squadron, which towards the close of the year 1814 cruised off the port of New York, was commanded by Captain John Hayes, of the 56-gun ship Majestic, who had under his orders the 40-gun frigate Endymion, Captain Henry Hope, and the 38-gun frigate Pomone, Captain John Richard Lumley. Between the time of her quitting Halifax and her junction with Captain Hayes, the Endymion had experienced a serious misfortune. On the 9th of October, when off the shoals of Nantucket, she fell in with the American privateer brig Prince-de-Neufchatel, of 18 guns and 120 or 130 men. It being calm, Captain Hope detached his boats, under the orders of Lieutenant Abel Hawkins, first of the Endymion, to capture the privateer. The boats were repulsed, after sustaining the loss of Lieutenant Hawkins, one midshipman, and 26 seamen and marines killed, the second-lieutenant, one master's mate, and 35 seamen and marines wounded: besides which the launch was captured, and the crew made prisoners. So determined and effective a resistance did great credit to the American captain and his crew. On the 31st the Endymion fell in with the 56-gun ship Saturn, Captain James Nash, bound to Halifax; and, sending on board, with her surgeon and his servant, 28 wounded officers and men, received from the Saturn, to replace the severe loss she had sustained, one lieutenant, four midshipmen, and 33 seamen and marines.

On the 13th of January, 1815, Captain Hayes was joined by the 38-gun frigate Tenedos, Captain Hyde Parker. Although at this time close off the Hook and in sight of the American squadron at anchor near Staten island, the British ships were the same evening blown off the coast by a violent snow-storm. On the next day, the 14th, the weather became more moderate; but, the wind blowing fresh from the west-north-west, the squadron could not get in with the Hook. Having no doubt that Commodore Decatur would take advantage as well of the favourable state of the wind as of the absence of the British squadron, Captain Hayes, in preference to closing the land to the southward, stood away to the northward and eastward, with the view of taking a station in the supposed track of the American squadron on its way out; and, singular enough, at the very instant of arriving at that point, about an hour before daylight on the 15th, Sandy-hook bearing west-north-west distant 15 leagues, the principal object of search to all the British captains made her appearance very near them.

Considering the chance of escape greater, by taking a separate departure with the ships of his squadron, Commodore Decatur, on the afternoon of the 14th, weighed and put to sea with the President and brig Macedonian, having left directions with Captain Warrington to join him at the island of Tristan-d'Acunha, with the Peacock, Hornet, and Tom Bowline. At 8 h. 30 m. P.M., owing partly to a mistake in the pilots and partly to the ship's increased draught of water, from the quantity of stores on board of her, the President struck on the bar, and did not get off for an hour and a half. Having, besides some trifling damage to her rudder, shifted her ballast and got herself out of trim, the President would have put back, but the strong westerly wind prevented her. Accompanied by the brig, the American frigate now shaped her course along the shore of Long island for 50 miles, then steered south-east by south, until, at 5 A.M. on the 15th, she encountered the Majestic and her companions. Three of the ships appearing right ahead, the President hauled up, and passed about two miles to the northward of them; and at daylight Commodore Decatur found himself, as he states, chased by four ships; the Majestic about five miles astern, the Endymion a little further in the same direction, the Pomone six or eight miles on his larboard, and the Tenedos barely in sight on his starboard-quarter. The Tenedos, indeed, having parted from her squadron the preceding evening, was taken for a second enemy's ship, and Captain Hayes ordered the Pomone, by signal, to bear away in chase of her. Consequently the President, at first, was pursued by the Majestic and Endymion only.

These and the American frigate were soon under all sail, steering about east by north, with the wind now at north-west by north. At 6 h. 30 m. A.M. the Majestic fired three shot at the President, but, owing to the distance, without effect; nor, for the same reason probably, were they returned. Towards noon the wind decreased; and the Endymion, in consequence, began to leave the Majestic and gain upon the President. At 1 h. 15 m. P.M., the American frigate commenced lightening herself, by starting her water, cutting away her anchors, throwing overboard provisions, spare spars, boats, and every article of the sort that could be got at: she also kept her sails constantly wet from the royals down. At 2 P.M. the President opened a fire from her stern-guns; which, at 2 h. 30 m., the Endymion returned with her bow-chasers. At 2 h. 39 m. P.M. a shot from the President came through the head of the larboard fore-lower studding-sail, the foot of the mainsail, and the stern of the barge on the booms, and, perforating the quarter-deck, lodged on the main deck, without doing any other damage. Towards 5 P.M., owing to the advance of the Endymion on her starboard and lee quarter, the President luffed occasionally, to bring her stern-guns to bear, and was evidently much galled; whereas the greater part of her shot passed over the Endymion.

At 5 h. 30 m. P.M., the Endymion having for the last 20 minutes maintained a position within half point-blank shot on her quarter, the President brailed up her spanker, and bore away south, to bring her antagonist upon her beam and endeavour to effect her escape to leeward. Putting her helm hard a-weather, the Endymion met the manœuvre; and the two frigates came to close action in a parallel line of sailing. At 6 h. 4 m. P.M. the President commenced with musketry from her tops, and the Endymion returned the fire with her marines; hauling up occasionally, to close her antagonist, without losing the bearing of her broadside. The two ships were now not more than half musket-shot apart; the Endymion with her rigging and sails considerably cut, and the President with the principal part of her damage in the hull, as betrayed by the slackened state of her fire.

At 6 h. 45 m. the President hauled up, apparently to avoid her opponent's fire. Profiting by this, the Endymion poured in two raking broadsides; then hauled up also, and again placed herself on the President's starboard-quarter. At 7 h. 15 m. the President shot away the Endymion's boat from her larboard quarter, also her lower and maintopgallant studding-sails. From 7 h. 18 m. to 7 h. 25 m. the President did not return a shot to the vigorous fire still maintained by the Endymion. Recommencing, then, the President shot away the Endymion's maintopmast studding-sail and main brace, and at 7 h. 32 m. hauled suddenly to the wind, as if to try the strength of her antagonist's masts. Having no fear for these, the Endymion trimmed sails, and, hauling up, bestowed another raking fire: to which the President, now evidently much shattered, replied with a discharge from one stern-gun. In 10 minutes the American frigate kept more away, firing only at intervals; and at 7 h. 58 m. ceased altogether and showed, or appeared to show (for we are doubtful of the fact), a light. Conceiving that the President had struck, the Endymion also ceased firing, and began to bend new sails, her present ones having been cut into ribands by the President's bar and chain shot; one of which had torn away 12 or 14 cloths of her foresail, stripping it almost from the yard.

While the Endymion was thus compelled to drop astern, the President continued her course to the eastward, under a crowd of canvas, much relieved, no doubt, by the absence of the former. At 11 h. 15 m. P.M. the Pomone gained a position upon the President's larboard quarter, and, luffing up, fired her starboard broadside, but did little or no damage. The President immediately shortened sail and luffed up also, as if to pour a broadside into the Pomone. Instead of that, however, the American frigate hailed that she had surrendered, and hoisted a light in her mizen rigging. Not hearing the hail, and mistaking the object of the light, the Pomone fired a second broadside, acknowledged to have been as ineffectual as the first. On this, the President luffed up still sharper, as if to lay the Pomone on board, and instantly hauled down her light, again hailing that she had surrendered. At this time the Tenedos, who had been hailed by the Endymion and informed that the only two boats her misfortune with the Neufchatel had left her were destroyed, ranged up on the President's starboard side, and, hailing, was answered: "The American frigate President: we have surrendered." Captain Parker immediately sent a boat and took possession; as did nearly at the same moment, Captain Lumley of the Pomone. At a few minutes before 9 P.M., having in the short space of 54 minutes, besides repairing her running-rigging, bent new courses, maintopsail, jib, foretopmast staysail, and spanker, and trimmed them to the wind, the Endymion went again in chase, as fresh as when she began the action. At 9 h. 45 m. the Endymion was hailed, as just mentioned, by the Tenedos, and was not very far astern of the latter at 11 h. 30 m. P.M., when the President struck.

The principal damages sustained by the Endymion have already been detailed. Her foretopmast was struck badly, but none of her other masts in any serious degree. Out of her 319 men and 27 boys in crew, the Endymion had 10 seamen and one sergeant of marines killed, and 12 seamen and two private marines wounded. If the high firing of the President displayed its effects in the disordered rigging and sails of the Endymion, the low firing of the Endymion was equally conspicuous in the shattered hull and lower masts of the President. The starboard side of the ship was riddled from end to end, particularly near the quarter. Almost every port-sill and port-timber, both on the main and the quarter-deck, exhibited marks of shot. Three shot had entered the buttock, one of which had passed into the after-magazine. Several shot had entered between wind and water, and some under water, which had cut the knees and timbers much. A great many shot had also passed through the ship, between the main and quarter-decks and in the waist; but, as a proof of the slight effect of the Pomone's fire, one shot only had entered on the larboard side: it passed through at the tenth port, and carried away the upper sill, clamp, and diagonal knees. With so many shot-holes in her hull, the President might well have six feet water in the hold. Five or six of her guns were completely disabled. Out of her 465 men and four boys in crew, the President had three lieutenants, and 32 petty-officers, seamen, and marines killed; her commander (slightly), master, two midshipmen, and 66 seamen and marines wounded; total, 35 killed and 70 wounded.

Of the Endymion's force in guns we have already given a full account. Her brass 18-pounder on the forecastle, we shall not include in the broadside force, because it could not, by possibility, be used there, without displacing one of the

32-pounder carronades.[1] The boat-carronade we shall also reject, for the reason formerly given: that leaves the Endymion with 24 guns upon her broadside. Her established net complement was 347 men and boys; but her loss by the Neufchatel, and the deficiency with which she had originally quitted port, left the Endymion with the number already stated.

The President had landed in all, four of her 24-carronades,[2] one pair at the beginning of the war and the other pair recently; but, like the Constitution, the President now fought one of her two upperdeck 24-pounders through a spare port on her quarter-deck, and the other through a spare port on the forecastle. She mounted also upon a travelling-carriage, a brass 8-inch howitzer; for which there was a spare port at the gangway. We shall consider this gun, although of a 68-pound caliber, merely as a 24-pounder. In her foretop the President mounted two brass 4-pounders, in her maintop the same, and one in her mizentop. These guns, although they were evidently used, and must have produced some effect on the Endymion's deck, we shall not reckon as a part of the President's force. This leaves the American frigate 53 guns on her decks, and 28 of them in broadside.

The number of prisoners delivered to the agent at Bermuda was 434. Add to these, beside the 35 acknowledged by the President's officers to have been killed, six or seven too badly wounded to be removed, and we have 475 as the President's complement; just two less than were named in her watch-bill. Yet Commodore Decatur and two of his officers swore before the surrogate, that the President had "about 450, but certainly not 460 men when the action commenced." The consequence of this oath, this American oath, was, that the captors got head-money for 450 men only; when there was proof positive that 469, and every probability that 477 men were in the ship at the time stated. We shall take the number of which there was that proof, 465 men and four boys. The President's ship's company were a remarkably stout set of men, and a great many British deserters were discovered among them; but, as the news of the peace very soon arrived, the men were not molested.

On the 17th, in a violent storm from the eastward, the Endymion lost her bowsprit and her fore and main masts; the latter chiefly from the shrouds giving way where they had been knotted after the action. The ship was also obliged to throw

[1] See p. 194. [2] See vol. v., p. 271.

overboard the whole of her quarter-deck and forecastle guns. In the same gale, the President carried away all three of her masts. Several of her guns were also thrown overboard; and, in the battered state of her hull by the Endymion's fire, it was considered a mercy to the people on board that she did not founder. On the 25th the two ships arrived at Bermuda. We will now give the

Comparative Force of the Combatants.

		Endymion.	President.
Broadside-guns	No.	24	28
	lbs.	664	852
Crew (men only)	No.	319	465
Size	tons	1277	1533

As soon as the gale of wind had dismasted and otherwise disabled the Endymion, so as to leave an inference that the shot of the President had mainly contributed to reduce her to that state, Commodore Decatur wrote his official letter. In a very few days after his arrival at Bermuda, the communicativeness of one of his officers made him regret that he had despatched the letter. Mr. Bowie, the President's schoolmaster, when deposing before the surrogate relative to the capture of the ship, says: "When the Endymion dropped astern, we were confident of escaping. Shortly after, discovered two ships coming up (Pomone and Tenedos), when Commodore Decatur ordered all hands below to take care of their bags. One of the ships commenced firing; and Commodore Decatur called out, 'We have surrendered,' and gave this deponent the trumpet to hail, and say, they had surrendered. The Pomone's fire did damage to the rigging, but neither killed nor wounded any person. The President did not return the Pomone's fire, but hoisted a light in the mizen-rigging, as a sign of submission." Again: "When the two ships were coming up, a light was hoisted in the mizen-rigging of the President, as this deponent conceived at the time, as an ensign or flag, but, as he afterwards had reason to believe, as a sign that they had surrendered; for this deponent observed to the commodore, that, as long as that light was hoisted, the ships would fire: upon which Commodore Decatur ordered it to be taken down." To counteract the mischievous tendency of Mr. Bowie's averment about the harmless fire of the Pomone, Commodore Decatur wrote from New York a supplementary letter, commencing: "I omitted to state, that a considerable number of my killed and wounded was from the fire of the Pomone." The one shot that entered on the larboard side might, to be sure, have killed and wounded a few men; but then, says, or rather swears, Mr. Bowie, "the men were all, just then, down below taking care of their bags." Oh! Mr. Bowie, Mr. Bowie, you were but half an American; and no wonder we do not find your name among the officers belonging to the United States navy in April, 1816.

Although Commodore Decatur's first official letter is a very long one, and contains a great many inaccuracies, we shall notice only two paragraphs. One is: "I remained with her (the Endymion) in this position for half an hour, in the hope that she would close with us on our broadside, in which case I had prepared my crew to board; but, from his continuing to yaw his ship to maintain his position, it became evident that to close was not his intention." The other: "It is with emotions of pride I bear testimony to the gallantry and steadiness of every officer and man I had the honour to command on this occasion; and I feel satisfied that the fact of their having beaten a force equal to themselves, in the presence, and almost under the guns of so vastly a superior force, when, too, it was almost self-evident that, whatever their exertions might be, they must ultimately be captured, will be taken as evidence of what they would have performed, had the force opposed to them been in any degree equal."

Passing over the illiberal insinuation cast upon a gallant British officer, upon one especially, who, as the commodore acknowledges, paid every attention to himself and his officers, "that delicacy and humanity could dictate," by the words, "it became evident that to close was not his intention," we come to an inquiry into the fact, of whether or not Commodore Decatur did intend "to board the Endymion." An extract or two from his own letter will, we think, establish the point. He states, that at 8 h. 30 m. the President "completely succeeded in dismantling her," the Endymion, whom he had previously shown to be on his lee-quarter; and yet it was not until 11 P.M. that "two fresh ships of the enemy came up." What was to have prevented Commodore Decatur, had such been his intention, from boarding the Endymion during this long interval? The truth is, such an idea never entered his head until some one, after the affair was over, pointed out to him what a chance he had missed of distinguishing himself. Admitting that Commodore Decatur had succeeded in capturing the Endymion, of which there is a very strong doubt, by boarding, he would, it is true, have been able to hold possession for only a quarter of an hour or 20 minutes. Still he would have had all the credit of the thing; and the subsequent capture of the President and recapture of the Endymion, by a force so overwhelming as that which was approaching, would not, in the slightest degree, have detracted from his merit.

Although the President did not inflict upon the Endymion above one-fourth of the numerical loss which she herself sustained; although, while the latter did not have a single warrant-officer touched, the former had three lieutenants killed, and her master and two midshipmen wounded; although the hull of the British ship was very little struck, and that of the President was shattered from stem to stern; although, in short, very little injury was done to the Endymion more than her own active crew replaced in less than an hour, still the President had "beaten" the Endymion. When Commodore Decatur was writing his official letter, he had been two days on board the Endymion, and had found time enough to discover, that her wounded men occupied "the starboard side of the gun-deck from the cabin bulkhead to the main-mast;" and yet he had the hardihood to declare to his government and the world, that the Endymion, the ship he had so "beaten," was equal in force to the President.

On the 17th of April a court of inquiry was summoned at New York, to investigate the circumstances under which the President had been captured. After what has already appeared in these pages on the subject of American courts of inquiry, after Captain Joseph Bainbridge could be honourably acquitted for the manner in which he gave up the Frolic, we cannot be surprised that the court should decree, that the "Endymion was subdued," that the "proposition to board her" was "heroic," and that Commodore Decatur "evinced great judgment and skill, perfect coolness, the most determined resolution and heroic courage," and so forth.

Although, by a sort of endemial tact at telling his own story, the commodore may have raised himself in the esteem of Americans, the manner in which he yielded up the President, coupled with the shifts and quirks, and the misrepresentations to which he afterwards resorted, have sunk the name of Decatur, in the opinion of every well-informed European, quite as low as that of Rodgers, Bainbridge, or Porter. The case of the Endymion and President has been compared with that of the Eurotas and Clorinde. Both the French and the American frigate, it is true, were about equally battered in hull; but there was this difference in the conduct of their commanders: Captain Denis-Lagarde, when he had surrendered, had only his foremast standing; whereas Commodore Decatur had all his three royal-masts an-end, and even the sails set upon them.

If we have been, or shall again be, a little more severe upon the Americans generally than accords with the impartial character of these pages, they have themselves, and themselves only, to thank. Have they not been trying to persuade the rest of the world that their naval officers and seamen surpass all others; that they are, in short, "invincible?" Who has ever heard an American acknowledge that any ship of his was taken by an equal force? Where can an American be found, who will not persist in declaring that an equal force captured the Guerrière, Macedonian, and Java, the Frolic, Peacock, and their sister-brigs? One fact is remarkable. Where the Americans have met a decidedly superior force, or an equal force that routed them about in an unexpected manner, they have invariably dropped their crests, and have lost the respect of their conquerors by the tameness of their surrender.

It would be an injustice to Captain Hope, not to notice the peculiar modesty of his official letter. He speaks of the cool and determined bravery of his officers and ship's company on the "fortunate occasion;" says, truly, that, "where every individual had so conspicuously done his duty, it would be injustice to particularize;" and in proof of the exertions and abilities of his men, appeals to "the loss and damages sustained by the enemy's frigate." In his letter to Rear-admiral Hotham, enclosing that of Captain Hope, Captain Hayes does ample justice to the Endymion; confirms every statement in her log-extract, which is the groundwork of our account; and emphatically adds: "When the effect produced by her well-directed fire upon the President is witnessed, it cannot be doubted, that Captain Hope would have succeeded either in capturing or sinking her, had none of the squadron been in sight." The senior lieutenant on board the Endymion, William Thomas Morgan, was deservedly promoted to the rank of commander.

On the 8th of March, after having undergone a partial repair, the President, accompanied by the Endymion, sailed from Bermuda for England; and on the 28th both ships arrived at Spithead. The President, of course, was added to the British navy; but her serious damages in the action, coupled with the length of time she had been in service, prevented her from being of any greater utility than that of affording to Englishmen, many of whom, till then, had been the dupes of their transatlantic "brethren," ocular demonstration of the "equal force" by which their frigates had been captured.

On the 26th of February the British schooner St. Lawrence, of 12 carronades, 12-pounders, and one long 9-pounder, commanded by Lieutenant Henry Cranmer Gordon, while proceeding with despatches from Rear-admiral Cockburn, relating to the peace between Great Britain and the United States, fell in with the American privateer-brig Chasseur, of six long 9-pounders, and eight carronades, 18-pounders, commanded by Captain Thomas Boyle. The brig attacked the schooner, and an engagement ensued; which, the Americans state, lasted at close quarters only 15 minutes, when the St. Lawrence was carried by boarding. No British official account has been published; but unofficial accounts state that the action continued much longer.

The St. Lawrence was a good deal cut up; and, according to a New Providence paper, lost out of her crew (exclusive of some passengers) of 42 men and nine boys, six men killed and 18 wounded. The Americans made the killed, as they generally do, much greater. The Chasseur was also injured in her hull and spars; and lost, by the American returns, out of a complement of 115 men, five men killed and eight wounded. Men are not in the best trim for fighting, just upon receiving the news of peace. Sailors are then dwelling upon their discharge from servitude, the sight of long absent friends, and all the ties of their homes and families. But even that, although it perhaps contributed to weaken the efforts, could not impair the courage of the crew of the St. Lawrence: they defended her, until nearly half their numbers were killed or wounded.

The British force stationed in Boston bay in the beginning of December, 1814, consisted of the 50-gun ship Newcastle, Captain Lord George Stuart, 18-pounder 40-gun frigate Acasta, Captain Alexander Robert Kerr, and 18-gun brig-sloop Arab, Captain Henry Jane. On the 11th, when the squadron was cruising off St. George's shoals, the Newcastle parted company, to reconnoitre the road of Boston. On the 12th Lord George discovered lying there the 44-gun frigate Constitution, Captain Charles Stewart, in apparent readiness for sea, and the Independence 74, with her lower yards and topmasts struck. The Newcastle then steered for Cape Cod bay; where, in a few hours, after having grounded for a short time on a shoal, she came to an anchor. On the 13th one of her men, from a boat sent on shore, deserted to the Americans. On the 16th the Acasta arrived, and anchored near the Newcastle.

On the 17th, having ascertained, in all probability from the Newcastle's deserter, that the two blockading frigates were not in a situation to offer him any annoyance, Captain Stewart put to sea. The Constitution stood across the Atlantic to the coast of Spain and Portugal, and cruised for some time off the rock of Lisbon. In the latter end of January, or beginning of February, Captain Stewart stretched over to the Western isles, and was tracked and followed by the British 38-gun frigate Tiber, Captain James Richard Dacres. The latter boarded two or three neutral vessels, which had been boarded by the American frigate only a few hours before. At one time, it appears, the Constitution actually got a sight of the Tiber, but did not shorten sail, because Captain Stewart, as he is said to have subsequently admitted, thought it probable that the ship was the Eurotas, or some other of the newly fitted 24-pounder frigates, detached in pursuit of him.

On the 20th of February, at 1 P.M., the island of Madeira bearing west-south-west, distant 60 leagues, the Constitution, steering to the south-west with a light breeze from the eastward, discovered, about two points on her larboard bow, and immediately hauled up for, the British 22-gun ship Cyane,[1] Captain Gordon Thomas Falcon, standing close hauled on the starboard tack, and about 10 miles to windward of her consort, the 20-gun ship Levant (18 carronades, 32-pounders, and two nines), Captain and senior officer the Hon. George Douglas. At 1 h. 45 m. the Constitution got sight of the Levant, then bearing right ahead of her. At 4 P.M., having stood on to ascertain the character of the stranger, the Cyane made the private signal; and, finding it not answered, bore up for her consort, with the signal flying for an enemy. The Constitution immediately made all sail in chase, and at 5 P.M. commenced firing her larboard bow-guns, but ceased soon afterwards, finding her shot fall short. At 5 h. 30 m., the Cyane having arrived within hail of the Levant, Captain Douglas expressed to Captain Gordon his resolution to engage the enemy's frigate (known from previous information to be the Constitution), notwithstanding her superior force, in the hope, by disabling her, to save two valuable convoys, that had sailed from Gibraltar a few days previous in company with the two British ships.

[1] For her force, see vol. v., p. 32.

At 5 h. 45 m. P.M. the Levant and Cyane made all sail upon a wind, in order to try for the weather-gage. In 10 minutes, finding they could not accomplish their object, the two ships bore up, with the view of delaying the commencement of the action until night; when they might hope, by skilful manœuvring, to engage with more advantage. The superior sailing of the Constitution defeating that plan also, the Levant and Cyane, at 6 P.M., hauled to the wind on the starboard tack, formed in head and stern line, at the distance of rather less than 200 yards apart. At 6 h. 5 m. the Constitution, all three ships having previously hoisted their colours, opened her larboard broadside upon the Cyane, at the distance of about three quarters of a mile on the latter's weather beam. The Cyane promptly returned the fire; but her shot, being all fired from carronades, fell short, while the frigate's long 24-pounders were producing their full effect. In 15 minutes the Constitution ranged ahead, and became engaged in the same manner with the Levant. The Cyane now luffed up for the larboard quarter of the Constitution: whereupon the latter, backing astern, was enabled to pour into the Cyane her whole broadside.

Meanwhile the Levant had bore up, to wear round and assist her consort. The Constitution thereupon filled, shot ahead, and gave the Levant two stern rakes. Seeing this, the Cyane, although without a brace or bowline except the larboard fore brace, wore, and gallantly stood between the Levant and Constitution. The latter then promptly wore, and raked the Cyane astern. The Cyane immediately luffed up as well as she could, and fired her larboard broadside at the starboard bow of the Constitution. The latter soon afterwards ranged up on the larboard quarter of the Cyane, within hail, and was about to pour in her starboard broadside; when, at 6 h. 50 m. P.M., having had most of her standing and running rigging cut to pieces, her main and mizen masts left in a tottering state, and other principal spars wounded, several shot in the hull, nine or ten between wind and water, five carronades disabled, chiefly by the drawing of the bolts and starting of the chocks, and the Levant being two miles to leeward, still bearing away to repair her heavy damages, the Cyane fired a lee-gun, and hoisted a light as a signal of submission.

It was not until 8 P.M. that the Constitution, having manned her prize and refitted some slight damages in her own rigging, was ready to bear up after the Levant, then in sight to leeward. At 8 h. 15 m., which was as soon as the Levant had rove new braces, the gallant little ship again hauled her wind, as well to ascertain the fate of her companion, as to renew the desperate contest. On approaching the Constitution and Cyane, the Levant, with a boldness bordering on rashness, ranged close alongside the Constitution to leeward, being unable to weather her; and at 8 h. 30 m. these two ships (the President and Little-Belt over again), while passing on opposite tacks, exchanged broadsides. The Constitution immediately wore under the Levant's stern, and raked her with a second broadside. At 9 h. 30 m., finding that the Cyane had undoubtedly surrendered, Captain Douglas again put before the wind; but, in the act of doing so, the Levant received several raking broadsides, had her wheel shot away, and her lower masts badly wounded. To fire her stern-chase guns, and steer at the same time, was impossible, owing to a sad mistake in the construction of this new class of vessel. Seeing the Constitution ranging up on her larboard quarter, the Levant, at 10 h. 30 m. P.M., struck her colours.

Out of her 115 men and 16 boys, the Levant had six seamen and marines killed, one officer and 15 seamen and marines wounded; and the Cyane, out of her 145 men and 26 boys, (making 42 boys between these two small ships!) had six seamen and marines killed and 13 wounded; total, 12 killed and 29 wounded. The Constitution had sailed on her last cruise with a complement of 477 men and three boys, but, having manned a prize with an officer and seven men, had on board only 469. Out of this number, she had six killed and mortally wounded, and six others wounded severely and slightly. The wounded are rather out of proportion, but they are all that the Americans have acknowledged.[1] The comparatively slight loss inflicted upon the two ships affords a clear proof, that the Americans had begun to relax in their gunnery; and, had the war continued, and the United States gone on equipping and manning new ships, some very unexpected reverses at sea would have followed.

The captain of an American frigate, who could solemnly declare, that a British frigate had run away from him, would naturally make a great boast of capturing these two sloops, as they may be called. Therefore Captain Stewart officially says: "Considering the advantages derived by the enemy, from a divided and more active force, as also their superiority in the weight and number of guns, I deem the speedy and decisive result of this action the strongest assurance which can be given

[1] [Fenimore Cooper admits the wounded to have been *nine*.—H. Y. POWELL.]

the government, that all under my command did their duty, and gallantly supported the reputation of American seamen." The term " speedy " may appear misapplied when, according to the "Minutes " published in the American papers, the action began at 6 h. 5 m. and ended at 10 P.M., or, as the British account states, at 10 h. 40 m.; but, by a mode of reckoning peculiar to himself, Captain Stewart declares that the action lasted only 40 minutes.

Let us suppose that the Peacock and Hornet, soon after leaving New York together, had fallen in with the Endymion, to windward of them, and (the only improbable part of the supposition) had stayed to engage the frigate until they were captured. How would the American citizens have behaved on this occasion? Why, they would have received Captains Warrington and Biddle precisely as they did Captain Stewart, and published accounts in every paper of the " heroic defence against decidedly superior force;" not failing to point out, as they did in the Essex's action, the great disparity between carronades and long guns, when the ship carrying the latter has the choice of distance. Mr. Madison, too, in his next speech to congress, would have declared, that the two little sloops continued the unequal contest, until, as he said of the Essex, "humanity tore down the colours which valour had nailed to the mast." How would Captain Hope have behaved? He would have told a plain tale of his good fortune, applauding the American commanders for having so long maintained a contest in which, from the nature of their armament, and from their leeward position, they could not have hoped to succeed.

Before we attend to the further proceedings of the Constitution, we will dismiss all we have to state on the subject of her action with the two sloops. On the 28th of June, a court-martial was held on board the Akbar at Halifax, Nova Scotia, to try the two captains and their respective officers and ships' companies for the loss of the Levant and Cyane. They were all, except three seamen of the Cyane who deserted to the Americans, most honourably acquitted for the surrender of their ships, and justly applauded for the gallant defence they had made against an enemy's ship so decidedly superior. With the exception of the three deserters, the two crews resisted the repeated offers made to them to enlist with the enemy. It was stated by the British officers, at the court-martial, that the crews of the two ships were for three weeks kept constantly in the Constitution's hold, with both hands and legs in irons, and there allowed but three pints of water during the 24 hours. This, too, in a tropical climate! It was further proved that, after the expiration of the three weeks, upon the application of Captain Douglas, one-third of the men were allowed to be on deck four hours out of the 24, but had not the means of walking, being still in irons; that, on mustering the crews when they were landed at Maranham, five of the Levant's boys were missing; that, upon application and search for them, two were found locked up in the cabin of the American captain of marines; and that a black man at Maranham was employed as a crimp, and enticed one of the Levant's boys to enter the American service.

On the 8th of March the Constitution, having in company, along with her two prizes, a merchant-brig of which she intended to make a cartel, anchored off the isle of Mayo, one of the Cape de Verds; and on the next day got under way, and anchored, a few hours afterwards, in the harbour of Porto-Praya, island of Saint-Jago. While on his way to these islands, Captain Stewart had caused the Cyane to be painted so as to resemble a 36-gun frigate. The object of this was to aggrandize his exploit, in the wondering eyes of the gaping citizens of Boston; not one in a hundred of whom, he knew, would trouble themselves to inquire any further on the subject. The American captain would doubtless have played off the same *deceptio visûs* upon the Levant, had he not been aware, that no efforts of the painter could make a low flush ship of 464 tons resemble a frigate. On the 11th, at 15 minutes past noon, just as Captain Stewart had sent his master to bring the cartel brig under the stern of the Constitution, in order that the prisoners might be removed to her, three strange ships were discovered through the haze, standing into the harbour. These were the British 50-gun ships Leander and Newcastle, Captains Sir George Ralph Collier, K.C.B., and Lord George Stuart, and 18-pounder 40-gun frigate Acasta, Captain Alexander Robert Kerr. We will now step back for a moment, and endeavour to show what had brought these three ships to a spot so distant from the station on which they had hitherto been cruising, the north-eastern coast of the United States.

On the 19th of December the Leander sailed from Halifax bound off Boston, and on the 24th fell in with the Newcastle and Acasta. By their captains, it appears, Sir George was informed, that the Constitution had sailed from Boston, and the Congress from Portsmouth, New Hampshire, and that the President was to join those ships "from the Delaware."[1] Unfortunately, although it had been stated over and over again in the Halifax papers, neither of the three captains appears to have been aware that the Congress had, some months before, been dismantled and laid up at Portsmouth, and that the President was not lying in the "Delaware," but in New York. On turning to the Newcastle's log, to see who it was that had been playing off such a hoax upon Lord George, we find that, on the 22nd, while the Newcastle and Acasta were lying at anchor in Cape Cod bay,[2] the 18-gun brig-sloop Arab, Captain Henry Jane, joined company, "with intelligence that the Constitution had sailed from Boston on the 17th instant." Not another word is there. This, however, was quite enough to hasten the two ships in getting under way, and to make their captains wish, no doubt, that they had kept under way in front of the port which they had been ordered to watch.

This story about the sailing of the American squadron, whether derived, in the first instance, from fishermen, cattle-dealers, or any other of the cunning New England folk, was credited by Sir George Collier; and away went the Leander, Newcastle, and Acasta, in search of the Constitution and the "two other heavy frigates" that had sailed "in her company."[3] On the 4th of January, when off the Western Isles, the three ships fell in with a brig-prize belonging to the American privateer Perry; and, having chased under American colours, were taken for an American squadron. The consequence was, that the prize-master of the brig voluntarily came on board the Leander, and pretended to take that ship for the President, the Newcastle for the Constitution, and the Acasta, not for the Congress, but for the Macedonian. In short, the fellow would have said or sworn anything that he thought would ingratiate himself with his hearers. Mr. Marshall says, "Nothing could have happened better"[4] than this farcical interview with the American privateer's-man. On the contrary, looking to the serious impression it appears to have made on board the Leander, we should rather say, nothing could have happened worse.

On the 11th of March, at 0 h. 15 m. P.M., when, as already stated, they first discovered the Constitution, Cyane, Levant, and cartel brig, the three British ships were standing close hauled on the starboard tack, with a moderate breeze from the

[1] Published letter of Mr. Thos. Collier.
[2] See p. 247.
[3] Marshall, vol. ii., p. 533.
[4] Ibid., p. 534.

north-east by north; and the ships in Porto-Praya then bore from the Leander, the leewardmost ship of her squadron, north-east by north distant seven miles. In less than 10 minutes after she had discovered the approach of the British ships, the Constitution cut her cables and stood out of Porto-Praya on the larboard tack, followed by the Levant and Cyane. At 1 p.m., just as the Constitution had got upon the Leander's weather-beam, the three British ships tacked in chase. At this time the strange squadron was about four miles in the wind's eye of the Acasta, the Acasta about one mile upon the weather-quarter of the Newcastle, and the Newcastle about two miles ahead of the Leander. At this time, also, the Acasta made out the strangers to be "one large frigate and two sloops." The Newcastle has merely noted down in her log, that one ship was larger than the others; and the Leander, in her log, describes all three of the ships as "apparently frigates." But the Leander's first-lieutenant on the occasion, the present Captain John M'Dougall, has subsequently stated as follows: " Weather very thick and hazy; took the two sternmost ships for frigates, the headmost, from appearance, a much larger ship, for the Guerrière; who, we understood, had long 32-pounders on her main deck."[1]

At 1 h. 30 m. p.m. Captain Stewart found that the Constitution sailed about equal with the ships on her lee-quarter, but that the Acasta, by luffing up, was gaining her wake and rather dropping astern. It was at the same time observed, that the Cyane was dropping astern and to leeward, and would soon be overtaken by the Acasta. At 1 h. 40 m., therefore, Captain Stewart made the signal for the Cyane to tack; expecting that the British commodore would detach a ship in pursuit of her, and that she would succeed in reaching the anchorage of Porto-Praya before the detached ship could come up with her; or, if no ship chased, that she would be able to double the rear of the British squadron and escape before the wind. The Cyane, just when bearing from the Leander north-north-east distant four miles, tacked accordingly; but no British ship tacked after her, Sir George rightly judging that she would reach the neutral port before either of the British ships could get within shot of her. The Cyane shortly afterwards bore away, and was seen no more. At 1 h. 45 m. the Leander hoisted her colours and fired a gun to windward; and then telegraphed that, in case of parting company, the Isle of Mayo was to be the rendezvous. Both the

[1] Marshall, vol. ii., p. 536.

Leander's consorts also hoisted their colours, and the Newcastle scaled her guns. The Constitution's log notices the circumstance thus: "The ship on our lee-quarter firing broadsides by divisions, her shot falling short of us." An officer of the Constitution, in a letter to a friend, says: "The shot fell short from 100 to 200 yards."[1] This would, indeed, have brought the ships near together; but the American officer must have greatly underrated the distance. For our part, we cannot see the necessity of scaling the guns at all: not only was the concussion calculated to check the ship's way, but it was very likely to calm the breeze, already beginning to slacken as the day drew towards its close.

At 2 h. 30 m. P.M., the Constitution having dropped the Levant considerably, the situation of the latter, in reference to the Acasta, became as critical as that of the Cyane had been. Captain Stewart accordingly made the Levant's signal to tack; and the Levant did immediately tack. At this time, says the Acasta, "the frigate had gained on us, but we had gained on the sloop." One of the Constitution's officers gives a different statement from that in the Acasta's log. He says: "The Acasta sailed faster than the Constitution, and was gaining on her."[2] At all events the Acasta, although she might drop a little astern, was weathering upon the Constitution, and had now brought her to bear upon her weather cat-head. The instant the Levant tacked, the Leander made a signal, the nature of which we shall discuss presently; and, in obedience to that signal, the Acasta "tacked in chase of the sloop." In a minute or two afterwards, according to statements that have appeared in print, the Leander and Newcastle successively did the same. When the Newcastle tacked, the Constitution was five or six miles to windward of her, and, "in the prevailing haze, nearly out of sight" from the deck of the Leander, from whom the Newcastle then bore south-east by east, and the Acasta north-east.

At 2 h. 50 m. P.M., which was just 14 minutes after she had tacked, the Newcastle lost sight of the Constitution, owing to the increased haziness of the weather as the former approached the land, and the opposite course steered by the latter. The Levant, shortly after she had tacked, bore away for Porto-Praya road, and at about 3 h. 15 m. P.M. received from the Leander in passing an ineffectual fire. "At 4 h. 30 m.," says the Newcastle log, "saw her (Levant) anchor. Acasta fired a broadside.

[1] Naval Monument, p. 182. [2] Ibid.

At 4 h. 56 m. tacked and fired our larboard broadside." An American account says: "The Levant ran into port, so as to run her jib-boom over the battery. The Acasta and Newcastle came in, and, although her colours were hauled down, fired at her a number of times. They were obliged to hoist and lower their colours twice; yet not a gun was fired from the Levant. Lieutenant Ballard, who commanded, had ordered his men to lie on the deck, by which they all escaped injury, although considerable damage was done to the town. It seemed unnecessary for two heavy frigates to fire into one sloop-of-war, who neither did or could make any resistance."[1] When the Leander opened her fire she discovered, clearly enough, the force of the ship in pursuit of which the squadron had tacked. Sir George then made the signal for the Acasta to take possession of her. The Acasta did so; and by 5 P.M. all three British ships had anchored in Porto-Praya road. On the 12th, at 6 h. 30 m. A.M., Sir George Collier went on shore to communicate with the governor, in consequence of the damage done to the houses of the town by the shot from the Acasta and Newcastle. At 11 A.M. Sir George returned; and shortly afterwards the British squadron, accompanied by the prize, got under way, and steered for the West Indies. We must now pay a visit to the Constitution.

The moment he saw how the Acasta was weathering him, and that he had no chance of escape by bearing up, as the Newcastle would inevitably intercept him, Captain Stewart considered the Constitution as within an hour or two of becoming a British prize. The American officers now questioned the British officers as to the manner in which the commodore of the chasing squadron would treat them; and, in short, began making, in regard to their clothes and other personal effects, such arrangements as they thought necessary in the change they were about to undergo from freemen to captives. All this while Captains Douglas and Falcon, and the late officers of the Levant and Cyane, were blessing their stars at the good fortune that awaited them, although, as we can readily conceive, their delicacy forbade them from making a display of it before Captain Stewart and his officers. When the Cyane tacked, and the three British ships still continued in chase of the Constitution, not a doubt could remain that the English commodore, whoever he might be, was determined to have her. The Levant tacks; and (can it be possible?) all three British ships tack

[1] Naval Monument, p. 182.

after her. Here is a change! The joy of Captain Stewart and his officers was now as extravagant as their fears had been well grounded. But what were *now* the feelings of Captains Douglas and Falcon and the other British officers? What were they indeed! "The British officers on board," says the Constitution's officer, "who had expressed the utmost confidence that the Constitution would be taken in an hour, felt the greatest vexation and disappointment, which they expressed in very emphatic terms."[1] From the following passage in the same account, it would appear that some one of the British officers, to save as much as possible the credit of the service to which he belonged, pretended to understand the purport of a signal that was hoisted by the Newcastle, and of which we shall speak presently. Thus: "After the other ships tacked, the Newcastle made a signal that her fore-topsail yard was sprung, and tacked also." In less than three-quarters of an hour after the Newcastle had tacked from her, the Constitution was becalmed or nearly so. As soon as a breeze sprang up, Captain Stewart steered towards the coast of Brazil, and through the West Indies home; and, early in the month of May, "lucky Old Iron-sides," as now she well might be called, anchored in Boston.

The three British ships, on being first discovered by the Constitution, were taken by the American officers for what, in reality, they were: the Leander and Newcastle for "ships of the line," or two-deckers, and the Acasta for a frigate. But the Cyane, according to her log, made out all three ships to be frigates, even before the Constitution cut her cables and made sail.[2] Yet, on board the Leander, the Constitution, of 1533, the Cyane, of 539, and the Levant, a flush ship, of 464 tons, all put on the appearance of "frigates." Hence, when the Cyane tacked, "Sir George directed the Acasta's signal to be made to tack after her, but countermanded the order, on observing that she would gain the anchorage before the Acasta could close with her."[3] It was, therefore, the respect which the British commanding officer paid to the neutrality of the Portuguese port that permitted the Cyane to go unpursued. But in less than an hour a second enemy's "frigate," the Levant, tacks, and the neutrality of the port does not save her from being pursued, or from being cannonaded, "with her jib-boom over the battery," by two of the three British ships that had tacked after her. How does Captain M'Dougall reconcile this?

[1] Naval Monument, p. 182.
[2] Ibid., p. 173.
[3] See Captain M'Dougall's paper, in Marshall, vol. ii., p. 536.

It appears, now, that it was not Sir George's intention that all three British ships should have tacked after the Levant. The signal was ordered to be for the Acasta alone to tack; but, according to the published letter of Mr. Thomas Collier, "the midshipman, Mr. Morrison, whose duty it was to make the signal, did, by mistake, hoist the general signal," or, according to another statement, and one which bears the signature of the Leander's late first-lieutenant, "in making the signal, the Acasta's distinguishing pendants got foul, and, before they could be cleared, the Newcastle mistook it for a general signal.[1] It is a point, we conceive, of very little consequence how the mistake arose. The fact is that, of all the three ships, the Acasta was the last that should have been ordered to tack after the Levant, even admitting that ship to have been the "Constitution, President, Macedonian, or Congress," simply because the Acasta was "weathering," "getting into the wake of," and the likeliest of any of the three to overtake and bring to action the "Guerrière." On the other hand, that the Leander herself, if any ship did, was the most proper to have gone in pursuit of the supposed Constitution, President, Macedonian, or Congress, is clear; first, because she was "falling to leeward" of the supposed Guerrière, and next, because she was the nearest of any of her squadron to the ship that, to the Leander at least, put on so fatal a disguise. Had we seen no other statement than is to be found in the three British ships' logs, we should consider that the Leander really did tack first; for thus says her log: "Tacked ship to cut off ship from anchorage, and made signal for ditto."

Sir George Collier was remarkable for the kindness with which he treated his officers, and for the, in this instance, most unfortunate deference he was in the habit of paying to their opinions on points of service. By whose suggestion he tacked, let his late first-lieutenant's own words determine: "When the Acasta had filled on the starboard tack, I observed to Sir George, that, if the ships standing in shore were really frigates, which it was impossible to ascertain, owing to the haziness of the weather, they would be more than a match for the Acasta He replied: 'It is true, Kerr can do wonders, but not impossibilities; and I believe I must go round, as, when the ship that tacked first hears the Acasta engaged, she will naturally come to her consort's assistance.'"[2] Captain M'Dougall here says,

[1] Marshall, vol. ii., p. 537.   [2] Ibid., p. 538.

"it was impossible to ascertain" whether or not a low flush ship, of 464 tons, sailing for more than an hour, at the distance certainly not of more than five miles, upon the weather beam of the Leander, and consequently with her whole broadside exposed to view, and every port, one might suppose, as easy to be counted as the ports of the Leander herself were by the British and American officers on board the Levant, was a "frigate;" and such a frigate as, with another like her, it would be "impossible" for the Acasta to cope with. Lieutenant Henry Richmond, who was a midshipman on board the Leander, appears to have sanctioned Mr. Thomas Collier in saying, that "all on board" the Leander fully believed that the Constitution, Cyane, and Levant were three American frigates. The only answer we shall give to this will be to subjoin the names of the five lieutenants who belonged to the Leander at the time. 1st. John M'Dougall, 2d. William Edward Fiott, 3d. Robert Graham Dunlop, 4th. George William St. John Mildmay, and 5th. Richard Weld. We believe it is not yet admitted by Captains Kerr and Lord George Stuart, that the Acasta was the first ship that tacked, or that the weather, at the time the Constitution was left to go her ways, was not sufficiently clear for the water-lines of all the ships to be seen.

Mention has been made of an optional flag. The following extract from the work of a contemporary will afford the requisite information on the subject: "Sir George Collier, confiding in the zeal and judgment of the captains under his orders, had previously informed them that, whenever a certain flag was hoisted with any signal addressed to either of them, they were at liberty to disregard the signal, if they considered that, by following the order conveyed thereby, the object in view was not so likely to be attained, as by acting in contrariety thereto. The flag alluded to was entered *pro tempore* in the signal books under the designation of the 'optional flag.' On its being hoisted with the Newcastle's pendants as above stated, that ship made answer by signal, 'The flags are not distinguishable.'"[1] We shall not stay to discuss this point, beyond suggesting the probability, either that the wrong flag was hoisted on board the Leander, or that it had got foul and was omitted to be cleared. If neither was the case, the Newcastle must have been nearer to the Constitution than she was to the Leander; for we observe by her log, that the Newcastle could

[1] Marshall, vol. ii., p. 537, note ‡.

distinguish the signal made by the Constitution to the Cyane, as being one not in the British naval code, also that the signal afterwards made by the Constitution to the Levant was "the same signal as before." We have now a word or two to submit on the part performed by the Acasta.

In two respects, the Acasta possessed a decided advantage over her consorts. She was far more advanced in the chase, and sailed better on a wind, than either of them; and she had, from the first, made out exactly the force of the three strange ships: they were, according to her log, "one large frigate and two sloops." We believe, also, that the "large frigate" was all along supposed by her to be the Constitution. When the Acasta saw the signal made by the commodore, so far to leeward, for the squadron to tack, how happened it that no signal was made in answer, expressive of the probability that some mistake had been made, in supposing that the two ships which had tacked were worth a moment's consideration, and communicating that the ship which they were all anxious to get hold of was ahead, and that she, the Acasta, was weathering her? Or, let us suppose that the Acasta had taken no notice of the Leander's signal, but had kept on her course, Captain Kerr, if we mistake not, had an honourable wound,[1] which would have served him for an excuse, as a similar wound, and on a similar occasion, had once served the greatest naval captain of the age. "Leave off action? Now d—n me if I do! You know, Foley, I have only one eye,— I have a right to be blind sometimes."[2]

On the subject of the "optional flag," in reference to the Acasta, we shall quote from a contemporary: "The Acasta's log informs us, that the enemy's force was discovered to consist of one large frigate and two sloops, so early as 1 P.M., the time when the British squadron first tacked to the eastward. If so we are sorry that a signal to that effect was not made, by which Sir George Collier's mind would have been set at ease as to the capability of the Acasta to cope with the two ships which had put back; and the Leander, having nothing else to engage her attention, would of course have continued in pursuit of the other. It was very natural for junior captains to feel a delicacy in addressing signals to their commanding officer when in the presence of an enemy; but, as Sir George Collier had formed his opinion of the American's force from the report of Captain Kerr and Lord George Stuart,[3] he certainly could not have

---

[1] See vol. i., p. 91.   [2] See vol. iii., p. 52.   [3] See p. 254.

taken offence had he been informed that the Acasta alone was more than capable of annihilating the two ships which she had tacked after."[1]

One part of this statement we consider quite nugatory. What would have been the utility of the Leander, a ship confessedly "falling to leeward," continuing in pursuit of the Constitution? No, the only ship that could have pursued her with any chance of success had been ordered by the Leander to tack from her. Most sincerely do we regret, on personal as well as on public grounds, that this last and most triumphant escape of the Constitution, the first frigate of the United States that had humbled the proud flag of Britain, had not long ago been brought under the scrutiny of a court-martial. The blame would then have fallen where it ought to have fallen; and, in the unpleasant task of detailing what, the more it is investigated the more it will show itself to be, the most blundering piece of business recorded in these six volumes, we should neither have had our statements called in question nor our motives misunderstood.

On the 20th of January, six days after the President and store-brig Macedonian had escaped from New York, the Peacock, Hornet, and store-brig Tom Bowline succeeded also in getting to sea. On the 23rd the Hornet parted company from her two consorts, and proceeded straight to the island of Tristand'Acunha, the first rendezvous for the squadron. On the 20th of March, Captain Biddle was informed of the peace by a neutral; and on the 23rd, at 11 A.M., when just about to anchor off the north end of the above island, the Hornet fell in with the British brig-sloop Penguin, of 16 carronades, 32-pounders and two sixes, Captain James Dickinson.

Before narrating the action that ensued, it will, we consider, prove useful to point out a few of the circumstances under which the parties met. The armament of the Hornet has already on more than one occasion been shown;[2] she now carried in lieu of her two long twelves, two long 18-pounders; and as these, owing to their great length, could not conveniently be fought through the foremost or usual long-gun ports, they were mounted amidships. She had musketoons in all her tops, each piece throwing 50 buck-shot at a discharge, and upon each quarter a 3 or 4 pound brass swivel, fitted on a chock. All this had been done to bring the Hornet nearer to an "equality" with the Loup-Cervier, in case the challenge,

[1] Marshall, vol. ii., p. 538, note*.   [2] See p. 44.

to which we have already alluded, had been accepted. Her crew, consisting at this time of 165 men (eight absent in a prize), had also, it may be presumed, been well culled preparatory to the expected contest. Each man had a boarding-helmet, similar to those we described as worn by the crew of the Constitution.[1]

The Penguin was commissioned, for the first time, in November, 1813; and, as a proof how much brigs of that class were wanted in the British navy, there were but 81 in commission on the 1st of the succeeding January. After having been run up by the contract-builder in the usual slight and hurried manner, to be ready on the emergency (there being, as already stated, no more than 81 such vessels in commission), the Penguin was to be manned with equal recklessness about consequences. In respect to captain and officers generally, the Penguin might compete with any brig of her class; but, as to men, when she did get them all on board, which was not until June, 1814, they were, with the exception, probably, of not being disaffected, a worse crew than even the Epervier's. Her 17 boys, poor little fellows, might do very well six or seven years to come. Her men, her misnamed "British seamen," consisted, except a portion of her petty officers, of very old and very young individuals; the latter pressed men, the former discharged ineffectives. Among the whole number thus obtained 12 only had ever been in action.

One might suppose, that a vessel so "manned," especially after a knowledge of the fact, that four of the same description of sloops had been captured each by an American sloop of the same nominal, whatever may have been her real force, would have been sent to escort some convoy from the Downs along the English coast; a service in which, as against the pickaroons that usually infested the Channel, the appearance of a force was almost as effective as its reality. Oh, no. The aforesaid emergency required, that the Penguin should be sent to the Cape of Good Hope, to traverse the very track in which the Java had met, and been captured by, the Constitution. Accordingly, in the month of September, the Penguin sailed for her distant destination. While on the Cape station, she lost several of her men by sickness; and, previously to her being despatched by Vice-admiral Charles Tyler, the commander-in-chief at the Cape, in pursuit of the American privateer-ship Young Wasp, the Penguin received on board from the **Medway 74**, as a loan for

[1] See p. 198.

that special service, 12 marines; thus making her complement 105 men and 17 boys, or 122 in the whole.

Had the vessel in sight to windward been rigged with three masts instead of two, and had she, on her near approach, proved by her signals to be a British cruiser, Captain Biddle might have marked her down in his log as a "frigate," and have made off with all the canvas he could spread. Had the ship, nevertheless, overtaken the Hornet, and been, in reality, a trifle superior in force to her, Captain Biddle, we have no doubt, would have exhausted his eloquence in lauding the blessings of peace, before he tried the effect of his artillery in a struggle for the honours of war. However, the vessel approaching was evidently a brig; and the utmost extent of a brig-sloop's force was thoroughly known.

When she first descried the Hornet in the north-west by west, the Penguin was steering to the eastward, with the wind fresh from the south-south-west. With all the promptitude that was to be expected from the gallant first-lieutenant of the Cerberus in the action off Lissa, Captain Dickinson bore up in chase. At 1 h. 45 m., P.M., Tristan d'Acunha bearing south-west, distant three or four miles, the Penguin hoisted her colours, a St. George's ensign, and fired a gun to induce the stranger to show hers. The Hornet immediately luffed up on the starboard tack, hoisted American colours, and discharged her broadside; and the Penguin, on rounding to upon the same tack, fired hers in return. Thus the action commenced within about pistol-shot distance. The Hornet's star and bar shot soon reduced the Penguin's rigging to a state of disorder; and a tolerably well-directed discharge of round and grape, meeting no adequate return, especially as the carronades, owing to their insecure mode of mounting, turned half round almost every time they were discharged, made a sensible impression upon the Penguin's hull. At 2 h. 15 m. P.M., as the Penguin drifted nearer, the Hornet bore away, with the semblance of retiring from the contest, but in reality to take up a more favourable position for doing execution with her gunnery. Captain Dickinson, on this, bore up with the intention to board. Before, however, this gallant officer could put his plan into execution, he received a mortal wound.

Lieutenant James M'Donald, who now succeeded to the command, aware of the brig's disabled state, saw that the only chance of success was to attempt his captain's measure Accordingly, at 2 h. 25 m., the Penguin ran her bowsprit between the Hornet's main and mizen rigging on the starboard side. The heavy swell lifting the ship a-head, the brig's bowsprit, after carrying away the Hornet's mizen-shroud, stern-davits, and spanker-boom, broke in two, and the foremast went at the same moment, falling in-board directly upon the foremost and waist guns on the larboard or engaged side. These guns becoming, in consequence, completely disabled, and the after-guns being equally so from the drawing of the breeching-bolts, an attempt was made to bring a fresh broadside to bear; but the Penguin was in too unmanageable a state to be got round. In this dilemma no alternative remained; and at 2 h. 35 m. P.M. Lieutenant M'Donald hailed to say that the Penguin surrendered. After a lapse of 25 minutes, an officer from the Hornet came on board to take possession.

Out of a crew, as already stated, of 105 men and 17 boys, the Penguin lost her commander, boatswain, and four seamen and marines killed, four others mortally wounded, and her second-lieutenant (John Elwin, very severely), one master's mate (John Holmes Bond), one midshipman (John Noyes, each of whom lost a leg), purser's clerk, and 24 seamen and marines wounded, for the most part slightly. Even the Hornet was beginning to fall off in her gunnery. Most of the Penguin's men were wounded by musketry; and the bowsprit, and the foremast along with it, fell chiefly owing to the two vessels getting foul in the manner they did, while so heavy a sea was running.

The Hornet received a few shot in the hull; one of which was so low down as to keep her men constantly at the pumps. Out of a crew of 163 men and two boys, the Hornet lost, by the acknowledgment of her officers, only two seamen killed and 11 wounded; but, according to the observation of the British officers, her loss was much greater. Just as Mr. Edward B. Kirk, one of the Penguin's midshipmen, and the very first prisoner that reached the Hornet, was stepping upon her deck, the crew were in the act of throwing a man overboard; but a struggle or convulsive twitch in the body occasioned his being hauled in again. The poor man's lower jaw had been nearly all shot away; yet he lived, and was walking about the deck in the course of a few days. This shows the hurry in which the American officers were, to get their killed out of the way before the arrival of the prisoners; and the time necessary to remove every appearance of blood and carnage contributed to the delay in sending for them. Even when the British did come on board, buckets of water were dashing about and brooms at work on all parts of the deck. The Penguin's second-lieutenant counted 16 of the Hornet's men lying in their cots; and several of her men told some of their former shipmates, whom they discovered among the Penguin's crew, that the Hornet had 10 men killed by the first and second broadsides.

We cannot, with any consistency, offer the trifling disparity of force in this action as an excuse for the Penguin's capture. The chief cause is to be sought in that which cannot be made apparent in figures—the immense disparity between the two vessels in the fitting of their guns, and in the effectiveness of their crews. A ship's gun, cast adrift, not only becomes utterly useless as a weapon of offence or defence, but in the very act of breaking loose, maims and disables the men stationed at it; and, if the sea is rough, as Captain Biddle says it was in the present instance, continues to cause destruction among the crew, generally, until again lashed to the ship's side. How much is the evil increased, if, as in the Penguin's case, instead of one gun, several guns break loose. In the midst of all this delay and self-destruction, the enemy, uninterrupted in his operations, and animated by the feeble resistance he meets, quickens his fire; and, conquering at last, fails not to ascribe solely to his skill and valour that victory which accident had partly gained for him.

We are inclined to think that the prize was not so "riddled in her hull" as to render her destruction on the morning of the 25th a matter of necessity. The fact is that, just after the action had ended, the Peacock and Tom Bowline hove in sight; and Captains Warrington and Biddle, having heard of the peace, were anxious to get to the East Indies as quickly as possible, in order to have their share of the few prizes yet to be taken.

The communicativeness of one of the American officers having conveyed to the ears of Lieutenant M'Donald the statement in Captain Biddle's official letter, that the Hornet had suffered so slightly in the action, Lieutenant M'Donald took an opportunity of mentioning the circumstance to the American captain; when, having drowned his native cunning in wine (some of poor Captain Dickinson's probably), Captain Biddle admitted the fact, but attempted to gloss it over by stating, that it was necessary to say so and so, and so and so, in order to make the thing be properly received in the United States. Here was an acknowledgment! How unnecessary, then, have been all our previous labours in detecting and exposing the misrepresentations contained in the American official accounts. Of course, we are saved all further trouble in showing how completely Captain Biddle has misstated every important fact connected with the capture of the Penguin. Before, however, we dismiss this action, let us make one remark on the circumstance of Captain Biddle having been informed of the peace on the 20th, three days previous to the action. If that information was communicated in such a manner as to have satisfied Captain Biddle as to the fact, there is no excuse his fondest admirers could make which should have screened him from the hands of the hangman. The action was disreputable; the slaughter criminal. His conscience, perhaps, at this moment is his best judge; and we are sincere when we say we hope he does not feel that sentence recorded against him, which he must feel if he fought that action, *knowing* the peace to have been signed.

On the 28th of April, at daylight, in latitude 39° south, longitude 34° west, the Peacock and Hornet bore down upon, in order to capture as an Indiaman, the British 74-gun ship Cornwallis, Captain John Bayley, bearing the flag of Rear-admiral Sir George Burlton, K.C.B. The mistake was soon discovered, and a chase commenced, during which the Peacock separated to the eastward. In the afternoon the Cornwallis, when gaining fast upon the Hornet, had to heave to and lower a boat for a marine that had dropped overboard. This delay, aided by the unskilful firing of the Cornwallis on the following day, saved the Hornet; but the chase continued until 9 A.M. on the 30th, when the 74, finding further pursuit useless, shortened sail and hauled to the wind. The closeness of the chase, however, had effected enough to render the Hornet, as a cruiser, utterly useless. She hove overboard her guns, muskets, cutlasses, forge, bell, anchors, cables, shot, boats, spare spars, and a considerable portion of her ballast, and was of course obliged to steer straight for the United States.

The Peacock, after she had been compelled to part from her consort, pursued her way to the East Indies; and, on the 30th of June, being off Anjier in the Straits of Sunda, fell in with the Honourable Company's brig-cruiser Nautilus, of 10 carronades, 18-pounders, and four long nines, commanded by Lieutenant Charles Boyce. On the Peacock's approach within hail, the lieutenant inquired if her captain knew that peace had been declared. Let us suppose, for a moment, that, just as the American commander was listening to the hail from the Nautilus, the latter became suddenly transformed into the British 22-gun ship Volage, Captain Joseph Drury, a sister-vessel to the Cyane, and at that time cruising in the East Indies. Captain Warrington would then have promptly hailed in turn, with the best speaking-trumpet in the ship, thanked Captain Drury for his politeness, and been the first to urge the folly, not to say wickedness of wounding and killing each other, while any doubt existed about peace having been signed. But it was a vessel he could almost hoist on board the Peacock. He therefore called out: "Haul down your colours instantly." This "reasonable demand" Lieutenant Boyce very properly considered as an imperious and insulting mandate, and, fully alive to the dignity of the British flag, and to the honour of the service to which he was acknowledged to be an ornament, prepared to cope with a ship whose immense superiority, as she overshadowed his little bark, gave him nothing to expect short of a speedy annihilation.

It will scarcely be credited that, about a quarter of an hour before this, Mr. Bartlett, the master of the Nautilus, and Cornet White, one of her passengers, in one boat, and Mr. Macgregor, the master-attendant at Anjier, in another, had gone on board the Peacock, in a friendly way, to communicate the news of peace. Scarcely had Mr. Bartlett stepped upon the American ship's deck than, without being allowed to ask a question, he was hurried below. Happily, Mr. Macgregor met with rather better success. The instant he arrived on board, he communicated to the Peacock's first-lieutenant, the most authentic information of peace having been concluded between Great Britain and America, grounded on no less authority than Mr. Madison's proclamation; which Mr. Macgregor had himself received from an American ship, passing the Straits on her way to China. What effect had this communication? Captain Warrington, whom the single word "Peace!" ought to have made pause, before he proceeded to spill the blood of his fellow-creatures, ordered Mr. Macgregor to be taken below.

Captain Warrington does not admit that Mr. Macgregor mentioned that peace existed; although the latter gentleman has sworn that he did, both to Captain Warrington's first-lieutenant and to his purser. As to the imputed silence of Messrs. Bartlett and White, would two officers, who had voluntarily entered on board the ship of a nation with whom they knew a peace had just been concluded, have acted in so senseless a manner as to suffer themselves to be made prisoners without some such words as, "Peace is signed," bursting from their lips? Even the ceremony of gagging, however quickly performed, could not have stopped an exclamation. which their personal liberty, and everything that was dear to them as men, would prompt them to utter. The same motives would have operated upon the two boats' crews; and there cannot be a doubt, that they all gave some sort of intimation, that peace had been signed. But Captain Warrington, as the Peacock's purser could not help saying, wanted to have a little brush with the British brig. He saw what a diminutive vessel she was, and, accordingly, ordered his men to fire into her. They did so; and the Nautilus was soon compelled to haul down her colours. But this the brig did not do until her gallant commander was most dangerously wounded, one seaman, two European invalids, and three lascars killed, her first-lieutenant (mortally), two seamen, and five lascars wounded. The wound of Lieutenant Boyce was of a most serious description. A grape-shot, that measured two inches and one-third in diameter, entered at the outside of his hip, and passed out close under the backbone. This severe wound did not, however, disable him. In a few minutes a 32-pound shot struck obliquely on his right knee, shattering the joint, splintering the legbone downwards and the thighbone a great way upwards. This, as may be supposed, laid the young officer prostrate on the deck. The dismounting of a bow-gun, and four or five men wounded, appears to have been the extent of the injury sustained by the Peacock.

Fearful that these facts would come to light, Captain Warrington had additional reasons for endeavouring to lessen the enormity of his offence, by stating, in his official letter, that "lascars" were the only sufferers. Poor wretches! and were they to be butchered with impunity, because their complexion and the American captain's were of different hues? Whose heart was the blackest the transaction in which they lost their lives has already shown to the world. Had the Volage, as we said before, been the vessel that had hove in sight, every man in the Peacock, in less than three minutes after the master-attendant at Anjier and the other British officers had come on board, would have been informed of the peace. Captain Warrington would have approached the stranger, if he approached at all, without opening his ports or displaying his helmets. In short, he that hectored so much in one case would have cringed as much in the other; and the commander of the United States sloop Peacock would have run no risk of being by his government "blamed for ceasing," or rather, for not commencing, "hostilities, without more authentic evidence that peace had been concluded."

The first-lieutenant of the Nautilus, Mr. Mayston, languished until the 3rd of December, a period of five months, when a mortification of his wound carried him off. About a fortnight after the action, Lieutenant Boyce suffered amputation very near his hip, on account of the length and complication of the fracture. The pain and danger of the operation was augmented by the proximity of the grape-shot wound. His life was subsequently despaired of; but, after a long course of hopes and fears to his numerous friends, this brave and amiable young man (or what Captain Warrington had left of him) survived.

Of course the American captain, who had himself escaped unhurt, the moment he was informed of the casualties on board his prize, either visited, or sent a condoling message to, her dreadfully mangled commander? Reader, he did neither. Captain Warrington, in the words of the poor sufferer, in his memorial to the court of directors, "proved himself totally destitute of fellow-feeling and commiseration; for, during the time he retained possession of the Nautilus," which was until 2 P.M. on the 1st of July, "he was not once moved to make a commonplace inquiry after the memorialist, in his then deplorable condition." No wonder that, throughout civilized India, the perpretator of this atrocious act is looked upon as a barbarian: let but the requisite publicity be given to the case of the Nautilus and Peacock, and the name of Warrington will be held in equal detestation throughout the civilized world.

On the evening of the 29th of December, 1822, the sloop Eliza, armed with one 18-pounder carronade, and with a complement of 24 men (including officers), commanded by Mr. Hugh Nurse, admiralty mate, anchored in compliance with orders received from Lieutenant Hobson, off Guajaba.

The next day (the 30th), a small vessel, felucca rigged, was observed standing towards the Eliza with a signal flying. Having approached her within five miles, the stranger tacked, and stood towards Green Key, still keeping the same signal flying. About five o'clock P.M. she was joined by a schooner, when both vessels stood towards the Eliza. Mr. Nurse, on perceiving this, immediately prepared to slip and make sail: at 7 o'clock the schooner having taken an advantageous position upon the larboard bow of the Eliza, opened her fire upon her. The Eliza immediately slipped her cable and made sail to close, keeping up a return fire upon the schooner. The felucca had now got into action, and warmly supported her friend. At 7 o'clock, after several cool and steady manœuvres, in order to clear the shoals by which the Eliza was surrounded, Mr. Nurse found himself close to windward of the felucca; he instantly bore up, poured in a round of grape, followed up by a volley of musketry, and boarded her on the larboard bow. The enemy made a smart resistance, but Lieutenant Nurse, although he had received a gun-shot wound in the right shoulder, cheered on his gallant crew, and in five minutes was in possession of the vessel. The schooner seeing her comrade disposed of in this summary way, made sail and escaped, and as the prize was quite ungovernable, on account of the loss of her bowsprit, Mr. Nurse judged it prudent to anchor for the night. The next day the Eliza, with her prize, made sail towards Green Key, to attack the schooner, which was ascertained to be a pirate of five guns, with a complement of 37 men: she, however, had escaped during the night. In this gallant affair, which reflects the highest credit upon Mr. Nurse, the Eliza lost two men killed (John White and John Goff) and eight wounded. Amongst the severely wounded were Mr. Nurse the commander, John M'Dermott, who died of his wounds shortly afterwards, John Welsh, Edward Bambrill, and Benjamin Inkpen; slightly wounded, William Adams, William Watts, and Henry Wilmot. We give below the relative force of each vessel, and by so doing we shall afford the reader a better idea of the gallantry of this exploit, in which the Spaniards sustained a loss of nine killed. The remaining part of the crew of the felucca, with the exception of four made prisoners, jumped overboard.

Eliza's Force.
One 18-pounder carronade.
Complement.
Midshipmen 2
Assistant Surgeon . . . 1
Pilot 1
Men 20
———
24

Felucca le Firme Union's Force.
One long 6-pounder on a pivot.
Four small carriage-guns, 4-pounders.
Crew 37
———
The schooner El Diableto, about the same force as the felucca.

In the official report Mr. Nurse mentions the services of Mr. George White, midshipman, whose bravery was highly conspicuous, and Mr. Clark, the assistant surgeon, who is since dead.

In March, in this year, Rear-admiral Sir Charles Rowley, the commander-in-chief in the West Indies, despatched Captain John Edward Walcott, in his majesty's frigate Tyne, having under his orders the sloop Thracian, Commander John Walter

Roberts, to endeavour to extirpate the piratical vessels which infested the West India station, and which generally made the different ports of the island of Cuba their rendezvous. Captain Walcott commenced his arduous task of searching 400 miles of coast, in order to examine the different creeks and inlets where small vessels could be sheltered and concealed.

If Captain Walcott failed in discovering the object of his search, he had the gratification of gaining information that a piratical schooner had been seen off the east end of the island of Cuba, and that she did occasionally visit a harbour in that neighbourhood, in which she disposed of her plunder to many of the residents. It may here be remembered that Captain Walcott, during his examination of the different creeks, found on an island, situated within the harbour of Nerangos, a cargo consisting of 1100 casks of wine and spirits; and upon his own responsibility, considering the concealment of the wine very suspicious, and believing it to be some of the captured property taken by the pirate, he embarked it. It was afterwards condemned, and sold at Jamaica for 6000*l*., two-thirds of which was deducted from the captors for government and colonial duties, thus leaving only 2000*l*. to be shared; whereas, had Captain Walcott failed to establish this cargo as the property of the pirates, he would have been liable to the full extent of 6000*l*.

On the 28th of March the Captain of an American pilot-boat confirmed the intelligence already received relative to the pirate. She was described as a schooner, named the Zaragonaza, of 120 tons, carrying one long 18-pounder on a swivel, four long 9-pounders, and eight swivels, commanded by a desperate character named Cayatano Arogonez, having a crew of between 70 and 80 men. Captain Walcott further learnt from the informer that he had been detained on board this vessel, and that during the time of his detention information reached the commander of the pirate that several men, a part of the crew of a piratical vessel, captured during a former cruise of the Tyne, had been hung at Jamaica. These men had given some proofs of a merciful disposition, for previously to their capture they had taken a small vessel tender to the Tyne in which were Lieutenant Hobson and 20 men. According to the general custom of the bloodthirsty savages they proceeded in their preparations to hang their captives, and actually placed the rope round the neck of Hobson and his men. The "still small voice" of conscience, however, seems to have awakened the last slumber of mercy, and ultimately they not only spared the lives of Lieutenant Hobson and his men, but after a few days' detention, allowed them to return to their ships. The execution of their brother pirates at Jamaica, after this rare mercy, was viewed by Cayatano Arogonez as an infamous, ungenerous, savage act; and he resolved to take ample revenge upon all unfortunate men who should fall into his hands. He summoned his crew, and, with barbarous ferocity, excited them to bind themselves by the most sacred obligation, under the form of an oath, that henceforth no Englishman's life should be spared, and that to avoid the retaliation which would certainly ensue in the event of their capture, they swore, rather than surrender to be hung, to blow up their vessel, their crew, and their assailants. To crown this horrid act of determination, it was requisite forthwith to procure a victim, that, passing the rubicon of crime, their consciences might become accustomed to the deed, and themselves cease to shudder at murder. A cry was raised to sacrifice the black cook, a native of Jamaica (and consequently if not an Englishman, one under the protection of the English flag), whom they had removed from a vessel they had captured. In vain did the poor fellow implore their mercy. They dragged him from his occupation, and instantly spritsail-yarded him, having secured him in a position to offer the fairest mark; these infamous villains amused themselves for 20 minutes, slightly wounding him at every shot before their savage pastime was surfeited, and the *coup de grace* inflicted. Against these men Captain Walcott had now to act. The pirate was cruising off the city of Baracoa, and was described as a very fast-sailing schooner; but as almost all the trade of Cuba, at least the coasting-trade, is carried on in vessels of this description, Captain Walcott became apprehensive that she might, by disguise, escape his vigilance; he therefore offered the American pilot 1000 dollars to remain with him; for, independently of the disguise which might be practised, two men-of-war schooners, belonging to the Spanish government, were cruising off the coast, and by pursuing these the pirate might escape. The pilot, however, refused; for he declared it impossible to capture the schooner by the boats, and that, failing of success, he would become known as the informer, and be obliged to relinquish his situation as pilot in the old Bahama channel. On the 31st of March the Tyne and Thracian, being off Baracoa, the pirate was discovered. The English men-of-war were instantly disguised as merchantships, their sails being set in a slovenly manner, and they stood in under easy sail to close with the schooner. For three hours this succeeded; at the expiration of that time the pirate was seen to crowd all sail for the harbour of Mata: the disguise was abandoned, and every stitch of canvas crowded in chase.

At 1 h. 30 m. P.M. the schooner anchored, and moored head and stern athwart the harbour, her broadside commanding the entrance which was not more than a cable's length, and wearing the royal colours of Spain. The boats of the Tyne and Thracian were instantly hoisted out, manned and armed, the total number of men being 47; and Captain Walcott duly considering all the consequences of failure from the information already given, resolved to head this desperate enterprise himself; leaving Captain Roberts in command of the ships, and desiring him to do his utmost to close with the pirate in order to afford all assistance. At 3 P.M. the boats arrived within gun-shot, when all thought of subterfuge was abandoned by the pirate, the black flag was hoisted, and a spirited cannonade commenced. Cayatano Arogonez, by way of strengthening his position, had landed some of his crew with small-arms, and these men, sheltered by the trees which grew close to the shore of the harbour, opened a very harassing fire upon the assailants. In the mean time the boats continued to approach, and the crowded deck of the schooner became visible; for three-quarters of an hour the English sustained the fire of the pirate and of the men on shore, when a favourable opportunity occurred, three hearty cheers were given, the boats dashed alongside, and the panic-stricken pirates endeavoured to save themselves by flight. Twenty-eight men, however, were secured, amongst whom was their commander. Every word of information given by the pilot was now proved correct: her description, size, armament, &c.; and the hand of retributive justice rid the world of Arogonez and his men, for they were all hanged at Jamaica, and received more mercy in their expeditious death than they had accorded to the poor cook.

It now becomes our cheerful duty to bestow on Captain Walcott and the officers under his command the praise they deserve. This attack took place in daylight, against a vessel advantageously moored, manned by a crew resolved to perish or to conquer; the boats were advanced in a calm, and for three-quarters of an hour they were under a heavy fire. Every man must have done his duty, and it has been well designated by a contemporary historian, as one of the most brilliant actions in boat-service he ever remembered.[1] Captain Walcott, in his

[1] Brenton.

official letter, mentions the excellent conduct of Lieutenants Amos Plymsell, and James Campbell, of Messrs. Robinson, Dawson, Shapland,[1] Gettings, and Dalyell, midshipmen; likewise of Mr. West the surgeon, and Mr. Graham assistant-surgeon, who volunteered their services. Of Captain Roberts he speaks in the highest terms, and Mr. Bull the acting-master of the Tyne, receives his warmest thanks for the manner in which he piloted the ships through the constant intricate and dangerous navigation, and finally got them within gun-shot of the captured pirate; the loss sustained by the English was one man killed and five wounded, the Spaniards lost 10 killed and 15 wounded.

In giving our account of this action we consulted Captain Brenton's history, but were discouraged from gleaning any information from him, in consequence of two mistakes in the first line: he calls Captain Walcott a commander and a C.B.; he had been post more than a year, and to this day, although he merits a higher distinction, is not a C.B. He calls the Tyne a sloop; she is a frigate. He says, "both the British commanders were made post," whereas one was posted a year previously to the action, and the other succeeded to an invaliding vacancy. He finishes by calling Mr. Thomas Bull, Mr. Ball.[2]

On the 31st of January, Captain James Ryder Burton, in command of his majesty's sloop Cameleon, of twelve 32-pounder carronades and 45 men, when in company with his majesty's ship Naiad, Captain the Hon. Sir Robert Spencer, off Algiers, made signal for a suspicious sail to windward, which ultimately proved to be the Tripoli, an Algerine corvette, of 20 long 12-pounders and 150 men. When the Naiad hoisted her colours, she fired a shot ahead of the stranger. The Tripoli, in showing hers, fired a shot *at* the Naiad; the signal was instantly made to chase, and both British vessels tacked to that effect with the intention of cutting off the Algerine from entering the mole of Algiers. The Naiad having the advantage of the Cameleon, after an hour's chase, passed ahead of the Tripoli and fired into her, then tacked and stood out to sea. By this time the Cameleon got close up under the enemy's lee, so close, as not only to receive the fire of the Algerine, but likewise the grape and canister of the Naiad, which ship was to windward of both the

---

[1] Mr. Shapland being the senior midshipman in this affair was promoted, and Mr. Bull was confirmed as master of the Tyne.
[2] These inaccuracies would not have been pointed out or noticed but for Captain Brenton's diligent search of our pages, out of 2000 of which he has discovered two typographical errors: unfortunately, the editor being more diligent, has found several more, which shall be rectified.

Tripoli and Cameleon. The fire of both ships, one so very superior in force as the Naiad, soon riddled the Algerine, but she still continued running towards the Mole, and was within gun-shot of the batteries, which opened their fire upon the Cameleon. As Sir Robert Spencer considered he had sufficiently punished the insolence of the Algerine, the Naiad stood out to sea, and the Cameleon was recalled, as that sloop was now closely engaged with a very superior force in the Tripoli. Captain Burton, on perceiving the signal, desired his helm to be put a-lee with the intention of boarding the Algerine, but having too much head-way, the Cameleon passed under the bows of the enemy, who put her helm a-weather and bore up close under the lee of the brig, receiving from the latter her broadside. In the mean time, the Cameleon braced her head yards round, and boxed off, then filled again in chase. Being now to windward, she availed herself of her position to run the Algerine on board, which she effected, placing her bowsprit between the fore and main mast of the Tripoli. Captain Burton headed his men, and soon drove the Algerines below; but in the act of taking his prize in tow, Sir Robert Spencer wore round, passed within hail, and desired Captain Burton to cut away the Algerine's anchor and abandon her. This was done, and both ships stood out. In this affair, it is necessary to state that the only credit which can be claimed by any one is by Captain Burton. It is evident that the attacking force was sufficient to beat five vessels of the size of the Tripoli, but in the moment of boarding, the Algerine was three times more powerful in men than the Cameleon, and, although the Tripoli had been cut up severely by the Naiad, and although it is probable that the crew of the former were already beaten, yet the act of boarding so very superior a force reflects the highest credit on Captain Burton, his officers, and men. For this action he received his post-rank shortly afterwards.

STATE OF THE BRITISH NAVY.

The totals in the two "ordinary" columns of the present abstract decisively show the peaceable state of the navy at the beginning of the year 1816;[1] and the totals, generally, differ but slightly from those of the abstract for the year in which the war had commenced.[2]

The number of commissioned officers and masters belonging to the British navy at the beginning of the present year was,

Admirals	67
Vice-admirals	68
Rear-admirals	75
,, superannuated 32	
Post-captains	851
,, superannuated 36	
Commanders, or sloop-captains . . .	812
,, superannuated 80	
Lieutenants	4064
Masters	693

And the number of seamen and marines, voted for the service of the same year, was 33,000.[3]

Having brought to a close the wars of civilized nations, we have now to record the particulars of a short but decisive war carried on against barbarians. Partly to settle some differences with the regencies of Algiers, Tunis, and Tripoli, and partly, no doubt, to astonish Europe with the extent of their naval force,

[1] See Appendix, Annual Abstract, No. 24.
[2] For the lists of casualties usually introduced in this place, see Appendix Nos. 8, 9, 10, and 11.
[3] See Appendix, No. 12.

the United States, the moment peace with England permitted them, sent forth, in separate divisions, as fast as the ships could be got ready, nearly the whole of their Atlantic or sea navy. On the 17th of June, off Cape de Gatte, the first division, consisting of three frigates and three smaller vessels, under Commodore Decatur, in the new 32-pounder 44-gun frigate Guerrière, after a running fight, by one account, of 25 minutes, and by another account, of nearly two hours, captured the Algerine 18-pounder 40-gun frigate Mezoura. Mr. Madison, in his speech to congress delivered on the 5th of December, when referring to this "demonstration of American skill and prowess," says, "The high character of the American commander was brilliantly sustained on the occasion." With examples of this sort from the head of the government, no wonder that the people of the United States are such unconscionable braggarts.

The American squadron also drove on shore near St. Xavier a small frigate or corvette. On the 30th Commodore Decatur concluded a treaty with the Dey of Algiers; by which all prisoners made on either side were to be restored, and all property given up, and no more tribute was to be demanded from the United States. The Algerine prisoners on board the squadron of Commodore Decatur amounted to 500, and the natives of the United States in the hands of the dey did not exceed 10; consequently his highness did not, in that respect, make a bad bargain. The American commodore afterwards sailed for Tunis and Tripoli, and obtained from those regencies payment of the few thousand dollars in dispute between the latter and some American citizens. In the case of Tripoli, 10 Danish and Neapolitan captives were given up by the bey, in lieu of a portion of the stipulated sum. In his letter to the American secretary of state, Commodore Decatur had the modesty to say, that the treaty he had concluded "placed the United States on higher ground than any other nation."[1] One of the officers of his squadron concludes a letter to a friend with the following piece of pleasantry:—"You have no idea of the respect which the American character has gained by our late wars. The Spaniards, especially, think we are devils incarnate; as we beat the English who beat the French, who beat them, who nobody ever beat before; and the Algerines, whom the devil himself could not beat."[2]

On the 23rd of May, at Bona, near Algiers, the crews of be-

[1] Naval Monument, p. 299.   [2] Ibid., p. 295.

tween 300 and 400 small vessels engaged in the coral-fishery while on their way to celebrate mass (it being Ascension-day), were barbarously massacred by a band of 2000 Turkish, Levantine, and Moorish troops. These atrocities committed on defenceless Christians having at length roused the vengeance of Britain, an expedition, of a suitable magnitude, was prepared to act against the forts and shipping of Algiers, and the command was intrusted to a most able officer, Admiral Lord Exmouth; who had already, a short time before, compelled the Dey of Tunis to sign a treaty for the abolition of Christian slavery, and to restore 1792 slaves to freedom.

On the 28th of July, at noon, a fleet, consisting, of the following 19 men-of-war, also a naval transport, a sloop with ordnance stores, and a despatch-vessel weighed from Plymouth Sound with a fine northerly wind:

Gun-ship		
100	Queen Charlotte	Admiral (b.) Lord Exmouth, G.C.B. / Captain James Brisbane, C.B.
98	Impregnable	Rear-admiral (b.) David Milne. / Captain Edward Brace, C.B.
74	Superb	,, Charles Ekins.
	Minden	,, William Paterson.
	Albion	,, John Coode.
50	Leander	,, Edward Chetham, C.B.
Gun-frigate.		
40	Severn	,, Hon. Fred. Wm. Aylmer.
	Glasgow	,, Hon. Anthony Maitland.
36	Granicus	,, William Furlong Wise.
	Hebrus	,, Edmund Palmer, C.B.
Gun-b.-sloop.		
18	Heron	,, George Bentham.
	Mutine	,, James Mould.
10	Britomart	,, Robert Riddell.
	Cordelia	,, William Sargent.
	Jasper	,, Thomas Carew.
Bb.	Belzebub	,, William Kempthorne.
	Fury	,, Constantine R. Moorsom.
	Hecla	,, William Popham.
	Infernal	,, Hon. George James Perceval.

At 5 P.M., when the fleet was off Falmouth, Captain Paterson was ordered to hasten on to Gibraltar, to have everything in readiness against the arrival of the expedition. On the 9th of August, at 2 P.M., Lord Exmouth anchored with his fleet in Gibraltar bay, and found lying there, in company with the Minden, which had arrived only on the preceding night at 11, the following Dutch squadron:

BATTLE OF ALGIERS.

Gun-frigate.
40	Melampus	. .	Vice-admiral Baron T. Van de Cappellan. Captain Antony-Willem De-Man.	
	Frederica .	. . . .	,,	Jakob-Adrien Van-der-Straaten.
	Diana .	. . . .	,,	Pietrus Zievogel.
	Amstel	. . . .	,,	Willem-Augustus Vanderhart,
30	Dageraad .	. . . .	,,	Johannes-Martinus Polders.

Gun-corvette.
18	Eendragt .	. . . .	,,	Johan.-Fred.-Chr. Wardenburg.

Immediately on being apprised of the object of the expedition, Vice-admiral Van de Cappellen solicited and obtained leave to co-operate in the attack with his frigate-squadron. No time was lost by Lord Exmouth in sending on shore all articles of useless lumber and in getting on board fresh supplies of provisions and ordnance stores, it being the admiral's intention to sail on the 12th. On the 11th, however, a strong levanter set in; and, continuing over the 12th, kept the fleet from moving.

Owing to the highly commendable regulations put in force by Lord Exmouth, an unusual proportion of powder and shot had been expended by the fleet since its departure from England. Every Tuesday and Friday the signal was made for the fleet to prepare for action; when each ship, according to directions previously given, fired six broadsides. Besides this general exercise, the first and second captains of the Queen Charlotte's guns were daily trained at a target made of laths, three feet square; in the centre of which was suspended a piece of wood of the shape and size of a bottle, with yarns crossed at right angles, so that a 12-pound shot could not pass through the interstices without cutting a yarn. This target, which was, in 1812, first introduced into the navy by Lieutenant George Crichdon, then belonging to his majesty's ship Rhin, commanded by Sir Charles Malcolm, and which was shown to, and approved by Sir James Brisbane, when fitting out the Queen Charlotte, was hung at the foretopmast studdingsail-boom, which was rigged out for the purpose; and it was fired at from abreast of the admiral's skylight on the quarter-deck. By the time the fleet reached Gibraltar, the target was never missed, and the average number of bottles hit daily was 10 out of 14. The confidence this gave to the ship's company was unbounded; and, of their expertness against stone walls and living targets, we shall soon have to display the terrible effects.

On the 13th the 18-gun brig-sloop Satellite, Captain James Murray, arrived from Algiers; and on this day every captain in the fleet received a plan of the fortifications of the place, with full instructions as to the intended position of his ship. On the 14th, early in the forenoon, the wind having shifted to the southward, the Dutch squadron, and the whole British fleet, except the Jasper sent to England with despatches, and the Saracen left behind, consisting altogether of 23 ships and brigs, five gun-boats, and an ordnance sloop, fitted as an explosion-vessel under the personal direction of Lieutenant Richard Howell Fleming, of the Queen Charlotte (who was to have the command of her), and Major Gossett of the corps of miners, weighed and stood into the Mediterranean.

Previous to the sailing of the fleet, each line-of-battle ship took charge of a gun-boat, and had their own launches fitted for howitzers. The flat-bottomed boats put in requisition were prepared for Congreve's rockets. On the 16th, early in the afternoon, just as the fleet had got within 200 miles of Algiers, the wind shifted to the eastward; and in the evening the ship-sloop Prometheus, Captain William Bateman Dashwood, joined company direct from the port, having on board the wife, daughter, and infant child of the British consul, Mr. M'Donell. The two former, disguised in midshipmen's clothes, had with great difficulty been brought off; but, owing to the treachery of Mrs. M'Donell's Jew-nurse,[1] the infant, while on its way to the boat concealed in a basket, was detained by order of the dey: as were also the surgeon of the Prometheus, three midshipmen, and the remainder of the crews of two boats, consisting in all of 18 persons. "The child," says Lord Exmouth, "was sent off next morning by the dey; and, as a solitary instance of his humanity, it ought to be recorded by me." The consul himself was put in irons and confined in a small room on the ground-floor of his house; nor could the most urgent remonstrances on the part of Captain Dashwood induce the dey to release his prisoners.

Captain Dashwood confirmed all that the admiral had previously learnt about the preparations making by the Algerines to resist the attack; of which they had received intelligence, chiefly, as was suspected, from the French 40-gun frigate, Ciotat, then at anchor in the bay. It appeared, also, that about 40,000 men had been marched down from the interior, and all the janizaries called in from the distant garrisons. The ships, consisting

---

[1] Upon the authority of Mr. Abraham Salamé in his very interesting "Narrative of the expedition to Algiers," p. 15, note; but, according to Lord Exmouth, owing to the infant crying in the gateway, although the surgeon had administered something to compose it.

of four frigates, mounting 44 guns each, five large corvettes, mounting from 24 to 30 guns, and between 30 and 40 gun and mortar boats, were all in port. The fortifications of Algiers, for so small a place, were of considerable strength. Upon the various batteries on the north side of the city, including a battery over the north gate, were mounted about 80 pieces of cannon and six or eight enormous mortars; but the shoalness of the water would scarcely admit a heavy ship to approach within reach of them. Between the north wall of the city and the commencement of the pier, which is about 250 yards in length, and connects the town with the lighthouse, were about 20 more guns, the greater part of them similarly circumstanced. At the north projection of the mole stood a semicircular battery, of two tiers of guns, about 44 in all; and to the southward of that, and nearly in a line with the pier, was the round or lighthouse battery, of three tiers of guns, 48 in all. Then came a long battery, also of three tiers, called the eastern battery, mounting 66 guns. This was flanked by four other batteries, of two tiers each, mounting altogether 60 guns; and on the south head of the mole were two large guns, represented to be 68 pounders, and nearly 20 feet long: so that the different batteries on the mole mounted at least 220 guns; consisting, except in the case just mentioned, of 32, 24, and 18 pounders. South-west of the small pier that projects from the city to form the entrance of the mole, or harbour, and bearing, at the distance of about 300 yards, due west from the south mole-head, was the fish-market battery, of 15 guns, in three tiers. Between that and the southern extremity of the city were two batteries of four or five guns each. Beyond the city, in this direction, was a castle and two or three other batteries, mounting between them 60 or 70 guns. Besides all the batteries we have enumerated, and which constituted the sea-defences of the port, there were various others at the back of the city, and on the heights in its environs: indeed, the whole of the guns mounted for the defence of the city of Algiers, on its sea and land frontiers, are represented to have exceeded 1000.

Having to beat against a head wind until towards midnight on the 24th, when it shifted to south-west, the fleet did not make Cape Cazzina, a high promontory about 55 miles to the westward of Algiers, of the bay of which it forms the northern point, until noon on the 26th; nor gain a sight of the city until daybreak on the 27th. The ships at this time lying nearly becalmed, Lord Exmouth took the opportunity of despatching Lieutenant

Samuel Burgess, in one of the Queen Charlotte's boats, towed by the Severn, to demand of the dey certain conditions, of which the following is the substance: The abolition of Christian slavery; the delivery of all Christian slaves in the kingdom of Algiers; the repayment of all the money that had recently been exacted for the redemption of Neapolitan and Sardinian slaves; peace with the king of the Netherlands; and the immediate liberation of the British consul and the two boats' crews of the Prometheus. At 9 A.M., the calm retarding the progress of the frigate, the boat, by signal from the Queen Charlotte, pulled for the shore, carrying a flag of truce. At 11 A.M., on arriving opposite to the mole, the boat was met by one from the shore, in which was the captain of the port. The demand was presented, and an answer promised in two hours. Meanwhile, a breeze having sprung up from the sea, the fleet stood into the bay, and lay to about a mile from the city.

At 2 P.M., no answer returning, Lieutenant Burgess hoisted the signal to that effect, and pulled out towards the Severn. The Queen Charlotte immediately asked, by signal, if all the ships were ready. Almost at the same moment every ship had the affirmative flag at her mast-head, and the fleet bore up to the attack in the prescribed order. At 2 h. 35 m. P.M. the Queen Charlotte anchored with springs about 50 yards from the mole-head. Just as the British three-decker was in the act of lashing herself to the mainmast of an Algerine brig fast to the shore at the mouth of the mole or harbour, and towards which Lord Exmouth had directed his ship to be steered as the guide for her position, a shot was fired at the Queen Charlotte; and almost at the same instant two other shot were fired from the opposite end of the mole at the Impregnable and ships near her, as they were advancing to their stations. Scarcely had these three guns been discharged, when Lord Exmouth, with characteristic humanity, waved his hand to a crowd of 200 or 300 soldiers and artillerymen, standing on the parapet of the mole, surveying the immense floating body so near to them. As the greater part of these were in the act of leaping through the embrasures into the lower battery, the Queen Charlotte opened her starboard broadside. Thus the action commenced, each British ship taking a part in it the instant she could bring her guns to bear.

Next ahead of the Queen Charlotte, or rather upon her larboard bow, lay the Leander, with her after-guns on the starboard side bearing into the mouth of the mole, and her foremost ones upon the fish-market battery. Ahead of the Leander lay the Severn, with the whole of her starboard guns bearing on the fish-market battery. Close to the Severn was the Glasgow, with her larboard guns bearing on the town batteries. In the rear of the Queen Charlotte, inclining towards her starboard quarter, at the distance of about 250 yards, and within a very few of her allotted station, was the Superb, with her starboard broadside bearing upon the 60-gun battery, next to that on the mole-head. This ship was not as close to the Queen Charlotte as her gallant commander intended her to be (by placing her flying jib-boom over the poop of the Queen Charlotte), owing to the signal having been made "to anchor" instead of "prepare to anchor," as was directed by Lord Exmouth. Close astern of the Superb, in a north-easterly direction, the Impregnable and Albion were to have taken their stations in line ahead; but, not being sufficiently advanced when the firing commenced, the Impregnable was obliged to bring to considerably outside, not only of her proper station, but of the line of bearing (about south-east from the south angle of the eastern battery) within which the attacking force had been ordered to assemble. The Impregnable thus lay exposed, at the distance of about 400 yards, as well to the lighthouse battery of three tiers, towards which she soon sprang her starboard broadside, as to the eastern battery of two tiers. Observing what an open space there was between the Impregnable and her second ahead, the Superb, the Minden stood on and took up a position about her own length astern of the latter. The Albion, following, brought up, at first, close ahead of the Impregnable; but, finding herself too near to the three-decker, she filled, and at about 3 P.M. came to again, within her own length of the Minden. The latter, quickly passing her streamcable out of the larboard gun-room port to the Albion's bow, hove the two ships close together. In this way the eight heaviest ships of the fleet took their stations; the Queen Charlotte, Superb, Minden, Albion, and Impregnable, from the mole-head in a north-easterly direction, and the Leander, Severn, and Glasgow, from the fish-market battery in a curved direction to the south-west.

The station assigned to the Dutch squadron was against the batteries to the southward of the city, and it appears to have been the intention of the Dutch admiral to place the Melampus in the centre of his five frigates; but the Diana's captain, not understanding exactly the orders given to him, did not go far enough to the northward. Seeing this, the baron gallantly pushed the Melampus past the Diana, and at about 3 P.M. anchored his frigate with her jib-boom over the taffrail of the Glasgow. The Diana and Dageraad anchored successively astern of their admiral. The two remaining Dutch frigates anchored further out; and the corvette Eendragt, as she had been directed, kept under way.

The Granicus and Hebrus frigates and the smaller vessels (except the bombs) being considered in the light of a corps de reserve, had not had any particular stations assigned to them, but were to bring up abreast of any openings they could find in the line of battle. Impelled onward by the ardent desire of filling the first of these openings, the Hebrus got becalmed by the heavy cannonade, and was obliged to anchor a little without the line, on the Queen Charlotte's larboard quarter. The Granicus, finding herself shooting fast ahead, hove to, with the intention of waiting until her companions had taken their stations. As, owing to the dense smoke which prevailed, nothing beyond the distance of a cable's length could be seen, except the Queen Charlotte's masthead flag, Captain Wise allowed 10 minutes to elapse for the ships to anchor. The Granicus then filled, let fall her foresail, set topgallantsails, and, soon gaining fresh way, steered straight for a beacon that, phœnix-like, seemed to live in the hottest of the fire. With a display of intrepidity and of seamanship alike unsurpassed, Captain Wise anchored his frigate in a space scarcely exceeding her own length between the Queen Charlotte and Superb; a station of which a three-decked line-of-battle ship might justly have been proud.

The different sloops attached to the squadron also took their posts; the Heron, Britomart, Prometheus, and Cordelia remaining under way, and the Mutine anchoring on the larboard bow of the Impregnable. The four bomb-vessels were soon in their stations, at the distance of about 2000 yards from the enemy's works, and began their destructive discharges; as did also the battering flotilla, commanded by Captain Frederick Thomas Mitchell, consisting of gun-boats, mortar-boats, launches with carronades, rocket-boats, barges, and yawls, in number 55.

Such was the precision and destructive effect of the Queen Charlotte's fire, that her third broadside levelled the south end of the mole to its foundation: she then sprang her broadside, until it bore upon the batteries over the town-gate leading into the mole. Here gun after gun came tumbling over the battlements; and when the last gun fell, which was just as the artillerymen were in the act of discharging it, one of the Algerine chiefs leaped upon the ruined parapet, and shook his drawn cimiter at the ship, whose fatally pointed cannon had so quickly demolished that which, by its brave defenders at least, had been considered impregnable.

The excellent position of, and the animated fire kept up by, the Leander very soon cut to pieces the Algerine gun-boats and row-galleys; whereby their intention of boarding the nearest British ships was entirely frustrated. Towards 4 P.M. the Leander, by orders from the admiral, ceased firing, to allow the Algerine frigate moored across the mole, at the distance of about 140 yards from the Queen Charlotte, to be set on fire. Accordingly, the flag-ship's barge, under the command of Lieutenant Peter Richards, assisted by Major Gossett, of the corps of miners, Lieutenant of marines Ambrose A. R. Wolrige, and midshipman Henry M'Clintock, proceeded to execute that service. A gallant young midshipman, Aaron Stark Symes, in rocket-boat No. 8, "although," as Lord Exmouth says, "forbidden, was led by his ardent spirit, to follow in support of the barge." His boat, being flat-bottomed, could not keep pace with the barge, and became exposed, in consequence, to a cannonade that wounded himself, and killed his brother officer and nine of the boat's crew. In about 10 minutes, Lieutenant Richards in the barge succeeded in boarding and setting fire to the Algerine frigate, and returned from the enterprise with the loss of only two men killed. The blaze was in a manner electrical; and Lord Exmouth testified his approbation, by telegraphing to the fleet, "Infallible."

At 4 h. 15 m. P.M. the Algerine frigate in flames drifting out towards the Queen Charlotte, the latter shifted her birth to let the vessel pass. At 4 h. 24 m. Rear-admiral Milne sent a message to the commander-in-chief, communicating, that the Impregnable had sustained a loss of 150 killed and wounded (including a third of the number by the bursting of a shell from the enemy's works), and requesting that a frigate might be sent to divert some of the fire from the ship. The Glasgow was immediately ordered upon that service; but, the wind having fallen in consequence of the heavy firing, she was unable to do more than take up, after the lapse of nearly three-quarters of an hour, a somewhat better position for annoyance than her former one. Here a short distance off the Severn, with her stern now towards that ship, the Glasgow became exposed to a severe raking fire from the fish-market and contiguous batteries; which dismounted two of her quarter-deck carronades, and in a few minutes did her more serious injury than all she had previously suffered. At 7 P.M. the Leander, being greatly cut up by the fish-market battery and others on her starboard bow, ran out a hawser to the Severn and brought her broadside to bear upon them. About this time, by the incessant and well-directed fire of the mortar, gun, and rocket-boats, all the ships and vessels within the harbour were burning. The flames subsequently communicated to the arsenal and storehouses on the mole; and the city also, in several parts, was set on fire by the shells from the bomb-vessels.

The ordnance-sloop, which, fitted as an explosion-vessel, had accompanied the expedition from Gibraltar, for the purpose of being sent among the ships in the mole, was now, as they were all destroyed, placed under the directions of Rear-admiral Milne. Lieutenant Fleming, who during the action had been commanding with great credit a battering-boat stationed close under the stern of the Queen Charlotte, proceeded, in company with Major Reed of the engineers, to take command of the explosion-vessel, and to place her where an officer, sent by Rear-admiral Milne, should point out. This officer was Captain Herbert Bruce Powell, a volunteer serving on board the Impregnable. In a short time the sloop was run on shore, close under the semicircular battery to the northward of the lighthouse. There, at a few minutes past 9 P.M., the vessel exploded; and, having been charged with 143 barrels of powder, must have operated very successfully as a diversion in favour of the Impregnable.

The whole of the ships kept up a tremendous fire upon the town and forts until about 10 P.M.,; when the upper tiers of the batteries on the mole, being in a state of dilapidation, the fire from the lower tiers nearly silenced, and the ammunition of the attacking ships reduced to a very small quantity, the Queen Charlotte cut her cables and springs, and stood out before a light air of wind, which, fortunately for the British, had just sprung up from the land. The remaining British ships, by orders of the admiral, began cutting also; but, owing to their disabled state, they made very slow progress, and the Leander, Superb, and Impregnable suffered much, in consequence, from the raking fire of a fort at the upper angle of the city. Before 2 A.M., on the 28th every British and Dutch ship had come to out of reach of shot or shells, the Algerine fleet and store-houses illuminating by their blaze the whole bay, and greatly assisting the former in picking an anchorage. As if to add to the awful grandeur of the scene, the elements began their war as soon as the ships and batteries had ended theirs. For nearly three hours the lightning and thunder were incessant, and the rain poured down in torrents. We are sensible that a diagram would have been particularly useful in this action, and had hoped to have been able to give one ; but, on consulting the logs, we found the positions of very few of the ships laid down with the requisite accuracy. Nor could we rely upon any of the few plans that have been published, having discovered mistakes in every one of them.

Now for the account of casualties sustained on the part of the assailants. The Queen Charlotte had seven seamen and one marine killed, three lieutenants (George Morison King, John Sampson Iago, and Frederick John Johnston, the latter mortally), one secretary to the admiral (Joshua Grimes), one captain of marine-artillery (Charles Frederick Burton), one lieutenant of marines (Patrick Robertson), her boatswain (William Maxwell), five midshipmen (George Markham, Henry Campbell, Edward Hibbert, Edward Stanley, and Robert Hood Baker), one secretary's clerk (Samuel Colston), 82 seamen, 24 marines, two marine artillery, five sappers and miners, and four boys wounded ; Impregnable, one midshipman (John Hawkins), 37 seamen, 10 marines, and two boys killed, one master's mate (George Nepean Wesley), one midshipman (Henry Quinn), 111 seamen, 21 marines, nine sappers and miners, and 17 boys[1] wounded ; Superb, one master's mate (Thomas Howard), one midshipman (Robert C. Bowen), three seamen, two marines, and one rocket-troop killed, her captain (slightly), three lieutenants (Philip Thicknesse Horn, John M'Dougall, and George W. Gunning), two midshipmen (William Sweeting and John Hood Wolseley), 62 seamen, 14 marines, and two marine-artillery wounded ; Minden, five seamen and two marines killed, one master's mate (Charles Calmady Dent), one midshipman (Charles G. Grubb), 26 seamen, and nine marines wounded ; Albion, one assistant-surveyor (Thomas Mends), one midshipman (John Jardine), and one seaman killed, her captain (severely), one midshipman (John Harvey, mortally), 10 seamen, and three marines wounded ; Leander, one captain of marines (James Willson), one lieu-

---

[1] An extraordinary number to suffer on board one ship. It is perhaps full as extraordinary that, out of a total of 210 persons killed and wounded, three only should be officers : this is partly accounted for by the havoc which the bursting of the shell caused among the sailors on the main or third deck; but the small proportion of officers, with even those fifty men deducted, is surprising.

tenant of marines (George Baxter), three midshipmen (—— Lowdon, Richard Calthrop, and P. G. Hanwall), 11 seamen, and one marine killed, two lieutenants (Henry Walker and John Stewart Dixon,) five midshipmen (Edward Aitchison, William Cole, Dawson Mayne, Henry Sturt, and George Dixon), one clerk (William W. Pickett), 69 seamen, 25 marines, four boys, and 12 supernumeraries wounded ; Severn, two seamen and one marine killed, five midshipmen (James Foster, arm amputated, Charles Caley, William Ferror, Daniel M'Neale Beatty, and William A. Carter), 25 seamen, three marines, and one boy wounded; the Glasgow, nine seamen and one marine killed, one lieutenant (Edmund Williams Gilbert), her master (Robert Fulton), one lieutenant of marines (Athelston Stephens), five midshipmen (John Duffell, George W. Hervey, Wynne Baird, George Henry Heathcote, and —— Keay,) 25 seamen, three marines, and one boy wounded; Granicus, two lieutenants of marines (William M. Morgan and William Renfrey), one midshipman (Robert Pratt), nine seamen, one marine, one marine-artillery, and two boys killed, one lieutenant (Henry Augustus Perkins), four midshipmen (Lewis Dunbar Mitchell, Lewis Tobias Jones, George R. Glennie, and Dacres Furlong Wise), 31 seamen, three marines, two rocket-troop, and one boy wounded ; Hebrus, one midshipman (George H. A. Pococke) and three seamen killed, one midshipman (Aaron Sykes Symes), 10 seamen, one marine, two rocket-troop, and one boy wounded ; Infernal, one lieutenant of marine-artillery (John James P. Bissett) and one seaman killed, one lieutenant (John Foreman), her boatswain (George Valentine), clerk (Matthew Hopkins), three midshipmen (James Barber, James M. Cross, and John H. Andrews), eight seamen, one marine-artillery, and two boys wounded.

None of the remaining three bomb-vessels, nor any of the sloops, appear to have incurred any loss. That sustained by the Dutch squadron amounted to 13 killed and 52 wounded; making the total loss, on the part of the allies, 141 killed and 742 wounded. The following statement will show, along with the names of the first-lieutenants (and of some of the others in the flag-ships) of the British ships, the individual loss sustained by the two squadrons, and the quantity of powder and shot which each of the British and Dutch ships expended in the action.

The quantities marked with an asterisk are doubtful: the others are officially correct. The Impregnable, it is understood, fired two shot at a time ; which accounts for her expenditure so greatly exceeding that of either of the other line-of-battle ships. The whole quantity of powder and shot expended in the engagement, according to Mr. Salamé's very interesting narrative, was upwards of 500 tons of the latter, and nearly 118 tons of the former. This includes, of course, the quantity expended by the sloops, most of whom fired when they could do so with effect. Mr. Salamé states, also, that the number of 13 and 10 inch shells thrown by the four bomb-vessels was 960.

SHIPS.	FIRST-LIEUTENANTS.	Loss. K.	Loss. W.	POWDER. lbs.	ROUND SHOT. No.
Queen Charlotte	Peter Richards, 1st F. T. Mitchell, 2nd J. W. Cairnes, 3rd	8	131	30,424	4,462*
Impregnable	J. B. Babington, 1st Roger Hall, 2nd	50	160	28,800	6,730
Superb	Ph. Thicknesse Horn	8	84	23,200*	4,500*
Minden	Joseph Benjamin Howell	7	37	24,536	4,710
Albion	Robert Hay	3	15	22,520*	4,110*
Leander	Thomas Sanders	17	118	21,700	3,680
Severn	James Davies	3	34	12,910*	2,920*
Glasgow	George M'Pherson	10	37	13,460*	3,000*
Granicus	John Parson	16	42	9,960*	2,800
Hebrus	E. Holling. Delafosse	4	15	9,780	2,755
Infernal	John Foreman	2	17		
	Total British loss	128	690		
Melampus		3	15		
Diana		6	22		
Dageraad		..	4	619	10,148
Frederica		..	5		
Amstel		4	6		
Total	Dutch loss	13	52		
	Allied loss	141	742		

Although none of the ships lost any spars, many, particularly the Impregnable, Leander, Superb, Granicus, Glasgow, and Severn, had their masts much injured. In hull, also, these ships, the first two especially, were considerable sufferers. The Impregnable, indeed, is stated to have received 233 large shot in her hull; a great many of them between wind and water. One 18-pound shot entered the bulwark, passed through the heart of the mainmast, and went out at the opposite side. The loss in killed and wounded, on the part of the Algerines, amounted, as represented by some accounts, to 4000 men. and, by others, to nearly 7000.

As soon as daylight came, Lord Exmouth despatched Lieutenant Burgess with a flag of truce and a note to the dey, repeating the demands of the preceding forenoon; and the bombs were at the same time ordered to resume their positions, to be ready to renew the bombardment of the city in case of a non-compliance. The Algerine officer who came off to meet the boat, and who had been captain of one of the frigates that had been destroyed, declared that the answer had been sent on the preceding day, but that no boat was to be found to receive it. On this subject, Mr. Salamé says: "When we opened over the mole-head, I saw, as I thought, a boat coming out, which I supposed was that of the captain of the port, and told his lordship of it; but, on looking with a glass, we found the mistake."[1] The fact of the boat's departure, was, however, confirmed by the captain of the port himself, when, in an hour or two afterwards, he came off with the Swedish consul, to acquaint the British admiral that all his terms would be agreed to.

On the 29th, at 10 A.M., the captain of the port again came off, accompanied by Mr. M'Donell, the British consul. On the same afternoon Captain Brisbane went on shore; and, by the aid of the interpreter, Mr. Salamé, a conference was had with the dey at his palace. Several other conferences took place, in the three last of which Rear-admiral Sir Charles Vinicombe Penrose, who had arrived on the 29th in the 36-gun frigate Ister, was present; and the final result was, the delivery to the British of upwards of 1200 Christian slaves, with an engagement (of no great value certainly) to abolish the practice of slave-making in future; the restoration of 382,500 dollars for slaves redeemed by Naples and Sicily; peace with the king of the Netherlands; the payment of 30,000 dollars to the British consul for the destruction of his effects, and a public apology to him, before the ministers and officers of the palace, in terms dictated by Captain Brisbane, for the detention of his person. Having thus accomplished, to the fullest extent, the object of his mission to Algiers, Lord Exmouth, at midnight on the 3rd of September, weighed on his return, leaving the Prometheus to attend the British consul, and embark the few remaining slaves that were then on their way from the interior.

Those only who may not be aware to what a pitch of extravagance the pretensions of the Americans have attained will feel any surprise that they should rank their performance at

[1] Narrative of the Expedition to Algiers, &c., p. 37.

Algiers very little if at all below the glorious exploit we have just done narrating: as if the act of Commodore Decatur, in exchanging 500 Algerine prisoners for 10 slaves, citizens of the United States, could be compared with the act of Lord Exmouth; who, with cannon-balls only to give in exchange, obtained the freedom of, including the 1792 given up to the admiral in his spring visit to the bay of Tunis,[1] upwards of 3000 slaves; not one of whom, as a proof how little of selfish feeling had actuated the framers of the expedition, was a native of the British isles. The release of so many Christain slaves from the iron fangs of barbarians was, indeed, an act worthy of Britain; an act calculated to raise the character of her navy, high as it already stood, higher still in the estimation of the world. Nor will the triumph at Algiers pass to posterity without the name of Exmouth as the leader of the brave band by whose prowess it was gained.

For the skill and valour he had displayed in consummating this glorious achievement, Lord Exmouth was created a viscount of the United Kingdom. Rear-admiral Milne, also, was made a knight-commander, and Captains Ekins, Aylmer, Wise, Maitland, Paterson, and Coode, companions, of the Bath. All the lieutenants named in the list in page 289, and some others, including Lieutenant Fleming who commanded the explosion-vessel, were promoted to the rank of commanders; and several of the master's mates and midshipmen obtained commissions as lieutenants.

The Dutch admiral behaved uncommonly well; and the following has been adduced as an instance of his self-possession in the heat of the battle: About an hour after the firing had commenced, a lieutenant of the Queen Charlotte went on board the Melampus with a message from Lord Exmouth. The baron himself attended the lieutenant to the gangway on his return, and rated the frigate's first-lieutenant somewhat sharply, for his inattention in not having shipped the best man-ropes for the British officer's accommodation. Among the meritorious individuals concerned in this expedition, the interpreter must not be forgotten. The zeal, talent, and fidelity of Mr Salamé appear to have merited all the praises officially bestowed upon him, as well by the commander-in-chief as by the officers, Rear-admiral Penrose and Captain Brisbane, present at the conferences with the dey.

See p. 278.

STATE OF THE BRITISH NAVY.

The abstract for the year 1817[1] differs from all that have preceded it in the series, by the double arrangement of its classification, owing to the revival, by an order in council, of the ancient and only reasonable practice of rating the ships of the British navy; namely, according to the number of carriage-guns of every sort which they respectively mounted. The memorial from the board of admiralty to the prince regent, recommending the alteration, bears date November 25, 1816: and the order in council establishing the new ratings, according to the plan submitted, issued in the month of February, 1817. Although this memorial of the board of admiralty was not seen by us until every abstract of the 28 was printed, and every note attached to them prepared, we find that we had anticipated nearly all the reasons urged by the board for the necessity of some amendment in the classification. The following are the two concluding paragraphs of this important memorial: " We trust that we shall be excused for observing to your royal highness, that it is wholly unworthy of the character of the royal navy of this kingdom to maintain this system, which though introduced by the accidental cause we have mentioned, and without any design of deception, yet may give occasion to foreign nations to accuse us of misrepresentation, when we state that a British frigate of 38 guns has taken a foreign frigate of 44, when in fact the British frigate was of equal, if not superior force. We therefore humbly recommend that your royal highness will be pleased to order, that the rule for stating the force of his majesty's ships, which prevailed prior to 1793, and which in fact never was formally abrogated, should be revived and established; and that in future all his majesty's ships should be rated at the number of guns

[1] See Appendix, Annual Abstract, No. 25; also, in particular, the notes belonging to it.

and carronades which they actually carry on their decks, quarter-decks, and forecastles."

A reference to the early pages of this work will raise a doubt as to the correctness of this passage, "which prevailed prior to 1793," unless we explain that, as "guns," were the only species of ordnance named in the original order, fixing the rates of the ships, no ship in the British navy, prior to 1793, nor subsequently indeed, did mount more "guns," that is, long guns, than her established or rated number; but that, as far back as January, 1781, 429 ships belonging to the British navy carried from four to 12 pieces of carriage-ordnance, or, as the French expressively say, "bouches à feu," more than their rated number, will not, we presume, be disputed.[1] We are sorry to observe that the new order confines the guns (for we must persist in including carronades within that term)[2] to the "decks, quarter-decks, and forecastles," because every ship belonging to the three higher rates of the navy still mounts six guns more than she rates. These guns, it is true, are 18-pounder carronades; but many of the 80s and first-class 74s have carried 24-pounders, and may again if a war breaks out. Moreover the public is informed by the Admiralty navy-list, that "the force of each ship is stated according to the number of guns and carronades actually carried," without any exception as to the poop, or roundhouse: hence, when it becomes known, that the Superb, of "78 guns," mounts 84, and the Bulwark, of "76 guns," 82, what will people suppose, but that the new rating system, like the old one, carries concealment in the background? The best remedy is, in our opinion, to disarm the poop of the six 18-pounder carronades, and to level the barricade: the ships will experience no sensible diminution of force, and be much more snug and seaworthy.

Viewed as a whole, the new rating system is a very important state measure; but as depending upon the guns which each ship is calculated to mount, the plan will require an active war to perfect it. Nor having used carronades to the extent of the British, the French have little if anything to alter in their system. If a French 74, when fitted out by the English, is mounted with 78 guns, it is not, in general, because she had carried that number in the French service; but because, for the accommodation of the far most important man on board a French ship, be the government a monarchy or a republic, two ports of a side were left vacant in the cabin. With respect to their

[1] See vol. i., p. 39.   [2] Ibid, p. 42.

frigates, the French more usually denominated them 44s than 40s; and even the latter came nearer to the mounted force of the ship than was the case with the British 38s. But the Americans, how did they act? Why their rating-system was founded upon deception, and deception alone. They built "44s," and mounted them with 56 guns; and they have since built "74s," and mounted them with 102 guns, on three flush decks: although, owing to inability to bear the weight, from some error in the construction of the hull, the two first-built ships went to sea with no more than 82 guns.

While on the subject of the American 74s, we will, having the means in our power, compare the force of one of the smallest of them with that of a British 74 of the middling class; a class that exceeds in number all the other line-classes in the British navy put together; and the only class of 74 which in the event of a contest the Americans would admit to be an equal match for a ship of theirs bearing the same denomination. Let us take the Albion. That ship mounts 28 long 32-pounders, weighing 55 cwt., upon her first deck, 28 long 18s upon her second deck, six-long 12 pounders and 12 carronades, 32 pounders, on her quarter-deck and forecastle, and six 18-pounder carronades on her poop; total, 80 guns. Her net war complement is 594 men and boys, including 32 of the latter; and her measurement 1743 tons. The American 74-gun ship Franklin mounts 30 long 32-pounders, of 63 cwt., upon her first deck, 32 medium 32-pounders, of 52 cwt., on the second deck, and two of the same guns and 18 carronades, 32-pounders, on the quarter-deck and forecastle; total, 82 guns. Her complement actually on board in 1818 was 786 men and boys, including but eight or 10 of the latter; and she measures 2124 tons. Admitting, then, these ships to be mutually opposed, the following would be their comparative force:—

Comparative Force of the Albion and Franklin.

		Albion.	Franklin
Broadside-guns	No.	40	41
	lbs.	982	1312
Crew	No.	594	786
Size	tons.	1743	2124

So much for the equality of force between an American 74 and a British 74 of the class of the Albion; and yet, were a war to break out to-morrow, Sir William Hoste[1] would consider himself peculiarly fortunate (and where is the captain of a British 74, indeed, who would not?) in falling in with the Franklin.

[1] The Albion's captain till June, 1825.

commanded by the most renowned of the American commodores.

We will now proceed to state a few particulars respecting the construction, equipment, and qualifications of the Franklin, the result of an inspection of the ship when she lay at Spithead in January, 1818; and which particulars, to the British public at least, are as novel as it is hoped they will prove interesting. The Franklin was laid down at Philadelphia in the summer of 1813, and launched in August, 1815. She is built of seasoned live oak, admirably put together, and, like the generality of Philadelphia ships, highly finished in every part; has a round bow, and works her cables, similar to other three-deckers, on the second deck. We call her a three decker, because, in fact, her upper deck is continuous from stem to stern, similar to the first and second, with chocks and fittings for five ports of a side along the waist: so that the ship can mount 30 guns on this deck (called "spar deck" by the Americans), similar to the 44s.[1] Her principal dimensions are as follows:—

	Ft.	in.
Length from the fore part of the stem to the back of the post at the wing transom	197	0
Breadth, extreme	50	0
First deck-ports apart	8	6
Height of ditto from water	4	7
Draught of water abaft, with nine months' provisions on board	24	0

After what has appeared in these pages respecting the American frigates, no doubt can remain, that this American line-of-battle ship is well found in all her stores, and that her guns are properly mounted and secured. She is, to all appearance, a very snug ship, and has been pronounced to be a very stiff one; an excellent sailer on every point, and a good sea-boat. She is steered with an iron tiller 16 feet long. Her lower masts, in their naked state, are not stouter than those of a British ship of the same dimensions, but they have each, as we noticed in the frigates, immense quarter-fishes, that make them appear of an extraordinary size; and the whole of the rigging, both standing and running, is far stouter than would be established upon a similarly-sized ship in the British navy. Her galley, dispensary capstan, and pumps, are all of the most improved construction; her pumps, indeed, are remarkable for their simplicity, the ease with which they are worked, and the quantity of water they discharge.

One error was committed by her architects. They did not

[1] See vol. v., p. 270

calculate properly the bulk of water that a hull so stoutly built, and so heavily laden with guns, would displace. Hence, her lower-deck ports are brought nearer to the water than was intended, or than is consistent with a due regard to the use of her lower battery in blowing weather. For instance, in the year 1818, the Franklin's midship lower-deck port was only 4 feet 7 inches from the water, while that of the British small-class 74 is usually 5 feet 10 inches; but the Franklin was then victualled for nine months, and had on board a quantity of stores for other ships in the Mediterranean. With six months' provisions on board, the height was stated to be about 5 feet 6 inches. The Independence, built at Boston, and launched eight or nine months before the Franklin, possessed the failing in a much greater degree; her ports were within 3 feet 10 inches of the water, and she was not considered safe to cross the Atlantic without half-ports.

However, the fault certainly increased the ship's stability; and the four last-built American line-of-battle ships, the Washington (the second), Ohio, Columbus, and North Carolina, are of greatly increased dimensions and, even with their full establishment of guns, 102 in number, carry their ports at a proper height. We have recently gleaned a few particulars respecting the last-named ship, which is now in the Mediterranean under the command of our old friend Commodore Rodgers. The North Carolina measures 206 feet on the gun-deck, and is 52 feet some odd inches in moulded breadth; which gives the ship about 53 feet 4 or 5 inches for her extreme breadth, and makes her measure about 2650 tons English. Her actual force at this time, according to the representation of a British officer who has recently been on board of her, consists of 34 medium 42-pounders on the first deck, 34 medium 32-pounders on the second deck, and 34 carronades, 42-pounders, on the third deck; total 102 guns. Her complement now on board is 1000 men. Her lower masts and topmasts are short, but of an immense stoutness. The mizenmast is within 4 inches of being equal in circumference to the Albion's mainmast. The masts have a fish on each side from the step to the head; and Commodore Rodgers told the post-captain who was paying him this visit, that, in an action in the Constitution when he commanded her, he had 32 shot through his mainmast, but did not lose it; which he attributed to the shortness of the mast, its size, and the strengthening fish. Had we been standing by the commodore when he made this bounce, we should almost have been tempted to ask him what action it was in which he commanded the Constitution.

We have already compared together an American and a British 74; we will now give a figure statement, showing the relative force of an American 74 (for so the North Carolina is officially rated) and a British 120. The force of the Caledonia has already been particularized; but her third-deck guns have since been changed from long 18 to Congreve's 24 pounders, and her present establishment gives her six, instead of two, poop-carronades, or 126 guns in all. The following, then, will be the comparative force of a British 120, and an American first-class 74 gun-ship:—

		Caledonia.	North Carolina.
Broadside-guns	No.	63	51
	lbs.	1648	1972
Crew	No.	891	1000
Size	tons.	2616	2650

It was given out as the intention of the American government, had the treaty of Ghent been broken off, to have cut down the Franklin and Independence to frigates, and have sent to sea, to meet the two-deckers of England, the ships then building of the class of the North Carolina. Had one of the latter captured or sunk a ship like the Albion, even the president, in his next speech to congress, would not have scrupled to tell the world, that an American 74 had vanquished a British 80.

The three remaining annual abstracts may be referred to together.[1] As they call for no particular remarks, we shall merely state that the number of commissioned officers and masters belonging to the British navy at the commencement of the respective years 1817, 1818, 1819, and 1820, was—

	1817.	1818.	1819.	1820.
Admirals	60	56	52	64
Vice-admirals	62	61	59	65
Rear-admirals	74	74	71	70
,, superannuated	20	27	27	20
Post-captains	854	883	865	837
,, superannuated	32	31	29	29
Commanders or sloop-captains	829	813	768	780
,, superannuated	100	100	100	100
Lieutenants	4012	3949	3901	3848
Masters	681	651	622	606

[1] See Appendix, Annual Abstract, Nos. 26, 27, 28; also Appendix 13.

And the number of seamen and marines, voted for the service in the same four years, was, for 1817, 19,000, for 1818 and 1819, 20,000, and for 1820, 23,000.[1]

We would most willingly give an account of the improvements that have of late years been introduced into the British navy; but our limits restrict us to a few superficial remarks. A great change has doubtless taken place, as well in the contour as in the arrangement of the materials that compose the fabric of a British ship-of-war. The principle of the change, as respects the arrangement of the materials or timber, consists in the substitution of the triangle for the rectangle, with the view of conferring upon every part of the fabric a uniformity of strength. The frame of the hold consists of a series of triangles, united by trusses; and the openings between the ribs, or outer timbers, are filled with slips of wood, calked within and without, and rendered quite impervious to water; so that, should a vessel so constructed, lose her main keel, and even a proportion of the plank from her bottom, she would still remain water-tight. As one instance, the British 20-gun ship Esk, Captain Edward Lloyd, while running between nine and ten knots, struck, near Bermuda, on a bank of coral and hard sand; where she lay, beating heavily, 48 hours. When got afloat, the ship was found with her main keel rubbed off nearly its whole length (at one part the dead-wood was crushed up to the keelson), and yet it was not until 11 hours afterwards that the Esk began to be, and that only in a slight degree, leaky. The Vigilant revenue-cutter, driven, and apparently wrecked, upon a bed of shingles in Douglas bay, Isle of Man, and yet got off and brought in safety to Plymouth, is another remarkable instance. As a still more recent case, the 10-gun brig-sloop Frolic, employed in the packet-service, after lying eight hours on her beam-ends, upon the rocks off Sable Island, beating violently, got safe into Halifax harbour.

The system of diagonal timbering, for which the British navy is indebted to Sir Robert Seppings, one of the surveyors on the establishment, was first commenced in the year 1800, upon the Glenmore 32. In 1805 it was further applied, at Chatham, to the Kent 74, to give auxiliary strength to that ship after her return from the Mediterranean. It was then introduced, to a certain extent, in the building of the Warspite 74; and, after the principle had been examined at the admiralty by a committee appointed for the purpose, directions were given to re-

[1] See Appendix, No. 14.

build the Tremendous 74 to the full extent of the diagonal principle. This was done, and the principle was extended even to the decks. The Tremendous was found so completely to answer, that the diagonal system,[1] both in building and in repairing ships, has since become general in the British navy. The Howe, launched March 28, 1815, was the first ship laid down and built upon the principle. A rumour for a short time prevailed, that this fine first-rate, just as she had entered one of the new docks at Sheerness, was infected with the dry-rot. So far from it, there is not at the moment we are writing this, from the best inquiries we can make on the subject, a sounder ship in the British navy.

Sir Robert's important improvement in giving to line-of-battle ships a circular bow, we have already slightly touched upon:[2] his ingenuity has since produced a more surprising, and an equally important change at the opposite extremity of the ship, a circular instead of a square stern. To convey an idea of the advantages of this plan we shall make a quotation from a work that treats professionally on the subject: "The sterns are also formed circular, and to add to their strength, as many timbers as possible are run up: this presents a very formidable stern-battery, enables the guns to be run out so far as to prevent accidents to the stern by their explosion; the danger arising from being pooped is considerably diminished, if not wholly prevented, and the obstruction to the ship's progress, which according to the old plan, was occasioned by the projection of quarter-galleries, when the ships were going on a wind, is removed. In fine, by this alteration, the ships are every way more seaworthy and better adapted for defence; qualities which are so essential and indeed indispensable in ships-of-war."[3]

As a proof of the good opinion entertained of this plan by the lords commissioners of the admiralty, an order of the board, dated on the 13th of June, 1817, directs, that all new ships, down to fifth-rates inclusive, are to be so constructed, and all ships of the same rates receiving extensive repairs are also to have circular sterns, provided the timbers in the old or square sterns are defective. By this alteration in her construction, the ship becomes, beyond a doubt, a stronger vessel and a more

---

[1] See a very valuable work recently published, with "Elements of Naval Architecture," entitled "An Appendix, containing the principles and practice of constructing ships, as invented and introduced by Sir Robert Seppings, surveyor of His Majesty's navy, by John Knowles, F.R S., secretary to the committee of surveyors of His Majesty's navy."

[2] See vol. iii., p. 509.

[3] See the work referred to in note [1] in the preceding column.

efficient man-of-war: advantages which it will require something more than an unsightly appearance (and even that, we presume, is a remediable effect) to counterbalance. The number of ships belonging to the British navy, which on the 1st of January, 1820, were repairing, building, or ordered to be built, with circular sterns, amounted to 67,[1] and the number of ships building of teak, at the same date, amounted to 19.[2]

On a former occasion, we ventured to suggest the advantages that might be derived, in the construction of ships-of-war, from the opinions of naval officers of experience.[3] A post-captain of acknowledged nautical skill, and of tried gallantry, has recently proved himself a very eminent naval architect. "Captain Hayes," says Mr. Marshall, "is the author of a pamphlet on the subject of naval architecture, his proficiency in which important science is the result of many years' professional experience and deep consideration. His proposed system, we understand, meets a point hitherto considered impracticable, viz.: that of building a thousand vessels, if required, from a given section, without the variation of a needle's point, reducible from a first-rate ship to a cutter, each possessing excelling powers and advantages of every description in their respective class. Since the publication of the above pamphlet, in which he carefully abstained from saying, or even hinting that he had made any progress in the formation of such a system, two vessels have been built, in a royal dockyard, on his projection: the first, a cutter of about 160 tons,[4] is said to embrace stability under canvas with little ballast, great buoyancy, better stowage, and swifter sailing qualities, than any model yet designed by known schools of naval architecture. The second, a sloop-of-war,[5] is at present absent on her first experimental cruise, in company with two other vessels of the same class, one of which was designed by Sir Robert Seppings, and the other built by the students of Portsmouth dockyard, under the superintendence of Professor Inman."[6]

In the former edition of this work, we were induced to give a brief account of the first two expeditions to the polar regions, in search of a north-west passage. Other expeditions to the same spot have since been undertaken; and if we broached the subject at all, we could not expect to make it interesting, or even

---

[1] For a list of names, see Appendix, No. 15.
[2] Ibid., No. 16.
[3] See vol. v., p. 437.
[4] The Arrow.
[5] The Champion.
[6] Marshall, vol. ii., p. 683.

intelligible, unless we brought down occurrences to a date far beyond the period to which this work, by its title, is restricted. Several works have been published exclusively on the subject of these expeditions, and they are in most people's hands: consequently there is the less occasion for us to deviate from our plan, and enlarge this volume to a much greater bulk than any of its companions.

THE BURMESE WAR.

NINE years had nearly elapsed, and Great Britain, her colonies and dependencies, had remained in the enjoyment of peace; but in the beginning of the year 1824, the governor-general of India, in council, decided upon attacking the territory of the Burmese, in consequence of their having committed, on the south-east frontier of the possessions of the East India Company, several unprovoked aggressions. In detailing the operations in Ava, during the Burmese war, it is our intention to confine ourselves as much as possible to those actions in which the naval forces were mostly employed, giving a slight sketch of the military movements, as far as is requisite to elucidate the subject.

At this period Commodore Charles Grant, C.B., in the Liffey of 50 guns, was the senior officer in India, and, on being informed of the determination to resort to war, a part of the squadron under his command was placed at the disposition of the governor-general, for the purpose of affording every assistance in its power. The Larne sloop, under the command of Captain Frederick Marryat, having under his orders the Sophie brig, Captain George Frederick Ryves, was desired to proceed to the river Hooghly, and to place himself under the directions of the supreme government.

The command of the military department was intrusted to Sir Archibald Campbell, K.C.B.; a division of troops was embarked at Calcutta under Brigadier Michael M'Creagh, C.B., and another division at Madras under Brigadier-general William Macbean. On the 8th of April, Sir Archibald Campbell embarked with his staff on board the Larne and made sail for the appointed rendezvous of the Madras division at Port Cornwallis thither the Bengal division had already sailed. Towards the end of April it arrived, and on the 2nd of May the Madras division convoyed by the Sophie hove in sight off the harbour of Port Cornwallis. A slight delay took place in the departure of ships for their ultimate destination, Rangoon, which is the principal seaport in the dominions of the King of Ava; during the interval between the 2nd of May and the 5th, on which day the fleet sailed, Commodore Grant, in the Liffey, anchored in Port Cornwallis and took command of the naval department, consisting of the Slaney, 20, Captain Charles Mitchell; Larne, 20, Captain Frederick Marryat; and Sophie, 18, Captain George Frederick Ryves. To these were added four of the Company's cruisers, under Captain Henry Hardy.

The whole force consisting, in addition to those already named, " of 18 brigs, schooners, and other small-craft (formerly pleasure-yachts on the Ganges), each armed with two light carronades and four swivels, and manned with 12 lascars, under the command of an European; 20 row-boats, lugger rigged (formerly Calcutta pilot-boats), each carrying an 18-pounder in the bow, and manned with from 16 to 20 lascars; the Diana steam-vessel; and about 40 sail of transports, only one or two of which had English crews. The Company's cruisers were manned with British sailors, Hindoos, and Mahometans, and all the row-boats were under the command of Mr. William Lindguist of the Bengal pilot-service. The total number of fighting men embarked at Calcutta and Madras in April, 1824, was 8701, of whom 4077 were British."[1] " On the morning of the 5th of May," says Sir Archibald Campbell in his despatch, "we finally put to sea, detaching a part of my force under Brigadier M'Creagh, in the Ernaâd timber ship, under the escort of H.M.'s sloop Slaney, against the island of Cheduba, and sending another detachment under Major Wahab of the Madras establishment, against Negrais, proceeding myself with the main body for Rangoon river, which we reached on the 10th, and anchored within the bar."

The principal point of attack, in the first instance, was Rangoon. This town stands on the Rangoon or Parnian river, and is situated to the eastward of Bassein or Negrais point; which latter place may be said to form the eastern point of the bay of Bengal, and is about 420 miles from Calcutta. Rangoon is 140 miles from Bassein point.

The Irrawaddi or Erawadi is a large and, in many places deep river; it takes its rise about the 27° of north latitude, and

[1] Marshall.

95° of east longitude; it runs nearly due south, gradually enlarging itself until it reaches Amarapura; there it turns in a westerly direction, running past the city of Ava, the capital of the country against which hostilities had been determined. It continues in this direction about 60 miles, when it inclines to the south-west for about 100 miles until it passes Pagahm-mew, when it again runs nearly south 250 miles to Kendowa, a town 70 miles to the southward of Prome; here the river branches off, the eastern arm running into the river Parnian, on which Rangoon stands, the western communicating with the Kendowa or Anowkiang, one branch of which becomes the Bassein or Negrais river. The town of Bassein stands mid-distance between Negrais point and Kendowa, the whole distance being between 150 and 160 miles; whilst Rangoon stands in the direction above named from Kendowa, and distant about 80 miles. It will be seen hereafter, how well and ably Sir Archibald Campbell's views and plans were acted upon; that the junction of his forces on the Irrawaddi by the rout of Bassein was effected nearly at the same time that the main body under his own command reached the point assigned. It is perhaps necessary to state, that, in consequence of the direction of the river, almost all operations were carried on near its banks, and that, as the army advanced, the boats or flotilla were always within communication, each supporting the other, and sharing the difficulties and dangers. The attacks were always made in conjunction, and we believe, throughout the whole war, there was not one place assaulted, attacked, or taken, at which assault, attack, or capture the flotilla were not present. Indeed, from the nature of the country, there being no roads, and only narrow footpaths through the woods and jungles, it would have required immense labour to render them applicable to military purposes, and to carry on the war inland; besides which obstacles, the army were unprovided with land carriages, and not half supplied even with water conveyances; and here, again, it was by no means probable that the Burmese could be induced to render any assistance, they being principally in the pay of the court of Ava, to which and to the golden-footed monarch, as their king is titled, they pay the most submissive obedience. We think it right to mention this, as any one perusing Major Snodgrass's book would be inclined to view the operations of the naval department as very secondary indeed to their gallant brethren in arms, who, we are quite certain, do not begrudge the laurels justly won by the indefatigable exertions and unremitting toil of his Majesty's and the Hon. the East India Company's navy.

The Liffey, preceded by the Larne, until she grounded on a bank at noon, led the fleet up the Rangoon or Parnian river on the 11th of May, and anchored abreast of the town, opposite a battery of 14 guns; the river about this part is calculated to be about 700 yards wide, the town being situated nearly 28 miles from the sea: its defences are described as being "an enclosure of palisades or stockades, ten or twelve feet high, strengthened internally by embankments of earth and protected externally, on one side by the river, and at the western end by a morass, over which there is a bridge. The palisade encloses the town, in the shape of an irregular parallelogram, having one gate in each of three faces, and two in that of the north: at the river-gate is a landing-place, denominated the King's wharf, where stands the battery opposite which the Lilley anchored."[1] From this battery a miserably directed and altogether insignificant fire was commenced, but which immediately was silenced by a few shot from the Liffey; in the mean time preparations were made to land the troops, during which the battery again opened its fire, and was as easily silenced as before; the troops were landed in three divisions, and the town was taken without the discharge of a single musket, the inhabitants, together with some British and American missionaries having been driven by the Burmese inland.

On the 16th of May, Captain Richard Birch, who had been despatched for the purpose of dislodging the enemy from the village of Kemmendale, a war-boat station three miles above Rangoon, was landed with the grenadier company of his majesty's 38th regiment, by the boats of the Liffey, under Lieutenant James Wilkinson of that ship, about a mile from Kemmendine, where a party of the enemy had stockaded themselves. The position was attacked and carried in a gallant style. The men being re-embarked, the boats proceeded further up the river, when a heavy fire from another stockade was opened upon them; the boats instantly pulled towards the point, the place was assaulted and carried in spite of numerous difficuties, and 400 men who defended it were driven from the stockade at the point of the bayonet, leaving 60 of the enemy killed. A third stockade was soon afterwards attacked and carried. In these affairs the army lost Lieutenant Thomas Kerr of the 38th regiment and one private killed, and nine wounded.

[1] Marshall

In the naval department Lieutenant Wilkinson and nine of his crew were severely wounded.

Commodore Grant left Rangoon on the 31st of May, in consequence of severe indisposition, which on the 25th of July following proved fatal; the command of the naval department in the Irrawaddi (on a branch of which river Rangoon stands) now devolved on Captain Marryat. In Sir Archibald Campbell's despatch, dated the day after Commodore Grant sailed, the following description is given of the enemy:—

"Every act evinces a most marked determination of carrying hostilities to the very last extremity; approaching our posts day and night, under cover of an impervious and incombustible jungle, constructing stockades and redoubts on every road and pathway, even within musket-shot of our sentries, and, from their hidden fastnesses, carrying on a most barbarous and harassing warfare, firing upon our sentries at all hours of the night, and lurking on the outskirts of the jungle, for the purpose of carrying off any unlucky wretch whom chance may throw in their way."

Major Snodgrass gives an equally unpromising view of affairs. "The enemy's troops and new-raised levies," he says, "were gradually collecting in our front from all parts of the kingdom: a cordon was speedily formed around our cantonments, capable, indeed, of being forced at every point; but possessing in a remarkable degree all the qualities requisite for harassing and wearing out in fruitless exertions the strength and energies of European or Indian troops. Hid from our view on every side in the darkness of a deep and, to regular bodies, impenetrable forest, far beyond which the inhabitants and all the cattle of the Rangoon district had been driven, the Burmese chiefs carried on their operations, and matured their future schemes with vigilance, secrecy, and activity. Neither rumours nor intelligence of what was passing within his posts, ever reached us. Beyond the invisible line which circumscribed our position, all was mystery or vague conjecture."[1]

From the period when the English flotilla anchored in the Irrawaddi, small cargo boats were continually captured, and these were cut down into more manageable craft, in order to move the troops with greater facility, each being well able to hold 60 men. These boats very materially strengthened the English force, and gave a facility of movement to the land forces excessively desirable in such a country, and with such

[1] See Appendix to the Burmese War, No. 1.

an enemy as Sir Archibald describes above. The enemy, ever watchful on shore, were equally on the alert afloat. The narrowness of the river, and the immense assemblage of vessels stretching from shore to shore, offered a fine opportunity for the employment of fire-rafts. These destructive engines were launched above Kemmendine, and it required all the vigilance of active officers and men to save the flotilla from nightly destruction. In order to frustrate, or rather effectually stop this annoyance, it was deemed requisite to occupy the stockades near Kemmendine, which commanded the river. They were attacked and carried on the 10th of June.

The division under Brigadier M'Creagh, having been successful against the island of Cheduba, the European forces were re-embarked, and joined Sir Archibald Campbell at Rangoon. Major Wahab, and Captain Goodridge, having executed their orders likewise, joined the commander of the forces. In the first of these operations, Brigadier M'Creagh thus speaks of Captain Mitchell:—" I must do myself the pleasure to acknowledge the cordial co-operation that I received from Captain Mitchell, of his majesty's ship Slaney, who accompanied me at the disembarkation, and to whose readiness in affording me every assistance his ship could supply, the service was importantly indebted ; and the exertions of his seamen, under the immediate command of Lieutenant Matthews, in getting the guns landed, and assisting in the battery, contributed essentially to accelerate the result." In the capture of the island of Cheduba, the naval department sustained a loss of one marine killed, and the first-lieutenant of the Slaney (Henry Bathurst Matthews) and four seamen wounded.

The rainy season had now set in, and that fearful malady, the cholera morbus, began to thin the ranks, and weaken the crews of the invading force. The enemy, as if aware that the climate was their best friend, and that the unremitting exertions of the English force, the constant exposure to the weather, the change of diet, and other circumstances would retard any advance, withdrew their forces to Donoobew, a town on the Irrawaddi, fortified strongly, and situated 20 leagues in a northerly direction from Rangoon.

With the exception of two fire-rafts destroyed by Mr. Henry Lister Maw, the naval aide-de-camp of Sir Archibald Campbell, and who had been left by Commodore Grant to fill that post, both the invaders and invaded remained without any offensive operations between the 10th of June and the 1st of July. On this last-named date, the Burmese forces were observed in motion; and, taking up a position so well covered by the jungles and thickets as to render doubtful their numerical strength, they occupied the left of the British lines, drawing up in front of the Kemmendine stockade. After a brisk affair, the Burman forces took refuge in the jungle, leaving 100 dead on the field. In this affair, the naval forces were not idle. The enemy meditated an attack by fire-vessels at the same time, but the zeal and activity of Mr. Lindguist, who commanded the boats stationed off Kemmendine, rendered that manœuvre abortive, and in counteracting the plan of the enemy, evinced great courage, coolness, and ability.

On the 8th of July, Sir Archibald Campbell embarked 800 men in order to gain possession of a point of land above Kemmendine, from which the enemy launched their fire-rafts. For the result of this expedition, and for the handsome manner in which Sir Archibald Campbell mentions the exertions of the navy, particularly as relates to Captain Marryat (who, although unable from severe indisposition to participate in the action, yet lent his powerful talent in arranging the plan of attack) we refer our readers to Sir Archibald's despatch, in the Appendix to the Burmese War, No. 2. It will be seen that the commander-in-chief refers to the forces under Brigadier-general Macbean, who had been detached on the 8th of July with 1500 men to Kummeroot, a stockaded position about five miles from the Shwe-da-gon pagoda, which stands about two miles and a half distant from the town of Rangoon. The naval department had eleven men wounded; but trivial as this may appear, it is evident from the letter addressed by Sir Archibald Campbell,[1] to Captain Marryat, and likewise from the despatch from the secretary of government to Sir Archibald, that a very high idea had been formed, and justly formed, of the services of the navy on that occasion.[2] The best record of the services performed, notwithstanding the severe illness which was prevalent in the squadron, will be found in Captain Marryat's letter to Commodore Grant, dated 11th July, 1824."[3]

On the 13th of July, Captain Marryat, in the Larne, dropped down the river to the Dalla creek, to recruit his ship's company, but returned to his position off Rangoon on the 27th, during which time Lieutenant Dobson had captured thirty-five large boats, with various cargoes.

On the 4th of August 600 men, with some gun-boats, were de-

[1] See Appendix, No. 3. [2] Ibid., No. 4. [3] Ibid., No. 5

tached up the Syriam river. Near the landing-place an old Portuguese fort was discovered, standing on the summit of a hill which commanded the entrance of the Pegu river. The troops were landed under cover of the fire from the Jessy and the Powerful. A deep nullah having for some time checked the advance of the British, Captain Marryat caused a bridge to be thrown across it, when, notwithstanding the heavy fire which the fort maintained, the advance was sounded, and the fort taken. The like success attended Lieutenant-colonel M. Kelly of the Madras European regiment, who was detached to the Syriam pagoda, which the Burmese seemed inclined to defend; but they were driven from their stronghold without much opposition, leaving behind them some artillery and stores.

Lieutenant-colonel Kelly was embarked with 400 men on the 8th of August, with directions to proceed up the Dalla river, the boats being under the command of Lieutenant Fraser. Of this expedition, in which, says Mr. Marshall, " finer or more characteristic traits of British soldiers and sailors were never witnessed, the officers, less encumbered than their men, forming line breast deep in mud and water, and passing the scaling-ladders from one to another to be planted against the walls of the stockade," the official despatch, in which Lieutenant-colonel Kelly bestows the highest encomiums on the naval officers employed, is the best history.[1] Captain Marryat, in his official letter to the commodore, speaks highly of the gallantry of Lieutenant Fraser, Mr. Atherton, Messrs. Duffil, Winsor, and Norcock.[2]

At this period, August, 1824, the following ships composed the naval force in India: Tees (26 guns), Captain Thomas Coe, who, after the death of Commodore Grant, became the senior officer; Alligator (28), Captain Thomas Alexander, C.B.: Slaney (20), Captain Charles Mitchell; Arachne (18), Captain Henry Ducie Chads; Larne (20), Captain Frederick Marryat; Sophie (18), Captain George F. Ryves; Liffey (50), commanded, *pro tem.*, by Lieutenant George Tincombe.[3] Of this force only the Larne was at Rangoon, the Sophie having been despatched to Bengal for provisions, &c.

The district of Tenasserim was now selected as the theatre of war, it having been found impracticable to carry on hostilities in the direction of Ava. A part of the 89th regiment and the 7th Madras native infantry, accompanied by the Company's cruisers, with some gun-boats, were detached on the 2nd of

[1] See Appendix, No 6.   [2] Ibid., No. 7.   [3] Marshall.

August, under the orders of Colonel Miles, C.B., from Rangoon. Tavoy was the first place attacked and taken; after which the forces embarked for Mergui, and arrived there on the 6th of October. The batteries were silenced in an hour, the troops were landed, escaladed a stockade, which defended the place, and took the town; after which Colonel Miles returned to Rangoon, having left a garrison in Mergui.

The enemy having returned and occupied some stockades in the Dalla creek, Captain Marryat, with two mortar-boats and some gun-boats, manned by the crew of the Larne, proceeded to dislodge them on the 2nd of September. Major Richard Lacy Evans commanded the land forces on this occasion. At 6 A.M. the boats opened their fire on the stockade, and by 9 o'clock the magazine was blown up and the guns silenced, but the enemy still held possession of the stockades, and kept up a very galling fire of musketry. The Burmese had learnt from former attacks the necessity of widening their ditches in front of their stockades, and on this occasion it was found impracticable to fix the scaling ladders, the place being secure by the river side. Major Evans landed with 150 men, and, approaching through the jungles, advanced in their rear; the boats instantly dashed forward towards the main stockade, and the whole was soon carried. Higher up the creek, Captain Marryat and Major Evans destroyed 30 boats, laden with arms and ammunition. In this sharp and brilliant affair, Captain Marryat speaks highly of Lieutenant Fraser, Mr. Henry Hodder, acting-master of the Larne, Mr. Duffill, and Mr. Alexander Cranley, midshipman. Sir Archibald Campbell, in detailing the account above mentioned, speaks in the highest terms of Captain Marryat.

The Burmese no sooner found the benefit which might accrue to their enemies, by the permanent occupation of a stockade which commanded the creek leading to Thontai (the capital of Dalla), than they resolved to attempt a recapture. They proceeded in their usual harassing manner, night after night, approaching under cover of the jungle, and keeping up a continued fire of musketry which kept the British always on the alert, until the 5th of September, when they made a resolute attack on the shore side with about 1800 men, at the same moment that their war-boats endeavoured to board the Kitty gun-brig, which was stationed off the stockade. The signal for more assistance having been made, Captain Marryat, with the boats of the Larne, arrived in time to give most effectual aid, and to turn the scale of victory which at that moment seemed trembling in the balance. The enemy seeing the reinforcement, instantly retired; Captain Marryat as speedily followed, and five vessels, which from their scattered state were unable to escape, fell into the possession of the boats' crews of the Larne.

In this affair the commander of the Kitty, Mr. Robert Crawford, behaved with uncommon bravery, and beat off the war-boats. "The spears," says Marshall, "remaining in her sides, the ladders attached to her rigging, and the boarding-nettings cut through in many places, proved the severe contest which had been maintained, and induced Captain Marryat to recommend the very meritorious conduct of Mr. Crawford to the favourable consideration of the governor-general in council." For the opinion of Sir Archibald Campbell upon this affair, and likewise on the general exertions of Captain Marryat and the officers and seamen under his command, we refer our readers to Nos. 8 and 9 in the Appendix. It will be seen by the letter of Sir Archibald Campbell, that, in consequence of the scurvy having broken out on board the Larne, Captain Marryat, knowing that active operations would be deferred for six weeks, had requested permission to remove his ship to Penang.

"At this period," says Marshall, "the European portion of the army, fit for active service in the field, was reduced to less than 1500: 749 British soldiers had fallen victims to the climate, and upwards of 1000 were in the hospitals. Nearly one-fourth of the Sophie's crew had died, and as many more were sick. On the death of Commodore Grant, Captain Coe assumed the command of the Liffey, and Captain Marryat was promoted into the Tees."[1]

On the 28th of August Captain Chads received the first intimation of the death of Commodore Grant. The former being then at Madras, he sailed with money for the use of the army on the 3rd of September, and, on the 15th, arrived at Rangoon, and took command of the naval forces.

Offensive operations began on the 19th of September against Penang, a point on which the enemy had established themselves, and from which they meditated, by fire-rafts, the destruction of the English naval force. Captain Chads commanded the naval department, consisting of nine gun-vessels and 16 row-boats, the boats of the Arachne and Sophie, and the Diana steam-vessel; this last vessel had been brought by the recommendation of Captain Marryat, and was of the greatest use during this harassing warfare. Brigadier-general Hugh Fraser commanded

[1] See Appendix, No 10.

the land forces. The expedition moved up the river on the 21st of September and returned to Rangoon on the 27th, having not only succeeded in their enterprise, but surveyed the river until it narrowed to 60 yards in breadth. Captain Chad's letter to Captain Coe gives an interesting account of the fatigues experienced on the expedition, and states that the naval casualty amounted to only four seamen of the Arachne wounded.[1]

It was now that sickness began to spread itself around; the incessant rains contributed much to increase the epidemic malady which during this month is so prevalent in India. The hospitals were crowded, and, although every precaution was taken which prudence and foresight could suggest, yet the fever increased, and the patients, after suffering from the most overpowering exhaustion, generally died. Major Snodgrass mentions, that at this time it became necessary to remove the convalescent to Mergui and Tavoy, before mentioned as having been captured by the English, and there the change of climate contributed much to re-establish the army in efficiency. Floating hospitals were established at the mouth of the Rangoon river, and by the beginning of the month of October a very beneficial change had occurred in both the naval and military departments.

The enemy occupied a stockaded position near Annauben, and likewise held possession of the pagoda of Keykloo; these situations are about 14 miles distant from Rangoon. It was judged necessary to dislodge them, whilst another detachment, under Major Thomas Evans, was despatched to Than-ta-bain to make a simultaneous attack upon that strong position, which was 30 miles distant from Rangoon. The best reference to the active part taken by the navy is to be found in Major Evans's[2] letter to the commander-in-chief; whilst the latter, in speaking of the meritorious exertions of the officers and seamen, pays the highest compliment to Captain Chads. The naval officers who were fortunate enough to participate in this expedition against Than-ta-bain were Lieutenants William Burdett Dobson, Augustus Henry Kellet, and George Goldfinch; Mr. Lett, master's mate, Messrs. James Ward Tomlinson, Archibald Reed, George Winson, Charles Mitchell, and Robert Murray, admiralty midshipmen.[3] Captain Chads speaks highly of Lieutenants Kellet, Goldfinch, and Dobson, and gives great credit to Mr. Winson of the Sophie, who had on this and on almost every occasion charge of the steam-boat.[4]

[1] See Appendix, No. 11.
[2] Ibid., No. 12.
[3] Marshall.
[4] See Appendix, No. 13.

Lieutenant-colonel Smith who commanded the force sent against Keykloo, after a series of successes against stockades and breastworks, was repulsed in his attack upon the pagoda of Keykloo, with a loss of 21 officers and men killed, and 74 wounded. It appears from the report of Brigadier M'Creagh, that the enemy, naturally ferocious, wreaked their vengeance upon the prisoners, and that 28 were found "fastened to the trunks of trees on the road-side, mangled and mutilated in every manner that savage cruelty could devise."

One hundred miles to the eastward of Rangoon stands the city of Martaban. Lieutenant-colonel Godwin has given a graphic description of the appearance of this city, which we place before our readers:—"The city rests at the bottom of a very high hill, washed by a beautiful and extensive sheet of water; on its right is a rocky mound, on which was placed a two-gun battery with a deep nullah under it. This battery communicates with the usual stockade of timber, and behind this is a work of masonry, varying from twelve to twenty feet thick, with small embrasures for either cannon or musketry. The stockade runs along the margin of the water for more than three-quarters of a mile, where it joins a large pagoda, which projects into the water in the form of a bastion. The defences then continue a short distance, and end at a nullah, at the other side of which all is thick jungle. The town continues to run in an angular way from the pagoda for at least half a mile, and terminates in the house of the Mayoon, close to a stockade up the hill. The whole defence is the water-line, with its flanks protected. The rear of the town and work is composed of thick jungle and large trees, and open to the summit."

Such was the place Sir Archibald Campbell determined to attack; for which purpose, 450 troops were placed under the command of Lieutenant-colonel Godwin. The naval part of the expedition, consisting of six gun-vessels, seven gun-boats, an armed transport which held the troops, one mortar-boat, and thirty men from the Arachne and Sophie, was intrusted to Lieutenant Charles Keele.

On the 27th of October, on which day the squadron arrived at its destination, Lieutenant Keele destroyed 30 of the enemy's war-boats. On the 29th the first regular fire was opened from the enemy's stockade, which was answered in a very spirited manner from the boats. During the night Captain Thomas Kennan, who had the mortar-vessel under his directions, kept up a destructive fire, and on the 30th Lieutenant-colonel Godwin made a regular attack. Some misunderstanding arose as to the landing-place, which occasioned some delay, but Lieutenant Keele, having discovered in the nullah a boat, over which it was possible to pass to the fort, the boats pulled in, and, under a heavy and well-directed fire of musketry, the fort was stormed and carried, but not without a brave resistance on the part of the enemy. Captain Burrowes of his majesty's 41st regiment, and Lieutenant Keele, R.N., had the honour of being first in the fort. The town was deserted by its inhabitants, and no resistance of any moment was offered after the fort had been captured. The whole was accomplished with the loss of seven killed and fourteen wounded. A vast quantity of stores, ammunition, &c., fell into the hands of the victors, and the Honourable Company's gun-vessel Phaeton, was recaptured. This vessel had put into Martaban by mistake; her captain was taken prisoner in Ava, and her crew were confined in irons. The navy lost, in this brilliant attack, two men killed and three wounded. In the official report made by Colonel Godwin, he speaks in the highest terms of the behaviour of Lieutenant Bazely of the Sophie, and of Lieutenant Keele; to the latter, the day following the engagement, the colonel wrote a note containing his warmest acknowledgments of the gallantry and judicious conduct of the lieutenant which tended so materially to the happy results of the day. Mr. Swinton, the secretary to government, conveyed the applause of the governor-general in council to those engaged in this affair, and, after paying a just compliment to Colonel Godwin, the letter concludes thus: "You will be pleased to convey to Lieutenants Keele and Bazely, of his majesty's sloops Arachne and Sophie, the acknowledgments of the governor-general in council for the zealous exertions of themselves and the British seamen under their command."

In the present account of the war against Ava, we have derived but little assistance from the perusal of the work of Major Snodgrass. In every one of his descriptions, he seems to have forgotten that the navy participated otherwise than in a secondary manner, and, speaking of this attack on Martaban, the whole notice taken of the naval assistance rendered with such happy effect, according to Colonel Godwin, is summed up in these few words: "The intricate navigation of a shallow winding river, presented many impediments to an approach by water; the latter course (the approach by water), however, was at once resolved on, and, by toil and perseverance, the vessels were finally anchored nearly abreast of the town;" not another word, not a hint that it was owing to Lieutenant Keele's recommendation, that Colonel Godwin availed himself of the enemy's boat, which became a bridge, and not one remark upon the gallantry of that officer, who with Captain Burrowes led the assault, and was first in the place! It is our duty, as historians, to notice these glaring oversights; and since Major Snodgrass has omitted to mention the gallant services of the navy, we have thought it our duty to refer to the commander-in-chief's letters, and to those of Mr. Secretary Swinton, as conveying the just reward due to the exertions, the bravery, and the talent of those naval officers who shared in all the difficulties and dangers of the Burmese war.

The town of Yeh, situated to the eastward of Martaban, was next captured without resistance. "By the capture of these places," says Marshall, "the previous reduction of Mergui and Tavoy, and the voluntary submission of the whole coast of Tenasserim, the British obtained possession of very large stores of grain, ammunition, and ordnance, together with numerous boats for the conveyance of troops, and the command of all the Burman sea-coast from Rangoon to the eastward, a district ultimately ceded by treaty."

The month of November was passed off without offensive operations of any moment. Mr. Greer, of the Bombay marine, in a gun-boat, beat off two war-boats in a gallant style, the enemy being very far his superior in force; and on the 29th Captain Chads, with Lieutenant-colonel John Mallet of his majesty's 89th regiment, made a reconnoissance as far as the ancient capital of Pegu; it does not appear, however, that the English forces were engaged during this four days' expedition. The city was found a heap of ruins, with a few houses inhabited by some poor men and women.

The King of Ava, far from being overcome by the repeated reverses of his arms, now made a desperate effort to change the fortune of the war. To Maha Bandoola he intrusted the command of his army, and this general of high repute, who had been desired to sack Calcutta, and bring the governor-general in golden fetters to Ummerapoora, was recalled, with orders from his king to concentrate his force, amounting in all to about 50,000 men, at Donoobew.

It was on the 30th of November that Maha Bandoola made his approach towards Kemmendine, and, although Major Charles Yates was exposed to a serious attack by land and water, owing to Captain Goodridge of the Teignmouth having slipped his cable to avoid the enemy's war-boats and fire-rafts, which were floating down the river to the attack; yet the gallant major with a handful of Europeans nobly defended his post and repulsed his assailants. This was merely a prelude to the grand attack which commenced on the 30th. The object of Bandoola was to surround the British army, and crush them by his numbers. On each flank of the British line, the enemy were discovered emerging from the thick jungle, and they took up their position uninterrupted by the British, who had now only the narrow channel of Rangoon open in their rear. To check a division of the enemy's force, which had crossed to the Dalla side, the Arachne, under Captain Ryves (Captain Chads not having returned from Pegu), was placed a mile in advance of the fleet, and the Teignmouth was ordered back to support Kemmendine. The enemy commenced throwing up works with their usual rapidity, but Major Sale, with a detachment of his majesty's 13th regiment, and the 18th Madras native infantry, soon forced them to abandon their position, and ultimately destroyed their works. A party of the enemy having approached the Shwe-da-gon pagoda, were driven back by two companies of the 38th, under Captain Hugh Piper and Captain Christopher Wilson, while two companies of the same regiment were equally successful the following morning in dislodging the enemy from a very strong position near the north gate of the pagoda.

On the night of the 1st of December, Kemmendine was again attacked, and at daylight the enemy commenced a regular attempt upon that place; in vain they approached this stockade, they were repulsed again and again. Our men, wearied with the incessant fatigue, as darkness closed upon them, sought their wonted repose. Short was the time allowed them; the enemy, recruited by fresh troops, now made the most desperate effort; the flames of the fire-rafts illumined the scene; far and wide appeared the devastating enemy, whilst the roar of the cannon, and the roll of the musketry, conveyed to the ears of those near the pagoda, the tidings of this fresh and vigorous assault.

On the river the navy gallantly enacted their duty. The flaming rafts were towed clear of the vessels, and the war-boats which were ready to avail themselves of the confusion, retired without daring to attack. The gallant defenders of the fort were equally successful against their assailants, who were beaten back; and Major Yates added to his well-earned fame, by his intrepid and successful resistance. In endeavouring to give a proper description of the attacks which followed, we feel convinced that all our exertions would only appear a kind of shadow to those given so ably, so faithfully, and so graphically by Marshall; we therefore borrow from him the following account, admitting our obligation to that officer, and gladly bearing testimony to his patient research, and the excellent manner in which he has compiled his history:—

"Things were in this state when Captain Chads returned from Pegu, at 8 A.M., on the 2nd of December. He immediately sent the Arachne's pinnace up, under Lieutenant Kellett and Mr. Valentine Pickey, admiralty midshipman, to gain information and reconnoitre; and shortly after, three row-boats, under Mr. William Coyde, midshipman, with a party of seamen to fight their guns. This assistance was most timely, the garrison being pressed in every direction; from which critical situation, Lieutenant Kellett's highly judicious and determined gallant conduct immediately relieved them, by clearing both their flanks of the enemy by showers of grape-shot. This service, performed by the pinnace, with a single carronade, in the face of hundreds of the enemy's boats, was the admiration of the whole garrison; and Major Yates expressed himself to Captain Chads in terms the most gratifying, 'for the able assistance Lieutenant Kellett had afforded him.'"

"The Teignmouth shortly afterwards resumed her station, and was constantly engaged with the enemy's war-boats, which had long guns in their bows, and annoyed her a great deal. In the afternoon, finding the Burmese were making every effort to gain possession of Kemmendine, and as that post was of the last importance, both in a military and naval point of view, Captain Chads ordered the Sophie up for its support, with three more gun-boats, and those already there, under Lieutenant Kellett, to remain. Observing, also, that the enemy upon the Dalla side had begun to throw up works, he likewise directed the Satellite, in charge of Lieutenant Dobson, with a party of seamen from the Arachne, to the support of the Good Hope transport, and several small gun-vessels, already for some time stationed there.

"Early on the 3rd of December, the Sophie took her station off Kemmendine. The enemy again brought fire-rafts down, with their war-boats firing shot over them, to prevent the approach of the British. The Sophie cleared the rafts, but the Teignmouth was touched by them, and on fire for a short time, sustaining, however, no serious damage. 'British seamanship, says Major Snodgrass, 'finally triumphed over every device of the crafty and ingenious enemy.' During this day the Burmese war boatmen became extremely daring, finding their shot went further than those of the British ; upon which Captain Chads sent Captain Ryves two long 9-pounders, and enabled him to keep them further off. Still, however, they continued to evince surprising boldness, and it was thought right to endeavour to give them a check. Accordingly, the latter officer placed the whole of his disposable force of Europeans, about 80 in number (including Lieutenant Goldfinch, Messrs. Pickey, Coyde, Scott, and Murray, midshipmen ; Lieutenant Curtis Clarke, of the Bombay marine ; Mr. Lindquist, in charge of the row-boats; and Messrs. George Boscawen, midshipman in the Hon. Company's service), under the orders of Lieutenant Kellett. This force was put into the Arachne's pinnace and eight other boats, and, as the moon went down on the morning of the 4th of December, they shoved off, and pulling upon the contrary shore to the enemy, by daylight came abreast of and boldly made a dash at them: the Burmese were completely taken by surprise, but did not run till the British were within pistol-shot, when their confusion was great, and they fled with all haste, keeping up a smart fire. Lieutenant Kellett, in the pinnace, came up with some of the rearmost, which were soon run ashore and deserted; and Lieutenant Goldfinch, passing him whilst taking possession, captured one bearing the flag of the Burman chief, her crew also flying into the jungle. The chase was continued three or four miles, when Lieutenant Kellett judged it prudent to secure his prizes, having an enemy of considerable force in his rear, up another branch of the river. The result of this gallant attack was the capture of seven war-boats, one of which was 96 feet long, 13 feet 6 inches in breadth, and 6 feet deep, pulling 76 oars, and, as did three of the others, mounting a long 9-pounder on the bow. 'Lieutenant Kellett's conduct on this, and on former occasions, speaks for itself, and,' says Captain Chads, ' I trust will meet with its due reward. Lieutenant Goldfinch is a valuable officer, and merits every praise ; Lieutenant Kellett reports the high gallantry of every individual under his command. On their return they cut adrift and brought down a large floating stockade from Pagoda Point; and what adds to the value of this service is, that it was performed without the loss of a man.' In Sir A. Campbell's report to the Supreme Government, of the operations of his army at this period, we find the following passages :—

"'During the 3rd and 4th the enemy carried on his labours with indefatigable industry, and but for the inimitable practice of our artillery, commanded by Captain Murray, in the absence, from indisposition, of Lieutenant-colonel (Charles) Hopkinson, we must have been severely annoyed by the incessant fire from his trenches.'

"'The attacks upon Kemmendine continued with unabating violence; but the unyielding spirit of Major Yates and his steady troops, although exhausted with fatigue and want of rest, baffled every attempt on shore, while *Captain Ryves*, with his majesty's sloop Sophie, the Hon. Company's cruiser Teignmouth, and some flotilla and row gun-boats, *nobly maintained the long-established fame of the British navy, in defending the passage of the river against the most furious assaults of the enemy's war-boats, advancing under cover of the most tremendous fire-rafts, which the unwearied exertions of British sailors could alone have conquered.*'

"Sir Archibald next proceeds to acquaint the governor-general in council, that the 'intrepid conduct of Lieutenants Kellett and Goldfinch merits the highest praise ;' and he then adds :—

"'The enemy having apparently completed his left wing, with its full complement of artillery and warlike stores, I determined to attack that part of his line early on the morning of the 5th. *I requested Captain Chads, the senior naval officer here, to move up to the Puzendown creek during the night, with the gun-flotilla, bomb-ketch, &c., and commence a cannonade on the enemy's rear at daylight. This service was most judiciously and successfully performed by that officer, who has never yet disappointed me in my most sanguine expectations.* The enemy was defeated and dispersed in every direction. The Cassay horse fled, mixed with the retreating infantry, and all their artillery, stores, and reserve depôts, which had cost them so much toil and labour to get up, with a great quantity of small-arms, gilt chattahs, standards, and other trophies, fell into our hands. Never was victory more complete or more decided, and never was the triumph of discipline and valour, over the disjointed efforts of irregular courage and infinitely superior numbers, more conspicuous.'

"The naval force employed in the Puzendown creek was composed of the steam and mortar vessels, a few of the gun-flotilla, and several transports' boats, with about 40 European soldiers to make an appearance. Mr. Archibald Reed, admiralty midshipman, was with Captain Chads, and 'rendered him much service. In the mean time, the Satellite was very closely and warmly engaged, as she had also been during the nights of the 2nd, 3rd, and 4th, with the enemy at Dalla, whose shot struck her in every direction, and greatly injured the rigging; but as Lieutenant Dobson had taken the precaution to stockade her all around with bamboo, she fortunately had not a man killed or wounded.

"The Burmese left wing thus disposed of, Sir Archibald Campbell patiently waited its effect upon the right, posted in so thick a forest as to render any attack in that quarter in a great measure impracticable. On the same day he wrote to Captain Chads in the following terms:—

"'My dear Sir,—A thousand thanks for the essential diversion you made this morning to the left and rear of the enemy. Their defeat has been, indeed, most complete; the game is, I think, now up with them, and the further conquest of the country easy—thanks to all the good and fine fellows under our command by water and land.'

"On the 6th, in the morning, finding the enemy still persisting in his attacks on Kemmendine, Captain Chads sent the mortar-vessel up there, which rendered the post very essential service, and relieved the garrison considerably. The war-boats still continued in sight in great numbers, but at a respectful distance.

"On the same day Sir Archibald Campbell had the pleasure of observing that Maha Bandoola had brought up the scattered remnant of his defeated left, to strengthen his right and centre, and continued day and night employed in carrying on his approaches in front of the Shwe-da-gon pagoda. This he was allowed to do with but little molestation, as it was rightly imagined that 'he would take system for timidity.' On the morning of the 7th, he had his whole force posted in the immediate front of the British army—his first line intrenched so close, that the men in their barracks could distinctly hear the bravadoes of the Burmese soldiers. Upwards of thirty fire-rafts and large boats, all lashed together, and reaching nearly across the river, were brought down against the shipping; but, although the Sophie was touched by one of them, they were productive of no mischief.

"The time had now arrived to undeceive the enemy in their sanguine but ill-founded hopes. Sir Archibald Campbell made his arrangements, and at 11 h. 30 m. A.M., everything was in readiness to assault their trenches. A short but heavy cannonade ensued, and at noon the British columns moved forward to their respective points of attack. They were saluted, after a momentary pause, by a very spirited fire, in spite of which they advanced to the works, and quickly put their defenders to the route. The Burmese left many dead behind them, and their main force was completely dispersed. On receiving this information, Captain Chads sent every disposable man from the Arachne, under Mr. James B. Manley, acting-master, with twenty sepoys, in the steam-vessel, up to Captain Ryves, to endeavour to intercept their boats and cut off their retreat; they had, however, already deserted the neighbourhood of Kemmendine.

" 'Thus,' says Captain Chads in his official report, 'has this formidable attack ended in the total discomfiture of the enemy; having called forth from the very small force I have the honour to command, in every instance, the greatest gallantry and uniform good conduct, *under the utmost exertions by day and night, the greatest part of them having been in the boats since the starting of the expedition for Pegu, on the 26th ultimo.*

" 'From Captain Ryves I have received all the aid and counsel that a good and valuable officer could afford; his determined perseverance in holding his ground, when the fire-rafts came down, merit the highest commendation; and from his ready and zealous co-operation with the post at Kemmendine, that place was greatly relieved in the arduous contest it was engaged in.

" 'Of Lieutenant Kellett I cannot speak in terms sufficiently strong to express my admiration of his uniform gallantry.

" 'Lieutenant Goldfinch's conduct has also been most conspicuous, together with that of all the midshipmen named in my reports, not one of whom but has shown individual acts of great bravery.

" 'Also to Mr. Manley, the master, who has, from necessity, been frequently left in charge of the ship during my absence, I feel much indebted.'[1]

" 'In another despatch, addressed to Sir Archibald Campbell, the commander of the Arachne says:—

" 'It becomes a most pleasing duty to me to recommend to your favourable notice officers in the Hon. Company's service, whose good conduct has been conspicuous in the recent

---

[1] Lieutenant Keele was then at Martaban, where he remained in command of the naval detachment until all the European troops were ordered back to Rangoon about the end of 1824.

attack of the enemy. The first I ought to name is Mr. W. Binny, agent for transports of the Bengal division, in charge of the Good Hope transport—that ship, sir, with the British crew of the Resource, who handsomely volunteered, did all the duties of a man-of-war, in silencing the enemy's guns as they mounted them at Dalla. Mr. Hornblow, agent for transports of the Madras division, in charge of the Moira, has also shown very great zeal in forwarding all the late arduous services; and the British crew of his ship, in charge of the mortar-vessel, have continued their usual good conduct. In the attack on the enemy's war-boats, Lieutenant Kellett speaks in high terms of the gallantry of Lieutenant Clarke and Mr. Boscawen, of the H. C. cruiser Teignmouth, and Mr. Lindquist, in charge of the row-boats; this latter young officer I have also had much reason to be pleased with.'

"The loss sustained by the Burmese, from the 1st to the 7th of December, is supposed to have been at least 5000 men killed and wounded; but they suffered most in arms and ammunition, which they could not easily replace; 29 guns (of which eight were brass), 200 jingals, 900 muskets, 360 round shot, 2000 spears, and 5000 intrenching tools, fell into the hands of the conquerors; besides which, 10,000 pounds of gunpowder, many muskets, spears, swords, and other implements, of which no account appears to have been taken, were captured and destroyed. The British had not more than 26 killed and 252 wounded.

"On the 8th of December Sir Archibald Campbell reported to the governor-general in council, that *his 'obligations to Captains Chads and Ryves, and the officers and seamen of H. M. navy, were great and numerous. In Captain Chads himself,'* says the general, '*I have always found that ready alacrity to share our toils and dangers that has ever characterized the profession he belongs to, and the most cordial zeal in assisting and co-operating with me on every occasion.*'

"On the evening of the same day, Sir Archibald Campbell found that the enemy's corps of observation on the Dalla side of the river had not been wholly withdrawn, probably from ignorance of what had taken place on the 7th, in front of the Shweda-gon pagoda; and as he was well aware they would not remain long after the news of Bandoola's defeat reached them, he at once determined to assault their works. Detachments from three regiments were immediately ordered under arms, and Captain Chads was requested to make a diversion up the creek upon the enemy's right flank. After dark, all the boats assembled alongside the Good Hope transport; and, just as the moon arose, they moved across the river; the troops, under Major Charles Ferrior, of the 43rd Madras native infantry, landed to the northward, whilst Captain Chads, accompanied by Lieutenant Kellett and Mr. Reed, proceeded up the creek, and opened his fire; the Satellite doing the same to distract the enemy: the troops then advanced, and jumped, without a moment's hesitation, into the trenches; many Burmese were slain in the short conflict that ensued; they were driven, at the point of the bayonet, into the jungle in their rear; and several guns, with many small-arms, taken. In this affair, the British had two killed, and several, including five of the naval detachment, wounded. Lieutenant Dobson having landed immediately after the troops, was one of the first to enter the enemy's works.

"In a general order, issued at Rangoon, on the 12th of December, Sir Archibald Campbell again 'acknowledges his highest obligations to Captain Chads,' and 'requests that he will communicate to Captain Ryves, who so effectually supported the post of Kemmendine, his warmest thanks.' The passage concludes thus: '*the conduct of both officers and men during the whole affair was characteristic of the British navy!* WHAT CAN BE SAID MORE TO THEIR HONOUR?'"

"On the evening of the 12th a deserter from the enemy informed Sir Archibald Campbell, that Maha Bandoola had recollected his beaten troops, and received considerable reinforcements on his retreat; which latter circumstance had induced the chiefs (to whom he had for the present resigned his command) to determine on one more great effort to retrieve their disgrace. For this purpose, it afterwards appeared, they succeeded in forming a force amounting to between 20,000 and 25,000 men; with which they returned to Kokeen, distant four miles from the Shwe-da-gon pagoda, and immediately commenced intrenching and stockading with a judgment, in point of position, such as would do credit to the best instructed engineers of the most civilized and warlike nations. The deserter also declared it to be their intention to attack the British lines on the morning of the 14th (pronounced a fortunate day by their soothsayers), determined to sacrifice their lives at the dearest rate, as they had nothing else to expect than to do so ignominiously, by returning to the presence of their monarch, disgraced and defeated as they had been. This information was too circumstantially given to be disregarded, and Sir Archibald

Campbell prepared accordingly: the enemy's movements, next day, left little doubt on his mind of the truth of the deserter's information. Previously to this, the Sophie had been recalled from Kemmendine, and the Hon. Company's cruiser Prince of Wales, commanded by Lieutenant William S. Collinson, ordered to relieve her. On the 13th the gallant defender of that post addressed two letters to Captain Chads, of which the following are copies:—

"'My dear Sir,—Mr. Midshipman Lindquist acquaints me, that I am to be attacked this night. May I beg Kellett and his brig, and his boats, and the Powerful? Alas! the dear Sophie has forsaken me, and no *prince* or potentate can replace her in my confidence and affection. Prithee keep the Prince of Wales, and cheer my heart again with the presence of Sophie. Believe me ever your obliged and faithful,
   (Signed)   'C. W. YATES.'

"' My dear Sir,—My little band are at their post. The fires of the enemy are all around me. I hope you will excuse my having detained Mr. Lindquist, and his three boats, until I hear from you. I have 200 natives short of the force I had the other day, and 27 Europeans. If the Prince of Wales comes, I can expect no aid, as her commander is junior to the captain of the Teignmouth, which ship, having twice deserted me, I cannot look for aid from.   'Yours ever faithfully,
   (Signed)   'C. W. YATES.'

"In consequence of this pressing request, Captain Chads sent the Sophie back to her former station; and with her the steam-vessel, the mortar-boat, the Prince of Wales, and a detachment of seamen under Lieutenant Kellett. The commander-in-chief also directed 100 sepoys to proceed thither with Captain Ryves.

"In the night of December 13th the enemy recommenced offensive operations, particularly by annoying the vessels off Kemmendine with immense fire-rafts, one of which consisted of upwards of sixty canoes, besides bamboo rafts, all loaded with oil and combustibles. On the 14th, about 2 h. 30m. A.M., their emissaries succeeded in setting fire to Rangoon, in several places at once, by which one-fourth of the town, including the quarters of the Madras commissariat, was destroyed, notwithstanding the utmost efforts of the garrison, the officers and men of the

Arachne, and the well-disposed part of the inhabitants, to subdue the flames.

"The 14th passed without any other attempts on the part of the enemy; during the day, however, he was seen above Kemmendine, transporting large bodies of troops from the Dalla to the Rangoon side of the river. For many urgent reasons, Sir Archibald Campbell determined to attack him on the following day, rather than wait his pleasure as to time and place of meeting.

"Thinking it probable that the enemy's preparations for fire-rafts might be destroyed, and as he had before sent a force up the Panlang branch of the river, without finding anything, Captain Chads now resolved to despatch one up the Lyne branch, under Lieutenant Kellett, consisting of the steam-vessel, with 40 marines and soldiers for her defence; the Prince of Wales, towed by the Diana; and the pinnaces of the Arachne and Sophie. He thus describes the result of this expedition, in an official letter to Captain Coe, dated December 16, 1824:—

"'Before daylight yesterday morning, they proceeded with the first of the flood, and at a short distance above Pagoda point, saw large numbers of the enemy's war-boats, at least 200, who retired in good order as they advanced, keeping up a smart fire from their long guns, five boats having them mounted, and taking their distance that the carronades should not reach them; when about seven miles up, a raft was drawn right across the river, and set on fire by them, to prevent the advance of our vessels; but an opening was found, and Lieutenant Kellett, now seeing the river quite clear, with great judgment decreasing the power of steam, deceived the enemy, and lulled them into security; when, putting on the whole force again, and casting off the Prince of Wales, he was immediately within grape and musketry distance; the enemy finding themselves in this situation, drew up in a regular line to receive him: this little band was not, however, to be daunted by their show of resistance, but nobly dashed on, although the Prince of Wales was out of sight; the heavy fire from the boat's carronades, and musketry, threw the enemy into confusion and panic, and they flew in all directions, leaving us in possession of three of their large war-boats; one belonging to the chief, mounting three guns, and pulling 60 oars; the other two, one in their bow, 9 and 6 pounders; with about 40 other boats of all descriptions, many of them loaded with ammunition and provisions for their army before Rangoon.

"'The securing of 30 of these boats, and destroying the others, took up the whole of the flood; when Lieutenant Kellett, having most fully accomplished my instructions and wishes, returned, destroying, on his way down, quantities of materials for fire-rafts, and a great many canoes laden with earth-oil. The enemy's loss in killed and wounded must have been very great; we, I rejoice to say, had not a man hurt, the steam-vessel having been stockaded to secure the people.

"'I cannot find words sufficiently strong in which to recommend Lieutenant Kellett's uniform gallantry to you; his conduct on this, as well as former occasions, proves him a most valuable officer. Lieutenant Goldfinch, of the Sophie, I have also frequently had occasion to name to you, and with pleasure I repeat my former recommendations; he was in the Sophie's pinnace, with Mr. Murray, midshipman. Mr. Tomlinson, admiralty midshipman, commanded the Arachne's pinnace; and Mr. Winsor, admiralty midshipman, was in charge of the steam-vessel, and showed his usual judgment and good conduct.

"'Lieutenant Kellett speaks in the highest terms of the determined steady conduct of every man under him, soldiers, sailors, and marines; and feels much indebted to Lieutenant Collinson, commanding the Prince of Wales, for the able assistance that vessel rendered him.'

"During these operations, of which Major Snodgrass takes no notice, Sir Archibald Campbell attacked the enemy in the same direction, and gained a most brillant victory. With only 1300 infantry, he stormed and carried by assault the most formidable intrenched and stockaded works which he had ever seen, defended by upwards of 20,000 men, under the command of the Maha Silwah, an officer of high rank and celebrity, late governor-general of Assam. In the despatch announcing this great achievement, Sir Archibald says, *Our gallant friends afloat were determined not to let the auspicious day pass without their share of its operations. Every day's experience of the zeal and cordiality with which Captain Chads, and every individual composing the naval part of the expedition, co-operates with me in carrying on the combined service, increases my sincere obligations, and merits my warmest thanks.*' The loss sustained by the British army, on the 15th of December, amounted to 18 killed and 118 wounded.

"Previously to the intelligence of Sir Archibald Campbell's last victory reaching Calcutta, the supreme government had issued a general order, of which we shall here give two extracts:—

" 'The official despatches already published in an Extraordinary Gazette having announced the late brilliant achievements of the British arms at Rangoon, the Right Hon. the Governor-general in Council now proceeds to the discharge of a most gratifying duty, in signifying, in the most public and formal manner, his high admiration of the judgment, skill, and energy manifested by Brigadier-general Sir Archibald Campbell, in directing the operations of the troops under his command, on that important and arduous occasion. * * * * *

" ' *The Governor-general in Council seizes this opportunity of expressing his warm acknowledgements to Captain Chads, of H.M.S. Arachne, the senior naval officer at Rangoon, and to Captain Ryves, of H.M.S. Sophie, for their distinguished personal exertions, and requests the former to convey to the officers and crews of H.M. ships, of the H.C. cruisers, as well as the officers and men of the transports who volunteered their services, the sense which government entertains of their gallant conduct in the several actions with the enemy's war-boats, when they so conspicuously displayed the irresistible and characteristic valour of British seamen.*' "

This last successful enterprise of Sir Archibald Campbell produced a decided change in the aspect of the war; the enemy returned again to Donoobew, and Maha Bandoola ceased to make any offensive demonstrations. The inhabitants, released from their worst enemies, their own troops, again occupied their habitations, and the country round Rangoon once more enjoyed the blessings of repose. Before the close of the year, the Larne returned from Calcutta; the naval force was augmented by 20 additional gun-boats, and the army received large reinforcements from Madras, Bengal, and Ceylon.

Although the arms of Great Britain had been everywhere victorious, very little progress had been made since the commencement of hostilities up to the opening of the year 1825: Sir Archibald Campbell now determined to advance, if necessary, even to the capital, which was 600 miles distant, or from the brilliant success of his arms, to force the enemy to accede to his terms. With this intention in view, it became necessary to despatch an expedition, to compel the enemy to evacuate the old Portuguese fort and the Syriam pagoda before mentioned, of which they had again possessed themselves, and doubly stockaded, making it a formidable post to be left in the rear. In order to dislodge the enemy from these strongholds, Lieutenant-colonel R. Elrington, of his majesty's 47th regiment, with 200 troops, were embarked on board some good boats, the naval part of the expedition being intrusted to Lieutenant Keele. We have had frequent occasion to speak in high terms of this officer, but in all his brilliant exploits he never was more conspicuous than on the attack of the Syriam pagoda, the day after the surrender of the fort. The seamen as they manned the scaling-ladders, were cheered on and headed by Lieutenant Keele, and he was the first person over the stockade: the enemy gave way before him, and the works were instantly destroyed.

In moving upon Ava it was decided not to take the road by Pegu and Tonghoo, for the army was destitute of sufficient carriage to enable it to advance in that line. It became therefore absolutely necessary to keep the troops on a parallel with the river, with a view to mutual co-operation and support, and likewise to receive by that communication supplies for the army.

Captain Alexander, in the Alligator, arrived at Rangoon on the 22nd of January, and, being senior to Captain Chads, the command of the naval department devolved upon him.

In order to command the navigation of the river Lyne, Lieutenant-colonel Godwin and Captain Chads were detached with a sufficient force to insure success. "The vessels employed consisted of the Satellite, Diana, Prince of Wales, 15 row gun-boats, seven boats belonging to his majesty's squadron, and several flats and canoes."[1] The officers under Captain Chads were Lieutenants Fraser, Dobson, Keele, and Kellett, acting-Lieutenants William Hall and Goldfinch; Midshipmen Pickey, Tomlinson, Scott, Reed, Norcok, Lett, Biffin, Wyke, Wimson, and Coyde. The surgeon of the Arachne, Mr. William Watt, volunteered his services and accompanied the expedition, which on the 5th of February, moved up the river towards Quangalee, or Than-ta-bain, a formidable stockade garrisoned by 2000 men; the place stands upon a peninsula, and every exertion of the enemy had been rendered to strengthen the position towards the water, but the rear was altogether unprotected. Neither the Diana nor Satellite opened their fires until within 40 yards of the stockade, although the enemy had fired upon them during their advance. The Satellite anchored by the stern and opened her broadside, whilst Captain Charles Graham on board the Diana, kept up a well-directed fire of rockets. The boats in three divisions, under Lieutenants Keele, Fraser, and Kellett, directly the enemy were observed in confusion,

[1] Marshall.

and the order was given to storm, pulled towards the stockade. Lieutenants Keele and Hall were the first to enter the position, and Captain O'Reilly, with the grenadiers of the 41st regiment, followed, and insured the victory. The loss sustained by the British in this affair amounted to three soldiers, four sailors, and two lascars wounded, one seaman was drowned. This formidable place having been taken, Captain Chads extended his operations up both branches of the river; one is called the Panlang branch, the other, the Lyne, being the main branch, was found perfectly navigable as far as Meondaga. In the course of this survey of the river, Captain Chads on the Lyne, and Lieutenants Keele and Kellett, on the Panlang, destroyed numerous fire-rafts, and captured or burnt great numbers of war-boats. That Captain Chads on this, as well as on every occasion in which he was employed, conducted himself with courage, coolness, and ability, the extract of the letter in Appendix, No. 13. will sufficiently prove.

Sir Archibald Campbell, on the return of the forces above mentioned, leaving Captain Ryves in charge of the shipping at Rangoon, began his march on the 13th of February. He had previously resolved on moving in two divisions, one of which consisted of 2468 men under his own immediate orders, the first and grand object being to drive Bandoola from Donoobew where that chief had concentrated his force. "The marine column under brigadier-general, now Sir Willoughby Cotton, consisted of 799 European infantry, 250 sepoys, 108 foot artillery, and 12 of the rocket-corps: these were embarked in the flotilla, consisting of two mortar-boats, six gun-vessels, 30 armed row-boats, about 60 launches, flats, and canoes, and all the boats of the men-of-war remaining at Rangoon, containing every disposable officer and man of the Alligator, Arachne, and Sophie, the whole escorted by the Diana and Satellite, and under the command of Captain Alexander."[1] This force was directed to pass up the Panlang river to the Irrawaddi, and driving the enemy from his stockades, to push on with all possible expedition to Donoobew.[2] A small division under Major Sale of 780 men, was destined to attack Bassein, and then to effect its junction with the other divisions at Donoobew. The Larne and Mercury co-operated with Major Sale. It will be seen by the above statement, that the whole force when concentrated, would only amount to 4417, and that, taking in the rear-guard left at Rangoon, under Brigadier M'Creagh, consisting of 3781 men, the greatest

[1] Marshall. [2] Snodgrass.

number of troops under the command of Sir Archibald Campbell, consisted only of 8198. The enemy had more than 40,000 men under the command of a chief highly respected for his talents and his bravery, and who had risen in the estimation of his countrymen, from his numerous victories; such was Bandoola. Against the man who had under his command ten times as many men as himself, in a difficult, nay, almost unknown country, every place being well stockaded, and every leisure moment having been turned to some account in strengthening the positions, Sir Archibald Campbell advanced; not with the intention of merely marching a few miles to return again to Rangoon, but, if it were requisite, to dictate terms of submission to the King of Ava, in his own capital, and that capital 600 miles distant! Such an undertaking might well have caused uneasiness; but such was Sir Archibald's confidence in the officers and men of both navy and army who attended him in this dangerous and difficult expedition, that he never wavered as to his determination to advance, but merely hesitated by which of the roads he should approach the capital.

Major Snodgrass has given a beautiful description of the hardships endured by the division under Sir Archibald Campbell, after their arrival at their first day's encampment. "On reaching camp," he says, "the scene which presented itself was at once grotesque and novel; no double-polled tent bespoke the army of Bengal, or rows of well-pitched rowties that of the sister presidency; no Oriental luxury was here displayed, or even any of the comforts of an European camp, to console the traveller after his hot and weary march; but officers of all ranks couching under a blanket or Lilliputian tent, to shelter themselves from a meridian sun, with a miserable half-starved cow or pony, the sole beast of burden of the inmate, tied or picketed in rear, conveying to the mind more the idea of a gipsy bivouac than of a military encampment. Nothing of the pomp or circumstance of war was here apparent, nor would even the experienced eye have recognised in the little group, that appeared but as a speck on the surface of an extensive plain, a force about to undertake the subjugation of an empire, and to fight its way for 600 miles against climate, privations, and a numerous enemy.

The naval department sailed on the 16th of February, three days after the departure of the commander-in-chief, and the day following, the detachment destined to operate against Bassein moved towards its destination.

The day after the division under Brigadier-general Cotton and Captain Alexander set forward, they destroyed an unoccupied stockade at Thesit, and as they advanced up the river, a firing commenced from a position which was instantly carried by the boats' crews of the Alligator. The division now continued its course, destroying some fire-rafts, which were rendered ineffectual from the activity and vigilance of the seamen. On the 19th the outworks of the stockade of Panlang, and shortly afterwards the stockade itself, was carried without much opposition; the garrison consisted, previously to the assault, of 4000 men, and a vast number of war-boats supported the stockade on the right. The place was afterwards garrisoned by the English; Captain David Ross, with 25 men, was left in command, and the Satellite was ordered to protect and shelter them.

Sir Archibald Campbell arrived at Meondaga on the evening of the 19th, and then taking the road by Sarrawah, continued his march in the direction of Donoobew. It was at Theeboon that Sir Archibald heard of the success of the second or marine division, and likewise that no delay had occurred, but that the boats had reached the Irrawaddi. On the 6th of March the white pagoda of Donoobew was seen by the flotilla. "Brigadier-general Cotton, and Captain Alexander proceeded to reconnoitre a succession of formidable stockades, commencing at the pagoda and increasing in strength until completed by the main work, which was lofty, and situated upon a very commanding site; surrounded by a strong abbatis, with deep ditches, and all the customary defences: the guns appeared to be numerous, and the garrison were seen in crowds upon all the works."[1] A reconnoissance was made on the left bank of the river, the enemy opening a heavy fire from about 30 pieces of heavy artillery. Bandoola himself was at Donoobew, and refused any kind of surrender which Brigadier-general Cotton thought fit to request by means of a flag of truce. The strength of the place having been ascertained, it was judged advisable not to attack the main work, and the landing was effected below the stockades, the flotilla commanding the river.[2]

The first attack was made on the morning of the 7th, by a division of 500 men, which were divided into two columns, one under Lieutenant-colonel O'Donoghue, and the other under Major James Basden. The boats supported the columns as they advanced to the attack, and although the enemy made a good resistance, and were nearly 3000 in number, they were forced

[1] Marshall, vol. v., p. 166.   [2] See Appendix, No. 14.

from the pagoda stockade, and according to the best accounts, about 450 were killed. The next attack was upon a second stockade, a few hundred yards from the pagoda, and here, although the British fought with a determination rarely if ever surpassed, they were met by an equal resistance, and after a long struggle, in which Captain Rose of the 89th was killed, and a heavy loss sustained, the attacking column was ordered to retire, and early on the morning of the 8th, after destroying the arms, and spiking the cannon captured at the first stockade, the troops were embarked, and fell back upon Youngyoun, a strong position, about nine miles below Donoobew. In this sanguinary conflict the naval department sustained a loss of two seamen killed and 13 wounded. The loss of the enemy could not be ascertained, but from the vigour of the assault, and the steady perseverance of the troops, the fire from the boats, and the good direction of the mortars, many men must have been swamped.

About 25 miles above Sarrawah, a town which stands on the eastern bank of the Irrawaddi, opposite Kewdowa, stands the town of U-au-deet: and here it was that Sir Archibald Campbell, on the 11th of March, heard of the unsuccessful attempt of Brigadier-general Cotton. The commander-in-chief instantly decided upon advancing towards Donoobew; and after overcoming all obstacles, he crossed the Irrawaddi, mentioned "as one of the widest and most rapid rivers of the East,"[1] on rafts and in canoes, and by the 18th the whole of his division had reached the right bank of the river. In the mean time Captain Alexander remained in great anxiety with the flotilla, about a mile from the white pagoda; by day great activity was required in the seamen, for not unfrequently batteries were opened upon them from positions hastily taken up by the enemy, and during the night the war-boats carried on a harassing, although unsuccessful attack. On the 25th Sir Archibald took up a position close to the main stockade, and from the judicious arrangements of Bandoola, it was evident that he intended making a serious resistance. The Burmese, flushed with their former success, opened their fire upon the English. The cavalry hovered on their flanks,[2] and it was evident that they courted rather than shunned the attack.

"The stockade of Donoobew extended for nearly a mile along a sloping bank of the Irrawaddi, its breadth varying, according to the nature of the ground, from 500 to 800 yards

[1] Marshall.   [2] Snodgrass.

The stockading was composed of solid teak beams from 15 to 17 feet high, driven firmly into the earth, and placed as closely as possible to each other; behind this wooden wall the old brick ramparts of the place rose to a considerable height, strengthening the front defences by means of cross-beams, and affording a firm and elevated footing to the defendants. Upwards of 150 guns and swivels were mounted on the works, and the garrison was protected from the shells of the besiegers by numerous well-contrived traverses and excavations."[1]

On the 27th the garrison made a sortie on the right of the British lines, during which the flotilla boldly advanced under a crowd of sail, and exposed to the fire of the enemy's works. The Diana with a mortar-boat and four gun-vessels, pushed by the stockade and formed a junction with Sir Archibald's division, whilst the infantry, cavalry, and war-elephants, advanced upon the English. "The British cavalry," says Major Snodgrass, "covered by the horse-artillery, was ordered to charge the advancing monsters: the scene was novel and interesting; and, although neither the elephants nor their riders can ever be very formidable in modern warfare, they stood the charge with a steadiness and courage these animals can rarely be brought to show. Their riders were mostly shot, and no sooner did the elephants feel themselves unrestrained, than they walked back to the fort with the greatest composure. During the heavy cannonade that took place between the flotilla and the stockade, Maha Bandoola, who was superintending the practice of his artillery, gave his garrison a specimen of the discipline he meant to enforce in this last struggle to retrieve his lost character and reputation. A Burmese officer being killed while pointing a gun by a shot from the flotilla, his comrades instantly abandoned the dangerous post, and could not be brought back to their duty by any remonstrance of their chief: when Bandoola, stepping down to the spot, instantly severed the heads of two of the delinquents from their bodies, and ordered them to be stuck up upon the spot "pour encourager les autres."[1]

Between the 28th and the 31st the time was employed on one part in the construction of batteries, and on the other, in improving their defences; the approaches were made, and on the 2nd of April the English took possession of the place without the loss of a man. Bandoola had been killed the night previously by a shell, and his troops, after the loss of their chief, made a

[1] Snodgrass.

precipitate retreat; leaving behind them 110 iron guns, 28 pieces of brass ordnance, and 269 jingals, mounted on the works, without disabling them in any way. A vast quantity of military stores fell into the hands of the conquerors, and the total loss sustained during the siege amounted to only 14 killed and missing and 69 wounded. The high sense of the services rendered by the naval department, during a period of six weeks, under every privation, surrounded by difficulties and dangers, exposed during that time in open boats, harassed day and night by the enemy with all the vicissitudes of climate, all the annoyance of their cramped situation, is ably put forth in the letter of Sir Archibald Campbell,[1] and in Captain Alexander's despatch to Captain Coe.[2]

Sir Archibald, profiting by the panic, marched on the 3rd of April towards Prome, while the water division kept up a constant communication with the land column, which had been increased by the junction of Brigadier M'Creagh, on the 12th of April, at Surrawah, the whole force having again crossed the Irrawaddi. On the 24th the columns arrived in the neighbourhood of Prome, and as the enemy did not wait to be attacked, but retired without any resistance on the approach of the English, the place was taken possession of the day following, although the different stockades mounted 100 guns, and were in excellent condition to withstand an attack. With Bandoola's death, all the energy or bravery of the enemy seems to have vanished, and the British columns marched through a hostile country unmolested; but, as the rainy season was now about to commence, the army went into cantonments, and as far as the land column was concerned, there was a total cessation of hostilities.

Major Sale's division, during the advance of the two former columns upon Prome, proceeded to attack Bassein, accompanied by the Larne, Captain Frederick Marryat, and the Mercury, Lieutenant Drummond Anderson. On the 20th of February the division arrived off the entrance of the Bassein river. It appears that on the 26th, as the ships advanced up the river, they were fired at from two stockades, which the enemy deserted directly the fire was opened upon them in return. On the 3rd of March the ships arrived and anchored within three miles of Bassein, having experienced much trouble in warping up the narrow part of the river, and from the vessels constantly grounding. Bassein was at this time a heap of ruins, having been destroyed by the Burman chief, who had fled from the first stockade near the entrance of the river. Major Sale advanced about 130 miles

[1] Marshall. [2] Snodgrass.

towards Lamina without opposition; finding the place deserted, he returned on the 23rd to Bassein, it being useless to attempt a pursuit of his flying enemies. The casualties in this expedition amounted to two wounded. Sickness and fatigue, however, decreased the ranks in a trifling degree.

Captain Marryat having dropped down the river to Naputtah, proceeded thence with a small body of men against Thingang. The enemy, however, declined all hostilities, and Captain Marryat's terms were accepted, by which 150 Naputtah men were released, and provided with canoes to return to their homes. The arms, &c., were surrendered, and the Wongee of the town, a chief invested with a gold chattah, was delivered up as a prisoner.

Lieutenant Fraser, on the 30th, was despatched to Pumkayi. The same terms were offered and accepted as at Thingang. The whole coast from Negrais to Bassein, being now in possession of the English, was ultimately added to the conquered provinces, and "the enemy were deprived of all maritime possessions from Cape Negrais to Tenasserim."[1]

Lieutenant Wilkinson having been despatched from Prome in order to reconnoitre the river, captured on the 1st of May, without any loss, eight war-boats, pulling each fifty oars, and laden with ordnance stores. It is a proof how inefficient the enemy were in regard to warlike operations, as practical gunnery for this service was performed in the face of, and under the fire of 500 musketeers, and yet not a man was hurt. Captain Alexander, in mentioning the gallant behaviour of Lieutenant Wilkinson, remarks, "that the capture of these boats liberated 3000 canoes, with families in them, driven before the retreating force of the Prince of Sarrawaddy."

The months of June, July, and August were passed by Sir Archibald Campbell at Prome. Captain Chads returned, after the occupation of that place, to Rangoon. Captain Marryat, who was promoted to the command of the Tees, left the Rangoon about the middle of May. Captain Ryves was invalided. Lieutenant Edward Blanckley of the Alligator, was promoted to the Sophie, and departed from the station shortly afterwards, leaving the Alligator and Arachne, the only men-of-war, at Rangoon. Captain Chads desired both ships, during the wet monsoon, to be unrigged and secured by means of bamboos thatched with leaves. "The gun-boats were placed at equal distances, forming," says Mr. Marshall, "a chain of posts between Ran-

[1] Marshall.

goon and Prome, by which means provisions were forwarded to form a depôt for the ensuing campaign under a safe protection.

The forces under Sir Archibald Campbell, previously to the opening of the campaign, amounted to only 6148 men. From this number he had to garrison Prome; he therefore ordered 2100 men to be sent from Rangoon and Donoobew, which would swell his effective force to 8248 men. The enemy, who viewed with increased alarm the approach of the English towards their capital, were not inactive spectators of the coming storm; 40,000 men, under Memia-boo, the half-brother of the king, were collected and stationed at various cities, the principal force being concentrated at Meaday.

Before hostilities commenced, Sir Archibald Campbell addressed a letter to the court of Ava, dated the 5th of August, offering to enter into pacific negotiations; but, previously to any answer being received, Memia-boo had advanced to Meaday, and it became necessary to check his approach to the British force at Prome. Brigadier-general Cotton was therefore sent in the Diana, with a small force, to reconnoitre. Captain Alexander commanded the gun-boats, and on the 15th of August the object of the expedition was fully answered. The town of Meaday stands on the left bank of the Irrawaddi; a nullah runs into the river immediately below it. The bank of the river was strongly stockaded, and the place altogether presented a formidable appearance. The force of the enemy was estimated at between 16,000 and 20,000 men, and a general activity prevailed in order to render the position secure.

On the 6th of September the answer to Sir Archibald Campbell's letter to the court of Ava was delivered by two Burman deputies, under the protection of a flag of truce; they declared their readiness to enter into negotiations, and requested that two officers might be permitted to visit the Burman commander-in-chief, in order to carry into effect the terms about to be proposed to him. Lieutenant-colonel Tidy, the deputy adjutant general, and Lieutenant Smith, of his majesty's ship Alligator, were appointed by Sir Archibald Campbell, and were accompanied by Mr. Sarkies Manook as interpreter.[1] The principal conditions of peace offered by the English were the following:—" The non-interference of the court of Ava, with the territories of Cachar, Munnipoore, and Assam; the cession of the four provinces of Arracan, and the payment of a certain sum as an indemnification for the expenses of the war, one moiety to be paid imme-

[1] Marshall.

diately, and the Tenasserim provinces to be retained until the liquidation of the other. The court of Ava was expected to receive a British resident at the capital, and consent to a commercial treaty, upon principles of liberal intercourse and mutual advantages."

There was a profusion of Oriental folly and extravagance in the reception of the English commissioners. All the pomp, the show, and the outward profession of sincerity, was abundantly showered upon Colonel Tidy and his colleague; a jetty was built expressly for their landing; 2000 troops escorted them to their abode; compliments from the Kee-wongee were duly presented by the late governors of Prome and Sarrawaddy. The time between the 11th and the 16th was thus occupied, when it was agreed that hostilities should cease until the 17th of October; that a Burman minister of high rank should meet Sir Archibald Campbell at Neoun-ben-zeik, a village equidistant from both armies: and that no advancing movement should be made by the Burmese troops to swell the forces of Memia-boo, but that all the troops of Ava should be considered as partaking of the present neutrality.

Before the conference took place, Sir James Brisbane, Knight and C.B., in command of the Boadicea, which ship he had left at Rangoon, arrived at head-quarters, bringing with him the boats of his ship to assist in future operations. Sir Archibald Campbell and Sir James Brisbane proceeded on the 30th to the village above named, and the conference took place on the 2nd of October. A house had been erected for the purpose, and two officers of rank were deputed by the Kee-wongee to wait upon the English commanding officers, and conduct them to the house. On the part of the British, Colonel Tidy and Lieutenant Smith were sent for the same purpose to the Kee-wongee; the first day was spent in useless compliments about the state of the king's health, and on the following day six officers, Sir Archibald Campbell, Sir James Brisbane, Brigadier-general Cotton, Captain Alexander, R.N., Brigadier M'Creagh, Lieutenant-colonel Tidy, and Captain John James Snodgrass, again met the Burman deputies. The principal objection, urged on the part of the Burmese, was the cession of territory, and much conversation took place upon the subject. The day finished by an extension of the armistice until the 2nd of November, when the determination of the court of Ava was to be made known. In the mean time all American and English subjects detained at Ava were to be liberated, the British, on their part, liberating all Burmese then confined in Bengal. On the 3rd of November Sir Archibald was informed that the court of Ava refused to listen to the terms; neither the cession of one inch of territory, nor the payment of the slightest pecuniary indemnity could be entertained. The answer given was, "If you wish for peace you may go away; but if you ask either money or territory, no friendship can exist between us. This is Burman custom!" The armistice was finished, and both parties proceeded immediately to active and offensive operations, which commenced on the 15th of November on the side of the Burmese, and which gave them some confidence from the success of the enterprise. A division of the enemy having advanced within 48 miles of Prome in a north-easterly direction, four regiments of native infantry, under Lieutenant-colonel Robert M'Dowall, of the Madras establishment, were despatched to dislodge them. This was attempted in vain. The Burmese out-numbered their opponents by more than six to one, and Lieutenant-colonel M'Dowall, with 53 men, were killed, 110 wounded, and the remaining force obliged to withdraw.

That the Burmese had not been idle during the long and fruitless negotiation, is evident from the fact that shortly after the recommencement of hostilities, Prome was surrounded by 50,000 men, and the centre of the active force began to stockade and fortify the height of Napadee. On the opposite side of the river the enemy were equally active, and pushed a strong detachment forward in the hopes of regaining possession of Padoung-mew, a town on the western side of the Irrawaddi, which was bravely defended by 200 troops and a division of the flotilla under Lieutenant Kellett. The enemy made their attempt on the 25th of November, but were repulsed with some loss, whilst the casualties of both army and navy amounted to one man being slightly grazed by a musket-ball.

In the naval department some changes had occurred. On the 7th of November, Captain Alexander died, and was succeeded in command of the Alligator by Captain Chads;[1] and on the 14th the squadron received the additional aid of Captain John Fitzgerald Studdert, who arrived at Rangoon in his majesty's sloop the Champion.

On the 1st of December, measures having been taken for an attack on the enemy's lines, Sir James Brisbane, with the flotilla, commenced the action by a heavy cannonading of the enemy's centre, which was intrenched upon the Napadee Ridge, strongly

[1] See Appendix, No. 15.

defended as to natural position, and consisting of 30,000 men under the Kee-wongee. This attack was intended to withdraw the enemy's attention from Sir Archibald Campbell, who immediately sailed forth to attack Maha Nemiow, who commanded the left of the enemy's forces, and had under his command 14,000 infantry and 700 cavalry. Brigadier-general Cotton, who commanded the right division of the British forces, moved on towards Simbike, whilst the other division, under the commander-in-chief, forded the Nawine river, and continued along its banks. Stockade after stockade was taken without much resistance; the enemy were panic-stricken and deserted their strongholds, falling victims to their opponents, who mowed them down without resistance. The massacre amounted to 300 killed, amongst which was Maha Nemiow himself.

The English advanced upon Meaday, after an attack on Zeouke the following day. It is impossible to give sufficient credit to the troops, who cheerfully and without a murmur marched 20 miles, and, on the morning of the 2nd of December, drove the enemy from all their strong positions. The flotilla gallantly performed its duties; 300 boats were captured, and stores, ammunition, and guns to a large amount taken.

The nature of this war of extermination can be well understood from the account of Major Snodgrass. We extract from his journal the account of the 19th of December:—" Marched upon Meaday, where a scene of misery and death awaited us. Within and around the stockades, the ground was strewed with dead and dying, lying promiscuously together, the victims of wounds, disease, and want. Here and there a small white pagoda marked where a man of rank lay buried; whilst numerous newly-made graves plainly denoted that what we saw was merely the small remnant of mortality which the hurried departure of the enemy prevented them from burying. The beach and neighbouring jungles were filled with dogs and vultures, whose growling and screaming, added to the pestilential smell of the place, rendered our situation far from pleasant. Here and there a faithful dog might be seen stretched out and moaning over a newly-made grave, or watching by the side of his still breathing master; but by far the greater number, deprived of the hand that fed them, went prowling with the vultures among the dead, or lay upon the sand glutted with the foul repast.

" As if this scene of death had not sufficed, fresh horrors were added to it by the sanguinary leaders of these unhappy men. Several gibbets were found erected about the stockades, each bearing the mouldering remains of three or four crucified victims, thus cruelly put to death, for perhaps no greater crime than that of wandering from their post in search of food; or, at the very worst, for having followed the example of their chiefs, in flying from their enemies."

A part of Sir James Brisbane's letter to the admiralty, in which he mentions the gallant services of all under his command, and records the death of Captain Dawson, of the Arachne, will be found in the Appendix, No. 16. The command of the Arachne now devolved on Lieutenant Andrew Baird, of the Boadicea.

Victory followed victory in all directions. Brigadier-general Cotton was equally successful against Sudda-woon, who occupied the high banks on the west bank of the river. The flotilla, under Sir James Brisbane, again lent its powerful aid, and is highly spoken of by the brigadier-general in his report to the commander-in-chief, and it is gratifying to find that on every occasion the different services lent to each other the most efficient aid and cordial co-operation.

No time was lost by Sir Archibald Campbell. The panic-stricken enemy fled before him; the English advanced in two divisions as before, whilst a small force, under Brigadier Richard Armstrong, was embarked to act in co-operation with the naval forces under Sir James Brisbane. A line of communication having been established between Sir Archibald Campbell and the flotilla, the whole advanced. Both services had numerous obstacles to oppose, and both overcame all difficulties: the boats were kedged or tracked up the river in many places, owing to the rapidity of the stream, which rendered the former perhaps less fatiguing than eternally toiling at the oars. At Meong a junction with Brigadier-general Cotton's division with the flotilla had been arranged, but it was useless. No enemy remained to be opposed; every work, however strong, was abandoned. It appears, from Major Snodgrass's description, that a few resolute and well-trained men might have kept back the whole invading force. The river, in some places, is described as being so narrowed by shoals that the boats must pass, and did pass, within 200 yards of the banks, and the natural advantages, which had been increased by art, if properly defended, might have effectually stopped all progress towards the capital. On the 17th the united force came within sight of Meaday. It was evacuated by the enemy. Captain Chads was sent forward to reconnoitre and although the enemy made sufficient resistance to kill two men and wound two others during the reconnoissance, they fled at the approach of the advanced guard.

Sir Archibald Campbell now marched upon Melloone, and arrived before it on the 29th of December. On the 26th a flag of truce had been received on board the Diana, by Sir James Brisbane, bearing intelligence that Kolein Menghie had arrived at Melloone with power to conclude a treaty of peace. The flag required a cessation of hostilities for 25 *days*, but as Sir Archibald had discovered the bad faith of his opponents, he offered 24 *hours* as the longest period, and in the mean time continued his march. Melloone was strongly occupied, but as the enemy did not appear disposed to exchange shots, Sir Archibald consented to an armistice, and once more negotiations commenced. The close of this year saw the British force of a few thousand men dictating peace as conquerors, although surrounded by an enemy nearly eight times their number, and threatening to advance upon a capital the population of which was above 150 times more numerous than our army. Such is the force of discipline, when opposed to lawless hordes. Sir James Brisbane, at the commencement of this year, was obliged, from severe indisposition, to retire to Pulo-Penang. He died on the 19th of December 1826

It was soon evident that the court of Ava was by no means disposed to fulfil its treaty. As long as the Burmese could gain time they were satisfied that some chance might turn the scale of victory, or that in the end, the tremendous superiority of number must triumph. Indeed, had they been commanded by any active man, with common sense, it is evident that Sir Archibald's small force might have been kept eternally on the alert, and fatigued into a retreat. To the extreme ignorance of military tactics, must therefore be attributed the fact, that a band of men, far below 8000 in number, could advance or dream of advancing into a populous country, with at least 60,000 men under arms, and concentrated, with strongholds in their rear, stockaded, fortified, every munition of war at hand, recruits to supply casualties, ample provisions, in short all that could be required to carry on a desperate contest. On the other hand, it is true, the river afforded conveyance from Rangoon, of ammunition, &c., but the enormous fatigue attending such transport must be considered, and that, from the smallness of the force the stockades, which stood on the banks of the Irrawaddi, and which were taken by the invaders, could not be retained, and again fell into the enemy's hands. We have seen in the preceding pages that hundreds of war-boats thronged the river, that fire-rafts were daily constructed and nightly used, that such was the scarcity of fresh provisions even at Rangoon, that mutton was sold at five shillings the pound, a duck at eighteen, and all other articles on an equal ratio. Of the luxuries of life there were none; to this must be added that the seamen were absent from their ships a whole year, and as Marshall remarks, " were employed rowing and tracking their boats by day against a rapid stream, sleeping in them by night, protected from the inclemency of the weather by awnings only; rarely meeting with a fresh meal, and at one period, upwards of two months without so great a luxury." These men well deserved the thanks which Sir Archibald Campbell and their own officers so frequently bestowed upon them.

On the 18th of January the Burmese commissioners again endeavoured to gain time, and requested a further delay of a week: it was refused; they had promised to evacuate Melloone on the 20th, they refused to comply with their own proposition, and war again became inevitable. Both parties laboured hard during the night; the English in landing 28 guns, which were in battery by 10 o'clock the next morning; the Burmese strengthening their already powerful defences. Before noon on the 19th the English opened their fire, and every prospect of any amicable arrangement had passed.

A brigade under the command of Lieutenant-colonel R. Sale, and a division under Brigadier-general Cotton were embarked in the boats under the command of Captain Chads. The first-named brigade assembled and carried the main face of the enemy's position; Major William Frith, of his majesty's 38th regiment, heading the party, the lieutenant-colonel having been wounded in the boats. The enemy gave way immediately, but were interrupted in their retreat by Lieutenant-colonel Thomas Blair, of the 87th foot, who boldly attacked and dispersed them with considerable loss. Such was the daring of one side and the imbecility of the other, that, in four hours after the opening of the battery, Melloone was in the possession of the invaders, and all the money, stores, ammunitions, and 300 cannons in the hands of the victors, and this chef-d'œuvre of Burman fortification, strongly garrisoned, was assaulted and taken with the trifling loss of nine men killed and 35 wounded.

The officers of his majesty's navy, who were employed in this gallant and apparently desperate service, were Lieutenants Grote and William Smith, of the Boadicea, Valentine Pickey, of the Alligator, and Messrs. Sydenham Wilde, William H. Hall, George Sumner Hand, George Wyke, Stephen Lett, and William Coyde (midshipmen).

Though the fall of Melloone convinced his majesty of Ava that his troops were unable, under any circumstances, to cope with his invaders, still it was considered that another chance should be taken, and Nie-Wooh-Breen (the king of hell), was in the well-fortified city of Pagahm-mew, with 16,000 men to turn the tide of victory. Sir Archibald Campbell now advanced to assault the place, and although the court of Ava had despatched Dr. Price, an American missionary, who was a prisoner at Ava, in conjunction with Dr. R. Sandford of the royals, also a prisoner, both of whom arrived at head-quarters on the 31st of January,—he did not delay his approach, although his force only amounted to about 2000 men to face this formidable warrior. On the 9th of February the king of hell was defeated and Pagahm-mew taken, the British loss amounting to two men killed, and fifteen wounded. The enemy were dispersed in all directions, and now sued for peace in all sincerity, imploring Sir Archibald not to approach nearer the capital. After considerable difference as to the amount of money to be deposited as an indemnity, it was finally agreed that 25 lacs in money should be paid, and this sum was brought to Yandaboo, a place only 45 miles from the capital, by the missionary above mentioned, and paid over.

The definitive arrangement was left to the commissioners already named by Sir Archibald Campbell, and Captain Chads was requested to lend his talent towards the completion of the treaty. On the 24th of February the peace was signed, the principal conditions being as follows:[1]—" To abstain from all future interference with the principality of Assam and its dependencies, and also with the contiguous petty states of Cachar and Jynteea; to recognise Ghumbeer Singh as Rajah of Munnipoore (should he desire to return to that country); to cede in perpetuity the provinces of Arracan, recently conquered by the British, including the four divisions of Arracan, Ramree,[2] Cheduba, and Sandoway, as divided from Ava by the Unnoupectowmien mountains, and also the provinces of Yeh, Tavoy, Mergui, and Tenasserim, with the islands and dependencies

[1] Marshall.
[2] The harbour of Kheauk-pheo, at the north end of the island of Ramree, is described as sufficiently large to accommodate the whole navy of Great Britain. The anchorage is from 8 to 15 fathoms throughout; and being land-locked on three sides, the west, east, and south, the harbour is completely secured against the south-west monsoon.

thereunto appertaining (taking the Saluœn, or Martaban river, as the line of demarcation on that frontier); to receive a British resident at Ava, and to depute a Burman minister to reside at Calcutta; to abolish all exactions upon British ships or vessels in Burman ports, that are not required from Burman ships or vessels in British ports; and to enter into a commercial treaty upon principles of reciprocal advantage; the King of Ava, 'in proof of the sincere disposition of the Burman government to maintain the relations of peace and amity between the nations and as part indemnification to the British government for the expenses of the war,' agreed to pay the sum of one crore of rupees, equal to about 1,000,000*l.* sterling (valuing the rupee at two shillings, the then rate of exchange), of which contribution the first instalment, amounting to 2,508,199 sicca rupees, was embarked at Yandaboo, brought down the Irrawaddi (a distance of 600 miles), and ultimately conveyed by Captain Chads to Calcutta, where it was landed from the Alligator, April 10th, 1826."

Thus ended the Burman war. On the 8th of March the troops were embarked, and by the 6th of May the whole force had returned to Rangoon, and sailed for their several destinations.

In conclusion, it becomes a pleasant duty to record the vote of thanks of both houses of parliament, to Sir James Brisbane, and the captains, officers, seamen, and marines, under his command, for their cordial co-operation, their skilful, gallant, and meritorious exertions, which greatly contributed to the successful issue of the war: and to add, that Captains Chads, Marryat, and Ryves, received the companionship of the Bath, and that every lieutenant, and passed midshipman, who were employed on this occasion, were promoted.

In the Appendix, No. 17, will be found the proclamation of the governor-general in council, and it is almost useless to add, that the Admiralty, and the East India Company, expressed their approbation of the zealous and gallant conduct, displayed by Sir James Brisbane, Captains Chads and Marryat, and the other officers and men, during the long and arduous service in which they were employed. Our men suffered all the privations incident to a hostile country, all the miseries of sickness, and want of common comforts, with constant exposure to harassing attacks from an enemy vastly superior in numerical strength, who disturbed them by night, and attempted to starve them by day, and every officer and man deserved the thanks which a grateful country returned them for their active, persevering, and meritorious exertions.

APPENDIX TO THE BURMESE WAR.

No. 1. See p. 306.

IN compliance with your orders, on the 9th instant, at 11 P.M., at the commencement of the flood-tide, I proceeded up the river in the Honourable Company's cruiser Thetis, accompanied by the Jessey [Penang cruiser], six of the gun-flotilla, six row-boats, and the Malay proa you were pleased to put under my command. At 2 A.M. the Jessey and the row-boats took up the position assigned them, about three-quarters of a mile below Kemmendine. The Thetis was anchored at the entrance of a creek about the same distance above Kemmendine, and abreast of the stockade from which the gun was taken on the 3rd instant, but which has since been greatly strengthened. The gun-flotilla were to have been placed abreast of the opposite point, forming the entrance of the creek (distinguished by a pagoda), on which, since the 3rd, there has been erected a formidable stockade; but in consequence of the ebb-tide making against them, with the exception of the Robert Spankie and two others, they failed in their endeavours to take up their position, and were brought up a short distance below the Thetis.

About 10 A.M. the batteries opened their fire against Kemmendine; the stockade on the pagoda point at the same instant commenced a fire of musketry, and from four small pieces, apparently 4 or 6 pounders, upon the Robert Spankie and the other two gun-vessels opposite to it, which was returned by them, and kept up on both sides for upwards of an hour. The stockades abreast of the Thetis not having fired a shot the whole time, and observing that the flotilla did not succeed in silencing the other, I took advantage of the flood-tide just then making, to drop abreast of it in the Thetis, and after a fire of half an hour, so far silenced the enemy that from this time they only fired an occasional musket at intervals when we had ceased, but altogether so badly directed, that we had only one man wounded, belonging to a row-boat at that time alongside the Thetis. Having observed a great number of boats, many of a large size, collected about two miles above us, and considering it possible that at night, during the ebb, they might attack any of the flotilla that remained in advance, when we, from the rapidity of the current, could not render them any assistance, I thought fit to shift the Thetis, at the last of the flood, about a quarter of a mile above the point, directing the flotilla to drop with the ebb below the stockade on the opposite point, which they accordingly did.

At noon on the 11th, observing the signal agreed upon, when the general wanted communication with us to be made, I sent an officer to answer it, who returned with intelligence of the troops having possession of Kemmendine, and with a request from the general, that two of the gun-flotilla and two row-boats might be left at that place; I accordingly directed the flotilla, with the above exceptions, to proceed to Rangoon with the evening's ebb. At 6 P.M. the Thetis weighed, and, with the boats ahead to tow, began to drop down the river.

From the place where we had been at anchor we had seen a great smoke and flame, apparently proceeding from the back of the stockade on the pagoda point; but which, on our opening the entrance of the creek, we discovered to be a very large fire-raft, composed of a number of country boats fastened together, and rapidly drifting down with the stream. By endeavouring to avoid the raft, together with the effect of the strong current setting out of the creek, the Thetis unfortunately grounded on the opposite bank of the river, where, in spite of every exertion, she remained until high water next morning.

The raft grounded on the pagoda point, where it remained burning the whole of the night; although occasionally large masses separated from the main body and drifted down the river. The most dangerous of these masses were towed on shore by Mr. [George] Winsor, of the Sophie, in the Larne's gig, who described them to be composed of canoes, filled with tar, matting, bamboos, &c. During the night there were some shot fired at the Thetis from the stockades, but without effect. At daylight on the 12th, having succeeded in getting her afloat, we proceeded down the river and anchored at Rangoon.

No. 2. See p. 308.

Having observed a disposition to recross part of their force to the Dalla side of the river, I determined, on the 8th instant, to make as general an attack as the very woody and inundated state of the country would possibly admit of. For that purpose I formed the force to be employed into two columns of attack; one proceeding by land, under the command of that excellent and indefatigable officer Brigadier-general Macbean, for the purpose of surrounding the enemy on the land side; while I, with the other, proceeded by water to attack their stockaded position, along the banks of the river in front. To this post the enemy appeared to attach the greatest importance, and the stockades were so constructed as to afford mutual support, presenting difficulties apparently not to be overcome without a great sacrifice of lives. *I therefore resolved to try the effect of shelling, and consulted with Captain Marryat upon the employment of such armed vessels as he might select to breach, in the event of our mortar practice not succeeding.* The shells were thrown at too great a distance to produce the desired effect, and the swampy state of the country would not admit of any advance. The armed vessels, viz., the Satellite, Teignmouth, Thetis, and Jessey, the whole under the command of Lieutenant Fraser, of H. M. S. Larne, now took their stations according to a disposition made by Captain Marryat, and opened a fire, which soon silenced that of 14 pieces of artillery, besides swivels and musketry from the stockades, and in one hour the preconcerted signal of "breach practicable," was displayed at the mainmast head. The troops, as previously arranged, entered their boats on the signal being hoisted. The assault was made in the best order and handsomest style: Major Wahab, with the native infantry, landed, and immediately attacked the breach, while Lieutenant-colonel (Henry) Godwin, almost at the same instant, pushed ashore a little higher up, and entered the work by escalade: the enemy kept up a sharp, but ill-directed fire, while the troops were landing, but, as usual, fled on our making a lodgment in the place. I now ordered Lieutenant-colonel Godwin to re-embark with the detachment of the 41st regiment, and attack the second stockade, which was immediately carried in the same style. The third stockade was evacuated by the enemy.

The cool and gallant conduct of all the troops on this occasion was, to me, a most gratifying sight. *To the officers and men of the breaching vessels every praise is due: and I much regret that severe indisposition prevented Captain Marryat from being present to witness the result of his arrangements.*

The inundated state of the country did not admit of any communication with Brigadier-general Macbean from the shipping, nor did I know the result of the operations of his column, until I returned to Rangoon in the evening. Nothing could be more brilliant and successful. He took, by assault, seven strong stockades in the most rapid succession, throwing the enemy into the utmost consternation; and he had also the good fortune to fall in with a large body flying from a stockade attacked by the shipping, of whom a great number were killed.

No. 3. See p. 308.

Sir,—I request you will accept my very best thanks for your able arrangement and disposition of the vessels employed in the attack of the enemy's stockades yesterday; and I beg you will do me the favour of conveying them to Lieutenant Fraser, R.N., Captain Hardy, and the officers in command of the Honourable Company's cruisers Thetis and Jessey.

I had the greatest satisfaction in observing the general good conduct of the row-boats and the boats of the transports; they carried the troops up to the assault in very handsome style, and Captain O'Brien, of the Moira, was the first man who leapt on shore, and entered the breach with the foremost of the troops. I am, &c.,
(Signed) A. CAMPBELL.

No. 4. See p. 308.

The Governor-general in Council unites with you in regretting, that the severe indisposition of Captain Marryat, the senior naval officer, prevented his witnessing the successful result of his judicious arrangements on the occasion alluded to. You will be pleased to assure Captain Marryat, that his lordship in council entertains the highest sense of his valuable services, and will not fail to bring them under the notice of his excellency Commodore Grant.

No. 5. See p. 308.

I must now call your attention to the condition of H.M.S. Larne, whose crew I am sorry to say have been rendered quite inefficient by disease. Since we have been on this expedition, we have had 170 cases of cholera and dysentery. We have had 13 deaths—we have now 30 patients at the hospital on shore, and 20 in the sick list on board; our convalescents are as ineffective as if they were in their hammocks; they relapse daily, and the surgeon reports, that unless the vessel can be sent to cruise for a month, there is little chance of their ultimate recovery. When I sent away the expedition, under Lieutenant Fraser, on the 7th instant, I could only muster three officers and twelve men fit for duty.

The conduct of Lieutenant Fraser, in the several expeditions which he has commanded, has been that of a gallant and steady officer; and I am under the greatest obligations to Mr. Atherton, not only for his active services in the boats, but for carrying on the whole duty of the ship, during the absence and sickness of the other officers. The behaviour of Mr. John Duffill, master's-mate of this ship, and of Messrs. Winsor and Maw, midshipmen, lent from the Sophie and Liffey, has been very satisfactory, and I trust, that when future opportunities may occur, they will so distinguish themselves as to have a fair claim for promotion.

No. 6. See p. 309.

I proceeded with the detachment you were pleased to place under my command, at 11 A.M., and after entering a large creek on the east side of Dalla, and proceeding about two miles, I observed two stockades, one on the right, and one on the left bank, immediately opposite to each other, both in commanding situations, particularly that on the left bank, which I instantly decided on attacking. The boats were hove-to for a short time, to make the necessary preparations for the attack, and as soon as these were completed, the whole moved on under a heavy fire from the guns and musketry of the enemy in both stockades. The landing was effected under an incessant fire from them, and after great labour and exertion in getting through the mud, which was remarkably stiff, and thigh deep, the scaling-ladders were placed, and the stockade stormed and immediately carried. Some of the troops then re-embarked, crossed the river, and took possession of the opposite stockade.

Our loss, although severe, is not so great as might have been expected from the nature of the ground we had to go over, and the sharp and severe fire kept up by the enemy until the scaling-ladders were placed. The loss on the part of the enemy was but small, in consequence of the vicinity of the jungle, into which they escaped the moment our men entered their works.

Of the conduct of the troops, I cannot speak in too high praise, although it will be impossible for me to particularize the officers who so gallantly led their men to the assault, as they are too numerous; many of them assisted in carrying the ladders to the walls.

I felt myself highly indebted to Lieutenant Fraser, and a party of seamen and marines of H.M.S. Larne, whose unremitting exertions throughout the affair, greatly contributed to the success of the day.

It is with regret I have to report that Mr. Maw, R.N., your acting aide-de-camp, was severely wounded in the early part of the day, whilst he and Captain John Campbell, H.M. 38th regiment, your (second) aide-de-camp, who was a volunteer on the occasion, were cheering on some of the seamen who accompanied us.

I have further to report, that the enemy, previous to their flight, threw some guns into a wet ditch that surrounded the fortifications. We found but two small ones, which were brought away. All the houses in both stockades were destroyed by fire, and a part of the palisade pulled down, before the return of the detachment to camp.

No. 7. See p. 309.

The gallantry of the officers employed in this expedition, viz., Lieutenant Fraser, Mr. Atherton, and Messrs. Duffill, Winsor, and J. H. Norcock, deserves the highest encomiums. I am sorry that our list of killed and wounded is so heavy, but it will be accounted for when I state, that in these attacks the Lascars, who man the other boats, will not pull into the fire unless they are led by the officers and men of H.M. sloop the Larne. The conduct of Mr. Maw, midshipman of the Liffey, has, during the whole period of his service here, been a series of gallantry. I have great pleasure in transmitting a letter from Sir Archibald Campbell, relative to his conduct, and adding my testimony to that of the commander-in-chief.

I regret, says Sir Archibald, the severe wound received by Mr. Maw. Of this young man's gallantry of conduct and merit I cannot speak too highly: he has repeatedly distinguished himself by the most conspicuous and forward bravery.

No. 8. See p. 311.

Sir Archibald Campbell will take an early opportunity of communicating to Captain Marryat, R.N., how gratified he was by his prompt support at the point assailed, and the gallant pursuit of the flying enemy by himself and his brave followers; and which he will not fail to request Captain Marryat to communicate to the officers and men of his majesty's navy, and also those of the transport service, who so handsomely came forward on this, as they have done on many former occasions.

No. 9. See p. 311.

Under these circumstances, I most fully coincide with you in opinion, that no time should be lost in proceeding to Penang, where those comforts essentially necessary for the recovery of your crew are at present most conveniently to be had; aware as I am, that the most urgent necessity alone induces you to suggest the removal of the ship under your command. I feel fully convinced that you will not lose a moment in returning to partake of the further, and I trust more active, operations of the approaching campaign.

In taking I hope a very short leave of yourself, and the officers and men of the Larne, I shall not dwell, as I otherwise would, on the valuable and ready aid I have invariably received from you all since the commencement of the present service, embracing duties of perhaps as severe and harassing a nature as ever were experienced by either sailors or soldiers, and under privations of the most trying nature. Any number of Malay sailors you may require to assist in navigating the Larne to Penang are at your service.

(Signed)   A. CAMPBELL.

No. 10. See p. 311.

I have the honour to enclose sundry despatches from Captain Marryat, of his majesty's ship Larne, in command of the naval force in the river Rangoon, detailing various successful attacks on the enemy, while co-operating with the army under Sir Archibald Campbell; and I feel much pleasure in recommending to their lordship's notice that officer, as well as those named in the margin,[1] to whose zealous exertions and cool intrepidity are to be attributed the successful results of the various attacks which they conducted against the enemy. I am pleased in having it in my power to recommend in the strongest terms Mr. Henry Lister Maw, midshipman of this ship, who volunteered his services to Sir Archibald Campbell, and who accompanied him in all his operations; and I trust, from the high encomiums passed on his conduct, their lordships will be pleased to consider his services, and his having been most dangerously wounded.

No. 11. See p. 312.

A chart drawn by Mr. Winsor, admiralty midshipman of the Sophie, to whom I feel much indebted for his exertion and ability, he having had the arduous charge of the steam-vessel during the whole of the time, will enable you to judge of our progress; the Satellite was on shore three times, and the Diana once, but without the slightest injury. It now becomes a most pleasing duty for me to express the high satisfaction I feel at the conduct of the officers and seamen I had the pleasure to command; their privations and harassing duties were extreme, under heavy rains, guards by night from fire-rafts with the enemy's war-boats constantly watching close to them, and incessant towing of the flotilla by day; their high spirits were unabated; and without the utmost zeal and fatigue in the officers commanding the divisions, it would have been impossible to have advanced, manned as they are, with natives only. Lieutenant Dobson rendered me every assistance, and was of great service; he was severely burnt on the 22nd. From the exemplary conduct of these officers and seamen, allow me, sir, to recommend them to your favourable attention. The casualties, I rejoice to say, have been very few—four seamen of the Arachne wounded.

---

[1] Lieutenant William Burdett Dobson and Thomas Fraser, acting Lieutenant George Goldfinch, Mr. Robert Atherton, and Messrs. John Duffill, George Winsor, and Charles Kittoe Scott.

No. 12. See p. 312.

ENCLOSURE.

Camp, Rangoon, Oct. 11, 1824.

Sir,—In obedience to orders I had the honour of receiving from you, to feel the strength and disposition of the enemy upon the Lyne river, and to attack him as often as opportunities might offer of displaying the valour of the troops under my command, I embarked, on the morning of the 5th inst., with 300 men of his majesty's 38th regiment, 100 rank and file of the 18th Madras native infantry, and a detachment of Bengal artillery, under Captain Timbrell, on board a flotilla of gun-boats, &c. &c., under the immediate command of Captain Chads. The first day's tide carried us as high as Pagoda-point, above Kemmendine, at the junction of the Lyne and Panlang rivers. Having been joined by the armed transport and flotilla, at 2 P.M. next day, the whole force proceeded up the Lyne river with a flowing tide. Bodies of the enemy were seen moving up on the right bank, while numerous war-boats hovered in our front, keeping up a continued but distant fire. After the flotilla anchored, the light boats in advance, under Lieutenant Kellett, of his majesty's ship Arachne, pursued the enemy's war-boats; and having closed with one carrying a gun and full complement of men, boarded and took her in the handsomest style, the Burmese jumping overboard to save themselves. On the 7th, after proceeding about four miles, I observed two stockades, which were taken possession of without loss, and we reached, with this tide, within a short distance of the large works and fortified village of Than-ta-bain, having in the course of the day destroyed seven of the newly-constructed war-boats. On reconnoitring the village, I found it was defended by three long breastworks, with a very extensive stockade, constructed of large teak-beams; and fourteen war-boats, each mounting a gun, were anchored so as to defend the approach to it.

Having consulted Captain Chads, we advanced to the assault, the steam-boat, with the Satellite and bomb-ketch in tow, and the troops in their boats ready to land when ordered. In passing the breastworks, we received a smart running fire from jingals and musketry, which was returned with showers of grape from the Satellite; and observing the enemy evidently in confusion, I directed the troops and scaling-ladders to be immediately landed, and in a few minutes every work about the place was in our possession. During this night, some fire-rafts, of a most formidable appearance, were floated down the river, but very fortunately they passed without touching any of the vessels.

At six o'clock next morning, we again moved with the tide, and in passing a narrow neck of land at the junction of two rivers, were received with a brisk discharge of musketry from a long line of breastworks, and a cannonade from a very large stockade on our right. The fire of the latter was soon silenced by the well-pointed guns of the Satellite.

The troops and pioneers were ordered then to land, and this formidable stockade was carried by assault without a struggle. It is, without exception, the strongest work of the kind I have ever seen—the length of the front and rear faces is 200 yards, and that of the side faces 150. It is built of solid timber 15 feet high, with a platform inside all round, five feet broad and eight feet from the ground. Upon this platform were a number of wooden guns, and piles of single and double-headed wooden shot, and many jingals; below, we found seven pieces of brass and iron ordnance. In front, the stockade is strengthened by breastworks and regular demilunes, and would contain with ease above 2000 men. In the centre of this stronghold we found the magnificent bungalow of the Kee-wongee, who, I presume, fled early in the day. I cannot doubt but the enemy's loss must have been severe, though we only found 17 dead bodies, which they had not time to carry off.

The advanced boats having pushed up the river some miles, without seeing any other works, I considered the objects you had in view fully accomplished, and we accordingly began to move back to Rangoon.
*　　*　　*　　*　　*I cannot adequately acknowledge my obligations to Captain Chads, for his zealous, judicious, and cordial co-operation; and the spirited conduct of Lieutenant Kellett, in command of the advanced boats, attracted the notice of every one.*　*　*　*　*

I need scarcely add, that every officer and man evinced, on all occasions, that cheerful readiness and determined valour you have so often witnessed.　*　　*　　*　　Much powder, and an immense quantity of petroleum oil, and warlike stores, were destroyed at the different stockades.

(Signed)　　　　　　　　　　T. EVANS.

No. 13. See p. 312.

Extract of a letter from George Swinton, Esq., to Sir A. Campbell, dated "Fort William, 18th March, 1825."

I am directed to acknowledge the receipt of your despatch relative to the capture of the strong post of Than-ta-bain, or Quangalee, by a detachment of troops under the command of Lieutenant-colonel Godwin, aided by a party of seamen under Captain Chads and Lieutenants Keele and Hall. The governor-general in council is happy to observe, in the signal and complete success which attended the operations against Than-ta-bain, the same judgment, energy, and skill, on the part of Lieutenant-colonel Godwin, which distinguished his conduct on the occasion of his being detached against Martaban, and which again demand the unqualified approbation and applause of his lordship in council.

To Captain Chads the governor-general in council desires to express his constant acknowledgments for the distinguished share he bore in the action. *His lordship in council has also noticed, with particular satisfaction, the characteristic gallantry displayed by Lieutenants Keele and Hall, who, with their boats' crews, were the first to enter the enemy's fort,* followed by Captain O'Reilly of the grenadiers of his majesty's 41st regiment. His lordship in council requests that these sentiments of the supreme government may be conveyed to Captain Chads and Lieutenants Keele and Hall, through the senior officer of his majesty's ships.

No. 14. See p. 331.

I now beg leave to acknowledge my obligations to Captain Alexander, C.B., senior naval officer, and commanding the flotilla, for his hearty and cordial co-operation on all occasions since we have served together, and for his very great exertions on the present occasion, in bringing up stores and provisions. Since we have been before Donoobew, 11 of the enemy's large class war-boats have been captured by our advanced boats, under his own immediate orders; making, with others, evacuated by their crews, 38 first-rate war-boats now in our possession; and I have every reason to think that only five of the large squadron, the enemy had stationed at this place, have succeeded in escaping. A vast number of other boats of an excellent description have also fallen into our hands. *By Brigadier-general Cotton, and all the officers embarked, the zeal and incessant labour of his majesty's navy are mentioned in terms of high admiration.*

No. 15. See p. 338.

In my former despatch, dated Feb. 24th, I gave you the names of all officers and young gentlemen commanding boats, and I again request you will be pleased to recommend them to the favourable attention of my lords commissioners of the admiralty, with the seamen and marines I have had the pleasure to command, their conduct having been such as to merit the highest encomiums—their privations, hardships, and fatigue, during upwards of six weeks, by day and night, in open boats, have been borne with cheerfulness, and every duty performed with alacrity.

Of Captain Chads I can only say, he has fully supported his former character, and has my best thanks. I trust I may be allowed to name my first-lieutenant, Smith, an already distinguished officer. Mr. Watt, surgeon of the Arachne, a volunteer, has been of most essential service in attention to the sick and wounded.

No. 16. See p. 340.

I have much satisfaction in stating, that the whole of the officers and men employed in the flotilla conducted themselves throughout this service in a manner that reflects the highest credit on each individual, composed as this force is of various establishments. The officers of the Honourable Company's marine vied with those of the royal navy in gallantry and exertion. Captain Chads, of the Alligator, who commanded the light division, displayed the same zeal, judgment, and intrepidity which have characterised his conduct since the operations in this quarter began. I have, however, the painful duty of announcing the death of Captain Dawson, of the Arachne, whose high professional character had induced me so recently to promote him to the rank of commander. The gallantry of this much-lamented officer was conspicuous on all occasions; inviting, by his example, the exertions of all under his directions, he fell just as success had crowned our efforts.

No. 17. See p. 344.

The relations of friendship between the British government and the state of Ava, having been happily re-established by the conclusion of a definitive treaty of peace, the governor-general in council performs a most gratifying act of duty, in offering publicly his cordial acknowledgments and thanks to Major-general Sir Archibald Campbell and the army in Ava, by whose gallant and persevering exertions the recent contest with the Burmese empire has been brought to an honourable and successful termination.

In reviewing the events of the late war, the governor-general in council is bound to declare his conviction, that the achievements of the British army in Ava have nobly sustained our military reputation, and have produced substantial benefits to the national interests.

During a period of two years, from the first declaration of hostilities against the government of Ava, every disadvantage of carrying on war in a distant and most difficult country has been overcome, and the collective force of the Burman empire, formidable from their numbers, the strength of their fortified positions, and the shelter afforded by the nature of their country, have been repeatedly assailed and defeated. The persevering and obstinate efforts of the enemy, to oppose our advance, having failed of success, and his resources and means of further resistance having been exhausted, the King of Ava has, at length, been compelled to accept of those terms of peace which the near approach of our army to the gates of his capital enabled us to dictate. Every object, the governor-general in council is happy to proclaim, for which the war was undertaken, has been finally and most satisfactorily accomplished.   *   *   *

To the consummate military talents, energy, and decision, manifested by Major-general Sir Archibald Campbell, to the ardour and devotion to the public service, which his example infused into all ranks, and to the confidence inspired by the success of every military operation which he planned and executed in person, the governor-general in council primarily ascribes, under Providence, the brilliant result that has crowned the gallant and unwearied exertions of the British troops in Ava. Impressed with sentiments of high admiration for those eminent qualities so conspicuously and successfully displayed by Major-general Sir Archibald Campbell, his lordship in council rejoices at the opportunity of expressing to that distinguished soldier, in the most public manner, the acknowledgments and thanks of the supreme government, for the important service he has rendered to the Honourable East India Company, and to the British nation. The thanks of government are also eminently due to the senior officers, who have so ably and zealously seconded Major-general Sir Archibald Campbell in his career of victory. * * *

Amongst those zealous and gallant officers some have been more fortunate than others in enjoying opportunities of performing special services. The ability with which Lieutenant-colonel Godwin, of his majesty's 41st, achieved the conquest of the fortified town of Martaban and its dependencies, appears to confer on that officer a just claim to the separate and distinct acknowledgments of the governor-general in council. In like manner, Lieutenant-colonel Miles and Brigadier-general M'Creagh have entitled themselves to the special thanks of government for their services; the former, in the capture of Tavoy and Mergui; and the latter, in that of the island of Cheduba.

The limits of a general order necessarily preclude the governor-general in council from indulging the satisfaction of recording the names of all those officers whose services and exploits at this moment crowd upon the grateful recollection of the government, by whom they were duly appreciated and acknowledged at the time of their occurrence. His lordship in council requests that those officers will, collectively and individually, accept this renewed assurance, that their meritorious exertions will ever be cordially remembered. * *

The conduct of that portion of the naval branch of the expedition which belongs to the East India Company has been exemplary, and conspicuous for gallantry and indefatigable exertion; and it has fully shared in all the honourable toils and well-earned triumphs of the land force. * * * The governer-general in council has not overlooked the spirit and bravery, characteristic of British seamen, manifested by several of the masters and officers of transports and armed vessels, in various actions with the Burmese in the vicinity of Rangoon.

It belongs to a higher authority than the government of India to notice in adequate and appropriate terms, the services of his majesty's squadron, which has co-operated with his majesty's and the Honourable

East India Company's land forces, in the late hostilities with the government of Ava. The governor-general in council, however, gladly seizes this opportunity of expressing the deep sense of obligation with which the supreme government acknowledges the important and essential aid afforded by his excellency Commodore Sir James Brisbane, in person, as well as by the officers, non-commissioned officers, seamen, and marines of his majesty's ships, who have been employed in the Irrawaddi. *Inspired by the most ardent zeal for the honour and interest of the nation and the East India Company, his excellency, the naval commander-in-chief, lost no time in proceeding, with the boats of the Boadicea, to the head-quarters of the British army at Prome, and directing, in person, the operations of the river force, rendered the most essential service in the various decisive and memorable actions which, in the month of December last, compelled the Burmese to sue for peace.*

THE BATTLE OF NAVARIN.

In the year 1827 Great Britain was at peace with all the world. Although the political horizon had been occasionally clouded since the year 1815, no act of aggression had been committed by any of the European powers, and a general tranquillity prevailed: Greece was the only nation excepted. The inhabitants of that country had long groaned under the tyranny of the Turkish government; frequent insurrections of its unhappy inhabitants, in order to shake off the yoke under which they laboured, had been attempted, and as often repressed: acts of atrocious cruelty were daily committed by the imperious master, until the slaves (for in reality the poorer class of Greeks had been slaves to the Ottoman Porte) rose in greater numbers, and made a more desperate, and ultimately successful, opposition to their former conquerors. The disordered state of Greece afforded ample scope for piracies; vessels of different sizes were manned and armed, and fell alike upon the Turkish ship or the unprotected merchantman of other countries, which chanced to cross their tract. Commerce was interrupted—thousands of helpless creatures were butchered—the loss of life was immense, until Great Britain, France, and Russia determined to interfere and to put a period to the ravages of both parties. The high contracting powers came to the following determination:—

"His Majesty the King of the United Kingdom of Great Britain, &c., his Majesty the King of France, &c., and his Majesty the Emperor of all the Russias, penetrated with the necessity of putting an end to the sanguinary contest, which, by delivering up the Greek provinces and the isles of the Archipelago to all the disorders of anarchy, produces daily fresh impediments to the commerce of the united states, and gives occasion to piracies, which not only expose the high contracting powers to considerable losses, but, besides, render necessary burdensome measures of protection and repression; having, besides, received on the part of the Greeks a pressing request, to interpose their mediation with the Ottoman Porte; and being animated by the desire of stopping the effusion of blood, and of arresting the evils of all kinds which might arise from the continuance of such a state of things, have resolved to unite their efforts, and to regulate the operation thereof by a formal treaty, with a view of re-establishing peace between the contending parties, by means of an arrangement which is called for as much by humanity as by the interest of the repose of Europe."

Plenipotentiaries were nominated by the different powers to carry their determination into effect; one of the first measures to be adopted being " a *demand* of an immediate armistice between the two parties, as a preliminary condition indispensable to the opening of any negotiation." To carry these *demands* into execution, Great Britain had a squadron in the Mediterranean, under Sir Edward Codrington; the French, one under Admiral de Rigny; the Russians one also, under Admiral Heiden; but at this period neither the French nor Russian squadrons had joined Sir Edward Codrington. The squadrons, when united, were placed under the orders of the first-named officer, who, with the ships under his command, was already actively employed in carrying his orders into effect.

It will be seen by the extract above, that the allied powers meditated a *mediation*, not an open warfare; the imposing force in the immediate vicinity to the scene of action was accounted sufficient to awe the Turks into submission, and no *positive* orders were, therefore, sent to Sir Edward Codrington, to have recourse to a violation of the peace existing between the Ottoman Porte and the high contracting powers; he was desired, as well as the other admirals, to correspond with the ambassadors at Constantinople, and to conform to their directions.

Feeling that a very great responsibility rested upon him, he applied to his excellency Mr. Stratford Canning for his opinion, apprehending that he could not prevent *all collision* between the contending parties, without actually having recourse to hostilities, or, by tampering with people in whom no trust could be reposed, lower the honour, the reputation of the British flag. The reply to his application was in these words: " You are not to take part with either of the belligerents; but you are to interpose your forces between them, and to keep the peace with your speaking-trumpet, if possible; but, in case of necessity, with that which is used for the maintenance of a blockade against friends as well as foes; I mean *force*." And in another confidential letter, dated 1st September, 1827, Mr. Canning further replied: " On the subject of collision, for instance, we agree, that, although the measures to be executed by you are not to be adopted by you in a hostile spirit; and although it is clearly the intention of the allied governments to avoid, if possible, anything that may bring on a war, yet the prevention of supplies, as stated in your instructions, is ultimately to be enforced, if necessary; and when all other means are exhausted, —by cannon-shot."

The object of this history is truth. We have endeavoured, from its first page to its last, to cast aside all party-feeling—all political controversy; our determination being to place before the reader, as far as our researches will permit, the truth, the whole truth, and nothing but the truth; and as differences of opinion have existed in a great measure concerning the battle of Navarin, and much obloquy been lavished upon Sir Edward Codrington, for what was termed "an untoward event," we feel it but due to him to place the answer of Sir Stratford Canning before the public; for although Mr. Canning's letter referred principally to the prevention of supplies, and in answer to a letter as to the power of using force, which the original instructions seemed, in some measure, to negative: yet it gave this authority—to use force, if the admiral judged it requisite; and throughout the whole paragraph above quoted, implies, if not orders, that the admiral should use endeavours, even to cannon-shot, to carry that part of such orders into execution, and, consequently, to make any hostile demonstration he might judge requisite.

That Sir Edward Codrington felt that the speaking-trumpet was not to be cast aside hastily—that cannon-shot were not to be used, but in extremity—may be gleaned from his own letter to the different officers under his command:—

" *Asia, at sea, September* 8, 1827.

" Sir,—You are aware that a treaty has been signed between England, France, and Russia, for the pacification of Greece. A declaration of the decision of the powers has been presented to the Porte, and a similar declaration has been presented to the Greeks.

"The armistice proposed to each, in these declarations, has been acceded to by the Greeks, whilst it has been refused by the Turks. It becomes, therefore, the duty of the allied naval forces to enter, in the first place, on friendly relations with the Greeks; and next to intercept every supply of men, arms, &c. destined against Greece, and coming either from Turkey or Africa in general. The last measure is that which requires the greatest caution, and above all, a complete understanding as to the operations of the allied naval forces.—Most particular care is to be taken that the measures adopted against the Ottoman navy do not degenerate into hostilities. The formal intention of the powers is to interfere as conciliators, and to establish, in fact, at sea, the armistice which the Porte would not concede as a right. Every hostile proceeding would be at variance with the pacific ground which they have chosen to take, and the display of forces which they have assembled is destined to cause that wish to be respected; but they must not be put into use, unless the Turks persist in forcing the passages which they have intercepted.

"All possible means should be tried, in the first instance, to prevent the necessity of proceeding to extremities; but the prevention of supplies, as before mentioned, is to be enforced, if necessary; and when all other means are exhausted,—by cannon-shot.

"In giving you this instruction as to the duty which I am directed to perform, my intention is to make you acquainted thoroughly with the object of our Government, that you may not be taken by surprise as to whatever measures I may find it necessary to adopt. You will still look to me for further instructions as to the carrying any such measures into effect.

"I am, &c.   (Signed)   ED. CODRINGTON."

On the 25th of September, Sir Edward Codrington, in the presence of Admiral de Rigny, had an interview with Ibrahim Pacha, at Navarin. The pacha commanded the Turkish fleet, and was likewise commander-in-chief of the land forces, a considerable portion of which was at Patras. At this conference the orders of the British admiral were made known to the pacha, and much pains were taken by Sir Edward to make Ibrahim perfectly understand that he should put those orders in execution in the event of his non-compliance. After a short conference an armistice was agreed upon between the Turks and Greeks by land and by sea; both land and sea forces were to remain in active at Navarin until further instructions should be received from Constantinople; and, in consequence of this armistice, a part of the Turkish fleet, then outside of the harbour, was allowed to join their admiral at anchor. At this interview Sir Edward Codrington wished the terms of the treaty, or armistice, to be placed on paper, but Admiral de Rigny mentioned that the request would be considered an insult by Ibrahim Pacha, the word of a Turk being considered by the Turks themselves, and generally so by those who have had intercourse with them, as an inviolable pledge. So cautious was Sir Edward Codrington not to give offence, that his own interpreter was not present.

On the following day the Asia, the flag-ship of Sir Edward Codrington, and the Sirène, a 60-gun ship, bearing the flag of Admiral de Rigny, were making preparations for putting to sea, when the dragoman of Ibrahim Pacha came on board the former ship. He stated "that his master had received information that Lord Cochrane had made a descent upon Patras, and requested to be allowed to send a competent force to frustrate his lordship's intentions." A most decided negative was given by Sir Edward Codrington, who inquired if by this message he was to understand that Ibrahim Pacha no longer considered the treaty as binding. The reply given by the dragoman was, "that if, at the expiration of an hour, he did not return, Sir Edward was to consider the treaty of the preceding day as still in force." About sunset the Asia and Sirène put to sea, the dragoman not having returned, and both admirals having the fullest confidence in the honour of Ibrahim. The Dartmouth was left to watch the Turkish fleet, and Sir Edward Codrington, having despatched some of his ships to Malta for supplies, shaped a course for Zante in the Asia.

On the 2nd of October the Dartmouth was seen in the offing, and communicated the intelligence that a strong division of the Turkish fleet had weighed from Navarin, and were standing to the north-west towards Patras. Immediately the Asia, Talbot, and Zebra weighed, joined the Dartmouth, and soon came in sight of the Turkish squadron, consisting of 47 sail, amongst which were two double-banked frigates, one large frigate, seven brigs, and eight corvettes. The English squadron ranged up alongside, and the ships of both nations hove to. Sir Edward Codrington sent Captain Spencer, of the Talbot, to complain of this breach of faith, this sudden and unexpected violation of the treaty, and to make known the admiral's determination to fire into the first ship that might attempt to pass the Asia's broadside. The Turkish commander, Petrona Bey, replied that he was acting in obedience to the pacha's orders, and added that he was under the impression that Sir Edward Codrington had given Ibrahim leave to send a squadron to Lepanto. He then sent Reala Bey, the second in command, on board the Asia, to remonstrate, but without any effect; and when Reala Bey returned to his own ship, the Asia filled her maintopsail, and fired a gun, on which the whole fleet stood towards Navarin. Some of the smaller vessels evinced a disposition to pass the English ships, but in this they were thwarted. Sir Edward Codrington's squadron kept in their rear until they were all clear of the gulf of Lepanto, but no sooner had both divisions arrived at the south end of Zante, than the English ships made sail, and passed ahead of the Turkish squadron, in order to look out for some assistance.

On the morning of the 3rd of October the Turkish squadron were joined by 15 more ships, two having flags at the main, the whole under the command of Ibrahim Pacha, who came in sight round the north point of Zante; on his making a signal with a gun, the first division bore up to join him. Sir Edward Codrington immediately made the signal to prepare for action, and bore up also. A communication now took place between Ibrahim Pacha and the vice-admiral commanding the first detachment, after which the Ottoman fleet, in obedience to a signal from their chief, made sail for Navarin, although the wind was fair for Patras. The Asia and Talbot anchored in the entrance of the bay of Zante, in order to obtain coals, water, and other supplies of which they were much in want, the Dartmouth being desired to watch the Ottoman fleet.

The next morning the Dartmouth communicated that several of the Turkish ships had again sailed towards Patras. The English admiral immediately put to sea, and at 6 P.M. was off Cape Papa, having the Talbot and Dartmouth in company. The largest of the Turkish ships were at anchor, the rest were working up to the anchorage, but without any colours flying. Several shots were fired by the English, in order to force the Turkish ships to show their flags; indeed, in this affair, the Asia fired 96 shots, and the Dartmouth 100.

That Ibrahim Pacha had no intention of fulfilling the treaty was evident. On two occasions his sacred promise had been violated, and now, finding that he could not succeed in effecting a junction with his army at Patras, and in relieving that place, he, on his arrival, with his whole fleet at Navarin, landed the troops he had embarked on board his ships, and wreaked his vengeance on the unfortunate Greeks of the Morea; neither women nor children escaped his fury, villages were pillaged and burnt, the trees were destroyed, and a devastation commenced which would have ended in rendering the whole Morea a desert.

Captain Hamilton, in the Cambrian, was despatched to ascertain the truth of these reports, and, in his official letter to the English admiral, he thus describes the miseries of the poor unprotected wretches :—" I have the honour to inform you that I arrived here yesterday in company with the Russian frigate Constantine. On entering the gulf we observed, by clouds of smoke, that the work of devastation was still going on. The ships were anchored off the pass of Ancyro, and a joint letter from myself and the Russian captain was despatched to the Turkish commander. The bearers of it were not allowed to proceed to head-quarters, nor have we as yet received any answer. In the afternoon we went on shore to the Greek quarters, and were received with the greatest enthusiasm. The distress of the inhabitants, driven from the plain, is shocking; women and children dying every moment of absolute starvation, and hardly any having better food than boiled grass. I have promised to send a small quantity of bread to the caves in the mountains where these unfortunate wretches have taken refuge. It is supposed that if Ibrahim remain in Greece, more than a third of its inhabitants will die of starvation."

On the 13th of October, Sir Edward was joined by the Russian squadron. On the 14th he arrived off Navarin, where the allied squadrons of France, Russia, and England were concentrated, and placed under his directions. We have thus far endeavoured to give our readers a perfect knowledge of events prior to the action, and we have entered into some details in order to show that Sir Edward Codrington evinced the greatest forbearance, and used every means in his power to avoid a collision, which an unpremeditated circumstance afterwards occasioned.

The combined squadrons consisted of the following ships and sloops :—

English.

Gun-ship
84 Asia . . . . { Vice-admiral Sir Edward Codrington.
Captain Edward Curzon.
Commander Robert Lambert Baynes,

THE BATTLE OF NAVARIN.

English—continued.

Gun-ship.
- 74
  - Genoa . . . { Captain Walter Bathurst. / Commander Richard Dickenson.
  - Albion . . . { Captain John Acworth Ommanney. / Commander John Norman Campbell.

Gun-frigate.
- 50 Glasgow . . . . Captain Hon. James Ashley Maude.
- 48 Cambrian . . . . ,, Gawen William Hamilton, C.B.
- 42 Dartmouth . . . ,, Thomas Fellowes, C.B.
- 28 Talbot . . . . ,, Hon. Frederick Spencer

Gun-brig.
- 18 Rose . . . . . Commander Lewis Davies.
- 10
  - Mosquito . . . . ,, George Bohun Martin.
  - Brisk . . . . . ,, Hon. William Anson.
  - Philomel . . . . ,, Viscount Ingestre.

French.

Gun-ship.
- 74
  - Scipion . . . . Captain Milius.
  - Trident . . . . ,, Maurice.
  - Breslau . . . . ,, De la Bretonniere.
- 60 Sirène . . . . . Rear-admiral H. de Rigny.

Gun-frigate.
- 44 Armide . . . . Captain Hugon.

Schooner, Alcyon: Dauphinoise.

Russian.

Gun-ship.
- 74
  - Azof . . . . . Rear-admiral Count de Heiden.
  - Gargonte.
  - Ezekiel.
  - Alexander Newsky.

Gun-frigate.
- 50 Constantine.
- 48
  - Provernoy.
  - Elena.
  - Castor.

The Ottoman and Egyptian fleets amounted, according to the statement made by the capitan bey's secretary, to 65 sail; of which two were Turkish 84-gun ships, one 76-gun ship, fifteen 48-gun frigates, 18 corvettes, and four brigs. The Egyptian fleet consisted of four double-banked 64-gun frigates, eight corvettes, from 18 to 24 guns each, eight brigs, and five fire-vessels; making a total of 65 sail. There is a considerable discrepancy between the number of the Turco-Egyptian fleet as mentioned by the secretary of the capitan bey, and in Sir Edward Codrington's letter, dated 24th of October, addressed as a general order to the captains, commanders, &c., in which he states that "out of a fleet composed of *eighty-one* men-of-war, there remain only one frigate and 15 small vessels in a state ever to be again put to sea." The comparative force in guns has been mentioned as 1324 on the part of the allied fleet, and of 2240 on the part of the Ottoman fleet. It must, however, be admitted, that this calculation cannot be relied upon, the comparative force being,

Allied Fleets, English, French, and Russian.		*Turco-Egyptian Fleet.*	
Sail of the line, including one 84,	11	Ships of the line, one of 84 guns,	3
Large frigates	8	Large frigates	15
Small ditto (the Talbot) . .	1	Corvettes	18
Brigs	4		—
	—		36
	24	The rest of the force is made up in gun-boats, schooners, and craft of all descriptions.	

In former warfare, frigates never took part in a general engagement, and sloops, schooners, gun-boats, &c., were never fired upon without they were rash enough to court a return of shot. It will be in the memory of our readers, that at the battle of the Nile a frigate was sunk by one broadside of a line-of-battle ship, and that consequently the vast superiority of force in the 11 sail of the line in still water, must be obvious to any man at all conversant in the destructive fire of an 80-gun ship; four line-of-battle ships were more than ample to destroy the 18 corvettes, when those corvettes were at anchor, and we state this without any fear of contradiction. We have seen the Glatton beat off six frigates; and the splendid attack of Captain Prowse in the 18-pounder 36-gun frigate Sirius, off Civita Vecchia in 1806, where he attacked one ship-corvette, three brig-corvettes, one bombard, one cutter, and three gun-boats, took the largest and drove the rest to seek shelter, may be found in our pages. The action of the Spartan in 1810, in the bay of Naples: and many, many other instances might be produced to show the destructive fire of one large vessel, against ten times the number of guns in smaller vessels; but it is likewise to be borne in mind, that for five days previously to the action of Navarin, M. Letellier, a French naval officer in the service of the Pacha of Egypt, had moored the Turco Egyptian fleet in such a manner, that every broadside of both large and small vessels was directed towards the centre of the circle in which they were moored, and, as far as small vessels could be made effective, they certainly were rendered so on this occasion.

It was evident to the allied admirals that to keep an efficient force as a blockade, ready to thwart the intentions of Ibrahim Pacha during the winter, would be attended with great risk, if it was not physically impossible, and would also cause an enormous expense to their respective governments; and as the bay of Navarin was, at any rate, to them a neutral port, if not partially an English anchorage (for the island of Sphacteria, which belongs to the British, forms part of the bay of Navarin), it was resolved by the commander-in-chief, on the grounds which will be seen by a reference to his official letter, to anchor the three fleets in the bay, alongside of the Turco-Egyptian force, and then be in readiness to use other persuasions than the *speaking-trumpet*, should Ibrahim continue to violate the treaty. On the 20th of October, the weather being fine, the combined squadrons stood towards Navarin. The Turco-Egyptian fleet were at anchor, moored in the form of a crescent with springs on their cables, the larger ones presenting their broadsides towards the centre, the smaller ones in succession within them, filling up the intervals."[1]

The printed instructions issued to all officers in His Majesty's navy, particularly desire that every ship approaching any ship of a different nation in time of peace or war, should be prepared for action, and it would be doing Sir Edward Codrington an injustice to state that he went into the anchorage unprepared; he *was* clear for action, but his lowerdeck ports, were not hauled flat against the ship's sides, but kept square as at sea in fine weather, and the ships were ordered not to anchor by the stern, which might imply a hostile intention, but to anchor with springs to their *anchors*. These little events we think proper to lay some stress upon, because they all prove to a certain extent a readiness to engage, but a determination not to become the assailants.

When three nations combine their squadrons, there must be, more or less, a jealousy; in regard to the English there could be none, because Sir Edward was a vice-admiral, and both De Rigny and Count de Heiden, were rear-admirals: but with the two latter, there might have existed some slight feelings of annoyance in regard to the post of honour, order of sailing, and so forth; to obviate this as much as possible, the vice-admiral determined that the order of sailing should be the order of battle; the English and French forming the weather or starboard line, and the Russian division forming the lee line. In this order they

[1] Sir Edward Codrington's official despatch.

entered the bay of Navarin. "The Asia led in, followed by the Genoa and Albion, and anchored close alongside a ship of the line;" she was instantly moored with 30 fathoms on each cable. The Genoa came next, and was about to place her bow towards the bow of the Asia, when she was hailed by the vice-admiral and desired to take up her position with her head in the same direction as the Asia's; this was done in good style, the Genoa passing very close to the vice-admiral, and taking up her appointed station. The Albion followed. The Asia's opponent was the flag-ship of the capitan bey; the Genoa anchored close to another ship-of-the-line, and the Albion close to a double-banked frigate. "The four ships to windward, part of the Egyptian squadron, were allotted to the squadron of Rear-admiral de Rigny; and those to leeward, in the bight of the crescent, were to mark the stations of the whole Russian squadron; the ships-of-the-line closing those of the English line, and being followed up by their own frigates. The French frigate Armide, was directed to place herself alongside the outermost frigate on the left hand entering the harbour; and the Cambrian, Glasgow, and Talbot, next to her, and abreast of, the Asia, Genoa, and Albion; the Dartmouth, and the Mosquito, the Rose, the Brisk, and the Philomel, were to look after six fire-vessels at the entrance of the harbour."[1] The Turco-Egyptian fleet did not witness this anchorage of the allied fleet without alarm; they were at quarters, their tompions out, and the guns nearly loaded to the muzzles, with shot, broken bars, rusty iron, and other materials.

On the fleet entering the bay, a boat was sent from a fort with a message from the commandant, "That as Ibrahim Pascha had not given any orders or permission for the allied fleet to enter, it was requested that they would again put to sea." Sir Edward Codrington in reply, said, "that he was not come to receive orders, but to give them; that if any shot were fired at the allied fleet, the Turkish fleet would be destroyed."

The ships of the allied fleet had now anchored; the sails of many of the ships were furled; and on board the Asia, the band was desired to be sent on deck, everything appearing to wear a peaceful aspect, when a firing of musketry was heard in the direction of the Dartmouth. This occasioned the action, and arose from the boats under the direction of Lieutenant Smyth being sent to one of the fire-ships, from the Dartmouth, to request that the fire-ships would move a little further from the allied fleet;

[1] Sir Edward Codrington's official despatch.

and if we, as historians, are inclined to make any observations as to the commencement of the action, we should say, that if a fleet of a strange nation came to anchor in a bay where another fleet was at anchor, they should have selected (that is if no ulterior measures were premeditated) such berths as would not in any manner have interfered with the vessels previously at anchor; and the only reason which can be given for the allied fleet anchoring to leeward of the Turco-Egyptian fleet (for the wind blew into the bay) is, that had they anchored to windward, they must have been placed in a position to receive the whole fire of the Turco-Egyptian fleet, in consequence of the crescent form in which M. Letellier had moored the fleet with their broadsides all directed towards the centre. Besides it appears that *boats* were sent, and the Turkish commander might be justified in believing that his vessel was to be taken possession of; for if a *request* is to be made, it would occur to a Turk or Christian, that one boat was as efficient as a dozen. The Turks, apprehensive that force was meditated, fired and killed Lieutenant G. W. H. Fitzroy and several of the crew. The Dartmouth immediately opened a *defensive* fire to cover her boats; the Sirène, Admiral de Rigny's ship, joined in the affray, with musketry only; one of the Egyptian ships fired a shot, which was the first round shot discharged, and struck the Sirène, "which, *of course*," as the vice-admiral states in his letter, "brought on a return, and thus very shortly afterwards, the battle became general."

"The Asia, although placed alongside the capitan bey's ship, was even nearer to Moharem Bey's, the commander of the Egyptian ships, and since his ship did not fire at the Asia, although the action was begun to windward, neither did the Asia fire at her. Moharem Bey, indeed, sent a message, that he would not fire at all, and therefore no hostility took place between Moharem Bey's ship and the English admiral's ship for some time after the Asia had *returned* the fire of the capitan bey. In the mean time, however, the excellent pilot, Mr. Peter Mitchell, who went to interpret to Moharem Bey, the vice-admiral's desire to avoid bloodshed, was killed by his people, in the boat alongside, whether with or without his orders is not known, but his ship soon afterwards fired into the Asia, and was consequently effectually destroyed by the Asia's fire, sharing the same fate as his brother admiral on the starboard side, and falling to leeward a mere wreck."[1] The action, now general, was

[1] Sir Edward Codrington's public despatch.

well maintained by the Turks, and for four hours the firing continued, until, at the expiration of that time, the Ottoman fleet had been nearly destroyed: each ship, as she became disabled, was deserted by the crew, after having set her on fire, and the frequent explosions rendered the situation of the allied fleet dangerous in the extreme.

Captain Fellowes soon cleared the fire-ships, and saved the French admiral's ship, the Sirène, from being burnt.. "The Cambrian, Glasgow, and Talbot, following the fine example of Captain Hugon, of the Armide, who was opposed to the leading frigate of that line, effectually destroyed their opponents and also silenced the batteries."

The smoke was so thick during the action that the guns of the Asia were pointed from the flag at the mast-head of the capitan bey's ship. It was the only object discernible; occasionally the Asia's fire ceased, in order to allow the smoke to clear away. At this interval her opponent fired single shot until the cable was either shot away or slipped, and she drifted to leeward out of fire. It was during the Asia's engagement with the senior officer's ship, that her stern was exposed to the raking broadside of a frigate, and she received more damage from her than from her regular opponent. About 3 o'clock the Asia, having disposed of the capitan's ship, turned her broadside to Moharem's ship and his second ahead, both of which were soon destroyed. Moharem's ship was sadly disabled, and her second ahead, burning to the water's edge, blew up at her anchors.

The French division, under De Rigny, displayed equal valour and seamanship with their old enemies, the English. The French admiral anchored athwart hawse of the first Egyptian frigate. The three line-of-battle ships were to have filled up the space between their admiral and the Asia, but owing to some unforeseen circumstance they were prevented taking their proper station. The Scipion, on coming to her berth, was obliged to anchor, owing to a fire-ship being nearly athwart her hawse. The boats of the Dartmouth and Rose went instantly to her assistance, and towed the fire-ship from her position. The Breslaw ran towards the end of the bay, near the Russian division, and there most gallantly took her share in the fight. The Sirène having set fire to her opponent, was in imminent danger of sharing the same fate; it is mentioned that a man from the French admiral's ship swam with a rope to the Dartmouth, and by that means the Sirène was warped from her perilous situation. The gallant conduct of Captain Hugon, of the Armide, we have before mentioned; his determination to place his ship in the hottest of the action rather blinded him to the disadvantageous position he took up. The Rose, Captain Davies, immediately went to his assistance, and this equally gallant conduct was acknowledged by Admiral de Rigny in a letter to the vice-admiral, bearing date the 23rd of October.

It is impossible to convey to the reader an accurate idea of the services of each ship when the names and force of their opponents are unknown; it must therefore be sufficient to state, that the Russian division took up their appointed station, and that by their gallant conduct, and unflinching bravery, they added their share to the ruin and devastation around.

About 5 o'clock the firing along the whole line ceased. All further resistance would have been unavailing; but the destruction did not end with the firing. The Turks, apprehensive that the vessels would become prizes to their victors, set fire to and blew up many which were still in a state of efficiency, and this wanton act of egregious folly was not confined to a few instances. We have before remarked the passage in the vice-admiral's letter relative to the almost total destruction of the Turco-Egyptian squadron, which letter was written whilst the devastation was before his eyes: he was, however, in error when he asserted that only "one frigate and fifteen smaller vessels were all that remained of this large fleet which ever again could put to sea;" for the Pelican sloop reconnoitred Navarin on the 14th of December following, and 29 sail were at anchor, amongst which was one line-of-battle ship and four frigates; two frigates fit for service, one of the Egyptian rasées in tolerable condition, five corvettes, 11 brigs, and five schooners; all, with the exception of the five first, which were reported much shattered, in a fit state for immediate service.[1]

In making our comments upon the battle of Navarin, we are bound to state that the circumstances connected with it must cause it to be considered in a very different point of view from a regular naval battle at sea, or in time of open war. The allies being obliged to enter the bay in apparent confidence of no hostile intention towards them, their being forced by circumstances not naval to expose themselves to the inner side of the

---

[1] We have given this report of the Pelican's rencontre from Marshall's excellent work, but it is well-known that several vessels joined the remains of the Turkish fleet at Navarin from Modon; so that the exact number of vessels left in a state "ever again to put to sea" remains uncertain, but, by *all* accounts, the destruction was not quite equal to the report.

circle formed by the Turkish fleet; the impolicy of anchoring in the centre of the bay, to which point the whole of the Turkish broadsides had been directed, and against which anchorage the fire-ships might have operated, are all circumstances not to be overlooked; but although Sir Edward Codrington states, in his despatches, that the object of the allied admirals was, by the imposing force of their squadrons, to cause a renewal of those propositions which had been broken through by Ibrahim going to Patras, and subsequently refused to be entertained by him, and as Ibrahim had submitted to be driven by so comparatively small a force from before Patras, there was no reason to expect that he would oppose the squadrons when united, and that their presence was the only chance of awing him into relinquishing his devastation of the Morea; yet it must be admitted that the action itself was occasioned by the allies having anchored to leeward of the fire-ships, and that their sending boats to remove vessels previously at anchor was the sole cause of the slaughter which ensued.

However much this country might have deplored the destruction of a fleet which would have materially assisted in checking the progress of Russian dominion in the East, yet they were not backward in the distribution of honours and the reward of promotions. The commanders were all advanced to the rank of captains; the first-lieutenants of each ship were promoted to commanders; the captains had honorary distinctions conferred upon them, and there were more orders given for the battle of Navarin than for any other naval victory on record.

It was impossible for such a number of ships to be so closely engaged for so long a period as four hours without considerable loss of men; indeed that loss, so severe in some ships, is the best proof of the gallant defence made by the Turco-Egyptian fleet. We regret we are unable to give the names of the French and Russian officers killed or wounded in this affair; but we are enabled to record the names of our own countrymen who fell or who suffered in the action. We therefore give the numbers of killed and wounded in the French, Russian, and English divisions, which were as follows:[1]

---

[1] An application was made to the admiralty to inspect the official returns, which was denied; we are therefore obliged to quote from the Gazette and the Annual Registers.

French.

Gun-ship.			Killed.	Wounded
60	Sirène	Rear-admiral de Rigny	21	42
74 {	Scipion	Captain Milius	2	36
	Trident	,, Maurice	..	7
	Breslaw	,, De la Bretonniere	1	14
Gun-frigate.				
44	Armide	,, Hugon	14	14
	Alcyone schooner		1	9
	Dauphincise ditto		1	8
			40	130
		Officers not included in the above	3	3
			43	133

Russian.

Gun ship.			Killed.	Wounded
74 {	Azof	Rear-admiral Count de Heiden	24	67
	Gargonte		14	37
	Ezekiel		13	18
	Alexander Newsky		5	7
Gun-frigate.				
50	Constantine		..	1
48 {	Provernoy		3	4
	Elena		..	5
	Castor		..	..
			59	139[1]

English.

Gun-ship.			Killed.	Wounded
84	Asia	{ Flag-ship, Captain Edward Curzon Commander R. Lambert Baynes }	19	57
74 {	Genoa	{ Captain Walter Bathurst Commander Richard Dickenson }	26	33
	Albion	{ Capt. John Acworth Ommanney Commander J. Norman Campbell }	10	50
Gun-frigate.				
42	Dartmouth	Captain Thomas Fellowes, C.B.	6	8
48	Cambrian	Gawen William Hamilton, C.B.	1	1
50	Glasgow	Hon. James Asley Maude	..	2
28	Talbot	Hon. Frederick Spencer	6	17
Gun-brig.				
10	Mosquito	Commander George Bohun Martin	2	4
18	Rose	,, Lewis Davies	3	15
10	Brisk	Hon. William Anson	1	3
10	Philomel	,, Viscount Ingestre	1	7
			75	197

The officers killed were, Captain Walter Bathurst, of the Genoa; Captain George Augustus Bell, Royal Marines; Mr. William Smith; Mr. Philip Dumaresk; Mr. John Lewis; Mr.

[1] Marshall.

Peter Mitchell; Captain C. J. Stephens; Mr. Edward R. Forster; Mr. Peter Brown; Mr. Charles Russell; Mr. A. J. T. Rowe; Lieutenant G. W. H. Fitzroy, of the Dartmouth; Mr. Brown Smythe; Mr. W. J. Goldfinch; Lieutenant Philip Sturgeon, and Mr. Henry Campbell. The officers wounded severely were, Mr. J. H. Codrington; Mr. W. V. Lee; Mr. R. H. Bunbury; Mr. C. Wakeham, Mr. William Lloyd; Mr. Frederick Grey; Mr. Thos. Addington; Lieutenant-colonel Carador; Mr. Henry S. Dyer; Commander J. N. Campbell, of the Albion; Lieutenant J. G. Durban; Rev. E. Winder; Mr. W. F. O'Kane; Mr. James Stewart; Captain Thomas Moore; Mr. H. B. Gray; Lieutenant H. R. Sturt: Mr. James Chambers; Mr. Launcelot Harrison; Lieutenant Spencer Smith; Mr. John Dellamore; Mr. Joseph Gray; Lieutenant R. S. Hay; Mr. Alexander Calton; Lieutenant Mr. Lyons; Mr. Douglas Currie; Mr. William Williams; Mr John Isatt.

The combined Turkish and Egyptian forces, with the list of vessels destroyed, is thus given by commander Peter Richards, who received his information from M. Letellier, the French instructor of the Egyptian navy:—

Line.	Double Frigates.	Frigates.	Corvettes.	Brigs.	Schooners.	Fire-brigs.	Austr.	Turk.	Total.	
2	..	5	12	..	..	..	..	..	19	Capitan Bey's division from Alexandria.
..	4	..	11	21	5	6	8	33	88	Moharem Bey's division, ditto.
..	..	2	..	1	..	..	..	..	3	Tunician division, ditto.
1	..	6	7	6	..	..	..	..	20	Tahir Pacha's division from Constantinople.
3	4	13	30	28	5	6	8	33	130	Total, transports included.
1	3	9	22	19	1	5	..	..	60	Destroyed.
2	1	4	8	9	4	1	..	..	29	Remain, besides transports.

The killed were estimated at 3000 and the wounded at 1109, perhaps, if for the wounded we read killed, and for killed, wounded, it would be more correct.

"LONDON GAZETTE EXTRAORDINARY.

"*Admiralty-office, Nov.* 10, 1827.

"Despatches, of which the following are copies or extracts, have been this day received at this office, addressed to John

Wilson Croker, Esq., by Vice-admiral Sir Edward Codrington, K.C.B., Commander-in-chief of his Majesty's ships in the Mediterranean.

"Sir, *His Majesty's ship Asia, in the Port of Navarin, Oct. 21, 1827.*

"I have the honour of informing his Royal Highness the Lord High Admiral, that my colleagues, Count Heiden and the Chevalier de Rigny, having agreed with me that we should come into this port, in order to induce Ibrahim Pacha to discontinue the brutal war of extermination which has been carrying on since his return here from his failure in the Gulf of Patras, the combined squadron passed the batteries, in order to take up their anchorage, at about two o'clock yesterday afternoon.

"The Turkish ships were moored in the form of a crescent, with springs on their cables, the larger ones presenting their broadsides towards the centre, the smaller ones in succession within them, filling up the intervals.

"The combined fleet was formed in the order of sailing in two columns, the British and French forming the weather or starboard line, and the Russians the lee line.

"The Asia led in, followed by the Genoa and Albion, and anchored close alongside a ship of the line, bearing the flag of the Capitana Bey, another ship of the line, and a large double-banked frigate, each thus having their opponent in the front line of the Turkish fleet. The four ships to windward, part of the Egyptian squadron, were allotted to the squadron of Rear-admiral de Rigny; and those to leeward, in the bight of the crescent, were to mark the stations of the whole Russian squadron; the ships of the line closing those of the English line, and being followed up by their own frigates. The French frigate Armide was directed to place herself alongside the outermost frigate, on the left hand entering the harbour; and the Cambrian, Glasgow, and Talbot next to her, and abreast of the Asia, Genoa, and Albion; the Dartmouth and the Musquito, the Rose, the Brisk, and the Philomel were to look after six fire-vessels at the entrance of the harbour. I gave orders that no gun should be fired, unless guns were fired by the Turks; and those orders were strictly observed. The three English ships were accordingly permitted to pass the batteries, and to moor, which they did with great rapidity, without any act of open hostility, although there was evident preparation for it in all the Turkish ships; but, upon the Dartmouth sending a boat to one of the fire-vessels, Lieutenant G. W. H. Fitzroy and several of her crew were shot with musketry. This produced a defensive fire of musketry from the Dartmouth and La Sirène, bearing the flag of Rear-admiral de Rigny; that was succeeded by a cannon-shot at the rear-admiral from one of the Egyptian ships, which of course brought on a return, and thus, very shortly afterwards, the battle became general. The Asia, although placed alongside the ship of the capitana bey, was even nearer to that of Moharem Bey, the commander of the Egyptian ships; and, since his ship did not fire at the Asia, although the action was begun to windward, neither did the Asia fire at her. The latter indeed sent a message "that he would not fire at all," and therefore no hostility took place betwixt our ships for some time after the Asia had returned the fire of the capitana bey.

"In the mean time, however, our excellent pilot, Mr. Peter Mitchell, who went to interpret to Moharem my desire to avoid bloodshed, was killed by his people in our boat alongside; whether with or without his orders I know not; but his ship soon fired into the Asia, and was consequently effectually destroyed by the Asia's fire, sharing the same fate as his brother admiral on the starboard side, and falling to leeward a mere wreck. These ships being out of the way, the Asia became exposed to a raking fire from vessels in the second and third line, which carried away her mizenmast by the board, disabled some of her guns, and killed and wounded several of her crew. This narration of the proceedings of the Asia would probably be equally applicable to most of the other ships of the fleet. The manner in which the Genoa and Albion took their stations was beautiful; and the conduct of my brother admirals, Count Heiden and the Chevalier de Rigny, throughout, was admirable and highly exemplary.

"Captain Fellowes executed the part allotted to him perfectly, and, with the able assistance of his little but brave detachment, saved the Sirène from being burnt by the fire-vessels; and the Cambrian, Glasgow, and Talbot, following the fine example of Captain Hugon, of the Armide, who was opposed to the leading frigate of that line, effectually destroyed their opponents, and also silenced their batteries. This bloody and destructive battle was continued with unabated fury for four hours, and the scene of wreck and devastation which presented itself at its termination was such as has been seldom before witnessed. As each ship of our opponent became effectually disabled, such of her crew as could escape from her endeavoured to set her on fire, and it is wonderful how we avoided the effects of their successive and awful explosions.

"It is impossible for me to say too much for the able and zealous assistance which I derived from Captain Curzon, throughout this long and arduous contest; nor can I say more than it deserves for the conduct of Commander Baynes and the officers and crew of the Asia, for the perfection with which the fire of their guns was directed: each vessel in turn, to which her broadside was directed, became a complete wreck. His royal highness will be aware that so complete a victory, by a few, however perfect, against an excessive number, however individually inferior, cannot be acquired, but at a considerable loss of life; accordingly I have to lament the loss of Captain Bathurst, of the Genoa, whose example on this occasion is well worthy of the imitation of his survivors. Captain Bell, commanding the royal marines of the Asia, an excellent officer, was killed early in the action, in the steady performance of his duty, and I have to mourn the death of Mr. William Smith, the master, admired for the zeal and ability with which he executed his duty, and beloved by all for his private qualities as a man. Mr. H. S. Dyer, my secretary, having received a severe contusion from a splinter, I am deprived temporarily of his valuable assistance in collecting and keeping up the general returns and communications of the squadrons; I shall therefore retain in my office Mr. E. J. T. White, his first clerk, whom I have nominated to succeed the purser of the Brisk. I feel much personal obligation to the Hon. Lieutenant-colonel Cradock, for his readiness, during the heat of the battle, in carrying my orders and messages to the different quarters, after my aides-de-camp were disabled: but I will beg permission to refer his royal highness for further particulars of this sort to the details of the killed and wounded, a subject which it is painful for me to dwell upon. When I contemplate, as I do with extreme sorrow, the extent of our loss, I console myself with the reflection that the measure which produced the battle was absolutely necessary for obtaining the results contemplated by the treaty, and that it was brought on entirely by our opponents.

"When I found that the boasted Ottoman word of honour was made a sacrifice to wanton, savage devastation, and that a base advantage was taken of our reliance upon Ibrahim's good faith, I own I felt a desire to punish the offenders. But it was my duty to refrain, and refrain I did; and I can assure his royal highness that I would still have avoided this disastrous extremity, if other means had been open to me. The Asia, Genoa, and Albion have each suffered so much, that it is my intention to send them to England so soon as they shall have received, at Malta, the necessary repairs for their voyage. The Talbot, being closely engaged with a double-banked frigate, has also suffered considerably, as well as others of the smaller vessels; but I hope their defects are not more than can be made good at Malta. The loss of men in the Turco-Egyptian ships must have been immense, as his royal highness will see by the accompanying list, obtained from the secretary of the capitana bey, which includes that of two out of the three ships to which the English division was opposed. Captain Curzon having preferred continuing to assist me in the Asia, I have given the charge of my despatches to Commander Lord Viscount Ingestre, who, besides having had a brilliant share in the action, is well competent to give his royal highness the lord high admiral any further particulars he may require.

"I enclose, for his royal highness's further information, a letter from Captain Hamilton, descriptive of the proceedings of Ibrahim Pacha, and the misery of the country which he has devastated; a protocol of the conference which I had with my colleagues, and the plan and order for entering the port, which I gave out in consequence.

"I have, &c.,
"(Signed)   EDWARD CODRINGTON, Vice-admiral.

"No. I.—(*Translation.*)

"The admirals commanding the squadrons of the three powers which signed the treaty of London, having met before Navarin, for the purpose of concerting the means of effecting the object specified in the said treaty, viz., an armistice *de facto* between the Turks and the Greeks, have set forth in the present protocol the result of their conference.

"Considering that after the provisional suspension of hostilities, to which Ibrahim Pacha consented in his conference of the 25th of September last with the English and French admirals, acting likewise in the name of the Russian admiral, the said Pacha did, the very next day, violate his engagement, by causing his fleet to come out, with a view to its proceeding to another point in the Morea:—

"Considering that since the return of that fleet to Navarin, in consequence of a second requisition addressed to Ibrahim by Codrington, who had met him near Patras, the troops of this

Pacha have not ceased carrying on a species of warfare more destructive and exterminating than before, putting women and children to the sword, burning the habitations, and tearing up trees by the roots, in order to complete the devastation of the country :—

"Considering that, with a view of putting a stop to atrocities, which exceed all that have hitherto taken place, the means of persuasion and conciliation, the representations made to the Turkish chiefs, and the advice given to Mehemet Ali and his son, have been treated as mockeries, whilst they might, with one word, have suspended the course of so many barbarities :—

"Considering that there only remains to the commanders of the allied squadrons the choice between three modes of fulfilling the intentions of their respective courts, namely:

"1. The continuing, throughout the whole of the winter, a blockade, difficult, expensive, and perhaps useless, since a storm may disperse the squadron, and afford to Ibrahim the facility of conveying his destroying army to different points of the Morea and the Islands.

"2. The uniting the allied squadrons in Navarin itself, and securing, by this permanent presence, the inaction of the Ottoman fleets; but which mode alone leads to no termination, since the Porte persists in not changing its system.

"3. The proceeding to take a position with the squadrons in Navarin, in order to renew to Ibrahim propositions which, entering into the spirit of the treaty, were evidently to the advantage of the Porte itself.

"After having taken these three modes into consideration, we have unanimously agreed that this third mode may, without effusion of blood, and without hostilities, but simply by the imposing presence of the squadrons, produce a determination leading to the desired object.

"We have in consequence adapted it, and set it forth in the present protocol.—Oct. 18, 1827.

"(Signed) EDWARD CODRINGTON, Vice-admiral and Commander-in-chief of his Britannic Majesty's ships and vessels in the Mediterranean.

LOUIS, Count de HEIDEN, Rear-admiral of his Imperial Majesty the Emperor of the Russias.

Rear-admiral H. de RIGNY, commanding the squadron of his most Christian Majesty."

"No. III.

"*Statement made by the Secretary of the Capitana Bey in the Port of Navarin, Oct.* 21, 1827.

"3 Turkish line-of-battle ships :—1 Turkish admiral—84 guns, 850 men—650 killed—1 ditto, 84 guns, 830 men—1 ditto, 76 guns, 850 men, 400 killed.

"4 Egyptian double-banked frigates, 64 guns each, from 450 to 500 men.

"15 Turkish frigates, 48 guns, from 450 to 500 men.

"18 Turkish corvettes,—8 Egyptian ditto,—from 18 to 24 guns, 200 men.

"4 Turkish brigs,—8 Egyptian ditto,—19 guns, from 130 to 150 men.

"6 Egyptian fire-vessels.

"40,000 Egyptian troops in the Morea, 4000 of whom came with the above ships."

Since the battle of Navarin no other action has occurred ; our pages will therefore close with the strength of the navy in 1827, immediately after the promotion which took place on the 10th of January in that year.

Flag-officers	154
Captains	759
Commanders	1105
Lieutenants	2994
Masters	454
Medical officers	977
Pursers	758
Chaplains	69

APPENDIX.

No. 1.—See p. 116.

A List of the Ships and Vessels late belonging to the British Navy, Captured, Destroyed, Wrecked, Foundered, or Accidentally Burnt, during the year 1813.

Name.	Commander	How, when, and where Lost.
Gun-ship. 74 (O) Captain	(in ordinary)	Burnt, March 22, in Hamoaze.
Gun-frig. 38 (Z) *Dædalus*	Murray Maxwell	Wrecked, July 2, off the island of Ceylon: crew saved.
32 (H) Southampton	Sir Jas. Lucas Yeo	Wrecked, November 27 (1812), on a reef of rocks, near Conception island: crew saved.
Gun-sh. slp. 18 (R) Tweed	William Mather	Wrecked, November 5, in Shoal bay, Newfoundland: crew, except fifty-two, perished.
(S) Atalante	Frederick Hickey	Wrecked, November 10, off Halifax lighthouse: crew saved.
G.-bg. slp. 18 (Y) *Colibri*	John Thompson	Wrecked, August 22, in Port Royal, Jamaica: crew saved.
,, Ferret	F. Alex. Halliday	Wrecked, January 7, near Leith: crew saved.
,, Peacock	William Peake	Captured, February 24, by the American sloop Hornet, off Demerara.
,, Persian	Charles Bertram	Wrecked, June 16, on the Silver Keys, in the West Indies: crew saved.
10 (c) Sarpedon	Thomas Parker	Foundered, as is supposed, on the 1st of January.
,, Rhodian	John Boss	Foundered, February 21, on her passage to Jamaica: crew saved.
Gun-brig. 14 (f) Linnet	Joshua Tracey	Captured, February 25, by the French 40-gun frigate Gloire, near the Madeiras.

No. 1—continued.

	Name.	Commander.	How, when, and where Lost.
Gun-brig.			
12	(g) Bold . . John Shekel		Wrecked, September 27, on Prince Edward's Island.
	„ Boxer . . Samuel Blythe		Captured, September 5, by the American 16-gun brig Enterprise, off Portland, United States.
	„ Daring . William R. Pascoe		Destroyed, February 7, by her crew, to prevent her capture by the French frigate, Rubis.
	„ Fearless . H. Lord Richards		Wrecked, December 8 (1812), off coast of Spain.
Gun-cut.			
14	(i) Dominica . Geo. W. Barretté		Captured, August 5, by the American privateer Decatur, off Charlestown.
10	(l) Algerine . Daniel Carpenter		Wrecked, May 20, in the West Indies.
	„ Alphea . Thomas Wm. Jones		Destroyed, September 9, in action with French privateer Renard.
	„ Subtle . Charles Brown		Foundered, November 30 (1812), off St. Bartholomew's, in the West Indies, whilst in chase of an American brig: crew perished.
8	(m) Highflyer . Wm. Hutchinson		Captured, September 9, by the American frigate, President, off Nantucket.
S.S.	(s) Woolwich . Thos. Ball Sullivan		Wrecked, November 6, off Barbuda: crew saved.

ABSTRACT.

	Lost through the Enemy.		Lost through Accident.			
	Capt.	Dest.	Wrecked.	Foundered.	Burnt.	Total.
Ships of the line .	..	..	..	..	1	1
„ under the line	5	2	11	3	..	21
Total . . .	5	2	11	3	1	22

Although the total of this abstract corresponds with the total at the foot of the proper column of the Annual Abstract No. 22, the items do not quite agree; because, by mistake, the Peacock sloop has been inserted in the latter, and the Dædalus frigate in No. 23.

No. 2.—See p. 116.

A List of French and American Frigates, Captured, Destroyed, Wrecked, Foundered, or Accidentally Burnt, during the year 1813.

	Name.	How, when, and where Lost.
Gun-frig.		
40 {	(Z) Trave, F.	Captured, October 23, by the British frigate Andromache, latitude 46° north, longitude 7° west.
	,, Weser, F.	Captured, October 21, by the British sloops Scylla and Royalist, Rippon in company, latitude 47° north, longitude 9° west.
36 {	,, Chesapeake, A.	Captured, June 1, by the British frigate Shannon, in Boston bay.
	.. Rubis, F.	Wrecked, February 5, off the Isles de Los.

No Dutch or Danish vessel above a sloop, captured, &c., during the year 1813.

An Abstract of French and American Frigates Captured, &c. during the year 1813.

	Lost through the Enemy.		Lost through Accident.			Total lost to the American and French Navies.	Total added to the British Navy.
	Capt.	Dest.	Wrecked.	Foundered.	Burnt.		
F.	2	..	1	..	..	3	2
A.	1	..	..	..	..	1	1
Total	3	..	1	..	..	4	3

No. 3.—See p. 116.

	£.	s.	d.
For the pay and maintenance of 86,000 seamen and 31,400 marines for seven, and of 74,000 seamen and 16,000 marines for six lunar months	6,516,950	0	0
,, the wear and tear of ships, &c.	3,268,000	0	0
,, the ordinary expenses of the navy, including the salaries and contingent expense of the admiralty, navy-pay, navy, and victualling offices and dockyards; also half-pay and superannuations to officers of the navy and royal marines, their widows, &c.	1,730,840	12	8
,, the expense of sea-ordnance	532,000	0	0
, the superannuation allowances to commissioners, clerks, &c.	63,560	13	1
,, the extraordinaries, including the building and repairing of ships, and other extra work	2,086,274	0	0
., the hire of transports	2,980,623	13	2
,, the maintenance of prisoners of war in health and sickness, and of sick and wounded seamen	1,223,928	12	0
,, the salaries, contingencies, &c., in the transport-office	99,324	9	0
, the provisions for troops and garrisons for the year 1814	810,560	0	0
Total supplies granted for the sea-service	£19,312,070	19	11

No. 4.—See p. 133.

Letter from Captain Phillimore to Sir William Congreve, Bart.

H. M. S. Eurotas, Falmouth,
Dear Sir, October 11, 1813.

I am afraid you will attribute blame to me for not having written to you about your guns, but the fact is, I have been unwilling to give an opinion, till I had an opportunity of trying them; and the chasing, in a ship of this sort, looking out from a fleet, is so very frequent, and the attention requisite to a new ship's company occupies a great deal of time; but I hope you believe I am ready and willing to give any information you may like to write for. On the (my) arrival in the Brest squadron, I invited Commodore Malcolm, and all the captains, to come on board: we tried them eight times, with full allowance of powder, and double-shotted, which they stood remarkably well; indeed, every one of them went away pleased with the gun.

If well manned, I could fight both sides with ease, and I cannot express too strongly how delighted I am with them in a gale of wind; we had a very heavy gale coming in here, and I had to carry a heavy press of sail off Ushant; the guns did not work in the least, and the ship did not seem to feel the smallest inconvenience from them. A few days before I left the fleet, Commodore Malcolm mentioned (in conversation to me) he should like them on the Queen Charlotte's main and middle decks. I write this in haste, being anxious to send many letters by this post.

Believe me, dear Sir,
Yours faithfully,
(Signed) J. PHILLIMORE.

No. 5.—See p. 225

A List of French and American Line-of-Battle Ships and Frigates, Captured, Destroyed, Wrecked, Foundered, or Accidentally Burnt, during the year 1814.

Gun-ship.		Name.	How, when, and where Lost.
74		(M) Brilliant	Captured, April 18, at the surrender of Genoa to the British.
		.. Régulus	Destroyed, April 6, by the French in the Gironde, to prevent capture.
40		(Z) Alcmène, ,, Iphigénie	Captured, January 20 and 16, by the British 74 Venerable and 22-gun ship Cyane, off Madeira.
		,, Cérès	Captured, January 6, by the British frigates Niger and Tagus, off the Cape-de-Verds.
		,, Clorinde	Captured, March 26, by the British frigates Dryad and Eurotas, lat. 47° 40' north, longitude 9° 30' west.
		,, Etoile	Captured, March 27, by the British frigate Hebrus, off Cape La Hogue.
		,, Sultane	Captured, March 26, by the British 74 Hannibal, off Cherbourg.
		,, Terpsichore	Captured, February 3, by the British 56-gun ship Majestic, latitude 36° 41' north, longitude 22° 11' west.
		,, Uranie	Destroyed, February 3, by the French at Brendici, to prevent capture.
32	(D)	Essex, A.	Captured, March 28, by the British frigate Phœbe and sloop Cherub, off Valparaiso.
26		.. Adams, A.	Destroyed, September 3, by her crew at Castine, in the Penobscot, to prevent capture.

An Abstract of French and American Line-of-Battle Ships and Frigates Captured, &c., during the year 1814.

		Lost through the Enemy.		Lost through Accident.			Total lost to the French and American Navies.	Total added to the British Navy.
		Capt.	Dest.	Wrecked.	Foundered.	Burnt.		
Ships of the line	F.	1	1	..	..	..	2	1
Frigates	F.	7	1	..	..	..	8	7
	A.	1	1	..	..	..	2	1
Total		9	3	..	..	..	12	9

In the annual abstract to which this list belongs, there appear to have been eight foreign frigates of the Z class added to the navy. This is a mistake. The Melpomène, one of the number, was not captured until 1815.

APPENDIX. 387

No. 6.—See p. 225.

A List of the Ships and Vessels, late belonging to the British Navy, Captured, Destroyed, Wrecked, Foundered, or Accidentally Burnt, during the year 1814.

	Name.	Commander.	How, when, and where Lost.
Gun-p.-ship.			
22	(*M*) Laurestinus.	Alexander Gordon	Wrecked, October 22 (1813), on the Silver Keys, Bahana Islands: crew saved.
20	(*P*) Hermes.	William Henry Percy	Destroyed, September 15, in an attack upon an American battery at Mobile.
Gun-sh. slp.			
18 {	(*E*) Anacreon	John Davis	Foundered, February 28, in the Channel.
	(*S*) Peacock	Richard Coote	Foundered, in August, off the southern coast of the U. S.: crew perished.
Gun-brig-slp.			
18 {	(*Y*) Avon	Hon. James Arbuthnot	Destroyed, September 1, by sinking, at the close of an action with the American sloop-of-war Wasp, Channel.
	,, Crane	Robert Standley	Foundered, September 30, West Indies.
	,, Epervier	Richard Wales	Captured, April 29, by the American sloop-of-war Peacock, off the southern coast of the United States.
	,, Fantome	Thomas Sykes	Wrecked, November 24 on her passage from St. John's, New Brunswick, to Halifax: crew saved.
	,, Halcyon	John Houlton Marshall	Wrecked, May 19, on a reef of rocks in Anatto bay, Jamaica: crew saved.
	,, Reindeer	William Manners	Captured, June 28, by the American sloop-of-war Wasp, Channel.
16 {	(a) Goshawk	Hon. William John Napier	Wrecked, September 21 (1813), in the Mediterranean: crew saved.
	Vautour	Peter Lawless	Foundered, as is supposed, exact date unknown.
	Pictou	Edward Stephens	Captured, February 14, by the American frigate Constitution.

388   APPENDIX.

No. 6—*continued*.

	Name.	Commander.	How, when, and where Lost.
Gun-cut.			
14 (i)	*Racer*	Henry Freem. Young Pogson	Wrecked, October 10, in the gulf of Florida: crew saved.
10 { (1)	*Dart*	Thomas Allen	Foundered, latter end of 1813, or beginning of 1814.
„	Decoy	John Pearce	Captured, March 22, by what exact force unknown.
„	Holly	Samuel Sharpe Treacher	Wrecked, January 29, off St. Sebastian: crew, except the commander and five men, saved.
6 (n)	*Rapide*	(name unknown)	Wrecked, date unknown, on the Saintes.
4 { (o)	Ballahou	Norfolk King	Captured, April 29, by the American privateer Perry, off the coast of the United States.
„	Cuttle	(name unknown)	Foundered, exact date unknown, on the Halifax station.
„	Herring	John Murray	
„	Landrail	Robert Daniel Lancaster	Captured, July 12, by the American privateer Syren, Channel.
T.S. (r)	Leopard	Edward Crofton	Wrecked, June 28, near the island of Anticosti, gulf of St. Lawrence: crew, except a few, saved.

ABSTRACT.

	Lost through the Enemy.		Lost through Accident.			
	Capt.	Dest.	Wrecked.	Foundered.	Burnt.	Total.
Ships of the Line	..	..	..	..	..	..
„ under the Line	6	2	8	7	..	23
Total	6	2	8	7	..	23

Owing to the extreme inaccuracy of Steel's list of losses (in later years especially), and to the circumstance of the Annual Abstracts having been printed before the errors could conveniently be rectified, this abstract again differs, as well in its total, as in some of its items, from the Annual Abstract with which it corresponds in date.

No. 7.—See p. 225.

	£.	s.	d.
For the pay and maintenance of 55,000 seamen and 15,000 marines for three, and 70,000 seamen and 20,000 marines for ten lunar months.	4,759,125	0	0
,, the wear and tear of ships, &c.	2,386,500	0	0
,, the ordinary expenses of the navy, including the salaries and contingent expense of the admiralty, navy-pay, navy, and victualling-offices and dock-yards; also half-pay and superannuation to officers of the navy, &c.	2,278,929	11	11
,, the expense of sea-ordnance	388,500	0	0
,, the superannuation allowances to commissioners, clerks, &c.	67,232	16	0
,, the extraordinaries, including the building and repairing of ships, and other extra work	2,116,710	0	0
,, the hire of transports	3,309,235	3	0
,, the maintenance of prisoners of war, in health and sickness, and of sick and wounded seamen	337,653	16	5
,, the salaries, &c., in the transport-office	97,245	2	9
,, superannuations in ditto	2,811	12	6
,, the provisions for troops and garrisons	1,288,757	0	0
,, paying off navy-debt	2,000,000	0	0
Total supplies granted for the sea-service	£19,032,700	2	7

No. 8.—See p. 276.

A List of French and American Frigates Captured, Destroyed, Foundered, or Accidentally Burnt, during the year 1815.

Name.	How, when, and where Lost.
Gun-frig.	
40 (U) President, A.	Captured, January 15, by a British squadron, off Long Island, United States.
44 (Z) Melpomène, F.	Captured, April 30, by the British 74 Rivoli, off Ischia.

No. 9.—See p. 276.

RECAPITULATORY ABSTRACT

Showing the Number of French, Dutch, Spanish, Danish, Russian, Turkish, and American Ships of the Line and Frigates, Captured, Destroyed, Wrecked, Foundered, and Accidentally Burnt, during the War (including that of Elba), commencing in May, 1803, and ending in July, 1815; also the number of Captured Ships added to the British Navy during that period.

		Lost through the Enemy.		Lost through Accident.			Total lost to the F. Du. S. Da. R. & A. Navy.	Total added to the British Navy.
		Capt.	Dest.	Wrecked.	Foundered.	Burnt.		
Ships of the line	F.	26	9	1	..	..	36	13
	Du.	..	3	1	..	..	4	..
	S.	10	1	..	..	..	11	5
	Da.	18	..	..	..	..	18	15
	R.	1	..	..	..	..	1	..
	T.	..	1	..	..	..	1	..
Total		55	14	2	..	..	71	33
Frigates	F.	55	15	4	..	1	75	46
	Du.	5	1	1	..	..	7	4
	S.	6	1	..	..	..	7	6
	Da.	9	1	..	..	..	10	9
	T.	1	4	..	..	..	5	..
	A.	3	1	..	..	..	4	3
Grand Total		134	37	7	..	1	179	101

No. 10.—See p. 276.

A List of Ships and Vessels, late belonging to the British Navy, Captured, Destroyed, Wrecked, Foundered, or Accidentally Burnt during the year 1815.

Name.	Commander.	How, when, and where Lost.
Gun-frig. 38 (*Z*) Statira	Speelman Swaine	Wrecked, February 26, on a sunken rock, off the Isle of Cuba: crew saved.
Gun-p.-ship. 22 (*M*) Cyane 20 (*P*) Levant	Gordon Thomas Falcon Hon. George Douglas	Captured, Feb. 20, by the American frigate Constitution, sixty leagues west-south-west of Madeira: Levant recaptured March 11.
Gun-sh.-slp 18 (*S*) Sylph	George Dickens	Wrecked, January 17, on Southampton bar, North America: crew, except six, perished.
16 (*T*) Cygnet	Robert Russel	Wrecked (date unknown), off the Courantine river: crew saved.
Gun-brig-slp. 18 (*Y*) Penguin	James Dickinson	Captured, March 23, by the American sloop Hornet, off Tristan d'Acunha.
Gun-cut. 14 (i) *Dominica*	Richard Crawford	Wrecked, August 15, near Bermuda.
12 (k) *St. Lawrence*,	Henry Gordon.	Captured, February 26, by the American privateer-brig Chasseur, off Havana.
10 (l) *Elizabeth*	Jonathan W. Dyer	Foundered, October (1814), by upsetting in chase of an American privateer.
T.S. (g) Penelope	James Galloway	Wrecked, May 1, on the coast of Low. Canada: part of crew perished.

No. 10—*continued.*

ABSTRACT.

	Lost through the Enemy.		Lost through Accident.			Total
	Capt.	Dest.	Wrecked.	Foundered.	Burnt.	
Ships of the line . .	..	..	..	..	..	..
,, under the line .	4	..	5	1	..	10
Total . .	4	..	5	1	..	10

For the reason that this abstract falls short by two of the corresponding Annual Abstract (No. 24), see remarks at foot of the abstract at bottom of p. 388.

No. 11.—See p. 276.

RECAPITULATORY ABSTRACT,

Showing the Number of British Ships and Vessels-of-War Captured, Destroyed, Wrecked, Foundered, or Accidentally Burnt, during the War, commencing in May, 1803, and ending in July, 1815.

	Lost through the Enemy.		Lost through Accident.			Total.
	Capt.	Dest.	Wrecked.	Foundered.	Burnt.	
Ships of the line . .	..	..	8	3	2	13
,, under the line .	83	7	161	50	3	304
Total . .	83	7	169	53	5	317

No. 12.—See p. 276.

	£.	s.	d.
For the pay and maintenance of 24,000 seamen and 9,000 marines	1,839,337	10	0
„ the wear and tear of ships, &c.	922,350	0	0
„ the ordinary expenses of the navy, including the salaries and contingent expense of the admiralty, navy-pay, navy, and victualling-offices and dockyards; also half-pay and superannuations to officers of the navy and royal marines, their widows, &c.	2,689,931	18	3
„ the expense of sea-ordnance	150,150	0	0
„ the superannuation allowances to commissioners, clerks, &c.	72,707	3	4
„ the extraordinaries, including the building and repairing of ships and other extra work	2,102,563	0	0
„ the hire of transports	1,611,041	2	4
„ the maintenance of prisoners of war in health and sickness	69,820	0	0
„ the same of sick and wounded seamen	112,904	6	7
„ the salaries, contingencies, &c. in the transport-office	61,303	15	3
„ superannuations in ditto	3,080	15	10
„ the provisions for troops and garrisons	479,156	0	0
Total supplies granted for the sea-service	£10,114,345	11	7

No. 13.—See p. 297.

A List of the Ships and Vessels, late belonging to the British Navy, Wrecked, &c., during the years 1816, 1817, 1818, *and* 1819.

1816.

New rating.	Name.	Commander.	How, when, and where Lost.
Gun-frig. 42 (Y)	Phœnix	Charles John Austen	Wrecked, February 20, near Smyrna, during a hurricane: crew saved.
22 (Z)	Comus	J. J. Gordon Bremer, C.B.	Wrecked, Nov. 4, off Cape Pine, Newfoundland: crew saved.
Gun-sh.-slp. 20 (F)	Tay	Samuel Roberts, C.B.	Wrecked, November 11, off the Alacranes, Gulf of Mexico: crew saved.

394   APPENDIX.

No. 13—continued.
1816.

New Rating.	Name.	Commander.	How, when, and where Lost.
Gun-b.-slp. 10	(L) Bermuda	John Pakenham	Wrecked, November 16, on her passage from the Gulf of Mexico: crew saved.
	„ Briseis	George Domett	Wrecked, November 5, on the reefs of Point Pedras: crew saved.
Gun-cut. 14	(O) Whiting	John Jackson	Wrecked, September 21, on Dunbar sand, harbour of Padstow: crew saved.

1817.

Gun-frig. 46	(W) *Alceste*	Murray Maxwell, C.B.	Wrecked, February 18, off island of Pulo-Leat, China sea: crew saved.
Gun-bg.-slp. 16	(J) *Julia*	Jenkin Jones	Wrecked, October 2, off Tristan d'Acunha: 55 of crew, including all the officers but captain and two midshipmen, perished.
10	(L) Jasper	Thomas Carew	Wrecked, January 21, on the point of Mount Batten, at the entrance of Catwater, crew of Jasper, except captain, lieutenant, and two seamen, perished: Telegraph had but one man saved.
Gun-cut. 12	(Q) *Telegraph*	John Little, C.B.	

1818 none.
1819.

Gun-sh.-brig. 20	(E) Erne	Timothy Scriven, C.B.	Wrecked, June 1, on one of the Cape de Verds: crew saved.

APPENDIX. 395

No. 14.—See p. 298.

	1817.	1818.	1819.	1820.
Seamen	13,000	— — 14,000	— — 14,000	— — 15,000
Marines	6,000	— — 6,000	— — 6,000	— — 8,000
	£. s. d.	£. s. d.	£. s. d.	£. s. d.
Pay and maintenance	975,650 0 0	1,131,000 0 0	1,085,500 0 0	1,263,275 0 0
Wear and tear	531,050 0 0	559,000 0 0	533,000 ·0 0	612,950 0 0
Ordinary, &c.	2,476,150 4 8	2,480,680 17 3	2,483,013 12 7	2,480,566 3 11
Ordnance	49,400 0 0	91,000 0 0	91,000 0 0	104,650 0 0
Extraordinaries, &c.	1,391,645 0 0	1,787,181 0 0	1,631,628 0 0	1,594,480 0 0
Transport-service	119,026 16 6	178,948 0 0	284,321 0 0	245,924 0 0
Prisoners of war, and sick and wounded seamen	} 142,500 0 0			
Troops and garrison	300,000 0 0	320,000 0 0	419,319 0 0	389,500 0 0
Navy debt	1,660,000 0 0			
Total	7,645,422 1 2	6,547,809 17 3	6,527,781 12 7	6,691,345 3 11

No. 15.—See p. 300.

A List of Ships belonging to the British Navy, Building or ordered to be Built, and Repairing (the latter in italics), with Circular Sterns, on the 1st of January, 1820.

Gun-ship.
120 (A) { Prince Regent, Royal George, St. George, London.
110 (C) { PrincessCharlotte.
84 (G) { Asia, Bombay, Formidable, Ganges, Goliath, Monarch, Powerful, Thunderer, Vengeance.
80 (H) { Boscawen, Hindostan, Indus.
78 (1) { *Achille,* Kent, *Revenge.*
74 { (N) Carnatic.
     (O) { *Benbow,* Gloucester, Pembroke.

Gun-ship.
60 (Q) { Chichester, Lancaster, Portland, Southampton, Winchester, Worcester.

Gun-frig.
48 (V) { Druid, Jason, Madagascar, Manilla, Nemesis, Statira, Tigris.
46 (W) { Æolus, Amazon, *Aurora,* Cerberus, Circe, Clyde, Dædalus, Diana, Fox.

Gun-frig.
46 (W) { Hamadryad, Hebe, *Horatio,* Latona, Medusa, Melampus, Mercury, Mermaid, Minerva, Nereus, Pegasus, Penelope, Proserpine Thalia, Thames, Thisbe, Unicorn, Venus.
42 (Y) { Aigle, *Havannah, Owen Glendower.*

The orders to build the Bombay and Manilla have recently been countermanded; and the 60-gun ships have been reduced to 52-gun frigates.

No. 16.—See p. 300.

A List of Ships down to class Q inclusive, belonging to the British Navy built (in italics) or building of Teak, on the 1st of January, 1820.

Gun-ship.	Gun-frig.	Gun-frig.
84 (G) { Asia, Ganges.	48 (V) { Madagascar, *Seringapatam*, Tigris.	28 (A) { Alligator, Samarang
80 (H) { Hindostan, Indus.	46 (W) *Amphitrite.*	Gun-b.-slp.
74 { (N) { Carnatic, *Cornwallis.* (O) { *Hastings*, *Malabar*, *Minden.*	42 (Y) { Doris, Salsette.	10 (L) { *Chameleon*, *Sphynx.*

An ABSTRACT of the Ships and Vessels belonging to the British Navy at the commencement of the Year

Letters of Reference.	RATE.	CLASS.	For Sea-service.							No.		For Harbour-service.			
			In Commission.		In Ordinary.		TOTAL.		British Built.	Foreign Built.	In Commission.		In Ordinary.	
			No.	Tons.	No.	Tons.	No.	Tons.			No.	Tons.	No.	Tons.
A	Three-deckers. First.	120-gun ship — — — —	2	5124	—	—	2	5124	2	—	—	—	—	—
B	,,	112 ,, 18-pounder — — —	1	2351	—	—	1	2351	1	—	—	—	—	—
C	,,	,, ,, 12 ,, — — —	1	2457	—	—	1	2457	—	1	1	2398	—	—
D	,,	100 ,, 18 ,, — — —	2	4575	—	—	2	4575	2	—	—	—	—	—
E	,,	,, ,, 12 ,, — — —	1	2175	—	—	1	2175	1	—	—	—	1	2091
F	Second.	98 ,, 18 ,, — — —	1	2278	1	2276	2	4554	2	—	—	—	—	—
H	,,	,, ,, 12 ,, — — —	4	8275	2	4285	6	12560	6	—	1	1944	3	6195
K	Two-deckers. Third.	80 ,, — — — —	1	2265	4	8785	5	11050	1	4	3	6294	3	6365
L	,,	74 ,, 24-pounder — —	9	17227	2	3818	11	21045	9	2	—	—	2	3742
M	,,	,, ,, 18 ,, — large	12	22175	7	13329	19	35504	10	9	4	7360	6	11322
N	,,	,, ,, ,, ,, — middl.	52	90906	2	3500	54	94406	54	—	8	14011	7	12241
O	,,	,, ,, ,, ,, — small	12	19665	1	1615	13	21280	13	—	6	9716	12	19506
P	,,	64 ,, — — — —	1	1378	—	—	1	1378	1	—	16	22252	13	17972
Q	Fourth.	60 ,, — — — —	—	—	—	—	—	—	—	—	—	—	—	—
		Line — —	99	180851	19	37608	118	218459	102	16	39	63955	47	79434
R	,,	56 ,, flush — — —	3	4862	—	—	3	4862	3	—	—	—	1	1256
T	,,	50 ,, com. or quarter-decked	2	2202	2	2280	4	4482	3	—	3	3136	5	5326
U	,,	44 ,, — — — —	3	4516	—	—	3	4516	3	—	—	—	—	—
V	Fifth.	44 ,, — — — —	2	1779	—	—	2	1779	2	—	1	882	—	—
W	One-deckers.	44-gun frigate — — —	1	1384	—	—	1	1384	1	—	—	—	—	—
X	,,	40 ,, 24-pounder —	5	6249	—	—	5	6249	5	—	—	—	2	2787
Y	,,	,, ,, 18 ,, —	1	1142	2	2332	3	3474	3	—	—	—	—	—
Z	,,	38 ,, — — — large	49	53523	4	4277	53	57800	30	23	—	—	8	8891
A	,,	,, ,, — — — small	2	2044	2	1964	4	4008	3	—	—	—	4	3931
B	,,	36 ,, 18-pounder large	6	6215	—	—	6	6215	—	6	—	—	2	2041
C	,,	,, ,, ,, small	42	40432	3	2812	45	42244	44	1	1	926	7	6434
D	,,	,, ,, 12 ,,	3	2806	—	—	3	2806	—	3	—	—	11	10126
E	,,	32 ,, 18 ,, — large	2	1812	—	—	2	1812	2	—	—	—	2	1829
F	,,	,, ,, ,, ,, — small	1	816	—	—	1	816	1	—	—	—	1	791
G	,,	,, ,, 12 ,, — large	—	—	—	—	—	—	—	—	—	—	3	2414
H	,,	,, ,, ,, ,, — small	9	6107	—	—	9	6107	9	—	1	688	3	2087
J	Sixth.	28 ,, — — —	—	—	—	—	—	—	—	—	—	—	4	2471
K	,,	,, ,, 24-gun post-ship quarter-decked	1	587	2	1122	3	1709	1	2	—	—	3	1604
L	,,	,, ,, flush —	1	812	—	—	1	812	—	1	—	—	—	—
M	,,	22 ,, quarter-decked —	10	5341	—	—	10	5341	10	—	—	—	—	—
N	,,	20 ,, ,, ,, —	1	451	1	451	2	902	2	—	—	—	3	1305
O	,,	,, ,, ,, ,, —	12	5681	1	457	13	6138	11	2	—	—	1	513
R	Sloops.	18-gun ship-sloop, quarter-decked	33	14122	1	424	34	14546	34	—	—	—	4	1760
S	,,	,, ,, flush —	7	2713	1	399	8	3112	7	1	—	—	3	1212
T	,,	16 ,, quarter-decked, large	10	3755	—	—	10	3735	10	—	1	425	6	2271
U	,,	,, ,, ,, ,, small	—	—	—	—	—	—	—	—	—	—	1	326
V	,,	,, ,, flush — —	2	775	—	—	2	775	2	—	—	—	7	2479
W	,,	14 ,, quarter-decked —	—	—	—	—	—	—	—	—	—	—	2	604
X	,,	,, ,, flush — —	—	—	—	—	—	—	—	—	—	—	1	340
Y	,,	18-gun brig-sloop — — large	81	31142	2	772	83	31914	82	1	—	—	3	1151
Z	,,	16 ,, — — — small	32	9812	1	284	33	10096	13	20	1	234	12	3918
a	,,	14 ,, — — — —	14	3480	—	—	14	3480	12	2	—	—	—	—
b	,,	10 ,, — — — —	28	6649	—	—	28	6649	28	—	—	—	3	1009
c	Bombs, of	8 guns and 2 mortars —	8	2845	—	—	8	2845	8	—	—	—	1	425
d	Fireships, Gun-brigs.	14 ,, ,, — —	—	—	—	—	—	—	—	—	—	—	2	423
e	,,	,, ,, — — — —	3	657	—	—	3	657	—	3	—	—	—	—
f	,,	12 ,, — — — —	67	12057	2	362	69	12419	68	1	1	160	—	—
g	,,	10 ,, — — — —	1	158	—	—	1	148	1	—	—	—	—	—
h	Cutters, &c.	14 ,, — — — —	8	1699	—	—	8	1699	2	6	—	—	1	197
i	,,	12 ,, — — — —	8	1584	—	—	8	1584	1	7	—	—	3	415
k	,,	10 ,, — — — —	24	3471	—	—	24	3471	17	7	—	—	—	—
l	,,	8 ,, — — — —	2	264	—	—	2	204	1	1	—	—	—	—
m	,,	6 ,, — — — —	1	90	—	—	1	90	1	—	—	—	—	—
o	,,	4 ,, — — — —	10	774	—	—	10	774	10	—	—	—	—	—
		Cruisers — —	594	424609	43	55544	637	480153	531	106	48	70406	156	149770
q	Troop-ships — — — —		28	25933	—	—	28	25933	22	6	2	1295	13	12292
r	Storeships — — — —		15	10494	—	—	15	10494	14	1	1	176	3	1181
w	Surveying-vessels — — —		3	574	—	—	3	574	3	—	—	—	—	—
x	Advice-boats and Tenders — —		4	603	—	—	4	603	4	—	—	—	—	—
a	Hospital, Prison, Receiving ships, &c.		—	—	—	—	—	—	—	—	11	14373	8	8687
b	Royal Yachts — — — —		—	—	—	—	—	—	—	—	7	1288	—	—
		Troop-ships, &c. —	50	37604	—	—	50	37604	43	7	21	17132	24	22160
		GRAND TOTAL (f.) — —	644	462213	43	55544	687	517757	574	113	69	87538	180	171930

VOL. VI.

397

). 22.

Increase and Decrease in the Classes since the date of the last Year's Abstract.

ing, or ered Built.		GRAND TOTAL.		Built.			Purchased.				Converted from other Classes.		Ordered to be Built.		TOTAL of Increase.		Captured, Destroyed, Wrecked, &c.		Converted to other Classes.		Sold, or taken to Pieces.		TOTAL of Decrease.	
			King's Yards.		Merchants' Yards.		British Vessels or Enemy's Privateers.		Enemy's National Vessels.															
Tons.	No.	Tons.	No.	Tons.	No.	Tons.	No.	Tons.	No.	Tons.	No.	Tons.	No.	Tons.	No.	Tons.	No.	Tons.	No.	Tons.	No.	Tons.	No.	Tons.
13066	7	18190																						
4834	3	7185																						
— —	2	4855																						
2404	3	6979																						
— —	2	4266																						
— —	2	4554																						
— —	10	20699	—	—	—	—	—	—	—	—	—	—	—	—	—	—	—	—	2	3962	1	1945	3	5907
8325	15	32034																						
— —	13	24787																						
— —	29	54186	1	1809	—	—	—	—	—	—	1	1874	—	—	1	1874								
26251	84	146909	1	1746	1	1773	—	—	—	—	—	—	1	1768	1	1768	1	1639	3	4862	5	8266	9	14767
— —	31	50502	—	—	—	—	—	—	—	—	—	—	—	—	—	—	—	—	1	1388	1	1383	2	2721
— —	30	41582	—	—	—	—	—	—	—	—	—	—	—	—	—	—	—	—	—	—	1	1285	1	1285
54880	231	416728	2	3555	1	1773	—	—	—	—	1	1874	1	1768	2	3642	1	1639	6	10212	8	12829	15	24680
— —	4	6118	—	—	—	—	—	—	—	—	3	4862*a*	—	—	3	4862								
2426	14	15370	1	1173	—	—	—	—	—	—	—	—	—	—	—	—								
2779	5	7295	—	—	2	3128*b*	—	—	—	—	1	1388*c*	3	4586	4	5974								
— —	3	2661																						
— —	3	4171																			1	1388	—	—	1	1388
1260	6	7549																						
— —	3	3474	—	—	3	3761																		
9934	70	76625	1	1080	9	9701	—	—	3	3292	—	—	2	2314*d*	5	5606	—	—	—	—	1	1093	1	1093
— —	8	7929	—	—	—	—	—	—	—	—	—	—	—	—	—	—	—	—	1	1024	1	968	2	2022
— —	8	8256	—	—	—	—	—	—	—	—	—	—	—	—	—	—	—	—	1	1051	—	—	1	1051
2852	56	52456	3	2841	9	8528																		
— —	14	12932	—	—	—	—	—	—	—	—	—	—	—	—	—	—	—	—	—	—	1	906	1	906
— —	4	3641	—	—	—	—	—	—	—	—	—	—	—	—	—	—	—	—	1	919	—	—	1	919
— —	2	1607																						
— —	3	2414	—	—	—	—	—	—	—	—	—	—	—	—	—	—	—	—	1	751	1	827	2	1578
— —	13	8882	—	—	—	—	—	—	—	—	—	—	—	—	—	—	1	671	1	672	2	1398	4	2741
— —	4	2471	—	—	—	—	—	—	—	—	—	—	—	—	—	—	—	—	—	—	1	586	1	586
— —	6	3313																						
— —	1	812																						
— —	10	5341																						
3592	13	5799	—	—	2	902	—	—	—	—	—	—	9	4047	1	4047	—	—	—	—	1	509	1	509
4242	23	10893	—	—	9	4145*e*	—	—	—	—	—	—	11	5113	11	5113								
— —	38	16306	1	427	—	—	—	—	—	—	—	—	—	—	—	—	1	431	—	—	1	425	2	856
— —	11	4324	—	—	—	—	—	—	—	—	—	—	—	—	—	—	2	833	—	—	2	753	4	1586
— —	17	6431																						
— —	1	326																						
— —	9	3254																						
— —	2	604																						
— —	1	340																						
1539	90	34604	—	—	14	5410	—	—	—	—	—	—	2	772	2	772	4	1528	—	—	1	384	5	1912
— —	46	14248	—	—	—	—	3	912	—	—	—	—	—	—	3	912					2	459	2	459
— —	14	3480	1	233	—	—	1	214	—	—	—	—	—	—	1	214	—	—	2	481	—	—	2	481
713	31	7362	—	—	—	—	—	—	—	—	—	—	—	—	—	—								
1126	14	4980	—	—	3	986	—	—	—	—	—	—	2	749	2	749					2	618	2	618
— —	1	425																						
— —	5	1080																	1	197	—	—	1	210	2	407
— —	70	12579	—	—	8	1461	—	—	—	—	—	—	—	—	—	—	4	720	—	—	1	180	5	900
— —	1	148	—	—	—	—	—	—	1	148	—	—	—	—	1	148								
— —	9	1896	—	—	—	—	2	503	—	—	—	—	—	—	2	503	1	203	—	—	1	210	2	413
— —	11	1999	—	—	—	—	5	1125	—	—	—	—	—	—	5	1125								
— —	24	3471	—	—	—	—	2	327	—	—	—	—	—	—	2	327	3	433	—	—	—	—	3	433
— —	2	204	—	—	—	—	2	248	—	—	—	—	—	—	2	248	1	144	—	—	—	—	1	144
— —	1	90																			1	92	1	92
— —	10	774																						
85343	912	785672	9	9329	60	39795	15	3329	4	3440	5	8124	30	19349	54	34242	21	7280	12	16017	28	22477	61	45774
— —	43	39520	—	—	—	—	—	—	—	—	5	5054	—	—	5	5054	—	—	—	—	2	1337	2	1337
— —	19	11851	—	—	—	—	2	1147	—	—	1	751	—	—	3	1898	1	907	—	—	—	—	1	907
— —	3	574	—	—	—	—	1	139	—	—	—	—	—	—	1	139								
— —	4	603																						
— —	19	23060	—	—	—	—	—	—	—	—	1	2088	—	—	1	2088	—	—	—	—	2	2789	2	2789
336	8	1618	—	—	—	—	—	—	—	—	—	—	1	330	1	330								
330	96	77226	—	—	—	—	3	1286	—	—	7	7893	1	330	11	9509	1	907	—	—	4	4126	5	5033
85673	1008	862898	9	9329	60	39795	18	4615	4	3440	12	16017	31	19679	65	43751	22	8187	12	16017	32	26603	66	50807

2 D

No.

An ABSTRACT of the Ships and Vessels belonging to the British Navy at the commencement of the Year 1815.

| Letters of Reference. | RATE. | CLASS. | For Sea-service. ||||||| For Harbour-service, &c. ||||||| Building or Ordered to be Built ||
| | | | In Commission. || In Ordinary. || Total. || No. || In Commission. || In Ordinary. || No. || | |
			No.	Tons.	No.	Tons.	No.	Tons.	British Built.	Foreign Built.	No.	Tons.	No.	Tons.	British Built.	Foreign Built.	No.	Ton
	Three-deckers.																	
A	First.	120-gun ship	–	–	3	7741	3	7741	3	–	–	–	–	–	–	–	4	104
B	,,	112 ,, 18-pounder	–	–	1	2351	1	2351	1	–	–	–	–	–	–	–	2	48
C	,,	,, ,, 12 ,,	–	–	1	2457	1	2457	–	1	–	–	1	2398	–	1	–	–
D	,,	100 ,, 18 ,,	–	–	2	4575	2	4575	2	–	–	–	–	–	–	–	1	24
E	,,	,, ,, 12 ,,	–	–	1	2175	1	2175	1	–	–	–	1	2091	–	1	–	–
F	Second.	98 ,, 18 ,,	1	2278	1	2276	2	4554	2	–	–	–	–	–	–	–	–	–
H	,,	,, ,, 12 ,,	1	2155	4	8458	5	10613	5	–	–	–	5	10086	5	–	–	–
	Two-deckers.																	
K	Third.	80 ,, –	2	4546	4	8586	6	13132	2	4	–	–	5	10717	1	4	3	62
L	,,	74 ,, 24-pounder	6	11507	4	7637	10	19144	9	1	–	–	2	3754	1	1	–	–
M	,,	,, ,, 18 ,, – large	8	14826	8	15176	16	30002	9	7	1	1814	10	18737	7	4	–	–
N	,,	,, ,, ,, ,, – middl.	22	38286	30	52689	52	90975	52	–	1	1740	18	31433	7	12	13	227
O	,,	,, ,, ,, ,, – small	7	11486	3	4906	10	16392	10	–	4	6316	12	19649	14	2	–	–
P	,,	64 ,, –	–	–	–	–	–	–	–	–	5	6889	17	23589	13	9	–	–
		Line	47	85084	62	119027	109	204111	96	13	11	16759	71	122454	48	34	23	466
R	Fourth.	56 ,, flush –	2	3258	–	–	2	3258	2	–	–	–	2	2860	2	–	–	–
T	,,	50 ,, com. or quarter-decked	2	2221	2	2372	4	4593	4	–	2	2088	4	4240	2	2	1	12
U	,,	,, ,, flush –	3	4516	–	–	3	4516	3	–	–	–	–	–	1	–	2	27
V	Fifth.	44 ,, –	2	1779	–	–	2	1779	2	–	1	882	–	–	1	–	–	–
	One-deckers.																	
W	,,	44-gun frigate –	1	1384	–	–	1	1384	1	–	–	–	2	2787	1	1	–	–
X	,,	40 ,, 24-pounder	6	7549	–	–	6	7549	6	–	–	–	1	1038	1	–	–	–
Y	,,	– 38 ,, 18 ,,	1	1142	2	2332	3	3474	3	–	–	–	2	2103	1	–	–	–
Z	,,	38 ,, – large	43	46836	12	12966	55	59802	32	23	–	–	7	7709	–	7	8	87
A	,,	,, ,, – small	2	2044	2	1964	4	4008	3	1	–	–	1	1038	–	–	1	9
B	,,	36 ,, 18-pounder – large	2	2043	2	2069	4	4112	–	4	–	–	2	2103	–	2	–	–
C	,,	,, ,, 12 ,, – small	34	31934	11	10311	45	42245	44	1	1	926	5	4608	6	–	1	9
D	,,	32 ,, 18 ,, – large	1	942	–	–	1	942	–	1	–	–	11	10038	2	11	–	–
E	,,	,, ,, ,, ,, – small	1	894	–	–	1	894	1	–	–	–	2	1838	2	–	–	–
F	,,	,, ,, 12 ,, – large	–	–	–	–	–	–	–	–	–	–	1	791	1	–	–	–
G	,,	,, ,, ,, ,, – small	–	–	–	–	–	–	–	–	–	–	1	856	1	–	–	–
H	Sixth.	28 ,, –	4	2725	–	–	4	2725	4	–	–	–	7	4798	7	–	–	–
I	,,	24-gun post-ship, quarter-decked –	2	1122	–	–	2	1122	–	–	–	–	1	598	1	–	–	–
J	,,	,, ,, flush –	1	812	–	–	1	812	1	1	–	–	3	1669	2	–	–	–
K	,,	22 ,, quarter-decked –	9	4815	–	–	9	4815	9	–	–	–	–	–	–	–	–	–
L	,,	,, ,, flush –	1	539	–	–	1	539	–	1	–	–	–	–	–	–	–	–
M	,,	20 ,, quarter-decked –	8	3591	1	451	9	4042	9	–	–	–	1	433	1	–	1	45
N	,,	,, ,, flush –	16	7522	4	1886	20	9408	19	1	–	–	–	–	–	–	1	5
O	Sloops.	18-gun ship-sloop, quarter-decked –	29	12415	2	851	31	13266	31	–	–	–	5	2187	5	–	–	–
P	,,	,, ,, flush –	6	2305	1	399	7	2704	7	–	–	–	2	841	2	–	–	–
Q	,,	16 ,, quarter-decked, large	8	2996	–	–	8	2996	8	–	–	–	7	2688	7	–	–	–
R	,,	,, ,, ,, small	–	–	–	–	–	–	–	–	–	–	–	–	–	–	–	–
S	,,	14 ,, flush –	–	–	–	–	–	–	–	–	–	–	5	1865	5	–	–	–
T	,,	,, ,, quarter-decked –	–	–	–	–	–	–	–	–	–	–	1	302	1	–	–	–
U	,,	,, ,, flush –	–	–	–	–	–	–	–	–	–	–	–	–	–	–	–	–
W	,,	18-gun brig-sloop –	67	25750	6	2307	73	28057	73	–	–	–	7	2695	6	1	3	115
X	,,	16 ,, –	21	6424	1	284	22	6708	9	13	–	–	3	854	3	–	–	–
Y	,,	14 ,, –	13	3221	–	–	13	3221	10	3	–	–	1	256	1	–	–	–
a	,,	10 ,, –	30	7126	1	236	31	7362	31	–	–	–	–	–	–	–	–	–
b	Bombs, of	8 guns and 2 mortars –	7	2431	2	711	9	3142	9	–	–	–	3	1089	3	–	2	74
c	Fireships,	14 guns –	2	359	–	–	2	399	–	2	–	–	1	425	1	–	–	–
d	Gun-brigs,	,, –	35	6309	3	543	38	6852	38	–	–	–	17	3047	16	1	–	–
e	,,	12 ,, –	1	148	–	–	1	148	–	1	–	–	–	–	–	–	–	–
f	,,	10 ,, –	7	1768	–	–	7	1768	–	7	1	214	1	152	2	–	–	–
g	Cutters, &c.	14 ,, –	7	1444	–	–	7	1444	1	6	–	–	2	266	1	1	–	–
h	,,	12 ,, –	13	2029	–	–	13	2029	9	4	–	–	4	470	4	–	–	–
i	,,	10 ,, –	1	104	–	–	1	104	–	1	–	–	–	–	–	–	–	–
k	,,	8 ,, –	–	–	–	–	–	–	–	–	–	–	–	–	–	–	–	–
l	,,	6 ,, –	–	–	–	–	–	–	–	–	–	–	–	–	–	–	–	–
m	,,	4 ,, –	4	315	1	75	5	390	5	–	–	–	–	–	–	–	–	–
		Cruisers –	439	287936	115	158784	554	446720	470	84	16	20569	180	185957	135	61	42	6325
q	Troop-ships –		25	23862	–	–	25	23862	17	8	1	603	17	16163	10	8	–	–
r	Storeships –		14	10167	–	–	14	10167	13	1	1	176	2	857	3	–	–	–
w	Surveying-vessels		3	574	–	–	3	574	2	–	–	–	1	169	1	–	–	–
x	Advice-boats		4	615	–	–	4	615	5	–	–	–	1	169	1	–	–	–
a	Hospital, Prison, Receiving-ships, &c.		–	–	–	–	–	–	–	–	10	12537	6	6422	8	8	–	–
b	Royal Yachts		–	–	–	–	–	–	–	–	7	1288	–	–	7	–	1	33
		Troop-ships, &c. –	46	35218	–	–	46	35218	37	9	19	14604	26	23611	29	16	1	33
	Grand Total (b) –		485	323154	115	158784	600	481938	507	93	35	35473	206	209568	164	77	43	6358

VOL. VI.

398

	Increase and Decrease in the Classes since the date of the last Year's Abstract.																			
	Built.				Purchased.						Converted from other Classes.		Ordered to be Built.		Total of Increase.		Captured, Destroyed, Wrecked, &c.		Converted to other Classes.		Sold, or taken to Pieces.		Total of Decrease.	
	King's Yards.		Merchants' Yards.		British Vessels or Enemy's Privateers.		Enemy's National Vessels.														
	No.	Tons.	No.	Tons	No.	Tons.	No.	Tons.	No.	Tons.	No.	Tons.	No.	Tons.	No.	Tons.	No.	Tons.	No.	Tons.	No.	Tons.
90	1	2617a																				
45																						
55																						
79																						
66																						
54																						
99																						
92	1	2082	–	–	–	–	–	–	–	–	–	–	–	–	–	–	–	–	1	1942	1	1942
98	–	–	–	–	–	–	–	–	–	–	–	–	–	–	–	–	–	–	1	1889	1	889
53	–	–	–	–	–	–	1	1883	–	–	–	–	1	1883	–	–	–	–	3	5516	3	5516
55	2	3504	1	1758	–	–	–	–	–	–	1	1718	1	1718	–	–	–	–	1	1772	1	1772
57	–	–	–	–	–	–	–	–	–	–	–	–	–	–	–	–	–	–	5	8145	5	8145
78	–	–	–	–	–	–	–	–	–	–	–	–	–	–	–	–	–	–	8	11104	8	11104
61	4	8203	1	1758	–	–	1	1883	–	–	1	1718	2	3601	–	–	–	–	19	30368	19	30368
18																						
48	1	1199	–	–	–	–	–	–	–	–	–	–	–	–	–	–	–	–	3	3222	3	3222
95																						
61																						
71																						
49	–	–	1	1260																		
74																						
104	1	1155	1	1070	–	–	8	8599	–	–	1	1084	9	9683	1	1094	5	5477	3	3433	9	10004
46	–	–	–	–	–	–	–	–	–	–	–	–	–	–	–	–	–	–	3	2893	3	2893
15	–	–	–	–	–	–	–	–	–	–	–	–	–	–	–	–	–	–	2	2041	2	2041
53	1	949	1	949	–	–	–	–	–	–	–	–	–	–	–	–	1	976	3	2747	4	3723
80	–	–	–	–	–	–	1	867	–	–	–	–	1	867	–	–	–	–	3	2819	3	2819
32	–	–	–	–	–	–	–	–	–	–	–	–	–	–	–	–	–	–	1	909	1	909
91	–	–	–	–	–	–	–	–	–	–	–	–	–	–	–	–	–	–	1	816	1	816
56	–	–	–	–	–	–	–	–	–	–	–	–	–	–	–	–	–	–	2	1558	2	1558
23	–	–	–	–	–	–	–	–	–	–	–	–	–	–	–	–	–	–	2	1359	2	1359
98	–	–	–	–	–	–	–	–	–	–	–	–	–	–	–	–	–	–	3	1873	3	1873
91	–	–	–	–	–	–	–	–	–	–	–	–	–	–	–	–	–	–	1	522	1	522
12																						
15	–	–	–	–	–	–	–	–	–	–	–	–	–	–	1	526	–	–	–	–	1	526
39	–	–	–	–	–	–	1	539	–	–	–	–	1	539	–	–	–	–	–	–		
27	–	–	7	3140	–	–	–	–	–	–	–	–	–	–	–	–	–	–	2	872	2	872
19	–	–	8	3731	–	–	–	–	–	–	–	–	–	–	–	–	–	–	2	974	2	974
53	–	–	–	–	–	–	–	–	–	–	–	–	–	–	1	427	–	–	1	426	2	853
45	–	–	–	–	–	–	–	–	–	–	–	–	–	–	–	–	–	–	2	779	2	779
84	–	–	–	–	–	–	–	–	–	–	–	–	–	–	–	–	–	–	2	747	2	747
	–	–	–	–	–	–	–	–	–	–	–	–	–	–	–	–	–	–	1	326	1	326
65	–	–	–	–	–	–	–	–	–	–	–	–	–	–	–	–	–	–	4	1389	4	1389
02	–	–	–	–	–	–	–	–	–	–	–	–	–	–	–	–	–	–	1	302	1	302
	–	–	–	–	–	–	–	–	–	–	–	–	–	–	–	–	–	–	1	340	1	340
09	–	–	1	382	1	384	–	–	–	–	–	–	1	384	6	2311	–	–	2	768	8	3079
62	–	–	–	–	–	–	–	–	–	–	–	–	–	–	2	621	–	–	19	6065	21	6686
77	–	–	–	–	–	–	–	–	1	258	–	–	1	258	–	–	–	–	1	261	1	261
62	–	–	3	713	–	–	–	–	–	–	–	–	–	–	–	–	–	–				
80	–	–	1	377	–	–	–	–	–	–	–	–	–	–	–	–	–	–				
25																	1	258	2	423	3	681
99	–	–	–	–	–	–	–	–	–	–	–	–	–	–	–	–	1	181	14	2499	15	2680
99																						
48	–	–	–	–	4	1061	–	–	–	–	–	–	4	1061	1	250	–	–	3	573	4	823
34	–	–	–	–	–	–	–	–	–	–	–	–	–	–	–	–	–	–	2	289	2	289
10	–	–	–	–	–	–	–	–	–	–	–	–	–	–	3	480	–	–	4	492	7	972
99	–	–	–	–	–	–	–	–	–	–	–	–	–	–	–	–	–	–	1	100	1	100
04	–	–	–	–	–	–	–	–	–	–	–	–	–	–	1	90	–	–	–	–	1	90
90	–	–	–	–	1	75	–	–	–	–	–	–	1	75	4	306	–	–	2	153	6	459
805	7	11506	24	13380	6	1520	11	11888	1	258	2	2802	20	16468	20	6105	8	6892	112	72338	140	85335
628	–	–	–	–	–	–	–	–	6	6453	–	–	6	6453	1	1056	–	–	5	4289	6	5345
200	–	–	–	–	–	–	–	–	–	–	–	–	–	–	–	–	–	–	2	651	2	651
574																						
784	–	–	–	–	–	–	–	–	1	181	–	–	1	181	–	–	–	–	3	4101	3	4101
959																						
18																						
763	–	–	–	–	–	–	–	–	7	6634	–	–	7	6634	1	1056	–	–	10	9041	11	10097
568	7	11506	24	13380	6	1520	11	11888	8	6892	2	2802	27	23102	21	7161	8	6892	122	81379	151	95432

2 E

An ABSTRACT of the Ships and Vessels belonging to the British Navy at the commencement of the Year

Letters of Reference.	RATE.	CLASS.	For Sea-service.							For Harbour-service, &c			
			In Commission.		In Ordinary.		TOTAL.		No. British Built.	No. Foreign Built.	In Commission.		In Ordinary.	
			No.	Tons.	No.	Tons.	No.	Tons.			No.	Tons.	No.	Tons.
	Three-deckers.													
A	First.	120-gun ship	–	–	5	12972	5	12972	5	–	–	–	–	–
B	,,	112 ,,	–	–	1	2351	1	2351	1	–	–	–	–	–
C	,,	12 ,, 18-pounder	–	–	1	2457	1	2457	–	1	–	–	–	–
D	,,	100 ,, 18 ,,	1	2289	1	2286	2	4575	2	–	–	–	–	–
E	,,	,, ,, 12 ,,	–	–	–	–	–	–	–	–	–	–	–	–
F	Second.	98 ,, 18 ,,	1	2278	1	2276	2	4554	2	–	–	–	–	–
H	,,	,, ,, 12 ,,	1	2155	5	10633	6	12788	6	–	–	–	6	12177
	Two-deckers.													
K	Third.	80 ,,	3	6628	4	8643	7	15271	3	4	–	–	5	10717
L	,,	74 ,, 24-pounder	4	7670	5	9632	9	17302	8	1	–	–	3	5596
M	,,	,, ,, 18 ,, – large	4	7364	8	15084	12	22448	8	4	–	–	13	24444
N	,,	,, ,, ,, ,, – middl.	14	24416	35	61337	49	85753	49	–	–	–	17	29650
O	,,	,, ,, ,, ,, – small	2	3308	4	6586	6	9894	6	–	–	–	16	26953
P	,,	64 ,, ,, ,,	–	–	–	–	–	–	–	–	3	4240	10	13682
		Line	30	56108	70	134257	100	190365	90	10	3	4240	70	122169
R	Fourth.	56 ,, flush	1	1616	–	–	1	1616	1	–	–	–	2	2898
T	,,	50 ,, com. or quarter-decked	2	2256	2	2450	4	4706	4	–	1	1048	3	3218
U	,,	,, ,, flush	3	4516	2	2779	5	7295	5	–	–	–	1	1533
V	Fifth.	44 ,,	–	–	–	–	–	–	–	–	–	–	3	2061
	One-deckers.													
W	,,	44-gun frigate	1	1384	–	–	1	1384	1	–	–	–	1	1357
X	,,	40 ,, 24-pounder	1	1347	5	6202	6	7549	6	–	–	–	–	–
Y	,,	,, ,, 18 ,,	–	–	3	3474	3	3474	3	–	–	–	–	–
Z	,,	38 ,, – large	18	19623	25	27022	43	46645	31	12	–	–	14	15379
A	,,	,, ,, – small	1	944	1	1020	2	1964	2	–	–	–	3	3082
B	,,	36 ,, 18-pounder – large	1	1028	2	2069	3	3097	–	3	–	–	3	3118
C	,,	,, ,, ,, ,, – small	24	22364	20	18934	44	41298	44	–	–	–	5	4682
D	,,	,, ,, 12 ,,	–	–	–	–	–	–	–	–	–	–	6	5425
E	,,	32 ,, 18 ,, – large	1	894	–	–	1	894	1	–	–	–	2	1838
F	,,	,, ,, ,, ,, – small	–	–	–	–	–	–	–	–	–	–	–	–
G	,,	,, ,, 12 ,, – large	–	–	–	–	–	–	–	–	1	856	–	–
H	,,	28 ,, ,, ,, – small	3	2066	–	–	3	2066	3	–	–	–	3	2044
I	Sixth.	24-gun post-ship, quarter-decked	1	601	1	521	2	1122	1	1	–	–	1	598
K	,,	,, ,, flush	1	812	–	–	1	812	–	1	–	–	1	519
L	,,	22 ,, quarter-decked	3	1592	1	522	4	2114	4	–	–	–	4	2162
M	,,	,, ,, flush	1	539	–	–	1	539	–	1	–	–	–	–
N	,,	20 ,, quarter-decked	7	3140	2	902	9	4042	9	–	–	–	1	511
O	,,	,, ,,	13	6091	5	2294	18	8385	18	–	–	–	14	6021
P	Sloops.	18-gun ship-sloop, quarter-decked	15	6394	4	1698	19	8092	19	–	–	–	3	1240
R	,,	,, ,, flush	3	1200	1	399	4	1599	4	–	–	–	3	1898
S	,,	16 ,, quarter-decked	2	789	1	365	3	1154	3	–	–	–	3	1091
T	,,	14 ,, flush	–	–	–	–	–	–	–	–	–	–	–	–
V	,,	,, ,, quarter-decked	–	–	–	–	–	–	–	–	–	–	–	–
W	,,	18-gun brig-sloop	37	14185	30	11558	67	25743	67	–	–	–	7	2696
Y	,,	16 ,,	5	1562	–	–	5	1562	2	3	–	–	14	4213
a	,,	14 ,,	6	1436	2	504	8	1940	6	2	–	–	3	760
b	,,	10 ,,	22	5224	9	2138	31	7362	31	–	–	–	–	–
c	Bombs, of	8 guns and 2 mortars	7	2451	–	–	7	2451	7	–	–	–	6	2194
d	Fireships,	14 guns	–	–	–	–	–	–	–	–	–	–	–	–
e	Gun-brigs,	,, ,,	1	187	–	–	1	187	–	1	–	–	1	212
f	,,	12 ,,	3	546	16	2907	19	3453	19	–	–	–	19	3382
g	,,	10 ,,	–	–	–	–	–	–	–	–	–	–	–	–
h	Cutters, &c.	14 ,,	6	1565	–	–	6	1565	–	6	–	–	1	152
i	,,	12 ,,	2	490	1	197	3	687	–	3	–	–	2	348
k	,,	10 ,,	8	1350	1	150	9	1500	7	2	–	–	3	369
l	,,	8 ,,	1	104	–	–	1	104	1	–	–	–	–	–
m	,,	4 ,,	3	226	–	–	3	226	3	–	–	–	–	–
		Cruisers	233	164630	204	222362	437	386992	391	46	5	6144	204	197770
q	Troop-ships		11	9507	1	1090	12	10597	8	4	2	1482	19	17775
r	Storeships		13	9943	–	–	13	9943	12	1	–	–	3	963
w	Surveying-vessels		3	574	–	–	3	574	3	–	–	–	–	–
x	Advice-boat and Tender		–	–	–	–	–	–	–	–	–	–	3	495
a	Hospital, Prison, Receiving-ships, &c		–	–	–	–	–	–	–	–	4	2942	31	35866
b	Royal Yachts		–	–	–	–	–	–	–	–	7	1454	–	–
		Troop-ships, &c	27	20024	1	1090	28	21114	23	5	13	5878	56	55099
		GRAND TOTAL (c)	260	184654	205	223452	465	408106	414	51	18	12022	260	252869

VOL. VI.

	GRAND TOTAL.		Built.			Purchased			Converted from other Classes.		Ordered to be Built.		TOTAL of Increase.		Captured, Destroyed, Wrecked, &c.		Converted to other Classes.		Sold, or taken to Pieces, &c.		TOTAL of Decrease.	
			King's Yards.		Merchants' Yards.		British Vessels or Enemy's Privateers.		Enemy's National Vessels.													
Tons.	No.	Tons.	No.	Tons.	No.	Tons.	No.	Tons.	No.	Tons.	No.	Tons.	No.	Tons.	No.	Tons.	No.	Tons.	No.	Tons.	No.	Tons.	
5218	7	18190	2	5231a	—	—	—	—	—	—	—	—	—	—	—	—	—	—	—	—	—	—	
4834	3	7185	—	—	—	—	—	—	—	—	—	—	—	—	—	—	—	—	1	2398	1	2398
—	1	2457	—	—	—	—	—	—	—	—	—	—	—	—	—	—	—	—	—	—	—	—
2404	3	6979	—	—	—	—	—	—	—	—	—	—	—	—	—	—	1	2175	—	—	1	2175
—	2	4554	—	—	—	—	—	—	—	—	—	—	—	—	—	—	—	—	—	—	—	—
—	12	24965	—	—	—	—	—	—	1	2175	—	—	1	2175	—	—	—	—	—	—	—	—
6359	15	32347	1	2139	—	—	—	—	—	—	1	2255	1	2255	—	—	—	—	—	—	—	—
	12	22908																				
20917	25	46802	—	—	—	—	—	—	—	—	—	—	—	—	—	—	—	—	2	3661	2	3661
	78	136320	2	3505	—	—	—	—	—	—	1	1715	1	1715	—	—	4	6965	3	5285	7	12250
	22	35847	—	—	—	—	—	—	—	—	—	—	—	—	—	—	2	3249	9	3261	4	6510
	13	17872	—	—	—	—	—	—	—	—	—	—	—	—	—	—	1	1374	8	11232	9	12606
39732	193	356506	5	10875	—	—	—	—	1	2175	2	3970	3	6145	—	—	8	13763	16	25837	24	39600
—	3	4514	—	—	—	—	—	—	—	—	—	—	—	—	—	—	—	—	1	1604	1	1604
—	8	8972	1	1227	—	—	—	—	—	—	—	—	—	—	—	—	—	—	3	3176	3	3176
—	6	8828	2	2779b	—	—	1	1533	—	—	—	—	1	1533	—	—	—	—	—	—	—	—
—	3	2661	—	—	—	—	—	—	—	—	—	—	—	—	—	—	—	—	—	—	—	—
—	2	2741	—	—	—	—	—	—	—	—	—	—	—	—	—	—	1	1430	—	—	1	1430
—	6	7549	—	—	—	—	—	—	—	—	—	—	—	—	—	—	—	—	—	—	—	—
—	3	3474	—	—	—	—	—	—	—	—	—	—	—	—	—	—	—	—	—	—	—	—
10936	67	72960	—	—	—	—	—	—	1	1101	2	2143	3	3244	1	1080	1	1066	4	4442	6	6588
—	5	5046	—	—	—	—	—	—	—	—	—	—	—	—	—	—	—	—	—	—	—	—
—	6	6215	—	—	—	—	—	—	—	—	—	—	—	—	—	—	—	—	1	791	1	791
—	49	45980	—	—	1	954	—	—	—	—	—	—	—	—	—	—	1	882	2	1871	3	2753
—	6	5425	—	—	—	—	—	—	—	—	—	—	—	—	—	—	2	1791	4	3764	6	5555
—	3	2732	—	—	—	—	—	—	—	—	—	—	—	—	—	—	—	—	1	791	1	791
—	1	856	—	—	—	—	—	—	—	—	—	—	—	—	—	—	—	—	—	—	—	—
—	6	4110	—	—	—	—	—	—	—	—	—	—	—	—	—	—	2	1405	3	2008	5	3403
—	1	598	—	—	—	—	—	—	—	—	—	—	—	—	—	—	—	—	—	—	—	—
—	3	1641	—	—	—	—	—	—	—	—	—	—	—	—	—	—	1	563	1	587	2	1150
—	1	812	—	—	—	—	—	—	—	—	—	—	—	—	—	—	—	—	—	—	—	—
—	8	4276	—	—	—	—	—	—	—	—	—	—	—	—	1	539	—	—	—	—	1	539
—	1	539	—	—	—	—	—	—	—	—	—	—	—	—	—	—	1	433	—	—	1	433
452	10	4494	—	—	—	—	—	—	—	—	—	—	—	—	2	976	—	—	—	—	2	976
511	20	9407	—	—	—	—	1	464	—	—	—	—	1	464	—	—	—	—	3	1340	3	1340
—	33	14113	—	—	—	—	—	—	—	—	—	—	—	—	—	—	1	399	2	307	2	706
—	7	2839	—	—	—	—	—	—	—	—	—	—	—	—	1	365	2	791	4	1476	7	2632
—	8	3002	—	—	—	—	—	—	—	—	—	—	—	—	—	—	2	774	—	—	2	774
—	3	1091	—	—	—	—	—	—	—	—	—	—	—	—	—	—	—	—	1	302	1	302
—	74	28439	—	—	3	1157	—	—	—	—	—	—	—	—	1	387	—	—	8	3083	9	3470
—	19	5775	—	—	—	—	—	—	—	—	—	—	—	—	—	—	—	—	6	1787	6	1787
—	11	2700	—	—	—	—	—	—	—	—	—	—	—	—	—	—	—	—	3	777	3	777
—	31	7362	—	—	—	—	—	—	—	—	—	—	—	—	—	—	—	—	—	—	—	—
—	13	4645	—	—	2	749	—	—	—	—	—	—	—	—	—	—	—	—	1	335	1	335
—	2	399	—	—	—	—	—	—	—	—	—	—	—	—	—	—	—	—	1	425	1	425
—	38	6835	—	—	—	—	—	—	—	—	—	—	—	—	—	—	—	—	17	3064	17	3064
—	1	148	—	—	—	—	—	—	—	—	—	—	—	—	—	—	—	—	1	148	1	148
—	7	1717	—	—	—	—	—	—	—	—	—	—	—	—	1	203	—	—	1	214	2	417
—	5	1035	—	—	—	—	1	224	—	—	—	—	1	224	2	455	—	—	3	444	5	899
—	12	1869	—	—	—	—	—	—	—	—	—	—	—	—	1	121	—	—	4	509	5	630
—	1	104	—	—	—	—	—	—	—	—	—	—	—	—	—	—	—	—	—	—	—	—
—	3	226	—	—	—	—	—	—	—	—	—	—	—	—	—	—	—	—	2	164	2	164
51631	678	642537	8	14881	6	2860	1	224	2	1997	2	3276	4	6113	9	11610	11	4525	21	22698	91	58455	123	85878
—	33	29854	—	—	—	—	—	—	—	—	—	—	—	—	1	1051	3	3914	6	5809	10	10774
—	16	10806	—	—	—	—	—	—	—	—	—	—	—	—	—	—	—	—	1	394	1	394
—	3	514	—	—	—	—	—	—	—	—	—	—	—	—	—	—	—	—	—	—	—	—
—	3	495	—	—	—	—	—	—	—	—	—	—	—	—	—	—	—	—	2	289	2	289
—	35	38808	—	—	—	—	—	—	22	23536	—	—	22	23536	—	—	—	—	3	3687	3	3687
282	8	1736	—	—	—	—	—	—	—	—	1	282	1	282	—	—	—	—	1	164	1	164
282	98	82273	—	—	—	—	—	—	22	23536	1	282	23	23818	1	1051	3	3914	13	10343	17	15308
51913	776	724810	8	14881	6	2860	1	224	2	1997	24	26812	5	6395	32	35428	12	5576	24	26812	104	68798	140	101186

2 F

An ABSTRACT of the Ships and Vessels belonging to the British Navy at the commencement of the Year 1817.

Letters of Reference.	Old Rating. RATE.	CLASS.	Letters of Reference.	New Rating. (a) RATE.	CLASS.	For Sea-service. In Commission. No.	Tons.	In Ordinary. No.	Tons.	TOTAL. No.	Tons.	No. British Built.	Foreign Built.	For Harbo[ur] In Commission. No.	Tons.	In [Ordinary] No.
	Three-deckers.			Three-deckers.												
A	First.	120-gun ship — —	A	First.	120-gun ship —	—	—	5	12972	5	12972	5	—	—	—	—
B	,,	112 ,, 18-pounder —	B	,,	112 ,, —	—	—	2	4808	2	4808	1	1	—	—	—
C	,,	18 ,, 12 ,, —	C	,,	110 ,, —	1	2289	1	2276	1	2286	1	—	—	—	—
D	,,	100 ,, ,, —	D	,,	108 ,, —	1	2289	1	2286	2	4575	2	—	—	—	—
F	Second.	98 ,, 18-pounder —	E	,,	106 ,, —	1	2278c	—	—	1	2278	1	—	—	—	—
H	,, ,,	,, 12 ,, —	F	,,	104 ,, —	—	—	6	12788	6	12788	6	—	—	—	6
	Two-deckers.			Two-deckers.												
			G	Second.	84 ,, —	2	4546	1	2257	3	6603	—	3	—	—	1
K	Third.	80 ,, — —	H	,,	80 ,, —	1	2082	3	6386	4	8418	3	1	—	—	—
			I	Third.	78 ,, 24-pounder —	1	1927	4	7772	5	9699	4	1	—	—	—
			K	,,	76 ,, 18 ,, —	1	1901	2	3806	3	5707	2	1	—	—	—
L	,,	74 ,, 24-pounder —	L	,,	74 ,, 24 ,, —	3	5711	2	3809	5	9520	5	—	—	—	3
M	,,	,, 18 ,, large	M	,,	,, 18 ,, —	—	—	3	5645	3	5646	1	2	—	—	5
N	,,	,, ,, middl.	N	,,	,, ,, large	—	—	4	7374	4	7374	4	—	—	—	1
O	,,	,, ,, small	O	,,	,, ,, middl.	3	3229	47	82299	50	87528	50	—	—	—	15
P	,,	64 ,, — —	P	,,	,, ,, small	1	1677	3	4969	4	6646	4	—	—	—	8
		Line — —				14	27640	84	159448	98	187088	89	9	—	—	40
R	Fourth.	56 ,, flush —	Q	Fourth.	60 ,, —	2	3128	1	1458	3	4586	3	—	—	—	1
			R	,,	58 ,, flush, rasée —	—	—	2	3233	2	3233	2	—	—	—	—
T	,,	50 ,, com. or qr.-decked	S	,,	,, ,, regular	—	—	1	1321	1	1321	1	—	—	—	1
U	,,	,, ,, flush	T	,,	,, ,, quarter-decked	1	1199	2	2400	3	3599	3	—	—	—	4
V	Fifth.	44 ,, — —				—	—	—	—	—	—	—	—	—	—	—
	One-deckers.			One-deckers.												
W	,,	40-gun frigate —														
X	,,	40 ,, 24-pounder —	U	Fifth.	50-gun frigate —	2	2505	4	5044	6	7549q	6	—	—	—	—
Y	,,	38 ,, 18 ,, —	V	,,	48 ,, —	—	—	5	5777	5	5777f	4	1	—	—	2
Z	,,	,, ,, large	W	,,	46 ,, —	7	7426	31	33354	38	40780h	30	8	—	—	12
A	,,	,, ,, small														
B	,,	36 ,, 18-pdr. large	X	,,	44 ,, —	—	1028	2	2069	3	3097i	—	3	—	—	1
C	,,	,, ,, small	Y	,,	42 ,, —	11	10196	26	24509	37	34705	37	—	—	—	12
D	,,	32 ,, 18 ,, —				—	—	—	—	—	—	—	—	—	—	—
E	,,	,, ,, 12 ,, large				—	—	—	—	—	—	—	—	—	—	—
F	,,	,, ,, 12 ,, small														
G	Sixth.	28 ,, — —														
K	,,	24-gun ship, quarter-decked														
L	,,	,, flush —	Z	Sixth.	32 ,, —	4	2189	—	—	4	2189	3	1	—	—	—
M	,,	22 ,, quarter-decked	A	,,	28 ,, —	—	—	—	—	—	—	—	—	—	—	—
N	,,	,, flush —	B	,,	26 ,, —	5	2210	5	2254	10	4464	10	—	—	—	7
O	,,	20 ,, quarter-decked														
P	Sloops.	18-gun ship-sloop, qr.-decked	C	,,	24 ,, —	5	2125	3	1276	8	3401	8	—	—	—	10
R	,,	,, flush —	D	Sloops.	22-gun ship-sloop, flush	—	539	—	—	1	539	—	1	—	—	—
S	,,	16 ,, quarter-decked	E	,,	,, quarter-decked	1	432	1	365	2	797	2	—	—	—	2
T	,,	,, flush —	F	,,	20 ,, —	9	4188	10	4708	19	8896	19	—	—	—	1
V	,,	18-gun brig-sloop —	G	,,	18 ,, —	2	798	2	801	4	1599	4	—	—	—	1
Y	,,	16 ,, —	H	,,	18-gun brig-sloop —	17	6504	45	11339	62	23893	62	—	—	—	9
a	,,	14 ,, —	I	,,	16 ,, —	2	652	1	294	3	946	1	2	—	—	7
b	,,	10 ,, —	K	,,	14 ,, —	1	222	3	718	4	970	3	1	—	—	3
c	Bombs	— — —	L	,,	10 ,, —	14	3321	14	3329	28	6650	28	—	—	—	6
d	Gun-brigs of 14 guns		M	Bombs	— —	—	—	6	2112	6	2112	6	—	—	—	—
f	Cutters,	12 ,, —	N	Gun-brigs of 12 guns	—	2	363	14	2554	16	2917	16	—	—	—	3
g	,,	14 ,, —	O	Cutters,	14 ,, —	4	1016	—	—	4	1016	4	—	—	—	1
i	,,	12 ,, —	P	,,	12 ,, —	2	448	—	—	2	448	2	—	—	—	1
k	,,	10 ,, —	Q	,,	10 ,, —	6	1039	1	197	7	1236	5	2	—	—	—
m	,,	8 ,, —	R	,,	4 ,, —	1	75	—	—	1	75	1	—	—	—	—
o	,,	4 ,, —														
		Cruisers — —				114	79323	263	274560	377	353883	343	34	—	—	124
q	Troop-ships	— — —	S	Troop-ships	—	1	1107	6	5842	7	6949	7	—	—	—	9
r	Storeships	— — —	T	Storeships	—	5	3669	6	4176	11	7845	10	1	—	—	3
w	Surveying-vessels	— —	V	Surveying-vessels	—	4	523	2	492	6	1015	4	—	—	—	—
x	Tenders	— — —	W	Tenders	—	—	—	4	320	4	320	4	—	—	—	—
a	Hospital, Prison, Receiving-ships, &c.	X	Hospital, Prison, Receiving-ships, &c.	—	—	—	—	—	—	—	—	—	1	1452	65
b	Royal Yachts	— — —	Y	Royal Yachts	—	—	—	—	—	—	—	—	6	1290	1
		Troop-ships, &c. — — —				10	5299	18	10830	28	16129	26	2	7	2742	80
		GRAND TOTAL — — —				124	84622	281	285390	405	370012	369	36	7	2742	204

VOL. VI

	Building, or Ordered to be Built.		Grand Total.		Built.				Purchased.		Converted from other Classes.		Ordered to be Built.		Total of Increase.		Wrecked, Foundered, &c.		Converted to other Classes.		Sold, or taken to Pieces.		Total of Decrease.	
				King's Yards.		Merchants' Yards.																		
	No.	Tons.	No.	Tons.	No.	Tons.	No.	Tons.	No.	Tons.	No.	Tons.	No.	Tons.	No.	Tons.	No.	Tons.	No.	Tons.	No.	Tons.	No.	Tons.
–	2	5218	7	18190	–	–	–	–	–	–	–	–	–	–	1	2457	–	–	2	4834	–	–	2	4834
–	2	4834	3	7110	–	–	–	–	–	–	3	7110	–	–	3	7110	–	–	1	2457	–	–	1	2457
–	–	–	2	4575	–	–	–	–	–	–	–	–	–	–	–	–	–	–	1	2404	–	–	1	2404
–	1	2404	2	4682	–	–	–	–	–	–	1	2404	–	–	1	2404	–	–	1	2276	–	–	1	2276
–	–	–	12	25098	–	–	–	–	–	–	1	2088d	–	–	1	2088	–	–	–	–	1	1955	1	1955
1	2	4510	6	13544	–	–	–	–	–	–	5	11289	1	2255	6	13544	–	–	–	–	–	–	–	–
–	2	4104	7	14575	–	–	–	–	–	–	–	–	–	–	–	–	–	–	6	13420	2	4352	8	17772
–	–	–	5	9699	–	–	–	–	–	–	5	9699	–	–	5	9699	–	–	–	–	–	–	–	–
1	–	–	3	5707	–	–	–	–	–	–	3	5707	–	–	3	5707	–	–	–	–	–	–	–	–
5	–	–	8	15116	–	–	–	–	–	–	1	1917	–	–	1	1917	–	–	5	9699	–	–	5	9699
–	–	–	8	14978	–	–	–	–	–	–	8	14978	–	–	8	14978	–	–	–	–	–	–	–	–
–	–	–	5	9234	–	–	–	–	–	–	–	–	–	–	–	–	–	–	15	28202	5	9456	20	37658
2	8	13942	73	127650	4	6975	–	–	–	–	–	–	–	–	–	–	–	–	2	3407	3	5254	5	8661
1	–	–	12	19660	–	–	–	–	–	–	–	–	–	–	–	–	–	–	6	9632	4	6555	10	16187
–	–	–	–	–	–	–	–	–	–	–	–	–	–	–	–	–	–	–	6	8157	7	9715	13	17872
10	17	35012	155	294635	4	6975	–	–	–	–	28	57649	1	2255	29	59904	–	–	45	84488	22	37287	67	121775
1	4	5880	8	11999	–	–	–	–	–	–	4	6119	4	5880	8	11999	–	–	–	–	–	–	–	–
–	–	–	2	3233	–	–	–	–	–	–	1	1617	–	–	1	1617	–	–	1	1256	1	1642	2	2898
2	–	–	2	2577	–	–	–	–	–	–	2	2577	–	–	2	2577	–	–	–	–	–	–	–	–
–	–	–	7	7865	–	–	–	–	–	–	–	–	–	–	–	–	–	–	1	1107	–	–	1	1107
–	–	–	–	–	–	–	–	–	–	–	–	–	–	–	–	–	–	6	8828	–	–	6	8828
–	–	–	6	7549	–	–	–	–	–	–	–	–	–	–	–	–	–	–	–	–	3	2661	3	2661
2	2	2314g	9	10387	–	–	–	–	–	–	6	6913	–	–	6	6913	–	–	–	–	2	2741	2	2741
7	12	12939	62	66534	–	–	2	2140	–	–	5	5046	6	6457	11	11503	–	–	6	6913	10	11016	16	17929
1	–	–	4	4112	–	–	–	–	–	–	–	–	–	–	–	–	–	–	5	5046	–	–	5	5046
1	–	–	49	45862	–	–	–	–	–	–	4	3593	–	–	4	3593	–	–	–	–	2	2103	2	2103
–	–	–	–	–	–	–	–	–	–	–	–	–	–	–	–	1	884	1	926	2	1901	4	3711
–	–	–	–	–	–	–	–	–	–	–	–	–	–	–	–	–	–	3	2757	3	2668	6	5425
–	–	–	–	–	–	–	–	–	–	–	–	–	–	–	–	–	–	2	1812	1	920	3	2732
–	–	–	–	–	–	–	–	–	–	–	–	–	–	–	–	–	–	1	856	–	–	1	856
–	–	–	–	–	–	–	–	–	–	–	–	–	–	–	–	–	–	3	2025	3	2085	6	4110
–	–	–	–	–	–	–	–	–	–	–	–	–	–	–	–	–	–	1	598	–	–	1	598
–	–	–	–	–	–	–	–	–	–	2	1122c	–	–	2	1122	1	522	2	1122	1	519	3	1641
–	–	–	5	2714	–	–	–	–	–	–	–	–	–	–	–	–	–	–	–	–	1	812	1	812
–	–	–	–	–	–	–	–	–	–	–	–	–	–	–	–	–	–	4	2162	1	522	5	2684
–	1	503	1	503	–	–	–	–	–	–	–	–	–	–	–	–	–	–	–	539	–	–	1	539
–	1	452	18	7949	–	–	–	–	–	–	18	7949	1	503	18	7949	–	–	10	4494	–	–	10	4494
–	–	–	18	7671	–	–	–	–	–	–	1	422	–	–	1	422	–	–	20	9407	–	–	20	9407
–	–	–	1	539	–	–	–	–	–	–	1	539	–	–	1	539	–	–	10	4318	6	2546	16	6864
–	–	–	4	1595	–	–	–	–	–	–	–	–	–	–	–	–	–	–	6	2420	1	419	7	2839
1	–	–	20	9407	–	–	1	511	–	–	2	863	–	–	2	863	–	–	2	787	4	1533	6	2320
–	–	–	5	1998	–	–	–	–	–	–	20	9407	–	–	20	9407	–	–	–	–	–	–	–	–
–	–	–	71	27350	–	–	–	–	–	–	5	1998	–	–	5	1998	–	–	1	384	2	707	3	1091
3	–	–	10	3081	–	–	–	–	–	–	–	–	–	–	–	–	–	–	–	–	8	1089	3	1089
1	–	–	7	1732	–	–	–	–	–	–	–	–	–	–	–	–	–	–	1	277	8	2417	9	2694
–	–	–	31	7362	–	–	–	–	–	–	–	–	–	–	–	–	–	–	–	–	4	968	4	968
–	–	–	7	2449	–	–	–	–	–	–	–	–	–	–	–	–	–	–	6	2196	–	–	6	2196
–	–	–	–	–	–	–	–	–	–	–	–	–	–	–	–	–	–	–	2	599	2	399	2	399
–	–	–	19	3429	–	–	–	–	–	–	–	–	–	–	–	–	–	–	7	1234	12	2172	19	3406
–	–	–	5	1340	–	–	–	–	–	–	–	–	–	–	–	–	1	225	–	–	1	152	2	377
1	–	–	3	669	–	–	–	–	–	–	–	–	–	–	–	–	–	–	–	–	2	366	2	366
–	–	–	8	1386	–	–	–	–	–	–	–	–	–	–	–	–	–	–	–	–	4	483	4	483
–	–	–	–	–	–	–	–	–	–	–	–	–	–	–	–	–	–	–	–	1	104	1	104
–	–	–	1	75	–	–	–	–	–	–	–	–	–	–	–	–	–	–	–	–	2	151	2	151
31	37	57100	538	536002	4	6975	3	2651	–	–	99	105814	12	15095	111	120909	3	1631	135	141594	113	84219	251	227444
2	–	–	16	15545	–	–	–	–	–	–	2	2495	–	–	2	2495	–	–	6	5716	13	11088	19	16804
–	–	–	14	10081	–	–	–	–	–	–	1	178	–	–	1	178	–	–	–	–	3	903	3	903
–	–	–	6	1015	–	–	1	83	–	–	2	358	1	83	3	441	–	–	–	–	–	–	–	–
–	–	–	6	646	4	320	–	–	–	–	–	–	4	320	4	320	–	–	1	169	–	–	1	169
24	–	–	66	69079	–	–	–	–	–	–	38	40553	–	–	38	40553	–	–	1	2088	6	8194	7	10282
–	1	282	8	1790	–	–	–	–	1	218	–	–	–	–	–	218	–	–	–	–	1	164	1	164
26	1	282	116	98156	4	320	1	83	1	218	43	43584	5	403	49	44205	–	–	7	7804	24	20518	31	28322
57	38	57382	654	634158	8	7295	4	2734	1	218	142	149398	17	15498	160	165114	3	1631	142	149398	137	104737	282	255766

An ABSTRACT of the Ships and Vessels belonging to the British Navy at the commencement of the Year

Letters of Reference.	RATE.	CLASS.	For Sea-service.							For Harbour-service.				
			In Commission.		In Ordinary.		TOTAL.		No. British Built.	No. Foreign Built.	In Commission.		In Ordinary.		British
			No.	Tons.	No.	Tons.	No.	Tons.			No.	Tons.	No.	Tons.	
	Three-deckers. First.	120-gun ship	–	–	5	12972	5	12972	5	–	–	–	–	–	
A		112 ,,	–	–	2	4808	2	4808	2	–	–	–	–	–	
B	,,	110 ,,	–	–	1	2276	1	2276	1	–	–	–	–	–	
C	,,	108 ,,	–	–	2	4575	2	4575	2	–	–	–	–	–	
D	,,	106 ,,	1	2289	1	2286	2	4575	2	–	–	–	–	–	
E	,,	104 ,,	1	2278	–	–	1	2278	1	–	–	–	–	–	
F			–	–	6	12788	6	12788	6	–	–	–	6	12310	
	Two-deckers. Second.	84 ,,	1	2281	2	4522	3	6803	–	3	–	–	1	2231	
G	,,	80 ,,	1	2082	3	6386	4	8468	3	1	–	–	1	2003	
H	Third.	78 ,,	1	1927	4	7772	5	9699	4	1	–	–	–	–	
I	,,	,, ,,	18 ,,	1	1901	2	3806	3	5707	2	1	–	–	–
K	,,	76 ,,	24 ,,	3	5711	2	3809	5	9520	5	–	–	–	2	3695
L	,,	74 ,,	18 ,,	–	–	3	5646	3	5646	1	2	–	–	3	5574
M	,,	,, ,,	large	–	–	4	7374	4	7374	4	–	–	–	–	–
N	,,	,, ,,	middl.	3	5229	49	80814	52	91043	52	–	–	–	13	22667
O	,,	,, ,,	small	1	1667	3	4979	4	6646	4	–	–	–	6	9810
P			Line	13	25365	87	165238	100	190603	92	8	–	–	32	58290
Q	Fourth.	60 ,,	1	1572	2	3014	3	4586	3	–	–	–	1	1533	
R	,,	58 ,,	flush, rasée	–	–	2	3233	2	3233	2	–	–	–	–	–
S	,,	,, ,,	,, regular	–	–	1	1321	1	1321	1	–	–	–	1	1256
T			quarter-decked	1	1199	2	2400	3	3599	3	–	–	–	2	2166	
	One-deckers.	50-gun frigate	3	3765	3	3784	6	7549	6	–	–	–	–	–	
U	Fifth.	48 ,,	–	–	5	5777	5	5777	4	1	–	–	1	1135	
V	,,	46 ,,	3	3111	34	36557	37	39668	31	6	–	–	9	9659	
W	,,	44 ,,	2	2057	1	1040	3	3097	–	3	–	–	1	1015	
X	,,	42 ,,	7	6407	28	26376	35	32783	35	–	–	–	7	6491	
Y	Sixth.	32 ,,	2	1122	–	–	2	1122	1	1	–	–	1	538	
Z	,,	28 ,,	–	–	–	–	–	–	–	–	–	–	–	–	
A	,,	26 ,,	7	3113	4	1803	11	4916	11	–	–	–	6	2610	
B	,,	24 ,,	6	2552	2	849	8	3401	8	–	–	–	7	2983	
C	Sloops.	22-gun ship-sloop, flush	1	539	–	–	1	559	–	1	–	–	–	–	
D	,,	,, ,, quarter-decked	1	432	1	365	2	797	2	–	–	–	1	431	
E	,,	20 ,,	8	3728	10	4708	18	8436	18	–	–	–	1	511	
F	,,	18 ,,	1	399	3	1200	4	1599	4	–	–	–	–	–	
G	,,	18-gun brig-sloop	17	6354	45	17339	62	23693	62	–	–	–	5	1919	
H	,,	16 ,,	1	368	1	294	2	662	–	2	–	–	4	1282	
I	,,	14 ,,	1	252	3	718	4	970	3	1	–	–	2	511	
K	,,	10 ,,	12	2845	12	2854	24	5699	24	–	–	–	4	952	
L	Bombs,		–	–	6	2112	6	2112	6	–	–	–	1	337	
M	Gun-brigs, of 12 guns		2	363	14	2554	16	2917	16	–	–	–	1	183	
N	Cutters, &c.	14 ,,	3	787	–	–	3	787	–	3	–	–	1	229	
O	,,	12 ,,	2	448	–	–	2	448	2	–	–	–	–	–	
P	,,	10 ,,	7	1207	–	–	7	1207	6	1	–	–	–	–	
Q	,,	4 ,,	1	75	–	–	1	75	1	–	–	–	–	–	
		Cruisers	102	68260	266	283536	368	351796	339	29	–	–	88	94031	65
S	Troop-ships		1	1107	6	5842	7	6949	6	1	–	–	1	1032	
T	Storeships		6	4420	5	4025	11	8445	10	1	–	–	2	1173	
V	Surveying-vessels		5	894	1	121	6	1015	6	–	–	–	–	–	
W	Tenders		–	–	4	320	4	320	4	–	–	–	2	326	
X	Hospital, Prison, Receiving-ships, &c.		–	–	–	–	–	–	–	–	2	1756	57	59221	37
Y	Royal Yachts		–	–	–	–	–	–	–	–	5	1224	2	284	7
		Troop-ships, &c.	12	6421	16	10308	28	16729	26	2	7	2980	64	62036	49
		GRAND TOTAL	114	74681	282	293844	396	368525	365	31	7	2980	152	156067	114

VOL. VI.

			Built.				Increase and Decrease in the Classes since the date of the last Year's Abstract.														
ing, or ered Built.	Grand Total.		King's Yards.		Merchants' Yards.		Purchased.		Converted from other Classes.		Ordered to be Built.		Total of Increase.		Wrecked, Foundered, &c.		Converted to other Classes.		Sold, or taken to Pieces, &c.		Total of Decrease.	
Tons.	No.	Tons.	No.	Tons.	No.	Tons.	No.	Tons.	No.	Tons.	No.	Tons.	No.	Tons.	No.	Tons.	No.	Tons.	No.	Tons.	No.	Tons.
5218	7	18190																				
— —	2	4808																				
4834	3	7110																				
— —	2	4575																				
2404	2	4682																				
— —	12	25098																				
13530a	10	22564	—	—	—	—	—	—	—	—	4	9020	4	9020								
6196	8	16667	—	—	—	—	—	—	—	—	1	2092	1	2092								
— —	5	9699																				
— —	3	5707															1	1901	1	1901
— —	7	13215	—	—	—	—	—	—	—	—	—	—	—	—	—	—	—	—	2	3758	2	3758
— —	6	11220	—	—	—	—	—	—	—	—	—	—	—	—	—	—	—	—	1	1860	1	1860
— —	4	7374	—	—	—	—	—	—	—	—	—	—	—	—	—	—	—	—	2	3522	2	3522
10427	71	124137	2	3515	—	—	—	—	—	—	—	—	—	—	—	—	—	—	2	3204	2	3204
— —	10	16436	—	—	—	—	—	—	—	—	—	—	—	—								
42609	152	291502	2	3515	—	—	—	—	—	—	5	11112	5	11112	—	—	—	—	8	14245	8	14245
7348b	9	13467	—	—	—	—	—	—	—	—	1	1468	1	1468								
— —	2	3233																				
— —	2	2577																				
— —	5	5765	—	—	—	—	—	—	—	—	—	—	—	—	—	—	1	1048	1	1052	2	2100
— —	6	7549																	1	1161	1	1161
6962	12	13874	—	—	—	—	—	—	—	—	1	4648c	4	4648	—	—	—	—	6	6403	7	7504
29946	74	79273	2	2170	1	1066	—	—	—	—	29	20243d	19	20243	1	1101	—	—				
— —	4	4112																	7	6588	7	6588
— —	42	39274	—	—	—	—	—	—	—	—	—	—	—	—	—	—	—	—	2	1054	2	1054
503	3	1660																				
— —	1	503																	1	423	1	423
— —	17	7526	—	—	1	452	—	—	—	—	—	—	—	—	—	—	—	—	3	1287	3	1287
— —	15	6344																				
— —	1	539																	1	367	1	367
— —	3	1228													1	460	—	—	—	—	1	460
— —	19	8947	—	—	—	—	—	—	—	—	—	—	—	—	—	—	—	—	1	399	1	399
— —	4	1599																	4	1538	4	1538
— —	67	25812	—	—	—	—	—	—	—	—	—	—	—	—	1	284	—	—	3	853	4	1137
— —	6	1944																	1	251	1	251
2833	6	1481									12	2833e	12	2833	3	711	—	—	—	—	3	711
— —	40	9484																				
— —	7	2449																	2	329	2	329
— —	17	3100	—	—	—	—	—	—	—	—	—	—	—	—	—	—	—	—	1	324	1	324
— —	4	1016																	1	221	1	221
— —	2	448	—	—	—	—	—	—	—	—	1	151	1	151	—	—	—	—	1	150	2	330
— —	7	1207	1	151																		
— —	1	75																				
90201	528	536028	5	5836	2	1518	—	—	—	—	42	40455	42	40455	7	2736	1	1048	44	36645	52	40429
— —	8	7981																	8	7564	8	7564
— —	13	9618	—	—	—	—	—	—	—	—	—	—	—	—	—	—	—	—	1	463	1	463
— —	6	1015																				
— —	6	646	—	—	—	—	—	—	1	1048	—	—	1	1048	—	—	—	—	8	9150	8	1150
— —	59	60977																				
282	8	1790																				
282	100	82027	—	—	—	—	—	—	1	1048	—	—	1	1048	—	—	—	—	17	17177	17	17177
90483	628	618055	5	5836	2	1518	—	—	1	1048	42	40455	43	41503	7	2736	1	1048	61	53822	69	57606

2 H

An ABSTRACT of the Ships and Vessels belonging to the British Navy at the commencement of the

Letters of Reference.	RATE.	CLASS.	For Sea-service.					No.		For Harbour-ser			
			In Commission.		In Ordinary.		TOTAL.		British Built.	Foreign Built.	In Commission.		In Ordinar	
			No.	Tons.	No.	Tons.	No.	Tons.			No.	Tons.	No.	Tons
A	Three-deckers. First.	120-gun ship	–	–	5	12972	5	12972	5	–	–	–	–	–
B	,,	112 ,,	–	–	2	4808	2	4808	2	–	–	–	–	–
C	,,	110 ,,	–	–	1	2276	1	2276	1	–	–	–	–	–
D	,,	108 ,,	1	2289	1	2286	2	4575	2	–	–	–	–	–
E	,,	106 ,,	1	2278	–	–	1	2278	1	–	–	–	–	–
F	,,	104 ,,	–	–	6	12788	6	12788	6	–	–	–	6	123
G	Two-deckers. Second.	84 ,,	–	–	3	6803	3	6803	–	3	–	–	–	–
H	,,	80 ,,	1	2082	4	8442	5	10524	4	1	–	–	1	200
I	Third.	78 ,, 24-pounder	1	1927	4	7772	5	9699	4	1	–	–	–	–
K	,,	18 ,,	1	1907	2	3800	3	5707	2	1	–	–	–	–
L	,,	76 ,, 24 ,,	3	5711	2	3809	5	9520	5	–	–	–	2	36
M	,,	,, 18 ,,	–	–	3	5646	3	5646	1	2	–	–	3	55
N	,,	74 ,, – large	1	1874	3	5500	4	7374	4	–	–	–	–	–
O	,,	,, ,, middl.	3	3229	51	91247	54	94476	54	–	–	–	11	191
P	,,	,, ,, small	1	1677	3	4969	4	6646	4	–	–	–	5	81
		Line	13	22974	90	173118	103	196092	95	8	–	–	28	508
Q	Fourth.	60 ,,	2	3128	1	1458	3	4586	3	–	–	–	–	–
R	,,	58 ,,	–	–	2	3233	2	3233	2	–	–	–	–	–
S	,,	,, flush, rasée	–	–	1	1321	1	1321	1	–	–	–	1	12
T	,,	,, regular quarter-decked	1	1199	2	2400	3	3599	3	–	–	–	2	21
U	One-deckers. Fifth.	50-gun frigate	5	6272	1	1277	6	7549	6	–	–	–	–	–
V	,,	48 ,,	1	1148	4	4629	5	5777	4	1	–	–	1	11
W	,,	46 ,,	4	4179	33	35489	37	39668	31	6	–	–	7	74
X	,,	44 ,,	1	1029	1	1040	2	2069	–	2	–	–	2	20
Y	,,	42 ,,	9	8390	23	21573	32	29963	32	–	–	–	6	55
Z	Sixth.	32 ,,	2	1122	–	–	2	1122	1	1	–	–	–	–
A	,,	28 ,,	–	–	–	–	–	–	–	–	–	–	6	30
B	,,	26 ,,	8	3603	4	1323	12	4926	12	–	–	–	4	17
C	,,	24 ,,	5	2124	3	1277	8	3401	8	–	–	–	1	5
D	Sloops.	22-gun ship-sloop, flush	–	–	1	365	1	365	1	–	–	–	1	4
E	,,	,, ,, quarter-decked	1	3326	7	3326	17	7979	17	–	–	–	1	5
F	,,	20 ,,	10	4653	7	3326	17	7979	17	–	–	–	–	–
G	,,	18 ,,	2	798	2	801	4	1599	4	–	–	–	–	–
H	,,	18-gun brig-sloop	24	9274	36	13846	60	23120	60	–	–	–	6	230
I	,,	16 ,,	–	–	1	294	1	294	–	1	–	–	2	6
K	,,	14 ,,	1	253	3	717	4	970	3	1	–	–	1	9
L	,,	10 ,,	10	2367	11	2620	21	4987	21	–	–	–	1	9
M	Bombs	–	–	–	6	2112	6	2112	6	–	–	–	1	33
N	Gun-brigs, of 12 guns		2	363	14	2554	16	2917	16	–	–	–	1	18
O	Cutters, &c.	14 ,,	2	504	–	–	2	504	–	2	–	–	–	–
P	,,	12 ,,	1	224	1	224	2	448	–	2	–	–	–	–
Q	,,	10 ,,	6	1029	1	178	7	1207	6	1	–	–	–	–
R	,,	4 ,,	–	–	–	–	–	–	–	–	–	–	–	–
		Cruisers	110	74998	247	274810	357	349808	332	25	–	–	74	8119
S	Troop-ships		–	–	7	6949	7	6949	6	1	–	–	1	103
T	Storeships		6	4264	4	2777	10	7041	10	–	–	–	3	257
V	Surveying-vessels		5	811	1	204	6	1015	6	–	–	–	–	–
W	Tenders		–	–	4	320	4	320	4	–	–	–	2	33
X	Hospital, Prison, Receiving-ships, &c.		–	–	–	–	–	–	–	2	1990	58	6123	
Y	Royal Yachts		–	–	–	–	–	–	–	–	4	1039	1	6
		Troop-ships, &c	11	5075	16	10250	27	15325	26	1	6	3029	65	6523
		GRAND TOTAL	121	80073	263	285060	384	365133	358	26	6	3029	139	14642

VOL. VI.

27.

Increase and Decrease in the Classes since the date of the last Year's Abstract.

| Building, or Ordered to be Built. || Grand Total. || Built. |||| Purchased. || Converted from other Classes. || Ordered to be Built. || Total of Increase. || Wrecked, Foundered, &c. || Converted to other Classes. || Sold, or taken to Pieces, &c. || Total of Decrease. ||
| | | | | King's Yards. || Merchants' Yards. |||||||||||||||
No.	Tons.	No.	Tons.	No.	Tons.	No.	Tons.	No.	Tons.	No.	Tons.	No.	Tons.	No.	Tons.	No.	Tons.	No.	Tons.	No.	Tons.	No.	Tons.
2	5218	7	18190	–	–	–	–	–	–	–	–	–	–	–	–	–	–	–	–	–	–	–	–
–	–	2	4808																				
2	4834	3	7110																				
–	–	2	4575																				
1	2404	2	4682																				
–	–	12	25098																				
6	13530	9	20333	1	2056	–	–	–	–	–	–	–	–	–	–	1	2231	–	–	1	2231
2	4140	8	16667																				
–	–	5	9699																				
–	–	3	5707																				
–	–	7	13915																				
–	–	6	11220																				
–	–	4	7374																				
4	6994	69	120607	1	1718	1	1715	–	–	–	–	–	–	–	–	1	1772	1	1758	2	3530
–	–	9	14825	–	–	–	–	–	–	–	–	–	–	–	–	–	–	1	1631	1	1631
17	37120	148	284110	2	3774	1	1715	–	–	–	–	–	–	–	–	2	4003	2	3389	4	7392
7	10349	10	14935	–	–	–	–	–	–	–	–	2	3001	2	3001	–	–	1	1533	1	1533
–	–	2	3233																				
–	–	2	2577																				
–	–	5	5765																				
–	–	6	7549																				
6	6962	12	13874																				
28	29946	72	77107	–	–	–	–	–	–	–	–	–	–	–	–	2	2166	2	2166
–	–	4	4112																				
–	–	38	35491	–	–	–	–	–	–	–	–	–	–	–	–	–	–	4	3783	4	3783
–	–	2	1122	–	–	–	–	–	–	–	–	–	–	–	–	1	538	–	–	1	538
8	4008	8	4008	–	–	–	–	–	–	7	3505a	7	3505	–	–	–	–	–	–	–	–
–	–	18	7983	–	–	–	–	1	457	–	–	1	457								
–	–	12	5102	–	–	–	–	–	–	–	–	–	–	–	–	–	–	3	1282	3	1282
–	–	1	539															1	431	1	431
–	–	2	797	–	–	–	–	–	–	–	–	–	–	1	457	–	–	1	457
–	–	18	8490																				
–	–	4	1599															1	384	1	384
–	–	66	25428	–	–	–	–	–	–	–	–	–	–	–	–	–	–	3	998	3	993
–	–	3	951	–	–	–	–	–	–	–	–	–	–	–	–	–	–	2	511	2	511
–	–	4	970	–	–	–	–	–	–	14	3291b	14	3291	–	–	–	–	3	715	3	715
26	6124	51	12060																				
–	–	7	2449																				
–	–	17	3100															2	512	2	512
–	–	2	504																				
–	–	7	1207															1	75	1	75
92	94509	523	525510	2	3774	1	1715	–	–	1	457	23	9797	24	10254	–	–	4	4598	25	15774	29	20772
–	–	8	7981																				
–	–	13	9618																				
–	–	6	1015																				
–	–	60	63222	–	–	–	–	3	4541	–	–	3	4541	–	–	–	–	2	2296	2	2296
1	282	6	1397	–	–	–	–	–	–	–	–	–	–	–	–	–	–	2	403	2	403
1	282	99	83869	–	–	–	–	3	4541	–	–	3	4541	–	–	–	–	4	2699	4	2699
93	94791	622	609379	2	3774	1	1715	–	–	4	4998	23	9797	27	14795	–	–	4	4998	29	18473	33	23471

An ABSTRACT of the Ships and Vessels belonging to the British Navy at the commencement of the Year

Letters of Reference.	RATE.	CLASS.	For Sea-service.					No.		For Harbour-service.			
			In Commission.		In Ordinary.		TOTAL.		British Built.	Foreign Built.	In Commission.		In Ordinary.	
			No.	Tons.	No.	Tons.	No.	Tons.			No.	Tons.	No.	Tons.
A	Three-deckers. First.	120-gun ship	–	–	5	12972	5	12972	5	–	–	–	–	–
B	,,	112 ,,	–	–	2	4808	2	4808	2	–	–	–	–	–
C	,,	110 ,,	–	–	–	–	–	–	–	–	–	–	–	–
D	,,	108 ,,	1	2289	1	2286	2	4575	2	–	–	–	–	–
E	,,	106 ,,	1	2278	–	–	1	2278	1	–	–	–	–	–
F	,,	104 ,,	–	–	6	12788	6	12788	6	–	–	–	5	10363
G	Two-deckers. Second.	84 ,,	–	–	3	6803	3	6803	–	3	–	–	–	–
H	,,	80 ,,	1	2082	5	10618	6	12700	5	1	–	–	1	2003
I	Third.	78 ,, 24-pounder	1	1927	4	7772	5	9699	4	1	–	–	–	–
K	,,	18 ,,	1	1907	2	3800	3	5707	2	1	–	–	–	–
L	,,	76 ,, 24 ,,	3	5711	2	3809	5	9520	5	–	–	–	1	1853
M	,,	18 ,,	–	–	3	5646	3	5646	1	2	–	–	–	–
N	,,	74 ,, large	–	–	2	5500	4	7374	4	–	–	–	–	–
O	,,	,, ,, middl.	4	7016	52	91032	56	98048	56	–	–	–	10	17394
P	,,	,, ,, small	1	1677	3	4969	4	6646	4	–	–	–	5	8179
		Line	14	26761	91	172803	105	199564	97	8	–	–	22	39792
Q	Fourth.	60 ,,	2	3128	1	1458	3	4586	3	–	–	–	–	–
R	,,	58 ,, flush, rasée	–	–	2	3233	2	3233	2	–	–	–	–	–
S	,,	,, ,, ,, regular	–	–	1	1321	1	1221	1	–	–	–	1	1256
T	,,	,, ,, quarter-decked	1	1199	2	2400	3	3599	3	–	–	–	1	1052
U	One-deckers.	50-gun frigate	4	5021	1	1277	5	6298	5	–	–	–	–	–
V	Fifth.	48 ,,	1	1148	5	5781	6	6929	5	1	–	–	–	–
W	,,	46 ,,	5	5237	35	37677	40	42914	34	6	–	–	3	3228
X	,,	44 ,,	1	1029	1	1040	2	2069	–	2	–	–	1	1015
Y	,,	42 ,,	7	6533	25	23430	32	29963	32	–	–	–	3	2695
Z	,,	32 ,,	–	–	2	1122	2	1122	1	1	–	–	–	–
A	Sixth.	28 ,,	–	–	–	–	–	–	–	–	–	–	–	–
B	,,	26 ,,	9	4026	2	900	11	4926	11	–	–	–	4	1761
C	,,	24 ,,	5	2124	3	1277	8	3401	8	–	–	–	1	422
D	Sloops.	22-gun ship-sloop, flush	–	–	–	–	–	–	–	–	–	–	–	–
E	,,	,, ,, ,, quarter-decked	1	365	–	–	1	365	1	–	–	–	1	432
F	,,	20 ,,	11	5115	5	2407	16	7522	16	–	–	–	–	–
G	,,	18 ,,	2	798	2	801	4	1599	4	–	–	–	–	–
H	,,	18-gun brig-sloop	21	8097	39	15023	60	23120	60	–	–	–	–	–
I	,,	16 ,,	–	–	1	294	1	294	–	1	–	–	–	–
K	,,	14 ,,	1	253	3	717	4	970	3	1	–	–	–	–
L	,,	10 ,,	13	3081	7	1667	20	4748	20	–	–	–	–	–
M	Bombs	–	–	–	5	1737	5	1737	5	–	–	–	1	337
N	Gun-brigs of 12 guns	–	6	1099	8	1454	14	2553	14	–	–	–	1	183
O	Cutters, &c.	14 ,,	2	504	–	–	2	504	–	2	–	–	–	–
P	,,	12 ,,	1	224	1	224	2	448	–	2	–	–	–	–
Q	,,	10 ,,	6	1129	1	78	7	1207	6	1	–	–	–	–
		Cruisers	113	76871	243	278121	356	354992	331	25	–	–	39	52173
S	Troop-ships	–	1	692	6	6257	7	6949	6	1	–	–	1	1032
T	Storeships	–	5	3812	5	3229	10	7041	10	–	–	–	2	1773
U	Discovery-ships	–	2	557	–	–	2	557	2	–	–	–	–	–
V	Surveying-vessels	–	6	1114	1	83	7	1197	7	–	–	–	–	–
W	Tenders	–	–	–	4	320	4	320	4	–	–	–	2	326
X	Hospital, Prison, Receiving-ships, &c.	–	–	–	–	–	–	–	–	–	3	2528	58	61930
Y	Royal Yachts	–	–	–	–	–	–	–	–	–	4	1039	1	66
		Troop-ships, &c.	14	6175	16	9889	30	16064	29	1	7	3567	64	65127
	GRAND TOTAL		127	83046	259	288010	386	371056	360	26	7	3567	103	117300

VOL. VI.

28.

Increase and Decrease in the Classes since the date of the last Year's Abstract.

ding, or tered to Built.	GRAND TOTAL.		Built.				Purchased.		Converted from other Classes.		Ordered to be Built.		TOTAL of Increase.		Wrecked, Foundered, &c.		Converted to other Classes.		Sold, or taken to Pieces.		TOTAL of Decrease.	
			King's Yards.		Merchants' Yards.																	
Tons.	No.	Tons.	No.	Tons.	No.	Tons	No.	Tons.	No.	Tons.	No.	Tons.	No.	Tons.	No.	Tons.	No.	Tons.	No.	Tons.	No.	Tons.
10422	9	23394	–	–	–	–	–	–	–	–	2	5204a	2	5204								
– –	2	4808																				
4834	2	4834															1	2276	–	–	1	2276
– –	2	4575																				
2404	2	4682																				
– –	11	23151	–	–	–	–	–	–	–	–	–	–	–	–	–	–	–	–	1	1947	1	1947
20343	12	27146	–	–	–	–	–	–	–	–	3	6813	3	6813								
6177	10	20980	–	–	–	–	–	–	1	2276b	1	2037	2	4313								
– –	5	9699																				
– –	3	5707																				
– –	6	11373																	1	1842	1	1842
– –	3	5646	–	–	–	–	–	–	–	–	–	–	–	–	–	–	–	–	3	5574	3	5574
– –	4	7374																				
5285	69	120627	1	1709	–	–	1	1763c	–	–	–	–	1	1763	–	–	1	1743	–	–	1	1743
– –	9	14825																				
49465	149	288821	1	1709	–	–	1	1763	1	2276	6	14054	8	18093	–	–	2	4019	5	9363	7	13382
10349	10	14935																				
– –	2	3233																				
– –	2	2577																				
– –	4	4651	–	–	–	–	–	–	–	–	–	–	–	–	1	1114	–	–	1	1114
– –	5	6298	–	–	–	–	–	–	–	–	–	–	–	–	–	–	–	–	1	1251	1	1251
8134	13	15063	–	–	1	1152	–	–	–	–	2	2324	2	2324	–	–	–	–	1	1135	1	1135
26700	68	72842	3	3246	–	–	–	–	–	–	–	–	–	–	–	–	–	–	4	4265	4	4265
– –	3	3084	–	–	–	–	–	–	–	–	–	–	–	–	–	–	–	–	1	1028	1	1028
– –	35	32658	–	–	–	–	–	–	–	–	–	–	–	–	–	–	–	–	3	2833	3	2833
– –	2	1122																				
9028	18	9028	–	–	–	–	–	–	–	–	10	5020	10	5020								
– –	15	6987	–	–	–	–	–	–	–	–	–	–	–	–	–	–	–	–	3	1296	3	1296
– –	9	3823	–	–	–	–	–	–	–	–	–	–	–	–	–	–	–	–	3	1279	3	1279
– –	2	797																	1	539	1	539
– –	16	7522	–	–	–	–	–	–	–	–	–	–	–	–	1	457	–	–	1	511	2	968
398	5	1997	–	–	–	–	–	–	–	–	1	398	1	398								
– –	60	23120	–	–	–	–	–	–	–	–	–	–	–	–	–	–	–	–	6	2308	6	2308
– –	1	294	–	–	–	–	–	–	–	–	–	–	–	–	–	–	–	–	2	657	2	657
– –	4	970																				
6124	46	10872	–	–	–	–	–	–	–	–	–	–	–	–	–	–	–	–	5	1188	5	1188
2604	13	4678	–	–	–	–	–	–	–	–	7	2604	7	2604	–	–	1	375	–	–	1	375
– –	15	2736	–	–	–	–	–	–	–	–	–	–	–	–	–	–	2	364	–	–	2	364
– –	2	504																				
– –	2	448																				
320	9	1527	–	–	–	–	–	–	–	–	2	320	2	320								
113122	510	520287	4	4955	1	1152	1	1763	1	2276	28	24720	30	28759	1	457	6	5872	36	27653	43	33982
– –	8	7981																				
– –	12	8814	–	–	–	–	–	–	–	–	–	–	–	–	–	–	–	–	1	804	1	804
– –	2	557	–	–	–	–	–	–	2	557	–	–	2	557								
– –	7	1197	–	–	–	–	–	–	1	182	–	–	1	182								
– –	6	646																				
– –	61	64458	–	–	–	–	–	–	2	2857	–	–	2	2857	–	–	–	–	1	1621	1	1621
482	7	1587	–	–	–	–	–	–	– –	– –	1	200	1	200								
482	103	85240	–	–	–	–	–	–	5	3596	1	200	6	3796	–	–	–	–	2	2425	2	2425
113604	613	605527	4	4955	1	1152	1	1763	6	5872	29	24920	36	32555	1	457	6	5872	38	30078	45	36407

NOTES TO ANNUAL ABSTRACTS.

NOTES TO ABSTRACT No. 22.

(*a*) The Goliath, Majestic, and Saturn, three of the small-class 74s cut down, fore-and-aft, to the clamps of the quarter-deck and forecastle.

(*b*) The Leander and Newcastle, built of pitch-pine.

(*c*) The Akbar, late Cornwallis; had been a teak-built Indiaman, purchased in 1801.

(*d*) Ordered to be built of teak; the Seringapatam at Bombay, and the Tigris to be framed there and brought to England by the former.

(*f*) Number of hired vessels about 47.

NOTES TO ABSTRACT No. 23.

(*a*) The Nelson; began building at Woolwich in December, 1809, launched July 4, 1814. Except that the area of the line of flotation and the depth of hold in the Nelson were greater, her draught was similar to that of the Caledonia.

Principal dimensions of the Nelson.

		Ft.	In.
Length on the range of the first or lower gun-deck, from the rabbet of the stem to the rabbet of the stern-post		205	$0\frac{3}{4}$
Breadth extreme		53	8
Depth of hold		24	0
Burden in tons $2617\frac{4}{94}$			
Mainmast,	length	123	9
	diameter	3	5
Main-yard,	length	109	3
	diameter	2	2
Bowsprit,	length	75	1
	diameter	3	$C\frac{7}{8}$

It here appears, that the Nelson's depth of hold is 10 inches greater than the Caledonia's, and that the former's masts and yards, wholly on account of the alteration made in her hull, are considerably larger. The mainmast and yard of the San-Josef, a late Spanish three-decker of 2457 tons, were of the same dimensions as those of the Nelson; but the former's bowsprit was 2 feet 11 inches longer and two inches one-eighth thicker. The mainmast of the Commerce-de-Marseilles, the celebrated French three-decker brought from Toulon in 1793, was only one inch longer, and a quarter of an inch stouter, than the Nelson's; but the former's main-yard was as much as eight feet one inch longer, and two inches and a half stouter, than that of the latter.

The Nelson not having yet been at sea, her qualifications as a sailer and sea-boat, although the highest expectations are justly entertained of them, cannot at present be stated.

(b) The hired vessels appear to have been all discharged.

NOTES TO ABSTRACT No. 24.

(a) The Howe and St. Vincent; of a similar construction to the Nelson. The first, of 2619$\frac{35}{94}$ tons, began building at Chatham in June, 1808, and was launched March 28, 1815; the second, of 2612$\frac{28}{94}$ tons, began building at Plymouth in May, 1810, and was launched March 11, 1815. For the principal dimensions of these ships, and some account of their masts and yards, see the preceding paragraph.

(b) One of these was the Isis, first built as a quarter-decked 50, of 1190 tons, draught-measurement, from the reduced lines of the late Danish 80-gun ship Christian VII.; as were also the Salisbury, the single ship, of 1199 tons, in the first "Built" column of class T in No. 23 Abstract; and the Romney, the single ship, of 1227 tons, in the same column and class of the present Abstract. After the Isis had been constructed, it was thought advisable to cut her in two, and add an additional port and space to her length; and also, to take away her poop, forecastle, and quarter-deck, or at least as much of the latter as reached from forward to about a beam afore the mizenmast. This made the Isis a flush two-decker, with a short quarter-deck, or large roundhouse, merely intended as a roof to the captain's apartments, and increased her measurement to 1321 tons. The number of guns she was to mount, in her old and in her new state, was the same, 58; but the alteration in her construction gave the Isis nearly a double superiority in force, as the following statement will show:—

	Quarter-decked.			Flush.		
	Guns.		Pdrs.	Guns.		Pdrs.
First-deck	22	long	24	28	long	24
Second-deck . . .	24	,,	12	2	,,	24
Quarter-deck . . .	2	,,	6	28	carrs.	42
Forecastle	10	carrs.	24			
	58			58		
Broadside metal in lbs.		560			948	
Men and boys . . .		350			450	

According to this, the Isis gained two additional ports of a side on her first, and three on her second-deck, instead of one on each, as had previously been stated. The fact is, her foremost or bow-port (meant to be vacant) on the first deck was considered to be sufficiently aft to admit a standing gun, and a fresh chase-port was cut through further forward. This gave the ship 14 guns of a side on that deck. With respect to her second-deck, the substitution of carronades for long guns caused the ports to be altered, and admitted them to be nearer together; which at once gave the required number.

The second of the two ships in the "Built" column of this class was the Java, of 1458 tons, constructed from a draught prepared by the surveyors of the navy, and made a trifle shorter and narrower than the Leander and Newcastle, but established with precisely the same force in guns and men.

The principal dimensions of the Java were,

	Ft.	In.
Length of lower deck	171	11½
Breadth extreme	43	6
Depth in hold	14	3
Burden in tons 1458.		

NOTES TO ABSTRACT No. 25.

(a) Whatever remarks may have suggested themselves upon the eligibility of this plan of reform in a national point of view, will be found in their proper place in the body of the work. Our present business is with the details of the system, particularly as they affect that arrangement or classification of the ships which is the groundwork of these Abstracts.

How to effect the change from one plan of rating to the other without disorganizing the particular Abstract into which the new classification, from the date of its commencement, naturally fell, was long a subject of difficulty. At length I decided to arrange the old and new classes in the manner adopted in the Abstract before us, and to remove the ships to their new stations by the pair of converted columns; a method that, if not quite so intelligible as could be wished, possesses the merit of not disturbing, in the slightest degree, the arithmetical connection of the figures.

Class A is the same in each rating. B receives the San-Josef, and parts with the building ships, London and Princess Charlotte. C takes the latter, along with the Ocean, and gives up the San-Josef. D merely parts with the building ship Trafalgar. Old E is extinct. Old F, or new E, takes the last-named ship, and parts with the Ocean, and becomes exalted from the second to the first rate. Old G is extinct. Old H, or new F, receives, along with promotion, one ship, the Prince, from the last class but one (old a and new X) of the Abstract. Old K divides into new G and H, comprising the whole of the second rate; and old L and M distribute themselves into the first five classes of the third rate I, K, L, M, and N. Old O is new P; and old P, by transferring its six individuals, to the hospital and receiving-ship class, becomes extinct. It should here be remarked, that the official register of the new rating, as did that of the old, takes no note of the calibers of the guns, or of the size of the ships: hence the seven new classes, from I to P inclusive, form but three in the admiralty list.

The explanation just given of the process of removing the line classes may suffice, without investigating the remaining classes further than to point out where, by the new arrangement, a class is raised above the heads of any other class or classes. Q, the first new under-line class, is an instance of this, having formerly rated three classes lower. The strict numerical gun-force is here, indeed, a little defective; as the ships of the next, or R class, carrying heavier metal, and being, as well as larger, a full third stronger in frame, ought to have precedence of the ships of Q.

The comparison made in a former note between the Isis in her intended, and the same ship in her actual state of construction, will best explain why a flush ship, of any given number of guns, ought to be classed above, and not with, a quarter-decked ship of the same number of guns. Thus, R and S 58s, in the new rating, rank above T 58; that is, they do so in the Abstract before us. But in the official register, where no such distinction is acknowledged, the ships are all huddled together in one class; even although the ships of T are established with a less complement, by 100 men, than those of R or S. It is also worthy of remark, that, as the quarter-decked ships, now that they have the whole of their guns enumerated, rank much higher than formerly; so, except in the case (Q) cited in the last paragraph, and in any other (old and new R, for instance) wherein a pair of bow-chasers may have been omitted, the flush ships, mounting no additional guns, undergo no change in their classification. Thus, M and N, from being close neighbours, separate, the one into Z, the other into D, with three classes intervening.

In the old rating there are 50, and in the new but 42, cruising classes. According to the official register, however, there should be but 36 of the latter; the two classes distinguished by caliber (K and M), the two by size (O and P), and the three by decks (S, T, and E), not finding places in it, while a 34-gun class, of one individual, is added. The reason for excluding the latter from the Abstract will appear in a note to class Z, and that for admitting the whole of the former has already been stated. It should be mentioned that, when the new regulation was first adopted, two additional classes, an 82 and a 38, made their appearance in the list, and several of the ships in the other classes were differently arranged. But, shortly afterwards, the 82 was incorporated with the 80, and the 38 with the 42; and the other ships became, with the exceptions hereafter to be noticed, classed as they appear in this Abstract.

But, besides the classes arranged under the head of "New Rating," the official list still contained a set of classes of the "Old Rating," such as the 98, the 64, the 50, the 38, the 36, the 32, and some others. The alleged reason for this was, that the ships composing those classes, being laid up for permanent "harbour-service," had no armament belonging to them. If entitled to no armament, why were they designated as 98, 64, 50 gun-ships, &c.? None of the ships in the new rating carry any guns until they are fitted for sea; and yet all alike bear a designation significant, not of their "ordinary," but of their commissioned force. The term is meant as descriptive of a class, composed of non-effective, as well as effective ships: why, then, not include the harbour-service ships among the former; or else class them together as "harbour-service ships," without any reference to their original rank in the navy?

Having thus, in illustration of this rather complex Abstract, entered at a tolerable length into the minutiæ of the plan upon which the new classification of the British navy is conducted, I shall proceed to point out and explain two or three of the more important of those few cases in which I have been induced, chiefly for consistency sake, to remove ships from one class to another, without the authority of the official list.

(*b*) Until the new system, the San-Josef mounted, on every deck, the same number of guns as the Ville-de-Paris. It appears, however, that the former ship is to carry 30, instead of 32, guns upon the third-deck. Considering this either as a mistake in the register, or as an alteration not likely to be enforced when the ship is again, if she ever should be, fitted for sea, especially as the San-Josef is still allowed her 850 men (50 more than a 110-gun ship's complement), I have classed her as a 112-gun ship. The new plan of substituting Congreve's 24-pounders for the guns on the third-deck, by equalizing the calibers in the two ships, renders nugatory the distinction between the classes of old B and C, and occasions the Ville-de-Paris and San-Josef to approximate more closely than ever in their armament.

(*c*) The Impregnable registers as a 104; and yet the Trafalgar, the building ship associated with her, in constructing from the former's draught, somewhat enlarged it is true, but chiefly in breadth, to increase her stability. Of the two 106-gun ships in the official list, the second is the Royal Sovereign, of 2175 tons, a ship armed precisely as the 104s, except in being ordered two additional carronades for her quarter-deck; an alteration in a three-decker too insignificant and precarious to warrant the sacrifice of consistency. This consideration has induced me to substitute the Impregnable for the Royal Sovereign; and the latter accordingly remains with the 104s.

(*d*) The probability that the new plan of arming the third decks of three-deckers with Congreve's 24-pounders, instead of long 12 or 18 pounders, will extend to these ships, if any of them should hereafter be required, or be found serviceable enough to go to sea, is the reason that I have abandoned the former distinction between 18 and 12 pounder ships, and classed them, as in the official list, together.

(*e*) One of these ships, the Endymion, officially ranks as a 48. It is true that she mounts one gun of a side on the main-deck less than the other five ships; but the latter were built from the same draught, and merely differ in being pierced for an additional port on the main-deck. See vol. v., p. 432. As the Endymion is old and nearly worn out, and her five class-mates, being built of soft wood, are not likely to survive her, I have chosen to retain the former with them, rather than remove her to a class of which she would be the only individual. The official list contains a sixth 50-gun frigate, the Acasta; but as she carries 18-pounders on the main-deck, and is much smaller, I have ventured to assign her another place: moreover, she is an old ship, and cannot last many years longer.

(*f*) These five ships are the Acasta, Cambrian, Lavinia, Révolutionnaire, and Forte. The first is the ship referred to in the latter part of the last note, and the two next ships are officially classed as 48s: the two last-named, therefore, are the only cruisers of this class requiring to have their pretensions discussed. The Révolutionnaire, it is believed, usually mounted 18 carronades, besides two long guns, on her quarter-deck and forecastle, making 48 guns in all, and, being of 1148 tons, was well able to carry them; but she now officially classes as a 46. The Forte, measuring 1155 tons, was built, plank for plank, from the draught of the Révolutionnaire, and consequently possessed the same capacities. Most unaccountably, however (unless it be considered as a peace-establishment), the Forte has been assigned but 14 carronades, and on that account, though manned with a full complement of a 46, descends to a 44. Considering that a war would instantly restore the Forte to her proper rank by the side of her prototype, I have ventured so to place her.

(*g*) The Seringapatam and Tigris, building from the draught of the late French frigate Présidente, afterwards named Piémontaise. The two former, the first of 1152, the second of 1162 (occasioned by a slight increase in her length from being constructed with a circular stern) tons, are registered as 46s; and yet, in January, 1814, the Présidente appears to have mounted, along with her 28 guns upon the main-deck, twenty 32-pounder carronades and two nines upon the quarter-deck and forecastle, total 50 guns.

In fact, the Présidente could have mounted (she was broken up in 1815) 30 guns on her main-deck; and so can with ease (they being pierced for 32) the two ships building from her. The official register classes as 48s the Loire and Sibylle. It is true that these ships, obtaining two additional carronades each, did mount 48 guns; and so did the Amelia, Africane, and Madagascar. The latter, indeed, mounted 50 guns. There would be an end to all useful classification if such instances were not considered as accidental exceptions to the general rule.

(*h*) Take away the Naiad and Phaëton and two foreign-built ships, the Alceste and Madagascar, and, between any two of the remaining 34 frigates, no greater difference of size can be found than 39 tons. Nor does that occur in more than one instance. Generally, the ships do not disagree in size beyond 15 tons.

(*i*) Of these three ships, the only one officially classed as a 44 is the Andromache. The remaining two, the Pique and Unité, class as 42s. The latter certainly appears not to have mounted more than 42 guns (26 Gover's 24s on the main deck); but, being the largest ship of the three, the Unité can as well mount 44 guns as the Andromache herself, when named the Princess Charlotte, did 46, and the Pique the same. Such was the official oversight as to the latter ship's proper classification, that, in the old rating, she ranked only as a 32, from the time of her capture in 1800 until the 9th of April 1813, when an admiralty-order promoted the Pique to a 36, and this without at all augmenting her force, that already exceeding the establishment of her new class. Were these three ships to be transferred to the class next below them, the average difference in size between the 37 cruisers of the latter and them would be as much as 95 tons. Moreover, the 44 is a class that will soon disappear from the list.

(*k*) The Eurydice and Ganymede. The first, of 521 tons, from mounting on her quarter-deck two more 18-pounder carronades than established upon the 32-gun class, officially ranks as a 34. The second ship, of 601 tons, with more reason (though mounting, like all these ships, but 22 guns on the main deck), classed also, for a while, as a 34. Subsequently the Ganymede registered (by mistake, as it would appear) as a 26; and thus the Eurydice was left as the only 34-gun ship in the British navy. In point of size, the Eurydice is rather exceeded by each of the three ships, with whom she and the Ganymede are here associated. Upon the whole, these two ships cannot, with any regard to consistency or practical utility, be classed anywhere else than where I have ventured to place them.

NOTES TO ABSTRACT No. 26.

(*a*) These six ships, the Formidable, Monarch, Powerful, Thunderer, Vengeance, and Ganges (since built at Bombay, of teak, and with a circular stern), are from the draught of the Canopus, late Franklin, captured at the battle of the Nile, and are constructing with diagonal frames.

(*b*) Those five ships, the Chichester, Lancaster, Portland, Southampton, and Winchester, constructed with diagonal frames and circular sterns, agree in dimensions with the Java, except in being four inches broader.

NOTES TO ABSTRACT No. 27

(*a*) An improvement upon the old quarter-decked (R) ship-sloop class, and established with twenty 32-pounder carronades on the main deck, and six 18-pounder carronades with two long sixes upon the quarter-deck and forecastle. One of them, the Niemen, was built of Baltic fir; and the single ship of this class, in the "Building" column of No. 26 Abstract, the Atholl, was constructing of larch, cut from the estate of the Duke of Atholl.

(*b*) Surprising, indeed, that the navy-board should continue adding new individuals by dozens at a time (see the preceding Abstracts), to this worthless class.

There should have been a reference marked at the two "ordered" ships of class Q. One of them was named the President, built from the draught of the American frigate of that name. The other was the Worcester, similar to those noticed at (*i*), page 408.

NOTES TO ABSTRACT No. 28.

(*a*) The Royal George (first named Neptune) and St. George; the latter building at Plymouth, and the former at Chatham, upon the lines of the Caledonia, without, we believe, the alteration that had been adopted in the case of the Nelson. See p. 403.

(*b*) The Ocean. This ship was intended to be of the same dimensions as the Dreadnought, Téméraire, and Neptune, that averaged 2121 tons, but her draught was extended so as to make her 2276 tons. However, the plan was not found to answer; and, having failed as a 110, the Ocean is now to try her success as an 80.

(*c*) The Hastings, built in India of teak, and purchased by the British government. The first instance, we believe, of the kind, except in the smaller classes.

REMARKS UPON

THE NAVAL WAR OF 1812

WITH THE

UNITED STATES.

BY

H. Y. POWELL.

[*First published in the* 1886 *edition of* " *James's Naval History.*"]

REMARKS UPON THE NAVAL WAR OF 1812 WITH THE UNITED STATES.

MOST British readers will be surprised to learn that, notwithstanding the infinite pains* taken by William James to render his history a monument of accuracy, and notwithstanding the exposure he brought upon contemporary misstatements, yet to this day the Americans still dispute his facts, and still cling with fond tenacity to the romantic versions of their old writers. Fortunately, during the last seventy years many fresh authorities and new documents have come to light; and it will be the endeavour of this monograph to prove conclusively the correctness of James and the mistakes of his opponents. The earlier writers on the other side the Atlantic, as Clark, Bowen, Thompson, and others, were not men of any eminence, and were sufficiently disciplined by James in his work, " Naval Occurrences "—a laborious compilation of seven hundred pages, wherein he discussed all particulars of the war between England and America, giving exhaustive details, and fairly publishing the official accounts of both sides at full length. A certain amount of irritation is exhibited in this work, which was natural enough, as the author had to record various small reverses, and to deal with much exaggeration on the part of our opponents, while he himself was a sufferer in being for nearly twelve months a *détenu* in the United States. After the interval of many years we can now contrive to take a general view of all the transactions in a cooler spirit.

In 1839 a work was published (by Mr. Bentley), "The Naval History of the United States," written by Fenimore Cooper, whose high reputation gave promise of excellence, more especially as, from his having been a young officer in the American Navy, he had the practical experience which was wanting in other authors. It must be said, however, that this work was not altogether worthy of his

* " Almost daily toil among dusty shelves for several years."—Preface to vol. iv., edition of 1824.

eminent name. Written in a quiet style, and free from strainings after effect, it is deficient in statistics, and when dwelling on the war of 1812, there is a kind of *suppressio veri* and *suggestio falsi* which is surprising in a man of honour and culpable in a naval officer who should have been thoroughly acquainted with the subject. It is true that he was only a very few years afloat, and never appears to have risen above the rank of midshipman; retiring on succeeding to a landed estate. In his "Naval History" he affects not to take any notice of James whatever, but, it appears, had read both works by the latter, and in 1842 published articles in the "United States Magazine and Democratic Review," attacking them warmly, as we think with more heat than success, which will be shown presently. Unable to point out other than trifling errors, Cooper descended to hint that James was a man of dubious character, and really engaged in a grade of life quite below that of a solicitor or proctor; this calumny, however, has been lately effectually quashed by separate written certificates obtained from two legal firms now practising in Jamaica, where James resided from 1801 to 1813.

In 1882 a more candid and more detailed work was published by an American, Theodore Roosevelt, an octavo of five hundred pages, which has passed through two editions, and, if not extensively read in England, is likely to be popular enough in the United States; for, while admitting many errors on the part of predecessors, it labours hard to show that the war of 1812 was replete with glory for the Americans. It is impossible to deny that they gained some unexpected successes, and it would be ungenerous to dispute that they showed frequently a very respectable degree of efficiency; yet we still must contend that those successes, as shown by William James, were in nearly every case due not only to a superiority of force, but to a *great* superiority of force. In other words, that they were owing to the foresight and provident arrangements of the civilian and shipbuilding departments more than to extraordinary abilities of the naval officers and men. To prove this case it will be necessary for the present writer to take quite as much a naval architect's point of view as a sailor's; for discussions about relative skill, courage, endurance, manœuvres, etc., are interminable and indeterminable, while the materialistic facts of size of ships and other tangible matters are reducible to a fixed definite conclusion.

The incidents of this small war divide naturally into three classes—the frigate actions, the sloop actions, and the actions upon the North American Lakes. Respecting the frigate actions, the earlier American writers, from 1814 to 1836, endeavour to show that the three British ships separately captured by United States vessels were either superior in force or nearly equal; but Cooper states the American ships were rather superior in some cases, and in others "about equal"—a favourite mode of expression with him, the word "about" being peculiarly useful. And Roosevelt, who gives more statistics than Cooper, publishes the tonnage of the American frigates as 1576 each, and that of the British 1330. But James has stated that the average tonnage of the British frigates was only 1080 tons—a large and important difference. It may be added now that neither in the French nor the English service were any frigates ever built for 18-pounder guns, of a size reaching quite 1200 tons, and but few exceeding 1100. In Charnock's "History of Marine Architecture" (1801), and Derrick's "Memoirs of the Royal Navy" (1806), both reliable works and quite impartial, being published before this war, the sizes and tonnage of our "38-gun frigates" are clearly established. Since the times of James and Cooper various standard works have been published, both in England and America, affording overwhelming evidence on the subject, and these having been consulted, not without expenditure of time and pains, by the writer of these remarks, can now be brought as impartial witnesses into court. A very competent and credible witness is Fincham, who was master shipwright of Portsmouth dockyard, and who, in 1851, published a technical work, "The History of Naval Architecture," dedicated to the Prince Consort, tracing the development of naval construction from the earliest times to his own day; and under the year 1806 he gives the dimensions of La Guerrière, then captured from the French. These dimensions agree precisely with those published by James. Now, what says Cooper? "That the Constitution was a larger and heavier ship than La Guerrière will be disputed by no nautical man, though it is believed that the actual difference between these vessels was considerably *less* than might be inferred from their respective rates. It is understood that the Guerrière was nearly as long a ship as her adversary."

Here is vagueness—something indefinite, and then something unknown upon that! Why not have given the size or the tonnage? Simply because it would not have answered his purpose to state that one ship was 1090 tons and the other 1530, or nearly half as large again.

But Roosevelt gives the tonnage of Guerrière at 1338, without any explanation of where obtained or from what dimensions calculated. A witness at once impartial and crushing is the French

Minister of Marine, who, in response to a direct inquiry from the writer, in December last, with that courtesy which is so agreeable a trait of the national character, sent a letter with the precise dimensions of "La Guerrière of 40 guns, built in 1799 and lost in 1806." Those dimensions* are—Length on water-line, 47·10 metres; moulded breadth, 11·85; thus absolutely confirming James, when the thickness of the planking, omitted in the French mode, but included in English, is added. This evidence is of great importance, because English and American authors agree that the Guerrière, Macedonian, Java, and Shannon were all much of the same size. Again, the United States Navy List gives the "displacement" of Constitution as 2200 tons, and the British standard author, Edye, in "Equipment and Displacement of Vessels of War" (1832), gives the load displacement of frigates of Guerrière and Macedonian's class at 1470 tons—the nominal or usual tonnage agreeing with James. Load displacement or total weight of both ship herself and all on board is now adopted as the most satisfactory exponent of men of war. What answer have the Americans to this? Will they dispute their own Navy List or the written evidence of the French Minister of Marine? The lines of the British-built frigates of "38 guns" (so called), of which Macedonian was one, were published in Rees' Cyclopædia about the year 1820. The schedules of dimensions in "Naval Occurrences" of the frigates and of the sloops are always passed over silently by our opponents, and for very good reason—they are incontrovertible.

As American accounts state that the Java, 38, was of 1340 tons, and that she had more than 400 men on board on commencing action, also that the guns were French 18-pounders carrying balls of 19½ lbs. English weight, these statements have been submitted to the present Admiral Chads, son of the late distinguished Admiral Sir H. D. Chads, G.C.B., who so very gallantly fought the Java, and he is of opinion that they are quite incorrect, for his father "always considered the account of Mr. James and his statistics most exact, and if there had been any inaccuracies in them he would have pointed them out."

The next difficulty with the American authors is as to the weight of the shot used by the respective combatants. Anxious to explain away the inequality of general force, they seek to make out that their shot weighed seven per cent. less than the nominal amount, but that our shot were always full weight. The writer, determined to sift this subject, applied to the Carron Iron Co. at Falkirk, Scotland, who cast guns and shot so extensively for the

* In English measure, 154 ft. 6 in. by 38 ft. 10 in.

government during the wars of George III.'s time, and the present manager has replied that shot were cast to certain sizes by order, but that the weight was only approximate. The actual sizes are stated in the elaborate work on "Naval Gunnery," by Sir Howard Douglas,* an eminent authority, and at these sizes the British cannon-balls, by careful calculation, must also have been a little under weight—as nearly as may be five per cent. less. For proof of this reference can be made to Colonel C. H. Owen's scientific book on "Modern Artillery" (1871), where it will be seen that after the 18-pound shot had been increased of late years from 5·040 inches in diameter to 5·099, they even then weighed only 17 lbs. 11 oz., and therefore those of the smaller size would weigh little over 17 lbs.† As Colonel Owen was Professor of Artillery to the Royal Academy, Woolwich, and author of other cognate books, it is to be presumed his authority is final.

The second division of the subject, the sloop actions, comes next under discussion. Cooper suggests that American ship-corvettes, averaging 500 tons and 160 men, were "about equal" to British brigs of 380 tons and 120 men, and carefully avoids giving statistics of those sizes. Roosevelt states that the brigs measured 470 tons; but if the reader refers to J. Knowles's quarto book on Shipbuilding (1822), he will there find the drawings to scale of such a brig—the Raven, 18, built in 1804—and the dimensions exactly agree with James's figures, showing an actual tonnage of 382. Further, the American Captain Blakely, in sending in a formal list of captures to his government, enters thereupon the name of Reindeer, British brig of 18 guns and $382\frac{14}{94}$ tons (see "American State Papers (Naval Affairs)," in the British Museum). How remarkable that he should be at once so minute and so accurate, so different to published accounts in the United States.

One J. McCauley, in memorializing the Secretary to the United States Navy in 1815 on behalf of American officers, uses the argument that other actions had been well rewarded when gained by superiority of force; namely, that the Boxer, British brig, was inferior to the American brig Enterprise, and that the Macedonian, British frigate, was "not equal in any one respect to the United States, 44."

Respecting the third division of this subject, the actions upon the Lakes, it is difficult at this period to obtain such precise information, but items will be pointed out; and as American accounts have proved so fallacious on the other two divisions, we are entitled to

* Roosevelt has kindly raised him to the peerage.
† The weight of globes is in proportion to the cube of their diameters, and cast iron averages 444 lbs. to the cubic foot, according to the British "School of Naval Architecture."

assume that they are not more reliable on the third. Cooper and Roosevelt endeavour to show that the British ship Confiance, at the battle of Lake Champlain on Plattsburg, must have been 1100 or 1200 tons burden. James gives her size to an inch and her tonnage at 831. If we refer to the description of the American ship General Pike, we find that she carried much the same armament as Confiance, except that the latter had, with the like main-deck armament, several carronades extra, but on spar-deck one long 24-pounder less. Now, such long gun would weigh as much as three carronades; so the difference between the vessels need not have been more than trifling, especially as on the confined waters of Lake Champlain cruising qualities would be little available. Moreover, Lieutenant Emmons, in his "Statistical History of the United States Navy" ("by Authority"), gives the size of the General Pike as 850 tons. The conclusion, therefore, is that James, with his usual precision, was in all probability here quite right.

Regarding the affairs on Lake Erie between the squadrons of Sir James Yeo and Commodore Chauncey, there has now come to light, published in the American General Armstrong's "Notices of the War" (1840), the statement that the commodore was very backward in the eyes of his government, and that preparations were actually made to supersede him! This is in reference to the contemporary American fanfaronades, that Chauncey chased Yeo round and round the lake, but could not get him to fight!

There is now no ill feeling in England against our cousins on the other side of the Atlantic; we ask only that in writing history they will confine themselves to the facts, and not embellish with the fictions which have already been so often exposed. If, obdurate in error, they wish even now to contest the question longer, there will be yet further documentary evidence to be produced on this side. Readers who meantime wish to pursue the subject, will find additional details in "Colburn's United Service Magazine" for April, May, and August, 1885.

H. Y. POWELL.

17, BAYSWATER TERRACE, LONDON,
February, 1886.

THE END.